THE GREAT CROWD

To Marilyn

Part of the Greate crowd

Michael J [illegible]

The Great Crowd

A Love Story About a
Large Urban Parish

Michael J. Tan Creti

The Eighth Rector,
All Saints Omaha, Nebraska,
With the Help of Many

Library of Congress Control Number:		2014917955
ISBN:	Hardcover	978-1-4990-8098-8
	Softcover	978-1-4990-8099-5
	eBook	978-1-4990-8100-8

This book was printed in the United States of America.

Rev. date: 12/18/2014

To order additional copies of this book, contact:
Xlibris
1-888-795-4274
www.Xlibris.com
Orders@Xlibris.com
650945

To the unseen and unnamed

Contents

Preface

Author's Preface

I arrived in All Saints in the summer of 1977. I was hired to be the assistant to the rector by The Rev. Charles Pedersen. Immediately, I was treated to stories about All Saints past. Among these were personal memories about each of the previous rectors, save the first, Louis Zahner, who had been here for a rather brief stay. The stories also included memories of various lay members of the parish who had made unique and sometimes amusing contributions to the rich congregational life of the parish. The rector, for whom I worked, was himself a great *recounter*. He took great relish in the fables and foibles of his predecessors and of the notables of the parish.

With time, I myself gained a certain command of this repertoire; and of course, at some point, I became part of the story. In 1993, I became the eighth rector of All Saints and remained in that office until the end of 2005. After a period of separation, I returned to worship at All Saints, and since then, I have enjoyed a cordial relationship with my successor, The Rev. Thomas O'Dell. In 2011, I was approached by the members of the parish who had been charged with writing the history of the parish. They asked me if I would consider writing it. A history of the parish, in spite of the fact that the parish enjoyed telling its stories, had never been written. After some thought about my priorities and the special challenges of writing a history, when you are part of it, I offered the committee a proposal.

I told them that I would be interested in writing a social history of the parish, which would be different from a chronology or an annotated scrapbook, which often pass for parish histories. If I did it, I would tell the story with attention to the shifts in American culture and in the character of Omaha that had a hand in determining the parish's choices and outcomes. Similarly, since the parish's destiny was deeply interwoven with the conduct of the Diocese of Nebraska and the national church, I would have to make them part of the story as well. It would, I warned them, be a rather big story, perhaps more than what they wanted. Fatefully, they agreed, and so here we are.

While the reader has sufficient access to the history of the city and of the nation, it is less likely that they have the same access to the history of the Episcopal Church in the United States. For that reason, I have provided a foreword that contains a brief sketch of the Episcopal Church's story in the context of the American experience.

There is, of course, a special problem presented by the fact that I am part of the story. How can I be objective? Objectivity in history, however, is more of a pretense behind which "historians" hide than it is an absolute. Any story must inevitably be told from within, but a storyteller can hold himself accountable to truth and to candor. I will try to do that as best as I can. Fortunately, I have had access to archives that begin with the first vestry meeting on September 1, 1885, and continue down to the parish's most recent activities. The diocesan archivist, Jo Behrens, who worked on the archives at All Saints for a long period, has been a consistent and essential assistance to me. A large number of parishioners of All Saints have also been part of the process, and much is owed to them as well. A draft of each section has been presented to them for their input and critic. In addition, a number of individual parishioners have made large contributions to the research and editing of this text. Hopefully, this effort has kept the result both truthful and readable. In the end, of course, I am responsible for the final text.

If a history can only be written from some within it, it is also true that it will only succeed if others within it are committed to carrying it forward. This will not be the last story to be told about All Saints, and with that comes the comfort that whatever errors and omissions I have made will be corrected or amended with time.

Michael J. Tan Creti
2014

P. S.: Thanks!

I could not have brought this project to a fitting conclusion without the help of many people. I owe special thanks to Jo Behrens who laid the foundation for the archives of All Saints during the eighties and nineties. Also, I owe a great debt to those in the parish who have read this text and have helped it evolve into what I hope is a serviceable and accurate account of All Saints. These include Jean Lewandowski, Dr. Laura Palmer, Andrew Simpson, Marilyn Simpson, and Betty White. I have received crucial assistance with illustrations from Lavonne Past, Sooz Edwards, Elizabeth Encell, Robert Hall, Andrew Simpson, Brad Simpson, and Marilyn Simpson.

Over the past three years, Thomas O'Dell, the ninth Rector of All Saints, has provided me with support and inspiration. I am grateful to him and the parish for making available the archives and resources of the parish during this period of time. The current vestry has stepped forward and provided the support without which the publication of the result could not have happened.

For providing me with this opportunity and for all this help, I am profoundly grateful.

FOREWORD

A Brief Sketch of the History of the Episcopal Church in the United States

The story of All Saints is a story that sits within the larger story of the Episcopal Church. This story is driven by changes in American culture and by how its leadership navigated those changes.

It is well known that the Episcopal Church found itself in a difficult culture context in the colonial period and that difficulty became even more pronounced during the American Revolution and its immediate aftermath. The American experience began with an assertion of individual rights so much so that at times those rights trumped social responsibility. The Church of England transplanted in this country, on the other hand, valued social responsibility and associative behavior. That did not mean that its congregations did not succeed on American soil. It meant that where they succeeded, they were led by those who were both determined and skilled navigators of the difficult waters and prevailing head winds.

The bias of these early Anglican congregations was to resist the rush West, thinking that they needed to perfect the social order of the communities within which they lived before they proceed to the next step on the frontier. Other religious bodies in America, the majority in fact, considered the movement West an individual right. The Revolutionary War was compelled as much by a resentment of the monarchy's closing the Western frontier as by the inconvenience of any particular taxation. The resistance that these Church of England congregations met in the colonial period was compounded by the attrition of these congregations experienced during the war. Moreover, the political change caused these congregations to lose the church order upon which they had relied, tied as it was with the monarchy. Before they could move out on to the frontier, they needed to establish a church order of their own. This required them to bring bishops to this country and create a pattern of governance.

Meanwhile, those church bodies that were focused on individual salvation moved rapidly in the West. Suddenly, the Methodist and Baptist were the largest single identities in the new country. It was not until the second decade of the nineteenth century that the newly organized Protestant Episcopal Church in the United States of America launched a Western mission. Mainly, it did so with missionary efforts that sprung from its centers of strength, Virginia, New England, and New York City. Hobart, the bishop of New York, projected a high church mission across Upstate New York; and through Jackson Kemper, the first missionary bishop, the high church mission was projected into Wisconsin and Nebraska. In Nebraska, it merged with the work of Joseph C. Talbot from Virginia, giving Nebraska a rather divided identity. Philander Chase led a third trajectory that moved though Ohio, Indiana, and Illinois with a decidedly evangelical or low church orientation. In many ways, these early missionary efforts bordered on the heroic, if not saintliness, and they produced substantial results against great odds.

By the end of the 1840s, this effort began to bear a bounty that benefitted from a cultural change in American. Much of the country had been affected by revival movements, especially Upstate New York. There the revival, consisting of the Millerites, the Mormons, and Charles Finney, to name a few, had gone through successive waves responding to quests for individual salvation and for social regeneration. The movements were so extreme as to give the area the name "the burned over district." Such individualism and social polarization brought conflict into the congregations, including those of the Baptist, Presbyterian, and Congregationalist. By the end of the 1840s, it was more like the burned-out district. Religious individualism and social regeneration were in retreat. The Episcopal Church, which had been largely irrelevant to these waves of revival, now offered itself as an escape from the conflict that had engulf congregations; and it found itself front and center. The Episcopal Church began a period of substantial growth with the wind at its back for the first time in its existence in this country.

The trend away from individual freedoms to a social responsibility was intensified at the end of the Civil War. Once again after the fire, there was a feeling that American culture needed to avoid extremes and to promote a consensus. With this conviction came a new sense that Europe, formerly dismissed as the "old world," offered the new world patterns for those kinds of stable institutions that would enhance the social order for which it hungered. During the Civil War, the Episcopal Church was, for the most part, on the side line. Many Episcopal bishops, like Lee of Iowa, never officially commented on the war during its duration, nor had he allow his clergy to do so. Speedily, without recrimination or sanction, the Southern bishops were welcomed back into the House of Bishops once the war was over.

Historians have the habit of referring to the generation of this period as "American Victorians," which rather aptly describes them. It is certainly surprising that a nation whose identity began with the hatred of an English Monarch suddenly redefined itself with admiration for another. Mackay, All Saints rector at the time of Queen Victoria's death, published a stirring obituary in the parish newspaper, lavish with praise for her. The progressive movement in the hands of these American Victorians sought to enhance the commitment to social responsibility within the nation and to protect the sanctity of the home.

Even a radical reform, like that of the women's suffrage movement, was not aimed at the individual rights of women as much as it was in securing a role of women in the social action of the community. The attack on the double standard, which allowed men to get away with certain indiscretions, was not framed in terms as freeing women to enjoy the same freedoms but rather to reform men to a higher level of responsibility. This continued to be the nature of the women's movement up to 1915, when feminists like Margaret Sanger, Lillian Symes, and Winifred Harper Cooley broke with the older women's movement. These new leaders saw the world in terms of the individual, and the new emphasis became women should be able to do everything that men do.[1]

While it lasted, the Victorian-progressive era was a context in which the Episcopal Church found itself very much at home. It grew rapidly, so much that it could imagine itself as becoming the center of an American Catholic church. That possibility was drastically altered by the waves of immigration from Europe that began in earnest in the 1870s. The result was not so much a setback as the need for a course correction. The Episcopal Church would continue to grow well into the second decade of the twentieth century. But an undercurrent was at work that began to undercut the progressive era and the consensus that had sustained the country.

By the end of the second decade, the rise of a new individualism and the acceptance of a politics of conflict changed the fortune of the Episcopal

1 McGerr, Michael, *A Fierce Discontent, The Rise and Fall of the Progressive Movement in America*, Oxford Press, 2003, p. 167.

Church in the United States. Growth came grudgingly for the Episcopal Church, and it did well to sustain itself. This period of conflict continued through the Depression and the war. But the aftermath of the war was once again quite altered. People came home from war, wanting to get to work, start families, and build homes. They had seen enough conflict and were ready for a season of consensus. Moreover, the war had trumped individualism and taught people a sense of duty.

The Episcopal Church, to its surprise, found itself in a new climate where growth was possible and again entered a period of remarkable growth. It seems, however, that cultural swings in American life have accelerated, unless that is simply the problem of reflecting on history too close to one's own time. By the late sixties, America returned to a period of conflict politics and "me first-ism. There was a season of relief in the late eighties and nineties, but shortly after the beginning of the new century, community was dominated by conflict and individuals pressed for rights. Since what have happened in the last ten years are still current events, it is best left unexplained for now. Moreover, it is not my attention to take the story of All Saints beyond the year 2001.

Let us then embark on our story within the story: the story of a great crowd that All Saints began to assemble in 1885 and that has persisted with its witness to the end of the twentieth century.

PART 1

Growing in the Age of Progress (1885–1915)

Chapter 1

Laying the Foundation: 1885–1890

The Prelude

Our story begins with the death of the bishop. Robert Harper Clarkson died in his home on March 10, 1884. He succumbed to a bout of pneumonia brought on, one would suppose, by his relentless travel through the length and breadth of his very sizeable diocese. By sizeable, I am referring first to its geography. At the time of his death, the diocese consisted of the entire state of Nebraska, but before 1883, it had included the Dakotas as well. To this it might be added that Clarkson's ambitions for growth magnified the size of his diocese beyond its generous geography. His mission strategy was to plant an Episcopal congregation at every promising crossroad and for those congregations well under way to found a school to accompany their mission.

At the time of Clarkson's death, the diocese had twenty-one priests and 3,500 baptized members. A great portion of these individuals were part of the diocese as a direct result of Clarkson's work over the past nineteen years during which he serviced as bishop of Nebraska. The diocese was united in its disbelief and in its grief at his death, disbelief because he was only fifty-nine years-old and grief because he had put himself on the line in every venture the diocese had undertaken from the time of his arrival in 1865 onward. The Rev. H. B. Burgess wrote in the minutes of the standing committee, which met in March shortly after Clarkson's death:

> He was truly catholic in his sympathies, a lover of home and foreign mission, a lover of good men, a man of broad views—full

> of sunshine and true happiness, whether we consider his life or his death. As we look back upon both, they seem complete lectures, monuments [not] wanting in the single line of grace or loveliness.

Because Clarkson had been such a hands-on bishop, the diocese hastened to replace him, only to find that it was disunited by its needs and by its visions of the future. The constitution of the diocese required that notification for an electing council be given sixty days prior to its call to order. The diocese managed to assemble an electing council seventy-two days after the bishop's death, a mark of its resolve. Gathered in the newly completed Trinity Cathedral on May 21, they were called to order at 10:00 a.m. Completing the preliminary business inherent in organizing a council, the clergy sat down for the balloting that would continue on for twenty ballots. On that twentieth ballot, George Worthington emerged as the winner with a majority of one! Notification of his election was telegraphed to Worthington; and a delegation, which the council had elected for that purpose, hastily traveled to Detroit to plead Nebraska's case. After due consideration of the offer and the personal entreaties of the delegation, Worthington declined. He said that it appeared to him that there had been too much disunity in the election process for him to accept the election. He said he preferred to remain in his parish in Detroit where he was much loved and where he had been for nineteen years. His brother John, who was quite artistic, and his mother lived with him. When his mother had died, he and his brother gave a memorial to the parish, a magnificent high altar made of imported white Caen stone.[2] Clearly, he had reason to stay in Detroit. Moreover, he claimed to have heard—whether it was true or not, one cannot say—that Clarkson, in setting his house in order, had indicated his preference for a successor.

There is no indication that Clarkson had done so, but it is possible that someone else had been the source of the rumor, doing for the bishop what they thought he should have done. The existence of such a rumor could help explain the disunity that had plagued the first council.

Reacting to Worthington's rejection, a second council was hastily called by the standing committee. This council met in June in the basement of Trinity Cathedral, and in spite of the absence of some significant members of the diocesan clergy, it proceeded to organize itself. Having overcome an attempt from the floor to delay the election until the fall, this council

2 *Caen stone* or *Pierre de Caen*, is a light creamy-yellow limestone quarried in Northwestern France near the city of Caen. It was used in the building of Canterbury Cathedral as well as many other famous cathedrals and churches.

held a ballot and elected Eliphalet Potter, a prominent Easterner. Potter's father had been bishop of Pennsylvania, Alonzo Potter. His uncle, Horatio, was bishop of New York; and most recently, his brother, Henry Codman, had been elected assistant bishop of New York. Clearly, Potter represented the quintessence of the Episcopal Church's establishment; and the haste of the "rump council" might well have been driven by the opinion that the availability of Potter was an opportunity too good to pass up, indeed, one that might not remain if they did not act immediately. At this time, the personal finances of a bishop and/or his financial connects to wealth in the east were important, particularly to a Western diocese like Nebraska, and who was better connected that Eliphant Nott Potter. Potter was traveling in Europe at the time, and so there was a delay. When he could, he actually came to Nebraska but in the end turned down the election. Potter chose instead to accept the offer of Hobart College to be its next president, a job with prestige and a degree of comfort, which apparently better suited him.

In due time, a third council met in November, again at Trinity Cathedral. No less than ten names were placed into nomination in the course of the council's protracted proceedings. It is clear, however, that there were three primary contenders: William Walker, E. S. Thomas, and George Worthington.

William Walker was the newly elected missionary bishop of North Dakota. His diocese had been carved out of Clarkson's jurisdiction in 1883 by the House of Bishops. This brought a welcome relief to Clarkson and was a signal of his success as a missionary bishop. Since Walker's election had taken place in the House of Bishops, at which Clarkson was present, it is clear that he had played a part in the election of Walker to be his successor in the part of his missionary district which he was relinquishing. Walker had been born in New York City and educated at Columbia University. He was one of those bright and privileged young Easterners who entered the Episcopal ministry during the nineteenth century and who were willing to give themselves to the romance of the Western missions. He was cut out of the same mold as Jackson Kemper, James Breck, and Robert Clarkson, himself. We can conclude that his appeal would be to those priest and laity in the diocese who saw the Western mission as still the true frontier of the Episcopal Church. It is also likely that if Clarkson had indeed signaled a preference of someone to succeed him, it would have been Walker; and if he didn't, someone reading between the lines would have felt justified in attributing the preference to him. Without that surmise, it is hard to understand what a strong showing Walker made in the election.

The second contender was E. S. Thomas, who was the rector of St. Paul's in St. Paul, Minnesota. He had come to the Diocese of Minnesota as a professor of New Testament studies at the newly formed Seabury Divinity School. The divinity school was attached to the new cathedral that the Diocese of Minnesota had built at Faribault. It was this cathedral-school complex that had produced Frank R. Millspaugh, the dean of Trinity Cathedral, Omaha, at the time of this election. Thomas was held in the highest regard by his bishop, Henry B. Whipple, and he would go on to be elected bishop of Kansas. Clearly, this indicates that Thomas's qualifications for the episcopate were beyond question. His name had been placed into nomination at the first of the councils by Rev. A. J. Graham of St. Stephen's Grand Island, a signal that Thomas was acceptable to those out state and those interested in continuing the Western missionary effort. At this present council, it was Dean Millspaugh, who moved his nomination. Millspaugh knew Thomas personally and regarded him as his mentor. For Millspaugh, what was at stake in this election was what form the cathedral would take. It had been just completed, having been consecrated in November 1883, less than six months before Clarkson's death. The building phase was over, and it was time to live into the vision that inspired its undertaking. Millspaugh had been one of the primary forces behind the building of the Trinity Cathedral. The other was James M. Woolworth, who was chancellor of the diocese and who had been a long-time vestry man and senior warden at the Trinity. The other was, of course, Clarkson himself. While Millspaugh and Woolworth had been united in the building of the cathedral, their visions of its future were divergent. Clarkson, who was the master of mediation, had held the coalition together; but now he was gone. Woolworth's vision for the Cathedral had been clearly stated in his book, *The Cathedral in the American Church*, published in 1883. Woolworth's vision relied heavily on the ideas of Bishop Doane who had just finished his cathedral, All Saints, in Albany, New York. Doane's cathedral was a meticulous copy of an English cathedral, both in fabric and organization.[3] Millspaugh's vision, on the other hand, was the cathedral system in which he had grown up in Faribault, Minnesota; and he must have supported E. S. Thomas's election as the best means for actualizing that vision in Omaha.

Where the break between Millspaugh and Woolworth took place is difficult to pinpoint. Woolworth did not back Thomas in the elections. So

---

3 In The Cathedral in the American Church, Woolworth provides extensive quotations of Bishop Doane. He also cites the work of the recent Bishop of Truro, now Archbishop of Canterbury. Approvingly, he notes that this cathedral gives the first place to the education of candidates for orders and to a body of unattached clergy called Missioners, p. 123f. He gives a much more limited reference to Bishop Whipple and Faribault Minnesota, pp. 93–94.

the break must have come as soon as Clarkson's mediating presence was missing. Certainly, it happened by the conclusion of the election process in which, it seems, neither had gotten his way. Woolworth, after twenty-five years on the vestry of Trinity and seventeen of which he had been senior warden, left Trinity in the summer of 1885 to participate in the founding of a new parish church that would be called All Saints, apparently foregoing his vision of "an American cathedral" in Omaha. Millspaugh would battle discontent within the cathedral parish and would announce his resignation under fire in October 1885. His resignation took effect on February 22, 1886, exactly one year after the new bishop had arrived in Omaha.

The bishop who came to Nebraska in March was George Worthington, who upon being elected a second time said yes. Worthington had been born in 1840, in Lenox, Massachusetts, in the heart of the Berkshires Mountains. At that time, the area was already regarded as an art colony, and his mother had specifically chosen to live in the Berkshires for that reason. Worthington graduated from Hobart College and went to General Seminary in New York City. He was unmarried and energetically devoted to his work. He served in Troy, New York, and then Ballston Spa, a picturesque village just outside of Saratoga Springs. In 1868, he was called to St. John's Detroit, Michigan. At the time, Detroit was a burgeoning Western city. It was in a way a preview of what was happening in Omaha, which would grow from a city of thirty thousand in 1880 to a city of one hundred forty thousand in 1890. This kind of growth made these cities very different places from what they had been a few decades before. In the earlier period of steady growth, the population had been made up largely of New Englanders and Upstate New Yorkers who chose to come West; but in the period of explosive growth, the population would include Irish, German, Scandinavian, Czech, and Italian immigrants. Worthington's congregation in Detroit was known as the largest in the West, numbering one thousand four hundred communicants. In his first address to the Diocese of Nebraska, he laments the fact that in 1885, Omaha, a city of sixty thousand, did not have an Episcopal Church with the ability to seat one thousand people. Given Worthington's orientation to the emerging urban life, it is understandable that those priests and laity, who were interested in establishing more mission stations across the state and in building more institutions like Nebraska College to produce vocations for that mission, would find his candidacy threatening.

George Worthington, br. 1840 Lenox, Massachusetts, Second Bishop of Nebraska 1885 until his death in 1908.

The division of the diocese in the election process was the result of a difference over the paradigm for ministry. The dominant pattern of ministry, up to this time in the Episcopal Church, was to get out and plant missions wherever one could. It had originated with the efforts of Hobart and Muhlenberg and had been projected westward with missionary bishops like Kemper, Talbot, and Clarkson. Once there, the next step was to found institutions such as schools and hospitals. Beginning in the 1870s, the idea of building cathedrals was added to the list of institutions necessary for the advancement of the Episcopal Church. Clarkson was devoted to this blueprint and had executed it with a good deal of success.

This pattern of ministry, which had begun in the 1840s, brought to the Episcopal Church a significant measure of growth after the long static period in which the Episcopal Church had been cocooned following the Revolutionary War. The aftermath of the Civil War proved even more conducive for the growth of the Episcopal Church. The reason for this growth is complicated; but it is because, in some measure, of a desire on the part of the country to get beyond conflict and to restore an age of consensus. Episcopal communities epitomized consensus, and in the previous period, they had failed to grow, precisely because they proceeded from consensus. In addition to valuing consensus, a significant portion of the country also began to look at Europe in a different way. It saw the stable institutions of Europe as something that America needed to create in order to deal with the broad changes that it was undergoing at the time. The Episcopal Church had preserved its European ties, and what had formally made it suspect now commended it. The exception, of course, was the Roman Catholic Church; but it was broadly viewed as anti-American. There was a growing conviction that the Episcopal Church could become "the American Catholic church."[4] William Reed Huntington, the rector of All Saints Worcester, Massachusetts, formulated the idea in a book entitled *The Church Idea: An Essay toward Unity*. Huntington published his book in 1870 and advocated its agenda as one of the most prominent priests of the Episcopal Church. The General Convention meeting in Chicago in 1886 adopted the summation of these views in a formula eventually known as the Chicago Lambeth Quadrilateral. A central assumption of this vision was that immigrants, who were coming to this country with Roman Catholic backgrounds, would see that they were America Catholics, not Roman Catholics.

But even as Huntington's thesis was being adopted, its primary intent was being undercut. The new ethnic minorities, while quick to shed most of their European culture, held on to their church as the one thing that they hadn't given up or betrayed. Cities like Detroit and Omaha were quickly becoming populations that no longer shared a common culture. As long as Omaha's growth had been fed largely by people whose origins were in New England and Upstate New York, the Episcopal Church was recognized as an institution well known for its leadership in the community. But in the city that swelled with new immigrant populations, where overlapping and competing communities made up the city, the Episcopal Church was just another player. Like everyone else, an Episcopal Church would have to elbow its way to be notice. Institutions, schools,

---

4 As late as the 1920s, Bishop Williams of Nebraska advocated that the Episcopal Church should change its name to "the American Catholic Church."

hospitals, cathedrals, would not produce congregations; congregations would produce institutions. Grasping what had changed in its environment would not come easily or uniformly, but the results of the 1884 election put Episcopalians in Omaha on notice.

Woolworth, grieving for the loss of his personal friend Robert Clarkson, was quick to read the consequences of the election of Worthington and seems to have begun to create a plan "B" with a group of his friends at Trinity Cathedral and in the city at large.[5] When the plan for a new parish to be called All Saints entered into the light of day at a meeting of a newly formed vestry on September 1, 1885, it is obvious that its conception had begun well before Bishop Worthington's arrival. Worthington arrived with his own plan for urban mission, and shortly after he arrived, he formed the City Mission Committee. Worthington's approval of Woolworth's proposal to establish a new parish in the city may have been in part motivated as a means of getting some "dissident interests" in the cathedral out of the way of his own ambitious high church adventure. The bishop launched his own urban strategy; and as he had in Detroit, he recruited a group of young celibate priests, who were idealistic and ritualistic-minded, and organized them in effort that he called the Associate Mission. At its peak in 1897, the Associate Mission served eleven congregations in the Omaha area.[6] The apparent success of the Associate mission at the time and the romantic aspect of its story have often attracted notice.[7] An assessment of its long-term effect, however, must be tempered by the fact that only a couple of its congregation have survived, the most important being St. Andrew's, whose success came largely at the expense of the ritualistic traditions that characterized the Associate Mission. The irony, of course, is that it was the effort that began with the laity and not the bishop, which came closest to fulfilling the bishop's vision of a large urban parish.

---

5 For example, he included Dr. George Miller, who he had known in Syracuse, New York, before they had moved to Omaha, on a list of petitioners for a new parish church, not because he was an Episcopalian, but because he was financially important in the city.

6 The Associated Mission in 1887 founded four missions: St. Andrew's, Forty-Second and Nicholas; St. Augustine's, Thirty-Third and Francis; Good Shepherd, Nineteenth and Lake; and St. Martin of Tours, Twenty-Third and F.

7 Dennis Paz, Social Catholicism in Omaha, 1877–1914, paper Missouri Valley History Conference, 1980.

Conception

Late on the afternoon of September 1, 1885, six laymen sat down with their new bishop in a suite, numbered 23, 24, and 25, in the Paxton Building. The Paxton Building, on Sixteenth and Farnam, was the common meeting place for Omaha's businessmen, and many of the city's deals were cut there. The bishop took charge of the meeting, and the group duly passed a motion to organize a new church to be called "All Saints Church Omaha." The next order of business was for the group to elect wardens and vestrymen to serve until the coming Easter, the time when parishes were canonical obliged to hold their annual meetings, at which time the new parish would hold its first regular election of wardens and vestry members. That same day, the papers of incorporation were filed with the Douglas County Clerk; the name of the new parish was officially recorded as "All Saints Church of the City of Omaha." Twenty-four hours after meeting with the bishop, the group reconvened with James M. Woolworth, their senior warden, in the chair. They elected Carroll S. Montgomery as treasurer and moved to call a rector. The motion that they passed offered the position to Rev. O. J. Booth of St. Catherine, Ontario, and it offered him an annual salary of $2,600, a rather handsome sum at the time.

Farnam Street 1889. View from the tower of City Hall, The Bee Newspaper Building, the New York Building, two small unidentified buildings and the Paxton Building, at the corner of 16th and Farnam. It was here that the Bishop came to meet with the laity lead by Woolworth and approved the founding of the parish and it was here that Zahner was interview by the vestry prior to his call in 1886. Illustration Harpers Weekly, February 16, 1889, p. 138-139

The dispatch with which this new vestry acted makes clear that the origins of All Saints lay in events which happened long before any official meeting. The conception of All Saints took place among a group of laity, which makes it more difficult to uncover what had motivated them to found a new parish and what they imagined it would be. The positions of bishops and priests are more likely to be part of a public record or to be otherwise intuited from their background. The clues to the motivations for the founding of All Saints are to be found in the more private lives of the laity who had signed their name to the venture. These names begin with those laymen who met with the bishop on September 1. They were James M. Woolworth, Alfred Hopkins, Carroll S. Montgomery, Richard R. Ringwald, and Dana S. Saunders.

We have already encountered James M. Woolworth, chancellor of the diocese, heavily involved in the 1884 election but not on the winning side. Woolworth had a rich background in the Episcopal Church and was on record on a number of church issues to a degree that is unusual for a layman. In the short run, no one was quite as import to the foundation of All Saints, and from his history, we can fairly reconstruct something of his vision for the new parish.

Woolworth was born in 1829 in Onodaga Valley, New York, a village about eight miles south of Syracuse, New York. His father, Samuel B. Woolworth, was an educator and in time was appointed be the principle of the Cortland Academy, located in Homer, about thirty miles south of Syracuse. The Cortland Academy was one of several academies chartered by the state of New York in one of the earliest attempts in the country to advance public education. They specialized in preparing boys for college and were justified as a means for strengthening the state's economy. The academy at Homer was closely association with the Presbyterian Church as was Woolworth's family.

In 1841, James M. Woolworth matriculated at Hamilton College. Hamilton College itself had been one of these early New York State academies; but in the 1840s, it had become a college, similar to the academy in Hamilton, New York, which exists today as Colgate College. Hamilton's faculty was affiliated with the Presbyterian and Congregational churches. The education offered at Hamilton was topnotch, specializing in the classics and in rhetoric. At the time, the epitome of an educated man was his ability to assemble a persuasive argument and to deliver it in a convincing manner. Woolworth was a top student graduating in 1849. He would use his rhetorical powers honed at Hamilton, to great effect in his occupation as lawyer, as politician in Nebraska and in his various roles in the church.

James M. Woolworth: br. 1829, Onadaga, NY,
Omaha's first lawyer, Chancellor of the Diocese,
All Saints' first Senior Warden, 1885-1893, d. 1904.

After graduating from Hamilton, Woolworth went to Law School in Albany. While he was in Albany, the Episcopal Diocese of New York relinquished its jurisdiction over much of Upstate New York, forming the new Episcopal Diocese of Albany. This is a clear indication of the growth that the Episcopal Church was beginning to enjoy in the latter half of the nineteenth century, particularly in New York State. The formation of the new Episcopal Diocese and the leadership of its new bishop, William C. Doane, intrigued Woolworth, even though he had not yet become an Episcopalian, and it left a lasting impression on him.

When he graduated from law school in 1854, he moved to Syracuse, New York, to begin the practice of law. Shortly after arriving in Syracuse, he joined the Episcopal Church, worshiping at a new north-side congregation, called the Church of our Savior. The rector of the Church of our Savior was the charismatic Henry Gregory. Gregory was much taken by the Oxford

Movement in England, which sought to restore the catholic side of the Church of England. Gregory was described by his contemporaries as "a soul which by some mistake had escaped out of the thirteenth century into the nineteenth." "He was," it was said, "slight in build, delicate in health, and ascetic in habits, his one interest in the world being the up building of the Kingdom of God—as he understood it." In spite of his frail health, Gregory had a passion for the missionary efforts in the West and to the Native Americans. He came by this latter interest from living in an area where the Iroquois Indians were present, particularly those of the Seneca nation. He traveled to Wisconsin in pursuit of this interest and was said to be the first to celebrate a Book of Common Prayer service in Milwaukee. He extended this jaunt by traveling to Fort Leavenworth, and there he joined an army unit that was to explore the Nebraska territory. It is not clear that the expedition ever made it to Nebraska. Nevertheless, Woolworth held the conviction, which he repeated often, that it was Gregory who had celebrated the first Book of Common Prayer service in Nebraska in or near Omaha. Gregory's influence on Woolworth can hardly be overestimated. He imbued Woolworth with a love for the Oxford Movement; and he, no doubt, fostered the idea in the young lawyer's head that his destiny lay in the Nebraska territory.

At the Church of Our Savior, Woolworth met his first wife, Helen Marie Beggs. Helen was born in New York in 1829; though her father, Charles Beggs, had been born in Scotland as was her mother. Both appear to have come to the United States at the same time; and the 1850 census lists her father's home as Pomfert, Chautaugue County, New York, and his occupation as a druggist.

Helen moved as a young woman to Syracuse where she too had come under the influence of Henry Gregory. She was baptized by Gregory on May 2, 1852, at the Church of Our Savior. There she met Woolworth, and the two were married by Gregory on June 1, 1854. Their first child, Charles Peck, was born on June 25, 1855, and was duly baptized on September 1, 1855. A couple of years after the birth of their first child, Woolworth moved his young family to Omaha, Nebraska, which had only recently been opened as a territory. He was the city of Omaha's first lawyer and went on to become one of the city's most prominent citizens. By 1885, Woolworth was fifty-six. He enjoyed the largest legal business in the city, his cases being largely confined to the most important civil suits that came up in the courts. He was a large investor in business property and real estate and was one of the principal investors in the Union Stockyards Company, an institution that transformed Omaha. His wife, Helen, died in 1867. His devotion to her and to the Church of Our Savior was demonstrated by a gift in 1892 of a baptismal font in her memory to that parish in which they had met.

By 1885, Woolworth had married a second time to Elizabeth Stanton Butterfield. Elizabeth, like Woolworth, was a native of Upstate New York. She had come West to study and work at Racine, the Episcopal college in Wisconsin. There she made an intense study of Ecclesiastical history, sacred music, and the Episcopal liturgy and was not without strong opinions on the matter. Late in marrying—it is likely before Woolworth's proposal—she imagined herself as dedicated to church work. She came to Omaha, where her sister lived, the wife of Clement Chase, to serve as head mistress at Brownell Hall. Her subsequent marriage to Woolworth was, however, a different means of pursuing the same ends; and she was very much a partner with Woolworth in church work. He had recently moved into a handsome residence on St. Mary's Street, which he called "Courtland," a reference to where he had been raised in New York. When Woolworth called the meeting of the vestry to order, he did so with an authority that came from a record of leading and supporting every significant venture of the Episcopal Church in Nebraska for the past twenty-five years.

A second significant member of this group, which had gathered that afternoon in which the parish was organized, was Carroll S. Montgomery. Montgomery had been born in Juneau, Wisconsin, on July 25, 1851. His parents had migrated from Ohio to this Southeastern Wisconsin town, not far from Milwaukee. He was educated nearby at the University of Wisconsin. He graduated from the literary department of that institution in 1872 and from the law department in 1873. He began the practice of law in Lincoln, Nebraska, shortly after his graduation. He soon moved to Omaha and with his father, Milton Montgomery, a decorated veteran of the Civil War, and formed a law firm, Montgomery and Son, which continues to this day as Baird Holm. In 1875, he returned home to Wisconsin to marry Martha A. Gray, daughter of H. H. Gray and a native of Darlington, Wisconsin.

On coming to Omaha, Montgomery joined Trinity Cathedral, which was in the process of approving the final architectural plans and letting bids for the construction of the new building. Montgomery soon found himself on the vestry of Trinity and became a valuable lieutenant for Woolworth in that effort. Montgomery's background in the Episcopal Church had begun in Madison, Wisconsin, which provided him some links to Woolworth's experience. The first Book of Common Prayer services in Wisconsin, as we have noted, was conducted in 1836 by the Rev. Henry Gregory, the ubiquitous ritualistic missionary who had played such a profound roll in Woolworth's own spiritual journey. Jackson Kemper, the missionary bishop who had visited Nebraska at the time of its opening as a territory, had become the first bishop of Wisconsin. On November 1, 1869, Kemper laid the cornerstone of a cathedral in Milwaukee, which was called All Saints. It is said to be the first cathedral in the United States, though others contend for that honor. The impact of the cathedral project in Milwaukee on Montgomery was similar to the impact of the cathedral project in Albany, also called All Saints, on Woolworth. It is likely that this synergism was the source of the name for the new parish in Omaha, which these two men were instrumental in founding. The name, All Saints, was rather rare in the Episcopal Church up to this time, having no precedence in neighbors like Iowa, Minnesota, or Missouri.[8]

As Montgomery and Woolworth had worked together on building the cathedral, they were allied in the electing council of 1884. It is, therefore, little surprise to see them working together in the enterprise of founding a new parish. The importance of Woolworth to the foundation of All Saints is hard to overstate; but in the long run, Montgomery would have a far greater impact on the parish, succeeding Woolworth as senior warden in 1891 and continuing in the position for the next thirty years!

The third member of the core group was Alfred P. Hopkins, who was elected junior warden at the initial meeting founding the parish. Hopkins was a cashier at the Commercial National Bank, which had been recently organized by Ezra Millard. Upon the death of Millard, in the summer of 1886, Hopkins was elected president. His board of directors included prominent members of the community: William. G. Maul, Edward M. Andresen, Andrew Henry, L. B. Williams, E. M. Morsman, G. M. Hitchcock, and Joseph Garneau, Jr.

The fourth member of what seems to have been the original core of the vestry was Richard R. Ringwalt. Ringwalt was a freight agent for the railroad. He was born in 1850 in New York. He married in 1873; and he and his wife had their first child, a daughter, in Michigan prior moving to Omaha. In 1880, he established a home in Omaha. He was one of the younger and more modest members of the group, having a good job and a young family. While he did not qualify as "a mover and shaker," he played a significant role in the establishment of the parish. He serviced as secretary to the vestry from its first meeting with the bishop until he resigned and transferred to St. Matthais in the end of 1889. The reason he gave was that

8 The two parishes in Missouri named All Saints were founded in 1887 and 1951. The rise of the name in the Anglican Church is particularly marked by the London church, All Saints, Margaret Street, inspired by John Mason Neale, dedicated on 1859.

he was relocating his residence in the city to Tenth Street and was thus in close proximity to the new St. Mathias.

The minutes from the meeting with the bishop on September 1 indicate the presence of a fifth person, Dana Sanders. Since Sanders does not appear in any of the subsequent records of the parish, it is reasonable to assume that he was a layman present as a representative of the diocese and was not part of the original group interested in the founding of a new parish. Indeed, while the minutes treat this meeting with the bishop as a vestry meeting, it was, in fact, an ad hoc committee meeting convened by the bishop.

Woolworth and Hopkins were listed as senior warden and junior warden, respectively. The names of Montgomery and Ringwalt head a list of vestry men to which were added five additional names: George W. Ames, William A. Redick, William N. Babcock, George L. Miller, and Charles A. H. McAuley.

Ames was a realtor with an office at 1506 Farnam. He lived in a large home on the northwest corner of Park and Michigan avenues. His inclusion on the vestry was likely because of the wealth that he had accrued as a successful realtor. Ames emerged as an active member of the vestry continuing to serve until the annual meeting of 1891 when he did not get reelected despite having been nominated.

Redick was twenty-six years old and the deputy clerk of the U.S. Internal Revenue Office in Omaha. He was the son of John I. Redick, a contemporary of James M. Woolworth. Like Woolworth, Redick's father was a lawyer heavily involved in the Omaha real estate market. Unlike Woolworth, John was a self-made man from Ohio and with no connection to the Episcopal Church in his past. The senior Redick lived in a stately home set on fifty acres of ground, "beautifully improved," sitting just to the west of the city limits. The son seems to have been on the vestry as a kind of proxy so that "the Redicks" might participate in this great adventure which would develop a church on the west side of the city in which they had a stake. In fact, the young Redick became a valuable contributing member of the vestry, until he relocated his family in Los Angeles in 1888. He, however, returned to Omaha in a couple of years and rejoined All Saints and would again serve on the vestry and ultimately become one of its senior wardens.

Babcock was a freight agent for the railroad like Ringwalt. He was the general Western agent for the Chicago North Western and took office at 1403 Farnam. He was, in fact, living at the Paxton Hotel in 1885. At the time, he was about forty and his family was apparently still living in Denver. If he had plans at the time of becoming a permanent resident in the city, they seemed to have evaporated before long. After a couple of meeting, he resigned because of an impending move out of the city.

Dr. Miller attended the first meeting of the vestry on November 2, 1885, but subsequently resigned. Miller was a contemporary of Woolworth. He was born in Upstate New York and had actually crossed paths with Woolworth in Syracuse where Miller was completing his medical education and Woolworth was beginning his law practice. He had preceded Woolworth in moving to Omaha, and he recounts how he chanced to meet Woolworth on Woolworth's first visit to Omaha. He had, he reported to the newspaper, gone out of curiosity to river dock to witness the arrival of a steam boat, only to encounter his former acquaintance disembarking. On Woolworth's subsequent move with his family to Omaha, the family stayed as a guest for a while with the Millers. Miller's medical practice was in the process of changing into real estate development, politics, and publishing. In 1865, he founded the *Omaha Herald* (a precursor of the *Omaha World-Herald*). Miller had been instrumental in bringing the first congregational minister to Omaha in 1855, and there is no indication that he had ever belonged to the Episcopal Church. It seems likely that Woolworth had prevailed upon his friendship with Miller to allow his name to be put on the vestry list in 1885 as a means of giving it some prestige. That first vestry meeting that he attended authorized the purchase of two lots and called C. J. Booth as rector at an annual salary of $2,500. To the inner group who had been in on the conception of the project from the beginning, this would have seemed timely, but to someone on the outer edge of the group, these actions might well have seemed quite precipitous; and Miller sent his resignation.

Another member of the original vestry was McCauley, whose name was recorded as McAuley in the vestry minutes. He was a captain in the U.S. Army who was serving in the Quartermaster Core for the Department of the Platte. His residence at the time was 1026 S. Twenty-Ninth Avenue. McCauley has the distinction of never having shown up for a meeting, and like Miller, he tendered his resignation prior to the second meeting.

Stabilizing the Vestry

The new vestry was faced with three urgent issues that it had to face concurrently. They had to stabilize the vestry, arrange for a building, and call a rector. The stability of the vestry was immediately tested by the fact that McCauley was not present, and it was in short order further tested by the resignation of George L. Miller. It appears that neither man had more than a casual interest in the project of building a new Episcopal Church. They had been chosen on the hope that they would use their social standing and wealth to back the project. They were quickly replaced by A. H. Bishop and S. P. Morse at the November 14 vestry meeting, the same meeting that received the resignation of McCauley and Miller. Obviously, the vestry was prepared for their resignations. A. H. Bishop, who replaced Miller, was the manager of Consolidated Tank Lines and lived at 1917 Chicago. S. P. Morse was the head of a dry goods emporium. His store was located on Sixteenth and Farnam. In 1880, while establishing himself in Omaha, he lived in a boarding house at 1711 Jackson with his wife Isabel and their two children, Herbert, 4, who had been born in New York, and Samuel, 1, who was born in Nebraska, indicating the newness of Morse's enterprise to the city. By 1885, now thirty-three, he moved his family to their own residence, 420 S. Twenty-Third Street. Samuel would be a member of the first confirmation class presented to the bishop in May of 1887. Both Bishop and Morse were good additions to the vestry, and they would both be quite active in the ensuing months.

A third challenge to the stability of the vestry followed in short order when at the April 12 meeting, William Babcock turned in his resignation. The reason, he explained, was that he was moving from Omaha. In fact, Babcock was a resident in a hotel at the time of his appointment; and his family remained in Denver, raising from the beginning the question of whether he would become a permanent resident of the city. Nevertheless, his resignation was not anticipated by the vestry, which suggests that something had changed Babcock's plans. At the next meeting in May, the vestry elected C. A Potter. Potter's name had already shown up on the list of individuals who made a pledge to the parish capital fund drive. Potter was a law reporter and clerk with Groff and Montgomery as the firm was now known. He was thirty-two years old at the time and was newly married. In effect, Montgomery was his boss. Given Montgomery's prominence in the attempt to found the new parish, one might suspect a degree of arm twisting behind Potter's contribution to the capital fund drive and to his subsequent willingness to join the vestry. However, Potter emerged as an effective member of the vestry. His first child, Samuel, would be the third person baptized in the new parish; and a daughter, Edna, would be baptized a couple of years later.

With Potter's appointment, the vestry began at last to enjoy a degree of stability, at least as much as one can expect vestries to be. Its members range from prominent elders of the city, like James M. Woolworth and George Ames to young professional men at the start of their careers, like Potter, Ringwalt, and Redick. If they were long on lawyers and realtors, they included a couple of railroad agents, a dry goods merchant, a banker, and a plant manager.

The Location and First Building

The speed with which land was purchased for the new building again shows that plans where well on their way before a first vestry ever met. On November 14, at the second meeting of the vestry, a motion was made to buy lots 1 and 2 in the newly platted Clarkes addition. The Clarkes addition lay on the north side of St. Mary's Avenue, on the west edge of the city. The edge of the city on the west had for some time been defined by a line of hills, which presented a challenge to transportation and water supply. Nineteenth Street ran north and south at the bottom of the hill line, and Twenty-Fourth Street more or less negotiated the ridge. Imagine for a moment what a daunting task it would be to climb that hill, say on the upper end of Farnam Street, in mud season! In order to avoid that problem, Howard Street had stopped at Seventeenth and angled off to the south, becoming St. Mary's Avenue. It headed southwest toward a break in the hills in order to make a more commodious passage to the west. A historic picture gives us a view looking north from the corner of Seventeenth and Farnam. Taken in 1868, it provides a picture of the effect of the hills on the expansion of the city. Far in the distance, you can see the Capitol Building along with some other buildings clustered around it.

This rise, quite steep in places, had prompted the city's growth up to then to go south along Tenth Street or north along Nineteenth Street. This is a story that is often repeated in Omaha's development, as later along on Twenty-Fourth, Forty-Second, Seventy-Second, and Ninetieth. St. Barnabas, which had been founded in 1868, was located first on Ninth and Howard, then Fourteenth and Cass, and by 1885, at 510 North Nineteenth Street, a few blocks north of the Trinity Cathedral. St. Philip's was located a few blocks further north of St. Barnabas at 813 N. Nineteenth Street. The Mission of Good Shepherd, which at the time lacked a permanent location, was eventually settled at 1617 North Nineteenth Street. To imagine oneself over the ridge was to imagine a city whose most powerful impetus for growth was West, something that few could do at the time. The clustering of churches indicates that their leadership found it difficult to imagine a westward growth of the city; and those, like the vestry of All Saints and the backers of St. John's Creighton, whose cornerstone was laid shortly after All Saints was started, were thinking outside of the box.

The more impressive growth had gone to the south of the center of the city along Tenth Street, ascended to the heights of the Missouri River bluffs. The steep bluffs along the west side of the river were suspended at the point in the north where Sixteenth Street intersected them at Grace Street and where Tenth Street intersected them to the south at about Pierce Street. At the center of this basin, on the river's edge, the ferry had established a landing; and the rail road bridge followed later, a little to the south at Pacific Street. The main railroad tracks would cut southwest through a notch in the hills, carved by a creek, to reach the Platte corridor that had been chosen as the route of the transcontinental rail road. Secondary tracks ran north and south on the Missouri's flood plain to serve Omaha's developing industry such as the Metz Brewery located to the south or the Union Pacific shops to the north.

It was on these proximate heights to the south that Omaha built its first "Gold Coast." These included a number of great Victorian houses that had begun to appear shortly after the end of the Civil War. From this height, they looked over the river to the east and down on the city to the north. In the midst for them, the Episcopal Church created an enclave that consisted of Bishop Worthington's home, Brownell Hall, which was in 1886 in the process of building an impressive hall that would serve as residence and class room. In 1890, adjacent to the new hall, the school added a lovely stone chapel, St. Matthias. The location can still be recognized from the church, which is preserved as Dietz Memorial Methodist Church, and from the names of the streets, Worthington and Williams, which run between Tenth and Sixth streets, named for the second and third bishops of the Episcopal Diocese.

Those who were in the process of conceiving All Saints had a distinctly different sense of the city. They were a part of the city that looked at the possibility of pressing the city west by means of St. Mary's Avenue. This avenue has the distinction, among Omaha streets, of being the first attempt to break the pattern of the grid. It ran at an angle to Howard southwest, seeking an easier grade to the west. The angle that began at Seventeenth Street was a means of avoiding the steep rise by skirting the ridge line that ran south from the height on which the state capitol, originally, and Central High School, subsequently, had been build.

An alternative to skirting the rise was grading, which the city did extensively later on, as for example, on Harney and Dodge where houses were left ten feet above the new grade. In fact, shortly after All Saints completed its new building, the city graded the street on its north side, requiring the vestry to build a retaining wall. Woolworth, at his own his expense, supervised the construction of the retaining wall. In the end, grading won out, and the diagonal pattern of St. Mary's Avenue was relegated to a curious anomaly.

In the 1880s, several prominent homes were built along St. Mary's Avenue. One of these belonged to J. M. Woolworth. It sat at the corner of St. Mary's and Twenty-Second Street. None of these stately homes survived, with the exception of the two built by Thomas Kimball. A few blocks further west, the newly platted Clarkes addition began on the north side of St. Mary's. It ran north uphill for two blocks on what was Twenty-Sixth Street to what was roughly an extension of Howard Street, which was designated half-Howard until it was changed to Dewey.[9] From here, it ran west to Twenty-Seventh Street and returned south to St. Mary's Avenue. If one continued on St. Mary's, past the Clarkes addition, one dipped into the valley and passed along the south side of the large fifty-acre subdivision owned by J. I. Redick. It was here that he had built his mansion; and clearly, he and others had already come to believe that it was here where Omaha's next and greatest Gold Coast would arise.

The upper end of the Clarkes addition sat well above St. Mary's Avenue at the top of the hill. That meant that a church located there would be visible from all directions. It was, in short, a stunning location. The acquiring of such a fortuitous location is not all that surprising given the fact that Woolworth had been playing the Omaha real estate game for nearly thirty years.

The sale was executed in December. As it turned out, about half of lot 1, thirty-two feet, had been taken by the city for the extension of Howard Street, known as Half Howard. This resulted in the contract specifying the south half of lot 1, lot 2, and the northern thirty-two feet of lot 3. The total cost was $6,500. An escrow payment of $1,500 appears to have been paid, and the balance due was paid by means of a mortgage of $5,000. It is likely that the cash part had been paid by Woolworth himself at an earlier date.

The Building

Like the selection of the lots, the selection of an architect was never discussed by the vestry or at least it was never recorded in the vestry's minutes. Nevertheless on March 12, a set of plans, drawn up by Mendelssohn and Fisher Architects, at the time Omaha's most prominent architects, were

9 This was because Howard was not continued, and while the new street along the north border of Clarks addition was roughly where Howard would go if it had been extended, it was never called Howard, and it was eventually renamed Dewey.

shown to the vestry who had also just receive a favorable report on the status of the capital funds drive from the treasurer. The report showed that the vestry had pledged $3,100. Woolworth's name was on the top of the list, with the largest of the gifts. In addition to the vestry, thirteen members of the community were listed as having pledged $2,000, making the total amount to date $5,100. The estimated cost of the plan, which the vestry was shown, however, was $8,000. With the money left in the capital fund after the lots were paid for, the actual deficit was $5,000. Woolworth offered to pay half of this, effectively raising his pledge by $2,500, and he promised to personally secure the remaining from others. Woolworth's philanthropy toward All Saints is remarkably generous, keeping in mind that he also was committed to two other major efforts of the Episcopal Church at the time. Brownell Hall, where his second wife, Elizabeth, had served as principal for two years, was in the process of building its new hall on Tenth Street. It had been, and particularly now that he was married to Elizabeth, a beneficiary of Woolworth's charity. The second project was Child's Hospital, on whose board Elizabeth was also serving. The board headed by Medora Clarkson, the former bishop's wife, had also been a regular beneficiary of Woolworth's philanthropy.

It is clear that Woolworth's vision for All Saints was a stone church. He and his fellow vestryman Ames traveled at their own expense to Denver to examine the suitability of the red granite available from the well-known Castle Rock Quarry in Colorado. Upon their return, they reported at the next vestry meeting, April 12, that the stone was quite suitable for a church building. Holding out for stone construction, however, did not help with the gap between the funding that was available and the cost of building, and it would mean an inevitable delay in the completion of a building. The vestry initially proposed to deal with the inherent delay by proposing to build a temporary church building on the south end of the property, not to exceed $1,000, and/or to find a temporary space were worship could be conducted in the meantime. Most of the group must have continued to worship at Trinity Cathedral, which would explain how the $205 contribution had shown up on the altar of Trinity Cathedral in the Easter collection that year marked "for All Saints"!

With Easter came the annual meeting. On Easter Monday, April 26, 1886, All Saints at its first annual meeting received the report that the total subscription of the coming year as $5,995 and then proceeded to elect, for its first time, a vestry. Those elected were, in fact, the same as those who had been serving the past year. The vestry, duly elected, met immediately after the annual meeting adjourned. The subcommittee, which had been assigned to find temporary space, reported that none could be found in the city. That may be because of a lack of imagination on the part of the committee, but the rapid growth of the city in the Eighties might very well have made open meeting space a scarce commodity. The vestry, as a consequence, voted to rescind the motion for a temporary building; and a new motion was approved calling for the speedy erection of a church building to be constructed in the main of wood according to the plan not to exceed $5,000. Furnishings and heating were not included in the motion and were left for a solution at a later time. The motion was made by Ringwalt. Ringwalt, the young railroad shipping agent, with a wife and two kids and a pledge of $100 to the capital fund, was what one might call "a small stakeholder." He was the voice of practicality, and the motion prevailed.

Accepting wooden construction must have proven disappointing to Woolworth, but it did mean that construction could start immediately. Even more importantly, it meant that the primary goal of the design would not be compromised. The new space would seat five hundred persons, significantly larger than the capacity of Trinity Cathedral. This was a fateful decision that kept All Saints on track to become a large urban parish. Had the decision gone the other way, All Saints might have looked a lot like St. Matthias Church, build on Tenth Street in 1890. It was a charming stone structure that cost $10,000, more than All Saints, but it could only seat a couple of a hundred people. The choice of stone would have shrunk the size of the building and very likely would have locked it into a fate similar to St. Matthias, which was abandoned in the 1920s and ultimately sold to be used as a Methodist Church.

The large wooden structure that was begun in 1886 would serve All Saints for two decades when it would be replaced by a grand brick Tudor Gothic structure. It would remain in the history of the parish as that "great wooden arc" where a great congregation had had its beginnings.

The church structure was placed on the north side of the property running east and west along Dewey. The dimensions of the building are missing, but it appears that it ran the full length of the lot, giving it a length of nearly a hundred feet. The lot ran south seventy feet, indicating that the width was about sixty feet. Because the grade on Howard Street had been lowered to make the descent to the west less challenging for traffic, this large church structure sat well above the street, particularly on the west end of the lot. The exterior appearance of the church also must be guessed at as no picture of it survives. There does survive a picture of the interior taken about 1899. One is impressed by the breath of the space that it enclosed. The original seating was divided by a center aisle and two side aisles. This breadth was accomplished by large scissor trusses. At the same time, height had to be sacrificed. This resulted in windows that were more rounded than pointed as one would expect in Gothic architecture, which they were attempting. A contemporary source described the windows as "high round arches." The stained-glass windows were in the form of geometrical drawings with "blue heading." It would be best to think of this structure as a modified Gothic, the modification being the loss of vertical height driven by the desire to create the largest possible seating capacity.

Having committed themselves to action, the vestry faced yet another hurdle. The bid from the contractor, Hamilton and Woolsey of Omaha, came in at $5,200, exclusive of furniture, heating apparatus, and the construction of a room for the same and of glass windows and sashes. The vestry acceded to the new figure, and at long last, work began. The progress in the building can be marked by the report to the vestry on September 27. The vestry was informed at that meeting that the new church building had been insured for $5,000, indicating that there was something to insure. On September 28, the vestry met to award the subcontracts for heating, church furniture, ceiling, and for casing around the trusses. The latter item suggests that the trusses were iron, as the purpose of the casing was to make the trusses appear to be beams.

Canon Whitemarsh wrote in the diocesan journal of 1892 about the finished result. "The building seats five hundred people, and it has a considerably elevated choir. The parish is known for its excellent music program. The windows on the east and west are large and handsomely jeweled." Other sources tell us that the sanctuary was finished with highly polished oak. Woolworth had seen that the new church had a pipe organ. Covering the service at which the building was opened, the *Omaha Excelsior* wrote, "The sweet-toned Roosevelt organ was given by Ms. Meliora Woolworth in memory of her brother. It is one of Roosevelt's best instruments encased in a highly polished and carved oak."[10] The inscription read "In Memory of Robert Harper Clarkson Woolworth."[11]

On the south end of the property, a rectory was built. The rectory was started in August of 1886, which coincided with Louis Zahner's acceptance of the call to be the first rector of All Saints. Woolworth undertook the provision of a rectory and agreed to pay for it himself. The

10 *Excelsior*, January 29, 1987.

11 Robert Woolworth died in 1979 and is buried in Prospect Hill adjacent to his father's grave which is marked by a large Celtic cross. His name indicates the close relationship between his father and Bishop Clarkson. He was not yet five years old when he died and was survived by his parents and sister, Meliora, who was born January 13, 1973, being a year older than her brother.

way he accomplished this was to move his former residence, which stood for many years on Twelfth and Howard to the southeast portion of the church's property. His cost in the end was $8,000. Upon the rectory's completion, he donated it to the parish.

On January 22, the minutes reported that "a meeting of the vestry of All Saints Church, Omaha, had taken place at 7:30 p.m. this day in the Church." On the following day, January 23, an official opening was held. A difficult task had come to an end. The remaining task was the calling of a rector, which was not without its own drama.

The Call

The third task the newly formed vestry of 1885 faced was calling a rector. At its first meeting, on September 2, the name of a candidate was introduced. With the same kind of dispatch as land was purchased, a call was issued to Rev. O. J. Booth of St. Catherine's, Ontario, Canada. The motion was amended to set his salary at $2,500, a generous salary for the time. Upon approval of the motion, the vestry directed Woolworth to telegraph Booth; and apparently, Booth was inclined to accept.

There is good evidence that Woolworth had been the source of this name. Like many other things such as the site, building plans, and finances, much work had been done prior to the formation of a vestry, all of which can be traced to Woolworth. Booth's name likely was brought to Woolworth's attention by his daughter Jeanie and her husband Lt. Guy Howard. They had been married at Trinity Cathedral on February 11, 1884. The groom was the eldest son of Gen. O. O. Howard, commander of the Department of the Platte. Young Howard was serving in the Twelfth Infantry as aide-de-camp to his father. Following his marriage, Howard was posted at the historic Fort Niagara, New York, and was allowed to bring his new wife to live on the base. After the Civil War, Fort Niagara was expanded as a result of thriving industrial area of Buffalo and Erie. It was here that the army's equipment was being manufactured, and this was an important post for a young officer.

Immediately across the Niagara River from the fort was the Canadian village of Niagara-on-the-Lake, and a few miles further down the coast was the city of St. Catherine. The Howards' connection with the Anglican Church on the Canadian side is shown by the baptism of their first child, Woolworth's grandson, who was baptized at Fort Niagara. Otis Woolworth Howard was born at Fort Niagara on February 11, 1887, and was baptized on April 10, Easter, by Rev. E. Steward Jones. Jones is identified in the registry as an Episcopal minister of the Diocese of Niagara, Canada. Even though it was performed at Fort Niagara and officiated over by a Canadian priest, Woolworth saw to it that it was recorded in All Saints statistical registry, it being the second entry under baptisms. It is not difficult to conclude that the Howards had communicated to Woolworth their enthusiasm for the Canadian church and about the ministers that they had met there. Booth was likely recommended as someone who possessed exceptional abilities and who would be interested in serving in the American church, as a number of Canadians were at the time.

On November 14, 1885, a month after having issued the offer, however, the vestry passed a motion withdrawing its offer to Booth. The language is unusual if Booth had simply turned them down. Not long after the withdrawal, Booth accepted a call to Broken Bow, Nebraska. What had transpired between September 2 and November 14? From the evidence at hand, the apparent answer is that the vestry had begun to face the financial challenge that they had undertaken. The purchase of two lots in the Clark subdivision required them to secure a mortgage of $5,000. They also had to deal with the resignation of two vestry members, Dr. George L. Miller and Charles H. A. McCauley, from one of whom they would have expected to receive large contributions. It was also probably clear by then that there would not be for some months a congregation to lead. Woolworth was directed by the motion to notify Booth that the offer was withdrawn. It was not likely a pleasant task for him, and it is not clear whether he himself might have realized that a call was premature.

The issue of a rector remained moot until March 12. At their meeting, the vestry found itself presented with another name, William E. Wright of Somerville, New Jersey. There is no indication of the source of this name, and after a brief discussion, the vestry offered him a salary of $1,500. The delay and the reduced sum provide further evidence that the reason for the withdrawal of the offer to Booth had been, at least partly financial. Wright responded to the offer immediately in the affirmative and indicated that he would arrive in Omaha by May 9. All of this was duly reported to the vestry at its April 26 meeting, which had followed immediately after the parish's first annual meeting, and it is likely that the news about the prospect had been shared with those attending the annual meeting as well. The vestry, thinking that they had solved the rector problem, turned back to the serious business of building a church.

May 9 came and went without any sign of Wright. There was no official notice taken of Wright's failure to show up and no motion to withdraw the offer. It might be noted that when the next name came before the vestry, they decided to secure a railroad pass so that the candidate could actually come to Omaha before the vestry offered a call.

The new name before the vestry was Louis Zahner who was the incumbent in a small Episcopal church in the very rural town of Bloomsburg, Pennsylvania. In the 1880s, Bloomsburg had a population of about four thousand. The railroad pass, procured, one suspects, by one of the railway agents on the vestry, was promptly sent; and Zahner traveled to Omaha in July. There are no details of the visit available other than it had cost the vestry $45 to host him. Zahner would have seen work on the building under way, experienced the vitality of the Omaha community, and had been able to gauge the seriousness of the vestry with which he would work. In turn, the vestry would have been able to gauge what Zahner would bring to its effort and the likelihood that he would show up if said he would.

Shortly after the visit, on August 2, the vestry met, and Mr. Ringwalt moved that it be "resolved that the vestry extend to Rev. Louis Zahner of Bloomsburg, Pennsylvania, a unanimous call to the rectorship of this parish at an annual salary of $2,000 and the rent of a house." The motion was seconded by Potter. It was further ordered that his services were to begin at any date between October 15 and November 1 of 1886, as would be "most convenient to Mr. Zahner." Zahner responded without hesitation to the vestry's call. His reply came as a letter that the vestry had copied into the parish minutes.

Gentlemen:

> I have to acknowledge the receipt of your official action, communicated to me by Mr. Woolworth, inviting me to become your Rector, and to thank you for the honor you have thus done me. Having this matter before me for some time and having prayerfully considered the same, I am prepared to give you my decision at once. I hereby accept the rectorship which you have offered me and will try so to arrange my affairs that I may reach Omaha about October 15, prox. Trusting that under the guidance and blessing of the Great Head of the Church, my ministry in the new Parish of All Saints may be abundantly fruitful. I remain, Louis Zahner.

The third leg of the stool was in place, the vestry was as stable as one can expect a vestry to be, the construction of the church was proceeding, and a firm date had been set for the arrival of a rector. With Zahner's reply, Woolworth undertook the provision of a rectory to be located adjacent to the church building on the parcel of land the parish already owned. Zahner did arrive on October 15 and started to work immediately.

The First Rector

Louis Zahner, All Saints' first Rector, 1887-1891,
br. 1847, Shanesville, Ohio, d. 1908.

Louis Zahner, a large imposing man, sat down in the offices of the Paxton Building and assumed the chair for the first time on December 4. He had been in town little more than a month, and it was the first time for a vestry at All Saints to be chaired by its own rector. The following month, on January 22, he again chaired a meeting of the vestry; and it was another first. This time, it was the first time that the vestry met "in the church," that is, in its very own building. On the following day, Sunday, the twenty-third, he was installed as rector by Bishop Worthington, and the building was officially opened with a blessing. George Franklin Seymour, the bishop of the Diocese of Springfield, was present and preached the sermon at Worthington's request.[12] Seymour, before assuming charge of the Illinois diocese, had been a prominent professor of church history and then dean of General Seminary. He brought to the occasion an element of national prominence, something very much appreciated by Worthington. In the course of the service, Worthington installed Thomas Pennell as choirmaster. This was an unusual ceremony that signaled the importance that was to be given to the role of music in the new parish, something very highly valued by Woolworth and his wife Elizabeth.

After the festivities on the twenty-third, Zahner sat down in the late afternoon and began entering names of the families that had joined the parish in the parish's brand-new statistical record book. It was, it would seem, something he would not allow himself to do until he was officially the rector! When he had finished that day, he had listed thirty-eight families. Among those names were many which continued to be significant in the life of All Saints for many years to come. As Zahner reflected back over the three months that followed his arrival in October, he must have felt a great deal of satisfaction for prior to his arrival, there was no building, no membership, and no parish records. When he left four and half years later, the congregation counted 250 communicants, making it the second largest Episcopal parish in the city.

Zahner came to All Saints with an unusual background. He owed his ordination to the priesthood in the Episcopal Church to the Muhlenberg Memorial which had been passed by the general convention of the Episcopal Church in 1853. In that memorial, William Augustus Muhlenberg, the prominent New York City priest, argued that the Episcopal Church was faced with a crisis with which it would not be able to deal with by ordinary means. He proposed that:

> A wider door be opened for admission to the Gospel ministry than that through which her candidates for Holy Orders were now obliged to enter. Besides such candidates among her own members, it is believed that men can be found among the other bodies of Christians around us, who would gladly receive ordination at your hands, could they obtain it, without that entire surrender which would now be required of them, of all the liberty in public worship to which they have been

12 George Franklin Seymour was consecrated bishop of Springfield in 1878. He had formerly been elected as bishop of Illinois, prior to Dekoven, and like Dekoven after him, he was blocked by the House of Bishops because he was considered a ritualist. Seymour had been at General Seminary as professor of church history from 1865 to 1875 and then as dean from 1875 till his election.

> accustomed—men, who could not bring themselves to conform in all particulars to our prescriptions and customs, but yet sound in the faith, and who, having the gifts of preachers and pastors, would be able ministers of the New Testament.

Louis Zahner was precisely that kind of candidate. He was the son of a minister of the German Reform Church in United States. His father, John George Zahner, was born December 21, 1821, in Oberdigisheim, Baden-Wurttemberg, Germany. John George began his studies at the Mission House at Basel whose aim was to train young Lutheran and Reform men to go into the foreign mission field, particularly to pastor German immigrants. In 1845, before completing his degree, his father immigrated to the United States and completed his studies at Mercersberg in Pennsylvania. His mother was Whilhemina Cappel who had come to this country from Hesse when she was sixteen; she's well educated and quite refined. John George and Whilhemina married in Pittsburg in 1847, and his ordination followed quickly. Together they went into the missionary field in Eastern Ohio. He served a congregation in Shanesville, Ohio, for eleven years (1847–1858). It was here that Louis was born, the first of ten children. From there, his father moved to a congregation in Ragersville (1858–1868) and finally, for four years, to a congregation in Stone Creek, New Philadelphia, Ohio. John Zahner is highly thought of as one of the pioneer ministers of the reformed church.

Louis followed in his father's footsteps, matriculating in 1864 at Franklin Marshall in Lancaster, Pennsylvania. Franklin College had been founded by four prominent ministers from the German reformed church and the Lutheran Church, in conjunction with numerous Philadelphians. The school was established as a German college whose goal was "to preserve our present republican system of government" and "to promote those improvements in the arts and sciences which alone render nations respectable, great and happy." Marshall College, which was located at Mercersberg, Pennsylvania, began to explore the possibility of a merger with Franklin. On June 7, 1853, the combined college was formally dedicated at Fulton Hall in Lancaster, Pennsylvania. The merger created an all-male reformed church institution that combined the resources of both schools.

When Zahner arrived, the faculty was headed by John Williamson Nevin, a prominent theologian of the Mercersberg school. Nevin, with Phillip Schaff, led a "liberal catholicizing" movement within the reformed churches in the United States. Not only did the movement champion the adoption of English as the language for worship; it also advocated a revival of religious ritual much like the Oxford Movement had in England. Schaff had, in fact, carried on a correspondence with Edward Bouverie Pusey, one of the leaders of the Oxford Movement. Both men were tried for heresy by the reformed church, and both were acquitted.

Louis Zahner graduated from Franklin Marshall on June 27, 1872, with a doctor of divinity degree. There is no record that he attempted to be ordained in the reformed church, which suggests that his intension to seek orders in the Episcopal Church must have come about in the course of his studies. The school's ecumenical orientation must have suggested it to him, and his own father must have supported it, for he had himself a strong ecumenical orientation beginning with his early training at Basil Mission House in Germany.

Louis took additional courses at General Seminary completing yet another degree. He was ordained by the bishop of Central Pennsylvania in 1875. Soon after his ordination, he met Mary A. Lechler of New Castel, Delaware. Mary was raised in the Episcopal Church and was an organist and a trained musician, in the tradition of John Henry Hopkins.[13] By outward appearances, they seemed mismatched. Mary was very petite, and Louis was a very large man. Yet Mary's musical ability would always serve as a complement to Louis Zahner's ministry, and Mary seems to have consistently had an important share in his ministry. They were married June 27, 1877, at Immanuel-on-the-Greene in New Castel, the church in which she had been raised. While still in Delaware, a daughter, Margaret, was born to them. The fact that Immanuel-on-the-Green has no record of Margaret's baptism suggests that they resided somewhere else in Delaware. Within the year following Margaret's birth, they moved to Bloomsburg, Pennsylvania, where Louis had his first charge, St. Paul's Episcopal Church.

Bloomsburg, located along the storied Susquehanna River, was one of those small cities that boomed as a result of the Civil War. Its historic Episcopal Church founded in 1793 was located where Main Street was intersected by Iron St. The former indicated that the church was at the center of town, and the later indicated what made the city prosperous, its iron industry. The Episcopal congregation undertook a major building program in 1868, completing a handsome limestone Gothic church in 1870. The church was flanked by a large three-story brick rectory. Bloomsburg had both a small college and a German American population that attracted the young Zahner. By all measures, he must have considered himself fortunate to be rector of such a fine and established parish. The call

13 John Henry Hopkins taught music at General Seminary in 1855–1857 and authored and composed "We Three Kings." He was considered the dean of music for the Episcopal world.

to come to Omaha, to a congregation that was hastily building a church, a wooden one at that, without a congregation, must have appealed to a sense of adventure and to the sense of sacrifice that had characterized his father's ministry on the Ohio frontier.

When Zahner came to Omaha to join in the founding of a new parish, he found a city that was in a stage of rapid growth. A good deal of that growth was being fed by German immigration. By 1890, Germans comprised 23 percent of Omaha's population. By 1910, 57.4 percent of Omaha's total population of more than 124,000 was of German descent. It must have been part of what had attracted him to Omaha. He extended his ministry to this German-speaking population and held German language services on Sunday evenings throughout his tenure with the belief that the Episcopal Church offered the German immigrant the spiritual home they need in their new country.[14] These German language services were All Saints first attempt at an outreach ministry.

While we have little record of events from Zahner's tenure and no personal reminiscences, we have sufficient evidence to get a sense of what his ministry was like. The first baptism occurred on February 6, Septuagesima Sunday, 1887. Margaret Cornelia Saxe was a year and half old. Her father, Arthur W. Saxe, had been born in Sheldon Vermont and came to work in Omaha as a railroad clerk. When he first came to Omaha, he was twenty-four years old and lived in a boarding house. Having established himself in Omaha, he returned home to marry Mary M. Tillotson. He brought his bride to Omaha, and a daughter was born a year later in June of 1884. By the end of Zahner's tenure, he had baptized eighty-one individuals, about twenty per year, a substantial rate of such a small congregation.

On May 15, 1887, Zahner presented All Saints first class of confirmands to Bishop Worthington, eleven in all. By the end of his tenure, he had presented seventy-three individuals, which indicates that seventy-three of the parish's communicants in 1891 were new Episcopalians. The first marriage came later in the year, on October 11. The bride was Ida L. Remington of Omaha. She was a schoolteacher at the Leavenworth School. The groom was Dudley B. Natson of Washington DC.

These three firsts provide an interesting insight into the nature of the parish. The individuals involved in these events belonged to the very

---

14 Grace Church in New York, perhaps the preeminent Episcopal church in the country, began in 1877, holding two German language service on Sundays. It appointed an assistant minister of German origins and organized a German Missionary Association for lay support of this work and administration of aid to families in need.

ordinary rank and file of the city. It makes clear that if some of the parish's founders could be considered to be part of Omaha's upper class, it was by no means a general characterization of the parish.

Among the firsts in the parish, there is, however, a note of personal tragedy. The first burial service occurred at All Saints was in March of 1887. Zahner writes in the parish record his own daughter's name, "Margaret Duncan Zahner, eight years and five months, scarlet fever." Bishop Worthington presided at the funeral, and burial followed at Prospect Hill. It is difficult not to feel that the grief of this death would make it difficult for Zahner to continue his work long in Omaha.

In 1887, Zahner received an honorary degree of Doctor of Sacred Theology from Hobart College in recognition of his work with the original Greek text. Zahner was, indeed, a scholarly man and deserved recognition on his merit. This honor must have come about by means of a recommendation of Bishop Worthington who was a graduate of Hobart and who had received himself an honorary degree from Hobart in 1885. Worthington's honorary degree is not so surprising as institutions promote themselves and their agendas by granting honorary degrees to their alumnae in general and to bishops in particular. Saluting one's own undergraduates is, in part, self-congratulations and saluting a bishop is a means of enhancing one's means of recruiting students. There appears little reason on the other hand to honor a parish priest who graduated from a different college and who already had an earned doctorate. Worthington was no doubt impressed by Zahner's exegetical skills and more importantly wanted to keep Zahner in the diocese.

In turn, it would seem that Zahner was a strong supporter of the bishop's ministry. In a vestry meeting in May of 1889, he took the unusual step of turning over the chair to the senior warden in order to make a motion. He moved that at the forthcoming mission conference, the parish pledge $1,000 to the diocese's mission fund. He was, after all, the son of a missionary and knew how missionaries struggle with the insufficiency of funds. His motion was seconded by S. P. Morse. He was apparently thanked for his concern and had his motion amend by Hopkins, reducing it $500. Hopkins's motion was subsequently passed. When Zahner left All Saints in 1891, the *Omaha World-Herald* noted that "Bishop Worthington especially expresses regret at losing him and speaks of him as a most useful member of the diocese."

We have no sample of Zahner's preaching at All Saints; but his successor, Dr. Mackay, moved by the content of a sermon that Zahner preached in North Adams in 1906, entitled "Do This in Remembrance of Me," published the sermon in *Church and Home*.[15] It gives us an idea of Zahner's eloquence and theology. He begins: "Many of our parish need to have their conscience awakened in regard to the sin of neglecting the Lord's Supper." He identifies two groups who avoid communion. One group, he says, does so form "the inbred notion that only those who are perfect, only those who are saints can worthily approach the Lord's Table." The other group neglects the Holy Communion "because they have no worthy conception of their obligation to receive it." Zahner argues that "our Lord gave the explicit commandment to all his followers that they should receive it." He continues:

> The institution of the Holy Communion took place amid circumstances which made it the most deeply solemn and impressive act of His life. When the price of His life had already been agreed upon, when the dark spirit of betrayal had already enthroned itself in the heart of the son of perdition, when the mock trial, the scourge, the crown of thorns, the insults of the mob, when the dark deep, dreadful crisis of the cross were just before Him: when the little band were yet together, but would be only for a little while, when the ominous shadows of the coming separation and sorrow glided in sympathetic woe from face to face in that band of love; when men were raging around and hell was moving and howling from beneath, when nature was almost halting in surprise at the tragedy of the cross; when there was such an hour as there was not before nor shall be after, an hour of which the Son of God could say: "My hour is come—it was at this time and under these circumstances that 'Jesus took bread and blessed it and brake it and gave it to the disciples and said, "Take, eat, this is my body."

He concluded his argument with a flourish: "No wonder that the holiest hours and the deepest draughts of life which God's people enjoy this side of heaven are enjoyed at the altar of the Lord."

The argument of the sermon is classic Book of Common Prayer theology. It has a certain homiletic eloquence that suggests that Zahner's preaching was quite emotional. What is of particular interest is that he frames his position between two opposites, orthodox piety on the one hand and secular indifference on the other hand. He is working the vein of a mediating theology, which can be traced to his own teacher, Neville Nevin of the Mercersberg school, and to the emerging broad church theology of

15 *Church and Home*, vol. XII, no. 3, p. 1.

Muhlenberg, Henry Codman Potter, William Reid Huntington inspired by the English theologian, F. D. Maurice. Often disparaged as vague and eclectic, broad church could be, in fact, driven by a mediating theology that produced in several religious traditions an experiential catholicism, which was Eucharist-centered.[16]

We can see from this sermon that preaching was important enterprise for Zahner. He belonged to the tradition that believed that worship required eloquent preaching to drive it. Next in importance to Zahner was good music, which had the capacity to sustain worship. As we suggested, Zahner's wife, who grew up as church organist and student of music, was an important influence on him. We can get an idea of the importance he put in music by looking at announcements in the weekend editions of the *Excelsior*, a secular Omaha newspaper. In them, Zahner regularly published the music that would be used on the coming Sunday. For example, he makes the following announcement on February 28, 1891:

> On the coming Sunday, the Third Sunday in Lent, March 1, the services would be Holy Communion at 11:00 a.m. and a chorale evening song at 4:00 p.m. The music at Holy Communion will be 'Litany Hymn, Fiorio; Introit, "O, Savior of the World," Goss; Communion Service in F, Garrett; Offertory, "Come unto Me, Ye Weary," Dykes.' At the chorale evening song, the music will be 'Cantles, chants, Anthem for tenor solo and chorus "Withdraw Not Thy Merry," Atwood; Offertory (unaccompanied) "There is a Green Hill Far Away," Burstall.

His announcement concludes, "All are welcome." The young parish employed an organist, W. S. Marshall, who was paid $41.66 a month. It also employed a choirmaster, Thomas J. Pennell. Pennell as we have seen was formally installed; and it is clear that it was him, not Marshall, who was in charge of the music program. He was allowed $133.33 a month, with which he was to compensate himself and an adequate number of male choristers. The sentiment that a church choir should be made up of male voices was still quite strong at the time and was only beginning to be questioned.

16 In England, this mediating theology arrives with S. T. Coleridge and is developed by F. D. Maurice, whose classic *The Kingdom of Christ* first appeared in 1838. John Henry Newman evidenced this methodology in his classic *Grammar of Assent*, providing an example of its presence in the Roman Catholic tradition. The Danish Lutheran N. F. S. Gruntvig and the German Reformist F. Schleiermacher are part of this broad ecumenical movement.

While most of the money from pew rents and gifts went to the vestry, certain collections, first Sunday of the month, Good Friday, and special occasions, went to the rector for what we would recognize as a discretionary fund. Zahner carefully accounts for their receipt and expenditure. They are expended for communion supplies, Sunday school books, candles of the altar, and charities. The charity entries are sometimes marked "coal $4" or as "assist to another rector," or "For Ch. at Norfolk." The sum involved annually ran between $200 and $220.

The annual meeting of 1890 fell on April 14. The meeting in the church at eight in the evening, the group was called to order by the junior warden, Alfred Hopkins. Neither Zahner nor Woolworth was present to preside. Looking to the future, Montgomery moved that the meeting declare "lady communicants of legal age be permitted to vote." Outside of the parish, Montgomery, an active democrat, was associated with the suffrage movement. His motion carried. The meeting proceeded to elect Woolworth and Hopkins as wardens as it had dutifully done for the past four years. But when it came for nominations for vestry, something happened. There were for the first time in the short history of the parish more nominees than positions, which meant there would be a contested election. One of the past vestry members who failed to be elected was George Ames. This seems surprising since Ames had been an instrumental member of the vestry that had built the church.

The meeting also preceded to yet another unprecedented action for it was not the habit and perhaps not even canonically legal for the annual meeting to make a financial decision. Nevertheless, the annual meeting found itself debating the parish's contribution to the diocese's missionary budget. A motion was made by two active members of the vestry, Meday and Montgomery, to approve a donation of $500 to the diocese's mission fund, which must be seen as an attempt at an end run around the vestry. In the prior year, it will be recalled that Zahner had pushed for an acceptance of $1,000, and the vestry had settled on $500. That level must have been under attack on the vestry; it fared no better in an open vote at the annual meeting. Their motion failed; and quickly two other members of the vestry, Bradford and Guild, weighed in. They moved that the donation be $200. When their amendment did not carry, Montgomery, seeking for a compromise, amended the motion to read $350, which then passed.

The unprecedented actions at the annual meeting reveal a great deal about the tension that existed in the parish as it moved through the fifth year of its existence. Financial worries were foremost, and the debate about the donation to the diocese's mission fund is not only a matter of the parish's loyalty to the diocese but also a matter of the soundness of its own finances. During the past year, there had been a regular struggle with bills presented to the vestry by the choirmaster, for sheet music and other supplies. The majority of the vestry contended that Pennell, as he well knew, was supposed to budget such expenditures from his allowance. They also found themselves debating the water bill and ordering an investigation to determine if they were not, in fact, being over charge by the water company. The subject of why pew rents had fallen behind also was discussed. The mission donation was the lightening rod. The attempt to escalate the question of the mission donation out of the hands of the vestry into the open forum of the annual meeting put the parish's financial problems in the open for the whole parish to see.

There was also at this meeting a preview into the state of the parish's leadership. It is not clear why Zahner was not present and chairing the meeting. Since this was held on the day after Easter, when he would have presided at the liturgies, his absence seems to be a matter of choice. Woolworth's absence may be based on his absence for the city, but it is hard to get beyond the fact that this too was a choice. In the course of the meeting, it was Montgomery who emerged as the key parish leader, portend of the role he would soon play in the life of the parish.

The new decade that the parish was about to enter would bring all these issues to a head. The whole nation around it was sliding into a depression, which would come early and hard to the western part of the country and alter the fortune of many of the parish's members.

Chapter 2

Navigating the Nineties: 1890–1900

A Resignation

Hardly under way, the parish faced a sudden change of fortune. The country had entered into a serious recession felt first and foremost in the western states, Nebraska included. The start-up, launched in 1885, was by men whose jobs and fortunes were predicated on the growth of Omaha and the economy of the country in general. Like any start-up, they had borrowed money and made financial promises. As the new decade began, the financial difficulties of the parish were beginning to wear heavily on the new parish. They had surfaced in the prior annual meeting as a debate about their missionary contribution to the diocese, and they had continued throughout the year. The January vestry meeting at the beginning of 1891 had been preoccupied with financial issues, and as they gathered for the February meeting, the members of the vestry fully expected again to be immersed in their struggle with the finances.

Dr. Zahner took the chair; and the meeting began in a routine manner, receiving the treasurer's report, and then they received correspondence from Charles Harris, accepting his interim election to the vestry. Zahner then asked Mr. Meday to assume the chair and left the room, handing as he did so a letter to the secretary. The secretary then read a letter that was from Zahner. In the letter, he informed the vestry that he had received a call to be the rector of St. Mark's Church in North Adams, Massachusetts, and that he had accepted. He requested to be released from his responsibilities at All Saints by the end of the month, February 28. After a discussion, the vestry accepted his resignation and agreed to pay Zahner his March salary and to assume his coal bill. With that out of the way, the vestry turned to the routine of authorizing the payment of the bills. The vestry would go on at the subsequent meeting, noting that they had been completely surprised by Dr. Zahner's resignation. While they considered not accepting his request, they went on to say that they had "felt constrained by the urgency of the terms in which the resignation was communicated, to accept the same."

Perhaps they should not have been so surprised. It should have been quite clear that the financial stress in the parish was not about to abate any time soon. It is likely that Zahner had a clearer vision of the parish's financial difficulties than did the businessmen on his vestry. It is difficult not to credit the wearing nature of these financial pressures, as the primary reason for Zahner's decision to accept the call, and then it is worth remembering that Zahner's stay in Omaha had been clouded by his daughter's death not long after he arrived. On the other hand, the attractiveness of the call from North Adams would have made it hard for Zahner to resist even under more favorable circumstances. St. Mark's had been found in 1867 in a lovely city deep in the heart of Massachusetts Berkshire mountains, not far from where Bishop Worthington had been raised. Because of the industrial growth in the northeast stimulated by the Civil War, North Adams was a prosperous industrial town as well as picturesque. Its industrial growth had drawn German immigrants, engineers and mechanic, to the city; and St. Mark's had begun an effective ministry to them. The past rector had hired an assistant who could speak German and, at his retirement, told the vestry that their next rector should speak German, as over half of the active communicants in the parish were of German descent. It was a job that had Zahner's name written on it. He remained at St. Mark's the rest of his career, despite opportunities to move on. Among the calls he turned down was a call to Redeemer Church in Brooklyn, New York, a major parish with a substantial German population. He served in North Adams for twenty-five years and died in office. He was highly respected in the community of North Adams and was deeply loved in the parish, which stands as a testimony to Zahner's skill as a minister. The obituary for Zahner in 1908, written in North Adams newspaper, speaks of his ministry in Omaha as an important part of his life and of the many continued friendships with parishioners in Omaha that he had maintained over the years. It is telling that Zahner's burial monument in North Adams is a grand Celtic cross, much like the one identified with All Saints and which marked the graves of several of its parishioners in Omaha.

Still dealing with the shock, the parish leadership called for a special meeting on February 20 to pay tribute to Zahner. The vestry declared in a resolution:

> We cannot forget that Dr. Zahner came among us before more had been done in the organization of the parish than the election of a vestry: there were neither building nor services nor people nor any of the appliances for a parish. After four and a half years, today we see accomplished among us results which are largely because of the zeal, devotion, and energy of the rector. Dr. Zahner carries with him, to his new home, the gratitude, respect, and affection of the vestry and people of All Saints Church.

Zahner's departure was noted in the Omaha newspaper, the *Excelsior*:

> Rev. Louis Zahner, rector of All Saints Episcopal Church for about four years, has decided to accept a call to Adams, Massachusetts, where he will have a very fine church and very desirable congregation. Reverend Zahner has been in Omaha for about four years, but in that time, he has seen All Saints Church grow from almost nothing to a membership of 225 communicants and church property valued at $55,000. The departure of Reverend Zahner is deeply regretted by the members of his church and by his many friends throughout the city. His ministerial work here has been remarkably successful and could not ask for more flattering commendations than those furnished by his work at All Saints.

A New Rector

In the wake of Zahner's resignation, the vestry felt a sense of urgency. In the straits that they found themselves, they could hardly abide a vacancy. The passage of four and half years was not enough to erase the memory of the challenges of calling a rector from the minds of the vestry members. At the meeting on February 20, two names were brought up: Reverend Tuckerman of Chicago, Illinois, and Reverend Foster of Bangor, Maine. Three days later, they met and invited Tuckerman "to visit Omaha at a very early date, to preach in All Saints Church and visit the parish in a social way." For reasons not stated, they had moved on to Foster. On April 11, after an exchange of letters, they issued a call to Foster, offering him a salary not to exceed $2,000. On May 16, they received Forster's regrets, pleading ill health. They then in an abrupt change of direction turned their attention to Thomas J. Mackay, who was the rector of St. Paul's Council Bluffs, Iowa, immediately across the river.

The contrast between Zahner and Mackay could hardly have been greater. Zahner was tall and brawny, a large man/ Mackay was wiry and short, a slight man. Zahner had followed in the steps of his father. Mackay invented himself, including a father! Zahner was of German descent. Mackay, was Irish. And while stereotypes do not always prove true, in this case, it did. Zahner was a scholar. Mackay was a conversationalist.

Thomas Mackay, Second Rector of All Saints, 1891-1920, br. Ireland, 1844, d. 1920.

Thomas Mackay was born Thomas Jones in the small town of Westport, Ireland. Westport is in County Mayo, traditionally known for its beauty and its poverty, and lies on the northwest coast of Ireland. His birth on January 8, 1844, took place at the onset of the potato famine. His father, William Jones, was a young merchant and died of typhoid fever at the age of twenty-nine. He left his wife Eliza with three children, Thomas, William, and Robert. Shortly after his father's death, his mother married Henry Mackay, and together they immigrate to the United States. When they left Ireland in 1852, Thomas's health was poor, so they decided to leave Thomas behind with his maternal grandmother. In America, the Mackays settled in the area of Johnstown, Pennsylvania, where Henry worked as an engineer at the iron works.

Henry Mackay's father was a sea captain, and Henry had been born and baptized in Gibraltar in 1822. In the course of time, Henry became interested in the ministry and responded to the intensive recruitment of the Episcopal Diocese of Pennsylvania, headed by Alanzo Potter. Henry was ordained to the diaconate in 1856 and to the priesthood two years later. His bishop was a zealous evangelical, and since his preparation for ministry was within the diocese, we can assume that Henry was a zealous evangelical as well.

Thomas's mother, Eliza, died in 1889 in Fort Scott, Kansas. Henry lived on until 1905, dying in Las Vegas, Nevada, where he lived with a daughter. Thomas Mackay, the stepson, traveled to perform the service. When he returned home, he ran an obituary in *Church and Home*. praising his stepfather and his ministry. Curiously, Mackay does not make it clear in the article that Henry was his stepfather.

When Thomas came to this country with his grandmother in 1856, he rejoined the family, who was still living in the Johnstown, Pennsylvania, area. He took his stepfather's name, retaining Jones as a middle name, because his younger brothers had already done so. One senses that it was difficult for him, not only because he had to deal with a stepfather but also because his mother and two brothers had already adjusted to their new life in America and he had not. When Henry received ordination, he accepted the care of a couple of small missions and moved the family to Industry, Pennsylvania. Before long, a new call took them to Georgetown, Pennsylvania. At the time of this latter move, Thomas accepted an invitation from his maternal uncle, William Fitzgerald, to come and work in his dry goods emporium in Worcester, Massachusetts. At sixteen, Thomas was not confirmed, apparently keeping a distance from his stepfather's convictions. In Worcester, he encountered William Reed Huntington, who was destined to become one of the most prominent Episcopal priests of the nineteenth century. In 1862, Huntington organized a new Episcopal parish in Worcester along the lines of what he understood as a liberal catholic agenda. It was here that Thomas Mackay was confirmed and began a long-term relationship with Huntington. Huntington served as Mackay chief mentor to the end of his life.

It is likely that Mackay's decision to be confirmed was connected with his decision to enlist in the Forty-Second Massachusetts Volunteers in July of 1864. The unit existed for one hundred days, from July to December of 1864, after which Mackay was discharged. Following this brief period of service, Mackay returned to the dry goods business in Worcester, but this time not with his uncle. During this phase of his life, he drifted from one job to another until he found himself in Bloomington, Illinois. It was there that he decided that he would enter the ministry. Eschewing any short cut, such as his stepfather had taken, he sought an undergraduate degree, going to St. Stephen's College, in New York.

St. Stephen's College in Annandale on the Hudson, not far from Hyde Park, was founded in 1860 by John Bard as a training school for Episcopal ministers. John Bard was a successful New York City doctor whose family summer home was the original Hyde Park. His gift to the school included a church, called the Chapel of the Holy Innocents. The school was subsequently renamed Bard in honor of its founder and continues as a well-known private college. Upon graduation, he enrolled at the Episcopal Theological Seminary in Cambridge, Massachusetts. During his years in seminary, 1875, 1876, and 1877, he worked at St. John's Roxbury. The rector for whom he worked was George Converse, who became another of Mackay's lifelong mentors. Each of the summers in which he was in seminary, he returned and worked as an assistant to Huntington, the rector of All Saints in Worcester.

During his senior year in seminary, the missionary bishop of West Texas visited the seminary. Garrett, who had been for a time the dean of Trinity Cathedral in Omaha, a made an impassioned plea for young men to come West as missionaries. Mackay felt moved to do so and applied directly to Garrett. As a result, Garrett posted him in Fort Worth, which was Texas's most recent boom town, and charged him with the task of forming a new Episcopal congregation, the city's first.

In 1877, a small group of laity there, who had chosen the name St. Andrew's, had begun meeting in a room fifteen-by-thirty feet for services. Mackay's response upon being shown the room by them was that it was impossible for him to preach in such a place. "Are there no dance halls in Fort Worth?" he had asked. Indeed there were, certainly, more than there were churches; and in a short time, he arranged to use one and began preaching to his flock in a room that could accommodate six hundred. Mackay's sense of ministry was that the adults that he was trying to reach needed space for community. The dance hall not only provided space for him to preach but also provided space in which the laity could socialize. In a short time, he was in the position to build a church in Fort Worth, and he saw to it that it was not only built but paid for as well.

While Mackay was in Fort Worth, he met Georgia Coons. Georgia at the time was neither baptized nor confirmed, and it is unclear how they met. About the same time, his brother, William, who had also been ordained as an Episcopal priest and was the rector of St. Paul's Episcopal Church in Central City, Colorado, received a call to a parish in Pittsburgh. He told the vestry in St. Paul's that his brother would be an excellent replacement. In April of 1878, Mackay left Fort Worth and moved to Central City. However, he returned to Forth Worth to marry Georgia on September 17, 1878. Georgia, who was not baptized at the time they were married, was subsequently baptized and confirmed at St. Paul's. Mackay did not, however, feel sufficiently challenged by the position and asked Bishop Spaulding to consider placing him somewhere else. Spaulding, who would continue to be a close friend of Mackay's, sent him to Leadville, Colorado's latest boom town and charged him with organizing a new parish. Mackay took charge of the new work on December 12, 1879, naming the new parish St. George's. There he repeated the scenario that he had perfected in Fort Worth, using a dance hall to gather a congregation that could in turn build a church. Once again, Mackay was able to build a church, a charming Carpenter Gothic still in use, and pay off its debt. He stayed in Leadville until he received a call in 1883 to be the rector of St. Paul's Council Bluff, Iowa.

He arrived at Saint Paul's in January; and a year and half later, he was laying the cornerstone for a new building, the third in his career. The new building was completed by September 5, 1886. It was described in a history of Pottawattomie County in 1891 as "the only church in the city built of stone." The history continues: "It was erected at a cost for $50,000 and is the finest interior and exterior in Council Bluffs, and is surpassed by few in the West." Mackay's ministry at Council Bluffs included a close association with his parishioners, William and Amelia Bloomer, the suffragette. The membership of the congregation doubled during Mackay's stay. A new pipe organ was installed; and he hired a young English immigrant, Simms, as organist, giving St. Paul an outstanding music program. The combination of good music and adult society were hallmarks of his very successful ministry, a ministry from which there seemed little likelihood that he would leave.

By the time the vestry of All Saints sought him out, he had been at St. Paul's for more than eight years, and the need for adventure apparently had been subdued. It appears from a handwritten note that Mackay had received a call from the Episcopal Church in Dedham, Massachusetts, in 1889, where the family of the rector he worked for as student, George Converse, lived. His closeness with the Converse's is witnessed to by the fact that Mackay's first son was named Odin Converse. His choice then was to stay in Council Bluffs, reinforcing that sense that, now a man in his late forties, with a growing family and a congenial ministry, he was ready to stay put.

Mackay gave little encouragement to first inquiries from All Saints, and it would seem that he had laid down stipulations that he thought they would not be able to fulfill. He asked that any call be supported unanimously and that his salary would be $3,000. With an acute sense of urgency, the vestry sent a delegation to visit Mackay and instructed them to tell Mackay that its call had been issued with the unanimous support of the vestry and that he was offered a salary of $3,000, which he had requested. Mackay accepted immediately and took his seat as chair of the vestry of All Saints Omaha on June 29.

In spite of the obvious differences between Mackay and Zahner, they seem to have formed an effective sequence for the parish. In the end, more united them than divided them. Both men were broad churchmen, and both were American Victorians. The later term is used by historians to describe a dominant culture in the United States during the latter half of the nineteenth century, and it is based on the observation that these Americans shared a broad range of values with their English counterparts. Paramount for both populations was a sense of social duty, a commitment to the primacy of the family, and a belief in human progress. Mackay was perhaps a quintessential Victorian. One of his favorite references was Tennyson's "Idles of the King," quotations from which showed up in his parish paper and must have often done so in his sermons. When Queen Victoria died in 1901, he published a tribute to her in his parish newspaper, calling her "a pure and noble woman." "As woman! Wife! Mother! Queen! Victoria will ever live in the hearts of English speaking people."[17]

Mackay's respect for Zahner is shown by the fact that he maintained contact with him over the years. In his parish newspaper, *Church and Home*, he noted a change of residence for the Zahners. He reprinted a sermon that Zahner had preached "on not neglecting communion," and he republished a lengthy article that Zahner had published in his own *St. Mark's Church Monthly*, "Play-Time Is Over," in which Zahner outlined the serious demands that a "working church" made on its members.[18] When Zahner died, Mackay wrote a moving tribute to him, which also appeared in *Church and Home*.

Paying One's Dues

When Mackay took the chair of the new parish's vestry, he found a parish that was coping with severe money problems. Beside those of

17 *Church and Home*, vol. VII, no. 15, January 26, 1901.

18 *Church and Home*, vol. XII, no. 3, p. 1, October 20, 1907.

the parish's own making, they were being compounded by the troubled economy that gripped the country. While the panic that would mark the decade was yet a couple of years away, the economy was already falling into recession in 1891, particularly in the West, whose blistering expansion in the eighties had been financed with debt. Much of that expansion had been connected with the railroads who were themselves in trouble as credit was tightening. Western agriculture, which required credit to plant crops in the spring, would likewise find credit at a dear price if at all.

The vestry minutes throughout 1891 are replete with signs of financial stress. Unpaid or arrear pew rents, the primary income for the parish, regularly are brought to the vestry's notice. The system of pew rents had been the staple means of parish finance for American protestant churches since the Revolutionary War, when all but a couple of states retained establishment that was the alternative. Pew rent was an attractive idea in a free market economy because it looked like a normal business transaction, in the sense that something was given, a seating, in turn for something paid. In the 1880s, the system itself was being challenged by the idea that pews should be free so as to make those who could not afford a pew rent feel as welcome as anyone else at worship. In the Episcopal Church, this cause was fostered by the newly formed Brotherhood of St. Andrew. The brotherhood had, in fact, petitioned All Saints early on to make pews at the evening service free, a thing to which the vestry agreed, because as they opined, those who rented pews didn't usually go to that service. Pew rents had been established by the vestry meeting in January 22, 1887, the day before the building was publicly opened. Rents per annum ranged from $100 for the best seats, to $75 for the next best, and to $60 for the least attractive. The vestry agreed that the last ten rows should be free. The annual budgets of the parish ran between $6,000 and $7,000, and it was made up largely from pew rents. That suggests that little over half of the pews were subscribed and the rest remained free. A vestry committee was regularly assigned to deal with pew rents. While it was understood to be necessary for members to take their turn on the committee, it was never a popular or coveted assignment. When H. N. Meday, the head of the committee on pew rents, tendered his resignation at the meeting on March of 1892, the vestry expressed "surprise that he wishes to escape his duties."

Of course, there was an element of illusion in the view that a pew rent was a normal economic transaction, in that while it appeared to be debt, in the end, it was a voluntary contribution that could be walked away from with no financial consequence. It is interesting that there is just one occasion when the vestry minutes record that the vestry voted to vacate a pew for lack of payment. In 1896, the vestry authorizes the rector to "notify Mr. W. E. Clark that owing to the great demand for seating in the church, his pew would have to be declared vacant because of nonpayment." One has the impression that such an action could be taken only when the parish was recovering its strength and could accept the loss! It appears that Clark either paid up or accepted the loss of his preferential seating for he remained in the parish. By 1902, he was, at any rate, shown to have a seating.

The pressure on the budget was aggravated by the debt service on unpaid debts that amounted to about $5,000. Creditors in 1892 were becoming less lenient than they had been. Commercial National Bank, whose president, A. P. Hopkins, was All Saints junior warden, had been throughout the eighties a ready source of credit; but now it was less patient and less ready to extend credit. The vestry minutes note the approval, after the fact, of a withdrawal of $84, which the bank had made from the church's account in order to pay off a note that Zahner had left behind unpaid. It is likely that Zahner had borrowed the money to pay a church expense and considered it the church's responsibility. At any rate, the bank's action seems a bit precipitous and a sign of the parish's declining credit rating.

In October, the vestry decided that it was necessary to consolidate all of the parish's existing debts and to clear all the liens against its property. To do so, they sought to mortgage their property. Finally after much effort, they procured a loan from a local mortgage company, operated by Charles W. Rainey. The terms of the loan were five years at 6 percent, paid semiannually on a principal of $6,000. Over the next few years, the vestry frequently found it difficult to keep up the interest payments.

From October to February 1893, there were no vestry meetings, the work being carried out by the executive committee. The beginning of the new year must have brought with it a new level of foreboding, as it did for the whole country. Then within the parish, the unthinkable happened. A special meeting of the vestry was called to deal with a communication from the senior warden, James M. Woolworth. In the communication, Woolworth tendered his resignation and requested that he and his family be transferred immediately to the cathedral. The vestry expressed surprise, fear, and, in the end, settling down, gratitude for what Woolworth had done for the parish and to wish him and his family well in their new church home.

It is difficult to determine the cause for such an abrupt move on Woolworth's part. When someone leaves a parish without an explanation, it is usual to look to the rector as the cause. At that point, Mackay had been on the job about a year and half. Had Mackay proven too "low church" for Woolworth? Or was it that he was too extroverted or too glib to suit Omaha's paragon of dignity? But then Mackay was well known when he was called because he had been at St. Paul's Council Bluffs for eight years and had been a very public person during those years. Woolworth had participated in the search that led to Mackay's call and had joined, if not led, the decision to extend to Mackay a unanimous and enthusiastic invitation to become All Saints rector.

Mackay's views on ritualism were well known when Woolworth had participated in his call, and if in the end they were the cause for him leaving All Saints, it would have made more sense for Woolworth to transfer to St. Barnabas's, the city authentically Anglo-Catholic parish, than to return to the cathedral. The cathedral's liturgical practices at that time were hardly more Catholic or ritualistic than All Saints. When it came time for the election of a bishop coadjutor in 1899, the cathedral's delegates pushed for the election of their dean, Fair, and attacked his opponent, Arthur L. Williams, as a ritualist. It was Mackay who defended Williams against the charge of being a ritualist. He argued in *Church and Home*, "Mr. Williams is not a ritualist, his service in his own church being as plain and simple as that of All Saints . . . in Bishop Williams . . . they will have a wise, conservative, liberal churchman—not broad or low or high, as the words are used but a strong churchman, and Catholic-minded enough to unite us all."[19] In 1904, the cathedral again revealed its moderate position on the matter of ritualism in a contested election for vestry and wardens. Mackay explained at that time to the reader of his *Church and Home* that the disputed election at the cathedral had to do with ritualism. He commends the victory in which Woolworth was elected senior warden and attributes it to the fact that the cathedral liturgical practices were "old fashion" and in need of updating.[20] In other words, the cathedral under Fair had been less ritualistic than All Saints!

Henry W. Yates, who had succeeded Woolworth as senior warden at Trinity Cathedral in 1885, claimed that he told Woolworth when he left

---

19 *Church and Home*, vol. V, no. 4, p. 1, May 27, 1899.

20 *Church and Home*, May 7, 1904: "A new vestry was chosen for Trinity Cathedral, Omaha, in Easter week, on an issue, it is said, as to whether the services should become more 'ritualisitic' the affirmative side carrying the day Judge James M. Woolworth, Chancellor of the Diocese . . . was among those chosen. . . . Trinity is under the control of a local vestry, and it has long been a representative of what may be termed "old fashioned Churchmanship." From 1902 to 1905, no permanent Dean was named to replace Fair who had died in 1902."

Trinity Cathedral in 1885 that he could have his old position back when he returned.[21] The implication of Yates's remarks is that Woolworth had left the cathedral in 1885 with the intension of returning when he had completed the task of starting a much needed new parish. Yates's remarks overlook the feeling in 1885, in and around Woolworth's choice to leave the cathedral. It also ignores that while All Saints and Mackay put on the best possible face, there is evidence of hard feeling in 1893. In 1893, however, Woolworth was likely to be quite happy not to be a senior warden or a vestry member of any parish. He took ten years off from such responsibility, before he returned in 1904 to the vestry at Trinity Cathedral. Then seventy-three, Woolworth apparently was called upon by a group in the cathedral that felt the level of ritual was too low. Mackay, from his vantage point at All Saints, had dubbed it old fashion. Woolworth's willingness to service appears to have been more quixotic than a drive to be back in charge. At any rate, it was a short revival as Woolworth died in 1906.

The death of his second wife, Elizabeth, came within four years their departure from All Saints; and her funeral provides us with some additional clues for understanding why they had left All Saints. Her funeral was held at the cathedral; and it was described in detail in the *Excelsior*, whose publisher was her brother-in-law, Clement Chase.[22] Alexander C. Garrett, the bishop of North Texas, formerly the dean of the Trinity Cathedral, presided at a celebration of Holy Communion in the morning and then at the Burial Office in the afternoon and finally at the internment that followed.[23] At the communion service, Dean Fair read the Epistle; and John Williams, the rector of St. Barnabas, read the Gospel. Worthington assisted at the burial office; but it is hard not to conclude that he, like Fair, had been sidelined by Woolworth's invitation of Garrett. Other clergy participating in the funeral included Canon Robert Doherty, the chaplain at Brownell Hall at which Elizabeth had served a head mistress, and the Rufus D. Sterns.[24] Mackay's absence is conspicuous and a testament to the fact that there were feelings. He notes Elizabeth's passing in *Church and Home* with a polite and brief note: "Her death removes from church circles in Omaha a most devoted and faithful

21 *Omaha World-Herald*, June 17, 1904, Yates's comment in regard to Woolworth's election.

22 *Excelsior*, January 5, 1897

23 Garrett left Trinity Cathedral in 1874, when he was elected missionary bishop of North Texas, prior to the arrival of Elizabeth in Omaha or her marriage to Woolworth in 1885.

24 Rev. Rufus D. Sterns live at 2919 Mason in 1896. His assignment is unclear, but he is shown as active in Nebraska in the *Proceeding of the Platte in 1898*.

worshiper and a generous giver."[25] Later when Woolworth himself died in 1906, Mackay marked it with extensive and lavish praise for Woolworth, indicating that the focus of the tension had been Elizabeth not Woolworth.

Elizabeth Butterfield Woolworth br. 1836, Homer, NY, educated Racine Wisconsin, married Woolworth 1871, a partner with her husband in founding All Saints, d. 1897

This points toward the tension that surrounded the music program at All Saints as the nineties began, which would have put the Woolworths on one side and Mackay on the other. As is often the case, the parish's financial crisis had become focused on the music program. In fact, from the beginning, the parish's music program had been given substantial support, more than one might expect in such a new parish. The budget for the music program was $2,000, which meant that over 25 percent of the parish's income was devoted to the music program. Marshall, the organist, was anxious for a raise; and Pennell, the choirmaster, had ambitions for the program that invariably led him to overspend the budget. The rub came from these extras. As the vestry struggled to meet the parish's monthly expenses, it would inevitably encounter an unexpected bill for sheet music or for some other choir expense.

This must have been difficult for Woolworth for he had been from the beginning a patron of the music program. In the course of the building program, when church furnishings, like pews and prayer and reading desks were being

25 *Church and Home*, vol. IV, no. 4, January 1, 1898.

delayed for lack of available funds, a pipe organ arrived from New York. It had been built by the Roosevelt Organ Company of New York City and was considered a state of the art instrument. Trinity Cathedral, itself, would install a similar Roosevelt Organ a few years later, catching up, as it were, with the new upstart parish. The arrangements for the purchase and installation of the organ were made personally by Woolworth, and though it was recorded as a gift of his young daughter in memory of her brother, it is fair to assume that he had largely paid for the organ out of his own pocket. In the parish's second year, the music program was again a beneficiary of Woolworth's generosity. A room was added to the church to serve as a choir room, which would give the choir a place to vest and to rehearse, and it was furnished with a grand piano.

Clearly, the music program had a particular importance for Woolworth. If one reads Woolworth's book, *The Cathedral in the American Church*, published by E. P. Dutton in 1883, one gets the sense that what the Oxford Movement meant to him was beautiful worship. The key component of beautiful worship was that kind of English choral music that one might yet hear today if one were to visit St. Paul's in London or Christ Church in Oxford for an Even Song.

Woolworth's second wife, Elizabeth Stanton Butterfield, came to Omaha to serve as principal of Brownell Hall. Born in Homer, New York, she had migrated to Wisconsin, where as a single woman she dedicated herself to church work. She was profoundly given to ministering the sick and poor, and the church in Racine bemoaned losing her to Omaha. When she arrived in Omaha, she founded the Ladies Musical Society in the city and presided over it for many years. Her marriage to Woolworth, which followed a couple of years after her arrival, was not so much a change of direction as it was entering into a new partnership. She was very involved with her husband in church work in the city and in the founding of All Saints. At All Saints, she took a particular interest in its music program. Elizabeth had studied sacred music and the Episcopal liturgy when she was in college in Racine, Wisconsin; and she was not without strong opinions on the matter. The music program at All Saints was for the Woolworths a joint ministry.

It should not then be surprising that when the music program collided with the parish's financial difficulty in the fall of 1891, the parish paid a special deference to Woolworth. In spite of the vestry politely turning down Marshall's request for a salary increase in October and carefully explaining to him the limitations of the parish's finances, Pennell presented the vestry at the November meeting, with a new set of expenses for music outside of the agreed budget. It was one of the meetings at which Woolworth was absent, which provided the vestry with a dilemma. After a discussion, the vestry voted to hold off action on Pennell's request until Woolworth could be present. Woolworth was present at the December meeting and took the lead in dealing with the music problems. His solution was to offer a resolution that the annual music budget may not exceed $2,000. On the one hand, this upheld the vestry in that it makes clear that Pennell's $1,500 was meant to include his salary, any choristers' salary, and all other music expenses. On the other hand, it supported the music program by ratifying its rather large share of the general budget!

Woolworth's compromise did not solve the problem, and nine months later, it came to a head. The vestry meeting on September 10, 1892, received a communication from Pennell, this time about his salary, which was likely a request for a raise. Woolworth was again absent, as he had been frequently during the past nine months. This time, the vestry did not hesitate. A resolution was quickly passed.

> Whereas it is deemed necessary to reduce the general expenses of the church and to that end reduce the expenses in the sum of $500 per year by placing the choir under the charge of the organist and otherwise reorganizing the same, therefore be it resolved that from and after October 1, 1892, the services of Mr. T. J. Pennell as choir master be dispensed with and that the secretary notify him of this action.

Marshall, who had earlier that year asked for an increase in his salary, was now being asked to do more on the same salary. Hopkins, the junior warden, was appointed to work things out with Marshall. He must have been successful to a degree because Marshall continued until June of 1895. On the other hand, this was likely Hopkins's last service to the parish before he left for Chicago.

The cause then for Woolworth's decision to leave All Saints seems, therefore, not so much Mackay as the extended financial crisis that had been going on for the past year and half and the way that it had an impact on the music program. Woolworth had, in fact, had a role in creating the financial crisis, and there was a standing expectation on part of the vestry and parish at large that when necessary Woolworth would step in and solve it, as he had many time in the past. At the past annual meeting of the parish, it will be recalled that Woolworth's friend George Ames, who had been on the vestry with him since the beginning, was not reelected to the vestry. This was the first time that a vestry election had been contested at All Saints as before and largely after, vestry elections were uncontested. The lack of support in the parish for Ames was likely because of financial issues, either his or the parish's or both. A second partner, Hopkins, who had been junior warden from the founding of the parish, was becoming progressively disengaged from the parish. Business pressures at the Commercial National Bank were such that he was on the way out and he was progressively becoming more involved in new business opportunities in Chicago. In fact, at the meeting of the vestry in March, one month after Woolworth's resignation, the vestry recognized Hopkins's absences and the likelihood that he would soon move his permanent address to Chicago. They declared his position vacant and thanked him for his service to the parish. Of the crew that had signed up to the original venture in 1885 with Woolworth, only Montgomery remained. During 1891, Woolworth had a growing pattern of missing vestry meetings. In July, he asked that he be replaced on the vestry's executive committee as he would be absent from the city for some time. It would be November before it was noted by the vestry that Woolworth was back in the city.

As the year ended, Woolworth was confronted with the loss of his long-term allies on the vestry and a series set back in his cherished music program. It must have weighed heavy. As he pondered his role at All Saints, he would also have been confronted by the financial news not to his liking. To a Western Democrat like Woolworth, the news was bleak. The Western Democrats had fought for freer credit, in short, for an expansion of the money supply and had lost. The reelecting of Grover Cleveland assured the money policy would continue to tend toward tight money and high interest rates. On February 23, 1893, the Philadelphia and Reading Railroad filed for bankruptcy. Cleveland blamed easy money and convinced Congress to repeal the Sherman Silver Purchase Act, which set off the Panic of 1893. As we well know, economies are in recession well before it is recognized and they take time to work their way out of recession. Unemployment in 1893 was 11 percent; 1894, 18 percent; 1898, 12 percent; 1899, 6 percent. With the economy nearly paralyzed, Omaha's new subdivisions and the state's newly platted towns stood still. Stores, factories, and processing plants closed; thousands lost their jobs and eventually left the area. All new construction ceased, and many homes stood empty. While Omaha had grown from thirty thousand to one hundred thirty thousand during the eighties, it would actually contract in the nineties to one hundred ten thousand. If one was a player in Omaha's real estate game, as Ames and Woolworth were, one was flush as long as the eighties lasted, but in the nineties, one was suddenly under pressure. As surprising as Woolworth's resignation was to the vestry, it is perhaps not so difficult to understand after all. Woolworth was now sixty-four. Inside of the parish, he had lost colleagues and had lost his music program, a loss his wife shared with him and may well have been more incensed than he about it. Outside of the parish, he was facing with his peers financial pressures and, quite likely, needed to bow out. From the point of view of the parish, it couldn't have come at a worse time.

Recovery

More surprising than Woolworth's resignation was the way All Saints dealt with it. The leadership of the parish stepped up to the challenge, the most important of which was Carroll Montgomery. He had been there at the beginning of the All Saints adventure as one of Woolworth's original partners attending the meeting in the bishop's office on September of 1885 and remaining on the vestry ever since. Now at the meeting of the vestry in February of 1893, it was he who stepped forward and accepted the responsibility of replacing Woolworth as senior warden. He would continue in the office of senior warden until June 7, 1924. His continuous service on the vestry would by that time be approaching forty years, more than twenty of which he had spent as senior warden. If the name of Woolworth comes to mind when one thinks of the key laity who made All Saints what it is, one should quickly bring to mind the name of Carroll S. Montgomery. If Woolworth was essential to its founding, Montgomery was essential to its survival.

Carroll S. Montgomery br 1851 Juneau Wisconsin, Omaha lawyer whose firm continues as Baird and Holm at the founding meeting 1885, longest serving Senior Warden, 1893-1924

As people in the course of time made their departure, Bishop, Morse, Hopkins, and Woolworth, new people appeared. Such is the nature of parish life. One of these new people was Guerdon Wattles. His name appeared for the first time in the parish's records in the minutes of the annual meeting held on April 3, 1893. He was one of three new names nominated for election to the vestry. The first was F. T. Andrews. He was a real estate agent living in a boarding house near the church that year. He was elected and served for a couple of years. The second new name was J. P. Johnson, who also lived the neighborhood and was the junior partner in Sloan, Johnson & Co., a wholesaler grocery on South Ninth Street. He was not present at the annual meeting, but he also was elected. He declined to accept the election, suggesting that he had not been sounded out prior to the nomination. At the vestry meeting that followed the annual meeting, he was replaced by M. E. Smith, who headed a wholesale dry supplier and manufacture located on the corner of Howard and Eleventh. Smith continued to serve for some time and stepped up as one of the vestry who made a special pledge to the annual giving. Maday, who had been on the vestry for some time, moved up to the position of junior warden, replacing Hopkins; but by September, he resigned. All this turmoil suggests that the parish at that time was struggling to finds leadership.

The third name that was voted on at the annual meeting was Guerdon Wattles; and like M. E. Smith, Wattles would prove to be in there for the long haul, serving for the next twenty years, though he would never be confirmed in the Episcopal Church. His first assignment was to serve with Bradford and Hall to examine the insurance the parish carried on the church. Wattles's financial success and high profile in the city made him a luminary of Omaha business, which might lead one to think that he took his role lightly; in fact, he was, from the beginning of his term, one of the vestry's consistent work horses and was invariably present for meetings.

Wattles came to Omaha from Carroll, Iowa, in July of 1892. He had been born in Tioga County, New York, on May 12, 1854. After the Civil War, his parents moved to Western Iowa where they were among the earliest settlers. As a result, Guerdon grew up in Carroll County, Iowa, on a farm just outside of Glidden. He went to the nearby Iowa State University, graduating in 1876. There he met Jennie Leete, another student. On October 20, 1882, they were married in Jennie's hometown, Clarksville, a small town in Northeast Iowa.

After college, Wattles returned to Carroll County and began practicing law in the county seat, Carroll. In 1882, he opened a bank with the help of a silent partner, which specialized in making loans to the rapidly growing number of German immigrant farmers in Carroll County. By the mid-1880s, Wattles had become quite successful in his Carroll endeavors. His parents moved from their farm into town at his suggestion, and in turn, they suggested to their son that he give some land for the purpose of building of an Episcopal Church in Carroll. In 1885, the same year as the vestry in Omaha was undertaking to build All Saints in Omaha, a pretty white framed carpenter Gothic church was built to serve the small Episcopal community, which Bishop Perry had managed to assemble with the help of the elder Wattles.[26]

It is not clear that Guerdon Wattles, himself, ever attended Trinity Episcopal Church, in Carroll. Certainly, he grew up at time when no Episcopalian ministry existed in Carroll County; and while he was baptized before he left New York, the absence of an Episcopal Church in Carroll County meant that he was not confirmed as a youth. Once he was active at All Saints, Mackay would periodically encourage him to be confirmed as an adult, yet he chose to remain unconfirmed, never making his reasons for not doing so apparent.

Wattles had acquired significant capital from his Carroll banking venture and was looking for a larger stage for his enterprise. Ultimately, the choice was Omaha, and he moved his family to Omaha in 1892. In Omaha, he joined the Union National Bank, which had been founded in 1886 by W. W. Marsh and other principles. Union National had begun with a capitalization of $100,000 and up to that time had experienced only a modest growth. With Wattles's arrival, the capitalization of the bank was increased by $100,000. He was elected vice president and became deeply engaged in the management of the bank. As a result, the Union National entered into a period of rapid growth.[27]

Wattles had arrived in Omaha at the time at which the city was edging into recession. It might appear that this was extremely poor timing on the part of a budding capitalist; but, as is always the case with recessions, someone's loss is the possibility for someone else to gain. What caught Wattles attention was the disorganized state of Omaha's public transportation. Marsh already owned a piece of it, the Omaha Horse Railway Company, which he had bought in 1873. Wattles began a process of consolidating the various street car lines into a single efficient system,

---

26 Trinity Episcopal Church continues to worship in original church today. It was closed during the thirties and forties and reopened in the fifties. It is the church in which your author was baptized and confirmed in 1952.

27 Savage, James and Bell, John T., *History of Omaha, Nebraska*, Munsell & Co., New York, Chicago, 1894, p. 429.

not infrequently clashing with union labor as he did so. He would complete the effort in 1901 under the umbrella of the Omaha Traction Co. It is important to remind ourselves of the crucial role street cars played in the urban environment at the turn of the century. Only the very well off could afford to maintain their own transportation. Horse-drawn carriages came at the cost of high maintenance, and automobiles were yet a novelty. Most of the world walked. As a result, a fortune was made, and the reach of the city was extended to a new level of enterprise.

By 1895, Wattles employed Thomas R. Kimball, the rising Omaha architect, to build a home for him in Omaha's newest "Gold Coast." The house was a unique example of chateauesque architecture, and it remains to this day at 320 S. Thirty-Seventh Street. He also began to promote the idea of an Omaha exposition, and by the end of 1896, he was elected the president of newly incorporated Trans Mississippi Exposition.

How he and his family found themselves at All Saints is a mystery, but it is likely to do with the extroverted style of Thomas Mackay. His service on the vestry of All Saints began as we have seen in the pivotal year of 1893. His participation on the vestry seems to have been no less intense that he was in his business or civic ventures. Over the next six years, he seldom missed a vestry meeting. Even after he had assumed the role of president of the Trans Mississippi Exhibition in December of 1896, an intense time-consuming commitment, he did not decrease his level of participation on the vestry. He was clearly as engaged as anyone in the parish with the struggle to get the parish past its debt crisis and on to realizing its true potential. Like the other vestry members, he annually made a subscription beyond his pew rent, usually about $200, matching Montgomery's lead. In other words, he did his part, but in no way did he take on the role of the parish's rescuer.

It was not uncommon at this time for vestries of the Episcopal Church to be made up of businessmen who at the end of the year made up the difference between expenses and income out of their own pockets. The most storied example was St. George's Episcopal Church in New York City whose long tenured senior warden was J. P. Morgan. When the rector of St. George's wished to expand the vestry, Morgan, who was otherwise quite permissive with his liberal rector's wishes, baulked. He wanted, he said, a vestry small enough to meet in his library and able enough to step up at the end of the year to solve the financial problem. On the one hand, this was a limiting aspect of church finance; and on the other hand, it was the beginning of a pledge system that could spread to the active members of congregation, if and when a rector was prepared to make that happen.

Steady at the Helm

Amidst this constant flux of laity, which is the inherent nature of parish life, Mackay did not step back, but out, becoming intensely proactive. Sometime in 1894, probably October, he began publishing a weekly newspaper that he called *Church and Home.* The original printing was an eight-and-a-half-inch-by-eleven-inch sheet printed on both sides. Printing costs had been one of the contentious items on the vestry's agenda during the past couple of years, so it appears that Mackay's strategy was to make the paper self-sufficient. The subscription price is stated as $1 per year and included advertisements. These early editions state that cost for an advertisement was available upon inquiry, indicating that at this early stage, it was negotiable. The paper claimed to have a guaranteed circulation of eight hundred papers. It was originally printed by Nichols and Broadfield, and it was entered in the mail on Fridays, the assumption being that it would be delivered to the door of a subscriber on Saturday morning. By 1898, the format was expanded to a broad sheet, twenty-two-inch-by-eleven-inch, professionally printed, claiming a circulation of one thousand, well beyond the size of the parish. It could now be subscribed to for 50¢ a year, and names of new subscribers were regularly noted. This expansion seems to have been made possible by more extensive advertising.

By 1898, over half of the paper's columns are paid advertisements. The price is quoted at 25¢ an inch. Advertisers had to qualify as wholesome and appropriate to be accepted and could expect to receive the "good business certification of *Church and Home*." Sometimes this included direct testimonials by Mackay such as the advertisement for Union Brand's cereal, Wheatel. The ad reads, "Rector T. J. Mackay says Wheatel is the finest breakfast food he he has ever used." Ads by department stores were not accepted because Mackay was of the opinion that they were unfair competition against individually owned and operated shops.[28] Mackay regularly prods his parishioner and readers to patronize the advertiser in *Church and Home*, and when he can, he touts the value of advertising in it. "A notice," he writes, "was inserted that a good girl could be secured for house work by applying at the rectory. At least a dozen applicants appeared between the time of the issue of paper, Saturday morning and Sunday noon. It pays to advertise in *Church and Home*."[29] Mackay's younger years were spent, it will be remembered, working in his uncle's emporium

28 *Church and Home*, June 24, 1899.

29 *Church and Home*, vol. V, no. 21, February 25, 1899.

and in other emporiums. There he had learned the skills and values of advertisement and promotion. What he had learned there, he put to work in his ministry. The revenue from advertising, which would have amounted to about $20 an issue, probably covered the cost of printing and mailing. In other words, in a time of dire straits, Mackay had invented the means of projecting his ministry to the parish and indeed to a larger community beyond the parish.

The first page of the paper carried a lead article, occasionally filling the whole page, but more often, it was supplemented with a shorter article or two. Often these articles were borrowed from the national press. Mackay felt too few people ever saw the church news, such as they might, if they lived in a New York City or Philadelphia; and he sought to remedy that. His favorite national sources were the *Church Standard*, *The Living Church*, the *Church Union*, and the *Ladies Home Journal*, the latter of which had begun its long run as an American magazine in 1883 as the first of its kind. On the second page of *Church and Home*, there was a personal column, drawn mainly from the social and civic life of Omaha. On the third page, there was a column entitled "Parish Items," which included not only reports of baptisms, marriages, and funerals but also reports of visitors who stopped in the rectory, of the young people of the church who were off to school, parishioners on trips aboard, or holding family reunions. Occasionally, it exhorted better church attendance or attention to one's church giving. The first four volumes are represented by a small number of surviving copies, but once the newspaper hit its stride in 1897, each edition was carefully preserved and bound for posterity. They provide an exceptional opportunity to view Mackay's ministry and the growth of All Saints.

Church and Home, the name which Mackay chose for his publication, was intended to communicate his core vision of ministry. For him the value of a Christian ministry was that it produced character. That ministry had two crucial foci, the church and the home, the coordination of which was essential for a high level of success. The late nineteenth century was convinced that the home was undergoing a crisis, a view that Mackay himself held. Much of the progressive reform agenda with which Mackay identified himself, sought to reinforce the home. Jacob Riis, who exposed of nature of tenement living in the city with his stunning black-and-white photographs, wrote in *The Peril and the Preservation of the Home*: "Brethern upon the home rests our moral character; our civic and political liberties are grounded there; virtue, manhood, citizenship grow there. For American citizenship in the long run will be, must be, what the American home is." The temperance movement in a different way portrayed the evils of drink and the saloons as the enemy of home life. Carrie Nation's following was known as an army of home defenders. Josiah Strong argued, "There is an increasing population, which, though by no means shelterless, is really homeless." No less disturbing was the perceived rise of divorce among the middle class. Mackay launched his venture into a current that ensured that it would find a wide readership.

If his parish newspaper resonated with purpose, it was not driven by an agenda. It advanced like a conversation. One could not easily anticipate what would appear in a given issue. It mixed digests of articles from national publications, with Mackay's own editorializing and sermons. It picked up pieces from parish bulletins, newsletters, and newspapers like the *Excelsior*, the *Bee*, and the *World-Herald*. *Church and Home* cheered city projects and congratulated individuals and organizations for their civic success. It did not avoid controversial topics. For example, it supported the controversial ordination of Dr. Briggs, the "scandalously liberal New Testament Scholar, in New York City by Bishop Henry Codman Potter."[30] It sympathized with Bishop Johnson, backing his challenge to the church to speak out on the relationship of capital and wages.[31] It deplored the lynching of a group of African Americans in Georgia.[32] It took on theological issues such as the nature of the Eucharist,[33] the Resurrection,[34] or the role of God in natural disasters.[35] In all of these articles, there is no doubt where Mackay himself stood. He seemed to relish the label that he had gained for himself in the secular press as "one of Omaha's most independent and liberal preachers." Equally, he is likely to have enjoyed the stodgy Clement

30 *Church and Home*, "A Victory for Catholicity," vol. 5, no. 24, March 18, 1899; "The Briggs Case," vol. 5, no. 35, June 3, 1899. Dr. Briggs published an "Introduction to the New Testament," employing critical historical method which was fiercely denounced by conservative Christians.

31 *Church and Home*, "Christian Socialism," vol. 5, no. 41, 1899.

32 *Church and Home*, "The Horrible Butchering of Negroes," April 29, 1899: "No matter how horrible their crime, the law should have been allowed to take its course."

33 *Church and Home*, vol. V, no. 24, March 18, 1899 and again in vol. V, no. 34.

34 *Church and Home*, "Degrees of Glory," vol. V, no. 31, May 12, 1899. The whole text was published because the *Bee* had reviewed the sermon on the Monday after it was preached, April 23, 1899, in a derogatory way which incensed Mackay. Its theology was quite beyond the reviewer.

35 *Church and Home*, "Lessons from the Cyclone," vol. V, no. 40, July 8, 1899. The cyclone leveled the small Nebraska town of Hermon.

Chase's characterization of *Church and Home* in the *Excelsior* as Mackay's "saucy little paper."[36]

Still, such topics came and went, surrounded with the patter of society news, witty comments, and parish business, much as one might expect them to come up at the rector's dinner table. Week after week it was vintage Mackay. Before long, a reader would feel that they had come to know Thomas Mackay as an intimate friend.

Parish Work

The weekly publication of such a newsletter is a demanding discipline that must have consumed a significant amount of Mackay's time every week. While Mackay took a two-month vacation most summers, often closing the church during the period of his absence, *Church and Home* cranked out fifty-two issues a year, never without his input. One would be wrong, however, to conclude that Mackay relied on his verbal skills alone. *Church and Home* makes it clear that he worked actively in the area of parish education and visitation. He frequently spoke out on the education of children in the parish, encouraging better attendance at church school and better preparation for teachers and parents to make church school more interesting for the children. He advertised Wednesday evening meetings to be held in the choir room at which he promised to meet with teachers and parents to discuss the church school lesson for the coming Sunday. In an early edition,[37] the lead article is entitled "The Sunday School as a Nursery for the Church." It is an excerpt from a lecture that Mackay gave on the theory of Christian education to the Omaha Sunday School Union held at the First Christian Church. This suggests that Mackay was known in the city as both knowledgeable and passionate about youth education. "The goal," he argued, "is not to cram the child's head full of Bible facts, chronology, history, and the authorship of various books, etc., but to prepare him for intelligent entrance in the graduation school of the church." Then he concludes with an outline of his vision of what a Sunday school should be: "Given a godly man for superintendent, and an efficient corps of teachers, with the pastor of the church as the guiding spirit, the scholars, inspired by their teachers–from the moment they enter the infant class, are led to look forward to the day when they are to stand before the

36 *Omaha Excelsior*, March 7, 1903. Chase is reacting to Mackay criticism of Worthington refusal to retire and his retention of part of his salary.

37 *Church and Home*, vol. II, no. 17, February 1, 1896.

altar and take upon themselves the vows of a Christian in the Apostolic Rite of Confirmation."

It is also clear during these years that he was actively visiting in the parish, particularly new prospects. If his passion for educating the young is unalloyed, he frequently bemoans the expectations placed on him for visitation, clearly expectations that he equally placed upon himself as a story that he wrote for *Church and Home* makes clear. He cast his story as a report on "A Rector's Dream." He begins by recounting a rector's defensive reaction to the implied criticism of a parishioner who has commented that her rector had not visited her for some time. Musing over the pressure to visit newcomers and studying his parish list from A to Z, the rector asks, "What would a merchant think if he had to make regular friendly calls on his customers!" Then nodding off, the tired rector falls asleep at his desk, only to dream that he has been suddenly translated into Paradise. His first thought is what bliss, "no more parish calling." No sooner are those words out of the rector's mouth than he finds himself being asked by one of the celestial inhabitants if he was ready for work. "What kind of work?" the rector retorts with surprise. The celestial inhabitant explains that it only that which is most congenial, and as he had been a parish rector, that would be visiting on those who are new to Paradise to make them feel at home and upon the old residents who like to see new faces. The rector's first assignment is to visit the newly arrived sister "who had felt hurt by his apparent want of attention!" There is a charm in the story that is both a defense and a confession, and there is little doubt left that Mackay saw the ministry of visitation a key part of his ministry.

Church and Home gives us evidence of Mackay's untiring effort to build up the roles of the parish and to fill its worship service. He frequently scolds his flock about attendance and never tires issuing invitations. "Invitation for Strangers," an ad reads, "do you attend church anywhere? If not, All Saints extends a hearty invitation to you to attend services."

Things Begin to Move

By 1896, the number of communicants at All Saints had grown from one hundred twenty-nine to about four hundred or five hundred. The figure is unclear because Mackay, unlike his predecessor, was not given to keeping records. He appears to have attempted for a couple of years to follow Zahner's lead in carefully listing communicants, but after adding a couple of hundred new names, the effort seems to have abated.

At the annual meeting in 1896, the parish unanimously reelected the vestry and wardens, signaling a confidence that the parish felt that it was on the right track. At a vestry meeting in following November, the common problem of arrear pew rent was taken up, and the vestry took the unprecedented action of authorizing the rector to "notify Mr. W. E. Clark that owing to the great demand of seating in the church, his pew would have to be declared vacant because of nonpayment of the pew rent." Since 1890, the vestry had been stewing about unpaid pew rents, but it had never taken any action. The action taken in November is a sign of strength, not weakness. The church is full, and the likely consequence that dunning someone for an unpaid rent might result in that person leaving the church could be risked. At this same meeting in November, the vestry received a request from the rector for authorization to purchase Christmas Music. It was not that long ago that such a request for music had initiated the crisis which had ended in the dismissal of the choir director. In June of 1895, Mackay had replaced W. C. Marshall with James W. Simms, who he had hired to be the organist at St. Paul's, Council Bluffs not long before he moved to All Saints. Simms was thirty-two and had been born and educated in England. The quiet English man began to rebuild the music program and with a little over a year behind him, a modest request for some special music for Christmas signaled his confidence. Mr. Wattles removed any chance that this might initiate a replay the old debate over the music budget by "very kindly consenting to pay the bill for same." Music returned to the agenda in December. By a unanimous vote, the rector was authorized to maintain the music at its present standard of efficiency until the 1897 midsummer vacation unless sooner instructed to the contrary by the vestry. An estimate of the cost of music for the current year of $1,800 was approved, and the music committee consisting of misters Wattles and Kirkendall agreed to secure such attractions as would make All Saints Choir the best in the city. This is another sign that things are working! The budget was still less than the original music budget, but the results are labeled as quite satisfactory. The businessmen of the vestry provide it with an accolade dear to their hearts but seldom used as regards music programs. It is commended by them as "efficient," a curious but understandable accolade for a music program.

The result of this effort was celebrated with a photograph taken in December of 1897 by Lancaster–Hahnema. In the photograph, we see thirty vested choir members. Twelve of them are women, who were the only vested women in a choir of the Episcopal Church in Nebraska. The fact was so noteworthy that the *Boston Journal* ran the picture in its *Home Magazine* in the middle of 1998.

While things were encouraging, the parish's debt remained a problem. In 1896, they had been rolled over in the form of a new and somewhat larger mortgage. After several tries and some intervention on the part of Wattles, a new mortgage was secured from Peace Mutual Life Insurance Company of Philadelphia, the terms being similar, $6,000 for five years at 6 percent. As the year ended, there was more bad news, the loss of two important members of the vestry. Drake, who had been very supportive of the parish's effort and who had served from many years as superintendent of the Sunday school, moved Chicago permanently. On December 8, Louis Bradford died. Gathered at the end of the year, the vestry noted both losses and passed a touching testimonial in recognition of Bradford's service to the parish.

> Whereas, Louis Bradford, late junior warden of this parish, departed this life on December 8, 1896, and his connection with and service to the parish deserve special mention and record: Therefore, it is ordered that this preamble and the following recital and resolution be spread at large upon the vestry records and that a copy of the same be engrossed and presented to Ida A. Bradford, the widow of our deceased brother. Mr. Bradford was baptized April 24, 1889, and confirmed April 28, 1889, in All Saints Church. On April 22, 1889, he was elected a member of the vestry. He served in that capacity until September 4, 1893 when he was elected junior warden, which position he filled until Easter Monday 1895, when at his own request, he was succeeded by Mr. L. J. Drake. On September 30, 1896, Mr. Bradford was again elected junior warden to fill the vacancy caused by the removal of Mr. Drake from Omaha. From the last date Mr. Bradford served until the day of his death . . . from his earliest connection with the parish, our late brother was a regular attendant. As vestryman and warden, he was scarcely absent from a meeting, wherein his advice touching the affairs of the parish was highly esteemed. He was prompt and reliable in the performance of all his official duties, and he was exceedingly liberal touching the temporal affairs of the church. In his death, the Parish has suffered a severe loss, and each of us lose a friend and associate for whom we had great respect and affection. As a citizen, our brother stood in public estimation as a successful businessman of ability and strict integrity. In his domestic life, the deceased was a loving husband, a proud and affectionate father, and in every respect

> worthy. Therefore, resolved, that deploring our loss and that of the parish, we extend to the widow and son of our deceased brother, commending them to the care and consolation of our Divine Master who is our only sure hope and refuge in times of trouble and distress.

If the balance of good news and bad news within the parish still was tenuous, outside of the parish, the news was still clouded by the economy inNebraska, which was still far from recovered. Mackay writes in *Church and Home* about the departure of Rev. John Hewitt, the rector of Holy Trinity Lincoln. He reported that Hewitt accepted a call to Columbus, Ohio. Mackay expressed his regrets for Hewitt's departure but rejoiced in the relief it must have brought him from "the heavy burden of responsibility which he has carried for years." These have been a large parish debt and a boy's school, compounded by the failure of Mosher's bank whose employees had been among his best supporters in the parish and last year's crop failure.[38] The difference between Hewitt's burden and Mackay's was by no means so great as to cause Mackay to believe that a similar fate could not happen to him.

Omaha's Fateful Venture

In the following January's issue of *Church and Home*, Mackay gave a hurrah at the news that Omaha would build a Union Depot, a thing for which Mackay had campaigned for some time. "Now," he continues, "for the Trans Mississippi Congress!" "By the way," he adds, "we congratulate our esteemed vestryman, Mr. G. W. Wattles, on being elected president of the commission having the Congress in charge. *Push it, gentlemen*?"

The idea for an exposition began with the group of the Omaha businessmen who had lobbied the State Board of Agriculture to hold the Fair and Speed Association in Omaha. The success of that event provided the basis for imagining something even bigger. The original group of businessmen, John A. Wakefield, Z. T. Lindsey, Frank D. Brown, George H. Kelley, William Krug, and William A. Paxton, Jr., sought to expand the group and worked on the idea of a major exhibition. Their selling point was that by doing so, Omaha could create its own stimulus program to restart its flagging economy. Guerdon Wattles emerged as a chief salesperson for the exhibition, touting what the venture could do for the city's economy. It was Wattles who articulated a theme for the

38 *Church and Home*, vol. 2, no. 10, December 14, 1896.

exhibition, which was compelling. The exhibition, according to his plan, should show case the progress of the West and power of its agriculture, about which the nation, indeed, the world was unaware. In the course of January of 1896, an expanded group incorporated and began to sell stock, seeking a million dollars of capital! The lawyer for the group who drew up the original incorporation was C. S. Montgomery, All Saints senior warden. Montgomery became the group's chief counsel and would remain in that demanding role throughout the venture. The newly formed group had quickly chosen Guerdon Wattles as president of the organization. The choice is startling since Wattles at that time had been part of the Omaha business scene for less than four years. The choice indicates how much respect there was for his business and organizational skills as well as for how attuned he was to the vision of showcasing the progress of the West. Soon the group would be joined by other members of the All Saints vestry: W. A. Redick and Victor Caldwell were elected members of the board. Mackay, himself, was named the chaplain for the organization; and many others members of the parish joined the ranks of the numerous committees that carried off the event. There was certainly a measure of risk involved for a number of similar attempts around the country never managed to get off the ground and/or lost money. From the earliest work of creating an organization to its closing ceremonies on October 31, 1898, the exhibition was the focus of attention for many parish leaders, and the matters of the parish were put on hold.

Omaha's Trans Mississippi Exhibition, when it did happen in 1898, brought more than two million visitors to the city. The president of the United States, William McKinley, visited the exhibit and was hosted by Wattles. The exhibition was an extraordinary accomplishment for a city, which at the time was a little more than one hundred thousand. It was, as Guerdon Wattles had sold it, Omaha's own stimulus package.

The minutes record that "the rector opened the exercises on Chicago Day at the exposition with prayer and had the pleasure of meeting Chicago's famous mayor, the Hon. Carter Harrison." Mackay gave up his usual two-month vacation the summer of 1898 and kept the church open, filling it with overflowing with guests. In addition, the Mackays kept the rectory, their personal home, open for hospitality to many of the city's guests.

In the midst of the intense activity of the Trans Mississippi Exhibition, with all its crowds and all the buzz about human progress, Mackay managed to arrange for a nationally prominent speaker to give a public lecture at All Saints: David Starr Jordan, the president of Stanford University. Jordan was a prominent scientist and educator who attacked what he identified as the philosophy of despair. The philosophy of despair was the result, he maintained, of social Darwinism, which was being used to justified unbridled capitalism and to imply that progress was a determined outcome that had little to do with so-called moral effort. Against it, Jordan espoused a doctrine of progress, scientifically grounded, but one lift by moral effort. This doctrine fit the exposition's intent of celebrating the progress of the West. If not identical, it was sympathetic to Mackay own optimism and belief in progress. The church was packed when Jordan spoke, and the next day, his talk was given extensive coverage in the newspapers of the city.

When the final day of the exposition came on October 31, Mackay cheered with an exuberance that was a mixture of pride and relief. The final day had been designated Omaha Day, and the gate fee had been reduced as a way to payback to Omaha citizenry who had made in their own way contributions that had led to the success of the event. "Let every citizen, every man, woman and child turn out to swell the crowd: show your loyalty to Omaha by spending money at the Exposition," trumpeted Mackay in *Church and Home*. The mayor had declared a holiday, businesses hand out free tickets, and the school board closed the schools. When the day commenced, Mackay was on the podium, for the last time, to give the invocation.

An Election

As the nineteenth century drew to a close, Bishop Worthington faced up to the need for the election of a new bishop. Worthington had, for some time, been dealing with declining health, which was ultimately diagnosed as due to an ailing heart. He was told by his doctor that he would do better if he lived closer to sea level. This advice was the beginning of lengthening stays in New York City. Worthington, who was not without his own wealth, married Amelia Thibault Milton, a wealthy Easterner 1892. In spite of being financially secure, outright retirement did not appeal to Worthington; and in general at this time, bishops did not retire. They could do so only with the consent of the House of Bishops, which the house was loath to give. Among other reasons, they worried about what to do with retired bishops. Therefore in 1899, Worthington called for the election of a coadjutor, that is, a bishop who would serve under him and who would upon his death succeed him.

The cathedral promoted its dean, Campbell Fair, for the office. Mackay on the front page of *Church and Home* made clear that he would not support Fair. "If Dean Fair were a younger, more robust man, we could overlook all other deficiencies, and heartily support him, but the work to be done in this diocese requires a younger and stronger man, whose headquarters will be in the field, who will be a force in the city and in the state as well as the church, and who will be looked up to and respected by poor and rich, and beloved by those outside our fold as well as within." Whatever degree Mackay's opinion was, prompted by clerical rivalry, his judgment was born out by the fact that Fair did not outlive Worthington, dying in 1902. In the same edition of *Church and Home*, he charged the laity with the importance of their role in the election of a bishop. Clergy come and go, he argued, but the laity remained for the long run. More than the clergy, they deserved a say and should not merely defer to the wishes of the clergy.

In the next issue, Mackay had the audacity to question the salary proposed for the bishop coadjutor. Worthington's salary was $3,600, and he proposed to keep $600 of it for his travel to the diocese on occasions and to allow the new bishop the remainder. It is worth noting that $3,000 was the same salary that Mackay received at the time. He argued that was not enough for a new bishop to do his job and would severely limit the number of those who would be interested in the position.

Such candor did not go unnoticed. The *Excelsior*, published by Clement Chase of the cathedral, rebutted Mackay's argument. Mackay in turned published Chase's chastisement in his next issue as if it were a bag of honor and was self-evidently wrong. The *Bee*, in the meantime, challenged the orthodoxy of Mackay's Easter sermon. Mackay responded by publishing his whole sermon in *Church and Home*, and he challenged his reader to see if the *Bee* had come even close to understanding what he had said.

In the post-Easter season, while waiting for the episcopal election, Mackay had an outing which he described in *Church and Home*. He and his wife, Georgia, went to Kearney to visit their son Robert who was in school in the Kearney Military Academy. He reported on his positive impressions of outstate Nebraska and his respect for the academy. On their way back to Omaha, they spent Sunday in Central City, where one of the westernmost churches of the Diocese of Nebraska was located. Again, he described in glowing terms this out-state work. So excited was he with his reception at Christ Church, Central City, that he arranged an exchange so that the incumbent Rev. Arthur Marsh would take the services at All Saints, while he, Mackay, would preside at the services at Central City. To his congregation, he reported that Marsh "has a flourishing parish and a loyal loving people and is doing fine work in this and adjoining towns."[39] It is hard not to see in the timing of this outing and the subsequent altar exchange a certain amount of politicking aimed at the forth coming Episcopal election.

[39] *Church and Home*, vol. 5, no. 33, May 20, 1899.

When the thirty-second annual council of the diocese assembled in Trinity Cathedral, May 17, it was Marsh that put the name of Arthur L. Williams into nomination. The other names nominated were Campbell Fair and Frank N. Westcott. Mackay reported in *Church and Home*: "After a full and interesting discussion of the candidates which was conducted in a kindly spirit and free from personalities and bitterness, balloting commenced." The clergy voted 16 to 9 in favor of Williams. The laity confirmed the clergy's election, 28 to 23. Mackay could not refrain from commenting that the lay vote for Williams would have been far larger had it not been for a false rumor spread among them that Williams was a "ritualist." William Barnes's history of the diocese repeated the idea that it was "the high churchmen" that elected Williams. Mackay denied the validity of the rumor and claimed that Williams's churchmanship was little different from what one experienced at All Saints. Clearly, Williams was "higher church" than Worthington and his attempts to raise the level of ritual would in time be met with resistance, particularly at the cathedral. It may, therefore, seem strange that he was defended by the rector of All Saints. But Mackay's churchmanship was not that low, conforming as it did to the national norm at the time. Williams is usually identified as "Chicago priest," which carried the connotation of being high church. Actually, Williams originated in Colorado and was a product of Bishop Spalding, the same bishop that Mackay served and counted a lifelong friend. As such, his churchmanship, while advanced, was pragmatic. It is clear that Mackay had backed Williams from the beginning. That might explain why Mackay, who had never been that comfortable with Worthington, formed a close and special relationship with Williams. Williams's home was located near All Saints; and he was, in effect, a neighbor of the Mackays. Curiously, the flagon used on All Saints altar each Sunday belonged to Bishop Williams as did the ewer that is used at baptism.[40]

40 The items passed to All Saints at the death of Nancy Benolken.

A Final Look at the Arc on Hill

All Saints' Vested Choir by Lancastter-Hahnene, taken December 1897

As we leave the nineties, we might return for a moment to look again at a photograph of the choir at All Saints taken in December of 1897. In the center stands the rector vested in a cassock and surplus. Over the surplus is a stole, not unlike the one we see in the Wallace portrait of Mackay painted in 1913. On Mackay's right is a vested crucifer. The hymn board lists Psalm 12 and Hymns 516, 413, 607, and 522. There is an altar rail that Mackay had requested shortly after he arrived, something that neither Zahner nor Woolworth had felt necessary. A large prayer desk sits in the crossing; and one imagines that Mackay, who relished processions and solemn litanies, often knelt in it before the congregation leading their prayers. All these speak of an advance level of ritual practice. On the other hand, there are no candles on the altar, which suggests that Mackay operates in middle range of ritual, careful to have something quite visible that he didn't do!

The space, for all its attempts to look Gothic, is constrained and somehow transient. The floor grate in the crossing, the source of heat, must have been efficient for only a short range, leaving back and sides of the nave decidedly cool. The picture that Canon Whitemarsh painted of it in his history of the diocese, included in the 1890 diocesan journal, seems fanciful. No photograph exists of the exterior of the building, save for a piece of its south wall, which appears in a picture of the new rectory build in 1905. One is struck how low the eave appears in comparison with the rectory. A second photograph about the same time showed it badly damaged by wind, askew on the new foundation upon which it had been moved to make room for the new parish hall. It is difficult not to conclude that one reason for the absence of an exterior picture was that it was less than photogenic. Since its arrival, the neighborhood had grown around it and well past it. Clarkson Hospital was now a neighbor as was the Clarkson nursing school. Yet for all of its limitations, it had come to be the gathering place for a great crowd, and the hill on which it stood had made it a recognizable landmark in the city.

CHAPTER 3

Embracing the New Century: 1900–1915

Where Things Stood

When the new century began, the U.S. economy had recovered a full head of steam. The economy had, in fact, begun to recover as early as 1897; but as we know from experience, it takes some time for a recovery to become apparent to the general public. In 1897, the election of William McKinley, the Republican candidate, provided the business community with a sense of confidence; and more important, the Klondike Gold Rush, by then well under way, provided everyone with a virtual stimulus package by increasing the stock of gold! *Church and Home* noted the uptick, reporting to its readers in February 1899: "The Union Pacific since its reorganization is gradually winning back the branches or feeders it lost while the road was in the hands of the receivers." In the following April, Mackay, like a doctor reporting on a patient's recovery, shared the further observation: "From the report sent us from the U.S. National Bank of which our friend and vestryman, Mr. Victor Caldwell is a cashier, we glean the following satisfactory proof that the time of prosperity has at last reached Omaha." In fact, the economy had embarked upon a period of economic growth that would last for ten years, ending with the Panic of 1907.

The State of the Nation

The United States, shaken for a moment by the assassination of President McKinley, quickly recovered its stride with the ascension of the youthful and charismatic Theodore Roosevelt. Roosevelt's progressive reform agenda resonated with those who, like Mackay, had long pressed for such an agenda. While the period would be riven by contentious strikes, the flood of immigrants, and the emerging role of the United States in world affairs, the American people as a whole had a confidence that these problems would be solved with time.

Mackay commented on the labor movement from time to time in *Church and Home*. He does so even as one of his vestry members, G. W. Wattles, headed Omaha's Businessmen's Association, whose primary purpose was combating "unfair" labor demands. Mackay's general line was that he supported unions because they educated and lifted labor to higher levels of skill and morality. On the other hand, he supported capitalists because their enterprise produced prosperity for all. He, however, challenged businessmen to cultivate a spirit of trust with their workers and to bargain fairly. He admonished union leadership to avoid the use of strikes and especially violence. His conviction, one shared broadly in the progressive era, was that men of goodwill could with time work things out in a way that everyone would benefit. He was not afraid to weigh in on international issues in *Church and Home*, discussing, for example, U.S. policy in the Philippines and in Cuba, arguing for enlightened justice.

The State of the City

The city of Omaha began the century, for better or worse, with the reputation of being a wide-open city. Its rapid growth in the latter decades of the nineteenth century made it difficult for city government to order city services and to keep a burgeoning gambling and prostitution trade undercover. As in most American cities, this brought into existence bosses who mediated the various forces at work in the city in a way that city government could not. In Omaha, a Republican "machine" controlled the city. It was led by Edward Rosewater, the publisher of the *Bee*; Frank B. Johnson, the owner of the city's dominant printing shop; and Frank Moore, who served as mayor. In the 1890s, they brought Tom Dennison to town to be the fourth wheel of the machine. Dennison, a kid from an impoverished Irish family that had lived in Northeast Nebraska, had lifted himself out of poverty first by succeeding in the gambling parlors of Leadville, Colorado, and then graduating to managing gambling parlors in Denver. Dennison arrived in Omaha in 1892, the same year as G. W. Wattles. Dennison arrived with a stake of $75,000, which he deposited in a bank and told the bank president that $50,000 of it was for him to use as he saw fit. This too is reminiscent of Wattles's stake of $100,000 at the Union National Bank, except he had made his money in banking and Dennison in gambling. In keeping with its source, Dennison invested in gambling and in the under life of the city. By 1900, he was in control of the city's under life by various means and could deliver elections by various tricks he had mastered. His most powerful asset was his almost total control of the third ward, home to the city's under life. The third ward, which ran from the river to Sixteenth Street, between Leavenworth and Nicholas, would consistently produce supermajorities for the candidates that Dennison backed. In addition to his political power, he had resources in the police department through which he could harass competitors and those not willing to toe the line, which he had dictated. He also could keep crime away from the wealthy and powerful. The story is told of about the theft of jewelry from Mrs. Gallagher, the wife of the president of the city's largest wholesale grocer, Paxton Gallagher. A phone call by Mrs. Gallagher's brother to Dennison, with whom he was on speaking terms, resulted in the return of her jewels within twenty-four hours and with the explanation that the thief was from out of town and didn't know better.

Another newcomer to the city was James C. Dahlman. Dahlman grew up in Fort Worth, Texas. There he had shot and killed a man in a gun battle who had jilted his sister. It was said that the other man had drawn first, but Dahlman had not waited around to find out what the law would say. He went to work for E. "Zeke" Newman on his N-bar ranch twelve miles southeast of Gordon, Nebraska. As one of his first jobs, Newman sent him to round up stray cattle in the sand hills, which were considered at the time a desert in which cattle could scarcely survive. Instead of returning with a few half-starved cows, Dahlman returned with a large heard of sleek well-fed animals, proving for the first time that sand hills could support cattle. In another job for Newman, he took $300,000 cash in a shoe box to Oregon to buy cattle. Having bought the cattle, he then drove them back to Nebraska, covering over one thousand miles in the process. He conducted similar buying ventures for Newman in Texas, again resulting in cattle drives approaching one thousand miles.

Newman brought a young Wellesley girl, Harriet Abbott of Winterpoint, Maine, to his ranch to tutor his children. After a long courtship, James married Harriet. Settling down in nearby Chadron,

Nebraska, he was elected mayor and fell into his true vocation, politics. He was soon active in state politics, playing an important part in the promotion of the Trans Mississippi Exposition, through which he became associated with Guerdon Wattles. In state politics, Dahlman was a close ally of William Jennings Bryan and came close to being elected governor of the state, falling short, because, as a "wet" Democrat, he had less than Bryan's full backing. In 1898, he moved to Omaha to run a livestock commission house and bought a house at 2901 Hickory Street, located in Omaha's Hascom Park neighborhood. Once in Omaha, the Dahlmans joined All Saints and remained active members throughout the rest of their lives. When the Moore–Rosewater machine came apart in 1905, Dennison swung his support to Dahlman, the Democrat, and Dahlman became the "cowboy" mayor of Omaha.

The new status quo in the city was challenged from time to time by reformers who would claim that Omaha's reputation as was a wide-open city was well deserved. Mackay frequently defended Omaha as no worse than any other American city. The Civic Federation, which included many ministers of the city, made a particularly strong attack on the city government in 1904. Mackay took them to a task in *Church and Home*.[41] "Show what your charges are," he demanded. He argued that "closing saloons and not clubs is wrong." The saloon was the social venue of the working class, just as the club was the social venue of the wealthy, and if alcohol was served in the latter, it was according to Mackay's thinking hypocritical to proscribe it from the former and not the latter.

As part of their crusade, the reformers had passed the "Albert Law" to stamp out prostitution in the city. Mackay again charged that the law was hypocritical. It harassed women on the street and drove prostitution underground but did not stop anything. In an article in *Church and Home*, entitled "How to Make Omaha a Great City," he concluded, "I am not making excuses for the sin of these women, but I contend that the men are the greater sinners. Repeal the Albert Law."[42]

The State of the Episcopal Church

The Episcopal Church continued the growth that had begun with the end of the Civil War. In Massachusetts, William Lawrence had succeeded Philip Brooks. He was a new kind of bishop, not a charismatic

41 *Church and Home*, vol. 10, no. 32, May 7, 1904.

42 *Church and Home*, vol. 17, no. 33, June 8, 1912.

Victorian like Brooks, but a solid businessman. His mission as bishop, as he saw it, was to teach the church how to function as a well-run business. His credibility allowed him to call upon the businessmen of the church, beginning with J. Pierpont Morgan, to pony up. His ultimate and enduring gift to the national church was a clergy pension fund enacted by the Episcopal Church's General Convention in 1916.

The Episcopalians in the District of Columbia, having received a charter from Congress in 1893 to build a national cathedral, were trying to clear the way to build a Gothic cathedral on a European scale. Its cornerstone would be laid in 1907. In New York City, the Episcopalian had begun work on a cathedral, St. John the Devine, which was intended to be one of the largest cathedrals in the world. Bishop Henry Codman Potter, who was concerned that the laboring class in America was not attracted to the Episcopal Church, spoke frequently on social justice for labor with the hope that a report with the working class could be forged. He even, with a flourish, opened a saloon in New York City, which was intended to provide a wholesome environment for working-class men to meet and have a drink, just as businessmen had their clubs to do the same. One can see the resonance with Mackay's comments on saloons and clubs in Omaha. Potter's action was attacked as encouraging drink among the working class. Mackay came to Potter's defense in *Church and Home* praising his intention to create a wholesome space in which the working class might socialize. He also defended Potter's well-covered lecture at Yale, "On Labor and Capital." Potter had argued before the Yale audience: "The only safety for society lies in the removal of the mutual misunderstanding and caste spirit that now dominates capital and labor." And he concluded his remarks with the assertion: "In Christian socialism lies the hope of the future."

The Episcopal Church was, however, working in a very different demographic situation than it had in the previous century. There was rapidly growing number of Roman Catholics in the country. Moreover, Roman Catholics had a growing pride and confidence in their institutions in America. In Omaha, that was evidenced by the founding of Creighton University in 1878. Creighton remained Omaha's only college until the founding of Omaha University in 1908, largely by the Presbyterian Church as a Protestant alternative to the Roman Catholic college. That was followed in 1905, with the effort to build a massive new cathedral, designed by Thomas Kimball, St. Cecilia, which stood on the ridge along which ran Forty-Second Street.

The growth of the Roman Catholic population and its assertiveness was a catalyst for reigniting ritual controversy within the Episcopal Church, which had been dormant for some time. Some proposed that the way to cope with this change was by looking more catholic. These renewed ritualists argued that by doing so, one would draw a portion of this new population into the Episcopal Church. Others adamantly countered that only by emphasizing the difference inherent in a Protestant tradition could one hope to attract true converts.

Mackay regularly weighs in on the ritual controversy during the period. When Bishop Williams went to Fond du Lac for the consecration of its new bishop, he was lent a cope and miter to wear for the service. *The Living Church* published a photo of the twelve augustly attired hierarchs who had attended the consecration of Weller as bishop coadjutor of Fond du Lac.[43] To the high church party, it was a great comfort, a kind of milestone; but to the larger part of the Episcopal Church, including Mackay, it was an occasion for scandal. He wrote in *Church and Home* that it was a strange return to medievalisms and labeled it the Fond du Lac Circus.[44] He exonerated Williams by pointing out that Williams did not own a cope and miter and had been pressured into accepting them as a loan to wear for the service for the sake of brotherly regard! While from time to time the ritual controversy surfaced in the Diocese of Nebraska, it was usually restrained. Mackay praises the annual counsel of 1901, writing in *Church and Home*, "The council this year was most harmonious. Everyone seemed at peace with himself and each other. The Rites and the Broads, and the Lows were at once at peace."

During this time, *Church and Home* also regularly takes up an argument with Roman Catholic leaders. This argument is driven by the growing presence of Roman Catholics in this country and by the papal drive against modernism launched by Pius X in 1903 and again in 1907 when the decree "Lamentabili" and the encyclical "Pascendi" were issued. In 1906, for example, Mackay writes a long article that begins by stressing that the Episcopal Church is a branch of the Protestant Church and then charges that the Roman Catholic Church demands that its votaries "believe implicitly certain matters of their faith which to open minds are unreasonable as well as abhorrent." He illustrates this with a discussion of transubstantiation, the papal attack on modernism, and the piety related to St. Pelligino's blood.[45]

43 *The Living Church*, November 8, 1900. It appeared in the center of the issue as a double-page illustration.

44 *Church and Home*, "A Wonderful Spectacle," vol. VII, no. 8, November 17, 1901; "Echoes from Fond du Lac," no. 9; "The Fond du Lac Circus," no. 10.

45 *Church and Home*, vol. XII, no. 52, September 28, 1906.

Nevertheless, Mackay's attitude to local Roman Catholics was fraternal, and he charged that the more extreme ritualists in the Episcopal Church were seeking to win converts, a business that the Episcopal Church should not be in. In an article in 1915, he observes: "Most of us respect Catholic piety, bear witness to the good works and charities of the Roman Catholic church, and like many of the individual Roman Catholics of our acquaintance very much indeed. Nevertheless, there seems today to be a growing current of opposition to that church in politics."[46]

The State of the Diocese

The Diocese of Nebraska reported in 1901 that it had 18 parishes, 25 priests, 3,732 communicants, and 6,843 baptized individuals in its care. Remembering that the western part of the state had been separated forming the missionary Diocese of Western Nebraska, the growth during the sixteen years of Worthington's episcopate is substantial, amounting to approximately a 50 percent increase in membership. Since Worthington's absence from the diocese in 1899 for health reasons, Williams had vigorously attempted to care for the flock. Williams was, however, hamstrung by Worthington's continued unwillingness to actually retire, a thing Mackay had questioned from the beginning. In 1901, Mackay reported that he has learned from one of our Eastern church papers "that Bishop Worthington has purchased a $40,000 summer estate in the Berkshire Hills, near Lennox, Massachusetts where he intends to reside for the future." There is in Mackay's article an implication of scandal. In this article, Mackay expressed his wholehearted support for Williams. While Williams had both Mackay's sympathy and support, the Trinity Cathedral, which remained the diocese's largest congregation, reporting about one thousand baptized members in its care, frequently criticized Williams and gave him less than their full support. In a sense, they didn't need to, since Worthington was their bishop and all the better, from their point of view, that he was an absent one.

The State of the Parish

The parish of All Saints, which had lived for the past decade under financial restraints, found itself at the point where it could pay off its debt. On April 23, 1900, the treasurer, F. A. Ewing, reported there was enough

[46] *Church and Home*, vol. XX, no. 32, May 29, 1915.

cash from subscriptions to pay off the mortgage debt of $6,180, except for about $500, which would not come in until sometime in May or June. The vestry authorized that $500 be borrowed from the Union National Bank through Mr. Wattles in order that the books could be cleared. The following year marked Mackay's tenth year as rector. Looking back over those ten years, he reported that he had baptized 352 individuals, confirmed 275, married 180, and buried 201.[47] Communicants lost by removals from the city numbered 209, while communicants lost by death were 25. The disparity between the number of burials and number of communicants that had died in a given year points out that Mackay performed many burial services of individuals that did not belong to the parish. They include Anna Wilson, Omaha's well-known "madame" who died in 1911.

Mackay's assessment of the parish's situation is markedly upbeat.

> "For ten years," he says, "a steady stream of removals has been going on. (Remember that the city of Omaha declined in population during the decade of the nineties by about 15 percent.) Within the last year the stream has turned and now we are commencing to feel the setting in of a tide in our favor. Few parishes in this great West has such a favorable condition of affairs from the financial standpoint, for in all these years we have been able to meet each month our indebtedness in every direction since the beginning of Mr. F. A Ewing's remarkable work as treasurer several years ago."

Getting to this point had been made possible in a large part by the initiation of a pledge system in May of 1899. Mackay explained in *Church and Home*,

> Pledge cards have been distributed in the church which the rector requests every member of the congregation to inspect. He desires to have the three leading interests of the church sustained by the freewill offering of the people directly, instead of through dinners or entertainment events, these latter means being used only as incidental or as a means of bringing the members of the parish together.

The three that he identifies was interest on the debt, the contribution of the women's auxiliary to church mission, and diocesan assessment. The importance of this shift was that the pledges that had heretofore paid for

47 *Church and Home*, no. 37.

the interest on the mortgage would become a primary source of the parish's funding. Over the next several years, *Church and Home* continually drew attention to the use of pledge envelopes. Mackay reported in *Church and Home* that pledge income for the year of 1902 was $1,187.35

Parallel to the improved finances was an improved music program. Mackay heralded the choir in the *Church and Home* as the best in the West. This was important because it was considered that a music program was the key to growth. J. M. Simms had now been at the helm of the music program for five years and had established a reputation as a musician in the city. The four-o-clock service on Sunday was Evening Prayer with music. *Church and Home* frequently describes these services and reports that they filled the church. This is backed up by reports in the *World-Herald*, which describe the quality of the musical offering and strength of the attendance.

In general, attendance at All Saints ran high. The Sunday morning service was full. *Church and Home* implores those who rent pews to let the rector or ushers know if they are not going to be there, so that their pew may be used. At any rate, they are told that once the procession begins, their pews will be filled on a first-come-first-served basis. Easter and Christmas services always required extra chairs and sometimes resulted in turning people away. This attendance was not all because of parishioners who, by 1901, were reported as made up of eight hundred baptized members, three hundred of whom were communicants. Many people in the congregation were from other parishes and even from other denominations. Mackay liked to showcase the diversity of the parish. He ran, for example, a list of the railroad men in the parish. Starting with the Union Pacific, the list was headed by Lomax, general passenger and ticket agent; then Garrett, assistant general freight agent; and continued down to a locomotive engineer employed by the Chicago Great Western.

The Omaha business community continued to be well represented in the parish. One of the new additions was Freeman P. Kirkendall, whose boot factory was rapidly expanding to become the number one supplier of cowboy boots to the West. The company also boasted of supplying boots to such foreign dignitaries as King Gustav V of Sweden and the Emperor Yoshohito of Japan. The Kirkendall Company occupied the Millard Block, which still stands in Omaha at the corner of Eleventh and Harney. Kirkendall quickly became a leading member of the vestry, working hand-in-glove with Wattles as they had on the board of the Trans Mississippi Exposition.

This diversity that Mackay celebrated extended to politics. He reports proudly that "All Saints Church was well represented in the great political conventions. Mr. G. W. Wattles is the delegate at large to the Republican convention in Chicago and is one of the members of the committee chosen to notify Roosevelt of his nomination, and Mr. J. C. Dahlman is head of the Central Committee of the state in the great Democratic convention in St. Louis."[48] Dahlman was soon to become the "cowboy" mayor of Omaha, first elected in 1906. He continued in office until his death in 1932, with the exception of the 1918–1921 term. The mayor's daughter Ruth was married to Austin J. Collett on June 5, 1907, in the new building, shortly after its completion. Ruth's son Austin was baptized at All Saints on Monday, December 20, 1909, coinciding with the celebration of her mother and father's twenty-fifth wedding anniversary. Dahlman was listed in 1907 as the renter of pew 60 along with E. O. Hamilton and Dahlman was buried from All Saints when he died in 1932.

The parish recorded several firsts at the beginning of the century. The first bequest ever made to All Saints was made by Mrs. F. M. Ellis leaving the church a handsome diamond bar pin worth about $200. Mackay was quick to point out that "in the East, bequests are common." The first cookbook appeared in June 1901, named *What All Saints Eats*, costing 75¢. The parish sponsored its first candidate for Holy Orders, Mr. Bates, one of the parish's lay readers. Bates was ordained on June 7, 1902, at St. Martin's in South Omaha and continued to serve that congregation for some time. In 1904, Mackay informed his readers that Bates was in the East, doing well and about to assume the rectorship of a church on Long Island.

Envisioning a Response to the New Century

Under these favorable circumstances, the parish began to envision a new facility. This is startling since the parish buildings were at the time not yet fifteen years old. They were, however, seriously compromised from the beginning. The rectory had been Woolworth's old home before his move to St. Mary's Avenue. Once Zahner accepted the call to be rector, Woolworth had hastily moved it on to the church property as a gift the parish. It was a large wooden Victorian mansion, but it lacked modern amenities. Considering that a rectory served the parish as an office and as a location for parish meetings and entertaining, it also lacked enough space.

The church building itself had been shaped by a desire to have the largest seating capacity possible at the lowest possible cost. While the breadth of the building provided seating capacity, its lack of height dampened the experience of worship as did the limited area that it provided for a choir and altar. There was no parish hall. Mackay saw this as a severe

48 *Church and Home*, vol. IX, no. 41, July 9.

limitation on the program he believed that All Saints should be offering. He made up for this by renting public halls for parish suppers and events, but clearly this was not like having one's own venue. Originally, there had not even been a choir room. It had been hastily supplied by a modest addition of the south side of the sanctuary, another gift by Woolworth. The exterior of the building was without distinction. As early as 1895, Mackay put into print his opinion that All Saints needed a new church building, although he conceded at the time it was too soon.[49] A friend of Mackay, Senator Alfred Sorenson, would later offer an outsider's opinion that "the shack" should be replaced; and he personally offered to pledge $1,000 if the parish would build a new building. This description stood in stark contrast to the description which Canon Whitemarsh published in the diocesan journal in 1890. We, no doubt, should allow for a certain degree of hyperbole in both cases.

Meeting at the end of the 1901, the vestry, with all members present, appointed a committee consisting of Wattles and Kirkendall to consult with the architect Thomas Kimball as regards moving of the rectory and church building and to ascertain the feasibility of such a move and the probable cost of the same. Kirkendall and Wattles had both worked with Thomas Kimball who was the principal architect for the Trans Mississippi Exposition. Wattles's new chateauesque home in Omaha's new Gold Coast, 320 S. Thirty-Seventh Street, was designed by Kimball. In 1901, Kimball designed a home for Freeman Kirkendall in a Renaissance Revival style. It was among the largest in the Gold Cost and continues to stand at 3727 Jackson Street. In February, a building fund was set up, and pledges started to come in. The goal was set at $40,000 to be paid in over a five-year period. The sense of the vestry, however, was that nothing should be done until sufficient pledges were received. When the report drawn up by Kimball was received in March, the vestry, after an extensive discussion, went on record as choosing to hold the plan in abeyance.

A new attempt to move things ahead was made on May 26, 1902. The vestry explored the idea of selling its property on Twenty-Sixth and Dewey and relocating the parish to a lot on Park Avenue, between Dewey and Harney. This would have moved All Saints a few blocks further West, near to where the First Baptist Church would be built in 1904. This location would have been in the same neighborhood and would have allowed "the wooden arc" to be moved there from its present location. The same meeting asked for estimates on what it would cost to move the present church building to the east side of the lot and to build a new church on the land the

49 *Church and Home*, November 23 1895. Arguing for a Union Station, Mackay in passing mentioning that All Saints needs a new building.

parish already owned. One way or the other, the present church structure needed to be moved in order to make room for a parish hall.

Fire in the Rectory

The process continued to drag on, going back and forth between several different scenarios. Mackay at one point changed his opinion about a parish hall. What a great parish program required, he concluded, was a substantial worship space and a proximate rectory. Clearly, this was bargaining on his part in order to move things ahead. It doesn't seem to have worked, and things continued to drag on, until an event outside of anyone's control happened. In February of 1903, there was a substantial fire in the rectory. With insurance money in its hands, the vestry had to decide whether to make repairs on an old building, which was clearly inadequate, or to proceed with a new building, which it doubted it could afford. The Kirkendalls were close to taking possession of their new home in the Gold Coast, across from the Gallaghers and around the corner from the Davis's home. That made their old home at 402 S. Twenty-Sixth Street available as a temporary rectory, and the decision was made to proceed to tear down the old rectory and build a new one.

The architect for the rectory was John McDonald, which is a surprise, given the fact that Thomas Kimball had already done work for the parish. There was a degree of urgency that might explain why McDonald was chosen. The rector headed a committee to raise $10,000 to make it happen. On April 13, following the annual meeting, the vestry met and approved a bid by Walter Peterson to build a rectory for $7,965. The rectory was to be a stone building with a handsome portico on its front. In February of the following year, Mackay reported in *Church and Home*,: "The rector and his family are settled in the new rectory. It is almost a year since the fire occurred in the old rectory. The fire was on the morning February 21, which was the Saturday before Ash Wednesday. By strange coincidence, we moved into the new house the Saturday before Ash Wednesday."[50] The building program left the parish with a mortgage of $4,000. This was the apparent reason for the resignation of the junior warden, Knox. His resignation was followed by Updike's, but Updike resigned because he was moving from the city.

MacDonald's plan for the rectory also included a plan for a new church and parish hall. The plan for the new church was described in an April edition of *Church and Home*, entitled "Sketch of a Plan for the New All

50 *Church and Home*, vol. X, no. 21 February 20, 1904.

Saints Church." The article maintains that "this building and the parish house can be built for about $45,000. The plan is in keeping with the new rectory."[51] A detailed description was published in the *Excelsior*, the Omaha newspaper published by Clement Chase.[52] A picture of the newly completed rectory appeared on its front page with a headline, "The Plans for All Saints." In the article that followed, the report explains that plans for a new church and a parish house have just been completed but not yet passed upon by the vestry. The style of the proposed church and parish house will be Gothic, the material a gray pressed brick, with buff-colored limestone, similar to that so effectively used in the already completed rectory. It will have a slate roof. The interior finish will be Old English oak. The dimensions of the church building are 50 by 125 feet, with a handsome vestibule 18 by 18 feet. The parish house would adjoin the church, being a structure very much needed in the work of so large a parish as All Saints, will be 44 by 60 feet. It is proposed to have lecture rooms in the basement, a choir room, parlors, and toilet on the first floor, and on the second floor a large entertainment room. Mr. John McDonald is the architect. The cost is estimated to be $45,000.

Almost a Rockefeller in the Parish

Hoping to continue the momentum, Mackay renewed his call for a parish hall. In February of that year, he wrote in the *Church and Home*: "The need of some place where our people can meet for social intercourse is becoming more and more imperative in All Saints parish. If we only (we had almost said) a Rockefeller in our parish, who would build us a parish house, how happy we should be! But we don't need a Rockefeller and don't want one. All we need is the spirit of love and consecration among our people, and a new church and a parish house would speedily be erected."

The year passed, however, with no signs that a parish hall let alone a church would be built. Then with 1905 scarcely under way, the situation was suddenly transformed when Guerdon Wattles offered to build a parish hall, $10,000 to come from him and $5,000 from his wife. If the vestry accepted the offer, the church building would have to be moved to the west side of the property, reoriented on a north-to-south axis, in order to make room for the new hall. It was difficult at this point to hold back, and so the vestry undertook the responsibility of seeing that the church was

51 *Church and Home*. vol. IX, no. 30, April 22, 1904.

52 *Omaha Excelsior*, April 16, 1904.

moved and that sufficient repairs would be made to make it in order for it to be useable. The cost to do so was estimated to be on the order of a few thousand dollars.

It was understood that Wattles with his wife would personally build the parish hall, and upon its completion, they would deed it over to the parish. Moreover, they stipulated that the parish hall would be designed by Thomas Kimball. Wattles was in that way controlling the building and was in effect scuttling the MacDonald plan. The result was to shift the style of the hall from Gothic, which would match the rectory, to a distinctive different Tudor style. A buff stone trim matching the rectory would be used to provide continuity, but the hall would be built with red brick. This style broke with the current pattern of church building in Omaha. The most recent church building was Kountze Memorial, a couple of blocks north of All Saints. Built in 1904, Kountze was decidedly Gothic. Kimball's vision for All Saints was something distinctly new for the city.[53] Innovation was a primary characteristic of Kimball's work. His design for St. Cecilia's Cathedral, which was contemporaneous with that of All Saints, was also a radical break from the Gothic pattern. Work on this Spanish Renaissance masterpiece began in 1905. The new Tudor pattern chosen by Kimball would soon become a new vogue for church construction and can be seen in First Presbyterian, which was built at Thirty-Fourth and Farnam in 1917. Besides a fresher look, which appealed to Wattles, it also offered the possibility of a larger and more useable interior space. Kimball's design for the new church was for a floor 125 feet long and 43 feet wide surmounted by an apex of 70 feet.

The parish hall in his plan was stunningly attractive on the exterior and extremely well fashioned on the interior. The lower floor would contain a large refectory or dining room, which would also serve as a choir room and would accommodate various classes such as instruction in wood carving, sewing, and cooking. At the west end, which would eventually be joined to the church, there would be a wardrobe for the choir and a men's bathroom and lavatory on one side of a lobby and a well-appointed kitchen on the other side.

---

53 Examples of church building at the time are St. Martin of Tours, 1899, late Gothic; Sacred Heart Church, 1902; St. Mary Magdalene Church, 1903, Gothic revival; and Kountze Memorial Lutheran Church, 1904, Gothic revival; but St. Cecilia, designed in 1901, built in 1905, Spanish Renaissance revival.

Wattles Memorial Parish Hall built in 1906. On the right one can see the north end of the Church and on the left the new rectory designed by McDonnell and built in 1904. The neighboring home was also owned by the parish.

The lobby would have two stairways that would lead to the second floor. The second floor would feature a beautiful assembly hall with a high vaulted ceiling with exposed trusses. It would be used for Lenten services, Sunday school, lectures, and social entertainments. On the east end of the first floor of the parish hall, there was a shallow stage under a large stained-glass window divided into three units. On the west end over the entrance doors, there would be a gallery that would overlook the hall. From it a choir and/or musicians would be able to perform for an assembly. Also under the gallery would be a door that would lead to a lady's dressing room and lavatory on one side and child care room on the other. Beyond that, one would enter into a fine room, twenty-three feet square, over a porch that would connect the parish house to the church. This room would be used as a club room and sewing room. This new building was meant to be everything that the old wooden church was not a statement of eloquence and at the same time of modern efficiency. Certainly, it was one of Thomas Kimball's masterpieces.

When it was completed, the parish hall was to be named as a memorial for Frederick N. Wattles, the only child of Guerdon and Jean who had died on November 23, 1886. When it was completed, it cost the Wattles $30,000 instead of the original $15,000 that they had anticipated. Its completion would drag on into November 1907, but that resulted in the dedication falling on the boy's twenty-first birthday, which seemed particularly propitious.

There were a number of reasons for the delays. The party who had won the contract to move the church was slow in getting started, and Mackay's frustration was evident as the summer passed. His hope had been that the moving of the old building and its rehabilitation would be accomplished in the couple of months that All Saints was usually closed for the summer. Work in fact had not started until August. The church building was successfully moved and reoriented on the property. This made it possible to schedule the laying of the cornerstone for the parish house on September 1, a date that coincided with the anniversary of the founding of the parish in 1885. Dean Beecher of Trinity Cathedral presided at the elaborate ceremony. Articles placed in a copper box consisted of daily papers, a church directory, and a history of All Saints. Mr. W. F. Gurley, one of Omaha's noted orators, was chosen to give the address marking the occasion.[54] He spoke, he declared, as a layman in layman's terms with little knowledge or care for theology. He said that in this project he saw a response to a layman's desire. "What he wants the church to do, in the language of the street, is make good . . . He wants the church to make people good, to the alleviation of suffering and poverty." Gurley's theme could hardly have been more apt to the vision of Wattles or Mackay.

A Great Wind

Progress, however, was short-lived. On September 14, one of those fierce straight-line winds, characteristic of Nebraska, blew through town. It jarred the church building off its new foundation, damaged its pipe organ, and otherwise buffed the exterior. There would be some insurance, so once again the argument could be made that the cash in hand should not be put into a building that was less than satisfactory for the long run. Shouldn't they take this ill wind as a sign to build a new church to go along with their new parish hall? Mackay hinted at it, suggesting that God works in mysterious ways. The following issue of *Church and Home* under the bold banner headline: "God is our hope and strength. A very present help in

---

54 Gurley was an Omaha trial lawyer. He became well-known for a debate with Edward Rosewater in 1902 covered by the political cartoonist Guy R. Spencer, and he was orator of the day for the Lewis and Clark Centennial in 1904.

time of trouble." suggested that the parish should view the damage from the wind as a nudge and declared, "This is our opportunity."

His opinion announced in *Church and Home* was quickly seconded by Senator Sorenson, who was not a member of All Saints but a friend of Mackay's. In the *Examiner* under the headline "The Wreck of the Church," Sorenson offered the opinion that "the old shack" should not be rebuilt and mused about the mysterious ways of God. He personally offered to pledge a $1,000. He added that, in the spirit of J. D. Rockefeller who was well known for adding conditional string to his gifts, he would give half of the proceeds to All Saints as well, if any person or persons would within six months of the present date secure him a thousand yearly subscripts at $2 per year.

The congregational church on Twenty-Seventh and St. Mary's Avenue offered All Saints the use of its old building, which sat across the street from them. St. Matthias, which was without a priest at the time, suggested a temporary merger of the congregations; but Bishop Williams withheld his approval from the plan. The decision was made to persevere in the smaller building offered by the congregational church because it, among other things, would be the least disruptive as it was in All Saints neighborhood.

Meanwhile, the vestry struggled with the decision. Clearly, there were those that were anxious about incurring a debt. The insurance money was little more than $1,500, which suggests that Sorenson's label of "a wreck" was an exaggeration. The discussion of what to do dragged on into February. At the regular February meeting, Wattles raised the ante. He said that he would pledge up to one-fifth of any expense to build a parish house and church up to $50,000. The vestry set a date of February 27 for the final vote. On February 27, the vestry reassembled and voted unanimously to proceed. It was an audacious decision for the wherewithal was not on the table. In its place was the rector's conviction about the capacity of his laity, which they themselves doubted. It helped that the moment found the economy on a sustained rise that would last well past the end of 1907.

Kimball's design continued to evolve; and on March 10, 1906, he presented a new design to the vestry. A bell tower was eliminated, the roofline was steeper, and the north end was redesigned. By moving the entrance of the church to the side, the church could be lengthened by twenty feet. Above the additional pews in the rear would be a small rose window in the peak, and directly below the rose window would be "a stately English window." This window would have five lancets and would dominate the north end. Each of the lancets would represent one of five virtues. In these windows, the virtues could vary; but the core was always the three theological virtues, faith, hope, and charity. The style had become quite common in English churches built in the nineteenth century. Kimball's new design also called for a more extensive and elaborate use of the stone trim. In place of the bell tower, in the white stone work, which set off the windows and the entrance, a large Celtic cross would cap the northern gable. The stone cross, about six by four feet, would stand more than eighty feet in the air and would be visible on the Omaha skyline from all directions. This in itself was an important statement. At the time, having a cross on the top of a church meant for most people that the church was Roman Catholic. A Celtic cross signals not only "catholic" but also English. It resonated with Mackay's Irish background where Celtic high crosses were common and with Mackay's sense that the Episcopal was catholic without being Roman. The choice set a pattern for All Saints, which, from that time on, would use it repeatedly in various artistic expressions.[55]

No actual photograph of the exterior of the church exist. This is taken from the architect's water color rendering. The church, surmounted by a large Celtic cross, was link to the parish hall by a common entry way.

55 The Celtic cross is repeated in the Ritchie window commissioned in 1950 and was used by Ritchie to mark his wife's grave in Forest Lawn, as it was for a number of other parishioners. It is also the inspiration of the large modern cross that hangs on the north wall of the new building.

The plan met with the vestry's approval; and Mackay wrote in *Church and Home*: "Amount Needed for New Church $50,000; Subscribed to Date $28,255; Balance to be Subscribed $21,745. Let everybody work during the coming week to reduce balance to $10,000."[56]

On April 2, 1906, the vestry awarded the contract to Walter Peterson on the basis of his bid of $37,879, provided that he would also be awarded the contract on the parish hall; his bid for that was $15,845, the total now being $53,724. While dollar equivalents are difficult to calculate, it is clear that this was a major undertaking. Moreover, much of interior decoration and appointments were not included in this sum. Clearly, this was a brave undertaking.

On October 6, 1906, Mackay announced that he had secured financing of two of the five windows that would comprise the large north window from friends of his in Boston. With the one that was already provided for by the Parish Aid Society, he had in hand the money for the three center windows, faith, hope, and charity, each of which was to be represented by a classic lady. The work on the windows was to be done by Heaton, Butler, and Bayne of London, England, each costing $550. Under each of the figures, there was to be a scene from the Gospel illustrating the particular virtue represented in the window. Pledges for the other two lancets were made before long. The one on the right was to be Sir Percival, representing the virtue of courage, and the one on the left was Sir Galahad, representing the virtue of chastity. The male figures flanking the female figure at the center, both knights of the round table, completed Mackay's sense of virtue. Mystically for him, they tied the worship at the altar with the mission of going out in the world to transform it into the kingdom. When he announced the plan for the window, he quoted from his favorite poem, Tennyson's "Idylls of the King:"

> I saw the spiritual city and all her spires and her gateways, in a glory like one pearl and from the star there shot a rose red sparkle to the city, and there dwelt and I knew it was the Holy Grail which never I on earth again shall see.

This great window was the last thing that a worshiper would see as he left the church; and it was meant to be a message about what the worshiper was to carry into the world, namely, a noble character. Above this sermon in glass was another smaller rose window that depicted Jesus's blessing of the children. It was to be given by the parish's Sunday school.

---

56 *Church and Home*, vol. XI, no. 23, March 10, 1906.

Walking out of Church. The north end of the 1906 building was marked by a stained glass window with five lancets containing figures representing chastity, faith, hope, charity, courage, a selection which was expressive of Mackay's theology.

As the work was drawing to a close, the vestry authorized a mortgage of $25,000 to be held by the Rochester Loan and Banking Company. Wattles had a long business relationship with the Eastern company and actually served on its board. Mackay, whose previous building projects in Fort Worth, Leadville, and Council Bluffs had been paid off at completion or soon thereafter, had clearly hoped the same would be true this time; but this time, his project fell short on this account.

Easter 1907

On the other hand, what he accomplished was far from disappointing. He was determined to open the new church on Easter 1907 in spite of a good deal of interior work that remained to be finished in the church and even more work that remained on the parish house. The coverage of the opening, in the issue of *Church and Home* that followed, began, "Easter 1907 is a date which will be long remembered by the people of All Saints church as the day when we first worshiped in our new church."

The account continues,

> The day dawned bright and clear, and the weather was all that could be desired. At the seven-thirty celebration of the Holy Communion, more than two hundred of our communicants were present, and at the eleven-o-clock service, scores of people were turned away long before the opening of the service. The week preceding had been a trying one for all concerned, and at times, it seemed doubtful if we could possibly have the church ready for opening on Easter. Some of our organ pipes were lost in transit and did not arrive until Friday, and Mr. Benson, the organ builder, worked all night Saturday until the hour before the service Sunday morning to have the organ ready by eleven o'clock. Mr. Simms could not have a rehearsal with his choir until an hour before the opening service, and under the circumstances, it was wonderful how he managed to present such a splendid program of music. Our seats were not in place until 10:00 p.m. Saturday, Mr. Ewing and Mr. Miller remaining in the church lifting and arranging the heavy pews until the last seat was in place. Altogether, it was a trying time and little did the congregation know of the hard work and mental anxiety which had preceded the opening as they enjoyed the inspiring service and the beautiful building.[57]

The interior of the church was unfinished, much of the plaster decorations being incomplete, and no attempt had been made at coloring the walls. The coverage in the *Bee* trumpeted the building's prowess: "The new All Saints Church, at Twenty-Sixth Street and Dewey Avenue, which stands as a monument of architectural beauty, is lighted with 3,500 candle power of Nernst light, from sixteen Nernst lamps, specially designed for church lighting." Mackay's own assessment was that: "It is the most beautiful and complete plant, consisting of church and parish house, between Chicago and the Pacific Coast."

---

57 *Church and Home*, vol. XII, no. 27, April 6, 1907.

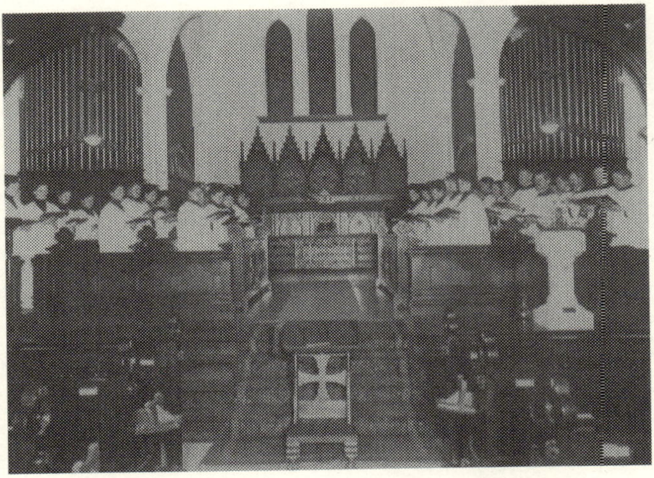

The Altar and Chancel of the 1906 building shortly after its construction. The Gothic style altar which was the original in the 1886 building was put in service in the new building.

The first child baptized in the new church and in the new baptismal font was Eleanor Smith, the daughter of Mr. and Mrs. Floyd Monroe Smith. Confirmation was held on May 5, and the list included Mackay's daughter Elenore and Edward and Irving Benolken. Irving had just served as crucifer for the dedication and would long serve in that role. The boy who had carried the cross on the first service of new church on Dewey, through the telling of his wife Nancy, who taught piano to many of the city's promising piano students and was a patron of music in the city, would remain an active presence in the parish well into the 1980s. In June came the first weddings, one of which was the marriage of the mayor's daughter, Ruth Dahlman, to Austin J. Collett, celebrated June 5, 1907.

The parish house, however, was not yet complete in May; and it was necessary for Mackay to turn down the bishop's request to hold the diocese's annual council at All Saints that year. In September, the vestry needed to borrow $1,000 to pay Thomas Kimball's final bill. Curiously, the vestry's minutes, up to this time meticulously kept, fall into disarray and leave us in the dark. It is unclear why this happened. Perhaps more of the work was being done by committees and have not been recorded. On the other hand, at this time, the minutes began to be typed and pasted into the book. Perhaps they had been put in a file with the intension of pasting them into the book, a thing that did not happen. It is only in 1920 that a record of regular minutes is restored.

The Spirit

Shortly after the dedication of the new church, Bishop Worthington died while traveling in the south of France on January 7, 1908. Mackay could not restrain from commenting about Worthington: "By nature and disposition, he was never intended for the hard work of a Western bishop, and the very qualities which would have endeared him to an Eastern diocese unfitted him for such a field as the Diocese of Nebraska." Of Williams, who he had always supported and regarded as a close friend, he said, "We believe that Bishop Williams will continue to be the bishop of all the people of the diocese as he has been in the past. That he will rise above partisanship and that his work for Christ in this diocese will ever be marked by the same frank fearless spirit we confidently expect and hope."[58] This transition too seemed like an opening to the spirit of the age.

In 1908, Clarkson Hospital joined All Saints on the hill at the end of Howard, a couple of block to the east. Mackay greeted the opening of Clarkson, which was dedicated on October 22, 1908, in an article in *Church and Home*: "The situation of Clarkson Hospital is ideal. Standing as it does on a high bluff, in the very heart of the city and yet free from all noise of passing cars, it commands a splendid view of Omaha north and south, while way to the east the city of Council Bluffs can be seen, and river winding for miles along the hills, all forming a panorama of rare beauty. Like a city set upon a hill." These are words that Mackay could have used to describe All Saints as well. Mackay was on the board of the Clarkson Hospital along with Dean Tancock and the bishop. His laity had worked hard on the hospital even as they were working on their own church. All Saints furnished a room of the hospital. He boasts of how well the women, led by All Saints women, especially Mrs. Noe and Mrs. Philip Potter, had managed to exceed their ambitious goal of $20,000. Mrs. Philip Potter served as secretary to Clarkson Hospital Association and Mrs. Noe as treasurer. This move opened up a long run of special associations between All Saints and Clarkson Hospital. Many nurses in training attended church at All Saints, where they found a warm welcome. Likewise, members of the staff also found their way into the parish. One of the long-serving choir mothers, Bessie Ohle, once explained to me how she had become an Episcopalian. Her mother was a cook at the hospital, and they lived in a small apartment close by. She said she used to play with the Mackay kids and was invited to be part of the church school.

---

58 *Church and Home*, vol. XIII, no. 15, January 11, 1908.

The visions of what could be done with a parish hall were soon fulfilled. Public lectures were regularly offered in the parish house. G. W. Wattles was frequently one of the scheduled speakers, which in today's terms would be something like having Warren Buffet speaking to your adult forum. The parish held dinners, the choir sponsored dances, and the various women's circles gathered for sewing. Particular emphasis was placed on working with the boys of the parish. A boys club was formed. A castle of the Knights of King Arthur was built to inspire them with virtue, the same virtue pictured in the great window on the north end of the church. Athletic events were scheduled to instill them with courage and discipline. The All Saints Athletic Club held its first meeting in 1909. Wattles personally funded the program. Mr. Morley Young, who had been one of Central High school's star athletes, was retained as the instructor and director of the club. The club met every Monday evening at seven o'clock. About twenty-five boys from the parish and the neighbor regularly participated in the program. Young listed some of its champs in an article published in the *Bee*. Paul Jones, not yet fifteen, is a wizard at high jumping, clearing five feet, ten inches. Gordon Grout is the lightweight wrestling champion of the club and Ronald Barrows the heavyweight. As for boxing, "no one dares claim to be champ, as the whole club would be on hand to knock his block off." Edward Mackay is a half-mile runner who will hold his own with any in the state, and John Metzger bids claim to the sprinting championship. The *Bee* concludes: "The All Saints Athletic club is a pretty classy junior athletic organization even if it does use a parish house for a gym and some of its youngsters will be heard from when they grow older and enter interscholastic and intercollegiate athletics."[59] The activities of the athletic club were regularly reported on in *Church and Home*. In a report on a boxing and wrestling exhibitions held in Wattles Memorial parish house, it concluded: "We wish more of our people could have seen these manly boys exhibit their prowess in athletic sports."

Mackay was always ready to mention the names of young people in *Church and Home*. He writes: "It was pleasant to see two of our boys at the early celebration last Sunday, Robert Storz and Frank Campbell." In another place, he recognizes All Saints golf champions, Mr. John Redick, Mr. Sam Reynolds, and Mr. Ralph Peters. "They are the leaders on the golf course." He often reports on the coming and going of college-age kids. "Robert Howe and Fred Clark for Yale, Herbert Davis for Cornell, and Drexel H. Sibbernsen and his brother Albert left for Dartmouth." In this same issue, he noted a baptism: Dana Cuthbert Bradford baptized on April 27, 1914, sponsors Mrs. G. Storz, Howard Balridge, and Thomas F.

---

59 *The Bee*, January 30, 1916.

Kenney. Sam Reynold's daughter and the Drexel Sibbernsen's and Dana Bradford's sons remain active at All Saints well into the twenty-first century, giving us a sense of the extent to which the legacy of Dr. Mackay has lived on.

Mackay was equally concerned to recognize the girls of the parish. He reports in the October 1912 issue of *Church and Home*: "Ms. Elizabeth Pickens, who was chosen for queen of Aksarben last week is one of our All Saints communicants and a faithful one at that." In 1914, Ms. Elizabeth Pickens is listed as president of the All Saints Altar Guild. Her wedding to Kenneth H. Patterson on June 3, 1915, is covered in detail in an issue of *Church and Home*, including the fact that the Aksarben Knights gave her a handsome hall clock as a wedding present.

Church and Home

The new volume of *Church and Home*, which was published at the beginning of October in 1912, reflected on the history of the paper. Mackay proudly announced:

> Last week's issue of *Church and Home* began the eighteenth volume of our parish paper . . . When *Church and Home* began its existence, it was the only weekly parish paper in the United States. It was a doubtful question whether a weekly paper could be sustained by the people of All Saints, but we began in faith, and though oftentimes discouraged by lack of interest and funds, we went ahead with the work and feel that our success as a parish has been largely due to the weekly visits of *Church and Home* in every home in our midst.

He went on in the article to thank the loyalty of those who advertise in the paper and listed seventeen advertisers who had been with the paper from the beginning. Two of these were given special notice: the Alamito Dairy and C. B. Brown Jewelry.

The original publisher had been Nicholson, but he was soon replaced by Waters. By 1912, Mr. Waters, who had led the firm for many years, was suffering from a number of health problems and was looking for time off. A printing company, which began printing a newspaper in Auburn, Nebraska, and several surrounding communities, had recently ventured into commercial printing. Its initial success led it to look for a way to expand into the Omaha market. The firm was headed by J. W. Barnhart, who had come to Nebraska from Lancaster, Pennsylvania. Waters's need for a partner came as the opportunity that Barnhart was looking for and he bought an interest in the Waters Printing Company and moved to Omaha. Beginning with the August 31, 1912, issues of *Church and Home*, the publisher of record is listed as The Waters-Barnhart Printing Co. located at 552 South Thirteenth Street. By November of that same year, J. W. Barnhart is listed as the manager of the company. Mackay noted the following April in *Church and Home*: "Since Mr. Barnhart has been reading the proof of *Church and Home*, we have had fewer typographical errors than ever before in the seventeen years the paper has been printed." It is clear the close relation Mackay had with Mr. Waters was extended to J. W. Barnhart, and with time, it became an even closer. That relationship would outlast *Church and Home*; and it has continued through his children, grandchildren, great grandchildren, and even the fifth generation who were still worshiping at All Saints at the beginning of the twenty-first century.

For a brief period, the parish's paper expanded to two broad sheets, making a total of eight pages. Advertisements grew and included such new businesses as Blitzen High Test Gasoline, 13½ cents a gallon, which had filling stations a Thirty-Eighth and Farnam, 315 South Twenty-Fourth Street, Seventeenth and Jackson streets; the L. V. Nicholas Oil Co.; and S. H. Buffett and Son Grocery, 315 S. Fourteenth Street. The issues between 1908 and 1913 represent *Church and Home*'s high water mark. A special testimonial to the importance of the weekly paper came with the death of a woman who lived in Brooklyn, New York, Mrs. Francis Helen Corney. Her sole connection with All Saints was a subscription to *Church and Home*, which she had started because of her first husband, Judge Clark, had a connection with All Saints through his friendship with Major D. H. Wheeler, an active parishioner and chorister at All Saints. Corney's daughter notified Mackay of her death and went on to say of her mother, "She spoke of you often, and she loved *Church and Home* which she called my little paper and said she got more good from it than from any other of her papers. When it came, she would say listen to this and read me such selections as pleased her." Mackay, of course, printed the daughter's remarks in the next issue of *Church and Home*.

Women's Work in the Parish

The significance of women's contribution to the life of any parish church and more particularly at All Saints is difficult to surface. Parish proceedings, particularly parish minutes, are filled with names of various men, but seldom with those of the women that worked alongside them. *Church and Home* was an exception, which from its beginning in 1896 regularly listed the names of women and their contributions to the work of the parish. We have already encountered the name of Mrs. E. G. Brabrook whom Mackay said was an indispensable aid in the publication of *Church and Home*. Her husband was a photo engraver, and she worked as agent collecting insurance payments for the Foresters, a mutual-aid society for English immigrants, such as herself and her husband. She retired from her work on the paper in 1902 and was followed by Ms. Julia Baker. Baker was the choir mother, no small task in itself, and soprano in the choir. She worked weekly with Mackay to pull the paper together, and during Mackay's absences, she took on the full responsibility for publishing *Church and Home*.

In 1906, the work of the women of the parish was recognized by a gift of a gold cross carrying the inscription "Women of All Saints." The gift was made by Blanche L. McKelvy. Blanche came to Omaha with her husband Russell from Pittsburg, Pennsylvania, in 1880. The daughter of a newspaper man, she began writing for the *Excelsior*. Before long, she was engaged more deeply in the newspaper business, becoming a full-time reporter and editor for the *Omaha Daily News* and then for the *Omaha World-Herald*. For the *Daily News*, she served as editor of the women's and children's pages, which often contain original fairy tales that she had authored. Subsequently, she served as women's editor for the *Omaha World-Herald* until her husband's death in 1915. In her personal life, she was a leader in civic and club life in Omaha. There is no record of membership at All Saints; but it is likely that she, like many, found themselves attending All Saints without ever formally joining, a thing that Mackay encouraged. Her motivation for making this gift is unstated, but coming from a woman whose reputation was that of being a spokesperson for woman in the community, her motivation must have been a desire to honor the contribution that the women of All Saints were making to the work in the parish and in larger civic community.[60]

One of the names that were frequently mentioned in *Church and Home* was Mrs. Albert Noe. Her husband was a commission livestock broker for the Clay, Robinson Company of Chicago. She often served as the head of the Women's Auxiliary and was particularly active on the diocesan level with missionary activities. Mackay published a long article by her

[60] It is unclear who was to wear the cross, as the parish had at the time four guilds and did not have a single women's chairperson. Subsequently, the president of ECW passes this cross down to each new president.

outlining the missionary needs of the diocese on the opening page of *Church and Home* in 1909.[61] The auxiliary also assisted various projects in the city and in particular with the work of the visiting nurses. Mackay regularly reported on and supported the work of the Visiting Nurses in *Church and Home.* Another outreach ministry in which All Saints women became instrumental was the creation of "Jean Home." "Jean Home" was a living situation for young, independent working-class women in the city, designed to relieve them from unsafe housing where they were often victimized. Mackay supported this ministry and asked the vestry to reserve pew number 7 for the young ladies of the "Jean Home." He said, "We hope to see it filled every Sunday."

At the beginning of the new program year of 1913, Mackay made a point of describing the parish societies, which were, in fact, the women's organizations in the parish. The first on his list was the Woman's Auxiliary, whose projects supported diocesan and national missionary aid programs. Then followed the Parish Aid Society, whose projects aided the work in the parish, such as paying for necessary repairs and, for a long time, making the semiannual payment of interest on the parish mortgage. Next in line were the Chancel Guild, whose role was to maintain things that pertain to the chancel such as choir robes, music, and other things necessary for the choir, and the Altar and Flower Guild, whose task was to robe the altar. The altar guild was considered at the time to be a guild for the younger women and was headed in 1913 by Ms. Elizabeth Pickens. It consisted of thirty young women, including Mackay's own daughter Eleanor. He completed his list of women's organizations by briefly noting a junior auxiliary, consisting of the girls enrolled in Sunday school, and a newly formed circle, the Dundee Guild, whose role was listed as social.

The formation of a Dundee Guild was a sign of the way the westward movement of the city was affecting the parish. Its first meeting was described with considerable detail in *Church and Home*.[62] The rector and Mrs. Mackay attended the meeting that was held in the home of Mrs. Joseph Polcar, the president.[63] Other officers were listed as Mrs. Rank

61 *Church and Home*, vol. XV, no. 1, September 25, 1909.

62 *Church and Home*, vol. XIX no. 1.

63 Emma Polcar was born in England and immigrated in 1894, naturalized in 1899. Her husband, Joseph, was the editor of *Omaha Daily News*. They lived on 4800 block of Cass Street.

Browne, vice president, and Mrs. W. W. Hoagland, secretary.[64] A second circle was formed in the Hanscom Park neighborhood, headed by Mrs. J. B. Reynolds. Mrs. Hoagland, who succeeded Mrs. Polcar in 1915 as president of the Dundee Guild, emerged as one of All Saints great workers whose memory was still fresh among the women of the parish when I arrived in the middle of the 1970s.

From the beginning, Mackay possessed an innate instinct for shared ministry with his laity and this instinct fostered the work of the women at All Saints. He saw trends at work in the church, particularly among the ritualists, which seemed to question his kind of ministry and the candor with which he entrusted himself to his own laity. Upon returning from his vacation in 1914, he preached a sermon and subsequently printed it in *Church and Home*, entitled "The Changed Relationship of the Christian Ministry." It is an interesting and skillfully crafted attack on rising clericalism. He began with the text: "Not that we lord it over your faith, but are helpers of your joy" (2 Cor. 1:24). One of the illustrations he used in the sermon was the fictional Mr. Hooper of Hawthorne's *Twice Told Tales*. Mr. Hooper is a Protestant minister who wears a black veil covering his face at all times. Behind the black veil, Hooper could see his laity, but they could not see him. Mackay concluded in the end:

> The laity both (men and women) will labor to lessen the work of their pastor by taking an active interest in its branches of work in the church. They will realize that it is THEIR church, not his alone, and that if it is a failure, it is as much their fault as his. His anxieties, his worries are THEIRS, and they will share them with him. And so will pastor and people work together, and live together as one great family, "knit together in the communion of the Saints."

Dissonance and Disconnecting

As the century progressed, Mackay found himself defending his laity. His parishioner William Gurley, the flamboyant and outspoken lawyer, found himself named in a federal indictment that had been prepared by a group of detectives and submitted to Congress by President Roosevelt in 1909. Mackay wrote in *Church and Home*: "We yield to none in our

[64] Florence Hougland on the corner of Forty-Eighth and Cass. Her husband William had succeeded his father George in a very successful wholesale lumber business.

admiration of the good qualities of our President. We admire the zeal and courage he has shown in the prosecution of offenders against the law of the land, but we fear that in his zeal he has allowed his temper to overcome his judgment."[65]

In the same year, the street car men went on strike. Mackay at first tried to mediate the issue. He began by stating sympathy with working men. "If I were a working man I should probably deem it wise to join a union for the reasons given." The reasons he has cited are that the unions provide a sense of belonging and they educate workers. It gave them an association that brought the best out of them and sheltered them against the inevitable hardships of life, often impossible for individuals to bear on their own. He concedes that strikes are sometimes necessary. He says: "I believe also with President Taft that sometimes strikes like revolutions, are necessary, but they should be adopted only as a last resort, and when all other means had absolutely failed."

On the other hand, he says, "I know Mr. Wattles and that he has a sympathetic attitude toward labor." His position, Mackay argued, has been misunderstood; and if the outsiders, who he refers to as "the walking delegates" would get out of the way, the workers and Mr. Wattles should be able to quickly solve the problem. It is not so remarkable that Mackay has a keen grasp of the situation as it is that he has the timidity wade into the issue in print. But then he has told us he is no Rev. Mr. Hooper with a black veil over his face.

In 1913, Mackay changed his opinion about women suffrage. All Saints had allowed women to vote at its annual meetings since 1891, and Mackay early on had a close relationship with women suffragettes beginning with his days in Council Bluffs. It is not clear what made him change his mind. In England, the suffrage movement spawned some high-profile violence that, like worker violence, was abhorrent to Mackay and would have certainly caused him to reconsider. He said in a *Church and Home* article, "The exhibition of the women of England is an excellent example to what women will descend to carry out her point. She will stop at nothing and is dangerous when given any power."

Perhaps his second thoughts had more to do with the anticipation of how women would vote. The struggle over prohibition continued to escalate on the state and local level anticipating national prohibition in 1920. The argument against prohibition with which Mackay had long cited was that such an attempt at controlling personal behavior would prove to be a self-righteous disaster, making things worse than they were. Progress demanded more reasonable steps. It seemed to many that this argument

65 *Church and Home*, vol. XV, no. 15, January 9, 1909.

would not carry weight with a female electorate, and if they had a vote, the approval of prohibition was a certainty.

Mackay attempted to carry out his change of opinion with good grace. He, for example, congratulated a Ms. Bronson on a particularly fine talk in favor of suffrage to one of All Saints circles. It surprised and hurt him, however, to find himself criticized for changing his mind. "When the rector of All Saints espoused the suffrage cause, he heard no criticism of his action among those opposing him, but the moment he became convinced of his error and became an anti-suffragist, the air was filled with base suggestion that he was influenced in his decision." The *Bee* poked its nose in on the issue, claiming that his well-known parishioner, Mrs. Polcar, had left All Saints because of his decision. He sets the record straight. She had simply moved to another part of the congregation to sit with friends. Moreover, he argued he could not, if he desired, be in agreement with every member of his large congregation on any subject. "There are ministers who live a clam-like existence, never expressing their real convictions, but the rector of All Saints does not belong to that class." Mrs. Polcar did, in fact, continue to be an effective part of All Saints; but the world in which Mackay had thrived was disappearing. It would be a world in which there would be progressively less tolerance for the other side of the issue and candor would have to pay an ever heavier price.

War

In 1914, Mackay left on one of his summer tours to rejuvenate himself. It was different this time in that Mrs. Mackay remained at home and that the steamer that he boarded was bound for Europe, not across the Great Lakes for Buffalo. Writing on July 18, 1914, in *Church and Home*, he noted that he had now been at the helm of All Saints for twenty-three years and announced that his address for the duration of his vacation would be the American Express office in Antwerp. He intended to travel in the Lowlands and was especially intent on visiting the battlefield at Waterloo, where Wellington's victory had brought a sustained peace to Europe.

When he arrived in Brussels in August, after his visit to Waterloo, he found the city bracing for war. He wrote from Brussels on August 5, "I feel that somehow or other the struggle will not last long. It would be frightful if it did. Christian nations thirsting for each other's blood in this twentieth century are not an edifying sight nor does it say much for the influence of Christianity."[66] Soon after these remarks were posted, Belgium began the

[66] *Church and Home*, vol. XIX, no. 49, September 26, 1914.

hasty evacuation of foreigners, and Mackay caught one of the last trains out. At home in Omaha, there was concern for Dr. Mackay's safety and parishioners worried that he might be interned for the duration of the war. With relief, *Church and Home* announced, "Dr. Mackay safe in London." A cablegram received Thursday noon by Mrs. Mackay conveyed the news that the doctor was safe in London and that he was in good health. The message was a source of great relief to his wife and many friends who feared he was in either Germany or Belgium and would be forced to stay there until after the cessation of Hostilities."

In London, he ran into his parishioners, J. W. Redick and his wife. On August 17 as he boarded the RMS *Royal George*, the first person he ran into was Mr. Arthur C. Smith, another of his vestrymen. This is a testament to how cosmopolitan his Omaha congregation was and at the same time to its naiveté about the world into which the twentieth century was about to introduce them.

Like most Americans, war in Europe had caught them by surprise, though few as dramatically as it had Mackay. Mackay struggled to find his old buoyancy, which had allowed him for so many years to ride out such storms. Logically, it was not difficult to argue for American neutrality. In *Church and Home*, he published the statements of the English clergy and the German clergy. But fairness, as he saw it, was being compromised. He condemned what he saw happening to Americans:

> They placed their dependence upon God, but we talk of increasing our standing army and building seacoast defenses, and we put our trust in our ironclad navy, rather than in the righteousness of our people and their devotion.

As time went on, it became clear that neutrality did not mean not profiting from the war. In January of 1915, he asks, "Are we keeping up the war?" After describing how the U.S. industry was supplying armaments to the war parties, he concludes,

> And we—we, the American people, who prate of peace and pray for peace and talk of brotherhood and helpfulness—we have helped to do it and are helping to do it every day. It was hard as time went on not to conclude that the country had been caught in "a horrible nightmare of a war."

On May 7, 1915, Mackay's position was further tried when a torpedo fired by a German submarine sank the *Lusitania*. An impassioned discussion of the event followed in *Church and Home*. Mackay, after labeling the sinking "an unthinkable barbaric act," attempted to convince his reader and even more himself that the German U-boat commander had not anticipated that his torpedo would do more than injure the vessel. Then he concluded:

> We hope and pray that the sinking of this great vessel and the fearful loss of life will bring both Germans and British to their senses and that the ocean may become free to all vessels employed in peaceful pursuits.[67]

Wilson's subsequent response and Bryan's resignation as secretary of state, however, made it very difficult to believe that anybody was going to soon come to their senses or that the United States would stay out of this war.

The Automobile

The identity of the twentieth century would also be marked by the most rapid deployment of technology in the history of the human race. This technological development promised relief from stultifying labor, which in turn could be better invested and/or better devoted to the exercise of personal freedom. No single technology at the beginning of the twentieth century was more exciting or more ambivalent than the rise of the automobile. Its growing presence is first noted in *Church and Home* with the reports of traffic accidents.

At first, of course, automobiles were for the wealthy; but by 1913, the circle of ownership was beginning to spread. Mackay noted with amusement that "three of our Omaha ministers are now the proud owners of automobiles—Tancock of Trinity, Jenks of the First Presbyterian, and Baltzly of Kountze Memorial. We congratulate our brethren, but we prefer the means of a locomotion provided by the street car company and Dame Nature. It's healthier and safer, and less expensive."[68] Nevertheless, he was in 1915 being assisted by parishioners with the loan of their automobiles. He writes in *Church and Home*, "Thanks to Mrs. Robert Trimble, the rector was able to make several long-distance calls last Monday. The automobile is surely a great convenience."[69]

---

67 *Church and Home*, vol. XX, no. 30, May 15, 1915.

68 *Church and Home*, vol. XIX, no. 3, November 7, 1914.

69 *Church and Home*, vol. XIX, no. 34, June 3, 1915.

His anxiety about the automobile, however, was reinforced on his summer vacation in 1913, which was spent on the Great Lakes at some of his favorite haunts. In a sermon, he takes as an illustration the precipitous decline in the economy of the resort hotels of the Great Lakes because of the way the automobile has changed what people do and where they go. You don't go sit on the front porch of a grand hotel and admire the sun setting over the lake if you can get in the car and drive out to Yellowstone or down to Kansas City. Then he argues:

> We have the same spirit of unrest even in the religious world. Men and women are not satisfied to walk in the old paths. The quiet religion of the Master of the Apostles, of the great religious minds of the past will not satisfy the restless spirit of this age. They must desert their churches for the crowded Tabernacle. The churches are not run on automobile principles.[70]

Mackay was quite intuitive on the way the automobile and other forms of technology were going to reshape American life, which among other things would cause the city of Omaha to spread out over a vastly greater area than ever imagined. By 1912, Omaha reached the peaceful town of Dundee and had begun considering the need to annex it. The developers of Dundee had made the principle selling points for homes in the new neighborhoods the priggish boast that the village was above and beyond the corruption of the city. There were, they pointed out, no saloons in Dundee. When the vote came for annexation in 1915, the developers enlisted the aid of the evangelist Billie Sunday who opened his crusade in Dundee with the challenge: "Come on, you forces of iniquity in Omaha, that made the church as thing to put your dirty feet on." Sunday's words were used by the citizen of Dundee to fight annexation. Mackay rose to the challenge and attacked back, disputing the validity of Billie Sunday's observations and pointing out that the result of his preaching was to sow division in the community whose life flowed from the city. Mackay saw that the emerging "suburban way of life" was quite different from the earlier "Gold Coast" developments. The residents of the Gold Coast enjoyed the privilege of living on the edge of the city, but their lives were deeply enmeshed in the city. But the suburb attracted people who wanted to dissociate themselves from the problems of the city. People might well come into the city to work; but their family life, cultural activities, and leisure time would be spent in the suburb. Why, asked Mackay, given this, would they choose to drive into the city to go to church? This was a threat

70 *Church and Home*, vol. XIX, no. 3, November 7, 1914.

to the premise upon which churches in general and more specifically All Saints had chosen their locations, built their buildings, and structured their programs for the past fifty years. In the May issue of 1915, Mackay wrote: "All Saints is now, or will be in the near future, in the condition of a downtown Church. It will need the earnest loyalty and hearty cooperation of every member of the parish to keep it at the front, as it has been for years, financially and spiritually."[71]

Church and Home Loses Its Voice

For some time the costs of publishing *Church and Home* were exceeding the money raised by subscriptions and advertisement. During 1914 and continuing on into 1915, even as some of the best editions of *Church and Home* were being produced, there is a plea for funding to allow the publication of the paper. A number of testimonials were elicited, but the problem remained unsolved. It was frustrating that a paper that had done so much to make All Saints what it was could not be seen as a legitimate part of the parish's expenses. But the parish budget itself was stressed, and it would take a long time for the concept of parish administration to develop and to come to terms with the idea that communications are as important as brick and mortar. Mackay managed to eke out the year. Precisely as he began the next volume of *Church and Home*, a fatal blow was struck. The Retailers' Association of Omaha announced a boycott of the religious press. The problem for the retailers was that the religious press had proliferated and they were being pestered for ads in all kinds of papers and newsletters. It was impossible to say yes to one whose advertising might actually pay and no to another whose would not, without being charged with bias. Mackay received notice that Burgess–Nass, Thompson Belden, and C. C. Brown Jewelry Co. were withdrawing their advertisements. He argued that *Church and Home* was different from the religious press. His paper was, he argued, intended for a public audience and ought to be considered equal to the secular press. The argument got nowhere and a last ditch attempt to raise the subscription price from 50¢ to $1 failed to produce the revenue necessary. In the end, he had to concede and *Church and Home* was reduced to a single sheet with a few announcements mailed periodically to members of the parish. In "Farewell" published in the last issue of *Church and Home*, date October 9, 1915, Mackay writes,

[71] *Church and Home*, vol. XX, no. 30, May 15, 1915.

> It seems like a light thing to say that *Church and Home* will cease to exist, but the words cause a choking of the throat as we think of the many pleasant and tender associations of the past. We have every year's issues bound, and as we look over the pages, what memories will arise. Twenty volumes of records of comedies, dramas and tragedies, every one of them closely linked to All Saints Church and its rector. It is like the tearing apart the most tender ties, and sweetest associations, to say, farewell.[72]

This was one of a number of growing signs that embracing the twentieth century as an age of opportunity for All Saints and for the Episcopal Church, in general, had been premature. By the end of 1915, there is much evidence to suggest that the Episcopal Church would have to step back from that embrace and to face the century as an age of struggle.

A Hospitalization

The year presented other difficulties for Mackay. As Easter of 1915 approached, Mackay was suddenly taken ill. He informed the parish that "On Saturday morning I awakened with a temperature of 103 and as oblivious of my surroundings as Nebuchadnezzar on the meadows of Chaldea." His diagnosis was streptococcus viridans or in layman's terms the grippe bug. Reverend Heaton was fortunately in Omaha because of his father's illness and could take the services at All Saints. On March 13, his doctor, Crummer, issued a statement: "The rector is improving nicely. As a complication of his original infection, he developed a thrombo phlebitis of his right leg, but fortunately, it was limited to the smaller veins of the calf muscles." Having become clear that Mackay's convalescence would be more protracted, Bishop Williams, who had taken one of the intervening services himself, announced that he had procured the services of Rev. George B. Adams of Chicago to serve the parish while Mackay recovered. It was not until the beginning of May that Mackay was able to be in church. He reported that he had taken the eleven-o-clock service, saying, "It was my first public service for nine weeks and the result was that I did a little more than I should have done, but no serious results have followed."

Mackay was not the only one in the parish who was hospitalized during the year. The junior warden, Victor Caldwell, had been under doctor's care during the year with several spells spent in the hospital. His

[72] *Church and Home*, volume XXI, no. 1, October 9, 1915.

condition was reported as asthma with which Caldwell had long suffered. In February, he returned to the small town in Upstate New York where his mother had been raised. From there he posted a letter to Mackay in which he had expressed the idea that he hoped that his life would be remembered as his mother's. He said his mother had spent scores of years giving herself to this little community, much like he thought his rector had at All Saints. He added this is "the work that counted."

Caldwell had risen rapidly in Omaha's banking community from a young teller in 1899 to president of U.S. National Bank in 1915. He was known for his knowledge and integrity and was instrumental in the development of the banking industry. He joined the vestry of All Saints in 1903 and went on to be elected junior warden, when the struggle over the future of All Saints was intense. He was allied with Wattles and Montgomery, with whom he had developed a working relationship during his service on the board of the Trans Mississippi Exposition.

He died the day after Christmas, at the young age of fifty-one, and was mourned by the banking community who closed their banks the day of the funeral. As a seasoned pastor, Mackay expected a death to fall during the holidays, but this loss threatened his equilibrium. The parish was losing one of its best givers and hardest workers. Indeed, he was losing a trusted adviser and a close personal friend. He had said in funeral sermon: "I loved him, friends, and in the mourner's place would I sit silent today–but his lips are still and I must speak."

The Last Sunday of 1915

Before leaving 1915, we might imagine Mackay at the end of the last service of the year. He would have followed the choir down the aisle as usual, but he would have been aware that he was exhausted by the service in a way and in a degree that was really different. He would after all, he reminded himself, celebrate his seventy-second birthday in little over a week. Earlier that year, a painful thrombosis had taken his beloved Easter celebration away from him. His legs, now free from pain, nevertheless lacked the spring that he had always been able to count upon. Midway down the aisle, he caught the eye of his wife, Georgia, standing in her pew. Their youngest son, Stanley, who had just turned twenty, stood to one side of her. Like his older brother, he had gone to work for Armour in Chicago, but thankfully, he had made it home for Christmas. The other boys had not. The oldest Odin, their Harvard graduate, was a successful businessman living in Chicago, working for the Amour Company. Ralph, having tried his luck with seminary, had chosen instead to go into business. He was living in St. Joseph, Missouri. Of the boys, Ralph always seemed to have the more difficult path to follow. Robert worked for the Fairmont Creamery that was putting Omaha on the map as the butter capital of the country. The company had stationed him in Pittsburgh, Pennsylvania. On the other side of his wife was their daughter, Eleanor. She was now twenty-two but still living at home. She had been a witness to many, many weddings, but she was yet unmarried. A smile flashes between Mackay and his wife, as he passes by.

As was his habit, he was assessing the congregation as he went out. He was pleased to see his vestry men there. Wattles, who had spent more than six months of the past year in his new mansion in Hollywood, was there that Sunday. He wondered how much he would see of him in the coming year. And then there was the empty pew of Victor Caldwell, the parish's junior warden. He prayed for Victor's soul as he past his empty pew, trying to put aside for the moment any further assessment of the loss to parish and himself.

Overall, the congregation had made a pleasingly strong showing for a winter morning. Congregations had run high all year. All the numbers had been good. Yet it had been a most difficult year. It felt to him like he had spent the year afloat on the "River of Doubt," which had been featured on the front pages of the country's newspapers for most of the past year. Who had ever known that there was a tributary of the Amazon River, which carried such an adverse name? It had become famous because his one-time political hero, Theodore Roosevelt, had nearly lost his life on it this past year, leading ill-planned and ill-considered adventure.

He could not keep out of his mind the thought that the country was progressively more conflicted about who it was. It couldn't get into the war and it yet couldn't seem to stay out of the war. It couldn't assimilate the massive immigration that had poured into the country, and yet it couldn't do without the cheap labor that they provided. President Wilson's reforms, generally just, were self-righteous and forced. The opposition to them seemed to be progressively more self-righteous in return.

His city, whose reputation he had so often defended, was endlessly conflicted between reformers who seemed more in love with condemning sin than preventing it and sinners who were not satisfied with enjoying their illicit pleasures but needed to flaunt them. Indeed, the city was changing rapidly in way that no one quite understood.

The church was more torn between the high church ritualist and the traditional low church Protestants than it had been in some time. Much effort was going into the debate whether to change its name from

Protestant Episcopal to American Catholic. What troubled him most was that the debate was being pursued more by threats that change or the lack of change would destroy the Episcopal Church. The civility of debate was missing there as well.

The parish was, despite its growth, incapable of paying off its mortgage. It seemed incapable of understanding the way that the country and the city were changing. Were they in the right place with the right building? How would they replace the leadership that they had depended upon for the last couple of decades and were now in the process of losing as he was only too well aware?

As he came to the end of the long aisle, he looked up at the great north window and recovered his balance. There, before him, were the five virtues—faith, hope, and charity—flanked by chastity and courage. It was just what he planned. Any one taking their leave from worship in this church would be encountered by the vision of these beautiful powerful virtues represented by the three stunning ladies and the two glorious knights. The whole work of worship, he thought, was to implant and revive these virtues in them and in himself. If he, if they, his most beloved people, would be so equipped as they went out into the world from this place, then he, they, would be well. If the world had become a "River of Doubt," they would be well equipped to deal with it.

Part 2

Holding on in an Age of Conflict (1915 to 1947)

Chapter 4

A Season of Disaffection: 1915–1927

The End of the Mackay Era

As new year began, Mackay's mind was preoccupied with many things. It was an election year. While President Wilson would no doubt run on the claim that he had kept the country out of war, it was hard to see what would stop him once he was reelected from involving the country in the European war. William Jennings Bryan, who had been Wilson's secretary of state and who had been a staunch advocate for neutrality, had resigned. The city also seemed likely to slip deeper into conflict over reforms. His parishioner James Dahlman had held on as mayor in 1912 and continued to be reelected, but with ever slimmer margins and ever fewer allies in city government. The election in 1912 had defeated the Citizen's Union Ticket, which Mackay had openly supported and elected a reform slate. Under the headline "Our City Election," Mackay had written at the time: "We confess to a feeling of disappointment over the result of the election last Tuesday. We expected the election of Dahlman, for he is very popular with the masses of the people who favor his home rule policies, but we confidently looked for the election of most of the Citizens Union ticket. When businessmen and men of integrity, such as W. A. Redick and Alfred C. Kennedy, are turned down by the voters of Omaha, we lose faith in the good sense and judgment of our people." Nothing had happened since then to alleviate his concern that things were somehow headed in the wrong direction. In 1918, Dahlman was not reelected. With the voice of *Church and Home* muted, this commentary in 1912 remains, for us, Mackay's valediction on Omaha politics.

The trend in the country continued to move in favor of prohibition. In general, the Episcopal Church had withheld its support from prohibition. Mackay, in particular, forcefully argued that prohibition was the wrong way to solve a real problem. Nevertheless, the Episcopal Church in Nebraska would yield to pressure and go on record at its annual council, held in May of 1916, in favor of prohibition. Bishop Williams moved the motion himself and announced as he did that his vote would be an "aye." Immediately, John Williams, the long-serving recently retired priest of St. Barnabas, rose to his feet and voted "Nay." The motion was overwhelmingly carried. The *World-Herald* reported that Tancock, the dean of the cathedral, and Mackay were "out of the room" at the time of the vote. The image of these two senior priests standing outside of the room to avoid having to vote on the motion provides a vivid representation of how Mackay began to experience his place in the church.

His last published assessments of the politics of the country were equally dreary. He had written in one of his final issues of *Church and Home*: "The most dangerous element in our country today is that rapidly increasing class of people who have no religion, and who have no knowledge of God in all their ways. If this country is to perish and our government to be destroyed, it will not be by the hands of anarchists, but by the failure of our people to realize their responsibility to Almighty God."[73] The comment was elicited by an article in the secular press that had caught Mackay's eye. The article was by Louis N. Hammerling, entitled "Personal Liberty, The Morbid Aspect of Social Reform." Mackay reproduced the article's argument in *Church and Home*. Hammerling argued that the reformer had in many cases crossed the line between social responsibility and personal liberty. "His ideals may be high enough and he may strive to cultivate a personal altruistic life, yet his studied desire to help AND REFORM OTHERS OFTEN ends in mischievous disregard of those who do not need development or protection or correction." The bottom line was that American life had become more conflicted than any time since the Civil War. A serious divide was being driven between social responsibility and personal liberty, which in the end would result in the replacement of an age of social orientation and duty by an age of individualism and personal rights.

Mackay's opinion about the Episcopal Church was quite similar. He was shaken by the claim, which he passed on in *Church and Home*, that the Protestant Episcopal Church in the United States was facing "a crisis with fourteen secret or semisecret organizations carrying on an active propaganda for what they call 'catholic' principles." "We hope," he said, "that this will command the earnest attention of the laity and that they

73 *Church and Home*, vol. XIX, no. 49, September 26, 1912.

will cooperate with those clergy who wish to do all in their power to check and gradually eliminate these insidious influences by legislation and the withholding of support." Mackay's heroes in the national church were Bishop Philip Brooks, the orator and poet; Bishop Henry Codman Potter, the author of Christian socialism; and Dr. William Reid Huntington, the author of the Lambeth Quadrilateral; but they were now all gone, having died in 1893, 1908, and 1909, respectively. The mantle had been passed to Bishop Lawrence of Massachusetts and Dr. James F. Freeman of Trinity Church, Minneapolis. Lawrence was very low church Protestant and very given to the idea that the church ought to operate like a business. At General Convention, Lawrence had declared that "the conventional language of the pulpit is Greek to the man on the street." He made an appeal for common sense churchmanship that would interest American men and women of the twentieth century. Dr. Freeman, equally low church, reported at the same convention: "I have traveled 7,200 miles on this continent declared Dr. Freeman, and I want to tell you that there is not a class of men in this country today more depressed and discouraged than the clergy of the Episcopal Church . . . We have to fight for the very life of this church and our religion."

The Diocese of Nebraska itself was troubled. Bishop Williams shared Mackay's uneasiness about the diocese and the nation. He sounded a somber note at annual council in 1916. His address was full of concern for the war in Europe. Brownell Hall had abandoned its location on Tenth Street for a location in the new suburb, Fairacres. It left behind a campus on Tenth Street, which thirty years before had been seen as the ideal facility in the ideal location, right at the heart of Omaha's future. It was now hanging out in the club house of the former country club which was quite inadequate and unsafe. Williams was forced to announce that the plan to build a fireproof building for Brownell Hall would have to be delayed because of the war. The same was true for a west wing for Clarkson Hospital. St. Barnabas, however, was building on Fortieth and Davenport, but this too was discouraging for Mackay. He had argued that instead of St. Barnabas building by itself, it should join with St. John's and St. Andrews to form a single large parish that could build a church that would seat five hundred, not three hundred. The city needed in his mind a third large parish not a number of small competing parishes. Like the move made by Brownell Hall, the move made by St. Barnabas's was a sign that the city was moving west. Dundee had been annexed in 1915, and beyond it, Fairacres was opening up. It was not just another Gold Coast, but something new, a suburban neighborhood. All these changes, Mackay recognized, had repercussions for All Saints.

By 1915, All Saints was approaching parity with the cathedral, and these two congregations were providing a major part of the diocese's support. There were seventeen parishes in the diocese and thirty-nine missions. Of the seventeen parishes, only three had any real size, Trinity Lincoln being a distant third to Trinity Cathedral and All Saints. The burden was heavy, and it looked like it would get worse. Despite All Saints growth, a sizable mortgage remained unpaid. Mackay's stamina was not what it was. From 1915 on, the vestry had instructed him to hire an assistant and provided a salary of $1,000 a year for an assistant. Mackay was also instructed by them to take his full two months of vacation in July and August without fail. He knew that he would have to accept the aid of an assistant supplied by his vestry, but this simply aggravated the financial problems of the parish. As it was turning out, the century, which he had embraced with such optimism in 1900, was fraught with conflict; and he and his church were progressively feeling disaffected.

The one thing that did not enter into Mackay's mind was his retirement. He would, no doubt, like his predecessor, Louis Zahner, die in office. In general, the clergy of this period did not retire. It was financially inconceivable for most. Not only did low salaries make saving difficult, but the fact that one had spent his career living in a rectory also meant that one had no place to go and no equity to take with you. The national church was working on the creation of a pension program, but it would take years before it could actually offer someone a real retirement.

The year 1916 was a particularly difficult year for Mackay. His health had not, in fact, ever returned. Outside of the joyous preparation for his daughter's wedding, which took place in January of 1917, to Austin Gailey, there was little to cheer him. By the time the annual meeting was due in the spring of 1917, Mackay's frustration with his health boiled over. He appeared at the annual meeting with Mrs. Mackay, which had been delayed to accommodate him. After opening the meeting, he stated that, hereafter, because of the immense amount of work he had on his hand and his feeble condition following his recent illness, all of the business connected with the church would be left by him to the vestrymen and officers where it belonged. He then rose with Mrs. Mackay and left the meeting in the charge of the senior warden. C. S. Montgomery told the gathering that they had too long relied on the "overwillingness of the rector to do it for them." Montgomery went on to state that the present condition of the church was quite good and that in his opinion "there was more good feeling in the parish at this time than for a long time before." The meeting then proceeded to reelect Montgomery and Redick as wardens and to reelect F. A. Ewing, G. W. Wattles, J. S. Brady, E. S. Burke, and A. C.

Smith and F. P. Kirkendall as vestrymen. It then replaced W. D. Williams, who had resigned, with John T. Yates.

Montgomery's assessment about the parish seems to have been right. The Easter offering the following year was $4,000. On previous years, Mackay had set the goal for the Easter offerings at $2,000 and had a hard time reaching it. In 1917, All Saints annual expenditures reached $9,097, exceeding those of the cathedral, which were $7,627. Rising expenditures, however, meant rising assessments for the diocese, which had been set at 14 percent of the expenditures. The assessment in 1917 was $1,288, the largest All Saints had ever paid. There was a certain sense of accomplishment in have done so.

A String of Deaths

The country, as Mackay had feared, continued to slide into war. In December of 1916, Congress passed the National Defense Act that authorized raising the strength of the regular army from one hundred thousand to one hundred sixty-five thousand and the National Guard to four hundred fifty thousand. It also made provision for a selective service draft. On February 3, 1917, the United States broke diplomatic ties with Germany; and on April 6, 1917, war was declared on Germany and its allies. The draft went into effect in June. Mackay moved with the country as it prepared to participate in combat. He had a vision of the pain that would inevitably come for parents of the young men that join the service and came up with the idea of founding an order to recognize this anticipated sacrifice and loss. Every participant in the army service would be honored with a blue star, and those who lost their lives in the service would be recognized with a gold star. The idea took hold nationally, and Mackay participated in a national convention founding the order in Boston that year.

Patriotism led many young men to volunteer. In all, fifty-one young men from All Saints entered the armed services and were awarded their blue star. Among these was Mackay's youngest child, Stanley Brooks, then twenty-four. Mackay had named him after Dean Stanley of Westminster Abbey and Philip Brooks, the bishop of Massachusetts.[74] After graduating

74 Mackay's son was born in the year that Philips Brooks was elected bishop, and as Mackay was paying honor to Philips Brooks, Bishop A. C. Seymour of Springfield, who had preached at Zahner's installation, was carrying on a letter-writing campaign to block the confirmation of Brooks's election in the House of Bishops.

from public school in Omaha, Stanley went to Holderness School in New Hampshire and then at age eighteen entered the business world with Armour and Company in Chicago. He was rapidly advancing in the company but felt that he should join his country's war effort. After all, his father had left business to join the Union Army in 1864. Stanley enlisted in the Sixth Nebraska National Guard on June 20, 1917. His regiment, in which he had been made mess sergeant, was sent in September for training to Camp Cody, located at Deming, New Mexico. When he arrived, the decision was made to break up the regiment and merge it with other existing organizations, much to Stanley's disappointment. He was stationed at Camp Johnstone in Jacksonville, Florida, and he seemed quite pleased with the new situation. He, however, contracted blood poisoning and was admitted to the Base Hospital. A couple of days later, he died of what his family would always regard as improper attention at the Base Hospital. The death had occurred on January 8, 1918; and his body was brought home and was buried on Sunday, January 13, from All Saints. Bishop Williams presided; and a stirring funeral homily was preached by Charles McKnight, the parish's associated rector. After McKnight finished his homily, Mackay himself rose to his feet from where he was sitting in the congregation and added: "You must not think of Stanley as dead; but as going on." Afterward he thanked the community for its support and said that he "had little thought when in November in Boston, he brought the service flag from All Saints that the first blue star to turn to gold would be that standing for his own son."

The parish mourned deeply with the Mackays. On November 17, Mackay published an Honor Roll of the young men of the parish who had served in the armed forces during the Great War in *Church and Home*. They numbered fifty-one. The intention was to commission a bronze plaque that listed all their names, each with their own star, but only one would be gold. The bronze tablet was complete and hung in the church; and with time, it was brought to the new building and currently hangs in the Columbarium of All Saints, memorial of all of All Saints veterans. The trauma of returning veterans was quite dramatic, as it always is; and All Saints held an Employment Sunday, praying for the returning veterans, asking businesses to reach out and give them employment.

On top of the scars left by the war was the wave of illness that swept across the country. In 1918, All Saints recorded forty-five burials and in the following year, fifty. In both years, this was over double that of a normal year. All of these deaths weighed on Mackay, particularly the death of Bishop Williams. Mackay had been instrumental in the election of Williams and an unwavering defender of the bishop, even when Williams had blown Mackay's mind by appearing in cope and miter in the "infamous" photograph of the bishops at the Fonda Lac consecration. He was, in fact, a personal friend and neighbor. Bishopthope, as the bishop's residence was called, was located at Thirty-First and Farnam, a little more than four blocks from the rectory at All Saints.[75] Williams died of heart failure on January 28, 1919. Death came to the bishop unexpected. The bishop had spent the evening before at a meeting with the vestry at St. Andrew's parish. He was preparing to retire for the night when he was stricken. His wife and daughter, Lenora, who had married J. W. Benolken (All Saints crucifier), were at his bedside when he expired at noon.

An electing counsel met in May and elected Ernest Vincent Shayler, in rather short order. Shayler had been born in England near Oxford, and his parent immigrated to the United States when he was fifteen, settling in Ohio. He earned his bachelor's degree from Kenyon College, the historic Episcopal College located in Gambier, Ohio. He went directly on to study at the associated divinity school, Bexley Hall. Both institutions had been found by the militant evangelical missionary bishop, Philander Chase. Shayler served as curate in Colombus, Ohio, where he met and married Mignon Knight. His first charge was in Sandusky, Ohio, where he organized a mission and built a church. From there, he was called to Grace Church in Oak Park, Illinois. He took the congregation from five hundred members to one thousand two hundred and built a new building. In 1909, he was called to St. Mark's Seattle, which also grew dramatically under his leadership, and was preparing to build "a cathedral for Seattle," which according to his plan would be dedicated to the American Victory in Europe. Shayler had raised more than $100,000 for the project when he said yes to Nebraska's election.

It was said that he had taken Seattle by storm, which was as much a comment about his standing in the civic community as in his parish. His plan was to do no less in Omaha. When he arrived, he immediately began to cultivate a civic persona. He announced by way of the *Omaha World-Herald* that he desired to be "Bishop to All People," not just Episcopalians. At the first occasion to preach in the city, at Trinity Cathedral, before his consecration, he spoke forcefully about the necessity of the League of Nations. The topic was being hotly debated in the U.S. Senate, and Nebraska's Senator Gilbert Hitchcock was leading the effort to get it approved, without the help of Wilson who was by then ill. From here on, Shayler was regularly quoted in the *Omaha World-Herald*, whether he was

---

75 The name refers to the palace of the Archbishop of York which is known by that name and indicates an Anglophile orientation that both Mackay and Williams shared.

speaking on public morality, defending President Wilson's idealism, the need to reform city traffic control, the election of a mayor, or the approval a city manager. At one point, the *Omaha World-Herald* announced that Shayler would be a writer for the paper, referring to a series of dispatches he had agreed to do for the paper while he was traveling.

This special relation may well have been cemented by his bond with Gilbert Hitchcock, the owner and publisher of the *Omaha World-Herald*. Hitchcock was an Episcopalian who belonged to the cathedral. Clearly, both men had very similar political views, and the *Omaha World-Herald* still at this time had an unabashed political orientation. It thought of itself as a liberal Democrat voice, an identity held by Gilbert Hitchcock, E. V. Shayler, and their mentor President Wilson.

Shayler thought that it was the church's role to prepare its members for a role of militant citizenship, which was a sharp departure from Mackay's idea that it was the church's role to cultivate noble character. Mackay had never hesitated to make his view known, but he always had done so with an understanding that they were a part of greater whole. Mackay's statements were an invitation to dialogue, while Shayler's statements were declarations of truth. They called for action, which it was understood was part of the effort to build the kingdom of God on earth. This for Shayler was precisely what the Gospel asked Christians to do.

Shayler's understanding of the institutional church was much like his understanding of society. Like Bishop Lawrence, Shayler thought the church needed to be run like a good business in order to survive. He represented a change in direction that Mackay neither liked nor fully understood. Mackay had attempted to stop Shayler's election by nominating S. Mills Hays, the rector of Holy Trinity Church, Lincoln, who he counted as a personal friend. In the end, the death of Williams was more than a loss of a friend; it was the loss of the church as he had understood it.

In addition to those deaths among his peers that one expects when you reach a certain age were the even more troubling deaths among the young because of the influenza epidemic. One of these that hit Mackay particularly hard was that of Mary Virginia Megeath. She died on April 26, 1919, at the age of twenty-three. She was a graduate of Brownell Hall and had gone on to complete her bachelor's degree at Briarcliffe College on Long Island. She was engaged to Herbert Connell, and the wedding was set for May 6, 1919. In 1918, she had been chosen the twenty-second queen of Aksarben. Mackay had been thrilled that another one of his All Saints girls had been honored. She reminded him of one of his favorites, Elizabeth Pickens, who was queen in 1912. He had performed her marriage subsequent to her coronation in 1915. He expected to repeat the experience with this new young woman whose wedding would have surly been equally as grand as Elizabeth's. It was on occasions like these that he missed his voice in *Church and Home*. But then a few weeks before the wedding, Virginia was struck with influenza, which developed into a typhoid fever from which she died. Instead of officiating at her wedding, Mackay officiated at her burial. Her family had her laid out in her bridal gown. The church was full, and a large crowd stood around outside of the church. The *Omaha World-Herald* reported the service was markedly simple and that Mackay spoke briefly on the life and character of Ms. Megeath. "Never," he said, "in my whole life have I prayed more earnestly than I did for the recovery of this dear girl. And the Lord answered. 'You have asked for her life, and I have given her life eternal.'"

Finally to this growing lists of death came the chilling news of the death of William Brown on September 28, 1919. William Brown was a black man who was arrested for an alleged rape of a white woman. The local media, most notably the *Bee*, covered the story of the arrest with inflammatory rhetoric. A violent mob marched on the courthouse where Brown was jailed. Surrounding the courthouse, they demanded that Brown be turned over. The mayor, Edward Smith, locked himself in the courthouse and resisted the demands of the mob that numbered about four thousand. The mob soon set fire to the courthouse. They caught the mayor as he attempted to escape the fire and beat him so badly that he lay close to death for several days. Eventually, getting their hands on William Brown, the mob hung him from a telephone pole at Eighteenth and Harney. The violence was finally suppressed by the troops from Fort Omaha. On the next day, Major General Wood, commander of the Central Department, came to Omaha to take charge. Wood put the blame on the Industrial Workers of the World and claimed that violence was part of the Red Scare that was allegedly crossing the country the summer of 1919.

Unfortunately, Mackay's voice in *Church and Home* had been silenced, so we do not have an explicit expression of his opinion. He must have been thankful that his parishioner James Dahlman had failed to be elected in 1918. He had already spoken out in *Church and Home* at his abhorrence of Lynch justice, but it is doubtful when he had that he ever imagined it happening in Omaha.

Shayler on the other hand was in a position to speak out, and the *Omaha World-Herald* willingly gave him a voice. On October 1, the *Omaha World-Herald* gave Shayler's comments three columns on the front page under the headline "Bishop Shayler Sounds a Call to the Army for Right." Shayler began his comments by saying that the beginning of his residence in Omaha has been greeted by "the horrible blot of infamy and shame of

Sunday's terrible crime. There is he allows, mitigating circumstance in that it was mainly the work of a few and that 'the whole world,' in his assessment is at unrest. Underneath the surface of civilization lust, hatred, greed, bolshevism, riot, destruction and revolution are burning." The attempt to hang the mayor was, he argued, "the anarchist attempt at the destruction of law." He concluded:

> Responsibility fell to him to call all men in our city and state to ally themselves definitively upon God's side and particularly do I request that all members of that division of Christ's army over whom I have been placed, shall not only most strenuously live up to their bounden duty and service, but shall endeavor as never before to bring unfortunate men, women, and children into the usefulness, happiness and public service of the Christian life which they themselves may enjoy.

A few at the time might have faulted Shayler for failing to underline the element of racism, which had cause the event in the first place, but all recognized the strident character of his message. Many approved, but many other worried about what his claim to be the general would mean for them as they would continue to work within the church with Shayler.

Death Comes to the Rector

In July of 1919, Mackay announced that he would vacation on Belle Isles, Michigan, going there by way of Duluth. Unfortunately, the associate rector Charles McKnight resigned and made it necessary for the church to be closed for the remainder of the summer. Finding and keeping associates was difficult. The pay was limited, set at $1,000 and room and board with the Mackays. Fortunately, by October, Rev. Carl Worden accepted the call to serve as associate. He was the chaplain of Brownell Hall, which was undergoing change, and was also used by Bishop Williams as an office assistant. It was not, however, long before Mackay was sick again. His daughter, Eleanor, now Mrs. Austin Gailey of New York, returned home to be with him and assist her mother. By November 1, it was reported to the parish that Mackay was "now so far recovered as to be able to sit up and walk around the house. He hopes to be able to be out by Sunday." The slowness of his recovery, however, led him to offer his resignation in December. The vestry declined to accept his resignation, and the *Bee* commended the vestry for not accepting his resignation. It went on to offer the opinion that "the cause of religion in Omaha will sustain a great loss when Mr. Mackay no longer lifts his voice to advise or to comfort."[76] When Christmas came, "the rector vested and entered the sanctuary where he took the closing prayer and pronounced the final benediction."[77]

Clearly, Carl Worden was doing most of the work, including the editing of *Church and Home.* The January edition opened a window through which the parishioners of All Saints could view the state of the parish's finances in a way they had seldom been afforded. In all the twenty-three volumes that preceded this issue, such a thorough report on the finances had never occurred, not so much because of any secretiveness on Mackay's part but because the financial report was not all that interesting. Perhaps it had been restrained by the work that would have entailed to do so, but just as likely, it simply had never occurred to Mackay that such transparency would produce more good than harm. Carl Worden urged the readers of *Church and Home* to read the report carefully. Then he wrote, "Having been connected with the diocesan office for a number of years and receiving hundreds of financial reports in that time, he could testify that Mr. Ewing had the system reduced to an art. If their tribe might only increase, what an advantage it would be to the church at large."[78]

All Saints Church Treasurer's Report, January 1, 1920

Balance on hand January 1, 1919	$ 10.95		
Receipts as per general fund	$15,002.67	Payments as per general fund	$15,653.54
Receipts as per bills payable	$1,500.00	Payments on bills payable	$1,400.00
Overdrawn	$539.89		
Total	$17,053.51	Total	$15,653.51

General Fund Account

General Apportionment N Y	$ 725.60	Interest on Plowman Fund	$26.05
Diocesan Assessment	$1,269.80	Interest on Stanley Mackay Fund	$40.00
Clarkson Hospital	$40.73	Memorial Tablet Fund	$1.00

[76] *The Bee*, "A Church and Its Rector," December 9, 1919.

[77] *Church and Home*, vol. XXIV, no. 12, January 3, 1920.

[78] *Church and Home*, vol. XXIV, no. 12, January 3, 1920.

Wise Hospital	$25.00	Dundee Guild	$100.00
St. James Orphanage	$25.00	Parish Aid Circle No. 1	$100.00
Church Pension Fund	$318.75	Parish Aid Society	$400.00
Council Delegates	$40.00	Women's Auxiliary	$210.00
Bishop's Reception	$20.00	Communicant Dollars	$170.00
Memorial Tablet Fund	$1.00	*Church and Home*	$43.25
Paid on Mortgage	$600.00	Vacation Fund	$550.00
Interest	$1,083.00	Offerings	$3,105.34
Fuel, Water and Light	$431.83	Pledge Envelopes	$3,623.53
Music	$2,410.00	Pew Rent	$6,633.50
Salaries	$6,225.01	Deficit for 1919	$650.84
Expense	$332.68		
Total	$15.653.51	Total	$15,653.51

The laity of All Saints was doing an incredibly good job. From 1915, when Mackay had dramatically appeared at the annual meeting and turned the business of the parish over to the laity, the budget had doubled. In part, this can be attributed to the post war boom, but such a gain was not shared across the board in the diocese. It was also attributed to the laity's realization that their rector would not be with them much longer. The fact that they paid off the sizeable mortgage and increased the budget for the coming year lends one to suspect that they did this as a tribute to Mackay. Dr. Mackay would not die with his beloved parish in debt and his house would be in order!

Meeting in the parish house on February 22, with the senior warden presiding in Mackay's absence, the vestry noted that the outstanding mortgage stood at $17,400 and then unanimously adopted the following resolution moved by the junior warden, W. A. Redick:

> Resolved: That Mr. W. Farnam Smith, be and is hereby authorized to apply all money collected on the mortgage pledge to the payment of the mortgage and it is hereby authorized that a loan be negotiated sufficient to liquidate the entire mortgage at once and that all subsequent collections be applied upon the payment of the loan.

Without stating the reason, a second motion was made for the senior warden and one other vestryman to visit Pueblo on a tour of investigation.

The purpose, of course, was to see if the priest there would be a suitable successor for Mackay. So we should add that the additional reason for the financial diligence on the part of the laity was that they did not want the existence of an outstanding mortgage to cause a candidate for rector of All Saints to hesitate in answering their call! After all, this was a vestry made up of shrewd and successful businessmen.

Easter was approaching. On March 31, Wednesday of Holy Week, at four in the morning, Mackay died in his home with his wife and daughter at his side. By noon on that very day, Montgomery had gathered the vestry for a special meeting at the Omaha Club. Noting Dr. Mackay's death, the vestry instructed the treasurer to pay Mrs. Mackay the regular rector's salary of the next two months and appointed a subcommittee of Yates and Brady to see that a suitable floral design was sent to for the funeral. Then Montgomery and Yates both reported on their visit at Pueblo with Thomas Casady. Their report was so favorable that the vestry at once decided by unanimous vote to extend a call to Mr. Casady and invited Casady to come at the vestry's expense to visit the parish to help him make up his mind. That evening, Mackay's body lay in state in the church. A solemn watch was kept by the Knights Templar in full dress uniform. According to the *Omaha World-Herald*, "During this time people of all denominations—friends of the late rector—have visited his church to pay their last tribute to one of Omaha's best known clergymen." The funeral was held late afternoon on Thursday. The church was packed with representative of the Masons, the Elks, the Rotary Club, and the Grand Army of Republic seated in the front pews. The procession into the church was led by Rev. S. Mills Hays of Holy Trinity Lincoln, Bishop E. V. Shayler, the bishop of Nebraska, and Reverend Worden, the associate rector of All Saints. The casket followed with more than a score of vested clergy from the diocese coming after it. Hayes, who was a lifelong friend and whom Mackay had nominated as bishop in the recent election, officiated. It would seem that this was a choice that Mackay himself had made. No homily was preached. During the service, the choir directed by Simms sang "Blessed Be the Tie that Binds" and "O Love that Will Not Let Me Be," which Mackay had requested. At the recession, the coffin was draped with the United States flag, and full military honors were rendered as the body left the church. It was taken to Forest Lawn Cemetery by his three sons, Odin, Robert, and Ralph, where it was cremated. On Friday, Reverend Worden conducted a simple committal service with the family.

The diocese memorialized Mackay at the annual council, which followed shortly after his death:

> In the death of Rev. Thomas J. Mackay, the church in the Diocese of Nebraska has suffered a loss that will be felt for many years to come. For twenty-nine years, Thomas J. Mackay occupied a prominent place among the clergy of the diocese and had kept the eyes of the people of Omaha fastened upon the church. His personal consecration, his Catholic sympathy, his loyalty to the Lord Jesus Christ, and his belief in the divine Christ in humanity excited an incalculable influence upon the community in which he lived and brought back to the fold many who had strayed and had become indifferent to the claims of the Savior. His brethren in the diocese mourn his departure as a personal grief and recognize his great worth, and they thank God that his works do follow him.[79]

The newly operating national pension fund provided Mackay's widow a pension of $25 a month, less than a sixth of Mackay's salary and a mere quarter of what was considered a minimum living at the time. There was some hope that there might be some additional help from the diocese's clergy relief fund at some later date. Mrs. Mackay, who went to live with her daughter Eleanor, for her part wrote to the vestry in her own hand:

> To the Vestry and Wardens of All Saints Church
>
> Dear friends,
>
> It is with feelings of deepest appreciation that I wish to thank you for your great kindness to me and my dear husband during the past months. Words fail me when I try to tell you what it has meant to me, but I want you to know of my heartfelt appreciations and that I shall never forget your generosity.
>
> Most gratefully yours,
>
> Georgia C. Mackay
> June 24[80]

79 *Journal of Proceedings of the Fifty-Third Annual Council of the Diocese of Nebraska*, 1920, p. 75.

80 The letter is pasted into the minutes for July 1920.

Without Missing a Beat: The Calling of Thomas Casady

Without missing a beat, the parish held its annual meeting on April 5, Easter Monday, as usual, three days after Mackay's funeral. Present at the meeting were thirteen women and sixteen men. Brady and Ewing were the only members of the vestry present. After hearing reports, the meeting proceeded to reelect Montgomery and Redick as wardens and G. W. Wattles, A. C. Smith, W. F. Smith, Dr. O. C. Rich, F. A. Ewing, John T. Yates, and J. S. Brady. Four days later, on April 9, the vestry met in the evening at the Blackstone Hotel. The senior warden, Montgomery, reported that he had extended an official call to Mr. Thomas Casady who had been in the city looking over the church, the rectory, and other aspects of work at All Saints during the past day and was now present with them for a personal conference that would bear on his acceptance of their offer. Mr. Casady opened the proceeding with a statement of the consideration affecting his decision. The words appearing in the minutes described his statement as "very frank." He would, he stated, be giving up a very pleasant situation in Pueblo where his work was well organized and moving along very successfully. He then presented a series of questions to the vestry whose answers would determine his decision. Did they see the possibility of developing the parish into a bigger and more useful church? What were the relations of the parish with other Episcopal parishes in the diocese? Did the parish operate on a budget system as to its finances? Was the music program entirely satisfactory and how was it maintained? Casady also made it clear to the vestry that he would not be attracted by a larger salary or more pleasant conditions. For him the question was where he was most needed and of best use for the future of the church. His only expectation about salary would be that it was sufficient to support his family. At this point, Casady's family consisted of himself, his wife, and five children.

Casady conducted the regular services on the following Sunday at All Saints and returned to Pueblo. The vestry met the following Monday in the office of the senior warden and reaffirmed their offer to Casady, a salary of $4,500, the use of the rectory, and a commitment to meet his demands. Two days later, Casady wrote a very brief letter of acceptance and stated that he would start work on May 9, which was less than a month away. The vacancy between rectors would be less than forty days! The dispatch with which this was done is breathtaking. Clearly, Mackay's death had been anticipated, and groundwork was done well before the actual event of his death on March 31. This raises the question of what role Mackay played in the process. Clearly, he planned his own funeral, chose the music, expressed his wishes about details such as flowers, and had given the very explicit direction that his close friend, the rector of Holy Trinity Lincoln, should officiate at his funeral and not the bishop. At a minimum, he must have given permission and encouragement to the vestry to begin a search for a new rector while he was still alive.

How did Casady's name come into play to begin with? There was an associate, Carl Worden, who had served the parish well and might well have hoped that he would be considered. The new bishop, Shayler, had assumed office in Nebraska less than six months prior to Mackay's death and was not in much of a position to influence the parish's decision. Shayler, who had started his ministry in Ohio and then served Oak Park, Illinois, and Seattle, Washington, had no apparent contact with the Diocese of Colorado where Casady was serving or the Diocese of Iowa where Casady had been raised up. On the other hand, Mackay, who had a way of cultivating and retaining friendships, had many ties to Colorado and Iowa, having served in both dioceses. Even in his infirmity, he was likely have been up to date on the news in both of these dioceses. Another link between this young up-and-coming priest and Mackay was provided by Bishop Williams with whom Mackay had enjoyed a close personal relationship. Williams had, in fact, ordained Casady in 1906! Apparently, he substituted for Bishop Morrison, Casady's bishop, as a courtesy for Morrison, who was dealing with health problems at the time. Moreover, it is hard to imagine whose recommendation would have been so well received by Montgomery and the rest of the vestry if it was not Mackay's. While there is no direct evidence to prove it, it seems very likely from the circumstances that Mackay's hand was at work in the quest to bring Casady to All Saints.

A Young Man of Privilege and Promise

At the time of his call, Thomas Casady was thirty-nine years old. His family consisted of himself, his wife Francis, and five children: Phineas, 12; Simon, 11; Thomas, 8; Frances, 7; and Richard, 4. Casady was born and raised in Des Moines, Iowa. His father Simon Casady was a successful Des Moines banker, as was his grandfather. Thomas went to the University of Iowa in Iowa City and majored in business. The presumption was that he would continue the family's line of bankers. In his senior year, he announced his intention to go into the ministry. The rector of his parish, St. Paul's Des Moines, was Jonathan Cathell. Cathell was a magnetic speaker and gave lectures around the country on a circuit organized for him by the Redpath–Slayton Bureau of Chicago. Unfortunately, he ran up enormous personal debts, which became so severe that in November of 1899, the vestry took over his salary, paid an allowance to his wife, and paid the rest of his creditors for him on a quarterly basis. Such an example, perhaps lampooned by his own father, might have stirred the young man's mind with visions of what a priest could accomplish for the church who knew how to run a business!

Thomas Casady, Third Rector of All Saints, 1921-1927. br. Des Moines, Iowa, elected Bishop of Oklahoma 1927, d. 1955

Casady chose to go to the Episcopal Church's most prestigious seminary, General Theological Seminary in New York City, following the lead of his bishop's son, Cammeron Swazey Morrison with whom he was friends. At the time, General enrolled very few Westerners. When Casady arrived at General, he found the morale of the seminary running high because of the impact of its new dean, Dr. Wilford Lash Robbins.[81] While the curriculum remained traditional, Dean Robbins made an effort to bring the students in touch with the affairs of the world. Robbins "persuaded laymen

[81] Powel Mills Dawley, *The Story of the General Theological Seminary, A Sesquicentennial History, 1817–1967*, Oxford University Press, New York, 1906, p. 297.

form different businesses and professions to speak at frequent informal assemblies in the gymnasium 'smokers,' as they were called—on subjects as varied as business methods in church affairs, religious philanthropy, the newspaper world, the church and social problems, and what the laity expect of their clergy."[82] Casady must have been inspired by these presentations, even as he struggled to compensate for his lack of classical preparation for seminary. Among other things, he was in the third of his class, which was dispensed from Hebrew. He graduated in 1906 not with a DD, but with a diploma of graduation. In June of that year, he was ordained as a deacon by Bishop Williams of Nebraska in his home parish, St. Paul's Des Moines. At the end of the month, he was married to Frances Labaron Kesson, a Des Moines girl, who had attended Baltimore Women's College. Like Casady, Frances was from a prominent Des Moines family. By the first of the next month, Casady was at work in his first cure, St. Mary's Oelwein, Iowa. One has a sense that Casady approached life with an orderly plan and with deliberate dispatch, something that would become quite evident in his ministry at All Saints and his subsequent ministry in Oklahoma.

He dutifully stayed at St. Mary's until he received a call from St. Marks, Des Moines in 1908. St. Mark's was a small parish on Des Moines's poorer east side, with great hopes for becoming Des Moines's number 2 parish. While at St. Mark's, he led the effort to build a sizable gymnasium on St. Mark's grounds in order to attract youth to the parish. The gymnasium was named Kesson Hall, which identifies that source of money had been his family, primarily in this case his in-laws.[83] Casady was at St. Mark's for four years when he received a call to the Church of the Ascension in Pueblo, Colorado. Pueblo was a small but important boom town at the time. In terms of his career, it provided young Casady with an opportunity to win spurs in a "western town" and to participate in a growth strategy rather than a maintenance effort which St. Mark's had become.

The Casady Years: 1921 to 1927

When he came to All Saints, he came to a parish that had been led by an extroverted personality for more than twenty-nine years. A newspaper article refers to Casady's task of replacing Mackay as "a delicate mission." He was, according to the article, "devoid of ostentation," "full of the milk

82 Ibid., p. 299.

83 St. Mark's struggled to maintain the hall and eventually sold the hall to the Iowa State government whose capitol building was close by.

of human kindness," and "lacking in ceremony in his contact with men." "When in a group of men," it reported, "he pulled out, filled, and lighted his pipe, and those around him were apprized of his geniality of nature. When he met and talked with a group of boys, they realized they were with a man who had not forgotten the time when he was a boy."[84] A similar impression comes from the editor of the *Oklahoma Churchman*, Rev. Joseph Carden. He comments on his first meeting with Casady and his wife in 1927: "Reverend Thomas and his engaging wife are as plain and matter of fact as an old shoe—or a pair of them—and they will fit comfortably as an old shoe fits the foot."[85] If Casady was somewhat of an introvert, he was also very disciplined and set very high standards for himself.

Out of the Starting Blocks

By any measure, Thomas Casady's beginning in his new parish was a fast start. On May 18, he sat down to preside over his first vestry meeting and led off by presenting the vestry with a list of six recommendations. The first was that a budget be made for all expenses and an allowance be made for a sinking fund of 8 to 10 percent for emergencies. The second was that pew rentals be forgone and that pledges, to be paid in a single envelope, should become the basis for the entire expenditures of the parish. Moreover, he urged that these pledges should be made for a three-year period and paid on a weekly basis. The third recommendation was that a list should be made of church families and something of their history and their pledges. Fourthly, he proposed that the parish be divided into districts of ten families each, each district to be headed by a captain. Next on the list was the recommendation that the parish should appoint a purchasing agent. Last on the list was the recommendation that the rector should receive each month $10 for petty cash. In addition to the list, Casady brought up the need for a parish secretary. The vestry responded favorably to his recommendations and voted to provide a salary of $100 a month for a parish secretary.

The next day, May 19, Casady went to the diocese's annual council. Since he had not yet been formally received into the diocese, the committee on credentials moved to give him the privileges of the floor, a common courtesy for new priests. The bishop had already appointed him to serve on the diocese's new Board of Education. Shayler was passionate about

84 *Omaha World-Herald*, September 29, 1927.

85 *Oklahoma Churchman*, vol. 30, no. 6, p. 4, June 1927.

improving Sunday schools and sought to establish a diocesan norm, which would be enforced. In his brief visit with Casady before the annual council, he had discovered that this was a passion Casady shared with him. As Casady sat at his first diocesan council in Nebraska, he listened to the new bishop, who was also attending his first council in Nebraska, present his vision. Shayler opened his address by declaring, "The world crisis is now. The church is doomed to failure if she relies upon the methods of past days. The world of sin is no longer the world of a pagan apathy, but the world of decisive combat. Forces are marshaled against the church and the Christian religion—defaming, stabbing, maiming, crippling. The lethargy and supineness which have been exhibited are sufficient no longer." He went on to say, "Political struggles in our land manifest the solidarity and union of those, who under one banner, rally around candidates who stand for radicalism, class-feeling, partisan selfishness and the hatred of a world peace treaty of any sort." Further, he maintained that "the foundations of home life are threatened," "the morals of youth are utterly degraded by many of the moving pictures of the present," and "a devilish greed is abroad in the land."[86]

Later in the council, Casady listened to the Committee on State of the Church present its report. The picture painted by the committee added to the somber note already struck by the bishop's address. The committee reported that "since the division of the diocese in 1891, the number of communicants had grown from 3,100 to 5,360, but the growth had slowed since 1911. In Omaha, the communicant strength of the Episcopal churches in 1891 was 1,215. By 1916 it had grown to 2,294, but by 1920 it had actually declined to 1,987. In 1891, the committee noted that there were four parishes and six missions, in 1920 there were five parishes and four missions. Closed or abandoned were St. Clement's, and St. Edward's in South Omaha, St. Augustine's, St. John's, St. Matthias' in Omaha, St. Mark's, Florence, and a mission start in Benson." "It is significant," the report continued, "that these missions have been abandoned while the areas in which they were situated have developed into well-populated sections of the city."

Reporting on Brownell Hall, the committee said that it "believes that as a distinct church school contributing to the cause of Christian education and reaching the general public, Brownell Hall has largely ceased to function."[87] The bishop's remarks on Brownell Hall in his address

86 *Proceeding of the Fifty-Third Annual Council of the Diocese of Nebraska*, p. 28–29.

87 *Journal of Proceedings of Fifty-Third Annual Council of the Diocese of Nebraska*, 1920, p. 62–65.

are more hopeful but nevertheless similarly concerned. The bishop said, "Under great difficulties, Brownell Hall has fulfilled a fruitful year, under the leadership of Ms. MacDonald . . . The Board of Trustees having sold the old property, are now selecting a site for the new buildings and have pledged themselves to the erection and opening of the first unit of the building by September 1921. The difficulties and discouragements of Brownell Hall in the past three years are more prominent in our vision than its glorious achievements in former years."[88]

To this, Bishop Shayler added the observation "that our Sunday Schools, which save for a few instances, are alarmingly and critically deficient and rapidly dying." He brought his consideration of the state of church to a close by proposing a new platform for the diocese, "Unity, Efficiency, Enterprise, and Enthusiasm." Shayler went on to specify these themes in Ten Recommendations. These ranged from the requirement that every parish be required to pay the diocesan treasurer, one-twelfth of its diocesan assessment upon the first of the month, to the requirement that every clergyman be required to read the bishop's message to his congregation the first Sunday after the same is printed in the Crozier."

The older priests, of whom John Williams, the retired rector of St. Barnabas, was the "dean," must have felt somehow uneasy, if not dismayed. A past in which they had participated had just been dismissed with faint praise, and a new rhetoric was introduced, which sounded like it belonged at a convention of businessmen rather than in a council of the ministers of the Gospel. A divide had come in American life. The elder priests knew that the formation of their ministry was on the other side of that divide, and they felt that it would be increasingly difficult for them to participate in the new order. To the young priests, like Thomas Casady, the bishop's words were square on with their own sense of church and world. They too were aware of being on the other side of a divide. They felt themselves to be without mentors trying to reinvent the church and wary of the clout of the dinosaurs that lingered on. Moreover, this new generation felt an urgency about acting before it was too late. This was not in other words the usual passage that takes place between generations. This was a radical discontinuity.

On January 3, 1921, Thomas Casady convened his first annual parish meeting. The date in itself was novel. Annual parish meetings up until 1921 had been held the Monday following Easter. The new January date had been mandated by the past annual council of the diocese, a date, as it were, more in line with the fiscal practice of the business world than with

---

88 *Journal of Proceedings of Fifty-Third Annual Council of the Diocese of Nebraska*, 1920, p. 33.

the liturgical rhythms of the church's life. Thirty-three men and seventeen women were present, which was a remarkably better attendance than in the past. The format that Casady introduced for the meeting specified parish reports would be read by the rector; treasurer, Mr. Townsend; Mr. Goodman, the Sunday school superintendent; and that the reports of the Women's Auxiliary would be read by Mrs. Trimble (Section A) and by Mrs. George Victor (Section B).

After the reports had been completed, the meeting proceeded to the election of the vestry. The meeting reelected the past vestry with the exception of Kirkendall, who, because of his continued health problems, had chosen not to run. Reflecting on Kirkendall's importance to the parish, the vestry elected him to the vestry emeritus.

Buildings and Grounds Issues

The fast start was soon confronted with some basic facts on the ground. The parish's buildings and grounds presented a significant challenge. Perhaps it is simply the fate of every new rector to struggle with the buildings and grounds that he finds at his disposal. Certainly, Mackay was confronted with buildings that presented needs and, at the time, presented limitation for the programs that he wished to run. While All Saints parish hall and church were less than fifteen years old, they were already being found wanting. Touted as state-of-the-art when the building was opened 1906, the lighting in the church was frustratingly inadequate. The lighting company had offered a plan to improve the lighting and had agreed to install four samples in the front of the church on a trial basis. The vestry was not ready to move, having only recently been allowed to enjoy the experience of being out of debt. The ventilation in the church presented problems as did the heating. The heating problem in the rectory was even more severe. The boiler had broken down and was in need of a major repair.

The rectory, which was built in 1905, was to serve two purposes, a shelter for a family and a hospitality center and office for the parish. It was decidedly too small for the new demands. Moreover, the 1905 rectory was not now, if it ever had been, in a family-oriented neighborhood. It was surrounded by apartments. Most of these were like the Old Judge Scott house, immediately south of the rectory on South Twenty-Sixth Street. The Scott house was a large wooden Victorian structure, in poor repair, subdivided into apartments. Casady favored purchasing this house for the land. Again, the vestry was not ready to move. Not only was Casady concerned to control the neighborhood around All Saints, but he was also very conscious of the fact that the parish's buildings had been shoehorned on to the existing property, leaving little outside space that could be considered "parish grounds."

The rectory seemed cramped in terms of the expectations put upon it, particularly since Casady's family was more expansive than Mackay's, five young children all at home. Moreover, it was very much the new nuclear style family that in itself required more room. A Victorian family, as Mackay's was, accepted the idea of living in a public arena; but the new nuclear family in America required privacy, and it experienced life in a rectory as living in a "fish bowl."

The parish hall also presented limitations that Casady struggled to overcome. It had been built for adult fellowship programs, which for Mackay and his contemporaries was the key building block for a great congregation. For Casady, the key to growth was a Christian Education Department aimed at children. He wrote in *Church and Home*, "All Saints is and should be preeminently a children's church. It ought to be a church that children understand and love, one that brings those He loved, nearer to Him in devotion and whole hearted service."[89] He was especially keen on assimilating non-Episcopal children from the neighborhood. Church school attendance ran about 170 children per week. What he needed were classrooms, not halls. Early on, he proposed putting up dividers in the parish hall only to find this too costly. Some relief came with the purchase of a house for the Casady family to live in. The house, located at 1116 Turner Boulevard, was a substantial middle-class house located in a suburban neighborhood, just a short distance from the field club. This allowed the old rectory to be converted into an office and classrooms and be renamed Mackay Memorial Hall.

Even under the category of adult fellowship, the parish hall had its limits. When Casady installed the practice of having a dinner as part of the annual meeting, it would work only if the group was divided between the two floors, a sit-down meal downstairs and a buffet upstairs. Various proposals were made to eliminate vesting and bathrooms, none of which proved suitable or doable. By the annual meeting of 1925, in an extensive set of proposals, Casady proposed that the present Mackay Memorial Hall (the old rectory) be replaced with an auditorium and dining room with the capacity of seating 450 people!

On the property south of the church, occupied by the Old Judge Scott home, which the parish had recently purchased, Casady proposed that the parish should someday build a new building, 72 feet by 132 feet. It would provide a workroom, living quarters for the rector's staff, a gymnasium

[89] *Church and Home*, vol. 28, no. 36, September 12, 1925.

for Boy Scouts and Camp Fire Girls, and rooms for various women's organizations.

Casady's vision was driven by his conviction that All Saints was becoming an urban church, a vision that Mackay had already noted with a degree of consternation. In searching for models for a successful urban parish, Casady had gone to Indianapolis to visit Christ Church. There he found a vibrant parish that had chosen to remain downtown. One of Christ Church's secrets was the very deep pockets of E. I. Lilley. Casady also studied Trinity Wall Street, New York City. There again he found that the key to the parish's success was a large endowment, this time nothing less than a large track of land on the Lower East Side of Manhattan known as the Queens Farm. Over the years, this gift made Trinity Wall Street one of New York City's largest landlords, and it enabled the parish to keep its property in repair and to field an extensive outreach ministry that drew people to it. The minutes of the 1924 annual meeting report that in Casady's remarks to the parish, he "pointed out that the opportunity of the parish was similar to the opportunity that had been well met by Trinity Church, New York City." This, Casady had continued, would imply "the gradual expansion of the personnel." This larger parish staff would consist of "a parish secretary, a curate, an assistant rector, a boys' welfare work director, a girls' welfare work director, deaconesses, etc."[90]

Parish Administration

Running All Saints also presented a serious challenge. The parish's records were seriously out of date. After an initial attempt to keep up the records that Zahner had initiated, Mackay had let the records fall progressively into abeyance. At a vestry meeting held on April 21, 1921, Casady reported:

> When he had come to the church a year ago there were supposed to be 469 communicants. The records were not in good shape, not even a definite or correct list of the church communicants and that up to January 1 last, after sending out information cards to be filled out by all the people whose names were on the list, and by careful checking and hunting up of members, he was able to locate 457. Despite the struggle with the records, he was pleased that at Easter there had been 379 communions and the number of communicants now numbered 612.

90 Minutes of the Annual Meeting, January 7, 1924.

While uncertainty about actual numbers was not a problem for Mackay, for Casady it was a nightmare. In part, this was because of Casady's personality, but both the national church and the diocese had begun to demand more accurate numbers. There was a widely shared view that long-range planning and assessments on the parish required that these numbers be accurate. The impact of this new record keeping on rectors, especially conscientious rectors like Casady, is revealed in a lead article in the volume of *Church and Home*, dated January 22, 1927. At the beginning of 1927, Casady was faced with reporting a slight decline in the number of communicants at All Saints. He was clearly upset. He confided in his congregation: "It is with unusual reluctance that they [rectors] find themselves compelled by canon law to make that list of the communicants under their oversight, and to make that list in accordance with certain rulings and arbitrary standards." The standard he is talking about is a lay person was required to make their communion three times in the course of a year to be counted as a communicant in good standing. He continued, "Even when one has an accurate knowledge of the individual's case, as has the rector of this parish, it is not easy to write off the communicant list a certain number of people whom he knows are essentially loyal and who would rally to the church in a real crisis." He confessed, "I have written them off, nevertheless." This had amounted to a hundred names, and he issued a plea to them to make the outward expression that the church requires so that he could restore them to the communicant roles.

Also, new was an acceleration of financial demands on a parish. It was no longer possible to support a parish with a core group of pew renters and the largess of a few vestrymen at the end of the year. The parish's expenditure grew from about $6,000 in 1885 to $8,500 in 1905, less than 50 percent in the course of twenty years. From 1905 to 1925, the next twenty years, they literally doubled. As Casady approached the end of his tenure at All Saints, he recorded annual expenditures of $47,000! While $17,000 of that was capital expense because of the parish's loan with Conservative Savings, the operating expenditure set a new record. The canvass for 1926 had sought to raise $30,000 but fell well short of that amount and several severe cuts were required to balance the budget. The resulting operating budget was $23,038.

Expenditures on this level required that a parish tap a wider range of participants thorough a pledge system. Mackay had begun an envelope system as a supplement to pew rent and other giving, but it was now incumbent upon Casady to complete the transition to a modern pledge system. He managed to succeed in this effort, but in 1926, he faced a backlash. Why the backlash came in 1926 is not entirely clear.

In reality, the very idea of parish administration was new. In Mackay's day, and almost as long as anyone could remember, the affairs of a parish were a quite simple matter. The rector and his family were an extension of the parish, and the parish in a sense was the rector's family. The parish's correspondence would have been in the form of handwritten letters and personal calls made by the rector. Daily, the rector inhabited the buildings, and with the help of a small group of men and women, he took care of things. The parish was a presence not an activity. Likewise, a diocese was a bishop whose presence was his ministry. A diocese did not have a program any more than a parish did. It didn't require much financing; and through most of Bishop Williams's years, it had continued to be financed by a $1 assessment on each active lay member of the diocese, some endowment income, and a special missionary collection. That would mean that the bishop's budget was fixed at $5,000 or $6,000, and a rector's responsibility was limited to bugging his lay people to send in their dollar. The missionary portion came from the projects of the parish auxiliary, the primary women's organization in each parish. While there was a great deal of pride in this effort, what was raised was sent and that was that. The new bishop, Shayler, who came in 1920, was aggressively changing the diocese into a business. Over the next decade, this would put a lot of pressure on parishes, precisely when they, themselves, were aggressively changing into a business, putting pressure on themselves.

Shortly after Casady arrived, he told the vestry that he thought that the work of the church was opening up in a way that would cause him to need the services of a secretary. What seems obvious to us now was a novel idea for the vestry in 1921. After discussion, they moved that Casady be authorized to hire a secretary whose salary would be $100 a month. The parish's first parish secretary, Ms. Marjorie Nye, was also a member of the choir. Marjorie had transferred to All Saints from St. Paul's Omaha with her father, Charles Munsen Nye; her mother, Mary Ann; and a younger brother, Charles Jr.

A little further into Casady's first year, the janitor who had been receiving $100 a month asked for a raise to $120 a month. It was granted. Not long after that, the janitor would explain that he could get a job in Wyoming at $140 a month. This too was a new kind of pressure for parish administration. In the past, a janitor/sexton was kind of a permanent fixture who seldom asked for anything.

Casady's conviction about the importance of Christian education put further demands on him. While Mackay had volunteers that assisted him with Christian education, he himself met children's classes and did teacher/parent education and confirmation instruction. Casady, in tune with his bishop and the national church, thought Christian education should be a professional discipline of its own. When he had been appointed by Bishop Shayler to chair the diocesan committee on religious education, he recruited a professional teacher, Louise E. Rich, to assist him on the diocesan level and in his parish. Louise had taught at St. Alban's School in Washington DC. She was the sister of Dr. Charles O'Neill Rich, a local surgeon and vestryman at All Saints.[91] In 1921, she began work for the diocese, the cathedral, and All Saints. Her salary at All Saints in the fall of 1921 was set at $100 per month. In 1923, she became full time at All Saints, primarily because the diocesan and cathedral budget had been cut back. Here her salary was raised to $200 a month. In the September 12, 1925, issue of *Church and Home*, Casady reported that Ms. Rich has been honored by an appointment to the faculty of the Faribault Summer School. There she had given a series of lectures on church school organization and management. "All Saints," he argued, "is and should be preeminently a children's church . . . Ms. Rich has sent out a card of greeting and invitation to all the children enrolled last year." The following issue reported that the church school opened on Sunday, September 13, with a total enrollment of 179.

In the field of Christian education, Casady's work for the diocese and in his own parish was so outstanding that he gained national recognition. On February 14, 1923, Casady was elected to the national council of the Episcopal Church of America. He was one of four clergy to serve on this committee. Mr. Casady was the youngest man elected to the council and the only Westerner serving on it at the time. Casady was put in charge of the national department on religious education for the country.

Back in the parish, Casady had initially suspended the publication of *Church and Home* to save money and perhaps to take some pressure off his own workload. It soon became clear to him, however, that "with the size of the parish it was necessary," so Casady asked the vestry to budget $1,000 a year for the publication. Publication was resumed in the fall of 1921.

The national church was putting pressure on dioceses and parishes to adopt a standardized financial reporting system. This meant that the parish's financial records had to be transformed. Ewing, who had been treasurer for twenty-five years and who had been trying to resign for some time, finally did so. A new treasurer, who in effect paid the parish's bills as well as keep the books, had to be found. W. H. Clark finally accepted the

91 Dr. Charles O'Neill Rich was a surgeon. He was born in Pennsylvania in 1876. His wife was Nelly, and he had two daughters Daisy and Sarah. He lived in Chicago St.

task. The vestry provided him with a paid assistant who would do the work of actually paying bills, who was in a sense the parish's first bookkeeper.

Changes in Parish Leadership

On November 10, 1921, the vestry received a letter from G. W. Wattles, sent to Casady, in which Wattles tendered his resignation "because of his absence from the city and consequent inability to be of much real service to the vestry." This was likely a relief for Casady since Wattles had never been confirmed and he should have ruled that Wattles could not serve on the vestry unless he was.[92] It is not clear if Casady had ever said anything, but if he did, Wattles had preempted him. Wattles went on in his letter of resignation to assure the new rector and vestry of his continued interest in the church. Wattles, a widower, had recently married. His new wife was Julia Vance. She was the director of the Department of Home Economic at the University of Nebraska. When they married in 1918, Wattles was then sixty, and Julia was thirty-three. For a while, they maintained their primary residence in Omaha. In May of 1920, a son was born, Guerdon Wallace Jr. The following year, Wattles moved the family to Hollywood. There the younger of his two daughters from his first marriage, Mary Louise, continued her education, graduating from the Marlbourgh School in Los Angeles and Pine Manor Wellesley. In 1930, Mary was married in the Hollywood mansion, which remains today a Hollywood landmark. Despite her education in Hollywood, Mary married an Omaha boy, Wilson Dunlap Bryans; and they subsequently made their home in Omaha.

The following March, the vestry lost another significant member. Arthur C. Smith died on March 3, 1923. A. C. Smith had been elected to the vestry on October 2, 1897, as a successor to his father, Monroe E. Smith, who had been on the vestry since 1893. His father had begun his service on the vestry the year that the parish was dealing a double loss on the vestry because of the sudden resignation of Woolworth and the removal of Drake from the city. The attempt that year to replace them proved difficult. Mackay reached across the river and prevailed on M. E. Smith, who lived in Council Bluffs. He had recently opened a second location in Omaha for his dry goods wholesale operation, specializing in overalls, jeans, and shirts; though he would not actually move to Omaha for some time. Mackay's resourcefulness in recruiting Smith is impressive if it is

92 Mackay held a different opinion, as he not only did not rule against Wattles serving on the vestry, but he also had a member on the vestry at Saint Paul's Council Bluffs who was not confirmed.

also a little irregular. It was a significant success for All Saints as Smith became an effective vestry man. Even more so was his son Arthur who was in business with his father. When Arthur Smith took over his father's chair in 1897, he, after Wattles and Kirkendall, became the most important member of the vestry during the building program. With Arthur's death in 1923, one of the final links to Mackay was gone.

At the annual meeting on January 7, 1924, Casady announced that C. S. Montgomery, past senior warden and chancellor of the diocese, could not be reelected as he was leaving the parish. Like a number of Omaha's leading business and professional men, he had established a residence in California. Montgomery had been active on the vestry the prior year. He was present at the May meeting of the vestry and participated in filling the vacancy created by the death of A. C. Smith. There were no meetings as usual during the summer, but when they recommenced in the fall with the September meeting, Montgomery was not present, nor again was he present for the November meeting. In 1923, Montgomery had turned seventy-two. He had been senior warden since 1892 when he had succeeded Woolworth. His time of service as senior warden was just shy of thirty-two years, and his continuous service on the vestry was a little over thirty-nine years. The annual meeting in January of 1924 proceeded to elect Judge William A. Redick as his successor. Redick would also succeed Montgomery as chancellor of the diocese within the next year. If Casady's soaring vision for All Saints had nudged Montgomery into retirement, clearly his age was the determining factor. As for leaving the parish, nothing more should be read into that than the need to distance himself from the action of the parish. His role as a long-term senior warden was much more like that of a past rector than that of a modern senior warden. If he had stayed in the parish, it would have been difficult for people, after all those years, to accept that he was not the go-to-person when there was a problem.

William Redick, br. 1859, Omaha, Present at founding meeting 1885, Senior Warden 1924 until his death in 1936.

While Redick had participated at the meeting in 1885, which founded the parish, he had been off the vestry for several stretches of time since then. He was, however, the last tie to the early days. The vestry in 1924 was John Yates, junior warden, J. S. Brady, W. F. Smith, George Morton, Robert Trimble, Dr. Lemers, Forrest Richardson, S. S. Caldwell, H. A. Scandritt, and Dr. C. M. Rich. They represented a new pattern of parish leadership. Moreover, Casady had hinted at the annual meeting that the parish should adopt three-year terms, which would allow for more rotation. In 1925, the names of Frank L. Adams and James L. Paxton replaced Richardson and Scandritt; and a truly Casady vestry had arrived.

Celebrating the Fortieth

On September 1, 1925, All Saints would turn forty. The thought stirred Casady's ambitions, and he declared that the theme for 1924 would be the preparation for celebrating the fortieth anniversary of the parish's founding. Later in the year, he published the goals that he hoped that the parish would adopt for the celebration:

> I hope, among other things, that we may be able to report eight hundred communicants in good standing and a church school of four hundred, including all departments . . . All Saints Church is unique in one respect among the parishes of this part of the country. Few, if any, have had such long rectorships . . . I am perfectly sincere in saying what I trust you also feel, that I hope the same comment can be made on the occasion of our fiftieth anniversary . . . The same thing might be said for the musical traditions of the parish which are generally recognized to be the best in the city . . . Our senior warden, as you will note from the minutes, was on the first vestry.

Casady's ambition can be measured by looking at the numbers at the beginning of 1924, which he had published in *Church and Home*. At the beginning of the year, the parish had 641 communicants, 1,090 baptized members, 566 Easter communions, and 251 kids out of a potential of 353 church school enrollment.[93] He set a very high bar for the parish and for himself. It is also clear from Casady's statement that he intended to be at All Saints for at least another ten years, affirming in his remarks the unique contribution to the parish that Mackay's long tenure had made, one he says he hoped he could emulate.

During 1924, Casady pursued a number of projects to enhance the ambiance of the church and the parish hall, capitalizing on the coming fortieth anniversary of the parish as well as celebrating it. He was particularly pleased with the relighting of the altar area. The most stunning opportunity in the course of the year was provided by the desire of the Megeath family for a fitting memorial for their daughter, Virginia, who had died in 1919. George W. Megeath (Magrath) was the managing partner of the Coal Exchange, which he soon owned and renamed the Megeath Coal Company. Casady proposed to Megeath that a fitting memorial would be a stunning new altar and reredos to replace the Victorian Gothic altar and reredos. It was the original altar-reredos placed in the old building in 1886, and it had been brought to the new building in 1906, and it was tired and dated. The design for the memorial was laid out and executed by Alois Lang. Lang immigrated to this country from Oberammergau, which is located in Germany's Bavaria Alps. In Oberammergau, famous for its Passion Play and as a center for wood carving, Lang had mastered the art of the wood carving that filled the churches of Europe. Intrigued by the American market, he immigrated and worked out of his studios in Detroit and Grand Rapids, Michigan. Lang was particularly noted in this

93 *Church and Home*, vol. XXVIII, no. 2, October 11, 1924.

country for his carvings of the Last Supper, which appeared in a number of American churches, including St. Mark's Pro-Cathedral in Hastings, Nebraska, where it was installed at about the same time.

The new altar was constructed out of oak and finished with a dark stain. It was covered with a contrasting slab of white marble. The altar was attached to an ornately carved reredos likewise finished with a dark stain. It set in the east end, typical of churches of this era. Into the niches of dark wood of the reredos were inserted a collection of hand-carved statues. Carved from blond oak and lightly waxed, they form a stunning contrast to the background. There were six large figures, John the Baptist, St. Andrew, St. Peter, St. John, St. Matthew, and St. Paul. The six were New Testament saints, the only saints recognized by the Episcopal Church at the time. They are accompanied by eight smaller figures: Ignatius and Polycarp, Athanatius and Augustine, Theodore of Tarsus, Stephen Langton, Bishop White, and Bishop Clarkson. The selection of these lesser saints seems to have been driven by Casady's own theology. They form an argument for the apostolic succession of the Anglican Church. The four figures on the right were early fathers. The martyrs, Ignatius and Polycarp, made an argument for an office of bishops independent of bishop of Rome. Athanatius and Augustine represent theologians who had taught a non-Roman theology. On the right were two archbishops of Canterbury. The first was Theodore of Tarsus, the second archbishop of Canterbury. One would expect that the choice would have been the first archbishop, Augustine, who had been sent by Pope Gregory the Great to revive the church among the Angles. In truth, Augustine had left behind a mission in a fragile state. Theodore, who came from the Eastern Church, followed him; and it was he that managed to organize the mission and save it from collapse. Again, this choice is of a figure who is non-Roman. Casady's second choice of an archbishop of Canterbury is also a surprise. More obvious choices would be Anselm, Thomas Becket, Thomas Cranmer or William Laud, who were known for their sanctity, at least in certain circles. His choice was Stephen Langton, not noted for his sanctity but for his role in the drafting of the Magna Carta. We can assume that Casady considered the Magna Carta as a forerunner of the American constitution; therefore, Langton provided a means for arguing that the Anglican Church had a particular relevance to American life. The last two figures are American bishops. Again, the primus, Samuel Seabury, is passed over. Casady chose instead William White, the first bishop of Pennsylvania. White, with his long tenure as presiding bishop, was arguably more instrumental in the formation of the American church than Seabury. His final choice was Clarkson, the first bishop of Nebraska, which was a way of tracing the apostolic ministry to Omaha.

The altar and chancel of the 1906 building after 1924. The Gothic altar has been replaced with the Megeath Memorial Altar. The design of the new altar gave an expression to Casady's theology.

One can imagine Casady bringing his confirmation class to the foot of the altar and tracing the descent from the apostles down through time and across the globe to the very spot they were standing in Omaha, Nebraska. The altar and reredos were dedicated, on the feast of St. Peter and Paul, June 29, 1924. It was from all points of view a stunning transformation of the sanctuary. It came with a cost. The *World-Herald* reported that it had cost the parish $35,000.[94]

Casady's study of successful downtown churches had led him to the conclusion that it was essential to establish an endowment. This too emerged as a project to be tied to the anniversary celebration. On December 20, 1924, Casady announced the intention to build an endowment for the parish. "We have paid in full our budget quota to the diocese and the general church. We have started an endowment fund." He argued,

94 *Omaha World-Herald*, November 21, 1933.

"Without an endowment, this parish cannot carry on during the next forty years as it has during the first forty of its existence. And yet our present building and our present location can be the scene of great service for one hundred years to come."[95] The parish was already experiencing its location as inner city; and Casady on this occasion pointed to Indianapolis and Akron, Ohio, for models of how a church could remain downtown and succeed.

In February, the vestry moved to establish a fund to be known as the All Saints Endowment Foundation. An exacting set of articles was adopted for the foundation. The principal was to be deposited with the United States Trust Company of Omaha and not to be withdrawn. The trustees were directed to pay the interest and earnings of the fund as the same are received every thirty days, to be used for the general support of the parish and for such special purposes as the vestry might order. The Articles of the Foundation specify that should All Saints ever cease to exist, the principle be paid to its successor, if any, or otherwise paid to the National Council of the Protestant Episcopal Church in America. The vestry set the goal as $100,000, and an initial deposit of $585 was dubbed by Casady the blade. Further progress with the endowment was reported in *Church and Home*. A year later, the vestry man William Farnam Smith died and left in his will a bequest that brought the total to $7,285.[96]

As the end of the anniversary year approached, much had been accomplished. Casady had held a summer camp in Wisconsin for parish youth in conjunction with his annual vacation at Wisconsin Rapids. Again, he was emulating the urban churches of the East in attempting to establish a summer camp. The experience of the first group to participate "Camp Casady" had been most encouraging. For Casady, it was an opportunity to train youth in "Christian Citizenship," a primary theme of his ministry. Part of the experience was roughing it and meeting challenges presented by rigorous hikes and canoe trips, all in Wisconsin's splendid outdoors. To get a sense of the spirit of the experience, it is helpful to remember that boxing was introduced by Mackay in 1907 as a key part of the parish's work with the boys of the parish and continued through the 1950s. This regime was to some of the parish boys quite attractive, but to not a few, one suspects, a serious put off. Dana Bradford II was one of the boys who were shipped off to summer camp that year, and in his eighties, he would offer lavish testimony to All Saints past rectors. McCallum scored high, Clayton was

95 *Church and Home*, April 17, 1926.

96 *Church and Home*, vol. XXX, no. 24, November 20, 1926.

outstanding, but Casady was—he would stop, roll his eyes, and mutter a few indistinct words that ended with the word *awful*.

During the past year, the church and parish hall had been strikingly redecorated. Property adjacent to the church had been purchased. A new rectory had been purchased, and the old rectory had been converted into much-needed office and meeting space. The cost, however, was a debt that in September of 1925 was consolidated into a single mortgage held by the Omaha Loan and Building Association in the sum of $29,000. As the parish leadership prepared for the Every Member Canvass for the coming year, they set for themselves a high bar. The goal would be $31,745. A. A. Lowman, a member of the vestry, stepped forward to be All Saints first true Every Member Canvass chairman. Lowman would continue to serve as Every Member Canvass chairman for several years, making an important and lasting contribution to All Saints.

Hitting the Wall: 1925–1926

As the new year began, the vestibule of the parish hall was still filled with a grand array of charts illustrating various aspect of church finances left over from the past Every Member Canvass, which had fallen significantly short of its goal. Casady painfully summarized the results:

> Our people desire to have the parish conducted on a more modest basis than heretofore: they do not believe that the work of the parish justifies such a budget as the vestry proposed . . . For five years, the rector and vestry have patiently waited in the faith that, as time went on, the people would feel as we feel about All Saints. Apparently, their faith was not justified.[97]

In December, pledges amounted to only $15,663.30, far short of the goal of 31,754. Meeting on December 10, the vestry, faced with the need to cut cost in the coming year, moved with regrets to dispense with Ms. Rich's services as director of Christian education and to make *Church and Home* a biweekly publication. Assignments were made at the vestry meeting for individuals to press the canvass further; but in January, the total had only grown to $16,073, still far short of the goal.

Casady was quick to dismiss economic conditions as cause; even though the economy, particularly in the farm states, had been stressed since the end of the war as the country transitioned to a peace time economy. Moreover,

---

97 *Church and Home*, vol. 29 XXIX, no. 9, December 5, 1925.

the recovery of agriculture in Europe came about much more quickly than had been expected, further aggravating the agriculture surplus that had been created by the war effort. While the numbers of communicants in the parish remained high, Casady complained that attendance was below reasonable expectations, and the activities of the men of the parish were at a low ebb. In some cases, the work in women's organizations, he asserted, was less effective than it was two and three years ago. "In short we are facing a real crisis." He went on to say that "he sadly takes his share of responsibility for our present situation but he does not propose to burden his conscience with all of the selfishness and indifference which the present condition reveals."

Perhaps the explanation lies not so much with the economic conditions as with sweeping cultural changes that, among other things, caused people to be anxious about the economic conditions. It was difficult to keep track of the growth in expenses that was experienced by individuals and institutions, which were caused by the new way of life. For John and Jane Doe, the need of a suburban home was on the way to becoming a necessity. With that came the need for a car, travel, and entertainment. Meeting these newly perceived needs not only took money but time as well. This supports Casady's observation that parallel to the lack of money was a decline in participation in spite of the fact that the parish had more members than ever before and nobody appeared to be particularly disaffected. The American Victorians had looked to the church for entertainment and socialization as well as spirituality. The new American individual progressively found entertainment and socialization outside of the church. This is reflected in Casady's decision that as of March of 1926, the parish would discontinue the evening service on Sundays. This service had traditionally centered on music and was more focused on entertainment and socialization than on spirituality.

As the expenses for individuals had expanded, so too had those for institutions. Parishes across the country, as All Saints in Omaha, thought that they needed more money to do their job. From 1919 to 1924, total parish giving across the country grew from $24 million to $41 million. Diocesan receipts grew from $1.5 million to $2.6 million. The very existence of these statistics was novel and signaled a new heightened concern in the church with money. Consistently, through the early twenties, the national church asked for more money from the dioceses, and the dioceses asked for more money from the parishes.

As it formulated the budget for 1926, the vestry sent a letter to the bishop. In the letter, they explained that they would have to limit the parish's contribution outside of itself, to $5,000. This was $663 less than their contribution for the previous year. The cut was far less, they explained to the bishop, than the cuts they were making to the parish's expenditure on its own programs. The senior warden, William A. Redick, who in his capacity of chancellor of the diocese attended meetings of the executive council, returned from its March meeting and reported to the vestry, with considerable dismay, that the diocese's executive council had not been informed by the bishop that All Saints total pledge for the year to the diocese was limited to $5,000. As a consequence, the executive council had made only nominal cuts to their budget.

The diocese, however, had requested relief from the national church's assessment; but the national church insisted that it receive the full amount. The national church was, it turned out, operating on a deficit budget like everyone else. To solve its problem, the national church had gone around the dioceses and made a direct appeal to parishes for assistance. The result was that the vestry at All Saints moved in its March meeting to pay its share of the national church's asking and to deal with the diocese's asking later in the year.

In May, the vestry acceded to the demands of the diocese and moved to pay six months of the assessment, stating that it was doing so under protest. The problem became more intense as the year continued. Casady, who had been a strong supporter of the national church and the diocese, now found himself on the other side of the issue. He visited with the vestry in September about a proposed meeting of six parishes within the diocese to create a common front to deal with the problem. In the end, he met with representatives from the cathedral and St. Barnabas in order to find a way for the diocese to adjust to the realities of the overall financial situation.

By October, the diocese's problem had become extreme. The treasurer of the cathedral chapter sent a letter to the vestry of All Saints. In the letter, H. W. Yates explained that the executive council had not only not made cuts, but that it had also added the bishop's salary of $3,000 to the diocese's budget. It had taken this action because the Episcopal endowment was presently without income. Property on Dodge Street had reverted to the chapter since the purchaser had declared bankruptcy. The former residence of Bishop Williams, Bishopthorpe on Thirty-First and Farnam, was likely to follow as the purchaser had ceased making payments. Yates concluded, "In its present condition, the principal account of the Episcopal Endowment Fund is practically non income producing . . . the result is an overdraft of more than $2,000 in the income account of the Episcopal Endowment Fund."

It is particularly ironic that the generation of clergy who had dedicated themselves to running the church on the basis of good business principles had managed in such a short time to plunge it at all levels into such a deep financial crisis. One might assume that the problem was that they had not been very good businessmen. As a matter of fact, American businessmen had been churning the American economy through cycles of boom and bust on the order of every eight to ten years. The difference was that businessmen could walk away from the mess and start over, while the clergy had to live with it.

As the year was ending, Lowman again took on the task of the Every Member Canvass. It was perhaps one of the most intense canvasses ever undertaken. He reported that "from one thousand to one thousand two hundred contacts have been made." He went on to say that as of November 27, the results had moved $18,000 pledged for 1926 to $20,000 for 1927. When 1926 ended, the parish had collected $23,000 of pledged income and $6,000 in additional giving, which totaled $29,000. This was remarkably close to the ambitious goal they had set for the canvass. To a great extent, the money had been there, but the anxiety of pledging in advanced had caused members of the parish to understate what they were willing and able to give.

In order to refinance its long-term debt, the parish borrowed an additional $17,000. It paid $4,615.43 to the diocese and $430 to the national church to assist it in paying its deficits. In a way, All Saints had performed remarkably well and yet strangely found itself, especially its rector, deeply disappointed. January would again find them struggling to find ways to cut their budget. Yet by the time the annual meeting came around, Casady reported that the parish found itself in an "improved condition."

New Leads

Casady continued to soldier on in the coming year. In many ways, things were better than anticipated. In March, he wrote to the parish:

> There is no question about it—the parish is growing . . . Although we have not raised the full amount hoped for our parish budget, the pledges are very considerably in advance of last year. New pledges keep coming in. Hence, it looks as though with a big Easter offering we may be able to meet all our obligations and keep out of debt this year. The parish organizations are larger and stronger without exception than

for some years. The spirit of the parish is better than it has ever been since I knew it first.[98]

It was with some relief and pride that he reported to the parish that Ms. Rich had found a new position at St. John the Divine in New York City. All Saints very own Ms. Rich had been hired by the Diocese of New York as the secretary of its Board of Religious Education. There, she had established a lending library at the cathedral and was working with rectors and church school superintendents throughout that very expansive diocese. Plans had been made for her to lecture on "The Principles of Teaching" at St. Stephen's College in Annandale, New York, and on "Church School Administration" at St. John the Divine in the coming summer.

Again, it was with pride that Casady recognized a member of the vestry with a special service cross. John Brady was honored for twenty-five years on the vestry. He had served with W. Farnam Smith on the committee that raised the money to pay off the parish's indebtedness in 1919. Among the reasons for praising Brady was listed the claim that "He is one of the men in the parish who gives a fixed proportion of his income to the church, thus following the recommendation of our national council."

In spite of this, Casady struggled with his disappointment. In a letter dated August 14, which was sent to the parish from "Camp Casady," he revealed his feelings at the beginning of the summer. "I went away considerably depressed over my condition." On top of that, he had had his tonsils and several teeth removed during the summer. News from the parish in his absence, however, continued to be positive; and he claimed he was feeling better and looking forward to getting back for the fall program. He asked the parish: "Please be as patient with my physical shortcomings as you have been with my spiritual defects and all will soon be running smoothly again. And thank you all for many things like loyalty, and encouragement and prayers."

One bright spot for him, however, was a growing involvement in a venture into the field of higher education. A small liberal arts college less than fifty miles south of Omaha had approached the Episcopal Church for help. Tabor College had been founded by the Congregational Church in 1852. The founders envisioned a liberal art college modeled on Oberlin, Ohio. Their commitment to the antislavery movement made Tabor a principal location on the underground railroad. The college had had a period of success, but it began to find it more difficult to prosper in the twentieth century. By the 1920s, it was reaching out for a lifeline and had found some interest in the Episcopal Church. Bishop Longley in Iowa became particularly enamored with the idea of an "Episcopal College" in

[98] *Church and Home*, vol. 29, no. 17, March 20, 1926.

the West. He had managed to get support from the bishop of Colorado and the bishop of Nebraska; and the college proceeded to hire a priest of the Church of England, Dr. Clayton, as its president. With this position, he also became the pastor of the Congregational church in Tabor. It was an impressive ecumenical venture driven by the ideals of a good business.

One might recall that at the beginning of our story, the election of Worthington, in effect, was the decision to close the Episcopal College in Nebraska City. It was closed because it was clear that the population of Episcopalians in the state would not provide a large enough pool of youth to build a student body nor would it be able to produce the finances to support a college, particularly when those finances needed to be directed at strengthening congregations. Revisiting the idea of an Episcopal College in the 1920 is simply a sign of how little we remember where we have been.

Casady, because of his Iowa connections, seems to have been among the first Episcopal clergy on the college's board. Casady was soon joined Wilfred Mann, the rector of St. Paul's Council Bluffs, on the Board of Trustees. In September of 1925, Casady invited Frederick Clayton, the president of the college, to preach at All Saints in his absence.[99] The following year, in May, Bishop Shayler invited Clayton to attend and address the annual council. In Shayler's address to a council, he briefly described the work at the college and concluded by saying, "It would be hard to find a better example of Christian unity in service or opportunity." Anticipating Clayton's presence at council, Casady, even while he was limiting the parish's pledge to the diocese to $5,000 and severely cutting the parish's own budget, asked the vestry to approve paying Clayton's pension for the year, a sum of $365. He defended his request by explaining: "The college was now being conducted under the Episcopal Church and is making splendid progress."

Shortly after annual council, Casady arranged for a group of women from All Saints to visit the college. On May 15, the women traveled with Casady to Tabor, Iowa. On their arrival, they were warmly greeted by the president of the college and were served a pleasant luncheon. Following the luncheon, they were escorted around the college and ended up in the auditorium where the college choir sang a cantata based on the Seven Last Words. They finished the afternoon by attending an interesting and illuminating talk on the life of Turkish women given by one of the professors. In the June 19 issue of *Church and Home*, Casady gave an enthusiastic appraisal of Clayton's first year at Tabor. He reports that it was the best year at the school since 1900. The school met its expenses and even made a payment on its debt, which is quite remarkable because

99 *Church and Home*, September 24, 1925.

it had been ready to close its doors and turn over its property for less than 15 percent of its value the year before. Clayton, he said, came to the situation because of the opportunity to do an important ministry, leaving a comfortable parish to do so. He concluded his report, "In the judgment of the writer, he is doing as much as any single man in the Middle West to revive and awaken the life of the Episcopal Church in small centers and to commend our church to those who through ignorance and lack of contact have misunderstood its life and spirit."[100]

A year later, as Casady was preparing for his usual summer vacation in Wisconsin, he arranged for Clayton to live in the rectory and office at Mackay Memorial Hall, "thus being more accessible than anyone we have ever had for our summer supply." In announcing this to the parish, he referred to Clayton as "an intimate personal friend" and praised "his personal charm and ability as a preacher." Casady was not one to speak casually of intimate friendships, unlike his predecessor Thomas Mackay who considered himself a friend with anyone he ever met. Casady was also likely aware that in praising Clayton's preaching skills, he was admitting his own limitation.

The venture with the college was not the only initiative in the parish. In spite of the financial struggle in which the parish found itself, there was an initiative to replace the organ. The need had surfaced during the envisioning year of 1924, which had been undertaken as preparation for the celebration of the fortieth anniversary of the parish. The women of the parish had responded and undertaken the task of raising the money for a new organ. The existing organ was the Roosevelt, which had been purchased in 1886 by Woolworth. It had grown progressively more limiting as it aged and as the style of church music changed. Casady presented to the vestry a letter from Mrs. Arthur C. Smith, recently widowed, on September 8, 1926, which outlined the plan. The Skinner Organ Company had offered to supply the organ for $25,000. The amount of $5,000 was required when the order was placed, a second $5,000 when installation began, and an additional $5,000 annually until the total was paid. In addition to the cost, Casady noted that a room to house the organ would have to be built at the cost of $8,000. Because of its deepening debt, the parish was not in a good position to proceed, yet not to proceed meant throwing cold water on the women's enthusiasm.

100 *Church and Home*, vol. XXIX, no. 24, June 19, 1926.

Casady Elected Missionary Bishop of Oklahoma

As the summer of 1927 approached, Casady dutifully worried about the mundane affairs of the parish such as replacing pews, which were not very attractive, and kneeling cushions, which were worn. He thanked the women for undertaking to redecorate the walls of the church during the coming summer while he was gone. He also continued to worry about the three years of heavy expense that would follow the installation of a new organ. There was, however, a wild card about to be dealt, which was not so much an added worry so much as a heightened anxiety. Theodore Payne Thurston, missionary bishop of Oklahoma, announced his resignation. He had been suffering from a heart ailment for some time; and on a temporary basis, the missionary bishop of North Texas, Seaman, had assumed jurisdiction over Oklahoma. The presiding bishop, Ethelbert Talbot, was set to convene a special meeting of the House of Bishops in June. Casady had come to national notice by serving on the national executive council, the only Western priest on the council. In the search from a new missionary bishop for Oklahoma, the majority of the House of Bishops saw Oklahoma as Western, not Southern. Coming out of the meeting, Bishop Seaman telegraphed his secretary in Oklahoma City:

> Please phone Mr. Carden (the priest who edited the *Oklahoma Churchman*) that Rev. Thomas Casady of All Saints Church, Omaha, was elected bishop of Oklahoma, subject to the approval of standing committees. Most excellent things are said of him, and I hope he will accept so that everything may move forward within a few months.[101]

Casady expressed no surprise at his election and quickly accepted. It is evident that Casady had been aware of the possibility; and even after his election, he moved ahead with the work of the parish in a methodical way, until consent was assured. He tendered his resignation in a succinct letter to the vestry devoid of any emotion, dated August 23, 1927, while he was still on vacation in Wisconsin. On his return, the vestry, meeting on September 20, accepted his resignation, and set Casady's last day as October 2, the Sunday on which his consecration was set to take place at All Saints. Meeting again on September 26, the vestry presented him with

101 *Building a Diocese: Thomas Casady as Missionary Bishop of Oklahoma, 1927–1937*, John E. Borrego, Norman, Oklahoma, 1999, p. 13.

a gold cross, likely his pectoral cross, and voted to march as a group in the procession at his consecration.

When the hour arrived in October 2, scores of people still waited outside of the church in hopes of getting seating. The procession down the aisle included the choir leading the hymn "Hail to the Lord's Anointed"; the vestry; the clergy of Oklahoma; the clergy of Western Nebraska and the clergy of Nebraska; Casady; and finally eleven bishops including the presiding bishop. The officiant was the presiding bishop, Murray, bishop of Maryland. With him were Bishops Seaman, North Texas; Roberts, South Dakota; Burleson, Missionary District of South Dakota; McElwain, Minnesota; Mize, Western Kansas; Morrison, Iowa; Longley, coadjutor of Iowa; Shayler, Nebraska; Beecher, Western Nebraska; and Johnson, Colorado, eleven in all.

Bishop Irving Peake Johnson, who had served St. Martin's and St. Andrew's in Omaha, from 1894 to 1901 and who had been Casady's bishop during the time that he served in Pueblo, preached. The bulk of the sermon was printed in the evening edition of the *Omaha World-Herald* and is quite stunning.[102] His text was Acts 20:28: "Take heed, therefore unto yourselves and to all the flock over which the Holy Ghost hath made you overseer to feed the church of God which he hath purchased with his own self." The main point of Johnson's sermon was a distinction between secular organizations and the church. He said:

> There are those who regard the church as a group of Christians who manage to get along with each other, but not essentially different from a lodge or a service club, a reflection of popular prejudice limited by artificial names.

The church, he argued, is a unique universal community. It cannot be bound by names like Rome, Geneve, Wesleyan, or even Canterbury. He made a plea for less sectarianism in religion and asked how could the church serve the world and the country, which was being driven apart by parties and groups, if it was just another party or group?

The day before, the evening edition of the *Omaha World-Herald* had informed Omaha that a "Tariff Deadlock is seen between France and US," that "Ruth hit 60," the Cornhuskers had managed to prevail over Ames in the first game of the season, and that eight sisters in Stromberg, Nebraska "spurn the Bob." Now it gave its readers an extensive account of Casady's consecration, devoting an entire page to it. The report began by observing that "the impressive yet not too solemn ceremony began at ten

---

102 *Evening World Herald*, October 3, 1927 p. 6.

o'clock and required nearly three hours." The article was accompanied by two large photographs. At the top of the page was a photograph taken after the service in the parish hall of the now twelve bishops in their vestments. Below was a picture of Casady standing with the presiding bishop.

In a separate article in the same paper, on the society page, it was explained that on the Monday following the service, Casady and his family had breakfast with Mr. and Mrs. Frank I. Adams. For lunch, they had met with a group at the University Club, hosted by Mrs. Gilbert Carpenter. Later in the afternoon, they departed from Union Station with three of their children. The two older boys were already in school at the University of Oklahoma.

Casady's contribution to All Saints was significant. Like his predecessors, he seems to have been the right man at the right time. He was able to continue the parish's pattern of growth, and he gave the parish what it sorely needed to keep up with the times, a pattern of modern parish administration. His own self-assessment of his All Saints years, however, left him with puzzles and regrets. In many ways, he had fallen well short of his vision for the parish. What he and his contemporaries failed to realize was how dramatically American life had changed. For a long period, the Episcopal Church had enjoyed a cultural orientation that had made its work easy. With the country's swing to a focus on the individual and his or her rights, already apparent in 1915, a religious community, like the Episcopal Church, which was inherently oriented to community and duty found itself navigating against the tide. The rise in the level of conflict, which was inherent in such a culture, was particularly hard for the Episcopal Church to deal with. If the Episcopal Church suddenly found its ministry being counter cultural, as Bishop Johnson had argued in his sermon at Casady's consecration, it had to expect harder times and to adjust the dreams it had nurtured in the great run from the end of the Civil War up to 1915.

Had Casady stayed at All Saints beyond the seven years, he would have had to radically alter his goals or he would have found himself progressively more frustrated. The thirties only compounded the culture shift by adding an economic disaster on top of it. Casady faced these harsh realities in Oklahoma. In the new field, his administrative abilities were much needed, and he could do for it what he had done for All Saints. His task was to make the missionary diocese an independent self-sufficient diocese, a thing that he accomplished. John Borrego, in his history of Casady's episcopate, comments: "Becoming a diocese required strong executive leadership and financial management skills perhaps even more than a gift for proclaiming the Gospel."[103] Much of his time was taken up with coping with a shortage of priests, particularly competent priests. He often found himself prodding them harshly and, not infrequently, removing them from office. Alongside his solid accomplishments, he entertained dreams. They included a million-dollar endowment and an exceptional cathedral for Oklahoma City. Borrego tells us that "no subject takes up more space among the bishop's surviving papers, or seemed to engage his passion as intensely as did All Souls Cathedral." The endowment struggled to reach $200,000, and the cathedral never came to pass. The dreams are parallel to those that he had once entertained for All Saints Omaha, an endowment and stunning additions to the plant, which also came to pass either greatly scaled back or not at all. The fate of such dreams suggest that Casady was a very private man, formulating plans that were belatedly shared and because of that they lacked an interplay with reality. One wonders if in his later years when he assessed his work in Oklahoma, if he recalled that he had placed, Theodore of Tarsus, the second "missionary" archbishop of Canterbury in the reredos at All Saints a quarter a century before, only to have found himself the second missionary bishop of Oklahoma, whose legacy was not so much to be the beloved bishop, as the bishop who gave the diocese its essential organizational structure.

When Casady died in 1955, two years after his retirement as bishop, the Diocese of Oklahoma commissioned a communion chalice to be given to All Saints in Omaha in his memory. The large chalice, executed in sterling by Louis R. Brasier and inscribed "Given to the Glory of God in Grateful Remembrance of Thomas Casady Bishop 1881–1955," is used regularly for Sunday Eucharists at All Saints. It is tangible evidence of Casady's regard for his ministry at All Saints.

Meanwhile, back at All Saints, Dr. Frederick W. Clayton began to function as an interim. He had been installed at All Saints for the summer by Casady and would have, presumably, returned to Tabor College in the fall. Despite two successful years there, the college's creditor demanded that summer immediate payment and the college collapsed. Without mentioning this disturbing news, Casady announced that after a brief vacation, Dr. Clayton would return and be in charge of the parish until a new rector was in residence. He would have charge of the services on the Sunday following the consecration and he would be in residence at Hotel Keen, Room 245.

---

103 *Building a Diocese: Thomas Casady as Missionary Bishop of Oklahoma, 1927–1937,* John E. Borrego, Norman, Oklahoma, 1999, p. 1.

Chapter 5

Individualists Holding On: 1927–1947

Clayton

The pendulum that governs the American life had reversed its motion sometime around the turn of the century. By 1920, it had passed, for the most part without notice, its center point and had begun to move American life into new territory. The assumption that the fortunes of the Episcopal Church could be repaired and/or extended by applying good business practices had for a time encouraged parishes, dioceses, and the national church to expand their programs. The legacies of the twenties were enlarged parish facilities, expanded budgets, and lofty ambitions. But as early as 1926, this legacy was proving problematic. In 1926, All Saints failed to fund its budget, which it had set at $33,000. From then on, the parish's annual budgets began a decline and would bottom out in 1936 at $16,500, a mere half of what it had once been. All Saints experience was part of a larger pattern. With a growing assertion of individualism and personal rights, the maintenance of communal structures, liturgically oriented churches among other things, was becoming progressively problematic. One might even venture so far as to say socioeconomic structures of all kinds were becoming progressively problematic, as laissez faire capitalism in America reached for its zenith.

An Obvious Call

As the All Saints vestry faced its need to call a new rector caused by the election of its ambitious rector, Thomas Casady, to the episcopate, it and those who were advising them, had little sense of what was happening. Numerous names were put forward to be considered as the next rector of All Saints. Casady suggested that the vestry consider Sam West of Greeley, Colorado, who he had invited to his consecration just so his vestry might have a look at him. Bishop Shayler, attending the vestry meeting the day after Casady's consecration, pledged his active assistance. He informed the vestry that "he considered it of importance that the man called should be of low church tendencies rather than one who favored high ritualism, that he should be a strong man from the preaching standpoint and one who would work well with the Bishop of the diocese and clergy."[104] He submitted several names: Rev. Ashley F. Gerhard of Winnetka, Illinois; Rev. John F. Plummer of Chicago, Illinois; and Rev. William W. Fleetwood of Salt Lake City, Utah.

In spite of all this advice, Senior Warden William Redick opened the vestry meeting two weeks later with the report that he had interviewed Dr. Clayton as to whether he would consider taking the position as rector if it were offered him. He went on to report the results of various other inquires, including two new names: Rev. Paul Roberts of Boise, Idaho, and Rev. P. M. Spencer of Kansas City. Spencer had indicated that he was not interested, but apparently all the others were. After all, All Saints was a well-resourced parish; and, above all, lightning had struck. One of its rectors had passed on into the episcopate! Arthur Lowman moved that Redick complete the correspondence and to report its results to the next vestry meeting set for November 14. Meeting in November, the senior warden made his report to the vestry, which was followed by a motion made by Robert Trimble to call Frederick W. Clayton as the fourth rector of All Saints. The vote was recorded as unanimous. By December 12, Clayton, now forty-two, presided at a meeting of the vestry as rector. The vacancy had been a little more than two months, quite remarkable even for an All Saints vestry, who have habitually acted with dispatch to fill vacancies. Moreover, they seemed to set aside a great deal of advice that they had been offered and had chosen to follow their own instinct. Perhaps the most important consideration was that they had experienced Clayton as a preacher. Against Casady's labored preaching style, he struck them as intellectually stimulating and emotional moving. Perhaps also they had a sense that Clayton had a very different understanding of what a parish should be than that of their bishop and their departing rector. What they did, in the end, was make the obvious choice, the one that was sitting there by default under everyone's nose.

---

104 Vestry minutes.

A Different Tack

Clayton immediately offered the advice that the parish should revise its property values on which the mission and national church assessments were based. They were, he thought, too high. This clarified one thing: Clayton was not going to be "one who would work well with the bishop of the diocese." Next, he advised the vestry that "he had no vision of increasing buildings or the accommodations in the parish." In other words, he was not going to be the heir to Casady's vision of a large urban parish with an extended modern facility. Hinting at his pragmatism, he also added the thought that the pipe organ, which had been commissioned, could be installed in a horizontal manner saving $10,000 on the expected cost of installing the organ.

If Clayton was not the business mind that Casady had been, he was, just as assuredly, not the Victorian gentleman that Mackay had been, though like Mackay he had come from the British Isles. It is true that he celebrated the literature of Charles Dickens, but that was not so much for Dickens's romance as for Dickens's anticipation of realism. There is nothing of the "Idylls of the King" resonating in Clayton's head. He had no sense of failure for not being a family man nor any guilt as Mackay would have of taking a drink in "a private club" while the working class was prohibited to do so in a saloon. Already deep into prohibition, Clayton drank and at times drank heavily. It was commonly said that after a vestry meeting, often held in the Omaha Club, a designated vestry man made sure that "Father" got home.

He was also unlike Mackay in that he was not a conversationalist. Clayton was a deep thinker, not shy in expressing himself, but always careful in choosing his words. Yet he took up the task of continuing *Church and Home* without hesitation, in contrast to Casady's reluctance. It was, however, a very different read than Mackay's version of it. Unfortunately, by 1934, funding in the parish was severely limited; and, as usual, the parish's communications budget was the first places to look for cuts. *Church and Home* became an occasional publication, depriving us of an important source for understanding a good deal of Clayton's ministry.

Frederick Clayton was born in Northern England in the town of Newcastle on the Tyne on February 22, 1885. He was the son of a coal mining official whose work was located in the grubby Durham area. As a boy, he saw a good deal of the seamy side of life. The experience ingrained in him sympathy for those who are cast in difficult circumstances. He completed his education in Durham, the great cathedral city of the north, known for its conservatism and Catholic tendencies. With his bachelor's degree in hand, he entered upon a journey to remake himself. His next step was to enroll in St. Augustine College at Canterbury, in the heart of the liberal and more Protestant south. Clayton characterized the college as an institution that turned out individualists and scholars. The college, at that time, was governed by Randall Davidson, the archbishop of Canterbury (1903–1928) who was a broad churchman, traditional, but sympathetic with nonconformists. There, Clayton was awarded a Doctor of Divinity in 1914. Subsequently, he left England to serve in Canada as a missionary. He was ordained deacon and priest by the archbishop of Ontario, Canada, in 1914 and 1916, who posted him in the wilds of Northern Ontario. There he served a population made up of metal miners, lumbermen, and struggling farmers settling on the Canadian frontier. After his stint in the mission field, he served as associate to the rector of St. Simon's parish in Toronto, Canada. Toward the end of 1921, he immigrated to the United States. His immediate destination indicated on his immigration papers was Burlington, Vermont. Shortly after arriving, he was called as rector of St. Andrew's Church in Princess Anne, Maryland. The church he served was a historic parish, the third Anglican parish church to be built in colonial America. His parishioners were made up of landed gentry, long on family and not so much with money. He served in Princess Anne until he was called in 1925 to be president of Tabor College, Tabor, Iowa. A story of his call to Tabor appeared in the *Omaha World-Herald* in January of 1926, likely the result of Bishop Shayler's special relationship with the paper, trumpeting his work. The headline read: "Episcopal Pastors Fill the Pulpit of a Congregational Church." Under a picture of Dr. Clayton, it quoted Clayton as describing the effort as "a practical experiment in church unity." The article explained that Tabor College was founded by Congregationalist in 1857, the settlement being made by a colony from Oberlin, Ohio. In addition to Clayton's role as president, a second Episcopal priest, Rev. LeRoy Weeks, served as dean. Both served as joint pastors of the Tabor Congregational Church.[105] His two years at Tabor were heady, but fraught with financial difficulty. While he made progress on the college's debt, its creditor would not wait and finally demanded full payment by the end of 1927. His supporters, the Episcopal bishops of Iowa, Colorado, and Nebraska, having not heeded the parable of the man who first counts the cost of building the tower before he started building it, were themselves overextended. The school was left with no choice except to close.

---

[105] *Omaha World-Herald*, January 31, 1926.

Dr. Frederick Clayton, Rector 1927-1947. Born 1885
Newcastle on the Tyne, England, d. 1950.

Bishop Shayler counseled the vestry at All Saints to seek a low churchman who did not favor ritualism as its rector. Clayton fit this bill as far as externals where concerned. He was not a ritualist, but he was surprisingly catholic in his teaching. In the first issue of *Church and Home* that he published, under the title *locum tenum*, before he was called as rector, he advanced the idea that

> The Church is a living body; it is that organism which continues the ministry of God's increasing incarnation. Let us be truly religious in our future outlook, for the religious man is the man who goes through life sure in his heart of the living God, and with the conviction that God will show him what that will is and, despite his constant and repeated failures, will enable him to perform it.[106]

In the following issue, now rector, he continued in a catholic vein: "The chief service of the church is the Holy Communion. It is Christ's own service: he himself is veritably there. Celebration of the Holy Communion will be held in this church on all of the greater festivals of the church, of which you will be reminded in *Church and Home*." He staunchly defended

106 *Church and Home*, vol. 31, no. 1.

the sacraments and the apostolic succession of bishops. All this suggests that he had a catholic spirit but that he had no need for extravagant ritual.

Clayton was also quick to reveal himself to the parish as an avid reader. His first issue of *Church and Home* opens with a book review, *Beauty in Religion*, by A. Maude Royden.[107] He apprises his readers that he had just finished reading the book with great pleasure. Royden was an English feminist theologian far ahead of her times. Her other books *Sex and Common Sense*, 1922, and *Church and Women*, 1924, issued a sharp challenge to the status quo of post war Britain. His attention to her writing shows Clayton's affinity for liberal thinking. Her book on beauty, which appeared in 1923, fits his sense of the need to recast of the mission of the parish from Casady's activist business model to the contemplative model focused on spiritual experience. Casady's keynote, you will recall, was "efficiency." Clayton's keynote, in a startling contrast, was "beauty."

Clayton's most common contribution to *Church and Home* was a book review. Characteristically, he reviewed books of serious intellectual and theological content. His next review was of *A Sketch of Church History*, by Frank S. Wilson, STD, which he described as a significant effort at understanding the nature of the church. The third review is even more startling. In it he reviewed *Does Civilization Need Religion?*, a new book by Reinhold Niebuhr. Niebuhr would emerge as one of the most respected voice in theology in America during the middle of the twentieth century. Clayton wrote that this latter book "is the first book from the pen of a brilliant young minister whose articles in the Atlantic Monthly and leading religious journals have aroused a keen anticipation of a fuller setting forth of the results of his fresh and original thinking." One of the best clues as to Clayton's perception of economic and political events is that he consistently refers to the writings of Reinhold Niebuhr. This suggests that, like Niebuhr, he was neo-orthodox in his faith and a realist in his ethics and his understanding of the world.

The importance of books to Clayton is made clear in some later remarks in *Church and Home*. In an article entitled "Something about Books," he wrote, "As I look at the books on my shelves now, I am particularly attracted to the original sayings and writings of great men." He goes on

---

107 Ms. Royden became well known as a speaker on social and religious subjects and, in 1917, became assistant preacher at the City Temple in London, being thus the first woman to occupy this office. In 1929, she began the official campaign for the ordination of women when she founded the Society for the Ministry of Women. Beauty in Religion appeared in 1923.

to say, “I always found that original documents are much more interesting than the books of other people concerning them.”[108]

When the new year began, Clayton initiated a new service register. The first service on the first day of January is a note with of the following entry:

> Circumcision, Jan. 1 8:00 a.m., H. C., $1.65, 15 below zero;
> 9:30 M. P.,
> 11:00 H. C., $24.40, “God’s New Year.”

January 1 fell on a Sunday in 1928, and obviously, it was a very cold one. According to the Book of Common Prayer’s calendar, the first of January is the Feast of Circumcision. Falling on a Sunday, however, presented him with a choice between lessons appointed for the Sunday and those for the feast day. He chose the latter, and as he had already announced, feast day would be marked by the celebration of Holy Communion; and so it was. Apparently, he said Morning Prayer that morning by himself as he listed no attendance and does not count it as a public service as he often did on other Sundays. The noted sums of money are the communion alms that would have gone into Clayton’s discretionary fund. The attendance is not noted as it seldom was, but on the following Sunday, he wrote “circum 340.” On Septuagesima Sunday, a few weeks later, he noted attendance as four hundred and the number of communions as two hundred. These figures give us a rather good idea of the congregation that he had inherited. The entry on the last line for January 1, “God’s New Year,” is the title of sermon that Clayton preached at the eleven-o-clock service. He dutifully registered the titles of his sermons for the next three years, giving us a clue as to how seriously he took his calling as a preacher. These titles also give us a sense of their content. The next titles were “Calculable and Incalculable Fact of Life,” “Truth and Tradition,” and “Individuality in Religion.” From them we can get a sense of Clayton’s agenda as a preacher, which seems remarkably attuned with the shifting culture currents of the day.

The early volumes of *Church and Home* expand our ability to understand Clayton as a preacher. He openly shares with his readers his views and methods for preparing sermons. Having been asked for the text of his last sermon, he explained that he did not write his sermons, but he would begin to print a synopsis of them ahead of time. Fulfilling his promise, he announced in the issue published on December 3, 1927: “I am hoping to preach a course of sermons which will deal with problems peculiar to this age and time. My subject on Sunday morning will be the spiritual

108 *Church and Home*, vol. XXXI, no. 14, January 7, 1928.

evolution. The text under discussion will be Ephesians 3:14–20." When he returned from his summer vacation in 1929, he announced a series of sermons to come: "(1) The Existence of God, (2) Can Man Know God? (3) The Nature of God, (4) Creation." Typically, Clayton's topics are weighty and unfolded in series. As a preacher, he is a thinker working through his own thoughts and finds himself in need of several steps to work through an issue to his satisfaction. He constantly worked at developing his preaching and was very moved by the thought, suggested to him in a book that he had recently read, that preaching that appeared to be a most public performance was, in fact, a most intimate form of communication. He invited his congregation into the work of making him a better preacher.

It might seem that the intellectual rigor of his sermons would have infringed on his success as preacher, but in fact, his preaching was well received. I have been told so by a number of All Saints parishioners that remembered him. One late afternoon, I happened upon a brother and sister sitting together in their mother's room in a nursing home, whom I had come to visit. Their mother was asleep, so they, breaking the boredom of their vigil, invited me to sit down and began to reminisce about growing up at All Saints. Nancy led off by saying that Dr. Clayton was an impressive preacher and that she still could recall a Christmas sermon of his that she thought was one of the best sermons she had ever heard. Her slightly younger brother immediately piped in, "He was a bore!" I took this as testimony to the strange conundrum with which preachers and pastors in general are faced. They are inevitably experienced differently by different people.

On another occasion, I was informed that in the opinion of one of Omaha's most distinguished lawyers, who was one of the young acolytes of the Clayton era, that Clayton's preaching was impressive, though it was often over of his head. It was inevitably long but always inspiring.[109] It should be remembered that this was a period when sermons usually ran from twenty to thirty minutes and that anything less might well be challenged by a parishioner as a sign the preacher apparently hadn't worked all that hard the past week. Moreover, considering the financial constraints of the time during which Clayton was rector, preaching was necessarily the best card he had to play.

The challenging themes he chose for his sermons were backed up with lecture series that he gave in the parish. The lectures were often given on Thursday mornings and repeated again for the professional women, the BPW, who met on evenings. In his first year, he offered a series of lectures that covered a general outline of the Bible. The titles of these lectures make

[109] A remark attributed to Robert Spire.

clear that their content had been drawn from modern critical studies. In 1928, the course of study concerned the conflict of religions in the early Roman Empire. The course identified the text for the course as "The Conflict of Religions in the Early Roman Empire" by T. R. Clover. Clover was a well-respected authority on the topic.[110] For the third year, he chose psychology as a topic. His text for that year was "The Ways of the Mind," by Henry Foster Adams, Associate Professor Psychology at the University of Michigan. He cited Adams's definition of psychology in the article announcing the series:

> Psychology is a science which has as its subject-matter the study of the consciousness and behavior of living organisms. In common with the other sciences, it obtains its data by observational and experimental methods. It has, in addition, a method peculiar to itself in introspection. For consciousness may be aware, not only of external events and objects, but of itself as well.

He concludes the announcement by saying: "I am anxious to make these courses useful in a spiritual sense. From time to time we will discuss some of the great problems of life and try to find solutions for them."[111] This choice of this topic should be seen against the background that psychology in the early part of the twentieth century was in its hay day and that it was seen as a major challenge to Christianity. It was the age of Freud, Jung, B. F. Skinner, and the scientific conviction that science could explain why people thought and did what they did. Casady had addressed a Phi Beta Kappa audience in Lincoln, declaring psychology to be a dangerous science. Clayton, on the other hand, believed in his capacity to reinterpret modern psychology and to bring out of it, fruits that would further the spiritual adventure of modern Christian spirituality.

From this and his announced sermons, one can see that Clayton had faith in the potential of his parish to wrestle with the most challenging intellectual challenges of the day. For him the congregation was a school, and his role was that of being its lead teacher. Clearly, his vision was

110 *The Conflict of Religions in the Early Roman Empire* by T. R. Clover, London, Methuen1920. Clover, 1869–1943 was a respected Cambridge scholar and a Baptist layman. His works were intended for a general reader, but were informed by serious scholarship. They were republished as late as 1960.

111 *Church and Home*, vol. 33, no. 3, September 21, 1929.

building castles in the minds of individuals, not ones along the streets of the city.

To balance his vision of his role as an adult mentor, he sought to hire an assistant. Bishop Johnson of Colorado, who was a personal friend of Clayton's and of the Diocese of Nebraska,[112] suggested that he consider the services of a young man, Richard Rohr.[113] Rohr was among other things an authority on Boy Scout work and was at the time leader of one of the largest troops in Colorado. Rohr was hired for the purpose of doing youth work and, particularly, for establishing Boy Scout work at All Saints. One of the new movers and shakers on the vestry, James Love Paxton, had a son James who was one of Rohr's first recruits. When his father died, James, Jr. took his father's place on the vestry. By then a successful businessman and the leader of the Boy Scout Troop number 9, Paxton began making a full report on the parish's Scouting program to each vestry meeting, a thing he continued to do for many years. Paxton remained active in scouting all his life and was an active force at All Saints well into to my own rectorship. He was remembered by those who grew up with him in the parish as "a Boy Scout," the epitome of a straight arrow. One of my informers loved to repeat the story of a time "when his halo slipped." He led a group of fellows into the sacristy one night for a sampling of the altar wine and subsequently made calls to the girls involved not to spill the beans.

Outside of the Parish

Nothing that I have said thus far should be understood in way that would make it seem that Clayton was antagonistic to the diocese or the national church. When the national church passed a revision of the Book of Common Prayer in 1928, even though it was viewed negatively by the lower and more protestant oriented end of the church, Clayton was supportive, and All Saints was apparently quick to adopt the change. Clayton informed the parish in *Church and Home*:

> Early in the year, the new prayer book will be ready for use. The revision of this book has been the work of a generation. The revisors did their work well. It is in keeping with the great

---

[112] Johnston had served as a priest in the Diocese of Nebraska, and he had joined Longley of Iowa and Shayler of Nebraska in the attempt to save Tabor College as an Episcopal college under Clayton's leadership.

[113] *Church and Home*, vol. 32, no. 32, April 13, 1929.

motto of the early writers, that everything be done *decently and in order.*

By November, the books were in the pews at All Saints, and again Clayton gave the new book a ringing endorsement.[114]

Clayton had no predilection against bishops. He was a friend and admirer of Bishop Johnson of Colorado and quickly bonded with Howard Brinker when he became bishop of Nebraska in 1936. He did find his relationship with Shayler, in spite of fact that they had both emigrated from England, strained. It was said that Shayler upon his first visitation demanded to inspect Clayton's books, particularly his record of services. This was not something that Clayton wasn't given to doing, and there were that year no entries in the column: number of attendees. Shayler chewed Clayton out and told him that he expected this to be corrected by the time of his next visit. When Shayler came the next year, Clayton dutifully produced his record of services; and there in the column, "number of attendees," he had dutifully written three hundred for every service!

The diocese continued to demand payments of assessments, which had risen steeply in the early twenties, as if nothing had changed in its parishes' capacity to pay. This caused the local level, All Saints included, to wonder if the bishop had any idea as to what they were up against. While Clayton never failed to remind the parish that it had an obligation to the national church, to whom an assessment was paid directly at that time, he had a great deal of sympathy for the dismay of his laity, particularly those on the vestry, at the demands of the diocese. Clayton was known to have referred to Shayler as "that little man."

An Uncommon Man

Clayton was unmarried when he came to All Saints and remained so for the rest of his life. He was known to date. Dr. Whitcomb, who considered Dr. Clayton one of the greatest influences on his life, passed on the memory that Clayton had dated his Latin teacher, among others. Clayton lived most of the time he was rector at the Blackstone Hotel. The Blackstone was originally built as a residence hotel, but in 1920, the building was purchased by Charles Schimmel and was converted into a regular hotel. It soon became a "symbol of elegance" and gained stature nationwide as the premier hotel between Chicago and San Francisco along

114 This is remarkably similar to the way All Saints dealt with the prayer book change in 1979 under the leadership of Charles Pedersen.

the Lincoln Highway. Nevertheless, some permanent residents remained. It would, however, be a mistake to see this as signs of an extravagant life. Clayton lived in what he described as a single room, which he admits in his letter of resignation in 1947 was a bit depressive. It was a practical solution for a bachelor; and, in reality, it was an economical solution for the parish.

After the 8:00 a.m. Holy Communion service, Clayton would return for breakfast at the Blackstone, a dozen blocks up Dewey. It was his custom to treat any acolytes who had been adventurous enough to make it to the early service to a full pancake breakfast. Two of these acolytes were Jack Barnhart and Galen Kelley. Jack's parents lived at 830 South Fifty-Second Street, and Galen's parents lived nearby at 912 South Fifty-Fifth Street. The two classmates would meet on Leavenworth Street where they would catch the trolley. They would ride to the stop in front of the Alamito Dairy and then walk up the hill to Dewey. Once at the Blackstone, the party would meet up with John A. Gentleman who lived in the Blackstone as well. Gentleman's funeral home, alongside Burkett's, sat a couple blocks east of the hotel on Farnam. As the boys had it, Clayton and Gentleman were "Mut and Jeff." Gentleman's catered to the Roman Catholic trade, and All Saints trade was largely Burkett's at the time. The two men's relationship seems to have been more personal than professional. Gentleman kept a personal supply of Vermont Maple syrup at the Blackstone, which he shared with Clayton and the boys, who would then wait around in privileged independence for the eleven-o-clock, where they would serve as well.

Shortly after Clayton's arrival, the *Omaha World-Herald* provided a glimpse of All Saints new rector. Under a headline reading, "Home for Sinners; School for Saints, Rector's Aim," the newspaper offered the following description of the new rector of All Saints: "Dr. Clayton while quick in action, is not quick in speech. He weighs each word just as he did when set forth the goal he set for himself in Omaha." In the article, Clayton expressed his broad church commitment to ecumenism; he had after all, served as the pastor of the Tabor Congregational church while he was president to Tabor College. He said, "We, Methodists, Catholics, Episcopalians, all are aiming at something fine, something great and because the other fellow chooses a different route than I, is no sign that he is not as good." The article went on to describe him as a scholar who scorned the ivory tower and his preaching as "tolerant, learned, practical to an extent that at time bordered on the unconventional. Leavening it all was a compelling, if salty at times, sense of humor."

Budget Struggles

At the helm for little more than a month, Clayton was confronted, by the other side of his job at his first annual meeting, January 10, 1928. From the very beginning of his tenure, it was clear that there would be struggles with the parish's budget. Clayton addressed his first annual meeting with a sense of ownership and direction, though he could little imagine at the time how difficult and protracted the struggle would be. Toward the end of his address, he expressed what we might recognize as the parish's mantra.

> As I said before, the position of All Saints Church is not discouraging. If we can keep up the increased interest, put first things first: the spiritual life of the parish. It seems to me our financial worries will melt away because of larger interests. It is much easier to give to something which you really and truly love than it is merely to try and finance something that has not got your entire absorbing interest. And I am convinced, from my contact with the people of the parish, that there is manifest an intense love for All Saints Church. It is your church. It has been your church for a long time. Some of you were baptized in it. Others have been married in it. Most of you have received the blessed Body and Blood of our Lord and Savior Jesus Christ at its altar. You owe the good things that you have received to the oncoming generation. We must try and pass over to them our own privileges, and we can only do this successfully by seeing that it is our duty to carry on the intensive work of the parish. I was, therefore, grateful to find a renewed interest at the annual meeting. Everybody seemed to think that the position of the church, while critical, was yet far from being discouraging. To me, it seemed most hopeful. The church is a fellowship; therefore, the parish which is part of the great church is also a fellowship. The Greek word, of which in the New Testament, it is translated *koinonia*, which certainly means not a general state of good will but a partnership with some common treasure.[115]

The clear sign that the parishioners shared their new rector's cautious optimism can be seen in the fact that when it came time for the nominations of wardens and vestry, the motion was made by J. W. Barnhart and quickly seconded by Robert Trimble, that rules be suspended and that the present

115 *Church and Home*, vol. 21, no. 6, p. 1, January 21, 1928.

wardens and vestrymen be elected by acclamation. But by May of the following year, Clayton gently laid out a more careful analysis as why the parish was struggling with its budget. He contrasted the past direction of the parish with that of the church during its first three hundred years. He had made this topic the basis for his parish teaching series for that year, apparently because he thought that this study would be helpful for his thinking and for his parishioners understanding the church of their own times. He argued:

> We have fallen into the fatal mistake of working the other way around. We usually begin with loading ourselves with the house and property and then spending a life time in struggling to pay for the property and in so doing lose a great deal of the spirit for which the property was built. I have thought about this a great deal and the more I think about it the more I distrust the mechanistic side of our church's life.[116]

If the castles of the mind that Clayton proposed to build were as grandiose as Casady's plans for a physical plant, no one, but Clayton himself, would have to pay for them.

At his first annual meeting, the financial report showed that revenue for local purposes had amounted to $20,846, that $3,640 had been raised for outside expenses and $1,850 for miscellaneous purposes by means of the rector's discretionary fund. Capital expenses for the years were $8,220, $4,500 of which was covered by a new loan. The total expenditures for the year had amounted to $33,518. Given the times, this was an impressive accomplishment for the parish. Nevertheless, the entire year that followed was spent scrambling to come up with money to stay current with the parish's expenses. There were a number of outstanding debts, the most significant of which was an $18,000 mortgage owned by the Omaha Loan and Building Association. Another looming obligation was the contract with the Austin Organ Company for a new organ. The women of the parish, led by Mrs. Hoagland, had been raising money for the project since its inception in1924. Most of the funds were raised by collecting and selling used paper. As all such well-intended projects, there were, however, considerable ancillary costs to installing the organ. For one thing, the plan required an addition to the building. Clayton had little choice but to support the effort. Praising Simms who had by then served All Saints as its organist with distinction for thirty-four years, he went on to say, "The organ had more than had its day. All Saints Church is worthy of the

116 *Church and Home*, vol. XXXII, no. 36, May 18, 1929.

best. Public worship without music is to us a thing almost impossible to conceive. It is the choicest implement of praise, and the new organ will add considerably to the perfection of musical offering which we believe to be precious and acceptable to the most High."[117]

The strategy for dealing with these obligations was in part the quick sale of the rectory that had been purchased for Casady. It was hoped that the sale of the rectory would bring in $25,000, but it sat on the market unsold. The real estate market in Omaha was clearly depressed in 1928, and it is important to understand that the parish's financial difficulty was well in place before the beginning of the Great Depression. To a large extent, it was because of the exuberance of the early twenties and Casady's "mechanistic" expansion of the parish. Fortunately, his election to the episcopate came before he could realize the lion share of his vision, or the parish debt might have been much larger and it might have been saddled with buildings, which it did not need. The fate of the gymnasium that Casady had built at St. Mark's Des Moines, his earlier charge, was that it was unused and eventually sold to the state of Iowa.

Both the national church and the diocese were in financial crisis as well. This suggests that the cause for the crisis lay in forces affecting the Episcopal Church as a whole and from a pattern of decisions broadly shared by Episcopalians across the country, which was out of sync with reality. It is not a little ironic that this financial difficulty had been produced by a generation of priests who thought of themselves as hard-headed businessmen, from Murray, the presiding bishop, who was touted as having been a successful businessman before entering the priesthood, on down.

The diocese and the national church were both attempting to collect obligations from the parish. Curiously, at this time, the parish's contribution did not pass through the diocese but was owed directly to the national church office. At the vestry meeting on October 17, 1928, it was moved that Dr. Clayton appoint a committee of two vestrymen who would meet with representatives of Trinity Cathedral and St. Barnabas Parish to discuss the amount of their diocesan assessments. "The purpose of said meeting being to make recommendations toward the reduction of diocesan cost of operation." The motion was made by Trimble and Paxton. Mr. Hurtz, when he made his vote, insisted that "all legitimate means be used to reduce diocesan expenses." Clayton appointed Carpenter and Whitcomb to undertake the negotiations, and the result of which was that the diocese's asking was cut in half.

Even with this help, little progress was made in balancing the budget and in March of 1929, the vestry was again hoping for a large Easter

117 *Church and Home*, vol. XXXII, no. 31, April 6, 1929.

offering to buy them some room. The rectory finally sold on June 4, 1929, for $19,000, netting the parish $3,000. The sale relieved the parish of the interest it was paying on the mortgage on the rectory, and the surplus made the interest payments on the other outstanding debts that year. The relief was temporary, and by the end of 1929, Clayton made the unusual gesture of pleading for support to complete the year from the pulpit. A letter was handed to the members of the congregation that morning, asking them to make a supplemental pledge to pay off $3,000 of unfunded obligation. It worked, and Clayton could announce at the end of the year with some pride "First of all, we have paid our diocesan assessment in full for the year 1929, and we have paid $1,000 to the national church." He continued, "This parish feels that it ought to be loyal to the diocese and to the national church. We are not independent but interdependent and, therefore, owe a sense of obligation to others." This was said at the end of 1929 without any appreciation of the fact that the country's finances, not merely the stock market, had driven over a cliff. The country had seen stock markets crash in the past and, in fact, the 1929 crash was not even reported upon on the front page of the *Omaha World-Herald*, but on the business page, presumably not of general interest or import.

The effects of the Depression were soon registered in the parish's consciousness as part of a good news bad–news story in *Church and Home* in 1930. A Ms. Olive Eaton had left the parish all of her life savings, which were by no means meager. The tribute to her in *Church and Home* describes her as "a Japanese communicant" of this church. It goes on to say that

> she came to church regularly and was a faithful attendant at the Parish Guild. She gave liberally . . . Her life, courage, and faithfulness make up a living sermon. May the souls of the faithful departed, through the mercy of God, rest in peace!

The bad news was that "much of it cannot be used owing to the failure of the bank in which the money was deposited."[118]

The financial report at the annual meeting 1931 showed $24,786 of expenditures and a balance of $243, but there was $3,200 owed to the diocese. On the other hand, there was some comfort taken in the fact that there were $3,941 unpaid pledges. The report estimated Sunday attendance the past year was had averaged 450, showing that while the

118 *Church and Home*, vol. 34, no. 9, November 15, 1930. Olive was born in 1879; her mother was Japanese, and her father was born in England. She spent her life as a live-in servant and had no family when she died. The church arranged for her burial at Forest Lawn with a simple marker.

parish's finances were sliding downward, it was managing to keep its congregation active and in place. The Every Member Canvass for 1931 was not yet complete. Arthur Lowman, who originated the Every Member Canvass at All Saints in 1925, was still the key force behind the Every Member Canvass. In 1931, Dr. Glen Whitcomb replaced him as chairman, but Lowman remained influential in the canvass as chair of the Finance Committee. The hope that the decline in income could be stopped was guarded. By May, however, it was necessary to announce that Rohr, the assistant to the rector, was leaving to become rector of St. Martin's South Omaha and would not be replaced. Clayton announced at the time that he himself would take over youth work. As the year progressed, Clayton provided the readers of *Church and Home* with the following assessment:

> We have certain obligations that cannot be curtailed; for example, our debt to the diocese and to the national church, which is of the utmost importance. Our budget, during my rectorship, has been reduced from $29,500 to $23,400. This year, we are facing a possible deficit of $2,614. This, I am certain, can be met because it is within the means of this congregation.[119]

At the beginning of 1932, Clayton had surgery, and the annual meeting was delayed to April 25. Once again the vestry struggled to hold the line. The budget was curtailed to no more than $23,218. The principal items to be reduced would be the janitor, compensation for the choir, publication of *Church and Home*, a reduced payment to Omaha Loan and Building (still $18,000), which had been possible by refinancing and ending the tenure of the rector's assistant. In spite of these budgetary pressures, the vestry found itself signing a contract with Austin Organ company of Hartford Connecticut.

Bishop Thomas Casady visited All Saints in June of 1932 and spoke to the parishioners of All Saints.[120] He called for hope in the difficult financial times. He suggested that the athletes preparing for the upcoming Olympics provided a good example. "They will think only of the glory to be theirs when the race is won. Despite hunger and woe and the cries of Communists and others, there are thousands of men and women in our country who are laboring with the last ounce of their brain power and

119 *Church and Home*, vol. XXXV, no. 1, October 10, 1931.

120 *Omaha Bee*, June 27, 1932.

strength of their bodies to bring back comfort and stability and peace to us all." He mentioned unemployment as only a temporary thing.

Yet rural Nebraska was suffering. Grain receipts reached an all-time high in 1930 of seventy-six million bushels and then plunged in 1931 to thirty-two million, reaching a bottom twenty-six million, which did not begin to recover until 1936.[121] Still within Omaha, no Omaha bank failed, population continued a modest increase, and significant civic facilities opened, such as Joslyn Memorial Art Museum and the Art Deco Union Station.[122]

By end of the summer, the long-awaited organ was installed and the official dedication was held on October 16. In the announcement of the dedication in *Church and Home*, Clayton made special mention of the effort of Mrs. Hoagland, "who for years has untiringly and quietly worked for this cause. A good deal of the money, as you know, has been raised by the sale of old papers."[123] Bishop Casady, who was instrumental in stirring up enough interest to start the fund, again came to Omaha and preached the sermon. In the following afternoon, there was a service under the auspices of the American Guild of Organists. The principal pieces were played by Martin W. Bush, an old choir boy of All Saints and student of Mr. Simms, and by Mr. Simms who had for so long labored with the old Roosevelt, given to All Saints in 1886.

As soon as the celebration concluded, the vestry turned to planning the 1932 Canvass. Again, they led with the announcement of a new round of cuts for the coming year: Salaries will be cut by 27 percent, music by 10 percent, and *Church and Home* by 47 percent; and no missionary apportionment would be budgeted. The cuts would make the 1933 budget 22 percent less than that in 1931. That resulted in a budget of $19,800. The committee reported that All Saints consists of 507 families; but in the past year, only 248 families, 49 percent of the parish, made a pledge for the support of the church. The parish would use a two-sided envelop in the coming year, which would allow individuals who want to make a contribution to the missionary apportionment to do so. Two-sided envelopes continually reappeared when the parish found itself divided over priorities.

---

121 Lawrence H. Larsen and Barbara Cottrell, *The Gate City: A History of Omaha*, Pruett Publishing, 1982.

122 Lawrence H. Larsen and Barbara Cottrell, *The Gate City: A History of Omaha*, Pruett Publishing, 1982, p. 197.

123 *Church and Home*, vol. XXXVIII, no. 8, April 9, 1932.

Death and Fire

As the first inklings of what the Depression would mean to the parish were registering, a death came to the parish, a death widely felt in the city of Omaha. The city's mayor, James Dahlman, died suddenly. He had filed for reelection and gone to Excelsior Springs, Missouri, for a rest. His complaints were confined to a cold and trouble sleeping at night. He spent the evening in the lobby visiting with old friends. They included the Carsons, ranchers from Irwin, Nebraska, whom he had known since the 1880s, and Fred Metz and his wife, members like the Dahlmans of All Saints since the Mackay era. Dahlman died in his sleep that night. He had served an unequaled twenty years as the city's mayor. He had skillfully navigated between the Dennison Political machine and the ever-demanding Businessman's Association and had somehow cultivated many friends along the way. That included Omaha's African American population. In a eulogy by Dr. John Singleton, president of the Omaha NACP, called him "a staunch friend of Negroes in Omaha." Whatever compromises he made, he did not enrich himself. He had lived in a modest house on Hickory Street across from Hascom Park where he enjoyed walking. His wife and daughter were left with little more than a very modest amount of insurance.

The mayor's funeral began with his body lying in state at the city hall. For twenty-four hours, people passed by the coffin. The chamber was filled with five hundred people seated and hundreds of other standing around in the balcony and hall. Outside the crowd was estimated at fifty thousand to seventy thousand people. The services there began at twelve thirty and included an "impressive Elks Rite." At fifteen minutes past three, the body, accompanied by Clayton, Dahlman's wife, and his daughter Dorothy, went to All Saints with other family members and close friends for a private ceremony. After the service, the interment was conducted by Clayton at Forest Lawn. It is clear that Clayton had in his short time at All Saints developed a warm pastoral relationship with the Dahlman's and would continue to support them pastorally for some time to come. Dorothy eventually moved to Washington DC, and in 1947, Clayton transferred her membership to St. John's Lafayette Square.

By 1933, despite the cuts in the budget, each month found the vestry struggling to pay the bills. Then came a fire in the church. The fire was noticed in the early hours of November 20. Neighboring Lord Lister Hospital was in a near panic. A great crowd from the neighborhood gathered to watch the dreadful sight. Among the watchers was a mother from the parish who brought her young son with her, who remembers to this day the sight of his parish church on fire, a thing that he has often recounted to me.[124]

Forty tons of coal, which had been stored in the basement of the church, started to burn ignited by means of spontaneous combustion. The fire burned through the floor of the nave and destroyed pews, prayer books, and hymnals. The chancel floor collapsed, dropping the brass litany desk given by William Redick in 1905 in memory of his father, into the basement. It now stands in the chapel of the new building. It also damaged the Austin pipe organ whose installation was not yet complete and whose cost was not yet fully paid. Firemen gained access to fight the fire by breaking stained glass at both ends of the church. Clayton upon arriving on the scene begged firemen not to break any more stained glass, and he organized neighbors and parishioners as volunteers to remove whatever could be salvaged. The great north window which had been made in England was broken about fifteen minutes before the fire was under control. Dr. Clayton said he knew of no reason for the breaking of the window, since the fire was at the other end of the church. "But I'm no fireman," he added diplomatically.[125]

Damage was estimated to be between $25,000 and $50,000. Fortunately, the vestry had maintained adequate insurance coverage, up to $65,000. On November 22, at an emergency meeting of the vestry, insurance damage was set at 75 percent, and services were moved to Wattle's Memorial Hall.

The budget problems did not, however, step aside, and so at this same meeting, they received a report that they were ending the year with money still due the diocese. While the diocese had finally cut its asking from $2,800 to $1,050, there remained $450 to pay. Freeman, who had long been the vestry's point man on finance, resigned as treasurer and chair of the Finance Committee, as his work meant that he would be absent from the city. This resignation led to centralizing bill payment in the office but left a large hole in the parish's leadership.

Clayton was pleased to tell the vestry that the nearby Temple Israel had offered it worship space to All Saints for the season of Lent. This offer came in part because Clayton was a close personal friend of the rabbi. Dr. Friedrich Cohen was a noted intellectual and liberal, much like Clayton. After presenting Temple Israel's proposal, Clayton went on to express his personal distress. He informed the vestry that he was quite distressed by the trouble incident to the financial condition of the parish and by the

124 Recounted to me by Larry McNichols.

125 *Omaha World-Herald*, March 31, 1934.

burden to the parish's expenses because of the work necessary to carry out the physical rehabilitation of the church. To help lessen the problem, he expressed willingness that his salary be reduced, even to half of its present amount and, referring to the fact that he had been rector of All Saints for seven years, that it might be wise for the vestry to consider a successor to him. He withdrew from the meeting which went on to accept the offer of Temple Israel and to work on the issues present by the rehabilitation of the church. Then the vestry turned to a discussion of Clayton's offer. They summarily dismissed it and expressed their complete confidence in him.

With careful attention to making every penny of insurance money count, the vestry managed to repair the church, procure new pews, prayer books, and hymnals; redo the lighting in the sanctuary; convert the heating plant to oil; repair the stained glass; and, with money to spare, they added a fashionable rood screen between the chancel and the nave, apparently a liturgical fashion favored by Clayton. Rood screens had become a liturgical fashion in the early twentieth century because of catholic revival and Anglophile nostalgia. They imitated the screens in medieval Western churches, which segmented the worship space in way that made a radical separation between the sanctuary and the nave, the holy and the secular. Rood screens varied in the amount of vision blocked from the nave and always had a cross on the top center. The screen at All Saints was moderate in that it allowed a rather clear view of the chancel and sanctuary. By separating the chancel from the nave, it added an element of mystery, as was common in English churches and cathedrals. The consciousness of the worshiper upon going to communion was impressed with the idea that one was passing under the cross to make that communion.

"The organ issue," as the vestry minutes put it, was solved by settling with Austin and hiring Kansas City Organ Service and Supply Company to complete the work. The settlement required borrowing from endowment. This was likely an attempt to make the repairs as economical as possible in order to stay within the insurance allotment, which in the end was $23, 341. Like the rood screen, the repair of the new Austin not only restored the instrument but also managed to add twenty-five chimes.

Clayton, summarizing the results of the refurbishment of the church, said: "I am hoping that All Saints Church will be a quiet place of retreat in a changing world, a sort of an oasis in the desert of depression. That is why we have endeavored to make it very beautiful." Curiously, the fire had given Clayton his one chance to leave a mark on the building! Cash in the depth of the Depression went a long way. When the building was reopened on April 1, 1934, the *World-Herald* said: "Interior Believed More Beautiful than Before Fire." "The church interior has been entirely redecorated, at a total cost of about $25,000. The committee in charge of restoration included Judge William A. Redick, Dr. Glenn D. Whitcomb, George T. Morton and Clarence T. Spier. The stained glass, only one of which had remained intact, had also been restored." It should be noted, however, not with the same quality of stained glass.

As the events of 1934 were working themselves out, the vestry found itself in the familiar position of writing a budget that was necessarily less than that of the one the year before. In fact, bottom would not be reached until 1936. The approaching year, 1935, was the parish's Golden Jubilee. Concurrent with the struggles in the parish; the city was experiencing growing agitation as the result of the stressed economy. This agitation had surfaced in April of 1934 in a strike at the Omaha Traction Company, the city's street car system. In many ways, it was a repeat of the strike in 1909 against the same company. Then the company was led by Guerdon Wattles, one of All Saints prominent laymen. We have seen how Mackay dealt with this in 1909. He supported his layman, condemned strikes, but supported the value of unions and called for mediation, which he argued Wattles really wanted. He dared to mediate the situation. The polarization in 1934–1935 was a completely different ball game. There is no ground for mediation, and Clayton has little to say directly about the strike. Nevertheless, he managed his way through the mine field with enough aplomb for both sides to recognize him to be fair and practical. In 1938, strikes would again be in the offing. The motor transportation union went on strike on September 8, 1938, affecting 550 workers. The union responded to a call for arbitration, and the *Lincoln Star* reported that an arbitration committee had been agreed upon which was to consist of Francis P. Matthews, president of the Omaha Chamber of Commerce; Mace Brown, president of the Omaha Central Labor Union; and Rev. Frederick Clayton, rector of All Saints Episcopal.

When the celebration of fifty years of existence came, it was, indeed, modest but heartfelt. Bishop Casady, making one of his many visits, attended All Saints annual meeting on January 9, 1935, and gave a talk. His talk took noted of the Depression, but he insisted that it was only temporary. As different as Casady and Clayton were, they show a pattern of collegiality and mutual respect that has characterized the rectors of All Saints. A Special addition of *Church and Home* was printed as November approached, recounting the parish's history. A large fellowship dinner was celebrated at the Blackstone Hotel. One thing to celebrate was that they could announce that the parish's debt was down to $15,000, a modest but steady decline despite all the financial struggles that had engulfed the parish from the beginning of Clayton's tenure.

Lay Leadership

During the thirties the lay leadership in the parish was also undergoing considerable change. Those who had been part of the early days of the parish were nearly gone. Of the leaders, only William Redick, who had sat on the first vestry in 1885, remained; and he would serve as senior warden until his death 1936. Next to him was John Yates, another long-serving member of the vestry from the Mackay years. He would replace Redick as senior warden in 1936. After them came George T. Morton and Gilbert E. Carpenter, both of whom had been on the vestry for a considerable time and went back to the late Mackay era. Both came from early Omaha families. Morton was a successful realtor. Carpenter's grandfather had started the very successful Carpenter Paper Company in 1888. His grandfather was a Baptist deacon. They were, however, greatly outnumbered by the new names on the vestry such as L. E. Hurtz, president of The Fairmont Creamery Co.; James L. Paxton, president of the Paxton Mitchell foundry; Dr. Glen Whitcomb, a medical doctor; Eugene McAuliffe, a special representative of the Union Pacific Coal Company; Clarence T. Spier, a relatively new lawyer in town; and Robert Trimble, the president of a growing fruit and vegetable wholesaler, all of who were new to the parish and the city.

Leonard E. Hurtz came to Lincoln just before the 1920 census. There he was listed as a manager of a phone company. By 1936, he was working for the Fairmont Creamery and was listed as a vice president. By 1940, he had become president. Omaha had emerged as the largest dairy processor in the country and had become known as the Butter Capitol. Hurtz's career was in management, and he was part of a new class of middle-class Americans on the rise because of their management skills. In 1940, Hurtz would lead the way in an effort to retire the parish's mortgage before it came up for renewal by pledging $1,000.

James Paxton is another of the new kind of businessman in the Omaha business culture. He came to Omaha from Missouri to work for William A. Paxton, taking charge of the Paxton Mitchell Foundry. William A. Paxton enterprises included interests in Paxton Vierling Iron Works, the stockyard, the retail enterprise known as Paxton Gallehger, and various real estate ventures such as the Paxton Hotel. Like his contemporary, Wattles, William A. Paxton listed his occupation on the federal census papers as "Capitalist." The new breed, like James Love Paxton, was proud to identify themselves as manufacturers.

The Whitcomb family was another important part of Clayton's support. The two brothers had been raised in York, Nebraska, and had come to Omaha to pursue their professions, one as a medical doctor, the other as a dentist. Glen Whitcomb, the medical doctor, was a personal friend of Dr. Clayton. He served on the vestry during all of Clayton's tenure and was parish treasurer from 1933 to 1938. His brother Fred Whitcomb was a dentist and shared offices with him. Fred's wife, Charlotte, was a nurse and was soon the supervisor of nurses in the Omaha Public School. Fred and Charlotte had an only child, Frederick, and asked Clayton to be the child's godfather. The closeness of the Fred Whitcomb with Clayton was demonstrated when their son's body was returned to Omaha in 2012 for burial, as part of his dying wishes. Young Fred had been educated at Hotchkiss, Yale, and Columbia Medical. His residency was at the Mayo Clinic where he developed a specialty in gastroenterology and became a prominent doctor spending the bulk of his career at the Lahey Clinic in Boston. In remarks he had prepared to be read at his funeral, he said: "My 'guardian angels' have been Dr. Fred Clayton, Minister of All Saints Episcopal Church in Omaha and my godfather, Oliver Townsend, my uncle; Dr. Harry Wieler, the Hotchkiss School physician, mentor and friend and the A. C. Nielsen family of Winnetka, Illinois." In a longer note appended to his remarks, he spoke of his religious training.

> My religious training was easy. The minister at All Saints Episcopal Church in Omaha, Dr. Fred Clayton from England, was also my godfather and friend. I was an acolyte who carried the cross and loved church. Dr. Clayton, along with my Dad, picked out my dog, Spotty, who was a faithful and loving dog . . . Dr. Clayton was single but dated my Latin teacher. He spent a lot of time in our house and would live in our great room when he was sick so my mother could take care of him.

Eugene McAuliffe was also new among the leadership, and like the Whitcomes, he seems to have become another of Clayton's personal support system. McAuliffe came to Omaha in 1924 as a mining engineer with a vision of mining safety, which he had learned at the University of St. Louis, Missouri. He was hired, upon graduation, by the Union Pacific to pioneer a safety program in their coal mining interest. He was a true pioneer in the field of mine safety, and his company in 1948 became the first underground coal mining operation in the United States to win a perfect safety record from the U.S. Bureau of Mining. McAuliffe rose in the ranks to become the president of Union Pacific Coal in 1940.

His wife Nell was confirmed at St. Michael and All Angels in St. Louis, Missouri, where they were married in 1924. Eugene was confirmed in 1926 by Casady, and he served on the vestry in 1929. He did not stay on the vestry long as his work required a great deal of travel, but he was a recognized lay leader in the parish. He had a particular rapport with Clayton, which was shown by the unusual courtesy Clayton showed him by printing a set of remarks by McAuliffe in *Church and Home*, something that Clayton did not afford anyone else during his tenure. McAuliffe's passion was Clarkson Hospital and, particularly, the Clarkson School of Nursing. He was instrumental in bringing a new reforming superintendent to Bishop Clarkson Memorial Hospital, Ms. Mildred Constantine in 1935. An Episcopalian, she transferred her membership to All Saints from Christ Church Cambridge, Massachusetts. Her presence in the parish along with McAuliffe's abiding interest intensified the parish's involvement with Clarkson

Clarence Spier who was raised in St. Joseph, Missouri, was yet another example of the new leadership of the parish. Clarence came from a German American family whose religious affiliation was the Evangelical Reform, a German version of Methodism. He chose to go out of state for college and enrolled in the University of Nebraska. He graduated in 1916 with a law degree. While at the university, he met Louise Coe from Nebraska City. Louise, raised in St. Mary's Episcopal Church, was a stellar student, graduating Phi Beta Kappa. Clarence was intent on marrying Louise and practicing law in Omaha. He had managed to establish himself with an Omaha law firm when the wave of patriotism that led young men around the country to enlist in the American Expeditionary Force swept through. Like Thomas Mackay's son, Stanley, he went off for training with the Nebraska Guard only to find the unit dissolved and folded into other existing units. Like Stanley, he was sent to the army base at Jacksonville, Florida. Unlike Stanley, he was deployed overseas with the First Division of the American Expeditionary Force arriving in France in January of 1918. As part of the division's supply train, he saw action at Cantigny, Aisne-Marne, St. Mihiel, and in the defense of Meuse Argonne, where he was gassed. When the armistice came, he took advantage of being in France and enrolled in the Sorbonne. Upon returning home, he married Louise and reentered the law practice that he had left. While a 1932 biography, *Nebraska 1932*, indicated that he was a member of the First Methodist Church, his first son William was baptized in Nebraska City in 1922 at St. Mary's and his second Robert at Trinity Cathedral in 1925. In 1926, Clarence became a deputy district attorney, in charge of most of the trial work in the city. By the end of 1929, he was featured in the *Omaha*

World-Herald Sunday magazine in a full-page story praising his work. The article noted that he was strict but fair. He had a record of standing up for the rights of the convicts and was active against capital punishment. The article said that many whom he had convicted had complemented him on the way that he had treated them. The article notes that he was an avid reader. While his penchant for reading detective stories was featured in the article, it is clear that his interest included literature as well. The article indicated that he was president of the Omaha Book Club, even though he was not a member. He was not a member because it was a woman's club. As his eldest son approached confirmation age, the couple became serious about joining a parish. Clayton's own affinity for books may well have been the thing that attracted Clarence to All Saints. At any rate, he formed a fast friendship with Clayton. By 1933, he was on the vestry.

Finally, this group counts among its numbers, Robert Trimble. Trimble was one of four brothers who had been brought to this country by their parents from Northern Island. The brothers had created a business in Omaha, Trimble Brothers, which employed eighty-six people and received about two thousand carloads of vegetables and fruits a year. He was listed as a communicant in 1923 along with his wife Bertha and his daughter Roberta. He was still active in 1962, participating at age 87, in the fund drive to relocate All Saints in the western part of the city. The common element of this new class of leaders is that they were new to Omaha and their qualifications came from hard work.

The change came rapidly to the parish, propelled by a series of death and moves, which moved these new names into the center of the parish's life. In June of 1936, W. A. Redick, the senior warden died. He had been on and off the vestry since the founding of the parish in 1885. The vestry elected John T. Yates, the last of the old-timers, to replace him as senior warden. James Love Paxton became junior warden. Within three years, Yates too would pass on to the larger life. In 1939, James L. Paxton succeeded him as senior warden with Leonard E. Hurtz becoming junior warden. James L. Paxton died unexpectedly at the end of 1939. He was replaced by Robert Trimble as senior warden; and his son James L. Paxton, Jr. took a seat on the vestry. It was not the first time that a son succeeded his father to the vestry. Arthur C. Smith succeeded his father, M. E. Smith, in October 2 1987. By the end of the thirties, the new class was in charge.

Another change came in 1936; the parish secretary, Marjory Nye Phulps, resigned. She was the parish's first secretary and came to work for Casady in 1924 just out of high school. Her family was important members of the parish. Her father, Charles, had served for a long time as superintendent of the church school, and the whole family participated in the choir. She had continued unmarried until 1934 when she married Robert Phulps. They lived with her parents, and when her parents decided to move to California in 1936, she and Robert went along. She had served eleven years as parish secretary.

The year of 1936 was a year of goodbyes, but it was also the year when the budget reached a new low, $17,000. While this was very near to the bottom, it would be 1943 before the parish's budget would begin again to grow. In spite of the financial straits, the parish's other numbers remained positive. The year 1936 was the first year that the national church required a parochial report, and as a result, it begins a more accurate set of statistics to measure the strength of a parish. All Saints first parochial report portrays an active parish in no way diminished from the size and activity of the parish in the days of Mackay and Casady. It reported fifteen children's baptisms, eight adult baptisms, thirty-four confirmations, ten marriages, twenty-six burials, and six hundred fifteen communicants.

A Troubled Diocese

Shayler, after ten years as bishop, continued to enjoy the favor of the *Omaha World-Herald* by means of which he continued project a strong persona in the city. The Sunday paper in November of 1928 gave Shayler the forum of its front page to express his hopes for 1929. In the article, Shayler said that he hoped that the city would adopt the idea of a city manager and build a new city county building. He decried boxing and Sunday movies. Churches, he hoped, would be "used as power houses and less as valves for escaping steam, or safety vaults for storage." Continuing his political involvement in the city, Shayler endorsed the mayor, Metcalf, for reelection in 1933, who was being challenged by Roy Towl, the reform candidate. Towl would, in fact, win the election. Turning to the churches in the city that year, he urged "churches to cease ambulance work" and "to engage in vigorous action."

When Shayler assessed what he had accomplished in the diocese after ten years, he pointed with great deal of pride to having given Brownell Hall a new lease on life, supporting its building program in Happy Hallow. In Omaha, he had founded a new St. John's on North Thirtieth, across from Miller Park. In Lincoln, he had founded a new parish, St. Matthew's on the south side, and the university church adjacent to the University of Nebraska. All of these efforts in the long run would prove to be valuable contributions to Episcopalians in Nebraska. Yet at the time, they were not without controversy. In Lincoln, the major parish, Holy Trinity, felt that it had been undermined and continued to lobby for the closure or limitation of the work at the university.

In spite of the bishop's virile persona in the press, he had a continual history of health issue. In 1926, after a strenuous year of activity, including his high-profile pilgrimage to the Holy Land, he was ill, missing annual council in January. The *Omaha World-Herald* explained that "during 1925 Bishop Shayler traveled more than 15 thousand miles on official diocesan business . . . A greater part of the mileage was covered in Nebraska." With the April pilgrimage, the *World-Herald* concluded, "This was one of the busiest years that bishop has spent since coming here."[126] It was difficult, however, for those in the parishes of the diocese to trust these numbers, remembering that Central City, a little over one hundred miles from Omaha, was his longest drive. In November of the following year, he suffered a mild heart attack and again had a period of convalescing.

The market crash did not register with Shayler, and his plans for 1930 continued to be expansive. He began the year by seeking to add a field secretary to his staff in order to reduce his travel in spite of the fact that his diocese covered only the eastern third of the state.[127] This led to the hiring of Rev. Luther Gramly, who might be called the diocese's first "canon to the ordinary." This help to send the diocese budget for 1930 to a new high of $17,639, before it would begin a precipitous decline to a low of $6,661 in 1938. Once again, Shayler would travel in 1930, this time to the Lambeth Conference in England. His time at the conference was extended three months to allow for "a residency" in England for the bishop and his wife and her sister Margaret Knight. During their stay, the party traveled to Germany to take in the mineral springs and on to Czechoslovakia where he was hosted by the president of that country.

In March of 1932, his wife, Mignon Knight, died. His wife was always heavily involved in church work and was a powerful support for her husband. Since their marriage, her younger sister, Margaret, had been part of their household and served as "secretary to the bishop." His daughter Ernestine remained a close member of the family circle even after her marriage to Robert Heath. The bishop was, in fact, surrounded by a circle of protecting women. After her mother's death, Ernestine began to struggle with her marriage. Her divorce was a front page story December 5, 1933. In 1934, she went missing for a period in Chicago, another drama played out on the front page of the newspaper.

---

126 *Omaha World-Herald*, January 19, 1926.

127 The diocese was composed of twenty parishes and twenty missions, the farthest of which was little over one hundred miles from Omaha.

Nevertheless, in 1934, Shayler spent three months of his summer on pilgrimage again in Palestine. At the annual council in January 17, 1935, the issue of university church was revisited. The former attorney general, Paul Good, senior warden of Holy Trinity Lincoln, led the charge on the floor of the council. He argued: "With University church scarcely a mile from Holy Trinity, and with one other Episcopal church in Lincoln, the field is not large enough for all." The *Omaha World-Herald* reported, "It was then that the bishop disposed of the question." Halting church controversy, however, did change the perception at Holy Trinity that the bishop didn't understand their side of the story. It is always difficult to surface the true feeling of rectors and laity toward their bishop as Episcopalians rather prefer this to remain unspoken. It is not hard, however, to imagine that the bishop's high social profile and controversial rhetoric created the impression that the bishop was unconcerned with what they were dealing with as congregations. Clayton on the surface always supported the bishop and stood as an advocate for diocesan causes. But there was a marked disconnect between Clayton preaching that stressed the development of an interior religious life and the bishop's preaching that invariably demanded exterior actions that would change the world.

As the 1936 council approached, the bishop found himself again not well. Council, which had been scheduled for January 15, was postponed and rescheduled to meet in May. On February 27, Shayler left for San Diego to further his recuperation. When the council finally met in May, Shayler made a brief appearance and suggested that by the fall he would be fully recovered. Having spent a good deal of 1937 recovering from a long illness, Shayler announced his resignation at the annual council, January 20, 1938. He was now seventy years old and had served as bishop for nineteen years. He said, "My physician told me I would live several years longer if I would give up my duties." William Barnes, the historian of the diocese, said that Bishop Robert B. Goodman, the retired suffragan of Los Angeles, wrote that Bishop Shayler "once told me that the greatest mistake of his life was his acceptance of the office of bishop."[128]

The office of bishop was left vacant while a discussion took place as to whether Nebraska and Western Nebraska should be merged before a new bishop was elected. By then it had become clear that the division of the diocese, if it ever had been, was not financially sustainable. In the end, it was decided to proceed with an election. Clayton served on the search committee with Dean McGinley, E. J. Secker, and C. C. Watkins. The laity were Paul F. Good, J. E. C. Fisher, J. S. Hedelund, and J. B. Maylard.

---

128 Barnes, *The Episcopal Church in Nebraska*, p. 103, Letter of the R. Rev. Dr. Roberft Gooden, November 27, 1964.

The report that they made, found in the minutes of the council, is the first of what we could call the modern search process. The committee listed three nominees: Howard Rasmus Brinker, rector of St. Bartholomew's Chicago; Thomas Neely Carrutheres, rector of Christ Church, Nashville, Tennessee; and the very Rev. John Warren Day, dean of Grace Cathedral, Topeka, Kansas. The council met on October 18, 1939, and elected Brinker and decided not to merge with the Western diocese, delaying the inevitable. Brinker was forty-six at the time. He had been born in Wisconsin and graduated from the University of Pennsylvania and Philadelphia Divinity School. His first charge had been in Douglas, Wyoming. Unlike Shayler, he chose to be consecrated in Omaha at Trinity Cathedral; and unlike Shayler's first sermon at the cathedral, which had dealt with the League of Nation, Brinker's first sermon dealt with the five factors needed in the service of the church.

The chancellor of the diocese, R. D. Neely, reflected over this period in an address to the council in 1950: "When Dr. Brinker arrived on the banks of the Missouri in 1940 the Diocese of Nebraska was in a pretty bad way. The old girl was really sick, rigor mortis had set in, and an emergency operation was the order of the day."[129] He added, "The whole diocese was in a bad way." Trying to explain the state of the diocese, he offered the opinion "Yes, we had a few outstanding and flourishing parishes with some money, but as far as I can make out, they were not interested in the diocese, and I really believe that the majority of the communicants throughout our diocese didn't realize or didn't know there was such a thing. No real program, no life, and no enthusiasm. They didn't really know that they owed any allegiance to the Episcopate."

In fact, the problem was Shayler of own making. It is easy to be impressed with Shayler's various causes. They were often socially astute and always high minded. They included going to the Omaha School Board in 1930 as head of a delegation demanding better education for Negroes. He handed the board a list of Negroes in the city that were qualified to be hired as teaches. He denounced demagogues like Coughlin and Townsend. But his positions were inevitably scolds and were always nonnegotiable. In the growing polarization of the nation, Shayler's positions resulted in a push back, which meant that parishioners on the local level frequently found themselves on the defensive. Moreover, they drew Shayler away from what was going on in his parishes.

As times changed, he was unable to adjust. Like many of his contemporaries in the Episcopate, he had staked out a vision of an expanded diocese, which required a large increase in parish giving; but he failed to see

[129] Barnes, *The Episcopal Church in Nebraska*, p. 43.

the shift in American economy that made that impossible and the shift in American culture that would prove difficult for the Episcopal Church to navigate. The signs of the cultural change, as we have suggested, were there as early as 1915; and by 1926, the money problem had begun in earnest. The Depression would confound the issue, but not cause it. The result was that parishes found themselves with oversized assessments beyond their capacity to meet.

With the election of Brinker, there was a different attitude, especially on Clayton's part. He wrote in 1940, asking his vestry men to support the diocese, even as the diocese was asking for a 25 percent increase, leaving it in their hands. At the annual meeting of 1943, the parish's treasurer was pleased to report: "This is the first year for some time that All Saints Church has paid its diocesan assessment and missionary assessment in full, and we, thereby, have fulfilled our obligation to the diocese. Special thanks are due to the womanhood of the church, who contributed $718.52 from their earnings from the St. Nicholas Festival to pay the balance due on our missionary assessment."

New Initiatives at the Clarkson Nursing School and at All Saints

There had been a long association of All Saints and Bishop Clarkson Memorial Hospital, which was strengthened when the hospital moved up Howard Street to become a virtual neighbor of the parish. The relationship was even stronger with the nursing school, which held some of its classes in Wattles Hall. The school of nursing could claim to have been in existence since 1888; but it had, in reality, undergone a number of changes, and in 1932, it was close to being closed down. In 1935, McAulife, an active parishioner of All Saints, became the executive vice president of the school upon the death of F. H. Davis, the long serving senior warden at Trinity Cathedral. McAulife quickly proved to be an incisive man who would, given time, act on his conviction that Clarkson needed a larger hospital and a new home for its nurses, the latter of which would serve both as a residence and as a school. While the hospital had bought property at Forty-Second and Dewey, near the University of Nebraska Medical School, on which it hoped to build, the money for a new hospital was not in the offing. The interim solution was to the purchase Lord Lister Hospital located on Twenty-Sixth and Dewey, immediately across the street from All Saints.

The history of the nursing school states that no Nebraska training school moved its students more frequently than Clarkson. When the hospital was at the 1716 Dodge Street, nurses had lived in one room on the third floor and in a very small house next to the hospital. When the hospital moved to the 2100 Howard Street in 1909, at which time Dr. Mackay had welcomed them to "the hill," the nurses lived in a small cottage east of the hospital. Later, a house on Twenty-Second Street was added, and ultimately, all the nurses were moved into F. H. Davis's home at 628 South Twentieth Street, when he moved into a new home in the Gold Coast. There they stayed for several years until it was declared a fire trap.

When the Lord Lister Hospital was bought by Clarkson in 1936, students were moved to the second floor, until the space was needed by the hospital. They were moved into the newly purchased Sweetwood Apartments, which, however, did not have adequate space. All Saints, at McAuliffe's request, made the wood framed Victorian home that it owned at 520 South Twenty-Sixth Street available to the nursing school.[130] The house had been bought as part of Casady's attempt to expand the parish facility. It was affectionately known as Nurses' Home No. 2. Appealing for funding for an entirely new residence for the nurses, McAuliffe provided a description of the proposed facility in the diocesan newspaper. The "makeshift living quarters for the nurses stationed at Clarkson Memorial Hospital" needed replacement. Nurses' Home No. 2 housed thirty-two nurses in the cramped sleeping quarters of twelve bedrooms, only three of which offered any privacy." When the hospital was ready to build a new nurses' home in 1944, All Saints deeded the building to the hospital, which made room for their new building that they completed in 1946. In reality, this building only served this purpose for seven years. When the hospital was relocated at Forty-Second and Dewey in 1953, it proceeded to build a new building for it nursing school.

Clayton maintained a special pastoral outreach to the nursing student, back by the women of the parish. Patricia Brooks was one of those students who have left a testimony about Clayton pastoral work. Brooks was a bright young woman from a small Western Iowa town. She had graduated at the top of her class in 1945 at Harlan Senior High. She had been active in Harlan's small but very beautiful Episcopal Church. While in school, she found herself participating in a very large and different kind of urban parish. Here, she also met her future husband, Samuel Perry, who was at the time in medical school. After their student years, life took them to Western Nebraska where Sam practiced medicine. In time, they returned to Omaha, and resumed a relationship with All Saints. Sam took up a specialty, and Pat continued her education. In 1976, she became president

130 *Learning to Care: A Century of Nursing Education Bishop Clarkson College*, Wendell W. Oderkirk, 1988, p. 141.

of the Clarkson nursing school and advanced it, ultimately, to the status of an accredited college. During this time, Pat was again active at All Saints, and she and Sam were particularly close friends of Charles Pedersen.[131] She was one of the first women to serve on the vestry and was All Saints first women warden. She enjoyed reminiscing about her student day. She would refer fondly of Dr. Clayton: "He was such a sweet man. He was such great help to Sam and me, while we were students in Omaha."

Facing War and a Serious Injury

Preparing for war had begun in earnest in Omaha in 1939. The most noticeable feature of this was the opening of the Martin Bomber plant, located adjacent to Fort Crook, south of Bellevue. Intense Nebraska lobbying in Washington DC, led the Baltimore armament company to locate the production plant in Omaha. It would prove in the long run the most important change in the destiny of Omaha since the decision, again made in Washington, to locate the Union Pacific Missouri River crossing at Omaha. In the short run, it was the first evidence that the economy was at last visibly improving. The evidence in the parish was more modest. The treasurer's report in 1940 indicated that the expenditures for the previous year had amounted to $16,781. This was only a slight improvement over the year before, but it broke the long pattern of decline and hopes for the coming year were high.

If 1940 was to be the beginning of the comeback, a personal injury suddenly threatened it. Clayton was vacationing in Canada where he had begun his ministry. On August 6, he set out to drive from Toronto to Montreal to meet up with an old friend, Rev. Gilbert Oliver. Having passed through the small town of Brighton some time past noon, his car collided head on with another. His condition was reported as good, but it was clear that he would be in the hospital about a month before he could travel back to Omaha. His primary injury was a broken right leg. Rev. Gilbert Oliver was immediately on the spot and continued to visit Clayton as he recovered in the Canadian Hospital. His close friend from the parish, Eugene McAuliffe, traveled immediately to see Clayton and brought back a report to the anxious parish. On August 24, Clayton underwent further surgery "to clear up congestion." This suggests that his chest had been compromised either from a blow in the accident or from

131 Pedersen spent an intern summer working at St. Christopher's Cozad and stayed with them at the cabin on Johnson Lake. They loved to tell stories about Charles from that summer.

a pneumonia contracted from being confined to bed, making it necessary to drain his lung cavity. Finally, at the end of the September, McAulife, who was also the vice president of the Clarkson Memorial Hospital Board, traveled with Edna Koop, Clarkson chief surgical nurse, to bring Clayton back to Omaha by train. The party arrived on September 21. A picture in the *Omaha World-Herald* shows him being removed on a gurney through the window of the train, since it would not fit though the doorway of the car. An inserted detail shows his face, which appears quite stressed. He was hospitalized at Clarkson, literally across the street from All Saints, for a protracted convalescence. While he worked from his hospital room, he was unable to assume his full duties for some time. On Christmas Eve, a phone line was set up between his room and the church, literally across the street so he could hear the service. When the time came for the sermon, he preached from his hospital bed what was termed his "usual sermon."

On January 7, 1941, he wrote a letter from the hospital that dealt with the need to appoint laymen to attend the diocesan council. He told the parish that the diocese would be asking for a 25 percent raise in its expenditures. He wanted to be on record as strongly supporting the request, which shows once again that he habitually supported the diocese. A renewed fervor is noticeable, however, now that the new bishop was in place. Clayton would have a substantially different relationship with Bishop Brinker than he had with Shayler. As was his custom, he left it to his laity to decide but had wanted them to know his opinion. The names he suggested to represent All Saints are Robert C. McClements, Dudley Colby, and Dr. Fred Whitcomb. He goes on in the letter to describe his condition.

> I do not want you to be duly alarmed about the condition of All Saints Church because I feel certain I will be back in the immediate future. I am already able to walk with the aid of crutches. Yesterday I walked from my room to the elevator and back, and each day I am able to add a little to my efforts. I hope you will bear with me for a week or two longer for I feel sure I will be able to at least to carry on the major part of the work then. I am deeply grateful to you for your courage and patience during my illness, but I do urge you at this time not to do anything of a radical nature because I am sure I will be able to carry on soon.

At last on January 13, 1941, he was brought to the church to preach from a wheel chair. An *Omaha World-Herald* headline announced, "Easter

Sunday Crowd Greets Dr. Clayton." The accompanying article reported that six hundred people were in congregation that morning and that since the weather was mild, many had put on their spring outfits. In a picture that ran in the *Omaha World-Herald*, a happy Clayton is pictured sitting in a wheel chair alongside of the pulpit. A sharply attired woman of thirty steps out of the choir and reaching across the pulpit to shake his hand. The caption read: "Dr. Clayton . . . receiving a homecoming welcome from Hazel Doane."[132] The sermon that he preached that morning was "Is the World Getting Better or Worse?" The five months that Clayton had lain in the hospital coincided with the beginning of the Battle of Britain. It was widely covered on the front page of the *Omaha World-Herald*. Clayton's sister lived in Newcastle on the Tyne, an industrial city, which had already been targeted by German air raids as it would be throughout the war. He received a letter from his niece living in Newcastle on Tyne and shared it with the parish. Subsequently, it was published in the *Omaha World-Herald*.

> It must be strange to live in America, as yet untouched by the far reaching effects of the war. To walk about at night and see electric lights in houses, to see electric signs flashing to hear no sirens. But perhaps after all you are missing something rather wonderful—the way people are kinder, more neighborly, one family—altogether it gives you a feeling one can't describe.[133]

It was obviously troubling for Clayton, and in the course of time, the Women of All Saints sent donations to Newcastle on the Tyne.

His argument in the sermon was that if the large picture was bleak, the fact was that the individual's worth was of more value now than at any time in human history. This claim might seem surprising, unless we recall that it was a theme that he had announced in one of his very first sermons at All Saints. He had said then in anticipation of that sermon: "I am hoping to preach a course of sermons which will deal with problems peculiar to this age and time. My subject on Sunday morning will be the spiritual evolution. The text under discussion will be Ephesians 3:14–20." The

132 Hazel Doane was a "working" girl who advanced to the role of Secretary for Guarantee Mutual Life. She was a pianist and was active with the Symphony Guild. She frequently presented papers on musical topics, for example one on the Firebird Suite. She also provided accompaniment for various soloist. She lived at the Wellington Hotel at Fifty-Eighth and Underwood. She never married and died in 1979.

133 *Omaha World-Herald*, March 3, 1941.

theme became the central element for opening up the text of the Gospel so it could be preached to the times. In this early series of sermon, Clayton had found his hermeneutic. The emergence of the free-self determined individual as a result of Christianity was for him the key for proclaiming the Gospel. It was a radical departure from the hermeneutic of his bishop and his predecessor, for whom building the kingdom of God on earth was the key to preaching the Gospel. Not only did the older hermeneutic stir up conflict in an age that had lost its sense of consensus, it also found itself at pains to differentiate itself from the totalitarian utopias whose appeal was growing so dramatically and whose implementation was leading to painfully destructive ends. Clayton's message offered a reason for hope in time when world economies were struggling to regain their momentum and national states to regain their internal unity and discipline. The individual would triumph, he was confident. His analysis was in some part the result of the thought of Reinhold Neibuhr, whose epic making book, *Moral Man and Immoral Society*, had appeared in 1932, and which he had at the time commended to the reading of the parish.

There was in this first sermon outside of the hospital, not a little of his own self, who had endured five months of medical treatment. It also was prophetic because, in a strange way, what ultimately happened was that an army of American individualists, resourceful young men who could think for themselves, defeated the Wehrmacht made of the best disciplined soldiers ever assembled. Never that impressive in parades and not that far from the farms or the neighborhood sand lots where they had played ball, these privates, corporals, sergeants, and first lieutenant could not be stopped on the battle field. He preached again the following Sunday from a wheelchair, returning immediately afterward to the hospital for continued care.

Toward the end of January, Guy S. Williams, the *Omaha World-Herald*'s personal columnist, paid Clayton a visit in his hospital room and featured him in his column. In it he gives us a snapshot of Clayton. He began by saying: "I've had some very good and beneficial friends among the clergy, but none who have been more a spiritual and mental tonic than Dr. Clayton." He goes on to say that "despite the weary months of pain, he was the same amiable smiling man I had known before the crack-up; with the same infectious laugh, the same sparkle in his eyes, the same lively interest in life and its goings on."[134]

Clayton never fully recovered, and it appears that he was plagued by doubts about his ability to continue as All Saints rector. This is suggested in a letter that Bishop Brinker sent to the bishop of Maryland in the

[134] *Omaha World-Herald*, January 20, 1941.

summer of 1941. In that letter, Brinker enquired about the possibility of Clayton finding a call to a small charge that would be easier for him to deal with. In the correspondence, Brinker writes, "Dr. Clayton is one of the outstanding preachers in the Middle West, and it will be very difficult to get an equal to succeed him if and when the time comes that he decides to leave." In the end, the correspondence was dropped, and Clayton continued at All Saints for the next seven years.

Continuing to Work at All Saints

The goals of the Every Member Canvass for 1941 were announced in a special issue of *Church and Home*, dated September 5, 1940. In it we have a picture of the parish's staff and their compensation. At its head was Clayton with a salary of $4,800. The parish secretary, Ms. Eleanor Robinson, had a salary $1,080. And the custodian, Homer Edmonds, had salary of $900. J. H. Simms, now in his fifty-sixth year of service to All Saints, had salary of $1,200 and an additional $600 to spend on soloists and music. Eleanor Sprague completed the staff as a lay assistant in charge of working with the parish children. She was paid $600. The staff's salary formed the core of the budget, with little left over for operating expenses.

On the surface, it seems like business as usual, but underneath there was the conviction on the part of Clayton that the United States would find itself at war in the not-too-distant future. When Nebraska's state guards were called up for nation service in the course of 1941, it created a void; and Nebraska, like other states, formed a home guard made up of volunteers generally too old for active duty. The mission of this volunteer guard was to provide disaster relief, riot control, and to meet other local needs that might occur. In October 1941, Governor Griswold signed the act forming a home guard and appointed Dr. Clayton the regimental chaplain of the First Infantry of the Nebraska State Home Guard, giving him the rank of captain. Clayton's appointment probably was owed to the fact that his parishioner and close friend, Clarence Spier, had been appointed at the same time as the captain of the same unit. In 1942, Spier, a veteran of WWI, was promoted to lieutenant colonel and in 1944 was promoted to full colonel, taking command of the guard. Throughout the duration of the war, Clayton provided religious services for the guard at its various training encampments.

Once the United States was involved in the war, there was a steady stream of memorial services in the parish from the casualties that resulted. None had such a high profile as that of Otto Jabelman, whose death came at the beginning of 1943. Jabelman was the vice president of research and mechanical standards at the Union Pacific. He had been called to assist in the war effort by W. A. Harriman, who was in charge of the lend-least effort in England. His sudden death in London was a staggering loss to the Union Pacific and to the parish where his family had been active since the mid-twenties. Jabelman's funeral was held at All Saints, and the church was packed. There was a large representation of dignitaries from the railroads, the U.S. Military, and Omaha's business community. Clayton's remarks show a close pastoral relationship with Jabelman and his wife. He had had firsthand knowledge of Jabelman's health problems prior to his departure for England, which might have dissuaded a man less driven by patriotism to turn down the assignment. Jabelman's wife continued to be active in the parish after his death and was presented for confirmation in 1947 by Clayton, showing a deepening relationship with the parish.

The following April came by far the most touching of the funerals that fell at this time to Clayton. Lieutenant Robert Moose was killed when his plane was shot down in the Pacific while engaged in combat. The young pilot was an All Saints Altar boy and a part of the parish's Boy Scout troop.

Glimmers of Hope

Amidst all the dark war news of 1943, the parish's long financial decline finally reversed, and for the first time in more than ten years, there was an increase in income and disbursements. The treasurer's report at the end of that year showed that the parish had spent $18,234 and ended the year with a balance of $127 and with an additional $668 prepaid pledge for 1944 in the bank. Moreover, the outstanding loan was now down to $7,700 and had been refinanced at 3 percent. The treasurer, looking ahead to1944, stated that "in December a very successful 'Every Member Canvass' was conducted by the following committee: Mr. C. Louis Meyer, chairman, Mr. Murray L. Champine and Mr. Vernon Smith, vice chairmen. The value of the pledges obtained in this 'Every Member Canvass' was $14,826, as compared with $11,657.20 for 1943, or an increase of $3,168.80." The treasurer concluded his report by saying: "This is the first year for some time that All Saints Church has paid its diocesan assessment and missionary assessment in full, and we thereby have fulfilled our obligation to the diocese. Special thanks are due to the womanhood of the church, who contributed $718.52 from their earning from the St. Nicholas Festival to pay the balance due on our missionary assessment." The progress continued throughout the year. At the December vestry meeting, L E. Hurtz, president of The Fairmont Creamery Co., pledged $1,000 for the retirement of the parish's mortgage and challenged the vestry to liquidate it before our annual meeting on January 15! Vestry's reaction to Hurtz's challenge was to initiate a fund drive at the annual meeting in order to retire the debt by its due date, which was March 1, 1945. While it took a little longer than Hurtz or the vestry had hoped, by 1947 Clayton could say that the parish was out debt and had restored to its endowment fund the money it had barrowed returning it to its original principal.

Clayton Resignation

Clayton was further cheered by being able to announce that Charles R. Johnson, the past lay assistant at All Saints Parish, would be ordained at All Saints on Memorial Day, May 30, 1945. Johnson was a local Omaha boy born in 1918. He was a graduate of Carroll College and of Nashota House. Johnson was raised at St. Andrew's and was a noted athlete at Benson High. The *World-Herald* reported that he had been known as a triple threat. He had played football, basketball and track. His father, who was the sales manager for an Omaha rubber company, went to work in the Martin Bomber plant and was killed in an unfortunate accident in 1942. Consequently, his mother had lived with him. This ordination was a glimmer of help for Clayton, who continued to struggle with his health and a shot of adrenalin for the young people of the parish. Johnson began taking services and appears to have been an able and hardworking assistant.

Good news continued in 1946, the first postwar year. The accounts of the annual meeting in January of 1947 reveal a vibrant parish that had returned to the budget level of 1929. Dinner was served in Wattle Memorial Hall to 187 parishioners. The buoyancy of the parish is further signaled by the fact that the parish took time for a speech form an outsider. A parishioner, Vincent Haskell, who was a member of the Board of Regents, introduced the chancellor of the University of Nebraska, Dr. Ruben G. Gustavson, to those gathered for the annual meeting. Dr. Gustavson is described in the minutes as "an erudite mind." His topic was identified as "science, religion, and the future of mankind." The speech took thirty minutes. It is not difficult to imagine how the presence of Gustavson; and his topic would have pleased Clayton, who had once himself been a college president. Gustavson's message was supportive of the very ideas that had been part of Clayton's teaching over the past nineteen years. It is hard to understand how the speaker and the topic fit an annual meeting, except as a statement of All Saints standing in the community (indeed the state!) and as a tribute to the rector who had done so much to earn its esteem.

With the speech out of the way, the meeting proceeded to the elections and reports. In the elections, Robert Trimble and Gilbert G. Carpenter were quickly elected as wardens; and Hyde, Burke, Scoular, and Judge Robert Troyer were added to the vestry. Reports were received by title and attached to the minute. The associate rector, Charles R. Johnson, reported seven hundred twenty-seven house and hospital calls, twenty-five Boy Scout events, nineteen funerals, ten baptisms, and nine weddings. He further described his work with the church school, the Young People's Fellowship and the Boxing Club. Yes, despite Bishop Shayler's desire to band boxing in Omaha, boxing had quietly continued at All Saints as a youth activity!

The president of the Executive Board of the Women, Mrs. Chester Cunningham continued, reporting a balance from its activities of $2,616. The altar guild, headed by Mrs. E. W. Bedford, reported raising and spending $1,904 on the care and dressing of the altar. The Chancel Guild, headed by Mary G. Knode, had raised and spent $1,737 caring for the needs of the choir and readers. This had included a new violet superfrontal, sheet music, and the laundering and cleaning that fell to that guild. The tireless Mrs. W. W. Hoagland reported for the Woman's Auxiliary. It had sent ten children's dresses and three coats and three quilts to the Booth Memorial Hospital, a hospital in Omaha that specialized at the time in the delivery and caring of unwed mothers, and to Holland, ten skirts and overalls and eighteen polo shirts, by means of a relative of a parishioner who was working in Holland with a relief agency. They had contributed $1,000 to the chapel fund, $400 to diocesan missionary pledge, $5 for St. Philip's organ fund, and $50 for the San Juan Indian Supply Box. Much of this money had come from four hundred quarts of minced meat, which had been made and sold by the auxiliary. The Parish Guild, which was charged with caring for the parish house and for Mackay Memorial Hall, had spent $1,070 during the year in the care and maintenance of these two heavily used facilities.

Most important, the treasurer reported the parish had disbursements during the past year of $21,058, that all bills had been paid, and that there was a balance of $1,968 in the bank. The budget set for the coming year was projected to be $23,026.

Successive vestry meetings in January, February, March, and April continue the sense that 1947 would continue to build on the successes of 1946. New people were incorporated into the work of the vestry; additional money was authorized to add new voices to the choir; and the associate, Charles Johnson, was given a raise. Moreover, the parish received a gift from the estate of Margaret H. Raffan, who had died on September 27,

1946. The amount was $4,000, which allowed the vestry to pay back money they had borrowed from their endowment fund, and put an additional $948 into the general fund for 1947. In April, the Men's Club stepped up and provided funding to publish *Church and Home*, which had been in abeyance since 1932.

An April edition, labeled volume 47, number 1, appeared in anticipation of Easter. It was obviously intended as a beginning of a regularly published newsletter. The issue carries a picture of Dr. Clayton on the front page. Clayton speaks in it of how important the resumption of the publication is. He quotes the late bishop of London's remarks made about World War I: "The song is true which says, 'Pack up your troubles in your old kit bag and smile, smile, smile,' but we, none of us, must forget the original purpose for which the bag was packed." He speaks of looking forward to Easter and quotes from a sermon, which he had delivered in September of 1934. In it, he had identified three central principles of why it was necessity for the Church to exist:

> The church is necessary in order to organize our own inner lives. Living outside of the church is like having a passing insight into a private world.
>
> Unless a man has learned to pray somewhere, the odds are many that he will not pray anywhere.
>
> The man who says that he is free to worship anywhere, as he surely is, usually worships nowhere, not having learned the art.

He concludes his remarks on the front page letter with a charge: "Now that we have taken a great step forward in this parish, do give us the necessary funds to keep this forward movement going."[135]

Easter went well, and ten days later, the vestry met for a brief meeting at which it authorized a railing for the steps leading from the parking lot behind the church and directed Dr. Clayton to write a letter to the parishioners recommending that they make a contribution to the Episcopal National European and Asiatic Relief Fund. There was, however, no May edition of *Church and Home* and no vestry meeting in May. Those are the only signs of the surprise which confronted the vestry on June 13. Robert Trimble, the senior warden, received a letter from Clayton tendering his resignation and asking him to call a vestry meeting.

---

135 *Church and Home*, vol. 47, no. 1.

Clayton opened his letter to the vestry, expressing his regrets: "I rather hate to leave Omaha and all my friends here. I love the city and my church. But I've decided that I've been in one parish long enough." Both of his doctors, he explained, had told him that his health could not handle the pressure of his work at All Saints. He had been offered a position at St. John's, Milwaukie, a small church in a suburb of Portland, Oregon. The parish had a small house with a garage. While his salary would be much smaller, he would have the satisfaction of doing what he loved in a small church setting. There was nothing in the present circumstances that had prompted this, he said, but he had been thinking about such a move for some time. In fact, he had entertained the idea in 1941, when he explored the possibility a return to Maryland.

The most important clue in his letter as to his motivation was the statement that he was depressed. This certainly would have surprised anyone who knew him for his outward appearance was as jovial and upbeat as ever. Yet it is often the case that persons who appear jovial and upbeat have a dark side. He said in his letter, "Things that have happened recently have not really weighed with me, it is just that living in one room at the hotel and with the pressure of a large pressure (He certainly meant to write 'parish') has somewhat depressed me." All he asked was that his salary continue until October first, that he might take September as his vacation in order to pack and say goodbye, and that the car that had been put at his disposal by the parish be given to him.

In spite of Clayton's protestation that "there was nothing in the present circumstances that prompted this, there must have been something which, at least, nudged Clayton decision. What was he referring to when he wrote of "things that have happened recently?" And then there is that uncharacteristic mistakes and confusion in the text of Clayton's letter that suggest that something unusual was going on. Perhaps the brain tumor that would ultimately cause his death was already there and affecting him. When Trimble called the vestry together to consider the letter on June 20, he invited Clarence Spier to be present. The vestry reacted to Clayton's letter with consternation. Clearly, they had not seen it coming and voted unanimously to ask him to reconsider. Reaching outside of themselves, they asked Clarence Spier to meet with Clayton in order to get him to change his mind. Spier represented someone who was noted as an honest negotiator, and he was a close personal friend of Clayton. Spier in a letter to Clayton said that "several members of the vestry addressed the group and expressed the substance of their recent conversations with you in respect to the matter and I may say that it was most apparent that every man present was mindful of the reason for your action and most sincerely regretful of such action." In his letter, Spier indicates that he had been appointed a committee of one to seek to get him to change his mind. Clayton's mind was not, however, changed; and on June 20, the vestry met and accepted Clayton resignation, granting him the terms that he had requested, with their regret.

Rev. Charles Johnson, the associate rector of All Saints for the past two years, tendered his resignation, as is *pro forma* with the resignation of a rector; but he offered to supply during the interim between rectorships. After consideration of his resignation, the vestry decided to accept it, effective October 1. Johnson went on to be rector of St. Andrews Church, Jackson, Mississippi.

Clayton died in 1950 of a brain tumor that his doctors attempted to remove with surgery. His funeral service was held at All Saints on September 29. Father Secker of Norfolk and Canon George Tyner, representing Bishop Brinker who was absent from the diocese, conducted the services. The organ was played by Cecil Neubecker, the newly appointed organist, and by J. H. Sims who had retired only recently. The Pall Bearers were Frederick O. Beck, Gilbert E. Carpenter, James R. Fields, George T. Morton, Robert S. Trimble, and Dr. Frederick F. Whitcomb, all friends of Clayton and all one-time vestry men of the parish. He was buried at Forest Lawn, and the *Omaha World-Herald* said that the service was a "tribute to uncommon man." Under his picture, they noted: "Dr. Clayton . . . tolerant, learned."

Part 3

Embracing the American Century

Chapter 6

A New Social Age: 1947–1961

The Transition

The Omaha that emerged from the Great Depression and World War II was greatly changed. As Larsen and Cottrell observed in their insightful history of Omaha:

> Less than twenty years earlier the same organizations had emphasized free enterprise and the open shop. Now they talked of building a better Omaha. While many of the same people who had fought for the older goals remained in key positions, there was a different attitude. Despite continued rhetoric about the virtues of an uninhibited city in which entrepreneurs would have a free hand in the market place—in practice the dominant economic groups in Omaha accepted the new age.[136]

The pendulum had once again reversed direction. The individualism of the twenties and thirties had run its course, and at some point, American life began to move back toward a sense of social responsibility and to a new consensus about what really mattered. After a long hard night, people wanted to return to normalcy, which was defined as going to work, having a family and enjoying a renewed sense of neighborliness. There was a restored consensus about what a fair deal was, which was evident in Truman's election victory over Dewey, and Eisenhower's victory over

---

[136] *The Gate City, A History of Omaha*, Lawrence H. Larsen and Barbara J. Cottrell, p. 210.

Taft. It had been created, to be sure, by means of bracketing out significant issues, particularly those of race relations and poverty. In 1947, a quarter of the population lived under the poverty line, thousands of children still contracted polio each year and fewer than one in twelve Americans had a college degree. African Americans came back from the serving in the armed forces to a rigidly segregated society, which was most evident in the Jim Crow south, but it was also true in the urban north, including Omaha. The cafeteria at Central High was segregated *de facto*, the school district had hired only a handful of African American teachers, and the flagship department store downtown hired African Americans as elevator operators and custodians but reserved the other jobs, floor clerks and professional staff, for whites. This racial discrimination was steadily, but cautiously being challenged.

Adam Clayton Powell Jr., who represented New York City's Harlem in the House of Representatives, was one of the few African American voices given any coverage the press. Regarded by the greater part of the nation as a kind of exotic nuisance, Powell, nevertheless, kept the racial issue from disappearing. For example, he challenged Congressman Rankin of Mississippi on the House floor in the 1940s for using the word "nigger." His challenge did nothing to change Rankin's mind or behavior, but it gave solace to millions who longed for at least some measure of change. Brown versus the Board of Education came along in 1954 and ordered the end of school segregation. The Supreme Court, led by Earl Warren, caused wide spread surprise by its decision. In 1955, Rosa Parks refused to go to the back of the bus in Montgomery Alabama and, for a moment, jarred the awareness of the American public, which preferred to be largely unaware of the quiet effort at incremental change. The more liberal side of the consensus convinced themselves that with time these incremental changes would yield to a substantial change in race relationships. The more conservatives side, however, were equally sure that it would never happen. This allowed the dawn of a new social age, which would flourish for a time before its contradictions caught up with it.

This presented new possibilities for the church, especially for the Episcopal Church, which could be used to reignite growth. The return of "foxhole Christianity" stateside meant that there were seekers looking for an open and practical presentation of Christianity. They did not want the "old morality," and they did not want conflict to be part of the religious community. The example of these new seekers gave currency to the view that everyone needed religion; particularly, it was needed if you were trying to raise a family. A considerable number of these returning vets sought to enter the ministry, with the result that there was a new surge in seminary enrollments. To benefit from these trends, however, churches, including the Episcopal Church, had to make adjustments to their message, their activities, and their physical plants and a new kind of priest began to show up in the parish. Their message was more pragmatic and less doctrinal. Activities aimed to be family-friendly, and physical facilities needed to add classrooms for children. Physical plants needed improvements to their comfort levels similar to those of the new American home. Many facilities were in the wrong place and had inadequate space for parking, which had been made into a crucial need as the spread of the city meant that most people drove to church. They lacked classrooms for Sunday school. They were hard to heat in the winter and hard to cool in the summer. The interior was cold and institutional, rather than warm and homelike. This orientation would, when the cycle had completed itself, give rise to the derisive term "the comfortable pew," which was aimed as a criticism at the era of church growth that marked the '50s.[137]

As this new age dawned, Dr. Clayton, now sixty-two and quite confirmed in his ways, must have sensed what kind of change would be required for him to continue to be as effective as he had been in the last nineteen years. Rectors, of course, generally have difficulty in letting go and are prone to hold on longer than they should. A lesser man than Clayton would have likely insisted that his message was still the Gospel and that the new patterns of parish ministries were nothing more than new fads that would pass. A vestry is prone to be drawn along by a rector who is holding on, since a vestry seldom relishes the idea of a search process. The vestry at All Saints had a special reason to feel reluctant to deal with changing rectors. Many on the vestry, like its senior warden Robert Trimble and its junior warden Gilbert Carpenter, had soldiered through the financial troubles of the Depression and the war with Clayton. Only in the last couple of years had the financial picture reversed. There had been times when Clayton had felt that he was failing the parish, and there had been times when the vestry felt it was failing Clayton. It was time at last for them together to enjoy the fruits of the long and hard labor in which they had shared. So they made an all-out effort to dissuade him. Clayton, however, insisted on resigning, citing personal reasons, mainly his health. There was a truth to this, of course. He died two and half years later from a brain tumor that might have already been affecting his health when he was still at All Saints. But above all, Clayton was a realist. Life after the war was greatly changed; and his personal life, his message, and his way of

[137] *The Comfortable Pew: A Critical Look at Christianity and the Religious Establishment in the New Age*, Pierrer Breton, January 1, 1965.

doing ministry would no longer work. At any rate, it was the right thing for the parish, and by resigning, Clayton forced the parish to deal with change.

The vestry of 1947 was led by Robert Trimble, who had joined the parish in 1923 and became its senior warden in 1939. The junior warden was Gilbert Carpenter. Together they represented continuity with the past. The others on the vestry presented the new face of the parish. They included Hyle G. Burke, Murray L. Champine, Dudley R.. Colby, Gale Davis, Frank S. Mellinger, Louis Meyer, Edward C. Reynolds, Judge Robert Troyer, Robert M. Scoular, and James. L. Paxton, Jr.

After accepting Clayton's resignation on June 20, the vestry prepared for the transition mainly by putting the parish's financial house in order. After his resignation had been tendered, Clayton stopped attending the meetings of the vestry and allowed the laity to carry on the administrative work of the parish. One of the first things they did was accept the associate's resignation and set his last day in the parish as October 1. Johnson clearly was not considered as a successor and not even as an interim, should one be needed. Johnson, for all his effectiveness as an assistant, had at that point been ordained little more than two years; and his formation at Nashota House would imply that he leaned distinctly toward the ritual side of the church. The minutes of the vestry meetings in the course of the summer were focused on putting the parish's financial house in order and give no evidence of a search process. At the October 14 meeting, the vestry arranged with Rev. George Tyner, the bishop's assistant, and Mr. Ernest Broad, a layman of the cathedral, to take the services while the position was vacant. Again, there was no sign of a search process taking place. Nevertheless, on October 30, the vestry met with Bishop Brinker who brought with him Rev. Gordon B. Galaty, the rector of St. James Episcopal Church, Dundee, Illinois. Following a prayer offered by the bishop, Robert Scoular moved that the wardens and vestry of All Saints call Rev. Gordon B. Galaty to become rector of All Saints Church on the following basis:

> That he be paid a salary of $6,000 per year, that he be furnished living quarters suitable for himself and his family free of rentals, that he be paid an appropriate automobile expense allowance, and that he be reimbursed for all expenses involved in his move from Dundee, Illinois.

Quickly seconded, it was adopted unanimously. In other words, the ducks were well in order. Galaty's words of acceptance "were most inspiring to all present" according to the secretary of the vestry, and the minutes go on to record that Galaty knelt and asked the bishop for his blessing.

Brinker, having blessed Galaty, went on to congratulate the vestry on its call and predicted "that in future years this event would come to be looked upon as of outstanding significance not only in the history of All Saints Church, but also in the Diocese of Nebraska."

Brinker, who had enjoyed Clayton's full support, had immediately perceived how important a successful call and the subsequent success of a new rector at All Saints were to the diocese. Galaty reported to the parish that when the acceptance of his call to All Saints was made public, he had received a broad response from across the Diocese of Nebraska.

> From all over the diocese, I have received letters welcoming me to All Saints Parish and telling me what a wonderful congregation you are. I infer from these letters that churchmen everywhere consider All Saints as the leading parish, not just in Omaha, but in the whole diocese. This is a tremendous responsibility for us to carry.[138]

It is not likely that this outpouring of support had happened without the orchestration of the bishop. Brinker must have played a primary role in the search process as it unfolded. Brinker, himself, had come from the Diocese of Chicago where he had been dean of St. Bartholomew's and had been active force in the diocese until he left in 1938. He was, consequently, in the position to identify strong candidates among the young upcoming priests of that diocese.

Brinker had written a letter to the bishop of Western Michigan in regard to Galaty's qualifications and received a prompt reply. The bishop, under whom Galaty had served before the war, praised Galaty and went on to say,

> The only faint doubts I have about Gordon would be his ability, even with the best intentions in the world, to adjust himself to a middle-of-the-road parish where, as you say, Eucharistic vestments are not used and people have the habit of addressing the priest as "mister." His churchmanship is such an essential part of Gordon that the fact that he is a decidedly Catholic churchman would stick out from the very first. There would doubtless come a very definite impulse toward changing the traditional churchmanship of the parish for that is exactly what happened at St. Paul's. It was marvelous the way he got 'away

[138] A letter by Galaty dated December 4, 1947, contained in the minutes of the vestry for December 4.

> with it,' but it did happen. He would probably get away with it in the same way in the parish which you have in mind, but I am just giving you what happened here where he went into a rather low church parish.[139]

Brinker appears to have no qualms about Galaty's churchmanship, even though Galaty's stay at St. Paul's, Grand Rapids, Michigan, had been for little more than two years. Most rectors can "get away" with just about anything for a couple of years! In any case, it is clear that Brinker initiated the consideration of Galaty and continued to back him.

Gordon Galaty was born in 1911 in Oak Park, Illinois, and continued his education through high school there. His father, Spiro, worked for the railroad in various middle-level management positions. His paternal grandfather, Zaffere Galaty, was an immigrant from Greece, who served in the Union Navy. He served on board a ship that participated in the blockade of the Confederacy in the gulf. After the war, Zaffere settled in Chicago and counted himself as the eighth Greek to do so. In spite of his Greek identity, or perhaps because of it, Zaffere raised his family at St. James Episcopal Church in Chicago. A Greek Orthodox congregation was not yet available in Chicago, and the Episcopal Church made him feel at home and at the same time gave him an American identity.

Gordon Galaty, Rector 1948-1950, br. 1905 Oak Park, Illinois, d. 1977

139 A letter in the Diocese of Nebraska Archives

In the twenties, Galaty's father, Spiro, moved his young family to the fashionable suburb in Western Chicago. In Oak Park, the family became members of Grace Episcopal Church. Galaty's mother, Edith Bird, taught eighth grade in the public school, which completed the picture of a hardworking upward mobile middle-class family. Galaty's heritage was an interesting mixture of ethnicity, middle class work ethic, patriotism, and loyalty to the Episcopal Church.

After graduating from high school, he went to St. Stephen's at Annandale-on-the Hudson, New York, for a year of prep school. St. Stephen's had a history of preparing young men intent on going in the Episcopal priesthood. In fact, All Saints earlier rector, Thomas Mackay, had been prepared there for seminary. His enrollment at St. Stephen suggests that Galaty had come out of high school with a strong sense of vocation to the priesthood. After a couple of years there, he continued his undergraduate degree at Michigan, receiving his degree in 1933. His father suffered a fall that year and died shortly thereafter. During the following year, Galaty suspended his education; but in the fall of 1934, he enrolled at Berkeley Divinity School, in New Haven, Connecticut. In doing so, he passed up Seabury–Western, his hometown seminary, as it were, and nearby Nashota House noted for its Anglo-Catholic orientation. Berkeley was the seminary of the Episcopal Church most clearly identified as liberal catholic. Berkeley's dean from 1933 to 1941 was Palmer Ladd, an astute liturgical scholar who was the forerunner of the generation of American liturgical scholars who would later in the century revise so superbly the American Book of Common Prayer.

Upon graduation from Berkeley, Galaty was ordained and served as curate at Grace Church, Oak Park, Illinois, where his family had been members. Rev. Harold Holt, the rector from 1937 to 1940, made him part of the family, literally, as Galaty lived in the rectory during his curacy. In 1940, Galaty was called to be rector of St. Paul's in Grand Rapids, Michigan; and at the same time, he served as the diocesan missionary directly under the bishop. Once the move was completed, he returned to Oak Park to marry Marguerite Craigie Holt, the eldest daughter of his former rector. They had two sons, David, born in 1942, and John, born in 1945.

Not yet two years in his new cure and with a child on the way, the country at last entered the war. The impact on Galaty was immediate, and he enlisted in the U.S. Navy as a chaplain. Clearly, Galaty's sense of national service was both intense and genuine. It is likely that his Greek heritage played a role in his decision. His storied Greek grandfather had been a "navy man" in the Civil War. In general, ethnic Americans felt a need to prove their loyalty by supporting the war and, if young enough, by joining up. Moreover, Greece had been invaded by Germany in April 1941 and had become in short order occupied territory.

Galaty, having completed his training, was stationed at the Advance Naval Base in the Pacific on the island of Efate, in the New Heberdies. When Vella La Vella in the Solomons fell, he was moved there with the Marine Air Wing whose task was to support the invasion of Bougainville. His service as a chaplain was in close proximity to the front and he was decorated for heroic service, being awarded the Navy and Marine Corps Medal. After a brief interlude at the Naval Station in Ottumwa, Iowa, during which time his second son was born, he returned to the Pacific. He was stationed on board the USS *Louisville*, a heavy cruiser, which had just been returned to service after repairs. The ship had been badly damaged when struck by two Kamikazes while on station in Lingayen Gulf. The USS *Louisville* was anchored in Hawaii when the war ended but was soon dispatched to the Far East, where Galaty spent the final period of his time on active duty. In January of 1946, Galaty was transferred into the inactive reserves with the rank of lieutenant commander. By March 1946, he had begun to serve as rector of St. James, Dundee, Illinois, where he was when he received the call to be rector of All Saints.

Brinker's engagement with the parish did not end with the completion of the search process. He continued to counsel the parish as it awaited the arrival of its new rector in January. He was insistent that the parish proceed with an Every Member Canvass. The parish, on the other hand, was reluctant to do so without the presence and guidance of its new rector. Nevertheless, the vestry yielded to Brinker and was pleasantly surprised with the results. D. L. Colby, All Saints treasurer, wrote to Brinker on January 6, reporting on the results of the drive. While they were still waiting to hear form forty-two units, which represented $2,086 of last year's income, they were already ahead of last year and projected an income of $19,500 for the new year as opposed to $17,400 for the past year. Colby went on to say to Brinker,

> It is the feeling of the committee that much of the success of the current canvass is due to the inspiration and assistance furnished by you, including your insistence that we adopt the form of pledge card generally used. Also, while we were reluctant to undertake the canvass without the guidance and assistance of a rector, it is our feeling now that this was the right thing to do and we are all very happy that you insisted on it being done prior to the arrival of our new rector.[140]

140 Letter attached to the minutes of the vestry meeting, January 6, 1948.

Galaty Arrives

Galaty's first services were held on the morning of January 11, 1948. In the evening on that day, he was installed by Brinker. The installation was followed by a parish dinner and the annual meeting. After the amenities were over, it was quickly apparent to Galaty that the parish had deferred maintenance on its buildings and grounds in order to live within the confines of the restricted budgets of the Depression and to reach its goal of being out of debt. In reality, little of the stained glass, which had been destroyed at the time of the fire, had been replaced by anything approaching the quality of the original glass and the very large north window, Mackay's pride, leaked air so badly that it made heating the church in the winter quite difficult. The parish hall and old rectory needed cleaning and painting, the replacement of their heating systems and other modifications to allow them to meet the needs of the parish. Galaty immediately set out on an ambition program to restore the parish's buildings and to make the alterations which would allow them to service the parish program as he envisioned it. The alterations were especially significant in the area of meeting the need for work with the growing number of children in the parish.

Church and Home was restored in May to a monthly publication, the first issue appearing on May 3. After a suspension for the summer, it resumed in September and continued to the end of the year with three more issues. Galaty used these issues of *Church and Home* effectively but chose in the following year to communicate with the parish by means of letters. This, it seems, suited his style of leadership. While Mackay and Clayton had a pattern that they used to sell themselves, Galaty, like Casady, communicated as needed and did little in the way of self-revelation.

In April, Dr. Clayton returned to Omaha for a brief visit, mainly for the marriage of Ruth Collins. Ruth's father was the manager of passenger traffic at the Union Pacific, and when Clayton died, he would arrange for Clayton's body to be brought by rail to Omaha at his expense. Galaty wrote in the May issue of *Church and Home* that Clayton attended the eleven-o-clock service and was received with excitement following the service. He assisted the rector at the marriage of Ruth Collins to Orville Olson on April 17 and did the funeral of Mr. Wesley P. Atkins on April 20, while the rector was occupied with officiating at a military funeral.

The May issue also carried an extensive discussion of the women's work in the parish. The Womanhood encompassed all the women in the parish. Its president that year was Mrs. George Morton, and she announced the commitment of the Womanhood to visit all the newly confirmed members of the parish with an invitation to participate in the work of the parish. At the top of the list of women's organizations was the Women's Auxiliary, in effect the working guild. The auxiliary was head by Mrs. A. E. Woodman, who had just taken over from the long-serving Mrs. W. W. Hoagland. It met the first and third Wednesdays of the month. During the year, it had made contributions to Clarkson Hospital, the Salvation Army, St. Francis's Boys School, foreign relief, and the diocesan assessment. The altar guild met the second Tuesday of every month and was headed by Mrs. Gale Davis. If one of the stalwarts of women's work, Hoagland, was in the process of receding, another was emerging. Margie Davis would remain a fixture at rummage sales long past the end of the century! The Chancel Guild was headed by Mrs. James Plumb, and it met every two weeks on Mondays. Sewing had been done for Clarkson and Booth Hospitals, also for missions and the annual bazaar. Financial aid was given to St. Christopher's Mission for the Indians, Rev. Robert Mize for his Boys' Home, the same charity as the auxiliary had given to, and to the Church of St. Philip's. There was a special committee within the guild, which provided entertainment for the Clarkson nurses, and the guild had sponsored a nursing student the past year. Another committee took care of the work in the chancel, providing several new vestments and veiling for the crosses.[141] The Parish Guild met on the second and fourth Fridays of the month. It had a particular care for the parish hall and the Mackay Memorial Hall. It was in the process of renewing the china, hanging drapes and reupholstering benches. It was headed by Mrs. Arthur Staubitz. This long list of organizations was completed by St. Anne's Guild, a relative new body. It was headed by Mrs. Stanley Blackburn, who had succeeded Mrs. Dana Bradford. Peg Blackburn reported to the parish that the guild was excited to have grown in the past year from ten to thirty-seven. They had taken an interest in the parish's new nursery, had hosted a dinner with their husbands and were looking forward to a picnic in the summer. They were obviously the younger women of the parish and concluded their report: "The future looks bright for St. Anne's. The possibilities are great, the spirit strong. We are happy to be of service to our church."[142]

Getting Things Organized

Prior to his arrival, Galaty presented the vestry with an elaborate scheme to reorganize its work, which bore the title: "Administrative

141 The reference to "veiling" suggests the innovation of veiling the crosses for Lent, a "high church" innovation by Galaty which was taken in stride.

142 *Church and Home*, vol. 1, no. 1, May 3, 1948.

Organization of Vestry."[143] The three-paged-document had the tone of a general order issued to a military staff. Calling attention to the canons of the diocese, it proposed that in addition to the senior and junior warden, there should be twelve vestrymen, which meant the addition of three members. The vestry would be organized into three departments, the Parish Relations Department, the Program Department, and the Finance Department. Each chairman was expected to have his own team, while the rector and two wardens would comprise an executive committee, which would integrate the work of the departments. Galaty concluded, "The meshing together of these teams determines how smoothly and efficiently the parish team will operate."

As the annual meeting approached, Robert Trimble announced that he would not stand for senior warden, clearing the way, as he put it for new blood. While Galaty had been present for the annual meeting in 1947, having just barely arrived in Omaha, this was in reality the first annual meeting for which he was responsible. The annual meeting elected Gilbert Carpenter as senior warden, and Clarence Spier came back on the vestry as junior warden. With a new vestry, organized according to Galaty's committee system, the parish began the new year by addressing a wide range of problems in a systematic way. Midyear, the effort suffered a setback when the parish secretary, Ms. Catherine Munro, died quite suddenly on July 12, 1948. She apparently had a heart attack while waiting for her bus. She had been parish secretary for five years and was highly regarded. The bulletin read: "Her passing will leave a lonely place in the hearts of her many friends for she had won the love and respect of every member of the parish. Here was indeed a most beautiful character." She was, however, quickly replaced by Agnus Munson, who would become one the parish's longest-serving secretaries.[144]

Despite this and other holdups, things fell into place. The need to deal with the nine windows along the side walls of the nave, whose stained glass had been destroyed during the fire in 1934, was suddenly advanced by the appearance of an initial donor, William Ritchie. He desired to do something significant as a memorial for his wife, Eunice Arthur Ritchie. A contract was signed with Willet Stained Glass Company of Philadelphia

143 The document is filed in the minutes following the annual meeting of January 1948. It is mislabeled by someone as "presented by the rector to the vestry meeting of Dec. 8, 1948." Glued in the minutes among the reports associated with the annual meeting of 1948 suggests that it was a mistaken date.

144 Agnus Munson retired when Pedersen arrived in 1971, making her tenure twenty-three years.

to produce a window called "All Saints and the Communion of Saints." The plan called for the new window to be installed on or before All Saints Day 1949. It turned out to be a splendid window of outstanding artistic merit and it was a perfect reflection of Galaty's "catholic theology" whose input in the content of the window is quite evident. Below the image of the enthroned Christ, crowned like a king and dressed like a priest, was a priest dressed in a chasuble (Chasubles were not yet being used at All Saints!) standing before an altar, flanked by a deacon and subdeacon in dalmatics, the long wide-sleeved garments worn by deacons as the counterpart of the chasuble. Below the priest was a mother pelican feeding its young, the common medieval symbol of the "Sacrifice of the Mass." With the contract, Willet agreed to produce proposals for the remaining eight windows. The All Saints window was installed in the rear west window, opposite the door from the entry way into the nave. This made it a very prominent statement because anyone who entered the church was immediately confronted by it.[145]

In the course of his first year, Galaty made a key innovation to the service schedule. He instituted a family service. It was scheduled at 9:15 a.m. on the third Sunday of the month. It was always a Holy Eucharist and was family friendly. This meant that it was somewhat shorter than the standard parish Eucharist on the first Sunday of the month, largely because of a more modest musical offering. Family services were coming into vogue in the Episcopal Church around the nation, responding to the resurgence in family life and values, not to mention the growing number of children in the aftermath of the war. Besides appealing to the family, it was also a place to make liturgical innovations. As 1948 ended, All Saints experienced its first Midnight Christmas Eucharist, beginning at 11:30 p.m. A children's service preceded it at 4:00 p.m. It was an instructed Eucharist, that is, a narrator explained the service as it was being performed. The instruction was read by Dr. Ralph Wardle, professor of English at the University of Omaha. Dr. Wardle, being a true Shakespearian, must have made this a most eloquent experience. Galaty explained that these two services would give the spiritual meaning of Christmas to the children and their parents who then would have Christmas Day free for the family.

In yet another change to the Sunday service schedule, he attempted to reintroduce a service of evening prayer. It was to be followed by a lecture given by the rector. His first topic was entitled "On the Life of the

145 The Ritche memorial also included a funeral pall, again is signal of Galaty's attempt to advance the ritual of the parish, purple with an elaborate Christ the King on its upper side.

Lord." As a lecturer, Galaty proved proficient and was invited by Omaha University in 1948 to provide a course on the Old Testament.

Galaty's formation in addition to providing him with a strong sense of liturgical revival, pointed him toward social ministries. In the church's new orientation of social ministry, the aim was not so much high-profile pronouncements, as it had been for Bishop Shayler's ministry, as it was to actually work on a significant social project in the city in order to make something happen. Galaty quickly found a role on the board of directors of the Child Welfare Association. In 1948, Mrs. E. C. Reynolds, the wife of his junior warden, was participating on this important civic board and must have facilitated Galaty inclusion on the board. This gave him the added satisfaction of "cominstering" with his laity in the work of the community.

His other community ministry, as he saw it, was with the Eighteenth Citizen Marine Battalion based at Fort Omaha. The battalion included young men from the parish as well as from a broad cross-section of the city. These young men were part of that generation that had missed the war, but which were affected by the residual patriotism. So they joined up and moreover they got to play baseball and were paid $10 a month. On November of 1948, 125 reserve marines in uniform attended church services, dividing themselves between All Saints and St. Cecilia's to mark the one hundred seventy-third anniversary of the United States Marine Corps. The size and discipline of the Omaha unit received special praise from the secretary of navy. The *Omaha World-Herald* quoted the secretary of navy commending the unit: "Although situated nearly 1,500 miles for the seaports of the Pacific and 1,200 from the Atlantic coastal cities, it has one of the first and largest Naval Reserve Marine Corps Training Centers commissioned in the postwar period."[146]

His local involvement in community affairs was complemented by a strong advocacy for the national church. The national office of the church launched an ambitious program in the postwar setting as it benefitted from increased funding and from renewed vision of American life. The success of the war effort and a national economy, which had moved forward instead of slipping back into recession, produced the belief that a national effort on the part of the church would pay off as well.

At the General Convention of 1943, a canon was passed, which required the presiding bishop to tender his resignation from his previous jurisdiction to take effect on the date that he assumed the office of presiding bishop. This had the effect of making the office a full time job for the first time. Up to this time, the office was limited to "presiding" at legislative and liturgical functions such as at the meeting of the House of Bishops or

[146] *Omaha World Herald*, September 3, 1949.

at the consecration of new bishops. This was a signal that the Episcopal Church expected the presiding bishop to be a national executive. Henry Knox Sherrill, the bishop of Massachusetts, was the first to be elected under this canon, taking office on January 1, 1947. While the presiding bishop, he organized the Episcopal Church Foundation and established the Seabury Press. Sherrill was the founding president of the National Council of Churches from 1950 to 1952 and one of the presidents of the World Council of Churches from 1954 until 1961. He resigned as presiding bishop in 1958 for reasons of health.

During Sherrill's tenure the Episcopal Church successfully projected a national image disproportionate to it actual size. In 1948, at the height of radio's power, the national church launched a sophisticated radio broadcast. Galaty announced the program in *Church and Home*: "The Episcopal Church Goes on the Air, KBON 'Great Scenes from Great Plays.' The effort was launched on October 1, with Cyrano de Bergerac, starring Walter H. Hampden. It reached seventy million listeners and cost $15,000 a week. The Episcopal Actors Guild, including such names as Basil Rathbone, Beatrice Straight, Jane Cowl, Ann Seymour, Boris Karloff and Joan Caulfield, lent the series their services. Future productions included 'The Corn is Green,' 'The Barrets of Wimpole Street,' 'Dark Victory,' 'On Borrowed Time' and 'Little Women.'" The series earned a high Hooper rating. Galaty saw to it that All Saints budgeted $850 in 1949 to support the series.

Galaty proudly announced to the parish that it would be the host of two national church functions: Rev. R. K. Yerkes and Rev. Don Fenn would present a workshop on the racial question. Galaty editorialized, "It is a crucial problem because it brings to the forefront the actual differences between peoples. We are all one family with one Father in heaven rather than divided." At the first of the workshops, priests were to attend from the fifth, sixth, and seventh provinces, an area encompassing everything west of Chicago with exception of the Eighth Province, the province that lay along the Pacific coast. The second workshop, "The Church in Urban America," was on a topic that related very directly to All Saints.

During Passion Week of 1949, Galaty hosted Rev. Canon Frederick Hood in the parish. Hood was principle of Pusey House at Oxford, England's noted Anglo Catholic seminary. He was on a national tour, and it was explained that he was an old friend of Galaty's, which made his stop here possible. Hood's tour began with a series of sermons for Holy Week to be preached at St. John the Divine in New York City. Galaty remarked to the parish that its ability to host such a distinguished visitor reflected well on its importance as a parish. While in Omaha, Hood also spoke to the city's Cosmopolitan Club and to the faculty of the University of Omaha.

The biggest impediment that stood in the way of Galaty's ambitions was the disrepair of the parish's buildings. As we have noted, they had suffered from deferred maintenance caused in the first place by the financial crisis that had begun as early as 1926 and when that crisis had abated from the conviction that the parish should be debt free. If, in 1947, Clayton could declare the parish debt-free, it was in part because of a non-monetarized debt of deferred maintenance. Galaty set to work on the problem stirring the vestry into action. It was action that the vestry was, in fact, inclined to take. As part of the administrative reorganization, a building and grounds committee was formed, consisting of Chester W. Cunningham, Dana C. Bradford, Henry D. Kosman, and Harrison Peddie. The chairman of the group was Hyle Burke.

As the canvass for 1949 approached, Galaty summarized the work done thus far.

> During the past year the Building and Grounds Committee has installed fire protection equipment, finished off the two basement rooms in the Mackay Memorial Parish House, recondition the heating plant in both buildings; had the sexton clean and wax the floors and woodwork in the church and parish house, repaved half of the rectory driveway and cleaned the rectory.

In other words, things were beginning to be somewhat shipshape. The cost at that point had amounted to $1,950, which at the time was a significant expenditure. Next year, the plans called for repairing the gutter and tuck-pointing the brickwork of the church and the parish hall, which has been affected by the elements. On the interior of the church, the list included decorating, installing radiator shields, painting the window frames and sashes, fixing the air vents, and in Wattles Hall, repairing, painting, and enlarging the vestment lockers.

When the annual meeting convened on January 25, 1949, it did so with a raft of detailed reports from the vestry's committees and from the Womanhood that were unequaled by anything in recent memory. Looking ahead into 1949, Galaty, in a lengthy report to the annual meeting, said,

> The vestry looks forward to completing the maintenance of the church building by tightening the north window which leaks and repairing a leak in the northwest corner. Once this is done, if our finances permit, we hope to redecorate the church. This is badly needed as you all can see. We have been given a substantial gift for this purpose but could use a few more.

The proposed budget for the coming year was $27,916. It included $1,500 for repairs, $850 for national radio broadcast, a diocesan assessment of $1,500, and a contribution to the diocesan mission budget of $3000.

Changes Begin to Register

Gilbert Carpenter stepped down as senior ward, though he agreed to continue on the vestry. Clarence Spier stepped up as senior warden, and Ned Reynolds became junior warden. Milton Clark who had been clerk of the vestry for twenty years resigned, and Harry H. McDuff was elected clerk of the vestry. This new configuration of the vestry seems to represent a confirmation of Galaty's attempt to move All Saints into the future. The impact of Galaty on the parish was beginning to register. In the vestry minutes of March 1949, under the hand of the new clerk, McDuff, comments made by Galaty are identified as having been made by "Father Gordon." This is a noteworthy signal of the direction and progress of Galaty's program. On the one hand, the catholic-sounding title father is used for the first time at All Saints. It would go into abeyance during the tenure of Mr. McCallum, only to return with "Father Pete," during the rectorship of Charles Pedersen, another Berkeley Divinity School graduate. It is also important to see, however, that this is not only a move in a catholic direction but also a move toward informality, as it made use of Galaty's first name. Mackay and Clayton had been "doctors" and Casady a "mister" as would be McCallum, preserving the decorum of polite society.

After the urgent issue presented by the state of the parish's buildings came the issue of the music program. The aging Dr. Simms, now eighty-five, was having trouble filling the needs of the parish as they were, let alone the needs created by the new directions in which Galaty hoped to take the parish. High on his list was the newly identified need for a "children's music program." At the June 10 meeting of the vestry, the music committee proposed a search for a new organist, preferably a younger man who can work with children. Richard Duncan, who had been hired as an assistant to Simms, seemed to be the obvious choice. By January of 1949, the committee announced the plan that they expected Simms would retire in June and that a search was beginning for a new organist choirmaster. Simms tendered his resignation on February 15, 1949, now being eighty-seven with an incredible record of fifty-four years of service in the parish. Duncan turned down the position, and so the search was extended outside of the city. The search led through Chicago to Eau Claire, Wisconsin. It is not without significance that the small cathedral at Eau Claire, which was at the center of the catholic movement in the Episcopal Church, was where it stopped. At a specially called vestry meeting on July 17, the music committee recommended that the young musician who was working for the cathedral by the name of Cecil Neubecker be hired. He was skilled both as an organist and as a voice teacher. He was, at the time, pursuing a master's degree, a thing that the contract with All Saints encouraged. The contract was lengthy including such details as offering a free voice lesson to any child in the parish whose voice was outstanding.

He arrived on September 1 and stayed at the rectory until the apartment in the new Carl Wilson housing development on Florence Boulevard would be ready for him at the end of the month. Until then, he had left his family, a wife and young son, in Eau Claire. His salary was set at $2,400 per annum, and the vestry agreed to provide moving expenses. With his arrival, it became apparent that the cost of the apartment would strain his budget, so Galaty provided him with an additional $15 a month from his discretionary fund, a sum that Galaty hoped that the vestry would assume by increasing Neubecker's pay before long. Galaty introduced him to the parish in a letter dated August 29, 1949, sent to all members of the parish. In the letter, he expressed the high expectations that he had for Neubecker. "Everything possible should be done to encourage members of the congregation to join the choir. Arrangements should be made as early as possible to introduce Mr. and Mrs. Neubecker to the congregation and the community."

In the same letter, Galaty spoke of a second initiative, which would affect the new program year. Work would begin on the church and Wattles Memorial Hall, which was largely aimed at facilitating the church school and the fellowship programs of the parish. The plan had been painstakingly prepared with the help of the architectural firm, Steel, Sondheim, and Steel. Actual work would begin after the annual meeting and would cost an estimated $25,000.

The church school was headed by Ms. Eleanor Sprague who had been in that position for many years. Now sixty-three, she very much desired to retire but had agreed to continue as religious educational director until her vacation while the parish looked for a replacement. The parish had trouble finding room in the parish's facilities for the growing number of young children and for someone to replace Ms. Sprague who, nevertheless, continued to soldier on. As the end of 1949 approached, the head of the Education Committee, Ralph O. Bartling, floated the idea to the vestry that an assistant priest be hired who would divide his time between Christian education, calling and office work. After a brief discussion, the proposal was tabled for the time being. Unspoken was the difficulty of finding the money that hiring an assistant would require. Despite not being able to find a new director and continuing to make do with space on hand, the church school continued to flourish with 21 teachers, 6 substitute teachers, and 186 pupils.

Two significant dedication ceremonies would bring a bright note to the fall of 1949. The long anticipated Ritchie Window, which had cost $4,962, was installed and was dedicated on All Saints Day by Bishop Brinker. Just before that ceremony, a memorial plaque was dedicated in memory of Margaret Helen Raffin, 1896 to 1946. Her death had resulted in a bequest, which helped create the momentum Galaty needed to keep his ambitious program on track. Margaret, who had never married, left her life savings to the parish. Margaret's parents had both emigrated from Scotland but had met by attending All Saints in Omaha. They both continued to be active at All Saints, particularly with the music program. Margaret was their only surviving child. She attended Brownell Hall for two years and transferred to Central High. She attended the University of Nebraska for one year. She was a librarian at the Omaha Public Library and later as the Secretary of the Veteran Administration, which had offices in Lincoln and Omaha. At the memorial service on October 16, the bulletin reported: "Margaret Raffan loved All Saints as did her parents. When she died, she bequeathed her life savings to the church." Her bequest, which amounted to $6,000, was used to establish a rectory fund. The picture of the rectory, located at 4818 Douglas Street, was printed on the card as well as Margaret's picture.

These two bright spots could not, however, overcome the growing anxiety that came with a need for a loan to do the work needed on the parish's buildings. The vestry, at its October 12 meeting, faced up to the task of paring down the list of work that was to be done on Wattles Memorial. The new list, which was presented at the November meeting, added up to a sum of $18,179, hauntingly similar to the mortgage the parish carried through the Clayton years. With it came a hand-penned letter dated November 8 from the Women's Auxiliary, signed by Maude A. Dreibus. She informed the vestry that the auxiliary would contribute $3,000; and its treasurer, Helen K. Shukert, was authorized to write the check whenever they were ready for it. This is a rather extraordinary gift, considerably larger than the typical gifts from the auxiliary for various parish, diocesan or community causes. It must have come from money the auxiliary had salted away, which rectors often suspect is there, but seldom get their hands on. The sudden appearance of this gift is a strong affirmation of Galaty's effort to clean up the parish's buildings and otherwise improve them.[147] Headed by Mrs. Murray Champine, who had replaced Mrs. George Morton at the beginning of the year, it represented an important group of parishioners and this has to be seen as an important vote of confidence. Having duly received the check, the vestry reduced its borrowing to $15,000, significantly below the $18,000 that it had anticipated in October.

Joining the Fifties

The end of the forties arrived at last. Omaha's new mayor, Glenn Cunningham, an Episcopalian, was midway through his term. The NCAA had moved the college world series to Omaha Municipal Stadium, later to be known as Rosenblatt. The city had become the nation's leading meat supplier, generating an annual business exceeding $5 billion and was well on its way to exceeding Chicago as the largest livestock yards in the world. The federal government had transformed the closed Martin Bomber plant located at Fort Crook into an air force base, naming it Offutt, after the young Omaha pilot killed in action in World War I. One minute after midnight on November 9, 1948, the Strategic Air Command came into existence under the leadership of Gen. Curtis LeMay. With that, Omaha had become an insider of the Cold War that no one really quite understood.

At the annual meeting in All Saints parish hall, held on January 14, 1950, the new organist choir director, Cecil Neubecker, recounted the beginnings he had made with the music program and the progress he had had in his attempt to attract choristers from within the parish. The rector, beginning his third year at All Saints, went on to present a glowing report about the new phase of work on the buildings which was about to be launched. The footnote to the report was that All Saints property was to again be mortgaged, this time to the tune of $15,000. While this was the parish's only debt and not disproportionate to the prospects of the future, it was clearly a jolt to the parish who had less than three years ago managed to get out from under a crushing mortgage. Nevertheless, the early months of the year passed with a deceptive calm as work got under way.

Well into the Cold War and having celebrated the success of breaking the Berlin Blockade, there was, however, little sense that a Cold War

147 The president of the auxiliary was Mrs. Murray Champine. She replaced Mrs. George Morton on January 10, 1949. Other officers were Mrs. Harold Peterson, vice president; Mrs. P. J. Dreibus, corresponding secretary; Mrs. E. R. Vierling, recording secretary; and Mrs. G. E. Shukert, treasurer. *Omaha World-Herald*, January 10, 1949.

could actually intrude upon everyday life. When North Korea crossed the Thirty-eighth parallel on June 26, it remained for most business as usual. Galaty had pushed very hard the past year to advance the parish into the state of readiness, which he considered necessary to meet the opportunities that the new era presented the Episcopal Church. He was ready for a rest. As he left for a summer vacation in Michigan, he hastily visited with Bishop Brinker and then with his senior and junior wardens about the vague possibility that Omaha's Eighteenth Marine Infantry Battalion might be mobilized. The *Omaha World-Herald* on July 20 made a routine announcement that the marine battalion was about to hold its summer camp. The article explained that the unit would be flown from Offutt Air Force Base to Little Creek, Virginia. There the reservists would get regular pay and have weekend liberty in Norfolk. The article indicated that there were still openings for physically qualified men, ages seventeen to thirty-two, and that they had until Saturday to sign up. There was no indication in the article that if you signed up, you might actually go to war.

Only well into his vacation had word come to Galaty that the Omaha unit would, indeed, be mobilized and him with it. The departure of the battalion for Camp Pendleton was set for August 26. Upon receiving news, Galaty had quickly sent a proposal in identical letters to Bishop Brinker and to the parish wardens, Clarence Spier and Ned Reynolds. In it, he asked,

> (1) That I be granted a leave of absence for a year. (2) That a *locum tenum* be brought in for this year. (3) That if it is at all feasible I be permitted to rent the rectory during this year and arrangements be made to rent other suitable quarters for the *locum tenums*. (4) At the end of a year, this arrangement be reconsidered in the light of the situation at that time.

As he ended the letter, he wrote, "I regret very much that this situation has arisen and I pray that it will be temporary. At present we leave on August 16 for Camp Pendleton."[148]

Spire advised the bishop that it was better that this letter not be presented to the vestry because it would certainly not be approved, and that if it became an official part of the minutes, it might make other possible offers more difficult. Moreover, Clarence Spier confided his doubts at the time to the bishop, saying,

148 Galaty's letter to the bishop is in the diocesan archives.

> I believe it was evident that Mr. Galaty is quite anxious to enter the service and upon being pinned down as to his desires in the matter he was rather evasive and indefinite. The most that he would say was that, of course, anyone would prefer to remain with his family and that he considered the work at our parish challenging and presenting great opportunity.[149]

When the vestry did meet on August 6, with Galaty presiding, two motions were passed, both made by the junior warden, and therefore, likely representing Spier's opinion as well. The first motion was that a committee be appointed to work on securing, "if possible, a deferment of Reverend Galaty from active military duty." The motion carried unanimously. Then Spier moved, with Reynolds seconding, that if Galaty was called up that he be given a leave of absence as rector from September 1 to December 21. At this point in the discussion, Galaty stated that if the motion was passed granting him a leave of absence, he would give his letter of resignation to the bishop effective December 31, 1950, should the leave of absence prove insufficient. The motion was passed unanimously. On his part, Galaty dutifully gave the vestry a letter of resignation to be activated should it be necessary. In it, he said, "I find that it will be impossible for me to return to my duties as rector of All Saints Church, Omaha, Nebraska, at the conclusion of my leave of absence. I, therefore, tender my resignation as rector of All Saints Church to take effect as soon as it is acted upon by the vestry of All Saints Church."

The vestry meeting had, in fact, taken three hours. Clearly, there were some strong differences of opinion that were thoroughly aired. From the vestry's point of view, it found the problem of raising money back in its lap. We have already noted its reluctance to carry out an Every Member Canvass in 1947 without a rector, even though it ended up being successful in doing so. But now, the circumstances for doing so were considerably more formidable. Galaty had pressed them into borrowing $15,000 for maintenance work and had set the goal for the general canvass at $29,000, representing a substantial increase. Galaty was sensitive to the predicament that he had put them in and used it as an explanation to the chief of naval chaplains why he ought to be deferred. The unanimity that resulted at this meeting was the kind that comes when a vestry decides that the stakes are so high that it cannot afford to settle for anything less. The operating rule was no one goes home until we have found a position that we can unanimously support.

---

149 Spier's letter to the bishop is in the diocesan archives.

On August 8, Galaty provided the vestry with a cover letter for his resignation. In it, he said: "It is with regret that I take this step for the months at All Saints Church were happy ones in my life. I want to take this occasion to express my appreciation for your cooperation and enthusiasm in developing a sound program in the parish while I was your rector. I also want to wish you well for the future."

On Sunday, August 13, Galaty handed out a statement at the 9:15 a.m. family service, the service that he had instituted and that in all likelihood gathered some of those in the parish who were most deeply attached to him. In that statement, he told the congregation that All Saints Church is one of the first parishes in the country to be called upon to make an adjustment to the declared war. "A half dozen men from this congregation are being mobilized with the Marines in ten days . . . Among those to be called up is your rector." Galaty goes on to explain that this presents the parish with various problems and that he had met with the vestry the previous Saturday. He explains at that meeting that a plan had been worked out, which granted him a leave of absence from the parish, but that he had given Bishop Brinker a letter of resignation, which the bishop was empowered to accept "whenever he and the vestry feel that it would be for the best interest of all concerned." He stresses that "it was not the vestry which had asked for this letter of resignation to be placed on file," but that he who had suggested it, "for I love All Saints Church and want to see her grow and develop through the years. If my absence—even though enforced by the government for military reasons—should in any way impede or hinder such growth and development, I would be the first to say to the vestry, "accept my resignation and get a new rector." He concludes his statement by asking the congregation to remember for a moment that the church belongs to Almighty God.

> It is His church—not yours or mine, and this is His parish—not yours and mine. For two and a half years, He has brought us together, and now He is separating us—temporarily we all hope. This temporary separation is a test of my ministry here and of your response to it. The question is, have I brought you closer to God? Have I made Him more real and personal to you? If I have, then when I am gone you will still worship and adore Him every Sunday in His Church. You will follow Jesus Christ and will work and pray and give for the spread of His Kingdom.

Thirteen days later, Friday night August 26, the officers and men of the Marine Corps Reserve Eighteenth Battalion assembled at Fort Omaha and boarded a special train which would take them to the West Coast. By Monday morning, they would be at Camp Pendleton. The *Omaha World-Herald* reported:

> Like good fighting men, the battalion left with a prayer on their lips. Before shoving off Major Glenn E. Martin of Council Bluffs, battalion commander spoke briefly. Then their chaplain, Lt. Comm. Gordon B. Galaty, led them in prayer. It was hard to say good-bye and to hold back tears as wives and families and sweethearts bade their loved one farewell.[150]

On September 1, shortly after arriving at Camp Pendleton, Galaty sent a letter to Bishop Brinker. In it, he describes his continuing effort to get a release from duty and described how things were going. At the end of this letter, he painted a vivid picture of the first contingent of his unit leaving for the war zone.

> I was with this group for the last couple of hours and am writing to their wives and parents. They are just kids–few with previous combat experience or training. It was like seeing David or John or Peter go. Does the Padre do any good? I don't know, but I know that the other offices couldn't take it. They came down said good bye and ran away—to cry. Only hardened NCO's, who had to stand by for other assignments, stayed but they clammed up and refused to talk for fear of crying. I mingled with them—took last minute messages—many, etc. to send home. Scared, I'll say they were and so was I. May God be with them. Do you see why I can't ask to get out.

The event was registered back home as well in the *Omaha World-Herald*. In a story under the headline, "Untrained Son Sent to Korea: Omaha Mother Wonders Why," a mother recounts that early in the morning of August 30 she had received a call from her son in San Diego. "He was crying," his mother said. "Have you ever heard a grown boy cry? He said: 'Mom, do something—I am being shipped to Korea, and I don't even know how to handle a gun." Galaty had found himself responding to the mother's frantic inquiry in a letter dated September 14. "This much can be said for those who fixed the policy, they not only had to think of your son, but also the thousands of their sons who have already been sent to Korea. The answer to your question . . . lies in recognizing that our

[150] *Omaha World-Herald*, August 26, 1950.

armed forces have been so cut down due to the economy that we do not have enough men available to handle the situation in Korea."[151]

Having been offered the use of a house on the base, Galaty moved his wife and children to Camp Pendleton on September 28. Nevertheless, it appears that Galaty continued to work diligently on being discharged in a timely manner, which would allow the vestry not to have to act on his letter of resignation. The vestry seems to have believed that he was continuing to work on a discharge as it held a review of the prospects of his release at its September 13 meeting. The minutes note that there was a "discussion of Reverend Galaty's situation in the armed services and of the prospect of his return to the parish." After the discussion, the vestry made provisions for Reverend Tyner for supply for the rest of the year.

In a letter to Brinker on September 14, Galaty reported, "I did send a personal letter to Chaplain Salisbury offering to request a deferment if the Chaplains' corps did not need me." Galaty must have felt that he had made some headway, even though it was becoming clear that a discharge would not come before the December expiration date of his leave of absence. In October, the vestry received a letter from him, asking that his leave of absence be extended. There is no record in the minutes as regards the nature of the discussion, but it was likely that Galaty might have thought at that time that he would be out the service by April or May. Given Spier's penchant not to put into the minutes anything that could later be used to make the vestry's job more difficult or, we might add, subject to question, we can assume that there was again considerable discussion.

There were various efforts in the parish to come up with a solution to the problem. There was an attempt to hold a brain storming session in the parish under the sponsorship of the women's organization. Galaty wrote about it in a letter to Brinker:

> I was informed that the vestry was advised or urged not to attend the "brain storming" meeting in October. The women covered it up by getting Mr. Trimble and Mr. Carpenter to attend at the last moment. I also was told that the wardens declined to make arrangements for the layman, Mr. Perrin, assigned to All Saints, to come and address them. I regret very much that this attitude prevails among a small group of the vestry. I do not feel that it is the true attitude of the congregation, and herein lies the basis for all the tension. This is why I am so eager to return to All Saints. For I feel that we are at a cross roads and

151 *Omaha World-Herald*, September 20, 1950.

> the old parish can now be brought into the fold and made a truly Episcopal Church.

Further evidence of the tension appears in a couple of letters appended to the November minutes. There is a copy of a letter to Spier from the Chancel Guild, which reads:

> Being cognizant of a certain amount of uneasiness among the members of All Saints Church, the Chancel Guild, as a most vitally interested body of the church, wishes it to be known to each member of the vestry that it is their desire to have Mr. Galaty retained as their rector and his leave of absence extended.

A similar letter was sent to the vestry's clerk, McDuff, from the Business and Professional Women:

> We know that Mr. Galaty has done excellent work in building up of our church. Also, we all feel very strongly that we should hold the position open for him the same as the stores, the banks, the telephone company, and other concerns are doing for their employees who are called to service. We realize, as does Mr. Galaty, the church cannot go on indefinitely without a rector. However, we do believe that his leave should be extended a fair and generous length of time. We are all willing to do our part to keep the church going.

The letter is signed by the president of the organization, Margaret Bromley (later Hughes), who explained that a secret ballot was taken at its last meeting; and all twenty-three present vote in favor to the proposal for a generous extension. The letter also is clear that the same letter had been sent by the guild to Bishop Brinker.

Brinker, who, like Spier, was cautious about getting things on the record that he did not want to live with, gave no indication that he had any position either way in regard to Galaty's tenure. His correspondence with Galaty was cordial and pastoral but never promised anything in terms of his position. Brinker's interest was, in fact, elsewhere. In anticipation of the parish's November vestry meeting, he sent a personal letter entreating the vestry to accept the diocese's asking of $4,752. He writes, "I am sure you realize without my mentioning it to you the great prestige All Saints has in the diocese and how important it is that the assigned quota be accepted by the vestry at least as a challenge to the people." He allowed that if the canvass does not reach its goal, an adjustment would be in order. It is the principle of the thing that is most important, he argued.

By December, Galaty had his answer from his superiors. In a letter dated December 12, 1950, Galaty reports: "I have been advised by Chaplain Salisbury, Chief of Chaplains, that in his opinion I have an obligation to the Navy which would not be fulfilled until May 1951. By that time he would hope to have secured another Episcopalian chaplain to relieve me. I could then be returned to inactive duty upon my own request, unless the situation changes radically. However, he does not give assurance that this policy will be carried out." Galaty is aware that this is a not sufficiently clear proposal to keep the vestry from acting on his resignation. Had he been able to say that he could be back at All Saints by June 1, it might have at least made the vestry pause. With this report, he added his own acquiescence to the vestry's inevitable action:

> Our hearts are heavy that anything should have disturbed this relationship. We are particularly sorrowful that the threat of another World War is the cause. The times however call for great sacrifices and I know that, with God's help, the members of All Saints Church will be in the vanguard as our Nation travels this road, following in the footsteps of our Lord and Savior, Jesus Christ.

Nothing in the sixty-six years of the parish's history prepared it for difficulty in which it found itself as 1950 came to an end. The termination of the rector's tenure had come with evident necessity, Zahner's dream job, Mackay's death, Casady elevation to the episcopate, Clayton growing disability, and his own insistence that it was time for a change. Nothing had as much potential to divide the parish since Woolworth's resignation as senior warden and his transfer to the cathedral. The parish was divided between those who had bonded with Galaty because of his catholic tendencies and those who had felt uncomfortable with his high church ways and were not sorry to see him leave. In the middle, the pragmatists worried that the forward movement of the parish, which had necessitated going into debt to the tune of $15,000, would be interrupted. Brinker must have suddenly been wondering if the pledge he had managed to get from All Saints vestry was worth the paper on which it had been recorded!

What is quite remarkable is that the parish did move on with little apparent cost. That is owed in no small way to Galaty's behavior. Once it was clear in the middle of December that he could not get a clear commitment from the service for his discharge, he ceased any attempt to extend his leave of absence, and he graciously thanked the parish and wished it and his successor well. Clarence Spier played a key role. He was a World War I veteran and had been a colonel in the Nebraska Home Guard during World War II. It was hard to accuse him of failing to be sympathetic with those in service. He had a reputation in his legal profession as tough but fair negotiator, though it seems from the beginning that Spier had little patience with Galaty's position. His second, Ned Reynolds, was a warm, friendly gentleman with an affinity for Galaty. His wife Laura had been instrumental in Galaty, gaining a position on the board of the Child Welfare Association. Yet throughout the whole process, Spier and Reynolds had never allowed anyone to see them divided. As they led the vestry, they never put the vestry in a position where it appeared to be divided; and, as usual, no decision was made until it could be recorded as unanimous.

Had Galaty been released as he had hoped in May 1951, it might have aggravated the division in the parish. As it was, he was not released until the end of 1952. In April of 1952, he was on board the USS *Philippine Sea*, an aircraft carrier from which sorties were attacking the shore batteries at Chongjin Harbor.[152] He was finally released from active duty on November 24, 1952. Immediately, he accepted a call to Emmanuel Episcopal Church in La Grange, Illinois. The suburban Chicago parish had nine hundred communicants when he arrived and 1,120 in 1965 just before he left. In early 1966, he retired because of his health and moved to Arizona, being fifty-five at the time. He died in April 1977 at age 65.

Galaty's Legacy

It might seem that after a tenure of no more than two and a half years, it would be impossible to speak of a legacy. But, in fact, in that brief time, Galaty left a legacy. In a tangible way, it might be represented by the Ritchie Memorial window, "the communion of the saints." More than just another pretty stained-glass window, it was a theological argument for the centrality of the Eucharist and a statement of its theology. It remains as the background for the chapel's altar to the present date. One of Galaty's few brides at All Saints has left a testimony to the way this window served her as a bench mark. Marie Savoda, a girl from a South Omaha Roman Catholic Czech family, and Bob Stitt, a boy from a North Omaha, Presbyterian family fell in love and were engaged to be married. They

[152] *Omaha World-Herald*, April 9, 1952.

sought a middle ground for themselves and their future family in All Saints. Galaty not only prepared them for the sacrament of marriage, but he also presented them for confirmation. They found, though Galaty's counseling and instruction, a spiritual home. Bob would soon be on the vestry and Marie on the altar guild. Some sixty-two years later, Marie would regularly visit with me about how much that particular stained-glass window meant to her. It helped her, she would say, feel at home and to reassure her that she is in the right place. Marie would added to her testimony how much she and her husband had like Galaty; and she would recall that when she had begun working in the kitchen with the ladies, she was aware of the chatter about the rector being too "catholic," which, of course, she would hasten to add with a wink was fine with her.

There were, of course, among the parish youth, those who had joined the Eighteenth Battalion to play baseball and get paid $10 a month, who would not forget that their rector had gone with them when they had been called up. While the Korean War was never a popular war, there was a general sense of pride in having been associated with someone who was willing to make such a significant sacrifice to serve his country.

His two initiatives, adjusting the parish facility to the needs of the postwar period and renewing of the music program, which had resulted in hiring of Cecil Neubecker, left permanent marks on the parish. While the physical efforts were in itself insufficient, they had managed to get the parish's leadership involved in envisioning the kind of plant that was necessary. It was easy for his successor to take it to the next level. Neubecker went on to create a music program that had a reputation of excellence citywide, and he continued to service All Saints for twenty-six years.

Back on Course

The Cold War, whose effect on American life was generally limited to putting a chill on attempts to bring about change to a number of social problems, which needed to be addressed, had blown All Saints off course. Now well into the fifties, the parish was without a captain. The impact of the fifties was already being felt in the destinies of Episcopal churches in Omaha. In 1944, William Reid had been called to replace the affable Ernest Secker in the combined fields of St. John's and St. Mark's. In short order, St. John's began to grow rapidly drawing from North Omaha neighborhoods, which were suddenly filled with young families looking for a church home. The highly personable Bill Reid, backed up by his untiring and immanently more practical wife, Emma, enabled a remarkable period of growth at St. John's. Extra chairs were regularly set up in the aisles to accommodate Sunday attendance. St. Andrew's in its small wood frame building in the inauspicious neighborhood at Forty-Eighth and Hamilton had moved on to become the third largest of the Episcopal parishes in the city surpassing the venerable St. Barnabas which sank to fifth place It was because of the family-centered program built by their new rector, Fr. Max Roberts. Following his lead, St. Andrew's made the dramatic decision to move itself to Eighty-Fourth and Pacific, the epicenter of Omaha's suburban development. In doing so, it would leave behind a decaying urban crossroad and plant itself in the center of a burgeoning upscale suburb.

From the perspective of Bishop Brinker, it was not a time to allow the diocese's number 2 parish to flounder. While the communicant numbers at All Saints were considerably less than those of the cathedral, its budget and, consequently, its contribution to the diocese was nearly equal to that of the cathedral and was far in excess of anyone else in the diocese. The vestry of All Saints had garnered from Galaty, if nothing else, a sense that the destiny of All Saints hung in the balance. Thus, both bishop and vestry faced the prospect of a search for a new rector with a sense of urgency and did not want it to become a "process." It is not surprising then that they met three days after Galaty's resignation had taken effect and issued a call to Rev. Mark Donald McCallum, rector of Grace Church Columbus, Nebraska. It is clear that the vestry resolution calling McCallum had been typed out before the meeting. The text, which was glued into the minutes, indicates that Judge Jackson B. Chase would move the resolution. The name of a seconder, however, had been left blank, presumably to allow for a touch of spontaneity. Chase, as it turned out, was absent because of unforeseen circumstances so his name was struck out and someone penned in the name of Mr. Hyle C. Burke. The same pen, which substituted Burke's name for Chase's, filled in the blank left for the seconder: Mr. Edward C. Pomeroy, who had served on the search committee. What was not left blank nor in need of any alteration was the result of the vote. The resolution typed prior to the meeting reported the result: "received the unanimous affirmative vote of the wardens and vestry."

Mark Donald McCallum was a native Nebraskan. He was born on October 21, 1905, in Morfield, Nebraska. Morfield was a small Western Nebraska village located along the Burlington Railroad's tracks. His parents, Duncan Ray McCallum and Nancy Gertrude Banta, soon moved the family a step further west down the Burlington tracks to Wauneta, Nebraska. Wauneta, named for the girl in the popular song "Jauneta," is a village in Chase County not far from Imperial, the county seat. It was there that McCallum finished high school and went on to try some courses at Colorado State Teachers College. He transferred, however, after a year to Nebraska Wesleyan University in Lincoln. In the fall of 1924, he became actively involved in all aspect of the school's life. He was class president his first semester. He went on to serve on the College Council and was president of the council during his senior year. He was honored by the college with an Oxford Fellowship. During his time as a student, he served as a lay pastor for Methodist churches at Wabash, South Bend, and Tamora, a clear signal of his growing interest in the ministry.

Mark McCallum Rector 1951-1971 in his new office
1964, br 1905 Morfield, Nebraska, d. 1988.

Following his graduation from Wesleyan in 1927, he matriculated to Garrett Biblical Institute in Chicago. Garrett was the Methodist Church's first seminary in the Midwest and had become quite prestigious. It was established in 1853 by the same church people who were instrumental in the founding of Northwestern University. The founders hoped that Garrett would be able to attract bright young men to the ministry and that school could shape in them ministries which would be noted for their education. Garrett was distinguished from the 1920s on for its advanced positions on race and women's ministries. This was, in other words, a long ways from the world of Wauneta, Nebraska!

In his junior year at Garrett, McCallum married Lucille Meek, of Ote, Nebraska, whom he had met at Wesleyan. Together they settled into life in Evanston for the duration of his senior year. As it turned out, a daughter was on the way. On May 29, 1930, as the academic year was ending, Lucille died in child birth, leaving McCallum with a daughter, Marilyn. The trauma caused his graduation to be delayed until September 3, 1930, after which he accepted a call to serve as assistant minister at the First Methodist Church in Decatur, Illinois. This worked only for a brief time. McCallum returned to Western Nebraska to be close to family and he took a job publishing a weekly newspaper in Scotts Bluff County. He lived in Lyman for nine years and edited and published its weekly. While there, he also edited and published the *Mitchell Index* and the *Merrill Mail*. While making his living in the newspaper business, he served as a supply pastor for a series of small Methodist churches in the area. During this time, he met Dolores Joyce Campbell of Wheatfield, Wyoming. They were married on January 19, 1935. Their first child was Kay, followed by, Kent, and Lynn. By 1944, Mark was the acting pastor of the First Methodist Church in Gering in addition to maintaining his publishing enterprises.

Somewhere in this time frame, he became interested in the Episcopal Church. St. Andrew's at Scotts Bluff was headed by this time by the charismatic Clyde Whitney. Clyde Whitney was a late vocation, something that was quite common after the war, and he had only recently been ordained. He had been a musician and bandleader prior to his decision to seek ordination and he brought to the ministry the charm and enthusiasm that one might expect from such a background. Nearby, Gearing had its own mission, St. Timothy's, which was served by Fr. William Stanton, a young energetic priest. He also served a new mission start in Mitchell. Besides the new mission at Mitchell, there was St. Mary's, the Japanese American church, founded and led by the revered Fr. Hiram Kano.[153] That is to say, by the forties, the Episcopal Church had established a high profile in Nebraska's panhandle. This, in part, must explain the lure that the Episcopal Church had for McCallum. The other facet of that lure was the general comfort at that time, which the Episcopal Church, even in an area as rural as the Nebraska panhandle, had in presenting itself as "a thinking man's church." McCallum, in fact, was a thinking man and his preparation for ministry at Garrett had done much to cultivate that aspect of his identity.

Father Whitney became McCallum's mentor, acting as a counselor and educator through the diocesan-based ordination process, which Bishop Brinker had established as the hallmark of his episcopate. Brinker's efforts in producing priests were so aggressive that young men came from as far

[153] Kano, by this time, was interned as a Japanese national in a federal prison, where he was kept for the length of the war despite the pleas of Bishop Brinker and others.

away as Philadelphia to serve as lay vicars in Nebraska's mission field in order to avail themselves of this path to ordination.[154] When it became apparent to Whitney that the bishop intended to send McCallum upon his ordination to St. John's, Valentine, he worried out loud about McCallum's fit. St. John's had most recently been ably led by an Anglo-Catholic priest. McCallum was not prepared for that style of ministry neither by way of knowledge nor temperament. Whitney in a letter to the bishop expressed this reservation and suggested that this might provide McCallum with a deep sense of insecurity in his first cure. The remedy that he and the bishop came up with was to send McCallum to Nashota House, the Anglo-Catholic seminary in Wisconsin, for a brief period of tutoring. This was, no doubt, some remedy to his lack of knowledge, but did little for his temperament, which would always remain staunchly Protestant.

McCallum was ordained by Brinker on January 21, 1945, and immediately began serving as clergy-in-charge of St. John's. He did acquit himself well at St. John's, staying for two years, before Brinker moved him to Trinity Cathedral in Omaha in June 1947. In Omaha, he lived with his family at 3852 Dewey and served as the assistant to the dean, Chilton Powell, as chaplain to Clarkson Hospital and as editor for the diocese's burgeoning newspaper. The latter assignment was, no doubt, Brinker's primary motivation for moving McCallum to Omaha.

McCallum's attraction for Bishop Brinker, in the first place, was his publishing experience. Episcopal dioceses around the country felt the need for a "newspaper" that looked like a real "newspaper" in order to convey the message that the diocese was a serious business. Brinker faced the particular problem of merging the newspapers of the Western missionary diocese, *Forward Together in Nebraska*, with that of the Diocese of Nebraska, *The Nebraska Churchman*. In 1946, the May issue of *Forward Together in Nebraska* was designated as volume 1, no. 1. It would be the paper of the merged dioceses; and McCallum would join its editor, Harold Shay, as the Departmental Editor. McCallum was there because of his expertise as a professional publisher, and it would be remembered by all that he himself was a "Western Nebraska man." Before long, *Forward Together in Nebraska* was edited by McCallum alone, and the name was changed to the *Nebraska Churchman*. The fluid situation in the diocese suddenly produced a vacancy at Grace Church, Columbus, and McCallum accepted a call. He began as rector on July 1, 1948. The care of Columbus also included the care of Trinity Church Schuyler. Two and half years later, All Saints Omaha was vacant and calling.

154 Roland Lindsey, who served at All Saints as an assistant for McCallum before returning to a church in Philadelphia, is an example.

McCallum Taking the Reigns

At his first vestry meeting on February 14, McCallum asked the senior warden, Clarence Spier, to preside, displaying a degree of caution. As the routine business came to an end, he asked the vestry to consent to mailing the Sunday bulletin to the homes of each member of the parish. These Sunday bulletins with a few revisions, which enabled it to carry some added information, would become McCallum's chief means of communicating with the parish. With the same cautious approach, McCallum set a slow steady pace for his first year at All Saints. He dealt with leftovers, like the ordination of J. S. W. Fargher, whom Galaty had recruited into the ministry. Fargher was from Missouri and was working in Omaha as a manufacture's sales representative when he became interest in the ministry. He was educated by the examining chaplains in Nebraska on the fast track that Brinker had established. After his ordination, he served at St. Thomas, Fall City, and before long moved on to serve a parish in Independence, Missouri.

Next, McCallum awarded God and Country awards to two of the parish's Eagle Scouts, Dick Barnhart and Larry Talmon, who had been prepared for the award by Galaty. He dealt with Walter Larson, the contractor who had been hired to repair and redecorate the rectory. In the end, he banned him from ever working for the parish again. Then he turned to negotiating the emotionally charged problem that had been created by the long-serving sexton, Jessie May. May, who lived in the old rectory, had allowed a member of his family who had been recently released on parole from the state institution for the insane to live with him. The concern was heightened by the fact that the old rectory was still being used for church school and meetings. McCallum's task was not made any easier by the fact that many of the women of the parish were of the opinion that Jessie had lost his ability to see dirt. By June, however, the course had steadied, and McCallum took a much-needed vacation.

With the arrival of September, the pace picked up rapidly. In the first place, the women of the parish were anxious about the fall. The vestry had received a letter from the Parish Guild, signed by Mardele Burke. The letter stated that, "The women are planning their annual Bazaar luncheon for this fall, and the Parish Guild feels that the interior of Mackay Memorial Hall is in such condition that it would be embarrassing to entertain outsiders." Where was the progress on such matters that they had been promised well over a year ago? By September 27, a special meeting had to be called to deal with the heating plant in Mackay Memorial Hall, for it had at last died. Hastily, arrangements were made to pipe heat in from the hospital as the parish was already doing to heat the church. By the November 13, the building and grounds committee reported on the progress and noted that the Parish Guild had taken over the painting of the kitchen in Mackay Memorial Hall. So much for their patience with the men.

McCallum was, however, ahead on one front. He had found a solution to the long pending resignation of Eleanor Sprague from her position as director of religious education. He reported that he had procured the services of Richard Miles as a part time employee, to serve as director of religious education. His monthly salary would be $40, with an additional $10 for car allowance. The attraction of the job for Miles was that it was an opportunity for him to explore a growing sense of vocation to the priesthood. Miles's vocation was quickly recognized by McCallum and fostered. By the end of the following January, Miles would tender his resignation, and McCallum would ask the vestry to join him in recommending him to the bishop for Holy Orders.

As it does every fall, the start-up was soon overtaken by the need to raise funds for the coming year. By the October meeting, the vestry concluded that the budget needed to be raised from $33,781 to $35,981. Joseph P. Muller, rather new to parish leadership, accepted the role of Every Member Canvass chairman. Joe and Bea Muller had come to Omaha from Rockford, Illinois, in 1932. Joe, after giving college a try, had gone into business with his father who owned a dairy in Rockford. In 1932, a Chicago Bond Company came to Joe's father and asked him to manage the Alamito Dairy in Omaha, which had gone into default. Joe's father agreed to the proposal if he could purchase the dairy. Receiving the company's consent, he asked his son to go and manage the business. Joe, who by then had a family of three young children, was reluctant but in the end agreed to give it a chance. Their oldest Lorenz, age seven, had recently been shot in the eye in an accident; and it would be necessary to leave him behind for surgery in Chicago. Nevertheless, the rest of the family moved to Omaha. Shortly after arriving, they set out on a search for a church in Omaha with little more to go on than that Bea's aunts had been Episcopalians. Bea's choice, after some searching, was All Saints, a few blocks away from the dairy on Leavenworth Street. Their son, Lorenz, joined the family before long and he was soon one of Dr. Clayton's acolytes. In 1937, the dairy's debt was paid off. A national fascination with the trademark "golden Guernsey" prompted the Mullers, now that they were out of debt, to build their own Guernsey herd and, consequently, to enter into farming. One of their first farms was located at Ninetieth and Maple, in close proximity to where All Saints would ultimately relocate. When it was sold to developers, the farm was moved to 108th and Fort. In the official records, the family is noted for the first time as communicants in March of 1939, which coincides with Joe's success as an Omaha businessman and his own more active participation in the affairs of the parish. The canvass that he led in 1951 was a remarkable success, and it put him in position to be considered for the position of senior warden the following year.

As 1952 began, the women were again up front pressing for change. At the annual meeting, the Women's Auxiliary Report was made by Kathryn Rhodes. She spoke out about "the need for expansion and for greater facilities for the church school, young people's work and parish activities." Then she called the meeting's attention to "a resolution of the Women's Auxiliary Council asking the vestry to take immediate steps to establish a building fund for the parish to meet the need for additional facilities." The women's concern was summarized in a graphic picture of the way the church school worked.

> At the present time the church school of 201 pupils and staff is divided into classes meeting in most inconvenient, time-losing locations. One Upper School class is meeting in the rector's office; another in the small front room on the first floor of Mackay Memorial; another in one of the classrooms of Clarkson Nurses' Home; another in the Rectors' Chapel. The prekindergarten department meets in the basement of Mackay Memorial, access to which is difficult, and the rooms themselves unlovely and unclean.

After receiving the report, the meeting proceeded to elect the successful Every Member Canvass chairman, Joseph P. Muller, as senior warden and the husband of the president of the Woman's Auxiliary, Varro H. Rhodes, as junior warden. It should be noted that both men were back by strong wives noted for their leadership in the parish.

After a year of wrestling with the building problem to little avail, and in spite of the remaining encumbrance on the property ($13,469), a new tack was taken. The vestry was asked at its January 30 meeting to authorize a new building committee with a building fund treasurer who would be authorized "to accept funds for a new building or for the improvement of the present building; to hold and invest them with the vestry's approval." However, it was understood "that no disbursements would be made without the sanction of the vestry." The Building Committee was headed by Joseph Muller. Its members included James Field, E. G. Pomeroy, Varro H. Rhodes, and M. C. Van Scoy. Arthur Pinkerton, a young businessman new to the vestry, was appointed the treasurer of the building fund. After approving the formation of the building fund, a motion was made to give the committee $1,000 from the general treasury. A discussion followed and was ended with a vote of seven to four rejecting the motion. This broke a long-standing tradition that the vestry did not register internal dissent in the minutes. If a vote was going to fail, it was not taken! This vote was duly noted. It was a clear signal of just how complicated the parish's building problem had become.

At the subsequent meeting in February, the vestry approved a motion to engage an architect for "future building as need develop." The Leo A. Daly Company offered to draw up a plan at no upfront cost and agreed to be paid only if the work went ahead at the standard architectural fee of 6 percent of construction. Turning from the building problem, the vestry approved a two-month vacation the following summer for McCallum in order that he would be able to avail himself of the opportunity to travel to Europe and authorized him to call an assistant. The salary for the assistant was set at $275 per month plus a $25 car allowance, pension, and living quarters, to start August 1, 1952.

By March, McCallum had offered the position to Mr. Roland S. Lindsay, a recently ordained priest who had been assigned to serve the mission in Bayard, Nebraska. Lindsey was one of many new priests who resulted from Bishop Brinker's aggressive recruitment. Brinker regularly preached on vocation to the priesthood in his parish visits. He established a "lay vicar program," whereby a man studied for orders under the Board of Examining Chaplains while servicing a church or a mission field as a lay vicar. Bypassing seminary education, allowed Brinker to recruit older men interested in the ministry as a late vocation and younger men not interested or equipped for seminary. Lindsay was an example of one of these younger candidates. He came from Philadelphia and worked as a lay minister in the Western Nebraska mission field, serving at Mullen and Hyannis. In exchange for his service, he was educated by the diocese's examining chaplains. For Brinker, this was a means for keeping vacancies in his hard to fill mission field at a minimum. The adequacy of these ministries was, as one might expect, uneven; yet over all, they seemed to serve the mission of the diocese rather well.[155]

Anticipating Lindsay's arrival in August, the parish leased a house for him on 2227 South Fifty-Ninth Street. Lindsey began his work as anticipated on August 1. His work was particularly aimed at expanding and improving the church school. By November, he could report that the church school now numbered 203, with an average attendance of

155 Barnes, William, *The Episcopal Church in Nebraska*, Omaha, 1969, p. 109.

143. Lindsey appears to have been a good assistant, but he submitted his resignation at the beginning of 1953, to take effect on July 31, meaning that his stay was just one year. The timing suggests that the cause of Lindsey resignation was the result of the growing commitment to build, which would have caused McCallum and the vestry to be nervous about whether an assistant's position could be funded. At his departure, it was announced that he accepted a call to St. Gabriel's in Philadelphia, where he continued to serve for the rest of his career.

By its regular May meeting, the vestry was ready to proceed with Leo A. Daly's offer to draw up plans for an addition to the parish's facilities. Cautiously, the vestry described the goal as a plan "to begin to meet the Sunday school needs of the parish." Leo A. Daly returned with a proposal, including tentative drawings at a special meeting on May 28. Daly's estimate on the basis of these drawings was that the project would cost $25,000 to $30,000. This first phase was conceived as a small addition that would come off the chancel of the church and connect to the back of Mackay Memorial House. It would provide a couple of new class rooms and a new sacristy. The proposed sacristy was an especially high priority among the women of the parish. The original sacristy off of the chancel had been lost when it was used to house the mechanisms for the Austin organ, a cost-saving measure at the time that allowed the parish to forgo a proposed addition to the building to house the mechanism. This money-saving move meant that the sacristy was relocated to the second floor of Wattles Memorial Hall. This required the members of the altar guild to traverse the entire length of the church, cross the narthex, and mount a flight of stairs in order to service the altar. An amazing inconvenience! The new sacristy was to be dedicated in memory of Mrs. George Morton, who served for so long on the altar guild and who had traversed that circuitous route more times than anyone else around. The following phases, which would require tearing down Mackay Memorial House, would add ten classrooms, an office, and a hall, which would be joined to the hall on the lower floor of Wattles Memorial Hall, giving the parish a hall at which they could seat more than two hundred.

On the advice of Joe Muller, the vestry postponed the push to raise the money to build until after the Every Member Canvass was complete. The launch date for the fund drive was to be the coming annual meeting in January. With the coming year's budget secured by a good canvass, those gathered for the annual meeting gave their support to the plan. Still cautious, the vestry waited for the following March before engaging Mr. Elliot of the Wells Organization, a national fund-raising organization with an Omaha office, to lead the fund drive. The goal was set at $75,000, and the fee to the Wells Organization was to be $3,500. The thought of raising $75,000, a year or two before, would have been unthinkable, and even now there was something quite daring in this decision.

The parish leadership for the fund drive was headed by Leonard E. Hurtz and James L. Paxton, Jr. In a handsome brochure, which had been produced with the help of the Wells Organization, the case was made for the building program with vivid pictures of the cramped and substandard spaces that were currently being used for the church school. The pictures of pretty little well-dressed girls and eager young boys attending to the instruction of their dedicated teachers in narrow carrels, basement rooms with low overheads or standing in narrow stairwells were calculated to spur action. The centerfold of the brochure was a rendering of the initial wing, which would provide a sacristy and two new classrooms. In the brochure, Hurtz declared: "The Opportunity is Now!" He explained that payments on the building pledges were to begin on July 1. Moreover, it was stressed that the word "pledge" would not appear on the card, and the card would be a simple expression of intent: "we will try to pay ______." The pace at which the plan was unfolding was to be decidedly slow and deliberate. There was a strong sense that the parish would not build before the money was in hand and that it would above all not incur any debt in the process. McCallum emphasized in his remarks for the brochure, "The vestry has determined further that the future will not be hampered by burdensome debts. Current income will be used in developing an expanding program to meet our increasing needs, not to service a heavy mortgage."

The summer surprise was that within five weeks the canvass had raised "pledges" amounting to $93,000, exceeding their goal by $18,000! The campaign had, in fact, outstripped Leo A. Daly's planning department for it was only with the arrival of September that they finished blueprints for the addition. Meeting on September 15, the vestry, encouraged by the success of the fund drive, voted to proceed not only with the first phase, but with tearing down the Mackay Memorial Hall and undertake the completion of the entire project. The estimated cost now stood at $101,000. The vestry accepted the bid of Shelton and Son for construction, Miller Electric Co. for electrical and John Anderson and Company for the plumbing. In order to allow work to begin in the fall, the vestry entered into an arrangement with U.S. National Bank to advance the parish money at 4.5 percent interest without a mortgage.

Ground was broken in October. The new building would have a brick exterior, matching that of the parish hall. It would be two stories high with a footprint, of thirty-five feet by ninety feet. This would add 6,200 square feet of new space and the upper floor of Wattles Hall would be turned into classrooms as well. On the north, the new addition would attach to the Wattles Hall, extending the capacity of the hall on the lower level of Wattles so it could seat 250 people. At the center of the new addition would be an entrance, appropriately Gothic in style matching the north entrance in to church. The entrance of the new wing would face Twenty-Sixth Street. Once inside of the new entryway, one would find a stairway to classrooms on the upper floor, a door opening into the parish hall to the north and one on the south to the parish offices. On the south end, behind the offices, was a new sacristy that opened into the chancel of the church.

The beginning of construction coincided with the annual effort to raise funding for the operation of the parish in the coming year. The Every Member Canvass chairman, Casper Whitney, outlined an extensive fall canvass. When the annual meeting came around, it was clear that fact that the parish was in the midst of construction, which would drag on until July, a total of ten months, had not harmed the parish's program. The treasurer reported that the past year had ended with all bills paid and a new canvass, which promised a successful year to come. McCallum reported that there had been more than fifty confirmations for the year. The parish now consisted, according to his report, of 1,125 baptized members, 920 communicants, and a church school enrollment of 161 children. Mrs. Gail Porter, church school superintendent, said in her remarks at the annual meeting that in spite of the building program, the church school program is going on. "The staff of the church school are doing a wonderful job in maintaining a high morale in the classes in spite of the handicaps created by the building program."

In March 1954, a full report on the Building Fund was made to the vestry indicating that the total building pledges paid after a year and a half had amounted to $39,258. Construction cost to date had amounted to $46,649. The difference had been made up by use of the revolving loan fund with the U.S. National Bank. The costs were now expected to total $105,984. This was an amazing and unprecedented response. One has only to remember that Galaty a few years prior was forced to borrow $18,000 to make basic repairs to the parish's building, a sum not yet paid off when the vestry began this new building program.

With the completion nearing, the vestry turned to the naming of the new facility. Apparently, there was no dominant donor to be consulted or honored. The past, whose "Mackay Memorial Hall" had been torn down to make way for the new structure, seems not to have such a hold as to require some notice; so after casting around, the vestry chose to call it "All Saints Parish House." This choice signified that the result was owned by the whole parish and that it was bravely oriented to the future not the past.

The total cost would reach $117,218, and the revolving loan would rise to $59,000. The good news was that the general budget, in spite of it being the end of the summer, had a large balance, $3,262. Expenditures were, in fact, nearly that much below last year's largely as a result of doing without an assistant and by McCallum's frugality. He, no doubt, operated with the conviction that the one thing that he did not want to do in the midst of a building program was to have to deal with an operating budget running into trouble. The restraint in 1954 made way for a more expansive plan for 1955. The canvass goal for 1955 announced in the October meeting of the vestry was to be a 7 percent increase over the past year. At the same time, McCallum announced that the church school would have a new leader, Ms. Cachules, a young woman who was presently majoring in religious education.

Much had happened during 1954 around All Saints. The year had marked the centennial anniversary of the founding of the Diocese of Nebraska. Clarkson Hospital had moved and sold its building, once Lord Lister Hospital, to Lutheran Hospital, giving the parish a new neighbor. Still, the focus in the parish was inward. It had turned the page and it was securely part of the Fifties. All Saints elder statesman, Robert Trimble, rose at the end of the annual meeting and asked permission to make some remarks before the meeting adjourned. Straightening his seventy-seven-year-old frame, he began with a smile,

> This meeting would not be complete without hearing from me. I attended an annual meeting in an Episcopal Church in California. They held their meeting in the dining room and that gave the people assembled a chance to applaud the reports and a better chance to discuss them and ask questions. We should really have a loud speaker so I could hear the reports. I want to complement the nominating committee. I think they made a very wise selection. I have been in this parish a good many years—during Mr. M. D. McCallum, then Dr. Clayton and Mr. Casady and back to the early days, there is no finer man than M. D. McCallum. The church has grown under his guidance. It takes tact and diplomacy—you need all those to keep members in the church satisfied. Mr. McCallum is on the job—he is getting skinny and run-down. We have to get him help; he has to have help. Our parish has grown. I used to know them all—don't know half of them by name now. I have a lot of respect for Mr. McCallum for carrying the load and I just felt moved to get up here and say so. Mr. Muller has

done a wonderful job. It is not an easy job being senior warden. A word about the altar guild ladies. While you are at home sleeping they are here getting the altar ready for the services. The church belongs to all of us. All Saints Church outshines all the churches—the women have done a wonderful job – its seems the women do all the work. I want to say my compliments to all the reports including those not read.

At Home in the Fifties

When 1955 arrived, it could at last be said that McCallum was at home at All Saints, and All Saints was at home in the fifties. The shakedown of the new building continued. There were problems with heating various rooms, with a couple of outside doors that fit so tight they resisted efforts to open them, and missing coverings on the stair treads to the second floor of the parish house. The vestry had withheld $500 from the payment to Shelton Construction until the work was done. The bank note held by U.S. National Bank needed to be paid off as soon as possible and the old mortgage of $18,000 for Galaty's work on the buildings was felt as a hindrance to the parish's future. Pinkerton, who continued to be in charge of the building fund, reported to the annual meeting that the building fund expected to collect $30,000 of due pledges. When those pledges came in, he concluded the parish would be short $17,000. Going into the summer of 1955, cash was low, and the list of things that need to be done long. Mr. Stitt advised that the windows in the east end of Wattles Memorial were in such bad condition that he suggested that they be bricked up! The issue of parking was a recurrent discussion at the vestry meetings. The last wrinkle was that the hospital across the street was charging parishioners 25¢ to park on Sundays. Remember the hospital was now Lutheran! Nevertheless, no one was registering any alarm.

The prospect of two memorial windows, one in memory of Dr. Frederick O. Beck, his wife Amy, and the other in memory of Clara and Oscar Goodman, provided a couple of bright spots for coming year. The bequest for the first had been received in March of 1952 from the estate of Dr. Beck. It provided for the purchase of an art glass window in memory of his wife Amy Lucille and himself to be consistent with the plan that had been adopted at the time of the commissioning of the Ritche window. The window had been set on the back burner, while the question of space for the Sunday school occupied the vestry's attention, but now it could be addressed. A second art glass window was commissioned by Gladys Hundley as a memorial to her parents, the Goodmans. In both cases, the theme of the window was developed from the propers of the 1928 Book of Common Prayer. The theme of the Beck window was a pictorial representation of the 1928 Book of Common Prayer lessons for Trinity Sunday, an eloquent three part sermon in glass and color. The theme of the Hundley window was drawn from the themes for the Feast of the Ascension. They provide an insight into McCallum who directed the execution of the windows. He had a very strong loyalty to the Book of Common Prayer. We might go so far as to say that the reason he had become an Episcopalian instead of remaining a Methodist was what he saw in the Book of Common Prayer a superior pattern of worship, a view widely shared in the Episcopal Church at the time. The Beck window was dedicated on Trinity Sunday in June of 1955. The Goodman window was dedicated on November 5, 1955.

The physical enhancement of the facility continued with a new set of doors for the main entrance of the church. The great wood doors at the entrance to the church were to be set off by a pair gold sculptured metal and stained-glass lancets presented to the parish by Mrs. Albert Pierson in memory of her husband, Ernest Pierson. Each of the doors would have the figure of an angel, and over the doors would be arranged three symbols representing prayer, worship and music. The effect was quite stunning, fit for the entrance to a spiritual fortress, as indeed the Victorian Gothic structure on Twenty-Sixth and Dewey presented itself.

As the parish entered the new year, two things continued to weigh on mind of the vestry: the backlog of debt and the fact that McCallum had been without an assistant since 1954 when Lindsey had resigned. Several leads were pursued, and finally McCallum had found a willing candidate. Leopold Hoppe was set to graduate in June from Seabury–Western in Chicago and was excited about the idea of returning to Omaha where he had been born and gone to school. In 1944, he joined the U.S. Navy and served until he was released in 1946. He had married Maxine Chapin from Omaha and enrolled at the University of Nebraska. He graduated in 1949 as a history major with the thought of continuing on into graduate studies. He enrolled in the prestigious University of Chicago to continue his studies, but gradually gravitated to the Federated Theological Faculty, originally Baptist, but by the forties, broadly Protestant. Hoppe had continued his evolution and, after two years there, took a third year at Seabury–Western. His journey was not that unusual in the postwar period when many found their way in the Episcopal ministry from the outside.

Mrs. Hoppe moved back to Omaha early to settle the family with the help of the vestry. After being ordained deacon on June 18 at St. James

Cathedral in Chicago, Hoppe arrived and made his first appearance at All Saints on Sunday, June 24. The following December, he was ordained to the priesthood at All Saints by Bishop Brinker.

By March of 1956, the balance owed on the debt was $24,000, with only $2,140 in the bank. Under pressure, the vestry raised the possibility that it should ask those who had made a three-year pledge to the building fund to extent their pledges to a fourth. The "Fourth Year Campaign" was launched in April. Gail Davis agreed to be the chair person and he defined the goals of the campaign: "Pay the note at U.S. National Bank, re-carpet and decorate the church, with other necessary repairs, such as new radiators, sanctuary lighting, etc." However, he continued: "It would not attempt to pay off the mortgage at this time. Any surplus, however, would go to reduce it. The goal was $35,000."

The drive was successful, and steady progress was made during the remainder of the year in reducing the note. By December 1956, the note was down to $6,000. As the new year began, the parish was still not out of the woods. The mortgage was due, and the parish's buildings continued to need work. Gale Davis sought to buy some relief for the parish by refinancing the mortgage. He turned to his own company, Guarantee Mutual Life Company, where he was a vice president. He secured a new mortgage for the parish of $24,000. The new mortgage allowed the parish to consolidate all of its debts and to have some additional capital with which it could deal with its more urgent physical needs. Bob Stitt was given the task of seeing through a redecoration of the parish's facilities. By May 12, 1957, the results were being widely praised in the parish, and the bill came to $16,774. Stitt's frugality and common sense had meant that the parish had gotten a lot for its money.

The slow but steady progress made during the year was, however, interrupted with the resignation of the newly hired assistant. Even though the vestry had assisted Hoppe by locating his family in Omaha prior to his completion of seminary, he had chosen to accept a call to St. Elizabeth's in Holdrege, Nebraska, and tendered his resignation to take effect at the end of the year. His tenure at St. Elizabeth's lasted through 1960.[156] By February, McCallum was once again pursuing new leads for an assistant. In March, a call was extended to Eldon C. Borell as assistant rector. The compensation offered was a salary of $4,500, a housing allowance of $125 to $135 a month and a car allowance. Borell made a counter offer, which

[156] Hoppe continued at St. Elizabeth's through 1960. He accepted a call to Grace Church, Ottawa, Kansas, where he also taught history at a local college. In 1973, he accepted a call to Good Shepherd, Kansas City, Missouri, and retired in 1989. He died in 2004.

the vestry declined, and in April, the search for an assistant was renewed. This was not the first time an assistant who had been offered a job turned down the job. It is clear that the parish had during this period a difficult time maintaining an assistant.

A new prospect was presented to the parish by Bishop Brinker. He had identified Jess Borg, a high school coach in Alliance, Nebraska, who Brinker thought was a great potential candidate for the priesthood. Warren Borg was born in Wakefield, Nebraska, in 1927, and he was a graduate of Wayne State College. Brinker managed to get the head master of Brownell Talbot to hire Borg as an athletic director. The missing piece of the puzzle was filled by convincing All Saints to take him on as a lay assistant. Borg began at All Saints on October 1 at a salary of $4,000 per year, a housing allowance not to exceed $135 per month and a car allowance of $600. He regularly attended vestry meetings, unusual for an assistant, and was in charge of the church school. He was ordained deacon on January 11, 1960. Shortly after his ordination to the priesthood, he accepted a call to St. Mark's in Omaha, a small historic parish located in the Florence neighborhood. While there, he led St. Mark's relocation to Sixtieth and Girard. His departure does not seem to have surprised or bothered McCallum or the vestry, who allowed him to continue to live in the house they had just purchased for some time. Assistants were expected to cycle through, and the parish conceived the "breaking in" of newly ordained ministers for their use in the larger church as part of its mission. Borg had stayed at All Saints for three years, rather a record for an assistant at that time. The relationship with All Saints and the Borgs would continue on and off over the years. After St. Mark's, Borg served as a chaplain at Brownell Talbot, and he returned to work as a part time assistant at All Saints, until he took a position in Houston, which entailed founding an Episcopal High School. After an absence, he returned to All Saints; and he, his wife, and some of their children rest in the columbarium at All Saints.[157]

McCallum, like Brinker, was keen on recruiting men into the ministry and quite successful. In the June 1959 edition of the *Nebraska Churchman*, McCallum ran the pictures of six men form All Saints who were in the process of becoming priests. Three were currently in seminary: Frank Faires, Charles Frandsen, and Robert Hall. Warren Borg, as we have mentioned, was studying in the field under the examining chaplains as he worked at All Saints. Arthur Staubitz and Jerry Jones, both of whom had grown up in the parish, were presently postulants. The impressive article

157 Warren Borg, 1927–2000; Annabel Lee Borg, 1929–1997, Collen, 1952–1987; and Kimberlee, 1956–1985.

explained that the parish maintained a theological education fund to assist such candidates in their studies.

Remarkably, the unity of All Saints held up throughout this effort to refashion its building and to create a staff that was capable of meeting the demands of the fifties. The numbers of communicants and annual giving grew during the period at a steady pace. As 1957 was coming to an end, McCallum could boast that the bishop would visit the parish for the third time that year for confirmation. The total confirmands for the year would be sixty, setting a new record. This was no mean feat. Trinity Cathedral, who faced the same problems as All Saints, had completed its new parish hall and church school in May of 1957. In the course of its project, Dean Barnhart resigned because of discord surrounding his leadership. The new dean, Robert Hewitt inherited the problems. Trinity's building project, also built by Leo A. Daly, was considerably larger than All Saints addition. The building, which replaced the cathedral's old Victorian parish hall, was twenty thousand square feet, nearly three times the size of All Saints addition. The total cost of its project was $300,000, and they found themselves underfunded by nearly $200,000. That was not the only bad news, for like All Saints, they continued to struggle with a Victorian building, which needed a lot of work to make it seem habitable to the taste of the fifties.[158]

Peace, Prosperity, and Then What?

The opportunity that the fifties presented had come so suddenly that it required a quick transition to take advantage of it. That meant letting go of a number of patterns of parish life that had existed for a long time. That transition was unsettling and created fissures within the parish community. The motto of the Eisenhower years was "peace and prosperity," and so it was in many ways. But many parts of American life did not participate in the prosperity. Even those that did had a growing sense that there was something more to be achieved. Like the country as a whole, religious bodies found that no sooner had they expanded and renewed their facilities, they were faced with a new round of questions about how they were to fill them and what they were to do with them. For many, the most challenging question was: were their improved facilities in the right place? An urban location, which that once provided a church with prestige, now saddled its members with the onus of a special out-of-the-way trip and the task at

158 Martin, Charles W., *The Church in the Middle of the Street 1838–1982*, Dilley Manufacturing Co. 1983, p. 76f.

the end of it of finding a place to park. Quietly, both the cathedral and All Saints began a discussion of whether they should remain where they were, and if they did, what kind of change they should make to their programs.

The discussion in Nebraska was fanned by a diocesan study. Returning from the annual council, McCallum explained to his vestry on May 14, 1956, that "starting in 1957 a survey of the diocese is to be made by the national council's Bureau of the Church to discover the strong and weak points in the diocese. Cost for the survey would be about $10,000 and it would take about 18 months to complete." The cost and the investment of time entailed in the proposed survey were an unprecedented challenge for the diocese, one that was not accepted without opposition. At the council of 1956, Brinker had behind him fifteen years at the helm of the diocese. He had been a judicious but forceful leader. He was, as we saw, on the spot when All Saints was in need of a rector, first because of Clayton's long in-coming resignation and then because of Galaty's precipitous resignation. Forcefully, he had told the vestry at All Saints in the fall of 1947 to proceed with an Every Member Canvass, even though they were without a rector. They objected, but in the end, they had done what he told them to do and thanked him for doing so.

The memory of his leadership was enshrined in a story that was frequently told to newcomers to the diocese so as to give them a clue as to what to expect from their bishop. Brinker, it seems, had advised a western parish in one of Nebraska's small towns to install a restroom in the church. When he showed up the next year for his visit, he asked to see the restroom. Finding it not done, he proceeded silently to vest for the service in a slow methodical manner. Having done so, with only minutes to spare before the service was to start, he proceeded to un-vest. Without saying a word, he walked out of the church, down the street to a filling station and used the restroom while everyone waited in the church. The next year when he returned, there was a restroom.

Bishop Brinker asked that the survey be approved and paid for by an assessment of $1 on each member of the diocese. So when it was all said and done, the council agreed to do what he had told them to do. The bishop asked McCallum to be the local director of the study. The temperaments of the two men were quite similar, and Brinker often chose McCallum as his point man. Through his work on the *Nebraska Churchman*, McCallum was well known in the diocese and was remembered as having originated and served in Western Nebraska where the survey was regarded with the most suspicion. McCallum accepted the task enthusiastically, but it is not clear whether he had any inkling of the impact that the study would have on All Saints and on his own life.

The head of the professional staff, which would carry out the survey, was Rev. Joseph Grasale Moore, the head of the National Council Staff of the Unit of Research. Moore was a priest of the Diocese of Chicago, ordained in 1930. He continued his education receiving a master's degree in anthropology from Northwestern University in 1946 and a doctorate in 1952.[159]

The competence of this study is impressive. The national church in the late fifties was at the high water mark of its prestige and of the resources that it had at its commanded. The survey made use of census tract material, local Chamber of Commerce material, and extensive parish surveys. The result was one thousand seven hundred sixty-eight pages, followed by eighty-two appendixes. It documented not only where the diocese was working but also where it was not. It provided an impressively detailed view of what the diocese was like at the close of 1957. The Diocese of Nebraska, it reported, was made up of seventy-four congregations, thirty-three parishes, thirty-eight missions, and three diocesan chapels. "In all three categories of membership, there has been a considerable net increase not only for the total diocesan area, but for both sections of the diocese. (The diocese had been divided east and west for the purpose of the survey.) Between the years 1936 and 1956, within the total diocesan area, the baptized membership had increased 70.7 percent from the 10,487 baptized members in 1936 to 17,904 baptized member in 1956; the communicant strength increased 52.8 percent, from 8,620 communicants to 13,175 communicants by 1956."[160] It provided a very encouraging picture of what the future might hold for the Episcopal Church in Nebraska, if the diocese could, indeed, build on this base. In retrospect, this survey measured what was very close to the high water mark of the diocese.

Based on the results of the survey of the Episcopal churches located in Omaha, the study concluded that the churches needed to work together in regard to the growing edges of the city. In 1958, the western limits of the city largely followed a north-south line along Fifty-Second Street. The

159 Moore attended both Seabury Western and Berkeley Divinity School. He also did studies at Garrett. By 1937, he was a deputy to the general convention. In 1942, he enlisted as a chaplain in the U.S. Army. He served as assistant professor and director of training (fieldwork) at Seabury from 1947–1951. His wife, Ruth, was an anthropologist. His research paper was published under the title "A Study of the Religion of Jamaican Negroes," 1953.

160 *A Study of the Episcopal Church in the Diocese of Nebraska*, The Unit of Research and Field Study of the Council of the Protestant Episcopal Church, September 1, 1958, p. 4.

primary exception was the Loveland/District 66 development along Pacific Street, which resembled an island tied to the mainland by a narrow neck of land. The survey began its discussion of Omaha by noting that at present the Episcopal churches are "located in a T-square: Six congregations are north and south along the eastern sector of the city, from St. Mark's in Florence to St. Martin's in South Omaha, and two congregations west along the Dodge Road addition, namely St. Barnabas and St. Andrew's." A look at the map that the survey provided makes the observation even more damming. St. Barnabas was little more than twenty blocks west of Trinity Cathedral and was really more a part of the north-to-south line than a real extension into the city's future westward growth. On the other hand, St. Andrew's at Eighty-Fourth and Pacific was barely on the city map. Its location was praised for being farsighted. Someday, the survey suggested, land should be bought at One Hundred Thirty-Sixth and Pacific. It is clear that to the survey this was thought of as so far off that even St. Andrew's was considered ahead of itself. The immediate recommendations for new church locations were five locations forming a second north-to-south line along the west edge of the city, more or less along Fifty-Second Street. The only exception was a proposal that one the new churches to be located on Seventy-Second and Maple. The strongest recommendation of this section of the survey was for the location of a church in the university area, more or less at Fifty-Second and Dodge.

> It would seem that a church should be located on or near Dodge Avenue and Fifty-Second Street. This could serve as an excellent location for a chapel of All Saints Parish and, eventually, the relocation center for this fine parish. If the rector, wardens, and vestry men of All Saints are willing, cooperative action here might call for the purchase of land by the diocese and by, perhaps, cooperation in the building of the first unit, after which time, however, the parish could develop the program and the property without additional help.[161]

However visionary, the research team grossly underestimated the drive of the western development, which had and would continually sap north-to-south development. Omaha's planners have consistently done this from the founding of the city. It also overestimated the ability of the churches

161 *A Study of the Episcopal Church in the Diocese of Nebraska*, The Unit of Research and Field Study of the Council of the Protestant Episcopal Church, September 1, 1958, p. 84.

to cooperate and of the diocese to actually execute a plan to acquire land apart from the action of an individual parish.

In spite of the thoroughness and competence of this study, its impact on the diocese was modest as most of its recommendations were ignored. William Barnes in his history of the diocese offered the opinion that

> Bishop Brinker hoped that the diocesan program for the next ten years could be planned and organized as a result of the survey's findings and recommendations. He strongly pleaded for the cooperation of everyone and especially wanted them to adhere to the time schedule. Following the survey, however, there were doubts registered as to its value, and it has been difficult to see many tangible results, although the removal of one Omaha church from downtown to West Omaha was a direct result of a survey recommendation.[162]

He is, of course, referring to All Saints. The impact of the survey on All Saints, however, unfolded at a slow pace. The first indication of its impact was registered in a terse note in the minutes of the vestry meeting of March 9, 1959. "The rector expressed his views relative to moving the church to some new location." It was apparently considered unnecessary and perhaps unwise to state his view in writing at this time. In an address to the parish on June 5, 1960, in which he announced the parish's purchase of land in West Omaha, McCallum makes the claim that three successive vestries had studied the recommendations of the study. According to his count, the vestry had begun its study in 1958. That suggests that McCallum had managed the study in an incremental way and had only gone on record with his own opinion in March of 1959. This apparently represented a change of heart. In this address, McCallum also reminded the congregation that he, himself, had originally taken "the stand that we could survive here and make a proper transition to fit those needs - conditioned upon the development of a strong lay-evangelistic program." Two things had led him to change his mind. First, the success of the ministry of an urban parish, much as Casady had argued in the twenties, presupposed the existence of a large endowment, at least a million dollars, McCallum thought, but there did not appear to be any reasonable hope that such an endowment would materialize. Second, the lay evangelism for which he had hoped, he was now convinced, was no more reasonable to expect from Episcopalians than a million-dollar endowment. Realism,

---

[162] Barnes, William J., *The Episcopal Church in Nebraska, Omaha*, 1970, p. 111.

he argues, had caused him to change his mind. The reasonable future of the parish lies in making a move.

With McCallum now on the side of moving the church, the next step was to form a formal study committee. Arthur Pinkerton, who had been chair of the past building fund drive, was chosen to chair the new committee. Pinkerton was the quintessence of a gracious man. He was liked by everyone and a natural born peacemaker. He was the perfect choice for a difficult task. In October, his committee brought a report back to the vestry. The minutes tell us that: "Mr. Pinkerton presented his report as chairman of the committee to study the church survey report. After considerable discussion, the committee decided to give further study to the report, and, due to the resignation of Crosby W. Wyman, the rector appointed Mr. Muller to serve on this survey committee." Again, no details were placed in the minutes. Wyman's resignation indicates that there was an element of dissent within the committee. That dissent, however, chose to step aside rather than to fight. The vestry had largely accepted the fact that a move was inevitable, as a junior member of that vestry recalled, "Oh, it was understood that we were going to move at some time."[163]

Dr. Moore's recommendation was that relocation should take place in the long run and that in the short run the parish should "purchase a site as soon as possible" and should proceed to build the first unit of its future plant and should begin "to develop a part of its total weekday and Sunday program at the new location." In his presentation, Moore stressed that "there was no urgency in moving the central activities of the parish immediately, but great need to secure property at a suitable new location, which would enable the parish to make an orderly transition over the years while it was relatively strong and able to do so."

Moore summarized his reasoning in a list of factors:

1. Declining membership in the normal parish area where the church is located.
2. Rapid and increasing removal of membership to West Omaha and suburban areas.
3. Disintegration of the area where the church is now located.
4. Increasing driving time to attend services and activities.
5. An unsolvable parking problem at the present location.
6. A prediction of financial difficulties.
7. Transfer of members to other parishes and churches in the areas to which they have moved.
8. Replacement of membership losses increasingly difficult to secure.

163 From an interview with L. K. Muller, January 2012.

Since its move to Eighty-Fourth and Pacific in 1951, St. Andrew's had been worshiping in its parish house. In 1957, Rev. Donald Haviland, having been its rector for three years, led a successful building program adding a strikingly up-to-date sanctuary at the new facility. Countryside Congregational down the street had a similar history and, like St. Andrew's, attracted new suburbanites. With the new sanctuary and Sunday school space, St. Andrew's beat them to the punch and succeeded in attracting people away from them. One of these key families was Ginny and Paul Wertz. Having started out at Countryside, they became strong Haviland supporters, eventually ending up at All Saints after Haviland's retirement. In fact, St. Andrew's was a classic model of the new suburban parish, having brought little of its Hamilton Street congregation and its high church ethos with it. A measure of its success is shown by the fact that on Easter of 1958, Haviland was running three choral Eucharist to everyone else's two. Leakage from the two downtown congregations must have been well under way as the vestry pondered Moore's arguments.

As the All Saints vestry began the process of responding to this challenge, by marvelous serendipity the parish received a significant bequest. In February of 1958, one month before the meeting at which McCallum registered his newly revised opinion on the relocation of the parish, the vestry received word that the parish would receive the gift of the Metz house, located on 3625 Dewey Avenue, from the Metz estate. The vestry greeted the news with a formal resolution which read,

> Whereas, Mr. and Mrs. Arthur Metz, faithful and longtime members of All Saints Church, where Mr. Metz was for many years official greeter of the parish, rendering incalculable service to God's church and to this parish; and
>
> Whereas, their daughter, Olga Metz Davis, and their son, Louis Metz, saw fit to memorialize their mother and father through the gift of their family home of All Saints Church.
>
> Now, therefore, be it resolved that the wardens and vestrymen of All Saints Church spread upon the permanent records of this parish, this resolution acknowledging the acceptance of this unusually thoughtful and handsome gift with the everlasting gratitude of the wardens and vestrymen and the entire parish, and that a copy of this resolution be forwarded to the family.

In fact, a generation of young people who grew up at All Saints would have among their chief memories of going to church the personal greeting by a little, some adding that he seemed as wide as he was tall, old man who was always cheerful and who always gave them the impression that he was glad to see them. By 1940, Arthur Metz's wife had become an invalid. Increasingly, his role as greeter which he saw as his ministry became more important to him. And what is more blessed than being a doorkeeper in your Father's House?

What was even more serendipitous was that an immediate offer on the house that came as soon as the gift was final. The parish was approached by Walter W. Peterson who wanted to make the Metz house his home. The sale was complete in June 1959 for the sum $40,000, and the legacy was deposited for the purpose of creating a permanent memorial to Mr. and Mrs. Arthur Metz.

Dr. Moore had suggested land in Western Omaha would progressively become more difficult to locate, more quickly, perhaps than he realized. McCallum explained to the congregation, "sites closer-in have become prohibitive in price or have evaporated entirely." Moore's original suggestion had been in the university neighborhood, which would have been comfortable for a large portion of the parish who lived in the nearby Dundee, Benson, and Aksarben neighborhoods; but by 1959, those potential sites were gone.

Meeting on April 11, the vestry discussed the advisability of inviting Mr. Moore to return to Omaha on May 18 and 19 "to resurvey and report on the church survey." The vestry apparently was looking for some reassurance as it waded deeper into the prospect of purchasing land. Having approved a visit by Moore, the vestry went on to approve a motion by Erhardt Edquist, which was seconded by John Moss, that the rector appoint a committee to obtain information and make recommendations on possible sites for the future location of All Saints Church. Gale Davis took on the responsibility of finding an appropriate site and looked at a wide variety of sites. Among these was a site at Seventy-Second and Western and the corner of Ninetieth and Dodge. This latter high-profile location, where the Embassy Office Building was built, struck McCallum as too busy and too confined.

By chance, some couples from the parish went for an annual fishing trip. The patterns of these trips have been described as fishing by day, cards and a bottle of scotch by night. In the course of one of these evenings, the question came up as to what was going on in the parish. The member of the vestry in the group began to elaborate on the parish's quest for locating land. One of the couples in on that fishing trip was William and Sarah

Spire. William's father, Clarence Spier,[164] had as we have seen often served on the vestry and had been a senior warden prior to his recent death in 1956. Currently, William's brother Robert was on the vestry. With some surprise, the Spires responded that they, in fact, owned ten acres, with a house and barn on the west edge of Omaha. They had bought it as a place so that they could keeping horses and as a good place to raise a family. Recently, they had been thinking about selling, and the price that they had in mind was $40,000.[165]

On their return to Omaha, things moved quickly. Gale Davis immediately saw the potential of the site which to his credit required breaking the mold in which the search had been cast. This was not the university neighborhood! In fact, it was not all that much of a neighborhood at all. Blondo Street was a two-lane paved country road, lacking the grade, curb and gutter and storm sewers of a city street. The city's sanitary sewer in fact stopped at Ninety-Third. Spot development was taking place around it. To the west, a Saxton Edition was being opened, which would produce before long a line of modest ranch houses along a block long gravel street on their own septic tanks. Northeast of the property at the corner of Ninetieth and Maple, land had recently sold to a developer. A number of businesses were looking at the location; the foremost prospect was Hinky Dinky, who was looking for sites for new grocery stores in the western edge of the city. Davis may have had some information about this as the former owner had been Alamito Dairy, owned by Joseph Muller. Joe and Bea Muller by that time, in fact, lived at Eighty-Eighth and Western, not far from where the proposed purchase was located.

When Davis took a close look at the property, he saw a unique opportunity for the parish to take control a large area of land, ten acres, which was neither affordable nor available in the more developed areas of the city in which the parish's search for land had been focused. It was there at this price because the area had been slow to develop. He had walked through the abstract, those ancient and nearly sacred paper documents, which maintained the title of the property recording of every change of ownership and every lien ever placed on the property.

Prior to 1901, it had been kicked around by a series of speculators who never physically saw the land. The original patent to the land had been

[164] William led the way for the change in the spelling of the family name. The original German spelling was often misspelled, stumbling over the i-e problem, and it was common after WWII for Americans of German background to disguise the German roots of their names.

[165] A story told by L. K. Muller.

granted to Robert Poynter in 1857 for his service in the U.S. Army. It had quickly passed through a number of owners, who were interested in making a buck off of it until it ended up in receivership. The final mortgage holder was John Marshall of Medona, New York. The occasion of his death in 1898 began the long and convoluted process of selling off his assets. The terce legalese in the abstract makes it possible to see a host of heirs locked in deadly conflict.

In 1901, a William F. Beckmeyer and his wife, Lena, appeared on the scene. They were German immigrants, following the wave of Germans who had come to the Midwest to find farm land, which they could own, something that was not possible in Germany. By 1901, the land in Western Iowa had been bought up, and these two late comers were forced to look for land in Nebraska. They were attracted by the prospering town of Benson just to the west of Omaha. Benson was growing steadily, and by 1907, it was declared by the state to be a "type two town." It was just the kind of small progress community that they wanted to be part of. In their search for land, the Beckmeyers had followed Blondo west out of Benson, on what was a rather primitive farm to market road. The northwest corner of what is now Eighty-Fourth Street and Blondo Street was the beginning of Section 10, right at the point where the land began a steep climb out of the river bottom. The bottom was subject to flooding from the creek, in spite of its diminutive size and beauty, and the Beckmeyers wanted to farm on level well-drained land, which they found just beyond the rise. Along the ridge ran Highway 133, later known as Ninetieth Street. By 1901, this location was just about as an ideal location for a farm as a family might want. It was a short trip north to Irvington, where there was a railroad depot, a mill, and a farm supply store. Not that much further east, one entered Benson, where one could find a bank, lawyers, doctors, and other amenities; and beyond that were the hungry markets of Omaha.

They had arrived at the point in the legal struggles over the Marshall estate had come to an end; and eighty acres, the perfect size for a man and his family to farm, had come onto the market. Their eighty was described as the south half of the southwest quarter of Section 10. It ran along Blondo from Ninetieth Street to Ninety-Sixth Street and north of Blondo, a quarter of a mile to about where Miami Street now runs. The Beckmeyers built the two-story house with eight rooms, a barn, other outbuilding, and planted an orchard and a wood lot. Robert, their oldest child, farmed with his dad, and gardened on the side for extra income. In addition to Robert, there were two daughters.

William Beckmeyer died suddenly in December of 1918 and left his property, valued at $30,000, to his wife for as long as she lived or as long as she remained unmarried. At either event, it was to pass equally to their children. Lena moved to town and lived in a small house three blocks north of Benson on Sixtieth Street. Robert remained on the farm for a while. Lena, however, pushed to have the property divided, no doubt feeling some pressure from her children to do so. In March of 1922, she sold off the house and ten acres to Christian Petersen and his wife. The Petersens, immigrants from Denmark, made the acreage their homestead. They worked in the city and supplemented their earnings with what they could produce. This was the beginning of the transformation of the area and a sign of the movement of the city westward. Christian died in 1935, and the house went back on the market. By 1935, a new kind of buyer was looking at the area. These were urbanites who wanted to live on an acreage on the edge of town. Jess and Elizabeth Thurmond acquired the property from the Petersen estate and made it their home. Thurmond was president and operator of Evan's Laundry and Zeric Dry Cleaners. By 1946, they had raised their only child, a son, Mallard, and they put the property back on the market. At the beginning of the postwar period, a new kind of buyer was interested in the property, speculators anticipating an acceleration of the growth of the city. In a short time, the ten acres passed through a couple of owners, as did the other sections of the Beckmeyer farm.

In December of1952, Bill and Sarah Spire was one of many young couples looking for the good life on the edge of the city. Bill was the older son of Clarence Spier, who had among other things been a senior warden at All Saints and who with his wife, Louise, had raised their two sons, Bill and Bob there. With the election of Eisenhower, for whom Bill had actively campaigned, came his appointment to the office of U.S. attorney for Nebraska, an office he held until the election of Kennedy in 1960. The return to private practice and other changes that had happened in the course of time caused Bill and Sarah to decide that it was time to move on from the homestead which had served them so well.

Davis was betting that now this land could pass on successfully to yet another purpose, ground on which a church family could grow and prosper, just as the other pieces of the Beckmeyer farm had passed on to other purposes as the fifties were coming to an end. Crucial to this possibility was the way the city was going to develop around it. Would the anchor dropped on Seventy-Second and Dodge, the stylish Crossroads Mall, direct the growth of the city north and south along Seventy-Second? Would it be the west end of the city, or would the city leap frog it? Davis was one of those who understood that the drive of the city was west, and felt that it would not be long before the city developed well past Ninetieth Street. The growth would press out Dodge, but Blondo running parallel to it would benefit from the growth and avoid the congestion. Indeed, it was possible to see how the city would with time grow around it. It lay close to the top of a hill, amenable to ecclesiastical imagination, which has long favored hill tops as the location for its sacred places.

Davis was quickly joined in his opinion by key leaders in the parish, and he took the proposal to the vestry at its regularly scheduled meeting on May 9. His motion to purchase the land was seconded by Jim Wells. This, however, was too sudden for the vestry. After some discussion, Davis withdrew his motion with the understanding that a committee would make further investigations and report to a special meeting of the vestry to be set for May 23, 1960. Such backpedaling was unusual for an All Saints vestry. The delay allowed for the meeting with Dr. Moore to take place on May 19, which had been asked for by the vestry in April seeking reassurance that it was on the right path. When the special meeting set for May 23 came, Davis again made the motion that the vestry approved the purchase of the property listed as 9140 Blondo.[166] In true form, it was approved unanimously. The parish's ability to do so was made possible by the Metz memorial. The new grounds upon which the parish would build in 1964 and upon which it has continued to live has become a permanent memorial to Arthur and Emma Metz.

Shortly thereafter McCallum chose a Sunday morning, as it turned out, Pentecost Sunday, to address the congregation to announce the purchase of the property and to provide the parish with the rational for the vestry's decision. He explained that his own resistance to relocating was overcome when he saw that staying in the old neighborhood would require an intense lay evangelistic effort and a million-dollar endowment or more. Neither he had come to believe were possibilities. "Apparently, it is beyond our abilities to stay interested in the problems in an area where our hearts and homes are no longer centered. It is sometimes difficult to get quorums on committees and groups even on Sunday mornings following services for important decisions."

His conclusion was that "It would be utterly foolish not to face the facts and plan for the future. This we owe to the Kingdom and to the posterity of the Church. Sentiment and deceptive strength must not blind us to the abiding obligation of a church to stay active and interested in winning people to the redemptive way of life as centered in the Body of Jesus Christ as the Savior and Redeemer."

On the other hand, he sought to reassure the parish that nothing precipitous was going to be done. Reading from his text, he said: "WE ARE

166 The address would be changed to 9302 Blondo, but at this time, neither Ninety-Second or Ninety-Third existed.

NOT ABANDONING THIS PARTICULAR SITE." As Dr. Moore had presented it, purchase of land was necessary now and time could be taken to carry out the actual move. McCallum continued: "Your vestry feels that this purchase gives us adequate insurance and protection. We will now have the time to develop a sensible and practical long-range plan aimed at serving the best interests of this parish and the Kingdom of God in this community." He concluded his address hoping to allay fears, some which might well have been his own as well: "I submit to you that this is the most challenging time this parish has ever had. And because that is so, it ought to prove the happiest and most fruitful time in our whole history." A very big step had been taken.

The vestry met on June 13 and set up a committee "to formulate the next steps relative to organizing the plans and program for the future of All Saints." They also made the provision that the assistant, Deacon Jess Borg, and his family should occupy the property, saving on the expense of the housing allowance and affording the Borgs a rather pleasant living experience. The final item of business that came before the vestry before their summer break was a report from John Moss on the negotiations with Lutheran Hospital concerning the sharing of its parking lot. Things look favorable, Moss reported and he thought that a deal was possible. The recollection that these negotiations had been going on for more than two years at this point, no matter how favorably they might presently be judged to be, must have made the possession of ten acres of land feel awfully smart, even if it was seventy-six blocks to the west.

Chapter 7

The Crisis of Prosperity: 1961–1971

On January 20, 1961, the youngest man in the history of the country was elected president. John F. Kennedy spoke in his inaugural address of "a new frontier" and issued a call for personal sacrifice in order to make the world a better place. "Ask not what your country can do for you, ask what you can do for your country." Five days later, an electing council of the Diocese of Nebraska elected Russell T. Rauscher as its new bishop. He would replace Howard R. Brinker, who had been bishop since 1940. The previous September, the city of Omaha had celebrated the opening of Crossroads Mall at Seventy-Second and Dodge Street, and it too began the new year a changed city. The city's center of gravity had shifted west in a way that was little understood at the time. Downtown Omaha's flagship store, Brandeis, was the primary investor in the Crossroads Mall and was one of the mall's two anchor stores. Like many of the initiatives of the sixties, the inherent conflict of interests was unseen or ignored. Brandeis's brave new initiative contained within it the inevitable closure of its downtown store. The gradual decline of the downtown store came to an end in 1980. With its closure, the primary reason that had brought generations of Omaha's citizens downtown was at an end, and the great majority of the people living in Omaha henceforth would seldom, if ever, find their way downtown.

All Saints began the new decade with a solid Every Member Canvass behind it. The church recorded 333 pledges totaling $54,403—an average of $168.38 per pledge. Heartened by these results, the vestry began to prepare its own radical initiative. Officially, it had been insisting that there was going to be no haste in the process of relocating the parish. McCallum, in his address to the congregation in June of the previous year, had explained that the purchase of the land was simply a means of ensuring the long range future of the parish. When it was needed, the land would be there. However, the preceding vestry had established a new account called the All Saints Church Memorial Fund, the purpose of which was to collect money for a future building program. On December 29, McCallum received a letter from Joseph P. Muller congratulating him and the vestry for creating the fund and informing them that he had transferred one hundred shares of Arkansas Louisiana Gas common stock to the fund. In January, a note of appreciation was sent to Joseph Muller, thanking him for his donation, as well as one to Jim Fields and George Morton, who had also made advanced gifts. If the nation was rushing toward a bigger and better future, so it seems was All Saints.

The new vestry met for the first time on February 13 that year. Its new senior warden was Erhardt Edquist, the president of Fairmont Foods. The junior warden was Gale Davis, a new vice president at Mutual of Omaha. With Joe Muller, the president of Alamito Dairy, they were at the core of All Saints strength, all hardworking and successful businessmen. The clerk of this vestry was Warren Howard. The vestrymen were Bernard Combs, George Devereux, Darwin Fallis, John Hanley, Charles Morton, Robert Plumb, Varro Rhodes, Bill Thomas, M. G. Van Scoy, Jim Wells, and Conrad Young. Hal Easton, John Moss, and Robert Spire had just gone off the vestry, but clearly they remained in the loop. For some time, All Saints had left behind the long, in many cases life tenures, in favor of a rotating membership on its vestry. Bishop Brinker had championed the change, and Galaty had initiated it at All Saints. However, no one who went off the vestry was off for long, and no one was ever out of the loop. The loop also included James Paxton, Art Pinkerton, Joseph Muller, Erhardt Edquist, and D. R. Colby. Pinkerton and Spire went back on the vestry in1962 and once again in 1970.

As the vestry broke for the summer, there was a broad discussion of a future move and concern about a request they had received from the diocese to approve a petition from St. Barnabas to allow it to establish a new mission in the western part of the city. They worried that they would approve a new Episcopal church in their own new backyard. At the June meeting, they expressed sympathy with St. Barnabas's intention to establish a mission but withheld approval until they knew where it was to be located.[167] A number of subcommittees worked throughout the summer, and a number of visits were paid to the new property.

A Visit to the Property

In 1885, James M. Woolworth, Carroll S. Montgomery, young Richard R. Ringwalt, and a couple of others members from the newly formed vestry of All Saints Church took a walk on a hill on the west edge of Omaha. Then the west edge of the city was more or less Twenty-Sixth Street, and the hilltop that they visited was in the newly platted Clarks addition that ran along Dewey, then know as Half-Howard. They were standing on ground that they had just purchased for a parish that was little more than a name on a piece of paper. From there they could look back into the city all the way down to the river where the city had begun and over it to the distant bluffs in Iowa. To the south, their eyes went down to where the new St. Mary's Avenue was working its way west. Stately new homes had begun to appear along it, Woolworth's included. Further to the south were the westbound tracks of the Union Pacific, which had assured the early development of the city. When they turned to the north, they could see the city's only high school perched on the same ridgeline on which they were presently standing. When they turned and looked west, they could see the beginnings of a new Gold Coast. It struck them that this hilltop was a perfectly splendid place to set a church. It would be a light on the hill seen from all who passed by.

Seventy-five years later, on a spring day of 1961, a similar delegation from the vestry of All Saints took a walk on a hill located on the west edge of the city, now Ninetieth Street, a distance from downtown, which the city of 1885 could hardly have imagined. This delegation consisted of the rector, Mark McCallum, the wardens, Joe Muller and Gale Davis, and several junior members of the vestry, including Chuck Morton. Morton's father and mother, George and Helen Morton, both passed, had been stalwarts of All Saints since Casady had been the rector. Young Morton

167 St. Barnabas was considering the land at the corner of Military and Crown Point. The parish had progressed a long way in considering a move when their new rector, James Bryce Clark, brought it to a halt and accepted the losses that it caused at the time. Clark rightly understood that if St. Barnabas moved, it could not stay the same as it had been, as All Saints would learn. By choosing to keep the church where it was, and thereby ensuring that it would stay the same as it has been, the leaders of St. Barnabas ensured its gradual demise, and All Saints would manage to thrive.

was a graduate of Iowa State University's Architectural School and was employed by Steele, Sandham, and Weinstein, the heir to Thomas Kimball and presently the leading architectural firm in Omaha.

They were standing on the southwest corner of the property that they had just bought for a parish who was worried they were falling behind the growth and change of the city of which they had been a part for so long. From the highest point on the land, they could look back into Benson, which had just recently moved beyond Seventy-Second Street into a broad valley, which had been formed by the Little Papillion (the Little "Butterfly" to translate the French) and its main tributary, Cole Creek. Technically, Benson Township stopped at the Little Papillion. Along the east side of the creek, the Fremont, Elkhorn, and Missouri Valley Railroad ran up the valley. There was an elevator where farmers brought their grain and purchased coal at the intersection of the railroad line and Military Highway. A short distance further up the line, at the nine-mile mark, was a train depot in the tiny community that went by the name of Irvington. From there, the railroad took off for Arlington, Fremont, and Chaldron. It was dubbed the cowboy line, supplying Western Nebraska and bringing cattle back into Omaha's bourgeoning stockyard.

Above Maple, the Keystone Drive followed the railroad until it cut back east over the ridge where it would intersect the Military Highway, a few miles closer to Omaha. The drive was originally part of the interior lanes of the Keystone Stock Farm, which had been established in 1884 as the home of William A. Paxton Jr. His father, William A. Paxton Sr., was one of Omaha's original capitalists and the founder of the Union Stock Yard, Paxton Gallagher, Paxton Vierling, Paxton Mitchell, owner of a deal of real estate, a huge ranch in the Sand Hills, and a number of other holdings in the city. His son was educated at the Episcopal College in Racine, Wisconsin, the effect of which was to bend him toward what he called "the bright side" of his father's business: real estate, theater, and horse racing. That can be taken as a compliment to the Episcopal Church, but it is likely that his more Calvinist-oriented father must have at times second-guessed his choice of colleges for his son.

The expansive farm with a long flowing system of internal drives was the base for raising young Paxton's prize horses and for his mansion, which was built in a location that is now known as Seventy-Ninth and Evans. He lived with his wife in that house until his father died in 1907. At much prompting from his wife and the new license of his circumstances, the younger Paxton built in Fairacres and replatted the farm, turning it into a subdivision, which he called Keystone Park. Midway through Keystone Park was a clubhouse that, in time, became one of Omaha's better known "speakeasy" before it passed on to the quieter existence of a family home. Around the flowing loops of the ranch's internal drives, a number of prominent homes were built in the early years of the century. In the postwar years, however, smaller more practical homes were built at an accelerating pace. In short, this well-known development served as a landmark for the committee by which they could locate their new property on Blondo. Our land? In Benson, just south of Keystone Park, they could answer.

The same view that ended somewhere in Keystone Park passed over open land, marked only by the intersection of Ninetieth and Maple. The southwest corner had recently sold to a developer, and as the committee was making its visit, a future member of the congregation, Tom Brown, was sitting in his car doing a traffic count at the intersection for an Omaha grocery chain, Hinky Dinky, who was looking for store locations in West Omaha.[168] When the group turned and looked south, the land fell off sharply to a bottom running east and west as far as one could see. In time, Maenner Meadows would flow across Ninetieth, where it had stopped in 1963 and would extend it way up this draw. Beyond the bottom, the ground rose to another ridgeline that was recognizable as the path that West Dodge took on its way out of town. To the west of them, at their backs, there was still a slight rise and a large ranch house, neither of which would obscure the visibility of anything that they chose to build. It struck them as a splendid place to set a church. It would be a place where they could lift high the Cross of Christ for all the world to see, at least, for several miles around in all directions.

At the heart of their property was a large two-story farmhouse with a couple of barns, which had been built in 1901 by William and Lena Beckmeyer and which had eventually passed to Bill and Sarah Spire. Behind them was a large ranch house with 2,200 square feet on the main floor and a small upstairs loft. It was built in 1957 on three acres, giving the Spires proximate neighbors for the first time. Since city improvements had not yet extended out Blondo Street, it had its own well and septic system.[169] To the west of the new ranch house was a 10-acre parcel, which had been purchase by a developer, Bessie Saxton. She envisioned a subdivision of up-to-date ranch homes, hers included. These would prove to be well built

168 As told by Thomas Brown, who, after All Saints was built, transferred from St. Andrews with his wife Martha and their three boys.

169 This three-acre property was bought by All Saints in 2003. The house was removed and the land incorporated into the parish's campus. The Saxon addition, which sits on ridge, is now the church's neighbor on the west.

but modest 1,800-square-feet ranches. They were as Saxton had planned an exceptional bargain because they were in the county and not subject to city taxes and building requirements. The Saxon subdivision, which was platted in 1961, was the first effort to move from a homestead model to a residential neighborhood model west of Ninetieth Street.

The vestry's committee felt reassured by these beginnings of residential development around them that they could see that day. They turned to the younger member of the gathering and asked, "Where do you see the church?" Morton began that day to sketch out a plan. Morton, in an interview in 2000, told me that McCallum's input was not very extensive except that he insisted the church should have a long center aisle to accommodate processions and that it should have a cross on top, which would be the highest of any in the area. With that in mind, Morton began by saying that he would locate the church on the west half of the property. The east half had a gentle slope, which took the water off the property to the east. With a minimal amount of grading, that part of the land would accommodate six parking bays, which could hold 250 cars, the number that the parish's survey had indicated as desirable. The southwest half of the property had the higher elevation, which could be taken advantage of in two ways. The end of the church on which the cross would be mounted would make use of this elevation. Set back from Blondo Street three hundred feet, the cross would set at the center of the property. From that point, the main building would run to the north, taking advantage of the slope of the land. This would allow basement area under the church to be build out of the ground, and it would be able to have full windows on each of its sides. Only the area under the narthex and the office wing would be a true basement. Moreover, the north door would provide a ground-level entrance for the lower level.

The front half of the land would be reserved for expansion. When it was possible, a church school wing would be built coming off the west wing of the building. It would run south for two hundred feet toward Blondo and then turn east, enclosing a courtyard in front of the church. At its farthest point south, it would be a hundred feet from the street. The church school wing would shield the courtyard and church from any street noise on Blondo Street, which would surely come with time.[170] Eventually, on the east end of the building, a second addition would be built to serve as a parish hall large enough to seat 250 people.

It would be a good idea, he thought, for All Saints to give the city land for a street down the east side of its property to serve as a buffer. When

170 Traffic studies in the nineties indicated that an average of fifty thousand cars passed the church each day.

houses would be built in that area, he reasoned, they would face the church across a street and not back up on it with a shared lot line.

What would the church look like? It would, in Morton's vision, be built of Wyoming fieldstone, unfinished cedar siding, and slate shingles. These natural materials would fit with the Nebraska prairie on which it was being built. The building would be tucked into the landscape in a way that it would become a part of it. In that way, it would be quite distinct from the old church, which had been intended, as the church buildings of that era were, to be monumental, a fortress on a hill, a bastion against time and place. The old building's Gothic decoration was meant to take you to a different time and place, but the new building would make you feel at home located in the time and place where you found yourself living, working, and raising a family. It would be a truly contemporary building and yet quite grand in its own way. As a contemporary architect, Morton wanted his structure to work with the land, as his professors at architectural school had taught him. But then what budding architect outside of the class room has such an opportunity as this presented Morton!

From Vision to Reality

When the summer break of 1961 was over, the vestry found itself faced with the need to repair or replace the furnace in the farmhouse that sat on their newly acquired property. Such were the burdens of holding property. A new extension of a gas main on Blondo Street made it possible to switch from coal to gas. The parish's assistant priest, Jess Borg, and his family were living in the house. That covered part of the salary and in turn their presence on the property provided the parish with a degree of security. It was, in short, a little too soon to abandon the house; and in any case, they reasoned, a gas line would have to be brought on the property when they built the church. The motion to repair the existing house was, however, followed by "a very interesting report on an All Saints survey." Apparently, the survey had been conducted during the summer of 1961. The results, however, were kept private for the continued study of the vestry, and they were not even recorded in the minute of the September meeting. The October meeting passed with no further mention of the study, but when the vestry came together in November, the results of the survey were recorded in the minutes and finally made public. Summarizing the survey, McCallum reported: "While pledging was up slightly from 1958, $50,400 to $52,800, attendance and membership was down. Sunday attendance had declined from 16,100 to 14,700; the number of received communions from 9,320 to 8,625; of families from 336 to 290." Anyone who has worked with church numbers knows that they are spongy, going up and down depending on how rigorous or how lenient the compiler happens to be. The Every Member Canvass, in 1961, would in fact produce 313 pledges, two less than 1960. That would be quite a feat if the family units were really only 290! One can conclude that the negative results of the survey served McCallum's purpose, though in a vague sort of way they probably accurately represented the likely trend with which the parish was faced. The survey concluded: "The City of Omaha has been showing a steady growth. All Saints Church is showing a steady decrease in membership and attendance . . . We recommend the present site be sold, and that a building program be started in the near future." The report was signed: J. M. Hanley, J. L Paxton, J. P. Muller, E. C. Reynolds, E. D. Edquist, and A. W. Pinkerton.

The vestry reacted to the report by commending the committee for "preparing an exceptionally fine report" and "by directing the rector to preach a sermon on the vestry's decision which he should announce in the bulletin ahead of time and that afterward a mimeographed copy of the sermon should be sent to the entire congregation." In addition, the vestry authorized the formation of a committee to study the various facets of the report "with the aim of implementing the program of the Planning Committee if possible." The minutes note that these actions were approved of by a unanimous vote of the vestry.

In December, McCallum announced that a committee had been formed to consider the sale of the property at Twenty-Sixth and Dewey. The members of this committee were Joseph Muller, Erhardt Edquist, and Gale Davis. He also announced the formation of the Preliminary Facilities Survey Committee. It was headed by Darwin Fallis. The committee members were each assigned a particular area: George Devereux, Kitchen and Women's Guilds; Robert Plumb, office facilities; Charles Morton and Mrs. Meyer, church school; Darwin Fallis and Cecil Neubecker, music department; L. K. Muller, parking and general information in regard to the property; James Wells, the procurement of information from the national church on building churches.

Their report was apparently made to the annual meeting held in January of 1962. In it, the survey committee stressed that its suggestions ought to be considered to be "the barest minimum" for initial construction. The building should provide a worship space capable of seating four hundred fifty to five hundred individuals and church school space capable of accommodating two hundred fifty children. The church school space should be easily expandable to accommodate five hundred children. The parking facilities should be able to handle two hundred fifty cars. Forced air heating and air-conditioning should be available throughout the entire structure. Art glass and the Austin organ should be moved from the old building if at all possible. The committee further urged that a formal property survey be completed as soon as possible, an architect should be selected, and a capital fund campaign should begin in the coming spring.

The growing momentum was further increased by an offer from Joseph and Bea Muller to buy the old church property at Twenty-Sixth and Dewey. While their Alamito Dairy was close to the old property and Joseph Muller was no stranger to the real estate market, there was little in it as a business deal for Mullers. It was, in effect, a second form of contribution to the building fund, following their gift of gas shares the year before. The arrangement was that the Mullers would buy the land as soon as building started. The Austin pipe organ, stained glass, books, prayer desks, and other appointments were excluded from the purchase. If the property was sold for more than $100,000, the agreed purchase price, any excess would be conveyed to the church.

At its regular meeting in February, the vestry passed the resolution "that All Saints Church of Omaha relocate the parish from its present location at Twenty-Sixth Street and Dewey Avenue to the new site at Ninety-Second and Blondo Streets effective as rapidly as the transition can be made." It was little more than a year and a half since the property had been purchased and the congregation reassured that nothing precipitous was going to be done. "We are not abandoning this particular site," McCallum had said, adding, "Your vestry feels that this purchase gives us adequate insurance and protection. We will now have the time to develop a sensible and practical long-range plan aimed at serving the best interests of this parish and the Kingdom of God in this community." It is not likely that McCallum had misstated his own position when he had given these reassurances. In all likelihood, he underestimated the energy inherent in the idea once it had been entertained. In fact, Omaha and the nation as a whole were rushing into the future with little sense of where it was going!

As 1962 got under way, the vestry moved quickly to select an architect. Charles Morton, who had been on the vestry for some time and who had been party to a number of visits to the property, was an obvious choice. The caveat against employing a member of the parish for any professional purpose was brushed aside. He was referred to as the parish's representative to the architectural firm, which implied that his role was that of a liaison. In spite of being a junior partner with Steele, Sandham and Weinstein,[171] the design was his creation. He was backed up by the senior partners. William Steele and J. D. Sandham, who had both gone to work for Thomas Kimball, and they continued his firm after 1946 under their own names. Alex Weinstein had been brought into the firm in 1959 to strengthen it with fresh new ideas from the outside. Weinstein quickly established a high profile in the city as its celebrity architect, frequently being featured in the *Omaha World-Herald* for his innovative work. A number of the design's special innovation are traceable to him.

With the architectural firm in place and hard at work, the vestry turned to the question of funding. The vestry set the drive to begin immediately after Easter, and they hired Burrill Inc. of Kansas City, Missouri, to assist the parish with a fund drive. The final step was to appoint a building committee. Its members were James Paxton, Gale Davis, Robert Spire, John Hanley, Joseph Muller, John Peacock, and Erhardt Edquist. This was truly a blue ribbon committee of men who had been deeply involved for the last five years with the parish's business affairs.

The dispatch with which this direction was being pursued is confirmed in a letter to the parish from Bishop Rauscher, dated May 7, 1962, giving the parish the official permission to proceed with its building program. In his letter, Rauscher wrote, "There being no objection by the three nearest parishes and the standing committee having given consent, I as the bishop of Nebraska, give full approval for the relocation of All Saints parish church." To that, he added his personal encouragement.

Not so encouraging, however, was a proposed commercial development of Ninetieth and Blondo. In September of 1962, the vestry was notified that Samuel Wolf had submitted a request to the planning commission of the City of Omaha asking it to rezone approximately fifteen acres of real estate on the northwest corner of Ninetieth Street and Blondo Street. He asked the commission to change it from First Residential to First Commercial and Seventh Residential. This parcel of land lay along the east property line of the parish's land. As it turned out, this was the stalking horse for an even-larger project. The proposal was part of a larger project called Williamsburg Townhouses, to be built by Kaufman and Broad Homes

[171] Steele, Sandham and Weinstien was an Omaha-based architecture firm originally formed by Thomas Kimball and William Steele Sr. in 1928. By 1946, it became Steele, Sandham and Steele when the younger Steele was made a partner. The firm was renamed Steele, Sandham and Weinstein in 1962 when it designed the prestigious Behlen Laboratory on the campus of UNL. Following Kimball's death in 1934, partners in the firm at various times were William Steele Sr., William Steele Jr., J. Dow Sandham, and Alex Weinstein.

Inc. of Southfield, Michigan. This proposal called for the development of fifty acres, the back half of the Beckmeyer farm, with apartments and various commercial buildings. The project not only lay along All Saints east boundary, but also along its entire northern boundary as well. The proposal was an $8 million development with a density of twenty units per acre. It was dubbed by the *Omaha World-Herald* as one of the largest Omaha apartment project in recent years. At the hearing, the parish was represented by Neil Hilmes. Hilmes was a lawyer, and he was on the vestry at the time. Charles Morton accompanied Hilmes as the parish's architect, and together they forcefully argued for the rejection of Wolf's proposal. While they managed to stall the project for some time and managed to reduce the proposed density to from twenty to twelve and a half units per acre, they, in the end, could not stop it. By the summer of 1963, the commercial strip on Ninetieth Street and the first apartments were under construction. Over the next two and a half years, the rest of the project would be completed, forming what is now known as Camelot Village. This is not what the leadership of All Saints had wanted as neighbors, but in retrospect, it must be said that the apartment complex, proved to be a good neighbor. While it did not produce families as a residential development might have, it did make Ninetieth and Blondo a significant crossroad in the city.

As the year of 1962 moved toward its end, there were regular reviews of the building plan. There is, however, little indication of any input from the vestry, except for a note that the music committee led by Robert Spire had decided not to use the Austin from the old church but to commission a new pipe organ.[172] An initial $4,000 was authorized to begin the effort to procure a new pipe organ. A latter note indicated that Neubecker, the parish's organist and choirmaster, favored an organ built by the Lewis Company. On April 28, 1964, shortly after the building was completed, Neubecker and Spire traveled to Lawrence, Kansas, to meet with the representative of the Reuters Company who was chosen to build the organ. The down payment of $4,000 was made. Another $8,000 was paid when the building of the organ began, and $16,000 was paid upon its installation, which was completed on August 1964.[173]

At the first vestry meeting of the new year, prior to the annual meeting, the design contract with Steele, Sandham and Weinstein Company was

172 The Austin was sold to Rockbrook Methodist Church where it is presently serving that congregation.

173 More extensive information on the Reuter organ can be found in the Appendix on Music, p. 541.

superseded by a contract to supervise construction with the same firm by the unanimous action of the vestry. The annual meeting that year looked at the building plans, heard a favorable financial report, and voted in the proposed slate of new vestry members. The Every Member Canvass had secured 285 pledges, a total of $50,646. The total number of pledges was down from 313 pledges of the prior year, approximately a 10 percent decline. No doubt this reflects the portion of the parish that was choosing not to follow All Saints to a new location. Nevertheless, the total amount pledged was an increase, and a healthy budget for 1964 was approved. The budget for the coming year was set for $64,076, of which $13,125 was the payment of interest on various loans. Building on the strength of the annual meeting, the vestry, at their regular February meeting, awarded contracts for the construction. The general contract was awarded to Hawkins Construction, the mechanical to B. Grunwald, and the electrical to Brite-way Electric. A second motion approved financing to be done through U.S. National Bank subject to a 40 percent amortization and that the limit on borrowing be raised to $225,000. The groundbreaking ceremony was set for March 3, 1963, at 3:00 p.m. A committee lead by Art Pinkerton was set in motion in anticipation of transportation need for parishioners who lived in and near the old neighborhood. Many of these were retirees and/or women who did not drive. The anticipation of this need at such an early point, before putting a spade in the ground, indicates that there was a sensitivity to issue and that the parish leadership was determined not leave anyone behind.

The Building of the Church

When the members of the parish walked into their new building for the first time on Passion Sunday, March 13, it had been almost exactly one year since they had broken ground. They walked through familiar wooden doors adorned with the lancets portraying two angels fashioned of gold-leafed tracery and stained glass. The doors had been moved from the old church but had been set rather oddly in a glass wall. Mounted in that glass wall were three of the old church's stained-glass windows, the All Saints Window, the Trinity Window, and the Ascension Window, similarly an odd fit.[174] Still, the combination of the three windows, flanking the old

174 Some of the other stained-glass windows, three in all, were sold to St. Thomas's Fall City, Nebraska. Other pieces came on to the open market and survive in private collections. Most was just lost, as it was considered too difficult and expensive to save. See an additional discussion in the Appendix I: Landscape, Architecture, and Art at All Saints, p. 513.

doors, was comforting and suggested that all had not been lost by the move. Once inside of the narthex, parishioners could turn and see the sunlight coming through them, as well as through the angels on the doors showing off their distinct artistry.

The 1964 Building shortly after its completion, staking out a new beginning in a very open space on the far west side of Omaha.

The new narthex ran the width of the church, fifty-six feet, and it was twenty feet deep. To the parishioners of the time, it felt quite spacious and bright. They had been used to passing through a much darker and smaller entryway on their way into the old church.

Once these members, making their first visit to the new church, crossed the narthex and stepped into the nave, they look down a long aisle to the altar, which was eighty feet away from them. Raising their eyes, they followed the skylight down the same path until it stopped at the north wall. There they would have seen a distinct finger of sunlight traced downward on a wall dramatically fingering the altar itself. At the time of this first visit, the skylight was clear glass shielded with a temporary wooden lattice. The parishioners were told that it would eventually be stained glass, similar to the glass that they could see in the sidewalls.

The wall behind the altar was a screen of vertical oak boards, stained dark, over a light-blue grill cloth.[175] The vertical grill rose to forty feet at the center and then stepped down to ten feet on either side. Behind the vertical oak boards and a grill cloth were three large cavities, which had been prepared for a future pipe organ. On the face of the screen were mounted the six large saints taken from the reredos of the Meagath Memorial Altar. The blond oak finish of the statues set them off, making an interesting contrast with the dark finish of the screen, much as it had in the original reredos. Above the row of saints was a large contemporary cross, continuing the Celtic form that had so often been used by the parish. The center of the cross was dark oak, but it was outlined with a blond oak trim, which matched the statues. The circle was filled with colored tile mosaic, picking up the colors in the new stained glass.

The interior north end of the 1964 Building, shown in 1978 after the chancel choir was removed and the altar brought forward.

The pattern of a vertical wood grill was continued in the pulpit, lectern, and altar. In the pulpit and lectern, the smaller blond oak saints from the Meagath reredos were used. The use of vertical wood members was quite common at the time, usually with a blond finish and can be

175 The dark color of the grill cloth today is the result of age and of a fire in the boiler room in 1993, which did a certain amount of smoke damage throughout the entire building.

seen in a number of churches built in the city at the same time.[176] It had a contemporary look, but the dark stain used at All Saints linked the look to the dark oak interior of the old church.

The openness of the worship space, 6,050 square feet, was also contemporary. The laminated wood beams supporting the roof are twenty-four inches by eight inches, and rise at a sixty-degree angle for forty-two feet, meeting forty-seven feet over the floor. This creates equilateral triangles at each end and an overhead which is an uninterrupted prism. Unlike the traditional tresses of the old church, this allows the vertical reach of the space to be maximized. Architect reinforced this effect by setting the lighting in the ceiling instead of bringing it down with a hanging light fixture. Morton confided to me that he had felt very strongly about the power of this openness and worried that suspended lighting would compromise it.[177]

Both the vertical and horizontal space was also augmented by starting each of the beams at the top of blasted concrete columns, which mean that the beams begin twelve feet above the floor and six feet in from the outside wall. The beams were tied to the concrete column by a heavy steel hinge that looks functional as well as secure. The columns, the beams, and the giant hinges, which joined them, exposed the working structure of the building, a common goal of architects at that time. The argument was that the exposure of the structure was interesting and contributed to the pleasure of being inside of a building.

The enhancement to the breath of space was important for Morton. In an interview, he said that he was anxious about McCallum's dictate that there be a long center aisle, fearing that it would make the worship space into an alley. He had striven to give the space as much breath as possible. He could only do so much with the slope of the ceiling and therefore had counter levered the church's floor six feet on each side. This added the breath he was seeking, and it allowed the side aisles to be outside of the columns, much like a cathedral ambulatory. In addition, he opened the outside walls with bays so that the stained glass could be pushed out an additional three feet on each side. This provided a sense of breadth and created a pattern of the bays and columns that give the eye a sense of rhythm as it moved down the aisle toward the altar end.

176 For example, the Presbyterian Church of the Cross.

177 Morton was critical about the hanging lamps which were added in the 1980s, but I think he would be pleased with the relighting of the space in 2012, which comes closer to preserving the openness of the ceiling than the fixture that Pedersen had put there in 1984.

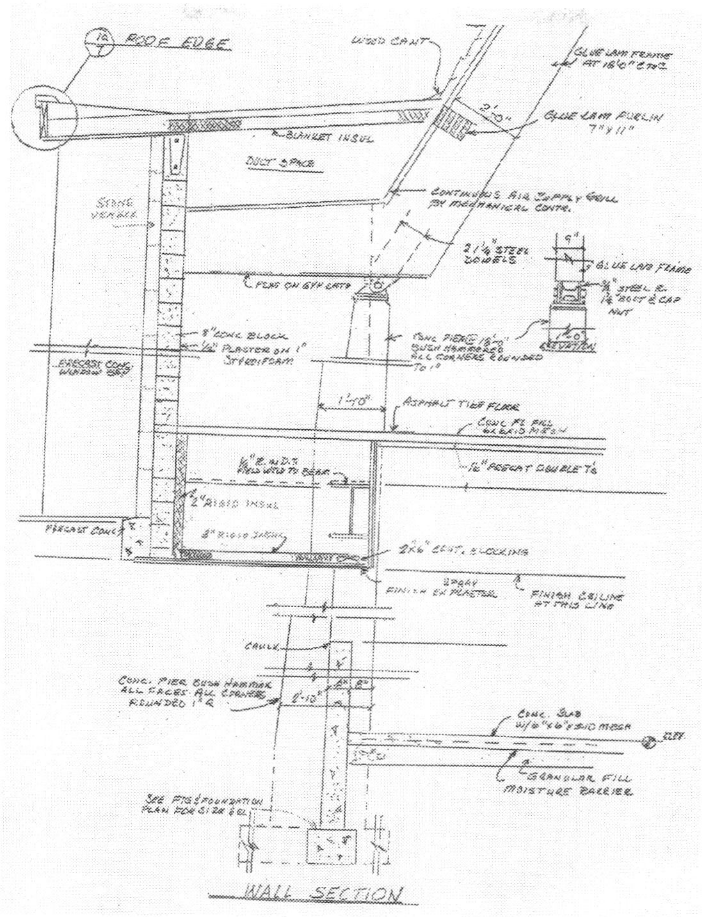

An architectural detail of the 1964 building showing column beginning below the floor of the lower level and extending above the main floor to support the tresses. Detail also shows the counter levered side aisles and window bays.

The parishioners that day would have been impressed with the idea that their new church was markedly more spacious than their old church had been. It could, in fact, seat a hundred to a hundred fifty more individuals than the church they were leaving behind. It had also benefitted from Morton's choices, which made it to seem even much larger than it was. Still, Morton had made a number of choices, which had kept the space from being starkly modern. The choice of a dark stain for the woodwork, when a blond wood finish was generally favored, gave the space a look, and even more, a feel, that was traditional. It appears that what the architect had aimed at was something that would feel like the old church without copying it in a way that would fan nostalgia or invite comparisons. One can see this careful balance struck as well in the choice of what was brought from the old church and what was left behind. In summation, to the parishioners, on the March morning, the new church was distinctly different from the old church without being shockingly so.

The natural light in the space was perhaps the most striking aspect of the new building. The stained glass situated in the six white marble bays on each side reflected the colors of the glass and pushed them into the room. The channeled light transformed the room with color constantly changing through the day. It was the conviction of the stained-glass artist, Gabriel Loire, who had designed and manufactured these windows, that the effect of stained glass in the great cathedrals was not so much as to be looked at as it was to bathe the space with a mystical light.[178] It was significant that the stained glass for All Saints was created as a whole so that there is a systematic variation of color as one moves toward the altar. Yet the greatest treat was reserved for the parishioners as they left the communion rail that morning. Upon turning, they looked back at the great triangular window in the south end. There they would have seen the noonday sun streaming through 221 slots filled with the red, blue, and yellow glass that matched the side windows.

178 The Gabriel Loire glass was a contribution of Alex Weinstein who had visited Loire in his home in France, in the cathedral city of Chartre. Loire's work is described in a book by Charles Pratt titled *Gabriel Loire: Les Vitraux* published in 1996, which includes a picture of All Saints triangular window.

The interior south end of the 1964 Building, shown in 2000
after the ceramic floor and mosaics were installed.

To say that it left everyone a little awed is not an exaggeration. Nevertheless, after the initial impression, the more critical eye could find fault. The altar was a simple large table made to the same vertical wood elements that covered the great wall behind it and that formed the pulpit and the lectern on each side of it. It was immediately dubbed the ironing board. It was, of course, perfectly defensible as precisely what the national church building guidelines had suggested as an altar, a plain table. In truth, it was a rather good execution of the national guidelines. Recognizing the power of the epitaph, the local leadership, however, reacted quickly. Four weeks after the opening of the church, at the vestry meeting of April 13, L. K. Muller moved that the altar from the old church be brought out of storage and incorporated into the altar area of the new church.

The choice to conduct the first church service in the new building on a March day also revealed a shortcoming of the building. As March days in Nebraska are bound to be, it was cold and blustery outside, and it was impossible to ignore the fact that it was just plain cold inside the new church. In the northwest corner of the building, a blast of cold air was coming up through the window bays, which were in fact designed to do just the opposite—return cold air to the furnace. The chairman of the building and grounds committee, L. K. Muller, had been in a running argument the night before with the contractors demanding that something be done. None of them was ready to own the problem as their own. Some remedy was found by blocking up the passage of outside air into the return air space that ran under the floor of the main church. Still, a year later, heating and cooling would be the primary problem with the building. A list, dramatically entitled "exhibit A," was presented to the vestry by the new buildings and grounds chairman, C. E. Whitney, along with a copy of the letter sent to the to the architects dated March 8, 1965. Nearly half of the twenty-four items on the tick list pertained to heating and cooling. The heating and cooling were labeled by Whitney as most urgent. In fact, a satisfactory solution was not reached until the mid-nineties in spite of a number of draconian attempts! Beside various design flaws, the problem was that the system was overly complex. For example, it had a complicated air-mixing system, which brought outside air into the space to ensure air freshness. It was the kind of feature that one might find in a large heavily used commercial space. It never functioned properly, and the outside vents around the building were soon covered with cardboard as an expedient solution. The operation of the heating/cooling plant really required a third-class engineer, and what was available was a number of well-meaning amateurs!

The list went on. The screening in the skylight rattled on a windy day. The sound system was not satisfactory. The report said, "We receive frequent criticisms from people that they have difficulty in hearing the sermon—that it seems garbled and indistinct, although 'plenty' loud. This is a critical situation." Again, this was a problem that was not addressed until the mid-nineties. The report continued, "Steps down to the various levels from the altar to the main floor of the church have resulted in several falls. This appears to be due to the fact that the slate floor and the lighting are such that people cannot tell where the step down is, or whether there is a step down. The exterior slate is cracking." These issues were dealt with over time and, like the heating and cooling, occupied the attention of several rectors.

Fortunately, some major issues were caught in time. When they had looked at the architect's plan for the bays, Hawkins's engineers disputed their stability. After a considerable fight, the architect accepted a need for more steel than he had anticipated. The bays have remained in place, in all likelihood, because of Hawkins's caution. The stability of the roof was also an issue. In a high wind, the roof rocked back and forth. Eventually, large steel plates were added to the ceiling beams where they joined the beams coming out of the sidewall to enhance the stability of the roof.[179] This helped a great deal, yet to this day, if one is in the space, one can hear the roof pop when a stiff wind comes along. The high steeple presented yet another stability issue. The tall aluminum-clad lance, rising seventy feet into the air, fastened to a pair of the forty-two-foot laminated ceiling beams, sways with a the wind. The stabilization of the roof helped to eliminate some of the movement, but it has never been possible to seal the joint about the steeple. The water problem that this created was eventually solved by building a large copper pan underneath it to catch the water where it is allowed to evaporate, which it does most of the time.

Living with What They Had Done

What the vestry had done was a really big thing. They had been convinced that if they started with a small or a temporary worship space, they would not carry their congregation to Ninety-Second and Blondo, and they would not grow. So they built a large and attractive sanctuary and left additional building for a church school and social gatherings to the future. To the accepted pattern of church development at the time, this was upside down. The common wisdom was to build a parish hall and classrooms first and then, in time, an appropriate sanctuary. This was the pattern used by St. Andrew's when it moved from Thirty-Eighth and Hamilton as it was for St. Timothy's in West Des Moines, Iowa, and Calvary, Sioux City, Iowa, all of which were built at approximately the same time as All Saints. But then these were congregations moving into or establishing themselves in a suburban area with the primary hope of building a congregation for the most part out of new people. All Saints, on the other hand, was a large established congregation trying to bring a citywide congregation into a new neighborhood and, secondarily, to benefit from new suburban families.

Phase 2, which was to be activated as soon as the building was paid for, was to be a wing of classrooms providing seating for 500 students. It was meant to come south from the west end of the building. Phase 3 was a parish hall capable of setting 250 at tables. It was to come off the east end of the narthex. In the meantime, the undercroft had to suffice for both purposes. It could be set up with dividers to accommodate 150 children

179 The steel plates were added in 1973. See page 326.

or with tables to seat 120 adults. Of the six parking lots called for in the plan, only two were paved, and the other four were graded and filled with heavy crushed rock but left in grass. They could be used in an emergency at least on a good day. In fact, forty years later, neither the parish hall nor the additional classrooms had been built. While the reasons they have not are more complicated than merely the question of money, it is still possible to ask what would have happened if it had been done the other way around.

As it was, the new facility provided the vestry with a full plate of challenges. To begin with, a lawn was barely established on the nine hundred square feet in front of the church, and the rest of the outlying areas were left in the natural state! Lawn care at Twenty-Sixth and Dewey had been minimal. The vestry was faced with a whole new ball game, not to mention expenses. At the May meeting, the motion was made to purchase a mower for $250 from a parishioner, Dr. Millett, whose home was down the road on the corner of 108th and Blondo. The image of someone sitting on a used rider lawn mower in the huge front yard that the church had acquired is somewhat comical. During the time when the spring rains in Nebraska push the hay crop, mowing the front yard with such equipment took nearly a week, at the end of which it was time to start again.[180] The maintenance of parking lots, which had not existed at the old location, was another new challenge and expense. The struggle to bring All Saints expansive grounds under control and to make them an asset to the parish, would, in fact, take well into the nineties, and even then it would continue as a significant concern and expense for the parish.

To succeed with what was on their plate, it was necessary for the vestry to solve two very large problems. It was necessary to provide McCallum with an effective assistant priest, and it was necessary to resolve the debt problem.

The Role of Assistant Priest

The role of an assistant priest was becoming more of a necessity than an interesting convenience. The size and the complexity of the parish made it difficult for a single priest to tend to its various needs. The rector was faced with new duties, which included the demands of the ongoing maintenance of the enlarged facility and the management of the large debt that had come about because of it. McCallum was approaching sixty.

180 Bishop Rauscher who came to All Saints as a business manager in 1976 use to mow the front law, as he had at the diocesan headquarters, spending many hours a week on the mower.

For a long time, he had dealt with a hearing loss that required him to wear hearing aids. In dealing with his hearing problem, McCallum had cultivated a rather brusque style. Once he had a sense of what was being asked, he responded with a precise reply, which was meant to minimize the need for conversation. This made him a very effective leader, one that cut to the chase. On the other hand, new people and young people in particular found him hard to relate to. Acolytes and even altar guild members proceeded with a degree of fear and trembling. His hearing also affected his preaching voice. While his preaching was clear and to the point, it was not easy to listen to.

The bet that the vestry had made with the building was that the new building and location would be the basis for an expanded church school and youth work, which, in turn, would mean new families who would help pay for the building. That made the need for an assistant priest urgent, even if it would be difficult for the parish to support one. The last assistant at All Saints had been Jess Borg, who had left in 1960. The vestry, now refocused on the need for an assistant, purchased a house at 8303 Seward. The house was a pleasant modern home that backed onto District 66's new junior high and city park. Sometime in the summer of 1964, the vestry approved the hiring of an assistant, though there is no record in the minutes of whom this was. The *Omaha World-Herald*, however, reported the arrival of Gerald Robertson in August. According to the article, Robertson had earned a bachelor's degree from Seattle University and had subsequently received a doctorate from St. John's University in music education. For the next fourteen years, he had taught science and music in various Episcopal day schools. Attracted to the priesthood, he entered the George Mercer School of Theology located on Long Island. Mercer had been found by the bishop of Long Island, particularly for the purpose of training late vocations. After his graduation, Robertson was ordained by the bishop of Albany. When he arrived in Omaha, he had a family consisting of a wife and two children ages seven and four. Expectation of his ability to contribute to the parish must have run high. There is, however, no further record of his work at All Saints. Without any explanation, the November vestry minutes record a motion approving the "immediate termination of assistant, 90-days of termination pay in the amount of $1,250, tenancy in the house limited to 30 days, pension premiums paid for the above period, subject to his removal peaceably from the parish and vacating of his present residence." What had caused this sudden dismissal and the rather threatening language used in this dismissal remains unclear. Clearly, this was a serious setback. The pursuit of an assistant fell in abeyance until April of 1966, when the vestry authorized the hiring of Jerry Steven Jones, who would graduate from seminary in May. Jones was a known quantity as he was an All Saints kid, and he had served as a seminary intern during the past summer. Jones served for a little more than two years and went on, like Jess Borg, to serve as priest-in-charge of St. Mark's Omaha.

On May 27, 1968, Robert Bee, recently graduated from General Seminary, began as McCallum's assistant. His salary was $4,400, $600 utilities, $600 car allowance, and his residence, 8303 Seward, was supplied by the parish. In the following year, he was given a significant raise: $5,700, a car allowance of $1,200, indicating the value of his contribution to the parish. However, on February 9, 1970, McCallum announced the resignation of Rev. Robert Bee to be effective April 1, 1970. Bee had been called as rector of St. Mary's Episcopal Church, Blair, Nebraska. The vestry unanimously adopted the following resolution: "That the vestry of All Saints Episcopal Church commends Rev. Robert D. Bee for his genuine devotion and outstanding service to the parish. Reverend Bee has served All Saints Church with integrity, wisdom, strength of character, and imagination and, in so doing, has profoundly contributed to the life of the parish." There is a sign that the vestry accepted Bee's resignation with real regret, but then it was not unexpected. The pattern of a new priest doing a two-year stint as curate with the expectation that he would then move on to a charge of his own was widely understood to be the way it should be. The result was that McCallum, now on the edge of retirement, would have to spend his last program year solo. The new rector, whoever he would be, would have no overlapping assistant; and therefore, he too would have to begin with a solo year.

Dealing with the Parishes Indebtedness

The need for an assistant to move the development of the parish ahead clashed with the debt problem. The unpaid debt was on the order of $250,000. The annual operating budget was making interest payments as high as $15,000, a sum equal almost to a quarter of the annual operating budget. Art Pinkerton, who had become the new senior warden, would often recount that his first job as senior warden had been to go to Cecil Neubecker and tell him that the parish could no longer afford paid soloists or sections. By March 1965, the decision was made that another capital funds drive would be necessary. The vestry turned again to Burril Inc. to direct the campaign. The campaign, called Our Next Step, is documented in detail in a scrapbook. Nothing else in McCallum's ministry is so carefully recorded, suggesting a heightened awareness of how crucial this undertaking was for the future of the parish. Burril assigned John Lane to All Saints, and he took a very hands-on roll as director, not only preparing the material, doing the advanced training, but also actually participating in the canvass and making its concluding report. The parish's chairmen were Gale Davis and Conn Young. Young, whose family was rooted in the parish and who was now on the rise in Mutual of Omaha, was an ideal partner for the old warrior, Gale Davis. Davis had been among the key leaders who had, from the beginning, pushed for the land purchase and building program. Training began immediately after Easter. The parish's situation was carefully described in the campaign material to be used to train the callers. "In short, it is thus: we are operating on a very conservative, cut down church budget of some $65,000 and nearly $15,000 of this amount is the interest we pay for our debt mortgage of a quarter million." The material outlined the goals of the drive:

> *We must* reduce the mortgage debt by $125,000. This will be stage no. 1 of consolidation: $150,000 is the *challenge goal.* When we reach this amount, it will allow us to have an assistant rector, air conditioning for our church, and meeting our goal in the outreach mission field. This will be stage no. 2 of consolidation: *Our faith goal is* $200,000. When we reach this sum, we're really in business, and we'll further reduce our debt mortgage liquidation, plus other things the vestry of our church has in mind. After we wipe out our debt and burn the mortgage, this will completely end our first initial big step capital building fund program and be stage no. 3 of our consolidation.

The campaign was launched with an attractive Next Step brochure, which contained statements by the rector, McCallum, the cochairs of the drive, Gale Davis and Conn Young, and Art Pinkerton, the parish's senior warden. Midnight May 2, the first count was completed and John Lane, who complied it at that late hour, sent the news off to the committee members. They had come close to $100,000 and were excited. By May 6, a week out, the total had reached $114,540. On May 14, Lane issued his last report: "161 pledge cards out of 413 had been returned totaling $129,828." Lane expressed hope that an additional $55,172 might yet come in. This was, in the end, not much above the minimum goal and left serious question marks over much-needed items, such as an assistant for the rector and air-conditioning. Needless to say, this was difficult money to raise. Retiring a past debt is not a very glamorous cause. Most of those who were solicited had participated in the capital fund drive just six years before. In addition, there were a number of other financial pressures on the parish. The parish was having a hard time meeting its missionary apportionment and had talked to the bishop about that. The diocese itself had a capital fund drive—"Builders in Christ"—which was building new facilities around the diocese and replacing outdated facilities. In the parish, the need for an assistant was urgent. McCallum had aged, had a full plate of problems that needed his attention, and the bet which required adding young adults and increasing enrollment in the church school was pressing. McCallum's talent had never been particularly strong in relating with kids. To accomplish this, the budget would require an income in excess of $71,000.

The good news was that the parish had managed to bring from the old church close to the whole congregation. This included working women, such as Helen Amos, who lived at 1530 Thirty-Ninth Street, and Mary Rankin in the apartment at 546 N. Twenty-Sixth Street. Mary was a Clarkson nurse who never married, never driven a car, and never moved more than a block or two from where she went to nursing school, which, at that time, was located next door to the old All Saints. In 1940, she had her hair styled in a fashionable "marcel" and wore it that way to the end of her life. In other words, Mary was not the kind of person who dealt with change. Yet for all the logistical inconvenience, she never faltered in her loyalty to All Saints and was buried from All Saints in 2004. Widows, such as Grace Bartel and her unmarried sister, Katherine Struve, who lived at 527 South Thirty-First Street, remained loyal to the congregation. For a long time, they rode with Helen Amos. After Amos had moved west, they would get a Sunday bus to Indian Hills, where parishioners would pick them up.

The hope that the new location would bring in new people also worked. New names were showing up. Tom Brown, who lived in Keystone and who was the one who made the traffic count for Hinky Dinky, which had led to their new store at Ninetieth and Maple, was summarily transferred by Father Haviland from St. Andrew's, along with Martha and the boys. Haviland, in his well-known dictatorial ways, explained that he had taken that action because they lived closer to All Saints than to St. Andrew's. Other names were Carroll Fredrickson, Joe Barker, and Robert Bell. Joe Barker was twenty-eight years old and newly married in 1964. He had been raised at St. Barnabas and married in the Presbyterian Church to which his wife's family had belonged for a long time. The compromise was that they needed to find a somewhat more temperate Episcopal church than St. Barnabas. When he and his new wife stopped in for a talk with Father

McCallum, McCallum enthusiastically greeted them with the statement that they were just the kind of young people All Saints wanted. This was more than a mere courtesy on McCallum's part, for within three years, Barker was on the vestry as was Carroll Fredrickson. Robert Bell would be called on as Every Member Canvass chairman in 1965. These new names were rapidly replacing the past generation of leadership, and they would have leading roles in life of the parish during the seventies.

The old building remained standing on Twenty-Sixth and Dewey until September of 1968. It had not been easy for Muller to sell the property, but he had at last found a buyer, Julius Novak. Novak's Cadillac dealership was one of the going concerns in the old neighborhood, which had, for a time, become "car alley." Novak initiated the demolition of the old building in September so as to clear the property for a sale to Lutheran Hospital, still living in the old Lister Hospital and hoping to build. When the cranes arrived on the morning of September 6, down on Farnam, two brothers stood in the windows of Barnhart Press, looking at the church in which they had been raised. Jack and Richard, who had taken over their father's business, could see the crane with a wrecking ball being readied to tear down the church building on Dewey.

The large stone Celtic cross on the top caught their attention, and they mused between themselves about whether it should have or could not yet be saved. Why not ask? Novak's office was next door, and so the elder of the two slipped over and asked if there was any way of doing so. "No problem. It'll be taken care of," Novak had replied. And sure enough, the crane was rerigged and the cross lowered and transported to Ninety-Second and Blondo to the field behind the new building. There it lay behind the building until the parish celebrated its centennial in 1985. As part of the celebration, it was set up in front of the new building. Saved, as were, by two ex-acolytes and a Jew.

With the old building down, one of the last pieces of nostalgia was removed. The church school and office wing, which had been built in 1954, however, was not torn down and is still used for offices. The actual location of the parish hall and the church remains vacant fifty years later. A new Lutheran Hospital built across the street in the seventies is now closed, and the surrounding area continues to be sadly blighted. The continued blight was ensured, in no small part, by the route of Interstate 480, which cut the neighborhood off from the west. It remains to be seen when the hill might again become a vibrant part of the city. This too has confirmed for the congregation at Ninety-Second and Blondo that the decision to move was the right decision, and it helped to consolidate support for the new location.

Return to Conflict

The life of a parish unfolds in the context of the larger community within which it lives, and this was undergoing a rapid change during the sixties. The consensus of the fifties was rapidly breaking down, and it was being replaced by a new level of conflict, which would define the era. Within days of the new building reaching the point where it could be closed in so that interior work could continue during the winter, the nation was shocked by the assassination of President Kennedy. When All Saints opened its new doors for its first service in March, Robert McNamara, the secretary of defense, had just returned from a trip to Vietnam. The coverage in the newspapers informed the country that his conclusion was that the new president of South Vietnam, Gen. Nguyen Khanh, was on the right track but that "the massive U.S. aid may have to be stepped up if the war is to be won."[181] Five months later, congress passed the Gulf of Tonkin Resolution, and United States was at war. With it was a bitter and growing division in the country that would have a serious impact on religious life in America and would, particularly, impact the Episcopal Church, which never had done well in such periods of conflict.

Simultaneously, the issue of race relations was moving toward its moment of crisis. Long held on the sidelines of U.S. politics, the massive March on Washington in August of 1963 put it at the center of the country's agenda. Martin Luther King was still firmly at the center of the growing movement, and President Kennedy had responded by meeting with King on the occasion of the march. It seemed, for a moment, possible that the postwar belief in progress was still in place. We would get there with some patience and hard work on everyone's part. But a year later, when All Saints occupied its new building, the country's newspapers were filled with the bitter fight going on in the U.S. Senate over the Civil Rights Act. The political power of Lyndon Johnson was pitted against the recalcitrance of the South's Democratic senators, who were filibustering and prophesying the end of America. By July, the Civil Rights Act had passed, and the controversy was refocused on the battle for the Voting Rights Act. If things were moving too fast for one part of country, they were moving too slow for another part. In July of 1964, a brutal race riot occurred in Harlem, creating a pattern that would find its way to Omaha in 1967 and burn itself out in Chicago in 1968.

The Johnson presidency added a third front in the growing internal conflict. Johnson announced a War on Poverty. In 1964, 25 percent of

181 *Omaha World-Herald*, March 13, 1968.

Americans lived below the poverty line. If this was tolerable during the Depression and war years, it seemed unacceptable after the postwar boom, which had so profoundly benefitted the rest of the country. Johnson's effort began in 1964 with the Revenue Act of 1964, which, among other things, created Medicare. The results of Johnson's programs were dramatic. Those living below the poverty line fell quickly from 25 to 12 percent. The easiest part of this, of course, was the way that Medicare and other programs reduced poverty among the elderly instantly.

None of these initiatives were out of line with what Kennedy had wanted to do, nor with the expectations of a majority of the country. It differed from what Kennedy is likely to have gotten done since he did not have Johnson's command over the political process. Johnson was willing to be ruthless in his drive to accomplish what he thought was right. Therein lay the problem. The legislative agenda outstripped the formation of a consensus that could support it in the long run. The stage for a new era of conflict was set. Johnson's over-size victory over Goldwater in the election of 1964 seemed to suggest that the conflict would remain substantially on margins of American life, but that would prove to be a false hope. The complicated configuration of the three crises—race, poverty, and war—set both ends of the political spectrum at odds with the national program.

In general, churches in America had benefitted from the consensus culture of the postwar era and no one perhaps quite as much as the Episcopal Church. Now the churches were being drawn in various ways into a culture of conflict, and no one was quite as uncomfortable with conflict as the Episcopal Church. In 1965, the presiding bishop of the Episcopal Church, Arthur Lichtenberger resigned. The national church office, by this time, had grown into a highly respected well-resourced office. Lichtenberger's quiet leadership, however, was judged by many as underutilizing the power of his office. Fairness and law and order were issues that the most conservative parts of the Episcopal Church could support, so the Episcopal Church did well with the early phase of the civil rights movement. In electing John E. Hines, the bishop of Texas, the general convention of the Episcopal Church had, however, aligned itself with the aggressive surge in American life of the Kennedy–Johnson administration and had called for bold leadership. Hines had, from the beginning of his ministry, been a social crusader, particularly in the area of race relations. While Lichtenberger had identified the Episcopal Church with the progressive advance in civil rights, Hines came into the office with a sense that he had to confront the church with the need to move forward at a much greater pace. Hines also found the war on poverty equally compelling. Hines argued that both of these issues presented the church with the need for urgent action, and he had no doubt that the church had ample resources to make a real difference. Not content with what was going on inside of the country, he reached out to involve the church in the struggle against apartheid in the Union of South Africa. This led the annual councils and conventions of various dioceses across the country to heated debates about divestiture in companies doing business with the Union of South Africa. Much like what Lyndon Johnson had done for the country as a whole, John Hines put an awful lot on the plate of Episcopalians and pushed them well beyond any semblance of a consensus.

Omaha was drawn into the struggle for racial equality as the sixties unfolded, rather uninformed about its own issues. For example, Central High School, which was the pathway to a college education, had a growing enrollment of black children, but it had only a single African American teacher, Wilma Stephenson, who taught typing and bookkeeping. It also allowed a de facto segregation of its cafeterias throughout the sixties. The near north side, which had once boasted of strong black middle-class neighborhoods and strong institutions, such as the *Omaha Star* and the Dreamland Ball Room, was losing ground. Its neighborhoods dealt with hostile police and city officials, crumbling schools, housing and services, and a lack of jobs and economic opportunities. On July 3, 1966, with the temperature at 103 degrees, the unthinkable happened. The near north side erupted in violence, frustration, and civil disorder. It lasted for three days, with as many as four thousand people gathered at the corner of Twenty-Fourth and Lake. In the end, order was restored with the use of National Guard troops.[182]

The documentation of the interface between Black Omaha and the churches, whose congregations were largely, if not exclusively, white, was documented by the film *A Time for Burning*. The film was broadcast by the three national networks in 1966. The project originated with the attempt of a young progressive pastor, William Youngdahl, who became the pastor of Augustana Lutheran Church. He set out to create in his parish a positive response to the challenges of race relations in Omaha. Augustana, the home church of Swedish Lutherans in the city, was located at Thirty-Sixth and Lafayette, and it was a close neighbor to the near north side. That put the congregation in the path of black migration moving West in search of better housing. The congregation's struggle was emblematic of the great majority of the Omaha congregations, which did little to refute Martin

182 A vivid picture has been provided by Steve Marantz's book, *The Rhythm Boys of Omaha Central High School Basket Ball at the '68 Racial Divide*, University of Nebraska Press, Lincoln, 2011.

Luther King's dictum. That Sunday morning was the most segregated hour in American life.

The Episcopal churches in Omaha had something going for it in the race issue. St. Philip's, the historic African American congregation located at 2532 Binney Street, had a strong congregation. While it consisted of only two hundred communicants, many of its members were articulate and well-placed members the city. St. Philip's served to keep Episcopal congregations grounded, if not integrated. Another plus was Dean Hewitt at Trinity Cathedral, who was providing effect leadership for outreach in the city. That, however, came to an end in 1968, when he left the cathedral under pressure. St. John's, on Thirtieth and Belvedere Boulevard, much like Augustana, found itself in the cross hairs of the race problem. Members of St. John's were moving west rapidly, and the African American population, looking for better and quieter neighbors, were moving north. William Reid, the rector, was approaching retirement and struggling with the leakage of his own parishioners who were moving west in the city and asking themselves why they were driving back across town to go to church. He was ill-prepared to be on the edge of the racial turmoil. The suburban parishes, St. Andrew's and All Saints, sat at some distance to the problem, but they both attempted in their own way to engage the growing problem with varying degrees of success.

This was driven in part by the presiding bishop of the Episcopal Church who was encouraging Episcopalians across the country to become engaged with the problem. Despite All Saints preoccupation with the problems that were created by its new building and its large indebtedness, it made an effort lead by McCallum. The effort shows up in vestry minutes in October of 1968. Joe Barker, a new member on the vestry, presented the report of the Steering Committee for Civil Rights, which had been formed by the Omaha clergy. In March of the following year, McCallum reported on the activities of a Community Action Committee. He informed the vestry that this committee was still meeting and that the movie *A Time for Burning* had been shown at its last meeting. At a later meeting, another of the new vestry members, Jack Sprague, presented the report on the progress of the Community Action Committee.

Much of All Saints program at this time was aimed at strengthening its relationship with St. Philip's. This included joint meetings and a joint summer school held on All Saints grounds. The first of these was held in August of 1969. Sixty children were enrolled, half black and half white. The All Saints effort was organized by Mary Wardle and All Saints assistant priest, Robert Bee. Mary's husband was Dr. Ralph Wardle, one of the University of Nebraska at Omaha's outstanding professors. We have encountered him when he assisted Galaty with an instructed Eucharist for the parish. He had subsequently served on the vestry of All Saints. Mary, in her own right, was an important force in the community and in the parish. An *Omaha World-Herald* article appeared in the August 4 edition with a picture of a group of children at one of the sessions. In the article, the reporter quoted a Metropolitan Association of Churches official as saying: "They cannot remember any similar programs in Omaha." The picture is a group of children being read to by Mrs. Artimese Ingram from St. Philip's, and the children listed are the following: Valerie Allis, Amy Barker, Kelly Horn, Ernest Steward Jr., Bobbie Barnhart, Saybert Johnson, Kathy Johnson, Kimberly Karnes, Jennifer Thornby. The vacation church school with St. Philip's continued several more years.

Following an eye-opening tour of Harlem with African American activists, the presiding bishop, John Hines, pushed through the regularly convened general convention of 1967 a "Special Program," which was commonly referred to by the initials GCSP. This program was intended to respond to the poverty and injustice of the American ghetto. The program directed the executive council to redirect the church's funds to community organizations and grassroots efforts aimed at the urban underclass throughout the United States. The disagreements over the GCSP and the Black Manifesto were greatly in evidence when a special general convention began on August 31, 1969. The argument of the Black Manifesto was that the exercise of rights and of voting were seriously, if not fatefully, flawed by the distribution of money in the society. It was hard to deny the logic of this observation at the time and the continuation of the poverty of a large portion of African Americans into the twenty-first century goes some way to confirming their argument. Bishop Hines's opening speech called for a renewed commitment to social justice and a "willingness to listen" to the differing opinions within the church. A confrontation erupted, however, when members of the Union of Black Clergy and Laymen (UBCL) wrestled the microphone from a speaker at the first joint session of convention and introduced Muhammed Kenyatta, a member of the Black Economic Development Conference, who demanded that the convention address the issue of racism and reparations directly. Ultimately, the convention voted to raise an additional $200,000 for development in African American communities, none of which sat well with the membership of Episcopal Church across the country.

James Paxton, from the parish, attended the special general convention and, on October 20, made a report to the vestry. Turning to local race relations, Joe Barker reported later in the meeting on the activity of the Community Action Committee, which had been formed by the Episcopal congregations of the city. Then after a general discussion, Mr. Barker moved, and Mr. Muller seconded a motion that carried putting the vestry on record as opposing the Black Manifesto contribution of $200,000. It would prove to be the bridge too far. As for much of the Episcopal Church, what happened in Indiana and the way that it had happened was asking too much. Confidence in the possibility of progress was shaken, and the seams of division appeared for the first time in a long while within All Saints itself. There was even hesitation about further participation on the local ministerial organization in the city. Darwin Fallis moved, Ira Couch seconded, and the motion carried that any action with regards to the Metropolitan Association of Churches be tabled until the next vestry meeting. However, by November, the vestry proceeded to approve membership.

A new young member of the vestry, not yet thirty years old, D. C. Bradford III, known as Woody, renewed the reports on the activity of the Community Action Committee. The results of the meeting were that seven joint meetings would be held on Wednesday evenings during Lent: four at All Saints Church and three at St. Philip's Church. By the end of the year, Bradford was also reporting on the results of the Every Member Canvass as its chairman. If this young leadership helped the parish move through the dark issues of racism, it was Bob Spire of the parish's senior leadership who held it together. An impeccable Republican and a gentleman noted for his ethics, Spire was well known in the city for his mediation of races issues in the city. He cultivated a personal friendship, Charles Washington. Washington wrote for *Omaha Star*, the African American newspaper in the city, and then became its editor. He was regularly quoted in the *Omaha World-Herald* as its best source at the time for the opinion of Omaha's African American community.

If tensions about the war and race made the task of the parish to raise money and membership difficult, there were other lesser troubles as well. Bishop Rauscher was approaching retirement. Concerned with his legacy, he was making a final push with a Centennial Fund Drive to mark the anniversary of Nebraska's transition from a missionary diocese to being a full-fledged diocese of the Episcopal Church. All Saints accepted a goal for itself of $40,000 and began on March 2, 1969, to raise the money to meet it. By April 14, they could report that with 152 pledges in, they had exceeded their goal, pledging $57,333 to the drive.

Closer to home the way the area around All Saints was developing was felt by the vestry to be disadvantageous. On April 14, 1969, Mr. Sheldon Harris and his architect attended the vestry meeting to present to them a new proposal for a commercial center and apartments at the corner of Ninetieth and Blondo and hoped for no objection from the church. Once again, on June 25, the vestry went on record opposing a commercial development; but by September 8, the rector had to report to them that the city had rezoned the corner commercial.

A Pair of Resignations

As the year ended, it was clear that the coming year would be McCallum's last. There is no official letter announcing his resignation in the minutes of the vestry. It appears that this was more of a general understanding than a surprise when McCallum brought it up. McCallum would turn sixty-five in October of the coming year, and his health was compromised by a slowly worsening emphysema. Had an earlier retirement been possible, it would have probably been beneficial for McCallum and for the parish, which needed some youth and freshness to fill the Sunday school and to attract young families. But early retirements were not common at this time, and McCallum's pension was limited. In the first place, it had begun to accrue with his ordination in 1945 in the Episcopal Church; and consequently, his time in service at the end of 1970 would be twenty-five years, fifteen years short of a full pension. His salary, which was the basis on which his pension was determined, had been modest. It had begun in 1951 at $6,000 and had grown incrementally to $12,000 in 1970. Like ministers of his era, he had lived in a rectory and did not have any equity in a home. Perhaps he had held on too long, but it was in some ways unavoidable.

The good news was that the Every Member Canvass, led by Woody Bradford, had produced a record result, $78,212, which was at the same time a testimonial for the emerging young leadership in the parish and for the parish's profound admiration of McCallum. The bad news was that the very effective assistant, Father Bee, resigned in February, and it was quickly determined that there would be no attempt to call an assistant until a new rector was in place. This was almost a necessity because an assistant priest worked for the rector, not the vestry or parish, and was expected to resign when the rector resigned. Whoever would accept a position as assistant at All Saints in 1970 would have had to tender his resignation effective next February. This would make it a hard year for McCallum, especially when it came to the launching of church school and fall programs the coming September. Adding to the bad news, the capital funding raised in the Next Step Campaign was just about exhausted. McCallum had to add to the report of a record canvass the warning "that under the present financing arrangement, the building fund would be depleted by approximately March 1971."

Fortunately, the parish had a very strong senior warden in place, Robert Spire, backed up with an equally strong new junior warden Carroll Fredrickson, both of whom belonged to the middle generation of the parish's leadership. Spire was forty-five and Fredrickson was forty, while the successful Every Member Canvass chairman Bradford was thirty, a representative of the next generation to come on. Losing no time, Spire, at the same February vestry meeting, presented a formal charge to the vestry of what it would need to do in the coming year:

1. The selection of a new rector incident to Rev. McCallum's retirement in January 1971. A calling committee will be selected shortly.
2. Revision of the current debt structure during the coming year. As previously indicated, the present cash flow will not cover monthly debt payments beyond the next twelve to fourteen months.
3. Vestry was charged to a close working relationship with the rector during this year of important changes. The vestry must give thought to more involvement in all areas of church activities with particular emphasis on youth activities.

Spire concluded his report by "emphasizing this year will be one of the most important and exciting years in the history of All Saints."

Bringing an already difficult year to an end, Bishop Rauscher also announced that he intended to resign and that he would call for a special council of the diocese to elect a new bishop coadjutor this coming January. He pointed out that he was due to complete ten years as bishop of Nebraska, and he thought that was enough. Rauscher had been an excellent bishop. He was inherently practical and actually mowed the lawn at the diocese office located in a home given to the diocese of Robert Storz on Sixty-Second Street just north of Dodge. Moreover, he was never overly impressed by the aura of the episcopal office, which rather sharply differentiated him from his peers. He said that he had found the office of bishop a lonely ministry, claiming he would sit in the office waiting for someone to call and that he frankly missed parish ministry.

The election, however, would prove to be more difficult and more seriously damaging for the diocese than anyone could have imagined. In part, this was because Rauscher had been both effective and unassuming. Rauscher had inherited Brinker's progressive administration and had continued it successfully building upon where he could and tempering it where it was needed. This was a thirty-year streak of competent, if a touch conservative, episcopal leadership. Rauscher was respected by everyone and liked by most. He had run a tight ship and felt a responsibility to see that his successor would extend this successful run of leadership. If any were to find a fault with him, it would be that he had not unleashed the latent potential of the diocese. This was a rather common theme among the younger generation of clergy in the seventies who were champing at the bit for their chance.

In some ways, the election had been set in motion by the resignation of Dean Hewett in July of 1968. Hewitt had been at the cathedral for twelve years, and the cathedral was at the peak of its success, boasting record numbers: 1,500 members and an annual contribution to the diocese of $10,700, by far the highest in the diocese. However, underneath these numbers, there was a growing division caused in part by Hewett's liberal urban strategy. Rauscher, as was his prerogative, steered the cathedral toward calling A. Donald Davies. Davies was a highly respected member of the Seabury–Western faculty, where he was the professor of Christian ministry. His name was already appearing on the short list of candidates for episcopal elections. He was both competent and conservative as his subsequent history as bishop of Dallas and Fort Worth would prove.[183] He was well known to both Rauscher and Don Haviland, the rector of St. Andrew's, who was a lifelong friend of Rauscher's. Rauscher and Haviland had grown up together in Iowa, had gone to college together, and then were classmates at Seabury–Western. Rauscher, with the knowledge of Haviland's support, saw this call as a means of bringing a highly qualified person into Nebraska who would be his logical successor, one on whom he could count on preserving the Brinker-Rauscher legacy. Davies arrived at the cathedral in December of 1968. It is unclear if Rauscher at that time had already made up his mind that he would resign at the end of 1971, but it was not long after that he announced that he would.

When the special council met at Hastings on January 25, 1970, no less than fourteen names were placed in nomination, Davies being one of them. Some of these may well have been courtesy nominations as Haviland's nomination by Fred Muller of St. James Fremont. Haviland was nearing retirement and could have hardly wanted to be bishop. Muller was another

183 Davies was elected the fourth bishop of Dallas and was consecrated on June 1970. In 1982, he divided the Diocese of Dallas and became the first bishop of Fort Worth. He retired in 1985 but became progressively more embroiled in the conservative Episcopal movement, particularly opposing women's ordination, and was drawn into supporting the Episcopal Synod of America and his deposition in 1994.

of the Seabury–Western graduates and was certainly in the loop. Unlike the famous election in 1884 following the death of Clarkson, the actual tallies of votes were not revealed or at least not made part of the public record. Nevertheless, those on the floor of the council had knowledge of the numbers. The last ballot of the morning put Davies very close to a concurrent majority, apparently a couple of votes shy in one house. When voting resumed after the lunch break, however, his support began to slip, and James Lee Stilwell, the rector of St. Matthew's Lincoln, began to rise. Obviously, some trading had been done during the break. Davies's difficulty was, from the beginning, that he seemed like he was being forced on the Diocese by Omaha. As Nebraska politics often does, things depended upon how Lincoln would pivot. A Stilwell candidacy seemed a way for the western part of the diocese to prevail. After the thirteenth ballot there was a motion to adjourn the council, but action on it was delayed to allow yet one more ballot. George Peek and Donald Haviland withdrew their names, hoping to make an election possible, but the fourteenth ballot again fell short of a concurrent majority. Frustrated, Rauscher abruptly adjourned the council with no date set to resume the election process.

On May 14, the diocese met for its regular annual council. The statistical reports portray a strong diocese. The diocese itself reported 19,961 baptized members and 14,883 communicants. The numbers in the key parishes also appear strong: Trinity Cathedral, 1,572, 1,200; All Saints, 1,276, 1,003; St. Andrew's, 1,268, 903; Holy Trinity Lincoln, 932, 794; and St. Matthew's Lincoln, 936, 771, to cite those of the leading parishes. But beneath the numbers, there were serious problems to which Bishop Rauscher gave voice to in his address.

> There is no doubt in my mind that the social revolution that is in progress throughout the world has permeated the life of the church. For this, we should be thankful, even though it is causing much travail and no little polarization. If these issues were not confronting us in the "Body of Christ" the church would, indeed, be dead already, and yet, there is evidence on many sides that the body is being torn asunder, and there is cause for concern and need for understanding and reconciliation. But even in these difficult days there is reason for that "sure and certain hope" so generously promised by Christ himself.

After talking about the struggle in the national church, which was the source of much of the contention, Rauscher turned to speak of the local effects of the crisis.

> We are faced today, within the diocese, by a crisis of fiscal affairs. The reasons for it are no doubt numerous, certainly one is dissent from the national program of social involvement. Whatever the cause, I must inform you of the results in the failure of many parishes and missions to accept fully the program apportionment for 1970. Of the seventy-four congregations in the diocese, for one reason or the other, twenty-four have failed to accept the apportionment in full.[184]

In his address, he expressed his disappointment that the special council had failed to elect a bishop coadjutor. Davies had, in the meantime, been elected bishop of Dallas, an opportunity that Nebraska had passed up. After a good deal of discussion, the decision was for the bishop to appoint a large representative committee to create a slate of appropriate nominees. They were to take as much time as they deemed necessary. When they were confident that they had done their work, they were to notify him, and he would set the date of a special council. Eventually, the electing council was set for January 24, 1971, to meet at St. Luke's Kearney.

When that council convened, the nominating committee headed by Edgar Wescot presented a lengthy report outlining the committee's work. At the conclusion of his report, he placed three names before the council: James De Wolfe Jr., Robert Varley, and Robert Witcher. A slide show introduced each candidate to the council. Along with the slides, a five-minute audio tape of each candidate was played. The results were that, on the first ballot, De Wolfe had twenty-one clergy votes and fifty-seven lay votes. Varley had twenty-six clergy votes and sixty-three lay votes, giving him a plurality. Witcher had six clergy votes and twenty-eight lay votes. In the second ballot, De Wolfe's support held, but Witcher's went to Varley, giving him a majority in both orders.

Father Varley, at the time of his election, was forty-nine years old and the rector of St. Peter's Church in Salisbury, Maryland. He was a member of the American Medical Association's committee on religion and medicine. He was also chairman of the Episcopal Church's committee on Christian social relations. His wife, Beverly, was an associate professor of Spanish at Salisbury College. They had two children: Douglas, nine and Barbara, nineteen, who was attending Roanoke College. In contrast to the reserved Rauscher, he was outgoing and highly social.

On May 5, Varley was consecrated at Trinity Cathedral and joined Rauscher at the annual council that convened at Trinity Cathedral the next day. Rauscher put Varley to work on the oversight of the parishes except for

---

184 *Journal of the Diocese of Nebraska*, 1970, The Bishop's Address, p. 73-73.

the two cathedrals. Rauscher defined his role for the time he had remaining before retirement as working with the missions of the diocese. His address was brief and somewhat lighter in tone than that of the previous council, but nonetheless, he underlined the tension and the polarization that were affecting the church's life. He argued that while there was no question that the church should be involved with caring for the poor, the tension had come about over methods, a tension that he expected that the church would be living with for some time in the future.

Within days of Varley's election, McCallum retired; and within a month, All Saints was under new leadership. Within the parish, a large residual debt had to be dealt with. Outside of the parish, the diocese was poised on the edge of a dramatic change, and the world was progressively more conflicted and less hospitable for the Episcopal Church.

Part 4

Completing the Century (1971–2000)

Chapter 8

Rising Above the Times: 1971–1980

Charles L. R. Pedersen turned off the lights and walked out of the west door of the church. He headed for his car, the green Volkswagen bus, which he had driven from Stamford, Connecticut, packed to the gills. Included were his wife, Frances; their five children, ages six through thirteen; Trooper, the family dog; and miscellaneous possessions.[185] The lengthy vestry meeting had continued well past 8:30 p.m. As February nights in Nebraska are wont to be, it was very dark and bitter cold. He had just presided over his first vestry meeting at All Saints. The minutes do not show anything remarkable by way of action taking place at the meeting, but it was quite likely that there had been a complete and open discussion about the parish's finances. Pedersen never did develop a taste for long vestry meetings or open-ended discussions, which to his mind were, at best, meaningless and likely worse. They had a way of spinning out of control. What he remembered most clearly about that night was a question that had assaulted his mind as he walked to the car. "What have I done to my family, bringing them all the way out here?"[186] That memory served him as a baseline with which he could measure what his ministry at All Saints had accomplished. To those outside of the parish, it appeared that his success was simply the result of his good fortune to have been called to a plum job, the rector of a parish with all the resources that anyone could

185 The Pedersen family consisted of Jennifer, 1958; Lee, 1960; Mary, 1962; Hugh, 1964; and James, 1965.

186 A story that Charles told me a number of times in the course of our time together at All Saints.

possibly desire. He could have hardly failed. To those on the inside, the combination of successes and ever new problems of the day had a way of erasing the memory of how perilous things had actually been during those earlier years at Ninety-Second and Blondo.

Pedersen's journey to All Saints had begun nearby, in Blair, a small town about eighteen miles to the north of Omaha. His grandparents were Danish immigrants who had settled on a farm southwest of Blair. There they raised a large family: six boys and one girl. Charles's father was Oscar, one of the younger boys. He left high school after a couple of years and went to work for the Nebraska Iowa Oil Company, selling and delivering fuel oil to farmers in the rural area around Blair. Oscar married Ora Dolan in 1931 and the new couple rented a house in Blair on Front Street. Charles came along on May 1, 1932, and he remained their only child. Charles often referred to his having been an only child as a special clue to his identity. He would marry an only child, and together they would have five children! Next to the marks caused by being an only child, he counted the marks derived from his Danish ancestry, particularly his closeness to their immigrant experience, as keys to his practical ability to get things done and to his impatience with the more pretentious reasoning why something couldn't be done. It was, of course, curious that Charles obscured the fact that he was half something else from his mother's side. He often referred to it as Irish, though it was more likely Norwegian. Given this ethic identity, one might assume that he would have been raised Lutheran, but his father sought out the Episcopal Church, apparently to free himself from the heavy hand of the Danish Lutherans who held a domineering position in the life of Blair. Charles was raised in the Episcopal Church.

Charles was an athletic, outgoing, popular kid. He was particularly proficient at baseball. What he lacked in size, he made up for with aggression. His father had not gone beyond his second year in high school. Charles would remember his father as a man who worked very hard and who fully enjoyed life.

In 1948, a new Episcopal priest came to St. Mary's, Blair. James Stillwell was twenty-seven years old, fresh from Berkeley Divinity. Stillwell was a native Nebraskan and found himself on the Lincoln campus in pursuit of a college education when the country went to war. He joined the B-12 naval officer training offered there and found himself in command of a PT-boat. He came out of the war with a sense of vocation like many of his generation, and he found his way into the Episcopal Church. The young Father Stillwell was a striking figure. He was poised, a benefit one suspects of officer training, and he was very bright, a member of the Mensa Society. He was, as his formation at Berkeley would indicate, high church, and he was very confident about his ministry. Instantly, he became a mentor for Charles, then sixteen, and would remain so for the rest of his life. Pedersen's own inclinations toward a priestly vocation were quickly solidified by Stillwell's influence. A second priest, Frederick Muller, rector of nearby St. James' Fremont, seconded Stillwell's encouragement. The two priests would remain an important influence on him throughout his life.

Charles L. R. Pedersen, Rector 1971-1993, br. 1932, Blair, Nebraska, d. 2007

The role of these two mentors in Pedersen's life became particularly important when his father was killed on June 30, 1951. Oscar was killed instantly when his tank truck skidded on a gravel road west of Kennard. He was on his usual route but was apparently unaware that gravel had been piled on the road preparatory to smoothing it out. The truck skidded fifty feet, knocking off the guard rail of a bridge and ending up in the creek below. Oscar was thrown another twenty-eight feet from the truck and suffered a broken neck and various head injuries. At the time, Charles was nineteen and away for summer school at the University of Wisconsin.

Returning home, he completed two years at Dana College and then went on to the University of Nebraska at Lincoln to finish his degree.

His athleticism and his extroverted personality made him quite popular on campus. He gave little indication to his fellow students that he was headed to seminary, and they certainly wouldn't have guessed it. Whenever occasions during his college years at the University of Nebraska seemed to take him off-course, his two watchful mentors were quick to set him back on it. He graduated from the university in June of 1954 with a degree in psychology and speech. The following September, he showed up at Berkeley Divinity School in New Haven, Connecticut.

The choice of Berkeley was due, no doubt, to Father Stillwell's influence. Berkeley was a liberal Catholic seminary with a high academic standard. While Berkeley was an ideal fit for Stillwell, with his high IQ, it was a challenge for Pedersen. Pedersen was not a traditional student. He did not do well when confronted with a pile of books that had to be read or with demands for term papers to be turned in. On the other hand, anything he heard he remembered. Years later, he could quote verbatim from the lectures that he had heard in seminary.[187] In the 1950s, Berkeley was on the cutting edge of liturgical renewal, and Charles was deeply influenced by E. R. Hardy, the seminary's church historian and liturgist. Another of Berkeley's fine scholars at the time was Dr. Elmer Cook, professor of New Testament. Dr. Cook was, in addition to being a scholar, a sensitive priest, and he took the struggling student from the West under his wings. As a result, Charles was often in the Cook's home. Dr. Cook and his wife, Esther, had a daughter, Frances, already a graduate nurse, living at home. In the course of time, Charles courted Frances, and they were married November 11, 1956. Graduation came in May of 1957, and the newly ordained deacon was posted by Bishop Brinker as vicar of St. Charles, Fairbury, and of two other small churches attached to the field in Wymore and Hebron.

His father-in-law, Dr. Cook, died in October of 1959, young and unexpectedly. The distance was difficult, and his wife, Frances, was, as you will recall, their only child. Frances's desire to be closer to her mother led Pedersen to consider looking for a call in that area. Shortly, he received a call to be the rector to Holy Trinity in Pawling, New York. Pawling was a charming Hudson River valley town not far from New York City, and Holy Trinity was a relatively new congregation sharing its ministry with Christ Church, Patterson. Pedersen left Pawling in 1963 to take charge of

187 I followed Charles at Berkeley Divinity School eight years later and had several of the same professors, particularly, Dr. E. R. Hardy, BDS's leading scholar at the time. Hardy had received his PhD from Columbia when he was sixteen and was a formidable lecturer. I was frequently amazed by Charles accurate recall of Hardy's lectures.

a new parish that was being founded in Stamford, Connecticut. There he had the opportunity to build a new church.

It is hard to convey what an incredible advancement it was for a young Nebraska priest to be the rector of an Episcopal church in Stamford, Connecticut, in the sixties. At that time, the Diocese of Connecticut was the powerhouse of the Episcopal Church. The bishop of Connecticut had two suffragan bishops to assist him with the management of the thriving diocese. The Connecticut clergy were among the best in the country, which meant there was an opportunity to learn by interacting with one's peers. Pedersen's outgoing nature helped him to take full advantage of what was on hand.

In addition to the strengths within the diocese, many of the executives of the national church lived in Connecticut, and they made available to the Connecticut clergy every new workshop on liturgy, ministry, and stewardship before they more or less filtered out to the rest of the country. Among these opportunities was a course on pastoral studies lead by Dr. Charles Taylor, the assistant director of Youth Programs in the Diocese of New York. Pedersen was also placed on the unique First Team Ministry founded by the Diocese of Connecticut to explore the latest theories on expanded ministries. Pedersen's verbal recall turned these resources into a powerful asset for the rest of his ministry.

Stamford was profiting from the suburban explosion of New York City. The new congregation of Trinity, which had called him as rector, counted among its parishioners a number of New York City executives, including Walter Cronkite of CBS news fame. It afforded Charles the opportunity to participate in a building project that made use of all the latest ideas promulgated by the Associated Parishes, which was the clearing house for the most up-to-date ideas about liturgy and church building.[188] Trinity's building was altar-centered, forgoing a long aisle and choir favored in traditional Episcopal churches. It is not easy to understand why Pedersen was persuaded to leave such a fine facility, which he had designed and built, in such a vibrant area of the country to come back to Nebraska.

The Diocese of Nebraska had, of course, kept its eye on Pedersen, and when an opening at Trinity Cathedral came along in 1970, his name was placed on its list by Bishop Rauscher, no doubt, at the urging of Stillwell and Muller. The cathedral, however, chose to call Jack Fricke, who had been the assistant to the prior dean of the cathedral. Whether Pedersen

188 Associated Parishes for Liturgy and Mission was founded in 1946. It was an advocate promoting the adoption of Eucharist as the main service on Sunday and for the revision of the American Book of Common Prayer. Their efforts were highly significant during the sixties and seventies.

would have said yes if he had been invited by the cathedral is unclear, but it was his habit to refer to the leadership at the cathedral as "that gang." A year later, when All Saints embarked on its search for a new rector, it is not surprising that Pedersen's name came up again. What was different this time was the search committee from All Saints pursued his candidacy with a great deal of enthusiasm. The committee, which visited Stanford to observe him celebrate and preach, were duly impressed. A snappy five-minute sermon caused one of the members to say in the midst of the service, "That's our man."[189] It did not hurt that he was a Nebraska boy, indeed, one who had played football at the university, and that he immediately struck anyone who encountered him as a high energy person.

The committee's enthusiasm, in fact, caused them to overlook some of its own guidelines in the profile, which it had prepared for its search. The most important of these was the advice that they had received from McCallum that the candidate be a low or middle-of-the-road churchman. Pedersen was quite Catholic in his churchmanship, and in a sense, it set up a replay of tension that surrounded Galaty's arrival at All Saints, 1948. There was little difference between Galaty and Pedersen except that Pedersen was perhaps more of a pragmatist than Galaty.

Pedersen, on his part, had never shed his Midwestern egalitarianism, work ethic, or nostalgia for Nebraska football, all of which, strange as it may seem, had contributed to his success in the East. The great mentors of his life, Stillwell and Muller, however, reminded him of a debt he owed to the Diocese of Nebraska and that he was being offered what was potentially the most important job in Nebraska. Again, one suspects enthusiasm was trumping guidelines.

So here they were, Pedersen and the parish, on the cusp of a great adventure.

Taking Hold of the Challenge

The debt and its effect on the operating budget was the parish's most urgent problem, and it would continue to define Pedersen rectorship until it was paid off in May of 1977. As 1971 came to an end, All Saints income was under budget by nearly $13,000. The actual income was $78,457 as opposed to the $91,000, which had been budgeted the previous January. Expenditures had been held down to $89,525, due in part to Pedersen's frugality, which gained for him the reputation in the parish of being a penny-pincher. He was, after all, a child of the Depression. In spite of

189 Told by Dr. Vale Sorenson, a member of the call committee.

the best efforts to cut cost, it was abundantly clear that this was a deficit budget, which was not sustainable. The debt, which was sucking funds out of the operating budget, the vestry reported as consisting of four outstanding loans:

9302 Blondo Unamortized	$87,000
9302 Blondo Amortized	39,195.23
8308 Seward	15,092.75
1838 No. 53rd	18,452.79
Total	$159,720.77

During the past year, the reduction of the loan had been limited to $8,512.22, providing little hope that it would be reduced to a manageable sum any time in the foreseeable future. Pedersen could see quite clearly that any modification of how the debt was impacting the parish would require a major fund drive. The participants in the previous capital fund drive, the Next Step, had finished paying on those pledges, for the most part, in June of 1969, not that far in the past to be forgotten. Moreover, the task of raising money to pay off debt that had been incurred by others in the past is notoriously plagued by negativity. It raised questions, such as "How did we get into such debt?" "Why aren't we growing?" or "Will we be any further ahead when we get out of this debt?" Pedersen began to try to cast the problem in a new framework: how could paying off the debt be clearly linked with moving ahead in a new direction?

Meanwhile, he had to face the pressure of the daily demands of maintaining the building and grounds. Preparing for the spring of 1971, the vestry received a report from Dr. Richard Peterson on lawn upkeep needs. Mar-H Nursery presented a bid of $750 for sod for the front of the church plus $60 to $70 per treatment for dandelions. Jack Sprague moved to accept this bid for sod and for the treatment of the remainder of the lawn with preemergence. By September, the parish was required by the city to provide a sidewalk along Blondo Street, more than six hundred feet of sidewalk. The expenditure was an unanticipated $1,475. By March of the next year, the vestry was again dealing with the lawn issues. It accepted a bid from Shur Lawn Service Co. to provide lawn care for the seventy-one thousand square feet of lawn located directly in front of the church for the sum of $432. This was the most sensitive area in regard to those coming to church, but it was less than 20 percent of the property. Large sections were being rough cut, with an aging and unwieldy mower usually operated by Pedersen's eldest son, Lee. An additional $1,000 was authorized for expenses to cover this outlying work without further action of the vestry. The constant expense was a problem, but from Pedersen's point of view, it was not so much the expense as in the time it was eating up at vestry meetings. It did not make sense to him that the vestry should be preoccupied with lawn problems when it should be dealing with larger issues, such as the debt and the growth of the parish.

Building issues also continued to surface. Heating and cooling continued to be a problem. There was a need to improve the existing Sunday school rooms. In June of 1971, the vestry approved remodeling the Sunday school rooms at a cost of $440 for material and $60 for paint. The most serious building issue was the stability of the supporting arches. The roof swayed too much in the wind for comfort. On June 3, 1973, the vestry took action to address this issue, moving that the senior warden and the building and grounds chairman are empowered to make such expenditures as are necessary in the repair of the faults in the arches and to incur such other expenses for consultants and other persons and function as are required for the proper and complete resolving of the situation and what other procedures are required for the protection of the church and its interests.

By November, the vestry retained Nicas–Goldstein Associates of Indiana and Dana Larson Roubal and Associates of Omaha to come up with a solution. This lead to the large metal plates being installed on the beams in the main church joining the main rafters to the shorter rafters, which were anchored into the sidewalls.

Another serious problem was the lack of help with which to deal with the complex demands of the parish. Agnus Munson, who had been the parish secretary since 1948, had resigned. Fortunately, Pedersen was able to recruit a newcomer to the parish as his secretary, Sue Caraker. Sue had recently moved to Omaha, and she and her husband had joined the parish. Dick had become active in the lay empowerment program called Doulos, which Pedersen had initiated. Their daughter Cathy played the guitar at the nine fifteen service. Sue proved to be an exceptionally competent and loyal parish secretary. Another parishioner emerged as communication secretary, Judy Henrichsen. Both she and her husband, Bob, were extremely active both in Doulos, Odd Couples, the lay fellowship groups, and like the Carakers, they participated in the square-dancing club, which met in the parish's undercroft on Wednesday nights. Judy's task as communication secretary was challenging. The ability to afford an outside printer for a newsletter had disappeared with Clayton, and for some time, parish communication was limited to occasionally duplicated letters. This was the age of the mimeograph, an inexpensive but crude technology, and Judy was quite expert at getting the most out of this limited technology.

Office space was a problem. The office core had been tightly configured on the north side of the west wing. The rector's office was thirteen feet by eleven feet located immediately adjacent to the secretary's office. It was not a little confining for a disciplined personality like McCallum's, but for a frenetic and easily distracted person like Pedersen, it was prison. The assistant's office immediately adjacent to the rector's was smaller yet, ten feet by ten feet.

New Directions

Pedersen had found some assistance with the building from a retired union carpenter, Beecher Jones. He was the father of Jerry Jones, whom the parish had sponsored for the priesthood and hired as an assistant priest in the early 1960s. Beecher Jones would build anything that Pedersen asked him to and would do it with uncanny economy. The two were perfect partners. The south side of the west wing had originally been largely devoted to the rector's chapel. As a chapel, it was neither attractive nor useful, and Pedersen set Beecher Jones on the task of turning the space into a sizable rector's office, sixteen feet by sixteen feet. This office boasted large mahogany panels, which Pedersen had personally salvaged out of the old First National Bank Building when it was being remodeled. Next to it was fitted an assistant's office, ten feet by twelve feet, and an even smaller but private office, for Sue Caraker, the rector's personal secretary.

That left Judy Henrichsen on the other side hall, dealing with a stream of volunteers, Ed and Eddie Wiedner; the money counters, Becky Frazer and Shirley Loring; Sunday school volunteer codirectors; and a variety of other drop-ins seeking to place announcements in the bulletin to procure posters and sometimes just for a visit. The realignment of the office was, in fact, a workable, if modest solution.

Henrichsen's expertise at cranking out mimeograph text allowed a publication to be mailed to the parish weekly, the first regular parish instrument of communication since the Depression had done in *Church and Home*. Styled the *All Saints Herald*, it was written by the rector and a string of volunteers, beginning with Arlene Hinchcliff and Peggy Sorenson. In it, Pedersen included personal often humorous revelations about himself. In the opening letter, he confesses: "I gained 10-pounds on going-away parties in Stamford . . . now I am in danger of gaining 10 more on welcome-here parties in Omaha . . . no hope for those with no will power . . ." Pedersen frequently used himself as the butt of jokes, which often turned on his lack of discipline or willpower. He liked to talk about his golf game, which would come to a head when the annually scheduled game with the past call committee was due. Having a competitive nature, he doubly hated the experience. He frequently joked that the key to succeeding at golf came down to the ability to concentrate on one thing for thirty seconds, and no one should be surprised that it wasn't his game!

The assistant's office, however, remained unfilled. In March of 1971, the lease on the house on Steward Street, which the parish owned and had been used for McCallum's assistants, came up for renewal. The vestry voted to lease for another year to the family living in it, precluding a search for an assistant until the following year. Finally, in December of that year, the vestry passed a motion authorizing the rector to hire an assistant as soon as possible after consultation with the senior warden as to the availability of the necessary funds. In all likelihood, the vestry envisioned hiring an assistant in May, when seminary graduates became available. In January, it was decided to sell the house. This was, in part, because the parish was still not in a position to proceed in hiring an assistant and, in part, because the church as a whole had begun to move away from owning housing for its clergy and toward providing housing allowances, which the clergy could use to make arrangements for their own housing. In the course of the year, Pedersen himself would buy the rectory located at Fifty-Third and Blondo from the parish. This took the parish out of the "landlord" business, for which parishes were never particularly well suited. It allowed the clergy to deal directly with their own housing and, at the same time, to acquire equity.

In the meantime, Pedersen had made an arrangement with Dr. George Barger to serve as a part-time assistant. Dr. Barger was a professor of sociology at the University of Nebraska at Omaha and had recently been ordained in the Episcopal Church after serving for some time as a Disciples of Christ minister. He did some preaching, counseling, and adult education, for which he was particularly well suited. Even when a full-time assistant was at last hired, Barger continued on. His service to the parish continued until 1979, when he found himself at cross purposes with Pedersen in a difficult divorce, which shook the parish in a particularly hard way.

A new direction particularly dear to Pedersen's heart was the possibility of an alternative service. At the March 1972 vestry meeting, Pedersen reported on a proposed 9:30 a.m. service. It should be remembered that the call committee had listed as a desirable trait for the new rector that he be "progressive in the sense of receptive to new ideas in development of church services and programs." Pedersen was frustrated with the constraints of the two services that he had inherited. The classic eight-o-clock was populated by those who sought the bare minimum, short, sweet, and unremarkable. At least it was the Eucharist. The eleven-o-clock service, on the other hand, was Morning Prayer, three Sundays a month, and it was dominated by the choir under the direction of Cecil Neubecker. McCallum had himself inherited Neubecker, and their mode of operation had been to split ownership of the service. McCallum, whose sense of liturgy was invested heavily in preaching, controlled the liturgy, and Neubecker controlled the music. The influence of Berkeley Divinity School and the Associated Parishes movement on Pedersen provided him with the conviction that the Eucharist should be the normative service for a Sunday, that the Eucharist should be celebrated from a table altar in the center of the worship space, and that music should be an integral part of the liturgy. The liturgy should control the music and not simply give place to it. Pedersen had, in fact, actually experienced the execution of these principles in his church at Trinity Stamford, which was altar-centered and had no formal choir. The altar at All Saints was at the far end of the church, separated from the congregation by a large antiphonally-arranged-chancel choir. The space could not have been more antithetical to the liturgy that he felt called to offer the parish. It was one of several struggles Pedersen had with the building he had come to work in. The proposed nine-thirty service would allow for a weekly Sunday Eucharist at an altar table to be set in front of the choir, with music drawn from the popular jazz and folk masses of the time.[190] It would be active, concise, and child friendly. The proposal remained, however, on the drawing board for lack of the resource to pull it off.

With the arrival of May, the rector could at last report that, after due consultation with the senior warden, he had hired Rev. George Martin as assistant rector on the following terms: "Salary $8,000, Auto $1,000 Ins. $800, Housing Allowance $3,600 and pension $1,800. Martin would begin on September 1, 1972." At last, help was on the way.

Martin had been raised in Toledo, Ohio, and educated at Hobart College, the historic Episcopal College in New York. From there, he had gone to Bexley Hall, the Episcopal seminary in Gambier, Ohio, famous for its low-church orientation and missionary zeal. Martin was ordained in Ohio on June 17, 1967. His first assignment was curate at St. John's Church, Cuyahoga Falls, Ohio. After two years, he returned to studies, enrolling at the University of Nebraska in a three-year program that lead to a master's degree in sociology. The University of Nebraska had the advantage of being near to his wife's home in Seward, Nebraska. There was, in the 1960s, a strong inclination among seminary graduates to seek

[190] Ian Mitchell, The American Folk Song Mass, 1967 FEL Record.

additional academic credentials, and many, such as Martin, did so. Perhaps this related to the sense that ministry was becoming more complicated and that the seminaries in themselves were not completely sufficient to prepare one to meet the challenge.

While Martin was enrolled at the University of Nebraska at Lincoln, he worked part-time at Holy Trinity. Upon completion of his master's degree, George accepted a call to come to All Saints. When he came to All Saints, he and his wife, Caroline Jones, had four children. Pedersen wrote in the *All Saints Herald*: "I feel we are fortunate to be able to obtain the service of such a qualified and energetic young man as part of the ministry here at All Saints."

In the fall of 1973, Martin took charge of the church school. He put into place an innovative open-classroom concept. The theory, borrowed from trends current at the time in secular education, was that each child learns at different rates and in different ways, therefore various choices needed to be presented to children in order to allow them to learn the material in their own way. The material of the Bible and Christian experiences were packaged as stories. The appropriate goal was to provide the children with an ownership of the stories, not to understand the story. The child would, according to the jargon, "be able to unpacked the stories" at a later time in his or her life when experience made them understandable. The material was presented by a storytelling team to the assembled Sunday school. After the story, the group was broken up into small interest groups. The chief resource Martin used as a source for his storytellers was the "Purple Puzzle Tree," which had been created by Concordia, the publishing house of the Missouri Synod Lutherans. It is clear that Pedersen gave his assistant an open hand in the creation of the educational program. Martin had a regular column in the *All Saints Herald* and regularly spent time brain storming with Pedersen on all aspects of the parish's life. In a short time, Martin developed a great deal of loyalty among the kids of the parish, the church school volunteers, and many of the young couples attending All Saints.

Martin had a beard. This was the period when beards were popular in youth culture but, on the other hand, controversial in the church. He also played the guitar, which was even more of an issue since, to many, the guitar was a means of inserting "radical" ideas into the church and society in general. These features of Martin's identity paved the way for the alternative service that Pedersen had wanted for some time, and a "9:15 Family Eucharist" was begun at the beginning of 1973. Amazingly, the ironing board that despised altar table, which had been built for the new church but which had been quickly displaced by the old altar, reappeared. It was dragged to the center of the crossing each Sunday at nine fifteen only to return to the wall after the forty-minute service. The quarter-hour difference had been suggested by Martin as a way to allow a more adequate church school for adults and children to follow the service, and it allowed them to be out of the building before the eleven-o-clock congregation started to arrive. This required a second church school session to be run for the eleven-o-clock service. By 1975, the nine-thirty regularly exceeded the size of the eleven, averaging about one hundred thirty-five, while the eleven averaged one hundred. This was not without some degree of rivalry, including an argument over which group was contributing the most money to the parish.

In the course of the year, Pedersen had another stroke of luck. Fred Lehmen moved to town with his wife, Lucille. His daughter Paula was active in the guilds, church school, and parish fellowship, and his son-in-law, George Rood, was active on the vestry and had already served as Every Member Canvass chairman several times.[191] Paula Rood's father was a retired executive of the large department store chain Macy's. Retirement never sat well with Fred. His last assignment for the company had been in Kansas City, where he regularly found a way to go back to work for Macy's on special assignments. The move to Omaha was supposedly going to solve this problem, but coming under Pedersen's radar, he was enlisted to help out by joining the staff in March of 1973 as business manager. This now gave Pedersen a considerable staff, something that was unprecedented in the history of All Saints.

Taking on the Debt Issue

Going into the fall of 1973, Pedersen felt that he had put into place a solid program with a new direction. James Paxton, an old-school gentleman and one of the last representatives of All Saints socially prominent old families, returned from the 1973 general convention held in Louisville with a positive message. The essence of his report was summarized in the minutes of the vestry: "In comparison with the confrontation and agonies through which we suffered at South Bend in 1969, this one was relatively harmonious and peaceful . . . The election of John M. Allin, bishop of Mississippi, as our presiding bishop was, in my judgment, the event which will have the greatest impact on the future of our beloved Episcopal

[191] George and Paula Rood joined the parish in 1966. George was an engineer who worked for Northern Natural Gas, subsequently Internorth, and ultimately Enron. They moved to Houston in 1980 and returned in 1986.

Church. He is quite the opposite of our present presiding bishop whose policies have brought about a serious split in our membership."[192]

This was a welcome relief, though the general convention presented the local parish with a wide range of issues that could not be ignored. In the following issue of the *All Saints Herald*, the plan to deal with these issues was laid out. Father Martin and Father Barger would begin an adult class dealing with some of the major issues faced by the recent general convention, which were listed as:

> Ordination of Women and Response to Change; Liturgical Renewal: the Green Book; the Green Book II; alternations proposed in Baptismal and Confirmation rites, etc.; the proposed budget; and putting money into program.

The parish's own fall program would be followed with an actual use to the Trial Rite, Number Two, communion service on Advent 1. In many ways, Berkeley Divinity School had prepared Pedersen for these changes in the prayer book, most of which were in line with his own goals, such as establishing the Eucharist as the normal worship for Sundays. With Martin and Barger, he had the support that he needed to sell it to the parish at least to give himself the cover he needed to get it done.

Leaving this task to his lieutenants, it was time for him to take on the elephant in the room, the parish debt. He proposed that the parish should not just retire its debt, but it should undertake a true "next step," an exciting new adventure. In March 1973, Pedersen presented the vestry with a preliminary report on a retreat center project. A retreat center, Pedersen argued, would bring a whole new concept to All Saints for the way it worked with its children and its adults. Pedersen had concluded this report with the announcement that "The committee has been selected and is researching possibilities, a further report will be presented next month."

By October 25, he could report that the parish has an offer of $55,000 if the church raised an equal amount for a new building to be built on church property for youth education. This was not a matter of luck but an intentional effort that had been under way since March to locate the significant advanced gift that would make the run for the money possible. It was precisely half of the anticipated cost of the retreat center. At the October meeting, the senior warden, L. K. Muller added to the report that the parish had an obligation to complete the organ at the estimated cost of $10,000 and that it owed, $80,000 on its mortgage. In a carefully orchestrated next step, Robert Bell moved that the vestry accept the offer

192 *All Saints Herald*, October 17, 1973.

of $55,000 and set out to raise a total of $250,000 to cover cost of the new building, finish the organ, and pay off the balance of the mortgage.

A motion followed that the vestry should conduct a study as to whether the facility would be best as an addition connected to the original structure or as a freestanding building. In fact, the plan for a freestanding building was already so far down the road that it is hard to imagine how the plan could be reversed at this point. The idea, which had originated with Pedersen, was an alternative to building classrooms. According to the master plan, which had been created by Charles Morton, the parish's architect in 1963, All Saints next step after paying off the mortgage should have been building a church school wing for which he had provided a design. That proposal had behind it the assumptions and methods of the fifties. The assumption in the fifties was that the church school population would continue to rise and the master plan had predicted that the enrollment would reach five hundred children. American demographics were changing rapidly, and that was something that was not going to happen. In fact, church school enrollment would never exceed two hundred fifty, and average weekly attendance has generally hovered around one hundred. The methods of working with children in the church also changed.

In the fifties, a number of graded curriculums were produced by the National Episcopal Church. Nationally, the premier curriculum was the Seabury Series, which was extremely well done but much beyond the competence of volunteers in most parishes. All Saints used the graded material of the St. James Series, which was easier to use but considerably less exciting. These curriculums envisioned a trained teacher working in a classroom setting with well-disciplined children who did what they were told to do. By the seventies, graded material was becoming unpopular as was the classroom model, not only in the church, but also even in the public school system. Children, it was said, needed to be engaged with storytelling and in experience-based activities and not sat down in classrooms in the same way that they supposedly spent their past week. This, as we have seen, had already been adopted as the model of All Saints Church School. Motivation had to replace discipline. Moreover, the premise that trained teachers could be recruited to fill the classrooms was always problematic. The retreat center promised to take children out of the classroom center and greatly enhance their contact with the clergy of the parish, who were "trained teachers" for the most part.

If one problem with classrooms was that they were passé, the other was that they had one and only one use. For the most part, they would stand empty except for an hour or two of use at most on a Sunday morning. The retreat center would provide overnight experiences for children combined with a breath of learning activities, but it also would provide a meeting facility for small groups of various kinds, for prayer, learning, and fellowship. The compelling argument in favor of a freestanding facility was that it would be accessible in a way that a room or rooms in the main building were not. Opening up a room in the main building for a particular group gave them access to the whole building. Heating and cooling such a room required heating or cooling most if not all of the building. That meant the need for a custodian to open the facility and oversee the activation of the complicated mechanical system and restoration of it afterward to the appropriate setback. Anyone with a single key and the knowledge of how to operate a thermostat in one's home would be able to open and close this proposed retreat center, raising no issue of the security of the rest of the building.

With the idea of a retreat center, Pedersen had found the way to give the necessity of raising money to retire the debt, a forward look. The fund drive was launched on February 19, 1974, with a seasoned parish leader, Joe Barker, as its chairman. The material for the drive announced three goals: $110,000 for a new retreat center, $87,000 to pay off the mortgage, and $15,000 to complete the pipe organ. Shortly after the drive opened, the *All Saints Herald* announced that the Retreat Center Drive had already received $125,000 in advanced gifts. By April, it reported that pledges had reached $225,000.

That was close enough to put things in motion. Pedersen drew on members of the parish to bring the project in on as small a budget as possible. One strategy that Pedersen used to get the most out of the money at hand was to use professionals within the parish who were either willing to donate their services or to work at a reduced charge. William Scott, who was a professional surveyor, provided, for expenses, a survey of the section of the property necessary for the building. Robert Stitt, another member of the parish who had done much for the parish over the years, took on the role of the general contractor. The architect was a freelance architect, Robert Amick, officed at 2507 S. Ninetieth Street, who had been under contract since April 10, 1974. The building would be 60 feet by 31 feet, giving it a footprint of 1,860 square feet. The downstairs would, for the most part, be above ground, making use of the slope on the north end of the property to minimize excavation. The lower level was to be divided into 12 individual rooms, a woman's bathroom and men's bathroom, each with a shower. The upstairs room was a large open space under a cathedral ceiling. At the north end was a stone fireplace, giving the room a comfortable lodgelike atmosphere.

The plan, however, quickly ran into trouble with the city planners. There was no bathroom upstairs, it was not handicap accessible, and the amount of bathroom space downstairs, they declared, was inadequate. The case for the facility was fought fiercely, and Pedersen, not necessarily right on all accounts, prevailed. Ground was broken on June 2, 1974. When the vestry meeting came around on December 16, 1974, Stitt promised it that the work would be completed on January 6. A great deal of plumbing remained to be done as did the painting of the interior, which was to be done by volunteers from the parish. The good news, Muller reported, was that the cash flow was on track with the help of the annual St. Nicholas Festival, headed by Dorothy Eckstrom, which had raised $2,000 for the completion of the center. By the end of January, it was announced that the building would be used on Ash Wednesday for the first time.

As the first retreats began in March of 1975, Pedersen provided a definition in the *All Saints Herald* as to what a retreat was to be.

> What is a Retreat? Retreat is perhaps not the best word for the small-group study, worship and fun sessions that we have in the new center. I just can't think of a better word. But what does happen at one of these things: The sessions run from 1:00 p.m. on Saturday until 9:00 a.m. on Sunday. In each of these sessions there are five hours of directed study, discussion and creative projects. There are two hours of formal worship and prayer with some silent time. The rest of the time is eating and sleeping. This setting of the new center and the fact that we are working in small groups makes it possible to have a great deal more depth in the working learning experience. The theme of the retreats are set to meet the interest and need of the various groups.

Things were on track. The retreat center had come in under budget. Parish groups such as St. Margaret's Guild, Odd Couples, and the vestry itself soon owned it as their preferred meeting space. Families used it for reunions, graduation parties, and receptions. The use exceeded expectation. Income from the drive continued to come in, making it possible to predict that the mortgage would be paid for by the end of the coming May; and even the organ project, which had a limited appeal to the practical-minded Pedersen, would be completed, although it would not actually be done until November of 1978.

Unfolding a New Order

Along with the good news came a number of new challenges. The income from the capital pledge drive, though coming in as well as was to be expected, would not be sufficient to pay off the mortgage for another twenty-four months. Only then would money be available for the addition to the organ. The addition was intended to be an antiphonal rank, including an eight-foot *trompette en chamade*. While the chests and pipes were under construction, the actual installation was only vaguely conceived with a great deal of room left for how expensive it would be in the end.

Then on March 7, 1976, Cecil Neubecker, who had been Organist and Choirmaster since 1941, died suddenly of a heart attack. His health had not been good for some time, and the previous September, the parish had given him special recognition at the eleven-o-clock service for twenty-five years of service as the parish's director of music. At the ceremony, Neubecker was given a paid winter vacation in Phoenix, Arizona, for himself and his wife, Virginia. Neubecker's death presented Pedersen with a difficult problem since probably next to money, nothing is so perennially contentious in the life of a parish as music. The laity are quick to defer when it comes to theology or ethics, but they are much more secure in offering opinions about dollars and cents and what they like and don't like in music. The choir itself, a significant group within the parish, entered into a time of grieving and was anxious about their future and about as to whether a prestigious music program would be maintained at All Saints. Pedersen was on the spot.

On the other hand, it was an opportunity to adjust the music program to the direction that he felt compelled to move the parish. Quickly, he announced that in the existing music program, the parish had a choir directress and organist, which were adequate for the time being. This was Lois Carlson, who had been recruited as a paid soloist, and Linda Shirk, the assistant organist. With their appointments, Pedersen bought some time, and he also made a shift, which would become permanent, from a full-time music director to part-time musicians. This was, in fact, an unprecedented change as All Saints had had a full-time music director since 1891! To Pedersen, this was in part a budget issue, and it bought space in All Saints budget for things that he considered priorities.

It also gave him an opportunity to reshape the music program to the new demands of the parish. Obviously, the alternative service, which had gained a strong following, often exceeding that of the eleven-o-clock, required nontraditional music. Even the eleven-o-clock, which was progressively more liturgical, required a different kind of music. In general, Morning Prayer was rather undersized for a Sunday morning, leaving plenty of room for a twenty-minute sermon and for extensive musical offerings. The music offering consisted of the chants that made up the Morning Prayer service and the classic choir anthem. Both the twenty-minute sermon and the large musical offering presented a problem, however, when the Eucharist was celebrated once a month. No one thought to blame the preacher or the music people for the service being overly long once a month and not a few simply avoided coming on communion Sundays.

Pedersen, however, was gradually working to replace Morning Prayer with the Eucharist. His preaching was oriented to a twelve-minute sermon, and he found it difficult personally to deal with a service that was lengthened by the music. It will be remembered that the search committee had been swayed by the conciseness with which he preached. Moreover, the music for him was meant to serve the liturgy by connecting directly with the lessons that were read and with the themes and traditions of the liturgical year.

Following in short order came another major loss. George Martin announced on April 4, 1975, that he had accepted the call to be rector of St. Luke's, Minneapolis. Father Martin had served All Saints since September 1972, and he had clearly been more than the average two-year curate. He and his wife, Caroline, and their four children, Kay, Susan, Timothy, and Michael, would leave Omaha on June 8. Pedersen wrote in the *All Saints Herald*, "During his almost 3-years at All Saints, Father Martin has served the parish with spirit, creativity and guitar. He has worked as priest, counselor, leader and friend. He has added a new dimension to the church school concept through the creation of the unique Interest Center Church School. Father Martin's Christian attitude and action have enriched the lives of all who know him." Again faced with the need to act quickly, he put Martin's two key volunteers, Becky Frazer and Shirley Loring, in charge of the church school.

At the vestry meeting in April, Pedersen outlined his progress on a search for replacement of Father Martin. September came, and the two volunteers launched the church school. The season when it was most likely to find an assistant, around the time seminaries graduated their seniors, was past, and a frustrated Pedersen reported to the vestry that he would suspend the search until December, when he would again begin contacting seminaries. The absence of an assistant had, however, saved about $7,000. George Barger had continued as a part-time assistant at $2,400 a year, and in February, Jess Borg was called back into service as a consultant to the church school.

Despite these problems, the rector's report to the annual meeting in January of 1976 was extremely positive and quite up front for Pedersen. It was printed and included in the *All Saints Herald* so as to reach as wide an audience as possible. "In twelve days I will have completed five years as your rector. It just doesn't seem possible that five years have gone by so quickly . . . My report this year is a special delight to me because 1975 has been a year that marked several important junctures in our work together." It was possible for him to announce that "the mortgage would be burned this coming May 1, that the retreat center has been completed and paid for, and the anticipated addition to the organ would be installed in the coming year."

In his report, he said that he anticipated that All Saints would achieve in the coming year a "team ministry." The concept of team ministries was being widely touted in church circles in the seventies as the wave of the future, and it will be remembered that he had participated in an early experiment with team ministry in Connecticut. A team ministry was a replacement of the rector-curate model in which an assistant priest worked circumspectly in the shadow of the rector who was in himself "the ministry." Yet for various reasons, team ministries seldom were attempted, and seldom lasted for any significant period. Pedersen said in his report:

> I expect that we will have a curate in the near future. This will be a younger man, and with Jess, George, and myself, we can assist him with more than sixty total years of experience in education. I see this man as being primarily directed to developing a fuller program in the area of retreats, newcomers, and Junior/Senior High work. Christian education at All Saints is really a full time job. I can envision the same sort of team effort from the past as being our thrust in the future. Although it has been difficult to locate a suitable curate so far, I am confident that we will accomplish our goal in the near future. For sure, we will not have someone here who is not totally committed to our programs and its direction.

An opportunity appeared in February, when Neil deRijik, from the Diocese of Nevada, was invited to come to Omaha for an interview in regard to curate position. It is not clear why, but the interview did not lead to a new assistant. At the vestry meeting the following month, Dr. James Kelsy pressed Pedersen to hire a woman curate. Pedersen replied "that the only woman candidates for the curate vacancy had not been willing to promise not to seek ordination until the general assembly approves ordination of women." A full discussion of women in the church ensued in the vestry.

The House of Bishops at that time had made it clear that they were nearly unanimous in their support of women's ordination. At the general convention in 1973, it was the House of Deputies that had not supported it. Pedersen had attended that convention as a deputy and had, in fact, voted no. In the meantime, irregular ordinations had taken place in 1974, the so-called Philadelphia 11. It was generally assumed, however, that it would be passed at the next general convention. Charles, in his pragmatism, was prepared for that to happen but had a great deal of concerns as to the practical implementation of women in the priesthood. The behavior of the Philadelphia 11 raised concerns for him as it did for those in the parish who were seeking to be in line for ordination when it was approved. This was all happening in the midst of a broader woman's movement and carried with it rather brash and vague predictions about the way the world would be changed.

Dr. Kelsey continued to press the issue by raising the question about women on the vestry, something that had not happened at All Saints up to that time. The minutes record that Pedersen had replied: "In regard to women on the vestry, however, the only reason this has not been done in the past is simply that none have ever been nominated." In answer to a question on how nominations to the vestry are made, he pointed out that they were made at the annual parish meeting and indicated that "such nominations in the future would receive impartial consideration." It was not, however, until the annual meeting of 1979 that such a nomination was made. In February of 1979, Gail Browning took her place as the first woman vestry member at All Saints. Hilda Swenson and Liz Kelsey followed before long, generally bringing the women's presence on the vestry to two where it stayed for some time. The succession continued in 1989 with Dr. Pat Perry and Sharon Kurger. It is noteworthy that these were all women who had active careers and impressive credentials.

Then on April 12, 1976, Pedersen announced that he had hired William R. Bagby, the present rector at St. Mark's in Wichita Kansas, as assistant to the rector. He would start on Pentecost, June 6, and would be introduced to the congregation at the parish picnic on the grounds, which had become a regular means of marking Pentecost at All Saints since 1972. Bagby was a native of Iowa and had graduated from Central College. Central College located in Pella, Iowa, was affiliated with the Dutch Reform Church. The college had strong religious emphasis, which affected Bagby but nevertheless led him into the Episcopal Church. He graduated from Berkeley Divinity School cum laude and was ordained in 1953. He served first as vicar of St. Paul's Durant, Iowa, and as an assistant at the same time to Trinity Cathedral, Davenport, Iowa. He was then called to serve the yoked field of St. Luke's Cedar Falls and St. Andrew's Waverly. He remained there until he was called as the rector of St. Mark's Wichita, Kansas.

Bagby did not, however, fit the profile that Pedersen had announced at the beginning of the year. He had, in fact, graduated from Berkeley Divinity School five years before Pedersen and could hardly be described as a younger man. The pressure to get the position filled, vacant since September of the previous year, including the unwelcome pressure to hire a woman, apparently provided Pedersen with a strong incentive to get this done. Another factor was that Pedersen was habitually drawn to the idea of rescuing individuals in trouble. Bagby had gone through a difficult divorce in Wichita and was pressured to leave. Connection through the Berkeley grapevine, which Pedersen had been actively using to locate a curate, would have brought Bagby's plight to his attention.

With the assistant-priest problem apparently solved, the parish turned its focus to the problem of a new program year with the looming September kickoff date. It did so in the face of a growing list of contentious issues centered on women's ordination, prayer book revision, and the social ministries of the national church. The general religious ethos in the country was being driven by the rising tide of the evangelical community, which poured oil on the women's ordination issue, made prayer book revision look irrelevant, and social ministries an attempt to avoid the gospel. In Omaha, the big news was that the Gospel Tabernacle would move to the Old Mill Business Park in a high-profile expansion. In doing so, a portion of the Tabernacle split off and formed Trinity Interdenominational Church, an equally expansive endeavor.[193] This evangelical expansion coincided with the losses in the mainline churches and in the Episcopal Church in particular. This new trend in religious development stoked the internal debates in the parish about its own identity and its capacity to survive. The claims for charismatic religion needed to be addressed. Pedersen allowed a group of charismatics, mostly women, to meet in the retreat center for a prayer group. This group was led by Evelyn Higgenson and included Ann Borg, Father Borg's wife; Edith Ray, the wife of Father Ray, former rector of St. Paul's Council Bluffs; Doris Taulborg; and various others.

193 By 2013, the congregation changed its name to Lifegate Church, suggesting that a strategy of appealing to mainline denomination conversion and to mainline theology had run its course.

Pedersen understood this as a safety value, and while he never attended, his assistants did.

Another contentious issue was court-ordered busing, which came to a head in 1975 and affected the Omaha Public School District. The *All Saints Herald* announced that Robert Spire would present a talk to an adult class entitled Desegregation of Schools—Past and Present. It went on to comment that "this subject, which is uppermost in the lives of many parishioners, should be of interest to all Christians." Realtors regularly steered people out of the OPS District, which was, in fact, the larger part of All Saints neighborhood. This included the Tan Cretis when they arrived, though they ended up buying in the OPS District not far from the church. Bussing would in fact suppress growth in the northwest quadrant of the city. This had a crucial effect on St. Mark's on Girard Street, which ultimately closed, and not a little on All Saints. If that were not enough, the Diocese of Nebraska added to the pressure with its request for more money for the coming year.

An Adversarial Relationship with the Diocese

The bishop's budget for 1976 called on All Saints to pay $20,000—$10,000 to the operating assessment and $10,000 to the mission fund. All Saints projected its income for 1976 would be $5,000 more than it was the previous year, a total income of $105,000. With that in mind, it had budgeted $3,500 for the diocesan assessment and $4,500 for its missionary contribution to the diocese. It also pledged that if the income exceeded its projection, it would give the surplus to the diocese. The parish's offer represented a substantial increase to its giving from the previous year, but it was far short of the figure the diocese was demanding.

The diocese, for its part, was responding to a national trend to "staff the bishop." Bishop Rauscher had never had an assistant, and his office was confined to a secretary and part-time bookkeeper. Staffing the bishop implied not only an assistant (canon to the ordinary), but also a canon missioner, a director of Christian education, a diocesan administer, a research and development officer in addition to the appropriate secretarial and bookkeeping personnel. The signal from the national church was that diocesan budgets should be expanding radically. The dioceses, not the congregations, were, in this view, going to be the driving force in the church. In 1973, Bishop Varley had paved the way for what he saw as a missionary imperative. He had called for an "Issues Council," which had met in February and discussed the activities of the diocese uninterrupted by elections, legislations, or budgets that usually kept the council from grappling with its ministry. The council had been expansive about its vision but unclear as to what, if anything, it had agreed to do. This was the basis for the push at the council at its coming meeting to pass a budget that was $40,000 more than the prior year's budget. The Omaha Clericus had gathered in preparation for that council and proposed an alternative budget for the diocese. Nevertheless, the bishop's budget was passed over the Omaha Clericus's warning carried by the weight of out-state missions and churches who thought that they would likely gain from the increase, and that little, if any, of the increase would be assessed against them.

This produced a standoff. All Saints lead the way by withholding funds from the diocese in 1974, and by January of 1975, two other major parishes in Omaha halted payments to the diocese. At the March 10, 1975, meeting of the vestry, Senior Warden L. K. Muller explained that the parish is withholding its contribution to the diocese until the meeting in April of the diocesan executive council. He explained, "Our policy is that we will make our parish contribution when the diocese presents a budget." The annual council had, in fact, adopted a budget, but acceptances of quotes had fallen far short. The result was that the diocesan executive council, which continued the authority of the annual council, had the responsibility of adjusting the budget to the pledged income, a thing that the bishop was loathe to have it do.

The issue, however, was not confined to money alone. By the end of 1974, it was clear that the bishop was hopelessly wallowing in addiction. It was primarily alcohol abuse, but "Dr." Varley had come to Omaha with a prescription pad; and from time to time, he penned off medical prescriptions for various pain medication, apparently for his own use. He had, by this time, frequently shown up for Clarkson graduations inebriated, and he had shown the president of the college his "privileges" apparently under the impression that she would be impressed.[194] He had become an expected visitor at the District 66 school board meetings, where his "liberal" opinions were well known as well as the likelihood that there would be alcohol on his breath.

On Christmas Eve of 1974, he showed up unexpectedly at Trinity Cathedral in high spirits and announced that he felt in the mood to celebrate and preach! He was obviously inebriated, and the assistant priest frantically placed a call to the senior warden. Wisely, the senior warden upon his arrival observed to the bishop that there was still time before the service and that perhaps they could go out for a little drink where they

194 This was recounted to me by Dr. Patricia Perry, who was president of Clarkson College.

could talk about it. The sacrifices we are sometimes called upon to make for the good of the order!

This resulted in an intervention led by the dean of the cathedral, Jack Fricke, clearly the priest most directly affected by the bishop's problem. Fricke had the help of Pedersen with whom Fricke had developed a close relationship in spite of their competition with each other. Varley checked into the Hazelden Foundation, the highly touted addiction treatment center in Center City, Minnesota, for a six-week stay beginning in January of 1975. No announcement was made to the diocese, including the clergy. Most of the diocese and clergy learned about his treatment from an interview that he gave to the *Omaha World-Herald* upon his return. It appeared on Sunday, May 25, 1975, on the front page. The headline read: "Hopes His Story Will Help Others, Bishop Tells of Struggle with Alcohol." The article was quite sympathetic. In it he attributed his alcohol abuse to his use of prescription painkillers used since 1947 and additional medication he began to use in 1972 for high blood pressure. Once he gave up the painkillers, he claimed he had no desire for alcohol. "In fact," he reported, "when he suffered a severe heart attack the day he came home from Hazelden, he refused painkillers "much to the consternation of the physician." The bishop asserted in the article, while he was told to expect to take four to six weeks to recover from the heart attack, he was back at work in two. "I was released in two weeks' time in far better shape than I'd been in the last five to six years." If the bishop's claim is to be trusted, his "illness" predated his election by four years.

To anyone who has had to deal with addiction in their family or close circle of friends, the article raised red flags. It was an easy medium in which to make a confession and, in a backhanded way, to receive attention and congratulations. The harder thing of addressing his clergy and his diocesan "family" whom he had let down was left undone. Moreover, the issues sitting in his office requiring his attention, the most important of which was the loss of approximately 25 percent of the diocese's revenue, were also unaddressed. In a manic mode, Varley was traveling throughout the diocese, seeking sympathetic ears wherever he could find them and telling whomever would listen whatever they wanted to hear. Clearly, the therapy was not complete.

For the pastors of the diocese, this was a difficult issue to address. In their own counseling, they regularly counseled individuals and families that addiction was an illness that needed to be treated and not punished. Treating their bishop pastorally seemed incumbent upon them. In the meantime, however, serious harm was being done to the diocese and, in turn, to their own work in their parishes. Pedersen often expressed resentment that had been forced into the role of being "the heavy" because no one else was ready to deal with the matter. In fact, Fricke was working with him and was probably more insistent than Pedersen that Varley had to go. At any rate, it was Fricke that would go on record in the *Omaha World-Herald* as having done so.

By August 20, Varley tendered his resignation. It was announced in another front page of the *Omaha World-Herald*. In an accompanying article, also on the front page, Fricke identified himself as one of the diocesan priests who actively sought his resignation. When asked if the bishop's interview in May, which the paper had published, had been held against Varley, Fricke replied that he had been incensed with the *Omaha World-Herald* article. He said, "I had asked him to talk to his own family (clergy and laity in the diocese) about it before airing it in public."[195]

Varley said in an article, which appeared on the following day in the *Omaha World-Herald*, that he had resigned because the interview he had granted the *Omaha World-Herald* had embarrassed some clergymen, and "there were disagreements over his handling of diocesan finances, style of ministry and liberal views on minorities, women priests and other matters." The standing committee, chaired by Rev. Ronald Wyly, accepted his resignation and made it effective September 1, 1975. Guided by a consultant from the national church staff, Rev. Charles Wilson, the standing committee granted him six months' salary as a severance.[196] The following December, Wyly presided over a tense annual council in Lincoln. When it came to dealing with the budget question, the council was presented with three alternative budgets, A, B, or C. Budget A, totaling $242,050, would continue the track proposed by Varley. Budget C, totaling $212,050, was in line with the restricted budget favored by Pedersen and the Omaha clergy based on what they considered was a realistic projection of diocesan income. The third alternative, budget B, attempted to reach a compromise by splitting the difference. When the council faced the vote on the budget on the last day of the council, it finally voted to adopt all three budgets! It is not difficult to imagine Pedersen's reaction, but it probably would be impossible to print his words if we had them.

The council to elect a new bishop was set for August 27 at St. Mark's Pro Cathedral in Hastings. At that council, three names were put in nomination: Rev. Thomas Carson, Rev. Willis Steinberg, and Rev. James

195 *Omaha World-Herald*, Tuesday, August 19, 1975, p. 1.

196 Rev. Charles Wilson of SALT, an entity of the national church, was present at the meeting of the Standing Committee, at which Varley's resignation took place and a settlement was arranged, which gave him six-month salary.

D. Warner. Warner managed to acquire a majority of clergy votes on the first ballot and was elected on the third. Warner was a marked contrast to Varley. He was an introvert, an expert on nothing except being a parish priest, and a self-deprecating man. He was a native of Sheridan, Wyoming. After graduating from Seabury–Western, he spent ten years in Wichita, Kansas. From there he had gone on to serve parishes in Mosinee and Marinetta, Wisconsin, before becoming dean of the cathedral in Oshkosh, Wisconsin. His own self-doubts were reinforced from the counsel of the national church office who labeled the Diocese of Nebraska as "a bishop killer." From its perspective, this nearly unprecedented event, meant that having tasted blood, it would be hard for the diocese to refrain from making a habit of breaking its bishops.

The result of this advice was that Warner worked scared. As it turned out, the warning was far off the mark. Warner was well accepted and served until 1989. He turned out, in spite of his limitation, to be a good bishop and one of the best imaginable after the debacle the diocese had just been through. His consecration took place as part of the upcoming annual council. On the first night of the council, November 30, the deputies with other guests assembled at St. Cecilia's Roman Catholic Cathedral in Omaha for his consecration. The next day, Warner waded into his first annual address to an annual council. He would have been better advised to have deferred on the ground that he had, at that point, little experience in the diocese and little time in the past two months, consumed with moving to Omaha, in which to prepare anything. As he was ending his remarks, he turned to a final topic: "And now a note of stewardship." He paused, apparently having lost his train of thought, and then continued:

> I am rambling today. I just want to share some personal thoughts . . . If I had a chance to give a title to this address of thoughts with you today it would be, "Don't forget, give God a chance. I am excited to be the bishop of this diocese, even though the responsibilities are overwhelming."[197]

These words, however, revealed much. It was not God, so much as himself, for whom he was making a plea; and in the course of his episcopate, he would ramble a great deal.

Once Varley's resignation was final, Pedersen moved to restore All Saints relationship with the diocese. At the vestry meeting in September, Pedersen discussed the resignation of the bishop and events leading to and surrounding it. He reported on the election of Warner and on the plans

[197] *Journal of the Diocese of Nebraska*, 1976, p. 89.

under way for his consecration and for the annual council. In the October meeting, a motion at the vestry was made to pay the diocese $5,000 immediately and the remainder of $8,000 assessment as soon as possible. The results of the Every Member Canvass at All Saints showed that the parish could anticipate a record income in 1977, which was projected to be $120,000. When the vestry took up the discussion of the parish's commitment to the diocese for the coming year, it, however, remained cautious. As a result of the discussion, All Saints accepted the largest assessment in its history, $16,814; and for the first time, its contribution to the diocese would exceed that of the cathedral.[198] It was not the $20,000 that Varley's budget had demanded in 1976, but it went more than halfway in meeting it.

Endowment Fund

The past year had been burdened by the problems of the diocese. The new year began with a laundry list of anticipated capital improvement: "North-end doors, undercroft, $1200—$1,400, Front entrance $3,000—$4,000, land and planting program $6,000, parking lot repairs." From the beginning, the building's greatest weakness had been its heating plant. The energy crisis, under way since 1973, had heightened the discussion and focused it around the high cost of fuel bills, which Pedersen had struggled to reduce by various means. The setback for the unoccupied building was allowed to drop into the forties, setting up a weekly struggle to reheat the building for the weekend activities, not always completely successful. Clearly, these things made the vestry wary; and when it returned in the new year to the discussion of the parish's contribution to the diocese, it expressed a need for caution. It was explained to the congregation that "The item for the diocesan support does not include provision for the additional faith offering which would add a considerable additional sum to our accepted allotment. Acceptance of this additional offering will be delayed at the suggestion of the rector." This acceptance would have taken the parish's contribution to the $20,000 level for which Varley had asked in 1976. In March, it was announced in the minutes that Pedersen would set up a meeting between the bishop and vestry after April to talk about All Saints relationship to the diocese.

For all this caution, however, the final report for the previous year showed that the income had been $16,000 to $17,000 higher than

198 Trinity Cathedral, Omaha, accepted $16,345; St. Andrew's Omaha, $11,674; Holy Trinity, Lincoln, $12,655, but paid $8,328.

expected, making it possible to carry over that amount into the new year. The capital pledge income had also continued on schedule, and the vestry could announce that it would pay $9,000 on the Building Fund and Debt Retirement, reducing the parish's debt to $27,000. If this good news had not made Pedersen and the vestry more optimistic about what they could do for the diocese, it did, nevertheless, allow them to begin an endowment fund. The fund was named the Witness and Endowment Fund, and it was described as a separate and special parish account under the control and management of the rector, wardens, and vestry.

> Funds and/or interest therefrom will be made available from time to time for capital, charitable and Christian programs, and other special needs. Funds and interest therefrom shall not be used to support or supplement the regular operational budget of the parish.

Pedersen had some ambivalence toward endowment funds, and it was his idea to add the concept of "witness" on to the purposes of the endowment, hoping that it would make it possible to use the endowment income for creative ministries as well as to ensure the brick and mortar needs of the parish. The fund opened with a balance of $65,000, which was registered as its protected principal. It will be recalled that Thomas Casady, in 1921, had called for All Saints to create an endowment fund. It had begun under Casady in a small way but had been interrupted by the Great Depression. An endowment fund had reappeared from time to time but only as a means to an end. At last, in 1977, All Saints, became an endowed parish, if only in a modest way. Only in 1980 did it begin to emerge as a significant factor when the bulk of the Gladys Hundley's estate was added, bringing its principal to a total of $236,731. One will recall Ms. Hundley gave the Ascension Window, presently in the chapel, in memory of her parents in 1954. She continued to the end of her life as a regular at the eleven-o-clock and was one of the last to wear white gloves and hats. By April 14, 1980, the endowment was handed over to the care of a permanent Investment Committee. Ike (Ira) Couch, married to one of Sam Reynold's daughters and an active member of the parish, was charged with the actual management of the account under the auspices of Kirkpatrick, Pettis, Smith, Polian Inc.

Opening Up a New Era

With the debt on the parish's new building at Ninety-Second and Blondo at last paid off, the consecration of the building could be set. The choice was May 29, the Feast of Pentecost, to coincide with the 11:00 a.m. service. The celebration was to be followed by what had by then become an annual tradition, a parish picnic on the grounds. The ceremony would take place precisely thirteen years after the dedication of the building. Rt. Rev. James D. Warner, bishop of Nebraska, would be present to consecrate the church in an indoor ceremony, which would feature past wardens and vestrymen, members of the various All Saints organizations, representatives of area parishes, diocesan officials, and other clergy as witnesses. Rev. Charles L. R. Pedersen, rector of All Saints for six years, was announced as the preacher. It was already clear that Warner could be counted upon to ramble, given time in the pulpit, a thing that Pedersen found hard to tolerate. Perhaps, more import, Pedersen felt that he owned the message to be given that day. It was to be, in his mind, a hardheaded charge for the work that lay ahead of the parish now that the crippling debt had been put behind them.

Two pieces of unfinished business, however, stood in way of the celebration that Pedersen wanted this to be. In the time remaining, he meant to bring both of these projects to completion. He wanted to fill the vacancy on his staff that had been caused by George Martin's departure and by the failed attempt to fill it with William Bagby. He had been trying since previous September to complete his staff by hiring an assistant whom he also hoped could be part of that celebration. The other project was launching a lay empowerment program, which he called Doulos. The name he had chosen was a reference to the Greek word that Saint Paul used in his letters meaning "servant" or, more literally, "slave." Pedersen hoped that the consecration of the building would also include the installation of the first class of Doulos ministers.

Lay empowerment was much in the air at the time. William Bagby, who was on his way out, sung the praise of the parish but suggested that Pedersen was afraid of "unleashing the laity."[199] It is true that Pedersen mistrusted some of the more common aspects of the lay movement. He did not like, for example, the term "lay ministry." He felt that the term lead to a confusion between the role of the ordained ministry and work of laity. The term "lay ministry," to his mind, pointed individuals toward the idea of putting on robes and cutting out roles in the liturgical life of the church

199 Comment made to me by Bagby on my visit to All Saints for an interview for the position of assistant.

rather than working with the elderly and poor, doing the work necessary for the physical operations of the church, or furthering the work that could make an impact on society in general. Characteristically, his instinct was to invent his own program, which he had manage to do with Doulos.

The *All Saints Herald* reported in an article appearing in the March 22 edition: "Empowerment and Outreach Program, begins Sunday, February 28, was the first meeting of 'Doulos'—those parishioners in phase 1 of the empowerment-outreach program at All Saints." The article went on to explain, "All Saints is striving for a new lay commitment. It is an exciting time in the life of the church and in the life of All Saints." The commitment consisted of three years of prayer, study, and service to the church. The group was divided into the following area of service: evangelism-fellowship, stewardship, Christian education, mission outreach, and pastoral support. In the *All Saints Herald*, Pedersen said, "The group will form the forward movement of the church as the consecration is the beginning process of the building of All Saints." If the syntax was a little unclear, the message came through that Pedersen viewed May 29 as beginning his era, an era which would, indeed, give him the opportunity to refashioning the building and grounds he had inherited into a pragmatic venue for the liturgy and ministry as he understood it.

The same March edition of the *All Saints Herald* announced that there would be a "Going away luau for Father Bagby" at the home of Berkeley Forsythe, sponsored by the "Odd Couples." There had been no written evidence that Bagby was leaving until the minutes of the March vestry meeting, which had preceded the announcement in the *All Saints Herald* by a few days. That makes it unclear when the decision that Bagby would leave was made. It was initiated by Pedersen. When he had hired Bagby, he asked for and received from him the assurance that there was not a third party involved in his divorce that would show up in Omaha. As it turned out, the divorce had involved a member of his former parish, and she was set to move to Omaha and join Bagby. It should be remembered that, at that time, the position on a remarriage after a divorce had only recently been altered. Pedersen's attitude toward divorce was pragmatic but conservative. He felt that he had been misled by Bagby. His explanation to the vestry made in a discussion labeled "staff searching and screening" was simply that "Father Bagby may be looking for other things." He continued that in any case, "we may soon need someone to work with the church school and young people. A committee should be formed for personal placement, made up of vestry and some non-vestry members who would be constantly in touch with potential staff members." Dr. Jim Kelsey again raised the question about a woman curate.

Within a couple of weeks, it was further announced that Bagby's departure was set for the end of May, when he would assume a position in a parish in Kansas City, Kansas. At the beginning of April, Pedersen invited a strong prospect to visit Omaha. He announced that "Fr. Larry Boyd and his wife, from the diocese of Fond du Lac, will be here next Monday for an interview." At the vestry meeting that followed, a report was made on Boyd's visit, and it was the consensus of the vestry that the salary that he had asked for was too high for the parish's budget. Another name had been received of someone currently in Ames, Iowa, but upon the parish's inquiry, he had decided not to move. A third name had been received of someone currently in Dubuque. The announcement says that "Father Tan Creti will be in town on Wednesday night, April 13. The vestry will meet with him Thursday in the Retreat Center."

Tan Creti had been in Dubuque the past three years in a doctoral program at Aquinas Institute. His family consisted of his wife, Jane, and their three children, Marcus, nine; Angelo, eight; and Marcella, seven. Michael Tan Creti was born in Carroll, Iowa, in 1940 and was raised in Carroll. He attended Dartmouth College, where he had encountered a number of Omaha boys in his class: Bob Brodky, Howard Weinberg, Russ Knot, Paul Brown, and Woody Bradford, the latter of whom was raised at All Saints. Upon graduation in 1962, he served two years in the United States Navy and then entered Berkeley Divinity School, graduating in 1967. Following graduation, he was married to Jane F. Warnecke of Worcester, Massachusetts. He returned with Jane to Iowa, where he was ordained by Bishop Gordon Smith. Smith posted him at St. Andrew's Clear Lake, Iowa, and after eighteen months, he asked him to be the vicar of St. Paul's Grinnell, Iowa, and chaplain to Grinnell College students. He spent five years at St. Paul's Grinnell, where he was noted for his work in the community, which included a recycling drive, founding a day care center, and promoting public housing. Drawn by a desire to deepen what he could offer the church, Tan Creti enrolled in Aquinas Institute, Dubuque, Iowa. Aquinas was a Dominican house of studies, which, in the hay days of Vatican II, had entered into an ecumenical relationship with University of Dubuque's Presbyterian seminary and with Wartburg, a Lutheran seminary, to offer a program of doctoral studies. While in Dubuque he was employed part-time at St. John's the Episcopal parish, and his wife, Jane, worked full-time as a hospital nurse. By the end of 1976, he had finished the course work requirements for doctor of theology and had begun writing his dissertation. At this point, it was possible for him to relocate his family and take on full-time employment, completing the dissertation in his spare time and summer vacations.[200] He had been working in Dubuque with the parish's church school and youth group on a part-time basis so that he brought experience to the need that was uppermost in the mind of All Saints leadership.

Michael J. Tan Creti, Rector 1993-2006, br. 1940 Carroll, Iowa.

The May minutes of the vestry indicated that Father Tan Creti has accepted the position and would start with a salary package of $19,000. The vestry also approved at this meeting the hiring of Joyce Thomas as director of Christian education. This had not been part of the discussion when Tan Creti had interviewed for the job. The parish had hired directors of Christian education in the past but not for a considerable time. Perhaps given his luck with assistants, Pedersen had second thoughts about what he had just done. He had hired a doctoral student who might find an

[200] The title of Tan Creti's dissertation was "The Ecclesiology of Romanticism: A Study of Three Nineteenth Century Essays in Ecclesiology in Three Church Traditions." The thesis had ecumenical implications, as it attempted to demonstrate that Roman Catholic, Anglican, Reform, and Lutheran traditions shared a common theological methodology at the beginning of the nineteenth century, and it had implication in parish ministry because these efforts within each tradition stressed the communal or ecclesial nature of salvation and, hence, of ministry.

alternative to All Saints in short order. He also was aware that, given the intensity of the church school, it was difficult, if not impossible, to make it work with volunteers. It was one thing to get someone to volunteer to spend an hour with a group of parish children on a Sunday morning. It was another thing to get the supplies the teachers needed ready for them, to give them reassurance that they were doing a good job, to deal with the inevitable, behaviorally challenged child, and to fill in for the teacher who, on a given morning, with little or no notice, didn't show up.

Perhaps he had found in Thomas someone who was too good to pass up. Thomas had exceptional qualifications and people skills, which make this an equally plausible answer. Joyce Thomas was born in Canon City, Colorado. She had attended schools in Denver and Council Bluffs. She worked in the Roman Catholic Diocese of Des Moines before coming to Omaha as parish liturgy consultant and religious education coordinator at Holy Cross Parish. In addition, Joyce had a great deal of experience in liturgy. She had served as cantor and choir director in Denver and had been appointed to the Omaha Archdiocesan Liturgy Commission the previous year. She was a member of RECOL (Religious Education Coordinators and Liturgists) which had grown as a result of Vatican II reforms in Roman Catholic life. Joyce had six grown children (four boys and two girls) who were ages seventeen through twenty-six. She was, at the time, caring for her semi-invalid parents in her home. In the *All Saints Herald*, Pedersen said to the parish, "We hope you will all take the opportunity to greet Joyce and come to meet our new DRE."

When at last the parish gathered for the celebration of Pentecost on May 29, it was a full house in more ways than one. The bishop congratulated the crowd that gathered for the liturgy, praising them for retiring the parish's debt, which allowed him to consecrate their building. The first Doulos class took its vow of service. The new staff was introduced. After the liturgy, the congregation spilled out on the grounds on a beautiful day to picnic, to meet the new staff members, Tan Creti and Thomas, and to enjoy each other's company. Altogether, there was a tangible optimism about the future that is hard to describe.

A Feeling of Entitlement

As 1977 reached its midpoint, two things were clear: a new era had indeed begun at All Saints and that what Pedersen had managed to accomplish in six years had exceeded all expectations. He had managed to pay off the parish's debt, added to the parish's facilities a unique new space that carried with it the promise of a new and exciting ministry with children, launched an endowment and outreach fund, and had even managed to get the long-delayed addition to the organ under way. In 1971, when he had taken charge of the parish, there was nothing under way to make any of this possible. Moreover, the climate surrounding the parish was troubled. The diocese was imploding under a flawed leadership. The national church was suffering from the conflict that had been engendered during the final years of Hines's controversial leadership as presiding bishop, which, among other things, had tried to put the Episcopal Church behind black empowerment. To these contentious social issues were added conflicts over prayer book revision and women's ordination. These national issues added new dimensions of conflict in the life of the parish. Large well-financed groups in the church ran negative campaigns aimed at parishioners. The Prayer Book Society's newsletter and an evangelical-charismatic newsletter called *Acts 29* was sent to growing mailing lists, condemning the scandalous implications of change and inviting rebellion within the ranks.[201] The nation as a whole continued to struggle with "energy crisis" and with the conflicted presidency of Jimmy Carter. The discontent of seventies was, for the Episcopal Church, the flip side of the consensus of the fifties. Nearly everywhere, the Episcopal Church was experiencing bad news in terms of growth. The exception was the South, where a very determined and conservative leadership had walked a fine line, creating a favorable position for the Episcopal Church. The election of John Allin as presiding bishop was a recognition of this, but it was not at all clear that Allin had the capacity to bring this favored status to the Episcopal Church outside of the South.

Pedersen's success at All Saints during a particularly troubling time for the Episcopal Church made it all the more amazing. It had not been easy, and it had not come without wounds. As Pedersen looked at his next five-year plan, it would be fair to say that he felt a certain amount of entitlement. To a large extent, what had been accomplished was due to a solo performance. That is not to say that Pedersen did it without some exceptional efforts from individual lay leaders and a general lay culture at All Saints, which supported its leadership, but it was quite evident that it

[201] Act 29 was a publication of a conservative group of the Episcopal Church who had a strong evangelical orientation. It disliked the new Prayer Book, which was too catholic, and women's ordination, which was unscriptural. Other mailing came to parishioners from the Prayer Book Society which were highly critical of the national church and implied that drastic consequence were resulting from its policies.

was his vision and his drive that had made it happen. He had help from other clergy who had made significant contributions, but they had come and gone according to their own needs.

Now he had assembled a team and was proposing to take on the future of All Saints at the head of a team ministry. Could it work? Pedersen, as we have seen, was exposed to the idea of team ministry in Connecticut. Tan Creti was exposed to it in seminary in Connecticut as well, and it was one of the implications for the dissertation on which he was working on at Aquinas Institute. The thesis was that priests should live and function as a community in order to minister to a community, community being intrinsically linked to salvation. The sticking point, however, was whether or not there were actually individuals in ministry who could live into the theory, and it would not be long before the concept of team ministry was out of vogue because the national church had discovered in a survey that there were not enough priests in the Episcopal Church who had the capacity to actually work together. Pedersen and Tan Creti began with a few things in common. They both had their formation in Berkeley Divinity School. They shared a work ethic that had been inherited from their fathers who had been profoundly shaped by the immigrant experience in America. Both of their fathers had worked very hard and never for a moment begrudged it. Both of their fathers had died young. Pedersen would remember his father as having said to his mother shortly before his accidental death, "Sis, it's been a hell of a ride!" And Tan Creti would remember that his father linked "priests" and "being lazy" as an invariable fact of life, having inherited this form of anti-clericalism from his Italian father. The lay member of the team, Joyce Thomas, also brought a strong work ethic to the potential team. She was raised by a German American couple in the midst of a large collection of brothers and sisters. She too was driven. Her second home had been a Benedictine monastery, which had reinforced a sense of fulfilment through work. She herself had tried a monastic vocation but left to have family. She now found herself a single parent used to making her own way.

Pedersen was by nature a fixer. He had special training as a counselor, and it should be noted that priests in the sixties and seventies considered counseling a very important component of their ministry, if not its central focus. Many sought additional credentials, and some parishes made counseling their chief identity.[202] Pedersen was gifted as a counselor and focused a good deal of his effort on marriage counseling and counseling

202 Such parishes were termed "pastoral parishes" in a somewhat unfortunate identification of "pastoral ministry," which is the shepherding of a community with personal counseling.

with troubled youth. He regularly devoted five to six hours a week to counseling, early evenings, and Saturdays particularly. He gained a reputation not only in the parish but also in the city as well as an effective counselor. A number of prominent individuals from other parishes sought him out and, as result, ended up at All Saints. His approach was pragmatic, and clearly it satisfied his need to be a fixer. If in theory being a fixer was a flaw, in practice, a number of individuals and marriages were greatly helped by his work as a counselor.

The Doulos community that he created was another attempt at fixing something that he felt was broken. The problem, in his estimation, was lay commitment to the work of the church in its broadest sense. Participation in Doulos by means of a third class in 1978 grew to more than sixty participants. His focus in the next few years would be to deploy these committed workers to meeting the crucial needs of the parish. They would be the backbone of such routine efforts as the Every Member Canvass and Sunday morning greeting. They would put on luncheons for newcomers, or they would undertake outreach programs, such as raising money for a van for St. Jude's Home for Abused Children in Nevada. They also visited the elderly, providing rides, and even changed lightbulbs.

The Builder

When he had commissioned the original class of Doulos, Pedersen referred to their work as "building" the parish. While he no doubt meant this metaphorically, the choice of the metaphor was not an accident, for the thing that needed fixing more than anything else in his mind was the building itself. He had fought the building from the day that he had arrived, and now it was his turn. In short order, the vestry found itself discussing a wide range of projects. It discussed the purchase of the field to the west of the church property. It was headed for the market, forced by an impending foreclosure. The large yellow house had declined, the ponies that the owner kept would periodically get out of the dilapidated fence, and they were usually emaciated. A columbarium was discussed, and a temporary facility was authorized to be located in a closet in the priests' sacristy, a location presumably least likely to spook anyone. Housing on the grounds for singles and elderly was discussed and deftly deferred to a committee on a motion by Jack Sprague "to report in 60 to 90 days." While there is no evidence of such a report, the idea would nevertheless return. The continued rise in the cost of utilities aggravated the discussion over the heating problem, and a study was pointed toward fixing the skylight and the windows on the east side. The altar needed to be closer to the congregation. This issue had been dealt with at the nine fifteen service by placing a temporary altar in front of the choir, but that was no solution for the eleven-o-clock and for Christmas and Easter services. In itself, it was a bit unsightly, and it was a bit of a struggle to get it in place and then out of the way each Sunday. The parish needed a chapel. The original chapel in the west wing, it will be recalled, had been quickly sacrificed in order to create office space, but now it returned as part of the energy discussion. A chapel could be used as a warm church in the winter, on weekdays when the heating and cooling of the main space was cut back, and it could solve the need for an altar-centered church. It could be a place where the liturgy could be done and experienced as it should be. Office space was needed not only because of the lack of space in the existing unit, but because it also was connected to the heating and cooling issue since the existing offices were heated and cooled by the central heating and cooling system. There was a need for an upstairs bathroom and for more church school space. The master plan for this lengthy list of fixes existed in Pedersen's head and was, as such, subject to constant revision.

Two things stood in the way. There was the leftover commitment for an addition to the organ. This had been planned by Cecil Neubecker and promised to him. Neubecker had died but the promise remained now as a memorial to him. The most evident thing missing on the organ was a trumpet. According to Neubecker's plan, a trumpet would be housed in an antiphonal organ located in the rear of the church. The problems incumbent with this had never been thought through, and so it was left to Pedersen to find a solution. While an antiphonal organ occupied a rather low rank in his priorities, he nevertheless understood that it had to get done to clear the way for those things that ranked higher on his list. Neubecker had begun the work with the Lewis Organ Company of Council Bluffs, Iowa. Pedersen's solution was to string out the progress on the manufacturing of the pipes and chests and to reserve considerations dealing with installation to the future.[203]

203 The antiphonal organ was dedicated on Sunday, November 26, 1978, at 11:00 a.m. The additional pipes were the dream of the late Cecil C. Neubecker who designed the organ in 1962 and in whose memory the antiphonal organ was dedicated. The memorial program was played by Mr. LaVahn Maesch, organist and director of music at the church of the Palms, Sun City. The final bill came in the December, and the vestry authorized a final payment to the Lewis Organ Co. of $3,810.

The second thing standing in the way was a national fund drive that had been launched by the presiding bishop, John Allin. Allin was caught in the divisive legacy of John Hines. A liberal with conservative restraints, such as opposing women's ordination, he sought to refocus the Episcopal Church on what it could agree on. He focused his energy on building the church as opposed to social action. He proposed that the Episcopal Church raise $100 million to strengthen missionary work in dioceses across the nation. According to his plan, called Venture in Mission, the national church would partner with the dioceses, and much of the money raised in any jurisdiction would stay within that jurisdiction for its missionary work. This reversed the Hines's fund-raising efforts, which had sought to raise money that the national church could use where it saw fit to further social justice, even if it was for a project in a diocese that that diocese did not support. The issue was analogous to the political issue over justice and state's rights and not a little colored by political tensions.

The Diocese of Nebraska was slow off the mark because of the turmoil caused by Varley's resignation. By 1978, however, Bishop Warner was attempting to follow through on the direction set by the national church. It came at a particularly bad time for Pedersen, and it was difficult for him to embrace because of the vagueness of its goals. It appeared to many that it was a cover for the national church, a way to claiming relevance without actually doing anything. Venture in Mission far exceeded its goal of $100 million. Yet Pedersen's assessment was that it had been done "with smoke and mirrors." In retrospect, the objective impact of Venture in Mission funding on the Episcopal Church was minor.

On October 9, 1978, Pedersen led a discussion on the National Venture in Mission Program. He reported to the vestry that he had been asked to submit a list of people in the parish he felt capable of making pledges at certain dollar levels. A motion was made by a member of the vestry who would have been one of those most likely to have been "fingered" in such a list, to "ratify Father Pedersen's decision against the program and not to submit any list of parishioners for advanced gift solicitation until we have further information."

Pressure to participate continued to be resisted, and the *All Saints Herald*, on January 11, 1979, made clear that what might have sounded like a conditional suspension was, in fact, a decision not to participate as a parish. Individual members could do so as individuals.

> We have informed the bishop that we are involved in our own development program and have commitments outside of the parish. It did not seem practical or possible to mount an all-parish drive at this time. At the same time, All Saints had

> accepted the largest parish quota for support of the diocesan budget in its history. In fact, it is the largest quota for any parish in the history of the diocese. The quota of $25,526 represents an increase of more than $5,000 over last year.

With the antiphonal organ and the national church drive satisfactorily dealt with, the addition on to the east side of the narthex won vestry approval as the year was coming to an end. The lower level of the space would be a new office core, and the upper level would be a chapel capable of seating 124 individuals. It was argued that this project would make a significant contribution to alleviate the heating and cooling problem, and it would make room for the Sunday school, which would inherit the old office core in the west wing. The new plan overrode the original master plan, which had reserved the space off the east end of the narthex for a parish hall. Bob Stitt again was called upon to work out a plan with the architect Robert Amick as they had done with the retreat center. The initial estimate for the addition was $124,000. By April, the estimate had risen to $165,000, which included $7,000 to $8,000 to furnish it and $15,000 for stained glass in the skylight in the main church. Petersen reported to the vestry in April that there was $51,000 already available in memorial funds and that a mailing in May would kick off the drive.

Ground was hurriedly broken for the chapel office wing on Sunday, November 5, 1978. Rev. Mark McCallum, the retired rector of All Saints, officiated at a brief service. Russell Rauscher, the retired bishop of Nebraska, now the parish's business manager, assisted. The presence of McCallum and Rauscher served to deflect any questions of whether the effort was consistent with the history of the parish and whether it was being built at the expense of the greater good of the diocese and the national church.

Pedersen, writing in the January 1979 edition of the *All Saints Herald*, reported:

> As you can see, progress is being made on the building of the Chapel, however slightly, in this frightfully cold weather, and we can see a rough timetable for the completion of this project. With another week's work the structure will be "closed" and with the coming of better weather we will look to have it complete by June. Our drive produced about $65,000 in income in 1978. The projected cash flow is such that we can meet the construction costs without extensive short term finance. Regular pledge payments for this drive are essential for us to accomplish this. With some modifications by the Building Committee,

> we have been able to alter the design and accomplish some savings and better use of space. Locating the altar in the north end of the chapel and using stone for the east wall meant that we were able to eliminate the need for a ramp or stairs in the chapel and still maintain the desired roofline. The size of the chapel was reduced slightly, but the potential seating remains at approximately 120. There is a revised rendering of the plan in the narthex. The other projects–the stained glass in the nave, (what a difference that made in sound and heat lost) the first floor lavatory, and finishing the sanctuary renovation are all complete and paid for. I think you will all be pleased with these new facilities and I encourage any who have not yet made a commitment to assist in this drive to do so.

The chapel that resulted was considerably more traditional than the original plan. In the original plan, the altar was to be located at the center of the west wall, taking advantage of its stone, which rose to a height of over sixteen feet. Chairs not pews were to be arranged in a semicircle around the altar. The revised plan yielded one thousand five hundred square feet, and a seating capacity closer to sixty than one hundred twenty. Steps and/or a ramp were eliminated by reversing the original plan of starting with the basement level and working up. This meant that what was eliminated upstairs was transferred to the lower level. This resulted in an office level that was two feet four inch higher than the basement and a chapel ceiling that was six feet lower than the original design. Instead of a ceiling that slopped from the high end on the west to the wall on the east, the ceiling was leveled at twelve feet throughout.

With the new orientation, there was a need for something dramatic on the altar end so the three stained-glass windows that were in the narthex—the Ascension Window, the All Saints Window, and the Trinity Window—were brought into the chapel. The windows have given the chapel a rich atmosphere, with the result that the chapel has been much used and much loved. It made possible a 5:00 p.m. Saturday Eucharist, which was begun shortly after the completion of the chapel and was one of the first Saturday services by an Episcopal church in Omaha. It also was a God-send for mid-week Eucharist, small weddings, and funerals.

Economizing, however, left the chapel with some flaws. Lighting was poor, and the lime green carpet was subject to puckering and more at home in a 1970s living room than a worship space. From the beginning, the pucker caused the worry that someone might trip. The lack of elevation meant the space felt cramped for larger services, and the vision of an altar-centered worship space was lost. The downstairs itself turned out undersized and provided a minimum number of offices, each a bit undersized and no provision for growth. Yet the project came off on budget, and the cash flow was sufficient to relieve the parish from having to borrow to meet its bills. In an era of high interest rates, this was not an insignificant accomplishment. It also made it hard to argue with the results since they were paid for, and then the chapel only confronted those who chose to use it. It was off the radar for most of the parish.

This was not the case of the alterations in the main church that were being pursued at the same time. The drive had identified the skylight as the key part of remodeling the church in order to deal with the acute heating problem. The Gabriel Loire workshop, which had designed and produced the rock glass windows in the bays, had also designed rock glass for the skylight. It had been delayed at the time because of cost. The Loire plan had a progression of color from blues to reds and golds, which paralleled and complemented the windows in the bay. The local stained-glass workshop Hautzinger was employed to complete this project. After living for a while without stained glass in the narthex, Bea Muller proposed a memorial for her husband, Joseph, and commissioned Hautzinger to produce a series of windows across the narthex windows. Each window was a depiction of a saint. While they were moved and added to at a later time, they continue to serve the parish in much the same way as they did originally.[204] Less up front was the decision to move the Loire glass in the bays, which had been deemed to be a significant cause for the problem of heating the church. The plan Pedersen presented was to move the glass in line with walls closing off the bays. This made more than a third of the stained glass redundant, and it was put into storage. The glass set in line with the wall line was not only reduced by a third, but it was also changed in the way that it worked in the space. In its new position, the glass did not transform the light so much as stand there as a tableau of color, a much less interesting effect than the original effect.

With the skylight and the alteration of the bays was a major change in the design of the worship space, which eliminated the chancel choir and moved the altar closer to the people. In the same January *All Saints Herald* that reported on the progress of the chapel, it was announced that during Lent, there would be a ten-week course on explaining the history of liturgy using characters and costumes. The demonstration liturgies were

[204] Joseph Muller, who had served as senior warden and as a crucial supporter of the move of the Parish to Ninety-Third and Blondo, died in April of 1983, and the design was approved by the vestry in May of 1984 and installed that following summer.

intertwined with an introduction and defense of the new *Book of Common Prayer*. Particularly, the design of the course argued for the historicity and superiority of the early church basilica-style liturgy presided over from a chair on one end of a central axis and a baptismal font on the other end. In between was an altar around which the congregation gathered.

Meanwhile, plans were made to remove the antiphonal choir and level the space for an altar platform. A selling point to the design was that it provided a longer altar rail almost all of which would be accessible without any steps. The wooden deck was installed with some compromise and covered with a blue carpet. The carpet was extended down the aisles of the nave as well. The music people had lost their antiphonal choir and been moved behind the altar, where they became part of the circle around the altar rather than the intermediary between the altar and the congregation. Moreover, the blue carpet was thought to have killed the sound in the room. That certainly was an overstatement, but it did have a definite effect, and the organ would progressively be judged to have been muted by the changes.

Like the chapel, the remodeling of the main worship space was a fait accompli and was hard to argue with, though unlike the chapel, there was no way to avoid being confronted by it. From the beginning of the project until its completion, Sunday worshipers picked their way around the mess. Its completion was set for Easter. On Palm Sunday, nearly complete, the procession gathered to do the liturgy of the Palms for the first time from the new *Book of Common Prayer*. It had been carefully scripted. Nevertheless, the choir, led by Lois Carlson, baulked at the last minute. Carlson, as a successor to Neubecker, had been a matter of default. It was easier to accept her than to mount a search for a new music director at the time. Her qualification was that of a soloist, and she had little background in liturgical worship. While things that morning, once under way, went as well as one might have expected, Pedersen dismissed her shortly after Easter. His plan was to move Robert Scheiblhofer to the position of director of music. Robert Scheiblhofer had been hired on September 1978 to handle the nine fifteen music. His salary was $50 per month, and it included a rent-free living in the custodian's apartment on the lower level of the building. Scheiblhofer was a Roman Catholic at the time and had little by way of formal credentials as a musician. On the other hand, he did have an understanding of and a natural flair for liturgy. Beginning on May 14, 1979, Scheiblhofer became the parish's full-time music director. It seemed implausible. Nevertheless, Scheiblhofer would prove to be a fine director of music and an equal of Sims and Neubecker. Yet the immediate result was rebellion, and a portion of the choir left, ending up for the most part at the cathedral.

Having had a very intense beginning to the year, Pedersen went off to the 1979 annual council. While council was never his cup of tea, he was unusually agitated. He never was very good at sitting and listening, and two things were on his mind. On the one hand, back in the parish, he had in progress an extensive building project on which he was betting his future; and on the other hand, he had stiffed the diocese's approach to participate in the Venture in Ministry Drive. The tickets for the banquet were, to his mind, overpriced, and the speaker underwhelming. Surprising everyone, including himself, he rose and invited annual council to meet at All Saints for the next annual council. The invitation went against all precedents but was nevertheless accepted.

So it was set that All Saints would host the 1980 annual council. It met on April 24 and 25. The meal was cooked and served by the women of the church led by Oral Couch. Through Oral, who represented the woman who had been the key workers of the sixties, a senior group of women were called back into service for what was understood to be a very special occasion. The banquet was served for half the price of the customary annual council banquets, making the point of frugality. Pedersen managed to engage for the speaker no one less than Tom Osborne, Nebraska's famed football coach. For Pedersen, Osborne, a Methodist layman, represented a way for the Episcopal Church to look outside of itself and, at the same time, to put itself on the map. He had also managed to arrange for the council to recognize Jim Paxton for his life of service to the Episcopal Church, an honor Paxton certainly deserved; but for Pedersen, it was a means of honoring All Saints and its contribution to the diocese. It was a splendid occasion that showcased Pedersen's accomplishments as builder, the hospitality of the parish family, and the efficiency of its staff.

The Educators

Pedersen had a great deal of confidence in himself as a salesman. His outgoing nature and energy made him a natural. He had sold the parish on two successful fund drives and two successful building projects. The areas in which he was less confident, he had tried to compensate for by putting together a team of individuals who were. This strategy would only succeed if the members of that team stepped up to the plate and only if he would provide them with the space and support for them to succeed. At the core of the vision was the concept of a large educational program whose slogan would be "Something for Everyone." Tan Creti had a great deal of confidence in himself as an educator. By nature, he was introspective and a thinker, a complement to Pedersen, who was an extrovert and doer. Tan Creti's orientation had already given him a good deal of success as a teacher in the context of parish life prior to coming to All Saints. Pedersen gave him the assignment to make this vision of a large educational program a reality.

The place to begin was the retreat program. This had been one of the promises Pedersen had made during the campaign to build the new retreat center. Overnight, retreats were scheduled for each age level of the parish's youth, beginning with the third grade. Each age level had two retreats a year. The format began with dinner on Friday night and ended by eleven on Saturday morning. Tan Creti and Mrs. Thomas stayed overnight with the children, did the cooking, and divided the instruction. There were also retreats for adults, one in the fall and one at the end of the school year.

Tan Creti took charge of confirmation instruction, which was scheduled for after school. Each child was paired with another child, and the two received ten weeks of personal instruction from one of the priests. Once again, this went a long way to meeting Pedersen's promise to the parish to vastly expanded number of hours, which would be spent with their children.

Mrs. Thomas was given the assignment of running the church school under the supervision of Tan Creti. She brought to the effort the educational theory and energy that developed in the wake of the Second Vatican Council. The educational creativity in Roman Catholic circles in this country, including art and music, was quite phenomenal during this period. This was the era of the artist, Corita Kent,[205] the Jesuit musicians,[206] and Franciscan Media, which perhaps produced some of the best media for religious education ever.[207] Mrs. Thomas had been an early recruit in the Roman Catholic

[205] Sr. Mary Corita Kent was born Frances Elizabeth Kent in Fort Dodge, Iowa. Her artwork, with its messages of love and peace, was particularly popular during the social upheavals of the 1960s and 1970s.

[206] Among the Jesuits were Dan Schutte, John Foley, and Bob Bufford. Rev. Carey Landry was also a contributor. Many of these hymns that were composed at the time are still used, like "On Eagle's Wings" and "Be Not afraid." This music was used not only on retreats and in church school but also through Scheiblhofer, who had been recruited by Mrs. Thomas, in the liturgies of the parish.

[207] Media was regularly borrowed for retreats and church school from the media center of the archdiocese. The productions of the Franciscan media were of a particularly high quality, regularly using well-known actors and actresses. The media was remarkably ecumenical.

effort to reenergize religious education and became a leader of a new class of professional educators organized under the name of RELCO. By the late seventies, the glow was coming off Vatican II. Moreover funding for religious education coordinators and liturgists was not keeping pace with the need, and it was coming under pressures from the stresses growing in the Roman Catholic world. While Mrs. Thomas never considered leaving the Roman Catholic Church, she greatly loved the freedom and support she found at All Saints. In quick order, she knew every child in the system and assembled a body of dedicated teachers. She did this primarily by being sure that each teacher had every resource possible at hand for a successful class and by being personally interested in each of them as individuals.

The Sunday school that she inherited was already a creative program built around the current storytelling method. This was easy for Mrs. Thomas to build on, and the sense of her effort was not to change it so much as to make it work the way that it should. The key problem that needed to be addressed was teacher training. Previously, this had been handled by a vote of confidence that anyone already knew everything they needed to know to be a successful teacher. This often did not cut it when the volunteer found himself or herself in the midst of a class period running out of ideas or being challenged by a child who thought that they knew more than they did. To remedy this, a curriculum was written over the course of the next four years. The format for the curriculum was a set of theological notes on the story followed by a set of themes entailed in the story that related to the religious readiness of each grade level. A second section was a set of comparable goals by which the teacher could evaluate the success of the class and contained a list of possible activities that could be used to reinforce the learning and/or at least fill the time. Teacher training itself was divided between a presentation by Tan Creti focused on the content of the story and a presentation by Mrs. Thomas, who talked about what children understood and offered a host of resources to the teacher to use to involve the children. Teacher training was held every six to eight weeks for alternating teaching teams and was well attended. Whoever missed was privately tutored by Mrs. Thomas. In short order, the success of the church school was well known both inside and outside of the parish, and it became a draw for new families. The close working relationship between Mrs. Thomas and Tan Creti that made this work remained in place for more than eighteen years.

The complement to the church school was adult education. While the children were at their studies, adults would be at theirs. Pedersen gave Tan Creti the charge to initiate an ambition adult education program. For example, the course plan for 1977 to 1978, announced ahead of time for the coming the year, would be divided into seven sessions. Each session was to have an offering in at least two of three categories: scripture, history-theology, and contemporary problems. The offering for that year read,

> The Scripture courses: Parables, Dr. Barger; Last Discourses, Dr. Barger; the Book of Revelation, Father Tan Creti; Book of Acts, Father Pedersen; and the Corinthian Correspondence, Father Tan Creti.
>
> The History–Theology courses: Identity of the Episcopal Church, Father Tan Creti; Prayer, Father Pedersen.
> Contemporary Problems courses: Marriage and Family, Father Pedersen; Children's Readiness for Religion, Thomas; Drugs, Father Pedersen; Sociology of Retirement, Dr. Barger; and Doulos presentations.
>
> During Lent: Five Ancient Liturgies of the Eucharist and Initiation; The Book of Common Prayer 1976 on Eucharist and Initiation. These will be presented by the whole staff and would include an instructed celebration of each of the liturgies in the study.

In the course of this inaugural year, a new identity emerged, which named All Saints as a "teaching church" analogous to a "teaching hospital." The specific intention of the programs was explained as training people for ministry. As children went off to their classes, adults did the same. There were, of course, suggestions that church school run the same time as service. Such a format was traditional and was appealing because it asked less time, and it eliminated the possibility of "disruptive" behavior by children in the service. For some time, this pattern continued for the eleven-o-clock service, meaning that two sessions of church school were being staffed and run every Sunday.

We have already seen that the Lenten instruction in 1978 was specifically intended to provide the rational for the changes that were being made to the building. In general, the educational program was used to sell the whole building program because it was the facility that made possible a unique educational and enrichment program. Under the slogan "Something for Everyone" and the concept of a "teaching church" a wide cross-section of the parish came to feel that they did not just come to church to have their own needs met, but that they were there to inform and improve on their own ministries.

As the seventies were coming to an end, the bet that Pedersen had made on a team was paying off. Even the bet that youthful Robert Scheiblhofer could revive the music program was paying off. Scheiblhofer's Roman Catholic training meant that he understood and complemented the liturgical direction Pedersen wanted to take All Saints. He quickly shed his guitar and proved commanding on the organ and thoroughly competent with the classical Anglican hymnology. It again is relevant to point out the special nature of the post Vatican II period. Roman Catholic parishes were quickly learning to sing hymns, and Scheiblhofer had created a hymnal for the archdiocese, which had borrowed heavily from the Anglican world as well as the general run of Protestant music. He also brought to the choir a great deal of fun that had long been missing. By the end of 1979, he was commissioned by parishioners to compose a mass setting for All Saints. His composition made its debut in 1980, and it has remained a hallmark of All Saints. All this was initiated by providing Scheiblhofer with a stipend of $1,000 and the use of the custodian's apartment to live in on the lower level of the church building.

The team soon included Russell Rauscher, the retired bishop of Nebraska. He had replaced Fred Lehman, after Lehman's death in 1978, as business manager; and in that capacity, he was an important council for Pedersen, whom he carefully nudged to deal with issues with which Pedersen had little patience. Just as important was the fact that a senior gray head was around who knew how to work the narthex. Rauscher offered reassurance by means of his calming presence to those who were worried by Pedersen's brashness, by means of his common sense shared with those who were anxious about Tan Creti's intellectualism, by means of his impeccable Anglicanism with those who were troubled by Mrs. Thomas's Catholicism, and by his mature wisdom with those who were fearful of Scheiblhofer's youthful zeal.

It was a remarkably balanced team. Each held him or herself to a high standard and enjoyed working with one another. Chance had, to some extent, put them together, and they were succeeding in one of the more difficult decades of the twentieth century to be in the ministry of the Episcopal Church. Few recognized at the time that the eighties that lay ahead would suddenly be much more conducive for the prosperity of the Episcopal Church than the past decade had been. All Saints had a ready-to-go team.

Chapter 9

Enjoying the Ride: 1980–1992

Fair Skies and a Favorable Wind

It is true that an ill wind passed through Omaha during the summer of 1980, which bent the cross seventy feet above the floor of the nave, which tops All Saints Church. But it is also true that the cultural winds of American life were suddenly more favorable for religious institutions, the Episcopal Church included. The culture of conflict, which had its origins in the late sixties, had burned itself out, and the country, in various ways, was embarking on "a head trip." If for some this was an escape into drugs, for others it was an exploration of spirituality. The bookshelves of the fifties and the sixties were filled with books on ethics, but those of the seventies and eighties were progressively filled with books on spirituality. They varied from the light, Scott Peak's *The Road Less Traveled*, to the profound, such as *Finding Grace at the Center* by Thomas Keating published in 1979. It wasn't the 1880s all over again, that favorable decade in which All Saints had been founded. No, it was not even a return to the fifties during which the parish had rebuilt its strength and cultivated the optimism, which enabled it to move to a new location and to build an entirely new facility. There was, however, a substantial change of attitude favorable toward religion in the 1980s, or better, toward spirituality, which provided the opportunity for religious institutions to reengage individuals.

The new climate did not, of course, translate into successful parish development automatically. But All Saints was ready. It had navigated the difficult waters of the sixties and seventies amazingly well, and when the eighties dawned, it had the resources to pick up on the new interest in spirituality and the nimbleness to do so.

For one thing, the periodic task of finding an assistant priest did not represent itself, even though the customary two-year tenure had been exceeded. Tan Creti's role as an assistant was, in fact, continuing to grow during 1980, beyond his initial role as an educator and youth worker. He had been appointed by Bishop Warner in the course of 1979 to the Commission on Ministry. The commission had just begun a study of alternative ministries, including the revival of permanent deacons. The presence of deacons in parishes was implied by the text of the new *Book of Common Prayer*, but there was the complicated question how candidates for the order should be trained as well as how suitable candidates could be identified. Among the possible means for training was the recently published Education for Ministry (EFM), a curriculum that was offered as an extension course by the University of the South. Tan Creti's participation in the diocesan discussion had the benefit that it gave the parish an up-to-date understanding of what was possible. In the course of 1980, the first EFM class was recruited at All Saints. When the seminars began meeting in October of 1980, it consisted of two groups of twelve each, both mentored by Tan Creti. Participation in the Commission on Ministry also meant that Tan Creti was able to supply the aspirations for ministry within the parish with the latest thinking in the diocese on the question of orders. By the end of the year, there were more than seven solid aspirants for "the life project" diaconate, as it came to be called in the diocese.

Another venture outside of the parish for Tan Creti was with a group in the community seeking to advance hospice care in the city. At the end of the year, Tan Creti accepted a position on the steering committee of the newly founded Omaha Hospice Organization. While this was understood as outreach work, like his participation in diocesan work, it brought back into the parish firsthand knowledge of the hospice movement. In the December issue of the *All Saints Herald*, a description of hospice care and its rational appeared. From that point on, courses on living wills, medical directives, and other aspects of medical decision making became part of the educational fare at All Saints. For example, on January 10, the parish began a six-session course on health, aging, and dying with six guest speakers, each of whom was a significant participant in the city's hospice movement.[208]

208 Rev. Judy Locke, chaplain at Immanuel Hospital; Sharon Van Butsel, hospital social worker at St. Joseph Hospital; Gary Bargetadt, Visiting Nurses Association; Virginia Gessert, occupational therapist; Dr. Ward Godsell, MD, Montclair Hospice; and Joyce Fox, RN, head of the Montclair Hospice team.

Inside of the parish, Tan Creti's role also began to expand into the area of pastoral care, newcomer calling, and visitation. It was the era marked by long hospitalizations and a growing population, particularly of women, who were homebound or in nursing homes. Visitation was a thing that Tan Creti did easily. The habit of calling extended to a number of marginal and nonmembers of the parish either because they were in the next bed or because there was some vague connection with the parish, which had caused them to be referred to him. Pedersen would say that whenever Tan Creti left town, he could count on one of Tan Creti's old women having a crisis or dying.

Pedersen had allowed an assistant to carve out a substantial space for a ministry that was both challenging and at the same time one that began to earn its keep. When Tan Creti began at All Saints, Pedersen had shared with him one of those old-school dictums of parish administration: assistants don't cause parish finance to expand enough to pay for themselves. The pattern of two-year curacies was generally followed by a six- to twelve-month search for a replacement, which, among other things, allowed finances to recover. But in 1980, that was changing because something else was happening that was quite different from the standard curacy. On Pedersen's part, he transcended the problem of being bothered by an assistant whose skills were broadly recognized in the parish. It would be naive to assume that there wasn't some sense of competition or tension between them. But as Pedersen told Tan Creti, whenever anyone on the parish was getting to him about the skills of his assistant, he would simply reply, "But who was it that was smart enough to hire that guy?" As for Tan Creti, his previous ministries in two small Iowa congregations with restricted resources caused him to appreciate the facility for ministry that he found at All Saints.

What was happening was noticed in the parish. One of the parish's elder statesmen approached Pedersen and asked him what was going on with Tan Creti. He had been there well beyond three years, and there was no sign that he was about to move on. Wouldn't he become indispensable competition for the rector or too much to afford? Pedersen shared the remarks with Tan Creti, and together they were amused by an opinion that they both considered to be based on an antiquated model of parish ministry: the two years and out curate who never paid his way and/or to whom the rector never gave enough space for a full-fledged ministry to take place. They felt that they were doing something very different. If how or why it was working was somewhat vague in their own heads at the time, nevertheless, it was.

In October of 1981, the doctoral dissertation, which Tan Creti had been working on, was defended at Aquinas Institute still located in Dubuque, Iowa. While the committee accepted the dissertation, it asked for a number of changes. The changes were problematic because Aquinas Institute itself was undergoing change at the time. The director of his dissertation, Thomas Amara, OP, had moved to the order's priory in Washington DC in 1979 and was not available. Aquinas's ecumenical partnership in Dubuque was in the process of dissolving, and it expected to move to St. Louis soon. The changes would have required considerable time and money. The result was that the dissertation was quietly shelved. Perhaps it had served its purpose. Its substance was being applied and taught in the parish. The response to his teaching from the parish apparently provided him with the sense that he was fulfilling his calling for which the dissertation was intended. There were little or no discussion about moving, though the absence of the dissertation implied that a curacy was no longer necessary for Tan Creti.

In the fall of 1983, the diocese was rocked by the arrest of the rector of Holy Trinity, Lincoln. Henry Burton was charged, along with a group of men, with disturbing the peace in an incident in the men's room at Antelope Park.[209] The sudden vacancy presented an opening, and Tan Creti, with the consent and coaching of Pedersen, applied. Tan Creti continued to be a finalist, but in the end, someone else was chosen. It was not clear that he would have accepted had he been chosen, but it had come very close to causing a change in the All Saints team. No serious attempt at a move would come along again until Tan Creti found himself a finalist among the nominees to succeed Bishop Warner when Warner retired at the end of 1989.

Pedersen's own ministry in this new period of expansion also grew dramatically, making greater use of his particular skills and in the parts of the ministry at which he excelled. As he marked the completion of ten years at All Saints, he addressed the congregation in a sermon preached on Sunday, February 1. The sermon was subsequently published in the *All Saints Herald*. There seems no better way to grasp the state of Pedersen's state of mind than to reproduce the text as it was published.

> Ten years ago to this very day, I came here as your rector. You as individuals and as a parish have extended yourselves to my wife and children as true friends, and the countless kindnesses you have shown us have done a great deal to make us a stronger family and have demonstrated again that the church is in its

[209] *Omaha World–Herald*, Tuesday, October 11, 1983.

essence a loving and caring family . . . I will mention a few things on my mind and in my heart. I consider All Saints Church one of the greatest parishes in the country. That is not just because Rev. Mark McCallum keeps telling me so, but for some of the following reasons: There is in this congregation a wonderful mixture of ages, types, interests, styles, backgrounds, and opinions. At the same time the one consistent factor I have seen is that around here almost everybody takes the church more seriously than they take themselves. Of course, there are some exceptions, but almost nobody takes them too seriously. This is no "secret spirituality" but it has something to do with the fact that we have leadership that has and is always able to commit. Among the leadership here, the dozens and dozens of lay people who have been and are now leaders, it is never a matter of rising to "higher position," but rather a matter of committing to greater service . . . Another important thing about this place is that we have shown ourselves a group not afraid of change. From the time we "packed up to go west from Dewey Street," and many times since. All Saints has looked at change not as some dreadful threat, but as a creative challenge. Because of this, the basics have gotten "more so" and we are freer with others and those who come to us. This very Sunday we lead the way in our diocese and as a parish church in this part of the country in terms of education, lay participation, stewardship, liturgy, and program. None of this is because we are brighter, or it is easy, but because priority was never personalized and almost each person has come to terms with the idea, "what is best for the church?' That is not to say that everything is perfect and that all changes are for the best, but it is to say we are in the business of being a faithful and caring Christian community and facing as best we can the challenges of our time. We are stronger than ever . . . Unless someone imagines that I have been a little too complimentary and in so being have complimented myself, let me just add this: you deserve a lot of credit, for you have had to live with one of the most stubborn priests God ever put on this earth and you have done so with good humor for ten years. Maybe that is because you have suspected rightly . . . he loves you deeply.

There was a steady flow of newcomers to All Saints, and Pedersen made an extraordinary effort at greeting and welcoming them into the congregation. A good portion of them was seekers from outside of the Episcopal Church. By far, the greatest number were disaffected Roman Catholic who were disappointed in that church's backlash against Vatican II and/or difficulties because of that church's position on divorce and remarriage. It should be remembered that the staff included two Roman Catholics and that the parish regularly advertised itself during this period in the *Omaha World-Herald* as "Catholic."[210] Episcopal congregations in the city were also in various forms of crisis. Holy Family, whose conservative rector, grieving the loss of his wife to cancer, entered a negative funk, which initiated a death spiral for the mission. A number of very attractive and talented young couples transferred from Holy Family to All Saints. St. Andrew's new rector, Robert Dunn, found himself struggling against entrenched interests in the parish left behind by the long tenure of Father Haviland. His rather indiscriminate combative style caused a number of members, some quite prominent, to transfer to All Saints. The cathedral itself had its own struggle going on. It found itself hard pressed to maintain a wide-ranging program, such as counseling, a creative and energized Sunday school, an intense confirmation preparation for children and adults, adult education, and just a welcoming atmosphere. Dean Fricke explained to his congregation: You can be either a program church or a worship-centered church. You can't be both. Fricke's aphorism may have been more of a salve for the predicament in which the cathedral found itself than an actual agenda for it. Clearly it contrasted with All Saints commitment to program and even to special services transcending program, such as lay and diaconal service ministries, health ministry, and advanced educational offerings. Another contrast between the cathedral and All Saints was that the cathedral was having a hard time sustaining an assistant priest both because of finances and because limitations on the vision and/or security of the dean, which would have allowed an assistant to exceed the model of two years and out. It was in the eighties that the destinies of the cathedral and All Saints took divergent courses, and as a result, a number from the cathedral found their way to All Saints. In addition to these was a small but steady trickle of refugees from St. Barnabas. The result was that services at All Saints were buoyed by excellent attendance. Not only did this increase the size of the congregation, but it also added dramatically to its diversity.

A frequent visitor to the parish pointed out to Pedersen that this attendance pattern made a profound impression on visitors and conveyed the feeling to them that something was happening at All Saints. The observer pointed out that if the nine-fifteen and the eleven-o-clock were

210 The text read, "a diverse community blending Protestant, Evangelical and Catholic Tradition."

put together, it would be one of the most exciting congregations in the city. Pedersen, without hesitation, did precisely that. In many ways, it was a substantial reversal; and had it been put to a vote at the time, it would have likely been defeated. Pedersen had little use for voting on things and had no fear of reversing his own direction. With the sanctuary remodeled and Morning Prayer gone from the eleven-o-clock, the need for two competing main services was gone as far as he was concerned. The announcement was made on August 21, 1980.

> Beginning September 14, we will change the schedule of services here at All Saints. We will continue with the 5:00 p.m. Saturday service and the 8:00 a.m. Sunday service. We will, however, have only one late Sunday service which will be at 10:30 a.m. Church school and adult education programs will begin at 9:30 a.m. and will finish in time for the parish Eucharist at 10:30 a.m.

Pedersen continued to explain his motivation: "To me the most impressive thing about all Saints is the congregation. The devotion, enthusiasm, mixture of ages, and pride in our parish is evident when we gather. Of course, such a gathering of our people has a strong evangelical impact on newcomers. Besides this, our own people want to know each other better and a single service provides a vehicle for this."

Attendance at this first reunited service was recorded as 323. For some time, this new ten-thirty Eucharist ran between 250 and 350 communions. The new expanded altar rail on the level of the nave made it possible to pass communion without lengthening the service. Dispatch was important for Pedersen, and yet with the new arrangement it was possible for the service to be unrushed. The crowd, which surpassed other Episcopal Church services in the city, was energizing and remained, for a time, a hallmark of the parish. Like a lot of things, it did have some unintended consequences. The most important of these was that the Sunday school space was packed with kids. The building project that Pedersen had walked around for so long was once again in his face.

Doulos, the lay service program that he had created, continued to be a focus for Pedersen's ministry. The Doulos community met many of the basic needs within the parish, and it made an extensive commitment to work outside of the parish. One project that claimed special attention was St. Jude's Home for Abused Children and received support, including the purchase of a van for the home in May of 1980, a beneficiary of the first big spaghetti supper. Doulos also began to work with Francis House and its sister, Siena House, which provide shelter for homeless men and women. Francis House's particular pride was that it would take men off the street unconditionally, that is, they were the stop of last resort. Doulos members, Walter Bacon, Don Amsden, and Frank Murphy, served on the board of Francis House; and throughout the eighties and nineties, they nurtured a bond between the two institutions.

Pedersen was drawn more deeply into Brownell Talbot School, where his older children, Jennifer, Lee, and Mary Francis, had attended. In the late seventies, under the leadership of a new headmaster, the school began to drift out of the Episcopal orbit, taking in progressively more non-Episcopal students. The board itself was more independent, and the bishop was progressively less of an active force on the board. Pedersen became anxious that the land that belonged to the diocese might be deeded over and/or mortgaged in a way that it might be lost. Pedersen heavily lobbied Warner to protect the land, which he considered part of the patrimony of the diocese. While a series of headmasters struggled, Pedersen built a relationship with the assistant administrator, Diane Desler. He would often comment that it was she that was holding the place together. When the board turned to her as the next headmaster, he was delighted. Soon he found himself as the school's chaplain, a role that had usually been given to junior clergy to supplement their income rather than as an assignment for a senior rector and particularly for one who was decidedly the busiest priest in the diocese. He quite enjoyed the work and was successful with the kids. His chapel was brisk, spontaneous, and filled with drama. In 1988, he established a food drive in the chapel, which was in turn distributed through the All Saints food program. The following May, he restored the custom of beating the bounds, marching the faculty and kids around the boundary of the property, and leading them in prayer and singing. He continued in the role of chaplain for some time even after he had retired as rector. In 1995, he was made a member of the Brownell Talbot board as the school was making a big push to expand, including considerable building.

In the parish, he also continued to expand his role as a builder. He turned first to the columbarium, which had been established as a modest set of shelves in the priest's sacristy. Eyeing space in the abandoned office core in the west wing, he came up with a plan to convert the old treasurer's office into a columbarium. A door, he contended, could be opened into it from the nave of the church, and it would create space for 250 niches. He put Rauscher, who was a master woodworker in his own right, in charge of designing the project and presenting it to the vestry. The establishment of the columbaria had come into vogue in the Episcopal Church during this time, and most were created by purchasing prefabricated structure. All

Saints columbarium, however, consisted wooden cabinetry built on site for a very modest cost. Pedersen turned to another parishioner, Don Olsen, to produce the urns. The urns were fabricated by Olsen Brothers' Roofing out of roofing copper, again at a great savings. The price for each unit was set at $300, and the construction was paid for by advanced subscriptions. Once the cost of construction was paid for, the additional income was to be retained in trust to care for and to relocate the facility if that ever were to become a necessity.

It was not so easy, however, to dispatch the building problem created by the combination of nine-fifteen and eleven-o-clock services. The problem of classroom space, which Pedersen had avoided for ten years, could no longer be ignored. The downstairs was bursting at the seams. In September of 1982, he put his old team, Amick and Stitt, on to the task of expanding the church school space. The expansion was an addition of nearly 2,400 square feet. There would be three small class rooms, each twenty-six by fourteen; one large room for audio visuals, twenty-six by twenty-eight; and a third large room, twenty-six by fourteen, which would be created by combining an existing room at that north end of the building with a room in the new addition to form a large preschool/kindergarten room. The design of the new addition specified a single story, the length of the lower level along the west side of the building. It would be poured concrete, and its roof would necessarily be flat so as not to interfere with the nave windows on the upper level. The exterior would be sandblasted concrete so that it would match the rest of the foundation. The problem of looks was largely muted by the fact that it was nearly hidden from view. It required no addition to heating and cooling system since the space adjoined the existing building precisely where a main forced air duct ran the full length of the building. Whatever additional heating and cooling needs this space put on the system was easily made up for by eliminating the wall of single pane glass set in metal frames along the west side. This wall of single pane glass, catching the prevailing northwest west wind, had made the lower level nearly impossible to heat during the winter. In summary, it was immanently practical solution.

Once again, the Stitt–Amick team had come through on the cost. When Stitt presented his final bid to the vestry, it was $113,000. This suited Pedersen well, for he had already acquired a bequest from the estate of Dr. Ralph Liukart, the doctor who had delivered Pedersen fifty years prior into the world. The bequest would amount to $45,000. Joined with other money already in the Capital Fund and Memorial Fund, it would suffice for the construction of the new classrooms. There would be no capital fund drive and, with that, not a great deal of discussion about the plan in the parish. Work could begin as soon as the weather allowed, and the space would be available for the coming September. With the completion of the Sunday school wing, Pedersen reputation as "a builder" was secure for better or for worse.

Expansion of the Team and Its Mission

As the parish moved into the eighties, Pedersen began exploring the idea of a third priest. It is not clear what was behind his thinking, but he had ambitions to expand the ministry of All Saints in new directions, convinced that All Saints had a formula to succeed where other in the Episcopal Church, at least in the immediate frame of reference, did not. By accident, an opportunity to expand the parish's mission presented itself to him.

In 1979, the diocese had fielded its own "team ministry," convincing the three struggling North Omaha parishes to form a single field to be led by a full-time priest in charge of the team. The parishes consisted of St. Mark's, on 6131 Girard St.; St. John's, 3004 Belvedere Boulevard; and St. Philip's, 2532 Binney. All three parishes had lost ground at least in part because of the impact of the cities racial issues, which had created flight and/or had crimped growth where it had been expected in the northwest. St. Philip's, the historic black congregation, was at the heart of the near north side, which was suffering from its own form of flight as upward mobile blacks moved West. This movement had a strong effect on St. Philip's, which was magnified by the north-to-south interstate that cut it off from its growing Western neighborhoods. St. John's neighborhood consisting of a lot of post-World War II housing was rapidly losing fashion. St. Mark's, the historic Florence church, with a new if small building, was located in the fashionable country club edition, which, however, was failing to match growth projections due to a great extent to the ordered busing. On the other hand, despite their common destiny, the three congregations were very different parishes. Each had, for some time, cobbled together their own part-time ministry. Father Muller, who had retired from St. James Fremont and moved to North Bend, was delighted to come in and do St. Mark's service for them. Jess Hansen and Ronald Wiley, the canon to the ordinary, filled in at St. Philip's and St. John's. Now with the backing of the diocese, Rev. Robert Manning Maxwell arrived in August 1979, hopefully bringing a solution to a difficult problem.

It was not long before there were signs of trouble. Having just completed the ten-thirty service and "worked" the narthex, Pedersen and

Tan Creti returned to the sacristy only to find Father Muller waiting for them. He was fuming. He had just driven forty miles to take the service at St. Mark's only to find out that he had done so because Maxwell had taken the Sunday off. "Could they believe it?" he asked Pedersen and Tan Creti, a priest taking a Sunday off. In fact, they, in spite of not being much more advanced on such issues, could because they were already over their surprise since Maxwell had been in their own congregation that morning. While they were both taken aback by a priest taking Sunday off, Muller was utterly confounded by the very idea. Muller had resigned on the spot, and Pedersen, forthwith, took his old mentor on to the staff. Now the narthex had two grey heads, to the delight of many in the parish, not a few of whom had grown up at St. James.

Maxwell's ministry from the beginning had the arc of crash and burn written into it. It was brought to a head by an extra-marital affair with a member of one of the parishes. The problem was compounded by the fact that Maxwell could not own the harm that he was doing. He was convinced that he was part of "exciting change." A psychiatric doctor attending one of the parishes remarked in passing, isn't there anything left that is just immoral? When his ministry came undone at the end of 1981, Pedersen stepped in. He told the diocese that he would take on the care of St. Mark's and St. John's. The diocese brought Jess Hansen in to care for St. Philip's and renewed its promise to find a black priest for them, a promise that was never kept. All Saints venture into the mission field was a way for Pedersen to call into question various diocesan lead efforts. All Saints could do what they couldn't, and All Saints could do it for much less money. Pedersen's role with the mission would focus on the business end. Tan Creti would take the baulk of the services and pastoral work. The educational resources of All Saints were put at the disposal of the missions. If for Pedersen this was a chance to show what good management could do for ministry, for Tan Creti it was an opportunity to show the strength of the communal-style ministry that he had written about in his dissertation.

This expansion of mission provided Pedersen with new arguments for hiring a third priest. In 1982, the diocese was about to graduate one of its best qualified candidates in years. Mitchell Lindeman was the son of an air force officer, born in Tacoma, Washington, and raised largely on the move. He met his wife to be Eileen at a Benedictine retreat in Arizona. Eileen Cornish was a Lincoln girl, and together they finished college in Lincoln, Nebraska. While both had an interest in a vocation, it was Mitchell who enrolled in Berkeley Divinity School. Eileen would complete her work later and be ordained. As the year was ending, the parish was told that Mitch Lindeman would visit the parish in January for an interview. The plan was that the parish would ask the diocese for 25–30 percent of his salary for work that he would do in North Omaha as part of All Saints mission there. In a follow-up to Lindeman's visit, the vestry, meeting on February 11, 1983, approved hiring Lindeman "anyway we can get him." The terms of his contract were defined as a three-year internship. With the agreement sealed, Lindeman's ordination to the diaconate was set for June 15, 1983, at All Saints. The parish, which had not experienced an ordination for more than sixteen years, attempted to make full use of his ordination to the diaconate and the one that followed in December to the priesthood as occasions to teach about ordained ministry. The two ordinations, in fact, set a stage for a rapid succession of ordinations over the next phase of All Saints life. The Lindemans, whose family included a young son, lived in an apartment in Maple Manor. Eileen complimented Mitchell's competence as a priest, and together they made a significant impact on the parish.

In the course of the next year, however, Pedersen's commitment to St. Mark's and St. John's lessened, and he ultimately came to the conclusion that he would not renew the covenant when it expired. By December of 1984, Lindeman had accepted a call to Fall City, Nebraska, and he preached for the last time at All Saints on June 30, 1985, a year short of the concluding date of his three-year internship.[211] It was not clear who pulled the plug, whether it was Lindeman that was ready for his own place or whether it was Pedersen that was ready for a different direction. At any rate, the recommendation to the vestry by Pedersen and Tan Creti was not to replace him. Pedersen announced at the same time that the three-year commitment to St. John's and St. Mark's would end in of 1985 as well. It had been a successful experiment, but it had not changed the future of the two congregations at that point in time. For Tan Creti, there were regrets that the experiment was ending, but Pedersen was ready to move on to something else. All Saints Centennial Year was on hand, and he had, as he often said, other fish to fry.

The Centennial Year

The discussion of the approaching centennial of the parish had begun in 1982. Pedersen understood that the centennial effort would define the decade and, for that matter, his legacy. At the end of the eighties, he would mark his twentieth year as rector of All Saints, putting him in a bracket with Mackay, Clayton, and McCallum. He was fortunate to be joined in his

211 Mitchell would go on to be the rector of St. Mattew's Lincoln and then Christ Church Coronado Island, California.

effort by a succession of highly competent and dedicated senior wardens—Carroll Fredrickson, 1979–1982; Dan Gardener, 1982–1985; Bob Bell, 1985–1988; and Bob Dickerson, 1988–1991. They were all businessmen at the top of their field. Fredrickson was the managing partner of KPMG's office in Omaha. He was from the small Nebraska town of Wakefield, famous for its Swedish days. He had an astute understanding of finance and a reputation for unquestionable integrity. His leadership provided the parish with a solid and trusted financial structure. Dan Gardener was an InterNorth executive who had managed the InterNorth Chemical Division and who was unimpressed with his own success or importance. A kid from Chanute, a small Kansas town, he remained interested in work, his family, and his church. Bob Bell was a South Omaha boy who grew up in St. Martin's. He saw combat in Korea as a marine, and his faith was deeply marked by that experience. In his early days at St. Martin's, he regarded All Saints as too low church and too socially upscale to ever imagine being part of it. Nevertheless, the decline of St. Martin's, including its failure to respond to the needs of his aging mother, led him and his family to All Saints. His wife, June, in her quiet way, became one of All Saints most valuable workers, tirelessly working on the altar guild, the rummage sales, and on the inner workings of St. Mary's Guild. Bell, like Fredrickson and Gardener, had served in the role of lieutenants to the lay leader of the McCallum era. Professionally, he rose to the position of the general manager of Omaha's gas and water utility, MUD, and was a highly respected leader in the city. He was well practiced in getting the right thing done in the context of conflict, which made him a great asset for Pedersen. Bob Dickerson was a lead engineer for Leo Daley. He was at the top of Daly's list as a contract negotiator, steady, quiet, unflappable, but capable of bringing the deals to a close when others despaired. He and his wife, Jan, had been loyal members of St. John's but found that All Saints, which was closer to their home in Benson, better served their needs. Jan was an outgoing activist among the women, though she had been crippled by a stroke not long after they were married. Bob was remarkably in the care that he provided for her and the mobility that his strong arms afforded her. The congregation was singularly impressed by them, Jan for her courage and Bob for his patience. Yet she was always quick to say, "But when we are alone we fight tooth and nail!"

All four men struck the members of the parish as spiritual leaders as well as good business leaders. All of their wives were deeply involved in the life of the parish as well. What Carroll had done for the parish's finance, Gardener and Bell did for the parish's management. Dickerson brought to the parish a pattern of successful decision making. Moreover, throughout the decade, they all stayed active and regularly counseled with one another, providing the parish with a special kind of "council of elders."

On March 2, 1984, Pedersen opened up the first formal discussion of a centennial celebration, speaking to the vestry about the hundredth birthday of All Saints, which would occur in September 1985. The minutes report that "He said this may be a once-in-a-century opportunity to say who we are and what we are about. Some ideas he gave were: being thankful for the past hundred years and being faithful to those growing old in the years to come; also scholarships for worthy students and staff housing for clergy. A circular drive out front and housing for the elderly also were mentioned." By June, he floated the idea that the parish should set out to raise a million dollars. In the end, the vestry settled on the goal of raising $500,000 for centennial projects. The greater part of these projects was built around an expansion of the endowment, but there was also the prospect for new building. Pedersen had, for a long time, entertained the idea of building housing on a part of the All Saints Campus. In the sixties and seventies, a number of major churches across the country had entered the subsidized housing market by means of HUD financing, which, at the beginning, was rather lavishly giving away funds. For rectors of this era, participation in such a project was the fulfilment of the dream of being "socially relevant" or, as it was often phrased, of actually doing something that made a difference. As early as November 14, 1977, a project of housing for single and elderly was discussed by the vestry. Jack Sprague, the senior warden at the time, suggested a committee be formed to look into it in sixty or ninety days, which was a rather successful means of pigeon holing it. Like many of the senior leaders of the parish, this struck him as an undertaking that it would be best to avoid. Nevertheless, Pedersen had a way of coming back to the idea. In February 11, 1983, the idea of housing on the property of All Saints was discussed in the context of the ministry being extended to St. Mark's and St. John's. It was further argued that the proposed duplexes would fill the need of someone being on the church property for the purpose of security.

Preparation for the Centennial Year also included an attempt to rebrand the parish. As usual, Pedersen looked within the parish for a resource. He identified Robert Ericson, a young graphic artist, who had worked for the large advertising agency in the city, Bozell and Jacobs, and had moved on as a freelance consultant. Ericson was a reserve air force captain who had also worked on various air force publications.[212] Pedersen asked him to design a centennial seal for All Saints, which could also become a new logo for

212 Erickson retired as a colonel. His wife, who was Australian, raised sheep, whose lambs began to appear at various services and occasions.

the parish. He charged Ericson to work with Helen Amsden, the editor of the parish's newsletter, and with Tan Creti. The result was a centennial seal, which picked up the interior of the worship space and on the idea of community. The graphic began to appear on letterheads, directories, special reports, advertisements, and on the cover of a redesigned parish newsletter. *All Saints Herald* was scrapped in favor of a new name, the *All Saints Witness*. While the word "herald" implied a newspaper, such as *Omaha World-Herald*, "witness" implied a ministry, which was a theme that had become the central identity of the parish. The new publication continued to be edited by Helen Amsden, but it was now a redesigned eleven-by-seventeen sheet printed in-house on a plain paper copier. Folded, it mailed efficiently; and opened up, it provided a generous magazine-style layout. Photographs were now possible because of digital photography, and they soon became a regular feature in the monthly publication. Articles were expanded as a means of keeping the All Saints story before the parish, filling anywhere from eight to twelve pages.

The next step in the centennial observance was taken in March of 1985, when the vestry named a drive committee. Dan Gardener, the present senior warden, was named to chair the committee; Carroll Fredrickson, the former senior warden and current treasurer, was to be in charge of finances; and Don Amsden would be in charge of the program. Don Amsden, who had served on the vestry, was a senior executive at Conagra whose career had focused on public relations. With the aid of his wife, Helen, he brought to the centennial effort a particularly strong competence for the task of telling the story. Two additional committee members were included, Bob Bell and Bob Dickerson, who were due to become senior wardens in the coming year, bringing the membership to six. The interesting thing about this group of men is none of them represent old Omaha, old All Saints families, or members of current Omaha society.

Somewhat buoyed by the initial reaction to the appeal, the goal was raised in April to $560,000 and the centennial drive now officially included the plan to build elderly housing. By now, however, HUD money was drying up, and the use of HUD money had always been problematic for Pedersen since he had no desire to relinquish control over the project as HUD financing would require. Fortunately, for Pedersen, there was a new resource in the parish. Frank Murphy had come to Omaha as a result of Conagra's acquisition of Blue Star frozen foods. Frank, a retired army colonel, was a passionate advocate for working with the poor. He quickly joined in with the parish's effort to support Francis House and was soon on its board. He brought some real expertise to the field of housing for the elderly from his previous experience. On February 22, 1985, Frank Murphy made a report to the vestry on an Elderly Housing Project. The proposed construction envisioned thirty to thirty-two units, which would sell 25 percent below market. One hot meal could be available from the church kitchen, which would meet both nutrition needs and fellowship needs. These meals would be prepared by volunteers recruited from the parish.

In the end, the celebration of the centennial passed quietly. Officially, it was celebrated on September 1, 1985, Sunday, at a ten-thirty Eucharist with a guest preacher. The preacher was Rev. Robert Dresser of Rye, New York, a high-powered suburb of New York City at the time. Dresser was a noted preacher and someone to whom Pedersen had looked up to during the years he had spent in the East. The primary publication for the event, passed out at the service, was a single-fold legal-size paper entitled the "SHIP'S LOG 1885–1985." Using a nautical theme, it traced the history of the parish with a series of brief entries, and it concluded with the summation: "To date, more than 3,800 have been baptized; 2,100 couples married; 3,400 burials; 32,000 worship services conducted, more than 850,000 Holy Communions; and in excess of 24,000 men, women and children have called this good ship their church home." It was quintessential Pedersen, brief, economic, and full of numbers. Following the service was a dinner and a slide show, which had been prepared by Don and Helen Amsden. The campaign chair announced at the dinner that the Centennial Drive had reached the mark of $412,470 of pledges. There was, however, still hope that it would reach $600,000. Part of Pedersen's boast was that the drive had been generated with resources already in the parish and had cost no more than $3,000. In general, the event was low key and low budget and could not, in any manner, be termed grandiose.

Pedersen's preoccupation for the rest of the decade was with the housing project. By April 1986, Amick, who was again enlisted as the parish's architect, reported that the Omaha Planning Board approved the parish's plan to build housing. In July, a bid to build the first duplex was awarded to Barry Larson. The actual building, however, was delayed while a plan was worked out for sewer and water. The reasonable solution called for bringing them in from Cady Street on the north boundary of the property, but this required an easement across city parkland. It helped that Bob Bell, the general manager of MUD, was the senior warden, and the easement was finally granted. Cedar Construction, whose bid was $19,741, went to work on the sewer and water once approval from the city came. Soon after Larson, whose contract was $121,000, began work. By October 14, the framing of the first unit had begun.

Each unit had a ground floor of 1,098 square feet. Its space was divided between a master bedroom with its own bathroom and a second small bedroom, also with its own bathroom and an open living area. The open room with a cathedral ceiling was divided between a living area and dining area, the latter of which was served by small efficiency kitchen. A washer and dryer were located in the first-floor hallway. Each unit also had a full basement which provided storage and the potential for being finished living space. The design was efficient and attuned to the needs of the elderly. The premise of the second bedroom-bathroom was that it might make possible live-in care. The units on Erskine, the name the city assigned the new street, backed onto a city park and had before them the broad campus running a full block on to Blondo Street. The setting was quite pleasant and parklike.

The vestry had agreed to build one unit as a staff house out of the existing capital funds, paved by the fact that Pedersen, by a number of means, memorial money, bequests, and a remarkable return on capital, had amassed a pool of undesignated funds, which could be tapped without any interior negotiations. For most of the vestry's attitude was, if the money was there, why not? For the parish at large, if it was not being asked to give anything, so what? The funds on hand could handle the infrastructure and the first half of the duplex. In order to proceed, Pedersen needed to find an additional $65,000. He was able to do this when he sold Ed and Edie Wiedner on the idea of buying the other half of the first unit. The arrangement made with them was that they would build the unit, and upon taking possession of it, they would deed the property back to the church. The Wiedner's stood to gain in three ways: they would be able to live in a pleasantly sized condominium as long as they were capable of independent living, they could have the satisfaction that they had made a major gift to their church, and they could enjoy a substantial tax benefit over the next decade of their life. There were implications, if somewhat vague to their extent, that while they lived in the unit the parish would provide them with special support.

At the time, Ed and Edie were seventy-three and eighty-two, respectively. Ed was very protective of Edie, and he was sure that it would fall to him to be her caregiver. Edie was raised on the south edge of South Omaha, an only child of doting and protective parents. She was a bright student and had gone into teaching. A student of hers provided the parish with the following description of her at the time of her death. "The last time I saw Ms. Merriman was June of 1937. I have tried to emulate her and became a high school English teacher as she was. She was so filled with zest, with the love of her students and the knowledge of her subject. She made learning an adventure and interesting, and she was so cute and peppy. Her mother designed her clothes and they were beautiful. She wore matching shoes and jewelry. She was "a darling and we all loved her!" At the height of her career in the fifties, she became a much-loved dean of women at Benson High School, which, at the time, was thriving.

Ed was raised in Dubuque, Iowa, in a broken home with a loose affiliation with the Episcopal Church. A self-reliant tall young man with an ironic sense of humor, he left home to make his way in the world on his own. Caught by World War II, he served a long and very bleak tour of duty on Attu in the Bearing Straits. Returning to the Omaha area, where some of his earlier adventures had led him, he landed a job with Greyhound Bus, the pride of the American highways. The advertisement slogan "Go Greyhound, and leave the driving to us" was ubiquitous and well received across the country. Edie's parents had been critical of any man who happened to get close enough to Edie to suggest that marriage might be in the offing. Ed's background was strikingly different from Edie's, and he was nearly ten years younger than Edie. Her parents were immediately and adamantly against their marriage. As it turned out, they were a perfect pair. Marked by the Great Depression, they lived a frugal, no-nonsense life, attending to both Masonic lodge and church work. They never had children.

They built a new home in Northwest Omaha, and in 1967, they transferred from St. John's and settled into a comfortable pattern of belonging to All Saints. Ed was a serial storyteller and few could outdo him, except perhaps "Father Pete." With that bond, he and Edie were drawn more deeply into actives of the parish. Soon they became the money counters and had "a second home" in the parish office. Their counting was legendary. It always came out to the last penny, even if it took long into Monday to complete the count. Those who overheard the process shuddered at the zingers that flew back and forth as only can be done by a genuinely loving couple. By the eighties, they were widely known as that very gracious and outgoing couple at the ten-thirty whose dedication to the church and to each other was an inspiration.

They were pleased with the plans for the unit as they had been drawn, except, Ed said, there had to be a drain in the garage. They waited through the winter, hanging on the news from the building committee, prepared for the adventure of living on the church's ten-acre grounds. When they came for the inspection, they discovered that there was no drain in the garage floor. Arguably, it wasn't code to have a drain in a garage. Nevertheless, the Wiedners withdrew their commitment. It is possible that in the intervening month they had grown anxious about leaving their home and taking on the venture of living on the church's grounds, but it is also true that for Ed, a deal was a deal, no matter how big or small.

Fortunately, for Pedersen, another interested party emerged. Ellen Black, whose son-in-law was an accountant associate with Carroll Fredrickson, wanted to buy the unit. With her son-in-law's help, the deal was made, and she was soon the resident at 9264 Erskine Plaza. Ellen would remain in her unit until 2006 and would be recognized for her pioneering spirit by being dubbed, in 1993, the Lord High Mayor of the village. A faithful participant in the life of the church, her presence on the grounds gave substance to the vision that a parishioner living on the parish's ground could contribute to the greater good of the parish. This stroke of luck, however, did not solve the problem that the staff house was without a tenant, and the possibility of a third priest had been put on the shelf. By November of 1987, Pedersen decided that he, with his wife's support, would move into the unit. The vestry authorized an additional $20,000 of work on the unit to make it fit for their needs, consisting mainly of finishing the unit's basement, with an additional bedroom, bath, and activity room.

By the time spring had rolled around, the Wiedners were back on track to purchase a unit; and this time, there would be a drain in the garage. By April 14, 1987, the senior warden could report to the vestry that the east side of the duplex had been closed in and that work inside was preceding. There was concern about wetness on the basement wall from the beginning, and in the long run, it was necessary to provide this unit with a sump pump. As the summer ended, the Wiedners moved into the unit, and they would end their days as residences of the All Saints campus, where they were regularly visited by members of the parish that had come to know them though worshiping with them.

The Wiedner's contribution to the parish would prove to be quite profound. They were an impressive presence at worship and suppers where they always went out of their way to speak to people. Over the years, they introduced a number of people to All Saints. Among these was a young couple, Tom and Cheryl Cline. Tom's dad was a Greyhound driver, and Tom was a fireman with the Omaha Fire Department. Cheryl was Roman Catholic, but once pointed to All Saints, they made a commitment to the parish and raise their family here. This provided a lead to a second young family to explore All Saints. Cheryl's brother, Jeff Pirruccello, and his wife, Lynn, would also join the parish.

The Wiedners, as has been mentioned, were a frugal couple. There investments were cautious but as regular as clockwork. For years their savings went into low-interest bearing savings certificates purchased through their insurance agent, Don Sharp. Don too would end up joining

All Saints with his new wife, Inessa, a Russian immigrant, both of whom made important contribution to the energy and diversity of the parish. Ed died on January 18, 1991, after about six months in a nursing home. Edie continued to live in the unit for three more years, dying in September 10, 1994, at the age of ninety. Their final impact on the parish was their decision to make All Saints the beneficiary of their estate. Their modest investment strategy in the end was valued at more than $1.5 million. A schoolteacher and a bus driver by means of their personal saving would make the largest single gift in the history of the parish.

In the meanwhile, the second unit of the new duplex remained unsold. The decision was made to complete the unit but not to carpet it until a sale was possible. Once again, the project was under stress. The unit remained empty for two years. Pedersen had identified Jim and Flo Wells as good prospects for the village. Jim had been on the vestry, frequently served on church growth/evangelism efforts launched by the parish, and had, in the seventies, taken on the role of head usher. His devotion to the task made him a successor to Artie Metz, the much-storied usher who had served in that capacity during the forties and fifties. Flo had grown up at All Saints and identified deeply with the parish. Flo was extremely active in the parish's women's work and fellowship, and when most of her generation moved on into a senior status to let the younger ones "take their turn" as it was explained, she continued to get involved in everything she could, especially if it involved cooking. Their presence on campus would add a dimension to the parish community, which both Pedersen and Tan Creti preached and was at the heart of the Christian experience. They were interested, but they did not have the money to buy the unit. After some time, an arrangement was made for them to move in for a stated rent that would apply to their purchase of the unit when that became possible. The vestry approved a five-year rental agreement, which would be set at $500 a month ($375 rent, $125 maintenance and utilities). They moved in November 1990, and it was understood that when they would realize a bequest from Flo's mother's estate, they would make the purchase. Mrs. Scott lived to be ninety-five, in church with hat and white gloves to the end, which came in December 17, 1995.

It is likely that the dissonance between the original housing plan, twenty to thirty units, and what had come about, four units and the latter of which was filled only by bending the rules, weighed on Pedersen's mind as he prepared himself for the final phase of his term as rector of All Saints, which he had frequently said would be when he was sixty-five.

Growing Ministry

As Pedersen pursued his projects and devoted himself to newcomer work, another facet of the parish's life came to fruition. For some time, Tan Creti had been working on the diocese's effort to restore the diaconate. He had brought this back to the parish with the hope that All Saints could establish its own pattern of diaconal ministry. The movement to restore the diaconate in the national church continued to strengthen, and with the support of the presiding bishop and the leadership of Ormonde Plater, it took on a tone of a crusade. It presented the Episcopal Church with the possibility of a more diverse ministry. In the previous form it had taken in the Episcopal Church, "the permanent deacon" was conceived of an assistant "priest" who was focused mostly on assisting in liturgical roles within the parish. After a brief revival early in the century, it had, by mid-century, become moribund. The new vision, which harkened back to the role of deacon in the early church, saw it as a service ministry in which a church ministry could be projected out from the congregation into the various avenues of life. It was also the means of moving women into a visible part of the ordained ministry, particularly in dioceses like Nebraska, where women priests were not accepted. Accepting this diversity, however, was a problem. Warner had, from the beginning, stressed his inability to support the ordination of women to the priesthood. His hesitation applied to deacons as well. The other hurdle for Warner was an answer to two related questions. What preparation was required for the diaconate and how could that be provided?

The first problem was overcome when Bishop Warner, attending the Lambeth Conference, talked to a Greek Orthodox bishop about women in the diaconate. That bishop had replied to him, "But there were always women deacon in the early church." Warner's reluctance was further abated when a national church consultant had asked him to imagine what deacons could do for his ministry. "Suppose you had a hundred deacons in Nebraska and you could put them anywhere you wanted, what would you do with them?" In the ancient city church, deacons were, indeed, the service arm of the bishop and did his bidding. The priests were the bishop's council, and they not infrequently told bishops what to do. The vision of an army of servants who saluted and said "yes, sir" stirred in the bishop's mind, like the sugar plums in the heads of children on the night before Christmas. It was more fantasy than reality. Still, it did open the door at last for those who had invested a substantial amount of time and self in the project, and they were not about to provide Warner with a dose of reality.

The question of preparation was more difficult to settle. James Barnett, the rector of Trinity Norfolk, Nebraska, had published a book as a part of doctoral study under the direction of Dr. Marion Hachette, the professor of liturgy at Sawanee. Hachette had been very involved in the final draft of the 1979 *Book of Common Prayer*, which had, as we have said, written an extensive role for deacon into the liturgy of the Episcopal Church. At the time, there were very few deacons in the Episcopal Church, and their extensive role in the new *Book of Common Prayer* owed a large part to the romantic imagination, which had driven liturgical studies the past fifty years. It was Hachette who gave Barnett the topic as a dissertation, and he turned over to him a great deal of material of his own and that of his predecessor, Dr. Massey Shepherd. Barnett's dissertation was published as "The Diaconate: A Full and Equal Order."[213] In it, he offered a simple but eloquent measure. A deacon should be expected to have the same level of knowledge as "a well-informed layman." This is quite adequate if "well-informed layman" is not reduced to "any old layman." Curiously, this simple common sense standard was continually being undercut in the diocese even in exams written by Barnett. The problem was that the issue was not simply about knowledge but about formation. Formation is a process through which a candidate for an ordained ministry achieves an identity that corresponded with ministry. The substitution of knowledge for formation is mistake.

With a great deal of difficulty, the diocese's Commission on Ministry finally managed to get the bishop to agree that EFM, the four-year, locally mentored extension course offered by Sawanee, would be acceptable or that, in places where it was not available, it would be taken as the norm for the theological knowledge and facility required. True, EFM had been conceived at Sawanee for lay education; but according to Barnett's norm, that was a good match for what was needed. EFM had begun at All Saints in 1980 as has been noted above. It was unusual in that the mentor was Tan Creti and that it included a number of participants that set very high standards for themselves. While in most places, EFM is process rich, at All Saints, it was also content rich. Moreover, from the beginning, those with interest in becoming deacons were involved in a parallel formation program, which was made possible by the rich community experience at All Saints.

Meanwhile, the parish at large was drawn into an understanding of the diaconal ministry as the program was unfolding on the diocesan level.

213 Barnett, James Monroe, *The Diaconate: A Full and Equal Order*, Trinity Press International, Harrisburg, Pennsylvania, 1979.

In February of 1984, Tan Creti reported to the vestry about how deacons would affect staff relations. The minutes explain that

> A handout was provided and included how a proposed assistant and diaconate would expand pastoral work. He explained the training process for the proposed diaconate. There are ten people now enrolled in the training course for the diaconate to be completed by October 1984. This course is also an educational course and not all participants will become deacons. Father Tan Creti said the long term goal is for ten to fifteen deacons at All Saints.

When the four years of EFM were up, the diocese was still struggling to put together an examination and the criteria for selecting candidates. It, in fact, required an additional anxious year of delay, which was hard on the aspirants. Nevertheless, when the way was finally clear, the All Saints aspirants were clearly among the most prepared candidates. As the day for the ordination approached, the *All Saints Witness* declared that "November 8 is going to be a milestone."

On November 8, 1985, the diocese's first class of deacons was ordained. They consisted of thirteen candidates from all over the diocese. Four of them were women. Three of the four women were from All Saints. They were Helen Prince Amsden, Mary Sue Coover Sturgeon, and Nancy Currey Wood. The service was held at St. Cecilia's Roman Catholic Cathedral, where Warner had been consecrated bishop on the basis that there was not a large enough facility in the diocese for such a large and historic ordination. As monumental as this goal was, it was hardly an end, but a beginning of a long rich diaconal ministry still flourishing at All Saints and around the diocese after twenty-five years.

In the original group of EFM graduates, there were three more possible candidates. On May 7, 1988, Berkeley and Mary Forsythe were ordained to service at St. Augustine's, Elkhorn. Samuel Morford was ordained to serve at All Saints on May 24, 1990. EFM at All Saints had been structured as a ladder, so a new tier was begun every two years. On the one hand, this provided a large number of lay leaders with a strong sense of ministry; and on the other hand, it continued to produce diaconal candidates. The second tier produced two more deacons: Betty Gaston, who served at Resurrection, and Ellen Ross, who served at Trinity Cathedral, both being ordained on May of 1988. Robert Scheiblhofer, who was part of that EFM group, with additional study, was ordained to the transitional diaconate on August 10, 1989. A third tier produced two additional deacons for All Saints:

Ernest Bowerman and Richard Landrith. They were ordained together on February 2, 1991. The fourth tier of the EFM produced another deacon, Lynne Bacon, who was ordained on September 25, 1993. The final tier taught by Tan Creti added two more: Frank and Oral Murphy, who were ordained on May 31. 1996. EFM continued at All Saints with a number of new mentors as a regular part of All Saints life well past its twentieth fifth anniversary.

The unfolding pattern of the diaconate created a complex set of issues that required constant tending. How could these ministries make use of their individual gifts and interests? And how could their efforts be coordinated with the overall ministerial needs of the parish? What would keep them from colliding with each other and other lay and ordained ministries? It was hardly automatic, and it was not without tension. Mary Sue Sturgeon's ministry was focused on hospital chaplaincies, and with time, she was a part-time employee of the Bergan Mercy Hospital's chaplaincy. Ernie Bowerman's ministry followed an interest in the city's police chaplaincy, even as he took on work in the parish as a custodian and a master of ceremonies. The Murphys were deeply involved with Francis Siena House, the city shelter, and with Together Incorporated, which worked with the city's food bank. All participated in parish visitation, and the parish's commitment to its elderly and shut-ins was greatly enhanced. All were regularly part of the parish's worship. Deacons were to be present at all of the Sunday liturgies to highlight service in the world as an essential component of Christianity. The effect of this decision put women at the altar for the first time, and the result was to open up the way for women's ministries to grow at All Saints.

An Ecumenical Ministry

As the eighties began, the pattern of participating with neighboring congregations in a dialogue during the Week of Prayer for Christian Unity, which began shortly after Tan Creti's arrival, continued. For All Saints, congregation-to-congregation ecumenism was more real or at least more enjoyable than the ecumenism, which happened between judicatories. To begin with All Saints dialogue partner was St. Robert Bellarmine, which had particularly receptive priests and, in some ways, was a similar congregation, both being a suburban congregation filled with business and professional people. However, the parish's dialogue was soon refocused and expanded into a trilateral dialogue including St. Leo's, a new Roman Catholic congregation in its neighborhood, and St. Timothy Lutheran, also a neighbor located on Ninety-Third and Dodge. During the week of Unity during 1980, there was the first pulpit exchange, beginning an exchange between Pastor Harmon of Trinity Lutheran and Pedersen of All Saints.

The parish responded to this interest in ecumenism, and Pedersen and Tan Creti not only valued it in itself, but also saw in it an opportunity to further adult education. If, for example, the dialogue topic was the Eucharist and what had changed in the Roman Catholic Church with the Second Vatican Council, it required the Episcopalians who participated to bone up on what the Anglican Church taught about the Eucharist and how that had changed.

The success of the initial trilateral dialogue lead to a wider range of exchanges, especially with Lutheran churches, such as St. Michael's, a newly founded congregation on Blondo Street; First Lutheran; Rejoice Lutheran; and Lord of Love. The Lutheran Church, as the Episcopal Church, had begun a dialogue with the Roman Catholic Church after Vatican II, which led to a series of impressive bilateral statements.[214] However, as the eighties began, there was a progressive retreat in the Roman Catholic Church from the results of Vatican II, and consequently, its dialogue with Lutheran and Episcopal bodies flagged. On the other hand, this led to the dynamic Lutheran Episcopal Dialogues: LED I, II, and III. The curious discovery was that the theology that Lutherans and Episcopalians had developed to be in dialogue with Roman Catholics put them in a position to be in dialogue with each other.

By the mid-eighties, this contact with Lutherans on a local level had become quite intense, and there was a desire to do something significant on the local level to further the growing sense of unity. Several years of dialogue with St. Michael's, Lord of Love, and Holy Cross Lutheran churches put All Saints in a leadership role. As Pedersen would observe, what the diocese gave lip service to, All Saints could make happen. This configuration of congregations on the northwest side of the city sought support from their judicatories to hold a major event in the city. The topic

[214] Episcopal-Anglican dialogue began in 1966 with the visit of Arch. Michael Ramsey to Pope Paul VI. The following year, the Anglican-Roman Catholic International Commission was established. Its first project focused on the authority of scripture. The commission has since produced nine agreed statements. Phase one of ARCIC ended in 1981 with the publication of a final report "Elucidations on Authority in the Church." The Lutheran-Roman Catholic Dialogue began in 1964 and has completed eleven statements. The two groundbreaking events of this dialogue were a joint statement on the doctrine of Justification by Faith in 1983 and the Joint Declaration on the Doctrine of Justification (JDDJ) on October 31, 1999.

proposed for the event was a conference on LED III, "Implication of the Gospel," which was due for its final review in June of 1987 and to be published by the end of that year. It was supposed to be the final round of the Lutheran-Episcopal dialogue, which would, if successful, lead to full communion between the two American denominations. As early as 1983, a local Episcopal-Lutheran committee was created. It was chaired by Harold Schmidt of First Lutheran and, in turn, by Tan Creti, who was the chair from October of 1985 until the summer of 1987, when the conference was held. The committee consisted of two Lutheran pastors, Norman Lillegard of Bethany Lutheran and David Zellmer of St. Michael's Lutheran Church, and Lutheran laity, Mrs. Donald Morin, Thomas Holtze, Harry Naasz, and Louise Vanzago. The Episcopalians were the Very Reverend Ron Wiley, canon to the ordinary representing the Diocese of Nebraska; Dr. Wally Bacon and Carroll Fredrickson of All Saints; Dr. Charles Wilhite, professor of music at Midland Lutheran College in Fremont; and Curt Youngman of Holy Trinity Episcopal, Lincoln. The strong presence of All Saints on the committee was backed up by the contributions of many other parishioners who worked behind the scenes. The night before the event, a group of volunteers cooked and served a dinner for the participants in the event in the retreat center. Robert Ericson, as he had done on several occasions for the parish, provided gratis an artistic design that was used in banners, vestments, and in "a very fine convocation magazine" published by Barnhart Press. The planning gained the enthusiastic support of Bishop Warner and Bishop Anderson, the head of the Nebraska synod, and both bishops participated in the event. The initial plan was to have the presiding bishops of the two bodies present, but Browning, having only recently been elected presiding bishop of the Episcopal Church, could not get his calendar in order in time. As a result, he appointed Grien, the bishop of Kansas, to be his representative; and the Lutherans responded by sending Weissenbuehler, their bishop of Denver, to be their national representative. The two scholars who were responsible for the drafting of "Implications of the Gospel" agreed to be present, Dr. William Petersen, dean of Bexley Hall, Rochester, New York, and Dr. Walter Bouman of Trinity Lutheran Seminary, Columbus, Ohio. When May 9, 1987, came, the event was blessed by a beautiful day, excellent attendance, and the animated presentations in the morning by Petersen and Bouman. In the afternoon, various workshops focusing around specific interests were held and were well attended. In the evening at Kountze Memorial Church, the site for the event, a jointly celebrated Eucharist was held in the main sanctuary designed to hold eight hundred people. The church was filled with a great crowd.

In the long run, the work of which this event was a small but meaningful part eventually produced a "Concordat," which became known as Called to Common Mission. Following a reception process by both churches, this document was brought before the governing bodies in the summer of 1999 (ELCA) and 2000 (ECUS). Having passed both churches' highest governing bodies, a relationship of full communion was celebrated at the National Cathedral in Washington DC on the Feast of the Epiphany 2001 and regionally in the following weeks and months.

While the implication of these actions has not been fully implemented, because of Lutheran reservations, altar exchanges now became possible; and in 2001, the pastor of Lord of Love, Donna Ward, was the celebrant at All Saints, and Tan Creti was the celebrant at Lord of Love. On a somewhat limited basis, Lutherans have served as priest-in-charge of Episcopal congregations, and Episcopal priests have served as Lutheran pastors. It remains an open question how significant the act of unity will prove to be.

The Election of a Bishop

A year after having been cohosts to the Nebraska Lutheran Episcopal Convocation, Warner announced to the annual council assembled on May 6, 1988, that he intended to retire at the end of the following year. He named a search committee for the election of a new bishop, which the council duly passed. All Saints had a strong representation on the committee. Dana Bradford, who had become the chancellor of the diocese in 1988 after serving for some time as diocesan treasurer, was chairman of the committee. In addition to Bradford, it also included Deacon Helen Amsden and Rev. Charles Pedersen from All Saints. Mitchell Lindeman, now the rector at Fall City, Nebraska, still carried his connection with All Saints, was named to the committee as well. Pedersen, whose parish was by this time hands above other congregations in the diocese, clearly intended to assert himself in this election.

With the council's approval of the committee, the bishop turned to his address. It rambled on for nine pages. It included thoughts on preparing a sermon for Palm Sunday, a rehearsal of the baptismal covenant, and then it concluded with a reference to his first address thirteen years before: "Again we are in a time of crisis. Let's give God a chance." There was nothing in the address that attempted to define what he thought the crisis was. When he had taken over, the nature of the crisis was quite evident; but now, if there was a crisis, it was the lack of clarity. Warner had come to the place where he had little sense about what needed to be addressed, and in this, he was perhaps joined by a large portion of the leaders of diocese and the national church.

Somewhat surprisingly, Tan Creti's name was placed in nomination, an anomaly in that he was not a rector. It was perhaps one way that Pedersen had of making a statement. Clearly, there were a number on the committee who knew Tan Creti well and others with whom he had worked in the diocese, which gave his name some degree of credibility. Other names included Rev. Carl Eugene Jennings, canon to the ordinary to the bishop of West Texas; Rev. G. Richard Lobs III, St. Mark's Geneva, Illinois; Rev. Loren B. McClanahan, St. Paul's, Canton, Ohio; and Rev. James Krotz, St. Matthew's Lincoln, Nebraska. There was a great deal of outside interest in the diocese, and the outside candidates where highly qualified men who had displaced some other equally well-qualified candidates. That two Nebraska priests held on in the field is a strong indication that a substantial portion of the diocese was oriented toward electing someone from within the diocese. Pedersen clearly was in this camp.

All five candidates were present and made presentations at annual council, which met at Holy Trinity Lincoln on May 5 to 6. The council adjourned and reconvened two weeks later at the Riverside Inn at Grand Island to elect a new bishop to be consecrated in late October. Two additional nominations to the already-large slate were made from the floor: John P. Bartholomew, dean of St. Mark's Pro-cathedral, Hastings, Nebraska, and Gary Young, canon to the ordinary. Clergy votes were rather evenly distributed across the six names, suggesting a lack of unity in the diocese. Lay votes were a little more focused on McClanahan, Krotz, and Bartholomew, with Bartholomew having the largest number, about 20 percent. Bartholomew had received full consideration by the nominating committee, and the choice to not include him among the nominees suggests that the committee felt he was not the right person at the right time. Certainly this was the opinion of Pedersen. A quick review after the first ballot caused Pedersen to visibly shift his support to Krotz. It took nine ballots to get Krotz over the line, but Nebraska would have a Nebraska bishop and a young one at that. In the end, Pedersen was quite pleased with the results and anticipated working with Krotz. They were, after all, both Nebraska boys, and he had been of pastoral assistance when the Krotzs sought to adopt a child. More recently, James Stillwell, who had long been Pedersen's mentor, had become Krotz's mentor. The bond was created when Krotz followed Stillwell as rector of St. Matthew's Lincoln. Pedersen's hope was, however, jarred when Krotz chose not to make Omaha his residence, either because of practical considerations or because it somehow signaled the western part of the diocese, that Omaha was not going to separate him from his roots among them. Pedersen was sure that this was a mistake, but more, he thought that Krotz should have made such a possibility known as he moved through the search process. Once again, the twist of diocesan fate would prove to further marginalize Omaha when what the diocese needed was unity. It returned Pedersen to a pattern of competition with the diocese, and often, his decisions in the coming years would be affected by the idea, to paraphrase Annie Oakley, whatever the diocese can do, All Saints can do better.

A Teaching Church

In the parish, the establishment of a diaconal ministry was quickly followed by the establishment of one of the very early parish-based health ministries in the Episcopal Church. In the late eighties, All Saints had a large and growing stake in health-related ministries. All of the newly ordained deacons had completed one or more clinical pastoral care units based in hospitals, the same as was required for priests. Sturgeon, in fact, completed three units and had an ongoing relationship with the hospital chaplains who had been involved in her training, eventually working as a coordinator at Bergen Mercy Hospital's chaplains. Tan Creti had, for some time, been involved in the Omaha Hospice Organization. This involvement led to a considerable interplay between the parish and a citywide movement in that field. Members of the parish became hospice volunteer and had, at their disposal, a variety of means of educating themselves on the use of hospice services for themselves and for the members of their family. Tan Creti also became an early and substantial participant in the AIDS Interfaith Network. On this issue, the synergism of Pedersen and Tan Creti was evident. Pedersen had become engaged with the issue when James Paxton's only child, Bill, was diagnosed as an early AIDS case. Pedersen as a counselor had been working for some time for a pragmatic reconciliation between father and son, a process that he accelerated when the diagnosis became known. He also provided support for Tan Creti, who had begun challenging in his sermons and classes the common accusation made at the time that AIDS was God's punishment for a corrupt lifestyle. This was particularly true in his Tuesday morning class in which he worked to create a civil understanding of homosexuality. He was invited to be a founding member of the AIDS Interfaith Network, which was being spearheaded by Bro. William Woeger of the Roman Catholic Archdiocese; Dana Banebridge, a Methodist minister at First Methodist and a chaplain at Methodist Hospital; and Nancy Brink, the pastor of Northside Christian. The committee had a wide range of ambitions and activities. It held monthly interfaith services in the Nebraska Chapel at St. Cecilia's Cathedral which was well attended by victims, family members, and caregivers. It worked at the creation of an activity center, complete with a coordinator with expertise in identifying the care required by AIDS patients and the training of volunteers. It also interfaced with the Omaha medical community and provided various educational resources as well.

In February of 1990, the vestry minutes record that Pedersen made the report that "Father Mike has been spending a great deal of time with the Interfaith Network on AIDS . . . and that he felt that All Saints needs to lead the way for AIDS victims." A motion followed made by Dr. Pat Perry to donate $500 to the network. Tan Creti's participation in the network funneled other resources from All Saints into the community effort, and at the same time, it returned to the parish the latest resource in the community.[215] This would prove helpful in the parish because, in short order, two more AIDS cases occurred at All Saints with whom the parish became pastorally involved.

Building on these early efforts, a pioneering parish health ministry was set in motion by the arrival of a young couple, Fred and Stephanie Ulrich. As is not uncommon for young couples, church had remained a moot part of their relationship until their child reached the age where she should begin church school in the early eighties. Fred had been raised at Good Shepherd in Bridgeport, Nebraska, and they had solved the question of baptism by taking their daughter back home to his mother's church. Stephanie had been raised as a Lutheran, but she had a great deal of exposure to the Episcopal Church while attending the Clarkson School of Nursing, where she had done her training. After being away for a while, the couple returned to Omaha, and she went to work for Clarkson Hospital, again reinforcing a relationship with the Episcopal Church as Clarkson, at the time, still had its historic relationship with the Episcopal Church. There she worked in intensive care, in the transplant lab, and finally as the head of the cardiovascular lab. It no doubt helped that Dr. Pat Perry, now on the vestry at All Saints, had taken a special interest in Stephanie from her student days on. The availability and skill of Pedersen as a counselor took their relationship with the parish another step further. Along with personal issues, Stephanie was questioning the growing tension and dysfunction in

215 Tan Creti was recognized on January 13, 1992, by the AIDS Interfatih Network of Omaha with the Jonathan C. Goldsmith, MD Caregiver Award in recognition and thanksgiving for outstanding service extended to people touched by AIDS.

the medical care community of which she was part. By February of 1988, Stephanie was confirmed at All Saints, and from that time on, both Fred and Stephanie were deeply woven into the parish community.

As part of this counseling, Stephanie began to explore with Pedersen her desire to leave the institutional model of health care and to explore what could be done from a community base, particularly that of a religious congregation. Pedersen was never one to let an opportunity pass by, and he began to follow up on her thoughts trying to imagine what a health ministry might be like at All Saints. The fact that it had scarcely been done anywhere else was, of course, appealing to Pedersen, who was convinced that All Saints could do anything it put its mind to. As part of the education program, Tan Creti invited the chaplain of St. Luke's Hospital in Davenport, Iowa, to come and do a program on parish participation in health care ministries. Marlin Whitmer, who also served as an assistant at Trinity Cathedral, Davenport, had developed a strong body of lay volunteers out of the cathedral and other Episcopal congregations in the area providing various services to the patients of St. Luke's Episcopal Hospital. He was also quite knowledgeable about health ministries based in parishes, and his input helped build a foundation for something at All Saints.

By December 12, 1989, Pedersen was ready to move ahead and presented to the vestry a plan for a Health Ministry Program in the parish, which Stephanie Ulrich would lead. The plan consisted of a first phase during which she would take a course in Des Moines under the direction of Dr. David Carlson at the Des Moines Lutheran Hospital. The parish was to pay her tuition, transportation, and other expenses involved with the course. The course, in turn, required that she be placed in an internship in a parish which would, of course, be All Saints. The parish would, in return, begin to experience the benefits of a parish nurse as she pursued her training. While the scope of the work would evolve with time, Pedersen argued, "parishioners would benefit from having a health professional as a counselor and advocate." This was understood to be of particular importance as medicine was undergoing radical changes in the eighties, including the growing complexity of various therapies, early dismissal from hospital stays, more options for assisted living, and the greater use of specialists. These changes challenged the capacity of patients and families to provide care, and it created gaps in the continuity of care. It was also expected that the parish nurse would do health screening in the parish and offer a number of educational programs in the parish for young people as well as adults.

It was not the intention for the parish nurse to become the pastor. The priests of the parish had a strong commitment to visitation as part of their pastoral ministry. The new deacons were trained for visitation as well. The nurse was to complement the visitations of priests and deacons and to provide them with medical expertise to understanding their pastoral ministry.

Ulrich's internship was completed in February of 1991, and All Saints was recognized as the first congregation in Nebraska to have an organized health ministry. During the bulk of the year, Ulrich served as independent contractor; but in September of 1992, her position was incorporated into the budget at twenty hours a week, making her part of the staff. By 1994, Ulrich extended herself to work in the city with a newly formed Health Ministry Steering Committee; and by 1996, she was active on the state level in writing standards and providing education for an expanding health ministries around the state. Her activities extended nationally by means of participating in the National Episcopal Health Ministries. This experience eventually led to the publication of a book, *Health Ministry in the Local Congregation*, of which she was the author. Her book is still regarded as a basic manual for Episcopal congregations seeking to develop their own health ministries.

Growing Ambiguity

As the eighties were ending, there were some losses that the parish seemed to pass over without losing its stride, and yet they also seemed to have lingered in the parish's unconscious. In April of 1988, McCallum, the parish's rector emeritus, died. While McCallum had long been unwell, he had periodically shown up in church, and he had served as friend and counselor for Pedersen. Pedersen had visited McCallum on a regular basis, and despite the difference between the personalities and churchmanship, they had built a close relation. Who, after all, understood the demands and stress of being the rector of All Saints better than an ex-rector? In May of 1989, Bishop Rauscher underwent a vascular surgery that went bad and which, subsequently, led to his death at the age of eighty. This again was both a personal and professional loss for Pedersen. Rauscher had provided cover for him on a number of issues during the past ten years. In January of 1990, Fricke, the dean of Trinity Cathedral, died after a struggle with a rapidly growing cancer. While the two priests had competed with each other, they had, over the years, become good friends. In the office, Deacon Helen Amsden, who had turned the flagging *All Saints Herald* into the *All Saints Witness*, resigned. Her resignation was followed by the resignation of the parish secretary, Helen Geisler, who had replaced long-serving Sue Caracter in 1984. The following July, a new secretary was hired, who needed to be trained, and it was too early to see how significant her contribution would be to the future of the parish. Sue Norman, who came from a pediatric doctor's office, was equipped with the discipline of diplomacy, patience, and confidentiality. She was up-to-date on computer skills, an area in which the parish was just beginning to explore.

Nevertheless, there were a number of expansive efforts that continued as the decade turned over, which seemed to compensate for the losses. Pedersen took great pleasure of welcoming Robert Spire to the pulpit in May 1988. Spire's services to the parish were innumerable and included having been chairman of the committee that had called Pedersen as rector. Spire had moved to Lincoln when Governor Bob Kerry called on him to replace the attorney general who had been forced to resign due to scandal. It was generally judged that Spire was the one person who could restore the integrity of the office. Spire spoke to a packed congregation assembled for ten-thirty Sunday service, which had been designated as a celebrating of Law Day. It was an opportunity for the congregation to express its deep respect and love for Spire, and for Pedersen, it was a way of servicing notice to the world of the significance of All Saints.

At the heart of the parish's program in the eighties, there was an ordination pipeline that it had constructed and had continued to be full. The diaconal ordination continued: Samuel Morford on May 24,1990, Ernest Bowerman and Richard Landrith, February 2, 1991, and Lynne Bacon was accepted as postulant, ensuring an ordination would follow in 1993. In addition to the diaconal track, there were vocations in the priestly track as well. Robert Scheiblhofer, the parish's organist choirmaster, was accepted as a postulant in June of 1987. He had an unusually strong foundation from his Roman Catholic training, including a period during which he tested his vocation with the Christian Brothers. This and his hard work made it possible for his theological education to be completed within the parish. That this was not an end run was proved when Scheiblhofer passed the general ordination exam with higher grades than the candidates that the diocese had recently sent off to seminary, several of whom failed sections, requiring them to do remedial work in the diocese. By the end of the year, Pedersen's son Lee (Charles LeRoy Jr.) was a postulant on his way to the Seminary of the Southwest in Austin, Texas. Needless to say, Pedersen was ecstatic when his son, after having proven himself in the business world by building a strong business in insurance sales in Phoenix, returned home and announced the desire to enter the priesthood. In many ways, the son was the clone of his father, and the two had a very close relationship. Pedersen was very supportive of his son, and as a result, the parish became involved in something that it had not heretofore done. Peaked by his visits to the seminary, Pedersen created a special link between the Seminary of the Southwest, sketching out a number of visionary possibilities for cooperation between the parish and the seminary. Dean MacDonald was hosted in the parish as a guest speaker for a Sunday liturgy at All Saints in 1989. His interest waned quickly after his son's graduation. Lee Pedersen Jr.'s ordination to the transitional diaconate was celebrated on December 12, 1990, at All Saints, and he was posted in the mission field at Lexington, Nebraska.

By 1988, a third young man raised at All Saints was approved for postulancy and entered seminary. Scott Barker was a native of Omaha and a Yale graduate. He enrolled in Berkeley Divinity School at Yale, the same seminary from which Pedersen and Tan Creti had graduated. Barker was ordained as a deacon on June 24, 1992, at All Saints, and twenty years later, he would be consecrated as the bishop of Nebraska, much to the pride of his family and parish.

Meanwhile, Emil Belsky, who was worshiping at All Saints with his wife, Cindy, began to explore the possibility of being received as an Episcopal priest. Belsky had been a Roman Catholic priest. He had received an exceptionally good theological education at St. Thomas's Denver and been a promising priest in the archdiocese. With a Vatican II-inspired education, he had found himself caught by the Roman Catholic reversal that stalled much of what council had begun. While he had married after he left the Roman Catholic priesthood, he claimed that it wasn't celibacy so much as the flawed authoritarian nature of parish life that drove him out. In a time when vocations had noticeably slowed, this pipeline added to Pedersen's sense that All Saints was on the cutting edge of the church.

Along with fostering the vocations of new priests for the larger church, Pedersen again became interested in the idea of adding a third priest to the staff. In March of 1989, he broached the topic with the vestry. He had been courting Rev. Thomas Miles for some time. Miles had been the rector of St. Elizabeth in Holdrege, Nebraska, and had been quite effective there. He had a great deal of talent, was outgoing and entertaining, and was passionate about evangelism. The problem was that he had done what he could at St. Elizabeth, and in a better time, when bishops looked out for the careers of their priests, he would have been helped to move on to another ministry. On his own, he had disengaged from the parish by going to work for the state educational services at Kearney, Nebraska. Pedersen was drawn by his paternalism to bring Miles back into active ministry and to do for him what, in effect, he thought that the diocese should do. He brought up Miles's name with the vestry in July of 1989, and Miles visited the parish that same month. Pedersen's pursuit of a third priest gained additional support from the fact that he had, by this time, moved out of the village house on the property, and a unit was again empty. That meant that the better part of the third priest's housing allowance could be paid for by providing the house, and at the same time, the question mark that a vacant unit placed upon the village project would be removed. It would be, to his mind, a demonstration to the parish of how it could use its existing resources for its own benefit.

Miles, whose father had been a postulant from All Saints in the fifties, fit in well, complementing Pedersen and Tan Creti. Pedersen put him to work in a number of aggressive evangelism efforts, and there was every reason to believe that he was carrying his weight. He also proved to be a good mentor for Belsky as he worked on the idea that he might seek to be received as an Episcopal priest.

Part of Pedersen's evangelism included fishing in the pond of new church starts. He became enamored with the idea of creating a parochial mission west of All Saints that would ultimately be spun off as an independent parish. At this time, there was a lot of talk in the diocese and the national church about church growth, and new mission starts. The national church proclaimed that the nineties would be the decade of evangelism. This was based in part by real growth for the Episcopal Church in the South and in part by the specter of declining membership in much of the rest of the country.

Nebraska's new bishop was anxious for church starts in the Lincoln and Omaha area, which he had made a point of declaring in his first address to the annual council. He argued that "The Episcopal Church in the Diocese of Nebraska is doing better in the western part of the state than in the East." "There we have held our own," he argued, but "that had not been so in Omaha and Lincoln . . . What makes this particularly alarming is the fact that we have suffered this decline in an area that has shown consistent population growth."[216] Shortly after annual council, the bishop brought Rev. Thomas Hansen from Broken Bow to start a new congregation in Omaha. Hanson was prepared for his task by being sent off to a wide array of national church growth conferences and seminars. He came back from the Home Reaching Conference in Minneapolis, the brainchild of George Martin, the founder of St. Martha's in Egan, Minnesota and one of All Saints own assistants, who had subsequently mastered the church growth

[216] Directory and Journal of the One Hundred Twenty-Third Annual Council, Diocese of Nebraska, p. 116.

jargon. This conference touted telemarketing and other contemporary evangelism techniques, such as advertising, door-to-door ministries, the interpretation of available demographic studies, and new patterns of the incorporation of new members into the congregation. Earlier, Hanson had participated in conferences in Florida, which espoused the use of strong lay ministry training and cell group's life.

After consultation in the deanery hosted at All Saints Retreat Center, Hansen proceeded with a foundation of a new parish in Papillion, Nebraska. Pedersen was skeptical of his expertise in church growth and cautioned that work in Omaha needed to begin by addressing the failing mission in West Omaha, Holy Family on One Hundred Twentieth Street and Shirley, and by strengthening the emerging, but by no means secure parish, Holy Spirit in Bellevue, before new work was started. New work, when it was undertaken, should be, in his opinion, in the Millard area of the city. The counsel that Hansen followed, however, was scripted by the national church's growth studies. Its demographics identified Sarpy County as the fastest-growing region in the metropolitan area and consequently the location for a new start. It argued that the new parish should downplay its Episcopal identity so that it would appeal to unchurch families seeking affiliation with an open-church community. This strategy also was meant as a comfort for existing Episcopal parishes since they had nothing to fear in terms of losing members to the new work. Highly skeptical of this model, Pedersen was prompted to think about how he would do it. A new start, sounding much like his predecessor Mackay, in his opinion, needed to lead from strength, which meant that it should begin as a parochial mission. As a result, Pedersen made several attempts to acquire land on West Maple, a part of the city that was finally beginning to develop and which would explode after 2000.

Another initiative of Bishop Krotz's was the establishment of a sabbatical leave policy for clergy. The diocese undertook the task of maintaining a fund for clergy sabbaticals. The parishes were directed to make a contribution to this fund, which would be matched by the diocese and to establish guidelines for their clergy. Again, in what appears to be a reaction, Pedersen declared that All Saints already had a sabbatical plan and would not participate in the diocesan plan. To prove the point, sabbatical leaves were about to be granted and properly funded for its clergy. Early in 1991, Pedersen approached the vestry with the plan that Tan Creti would go on a three-month sabbatical leave at the beginning of 1992. He would be gone for January, February, and March. Pedersen asked the vestry to appropriate an amount equal to Tan Creti's housing allowance, $10,000, for the purpose of enabling the sabbatical. The sabbatical was to be spent in Europe, one month of traveling in Italy and two months of residence in England. The purpose of the sabbatical was to allow Tan Creti to reequip himself with new skills and materials, which he would bring back and employ in the life of the parish.[217]

Yet in the context of these expansive efforts of the nineties came a series of hang fires, something that Pedersen had not previously experienced in his ministry at All Saints. As we have seen, his expectation that he would be the confident of the new bishop, a proverbial Dutch uncle, had not come about. Thinking that his success at All Saints qualified him as some kind of authority on church growth, he withheld full support for the missionary effort lead by Hanson in Sarpy County which, however, went ahead anyway. With the help of Dean Hokanson, a realtor and senior warden, he had identified, by October of 1991, a forty-two-acre parcel of land for sale on West Maple and proposed that the parish purchase the property. This and further efforts on his part to buy property for a parochial mission, despite the cogency of his argument, never found any support in the vestry.

Returning to his strong suit as a builder, he proposed an expansion of the narthex, which he argued was a crucial need for the parish. While the existing narthex was far grander than the narthex of the old building, its nine hundred square feet hardly allowed for an efficient emptying of the nave, particularly when the average attendance was running at three hundred individuals, let alone allow for any fellowship following the service. New standards insisted that a narthex, which was more likely called an entrance hall, should be a third of the size of the space it was serving. More important for Pedersen, he wanted to buttonhole individuals, leaving church and particularly newcomers. He saw the value of people lingering in the narthex for fellowship. He had begun to talk about this with the vestry as early as February of 1989. The response he got from the vestry in May 1988 was that "the project would be expensive and should involve professional input." The vestry's recommendation was that the "project should be postponed." He continued to work on it with Amick, the architect that had been the key to all of his former projects. Unfortunately, the other part of that team, Bob Stitt, had retired from the construction business. On May 5, 1990, he reported to the vestry that a committee had "determined that the narthex can feasibly be increased from

217 While on sabbatical, Tan Creti posted a journal which was published by the parish, and he created a lengthy poem titled "Six Modern Comedies" based on Dante's *Divine Comedy*. His Tuesday morning class had studied the *Divine Comedy* the year before. "Six Modern Comedies" was later published in his collection of poetry *To Make My Self a Word*.

940 square feet to 1,900 square feet by extending the narthex 20 feet to the south. The same study argued that it would not be feasible to include a basement under the addition. The glass would be removed (the Muller windows) and would be restored in the new addition identical to the way they currently appeared. Colorado moss stone would be used across the front of the church." Again, the response of the vestry was to wait. In February of 1991, two years after he had begun the process, he had a figure to add to the discussion. The expansion would cost $50,000. Still, the vestry was far from being convinced that it should act; and when a number of roof problems surfaced, it was clear to the vestry that they had to be dealt with before any further consideration of an addition should be entertained.

His other building agenda, the completion of the village, which anticipated another twenty units, was stymied as well. Pedersen had to struggle to keep the village that existed full. He had solved the problem by talking his wife, Frances, into moving into one of the units. It was an adventure that lasted only a couple of years. He had encouraged people to drop in and found that it was only too easy for them to do so. The worst part for him was that the unit was finished! He had no outlet for his favorite pastime, fixing things. The stay in the village had, however, served a purpose in that he and Frances had the opportunity to disengage from the house on Fifty-Third and Blondo and make a transition to a house that would serve as their retirement home. This had always been thought of as a house on the lake in Fremont, but instead they found a home on Candlewood Lake, which fulfilled all of their wishes, including the possibility of a number of remodeling projects! When they moved out of the village, however, there was again an empty unit, and the prospect of building more units was totally out of the question.

Other projects that presented themselves were more annoying than satisfying. There was unavoidable roof repair that had to be undertaken. This undercut more interesting initiatives. Similarly, the problem with the pipe organ had become so noticeable that it could not be deferred. The problem, in part, was that there was a substantial leakage of air pressure, which put a portion of the organ out of use and caused other portions to be unreliable and generally muted. The primary cause was that several of the wind chests were cracked. The cracks were in the chests on the northwest corner of the organ cavity, which had been most severely impacted by radical temperature changes. The cause of the temperature fluctuations was never clearly stated, but the evidence was that they were the result of Pedersen's draconian attempts to save on the cost of utilities during the energy crisis in the late seventies. He had ordered that, when the building was not in use during the winter, the temperature was set back to fifty degrees and rapidly reheated for Sunday, a struggle that usually started late on Saturday and was often insufficient. This actual damage was joined in the minds of those interested in the parish's music program with the opinion that the Reuter Organ was a lumbering dinosaur even on a good day. This opinion was strongly supported by the music director, Robert Scheiblhofer, whose training had convinced him of the superiority of tracker action. The study that he did for the parish with the consultation of the Canadian organ builder, Rosalis, put the cost of repair in the range of $200,000–$300,000. A totally new organ, a Casavant tracker, would, the report said, cost $900,000. On the other hand, a new organ that used 90 percent of the existing pipe work would be a bargain at $600,000. Organ building did not appeal to Pedersen, and he had already been through that with the antiphonal organ, which had not turned out very successful. Moreover, the kind of money that was being talked about would have seriously impacted the favorable financial situation, which Pedersen had managed to establish for the parish.

To the discontent aroused by the local issues in the parish was added the return of a growing dissonance on the national level of the Episcopal Church. The general convention in Phoenix, during the summer of 1991, featured a pitched battle between the conservatives led by Bishop Frey and the liberals led by Bishop Sponge. The liberal agenda had, if less vocal, the support of Browning, the presiding bishop. While there was a cluster of issues facing the convention, the main focus was on sexual issues, including the nature of marriage and the morality of homosexuality. What became clear at Phoenix was that these issues were not going to be solved by means of some kind of enlightened study on the nature of human sexuality but on the basis of political will. For Tan Creti, who attended the general convention in Phoenix, this was particularly disheartening. For Pedersen, dealing with a vestry, this was trouble that he did not need. Michael Yanney, new to the vestry, raised the issue at the September vestry meeting and offered a motion that was duly passed. The motion requested that the bishop be invited to the vestry in an informal setting whereby the vestry could voice its concerns about the national church. In the clear skies with which the eighties had begun, clouds were beginning to appear, and the fair winds began to grow turbulent.

It is difficult in this setting, marked as it was by both aggressive new initiatives and annoying hang fires, to assess Pedersen's state of mind. With the arrival of 1991, he marked his twentieth year as All Saints rector. Unlike his tenth, he made no extended comment about its passing. When May came, Pedersen turned fifty-nine. The clearest sign that he was getting ready for something was the shape of his vestry. Both wardens were personal friends. The junior warden had been an acolyte for him when he had started out in Fairbury. Michael Yanney, who had been a fraternity brother of Pedersen at the University of Lincoln, was new to the vestry. Yanney's remarkable success in business had moved him to the upper levels of leadership in the Omaha community, and he had begun to establish himself in the circles of the city's philanthropy. While Yanney was a devout participant at All Saints, seldom ever missing a Sunday, he had not, to that time, participated to any degree in other parish activities. His election to the vestry was, therefore, a surprise to many. It was perhaps somewhat of a surprise to Yanney, for whom the plodding rather low-level enterprise of a parish vestry must have been a stark contrast to the fast pace of decision making in his business world. He was there, no doubt, because Pedersen had asked him to be there. Clearly, Pedersen wanted Yanney on the vestry as a means of insuring his legacy, which would include his last hurrah as well as his eventual retirement. Since it was customary for a vestry person to serve two three-year terms, this observation does little more than suggest that Pedersen was already giving some thought to retiring.

An Unanticipated Resignation

When Tan Creti returned from sabbatical at the beginning of April, the first thing Pedersen did was to take him aside and indicate to him that he intended to retire, something he had not previously so much as hinted at. His words were: "You just wait and see. I'm going to hang it up." It was said with a hint of anger as if it had been prompted by a recent exchange, and it sounded more like a threat than a resolve. Nevertheless, Tan Creti did not dismiss this and began his own preparation for the consequences of such a retirement. According to the canons of the Episcopal Church, he would be required to tender his resignation, and a new rector would have been hard pressed to continue the services of an assistant who had been in place for sixteen years. He therefore set out immediately to update his deployment profile and put his name into the national search process. In the process of updating his profile, he required the help of Bishop Krotz and his newly appointed canon to the ordinary, Rev. Tim Vann. In a joint meeting, they encouraged him to proceed with the search, counseling him that parishes never made assistants their rector. Tan Creti did not count on the parish doing so, and yet he did not dismiss it as impossible.

As the Easter season concluded, only a very small circle of people had any inkling that Pedersen would resign. At annual council of 1992 held at the beginning of May, one of the deputies from All Saints recalls that he had his first indication that Pedersen intended to retire. It had come up in one of the late night "strategy sessions" that Pedersen habitually held at annual council in one of the rooms with a well-stocked bar. When other parish leaders became aware of his intention to retire is unclear. For everyone else in the parish, including the wardens, it was not until a month later on June 9. Faced with a very busy agenda, Pedersen suspended the agenda and asked the vestry to accept his resignation effective February 1, 1993. Following the motion to accept Pedersen's resignation, Yanney made a motion "to look into Father Pedersen's retirement," and he offered to serve on that committee and/or the search committee. It is likely that Yanney knew before the meeting. There was, however, nothing prepared, such as a motion or nominations for a search committee or any of the other thing that would need to be done by the parish in the ensuing months. Pedersen did say that Bob Spire, who had been chairman of the last call committee, was willing to serve as consultant. This would indicate that Pedersen, who had always kept a close relationship with his original call committee, had informed Spire prior to the June 9 meeting. There is little indication, however, of anyone else who knew ahead of time.

Little time was spent on the matter, and the vestry moved on to a very busy agenda, which included a report on the organ problem; a revised form of the Pastoral Care Position Paper, largely the work of Father Tan Creti; plans for the ordination of Scott Barker on June 24 at All Saints; and a report on an ambitious marketing plan, which was being designed for the parish by Bob Culver. Culver was a member of the parish and head of a very creative ad agency in the city, which was donating considerable expertise and printing for the project. It envisioned an extensive mailing to All Saints "market area."

Subsequently, a special meeting of the vestry was called for June 23 to appoint the members of the search committee. The members of the committee were Dean Hokanson, Doug Hokenstad, Jeff Pirruccello, Michael Yanney, Dana Bradford III, Carroll Fredrickson, Dan Gardner, Barbara Lacey, and Pat Perry. The search committee began meeting, and by August 11, it had produced a mission statement, which the vestry adopted at its August meeting. At that meeting, plans were made for a letter to the parish, which would contain a questionnaire that was to be returned with feedback. On the following Monday, August 17, the call committee met with Tim Vann, the canon to the ordinary, for the purpose of defining the parish profile, which would initiate a nationwide search. Vann told the vestry that the national church office would provide them with a list of names of interested and qualified candidates from the national church database. To that list, Bishop Krotz would add any names he thought appropriate; and of course, they should expect names would also come from parishioners as well as they returned their questionnaires.

The letter and questionnaire received by the parish in mid-July produced a wave of anxiety. One, of course, expects a parish to go through an anxious time when it faces the process of searching for a new rector. The level of anxiety, however, was much greater than anyone expected. Perhaps that was a result of the sudden unanticipated announcement of Pedersen's resignation. Pedersen had frequently spoken of working until he was sixty-five and was taken at his word. With the issue of having been caught unaware was the implication that in less than six months the decision would be made. For some time, vestry decisions had been rather opaque and tolerated because the results were positive, or at least they did not ask anything of the parish by way of special funding. The result of a call process, however, was more than most of the parish wanted to risk to such dispatch or opaqueness.

Adding to these issues was a rumor that Pedersen was bent on having his son, Lee, succeed him. Lee had been ordained a year and half before and was the curate at Lexington and Cozad, where he was doing an exceptionally good job by all appearances. The rumor appeared to be rather far-fetched. There is no doubt that Pedersen might have nursed the idea for some time. He had gone so far in April as asking one of the members of the parish's leadership if he would chair the search committee and, if he did, would he support his son as the next rector of All Saints. That person had turned him down. While there is no other evidence of any overt effort in Lee Pedersen Jr.'s behalf, it nevertheless added to a growing level of anger in the parish, which in turn fed Pedersen's own anxiety.

One reaction in the parish was to circulate a petition, which said, "We the undersigned members of All Saints Episcopal Church request that the search committee recommend to the vestry the appointment of Fr. Michael J. Tan Creti as the next rector of our parish." Attempts were made to stop the petition drive. Pedersen told a number of individuals that they could not sign it because of their position in the parish and a number of others that it was inappropriate for them to sign it. The senior warden, Dean Hokanson, sent a letter to the parish on September 1, asking for the parish to trust the process. He indicated that as of that time one name had been received, Tan Creti, and that it had been accepted as a nomination. Hokanson's letter was accompanied by a letter from Tan Creti supporting Hokanson's request. In that letter, Tan Creti stated his desire to be considered but went on to say,

> I think that it will assist the search process if my position is as clear and as open as it can be. I don't believe that the parish has any moral obligation to make me its next rector. I did not come to All Saints on that basis nor have I stayed here on that basis. I simply trust that the merits of my application will be considered openly and fairly along with others. It is important, from my point of view, that the search process be allowed to be carried out to its end, and I in no way mind being one among many candidates under consideration.

Hokanson's letter explained that it was the plan to continue to receive names and, in November, to reduce the names to five candidates at that time. The five candidates were then to be invited to All Saints for a personal interview with the committee after which one recommendation would be made to the vestry to approve or disapprove.

In spite of the request, the petition asking that Tan Creti be called as rector continued to circulate in the parish. It was presented to the search committee in early September signed by 288 parishioners asking that Tan Creti be called as rector. Copies were sent to the vestry, the search committee, Bishop Krotz, and Charles Pedersen.

When the vestry met on September 14, as vestries tend to do in September, it had a plethora of items on its agenda. The upcoming canvass was discussed, and Pedersen reported that Don Erikson had agreed to chair it, a report from the new scholarship committee was made, the new pension plan for lay employees was discussed, a letter from Tan Creti in regard to planting trees on the grounds as memorials to Grace Gould and Bart Brown, a young man, a new father who had recently died of cancer. Pedersen presented the request to make Lynn Bacon a postulant for the life project diaconate, which would bring All Saints deacons to five and concluded by reading a request from the diocese for –$2 per household assessment to allow it to continue publishing the *Nebraska Episcopalian*. Like the matters that preceded these requests, it was approved. Pedersen excused himself so that he could take the regularly scheduled Monday evening healing service.

The vestry then turned to its final item of business, a report from the search committee. Speaking for the committee, Hokanson, its chair, concluded his report with the summary that he handed out.

> Recent events within the congregation have created an emotional atmosphere of misunderstanding and mistrust. The committee feels that to continue the search process at this time

would not be in the best interest of the parish. Therefore, the committee offers the following options to the vestry:

1. Suspend the Search Committee. Consider the candidacy of Michael J. Tan Creti, schedule an interview with him this month and vote on his candidacy.
2. Suspend the Search Committee. Ask the bishop to appoint an interim rector and reconvene the committee at a later time.

In presenting the options, Hokanson "encouraged the vestry to adopt the first option." The motion to suspend the search committee and consider the candidacy of Tan Creti was made by Bob Knudsen and seconded by Michael Yanney. Pedersen's vestry meetings were always choreographed ahead of time. Phone calls ahead of time polled the strength of a proposition, the results of which determined if and how something was presented. Who would make a motion was not left to chance. If anyone on the vestry had reservations about Tan Creti as rector, it was Knudsen and Yanney, both of whom had close relationships with Pedersen. That they made the motion was a clear signal of Pedersen's position on the matter.

The vestry met on September 22 and prepared a set of questions appropriate for the interview. On September 27, the vestry met in the retreat center and conducted the interview with Tan Creti. At the conclusion, the vestry paused for discussion and proceeded to vote in favor of calling Tan Creti as the eighth rector of All Saints. The wardens stopped in Tan Creti's house after the meeting and presented him with the vestry's call and their terms of employment. The consent of Bishop Krotz to the call was received by the vestry at its meeting on October 13. At that meeting, Hokanson distributed a copy of a report made by Tan Creti outlining a job description for a new assistant priest. The efforts to secure an assistant was in fact already under way. That Tan Creti was already at work was a further indication of Pedersen's acceptance of him as the next rector. Pedersen put him in charge of drafting the budget for the coming year and for preparing for the annual meeting to be held in January while Pedersen intended to be on vacation.

If Tan Creti was preoccupied with the need for an assistant and for a workable budget for 1993, Pedersen was progressively more preoccupied with the nature of the retirement income that would be offered to him by the parish. The proposal emerged in the form of a motion by Yanney and Knudsen made at the October meeting. It called for the parish to lend $250,000 to an irrevocable trust set up as the Charles Pedersen Retirement Fund, the income of which was to be paid to Charles and Francis for their lifetime, after which the corpus would be paid back to the parish. This, in effect, would have entailed the income of a third of the existing endowment for a period, which would have likely stretched on for more than twenty years.

The surprise in June that Pedersen would retire at the end of the year was widespread but not shocking. On the other hand, it was both a surprise that parish was planning to provide him with a special retirement package beyond that of the church pension fund and a shock for many. Letters objecting to the proposal came from significant members of the parish, such as Don and Helen Amsden and Don Erikson. Bishop Krotz weighed in with a letter that stopped short of opposing the idea but indicated that, after research, he could say that such a benefit had no precedent and that the parish would be advised to ask the chancellor of the diocese if it was a legal possibility.

The preoccupation with his finances after his retirement was in part driven by the fact that early retirement did provide some special financial issues. The new rules of the church pension meant that there would be only a minor consequence for the generous lifelong defined benefit. It would be substantially equal to the income he was earning when combined with social security. Social security was, of course, three years off. More important was the expense of health insurance whose growing cost was already becoming punitive and enough to give anyone second thoughts about retiring prior to qualifying for Medicare. Perhaps more than the question of money, for Pedersen, it was a matter of recognition that he had done an exceptional job for the parish. This was all the more urgent because he had, in a way, sprung his retirement on himself as much as on the parish.

This added a new level to the "emotional atmosphere of misunderstanding and mistrust." The Every Member Canvass chair, Don Erikson, resigned, and a delegation of laity came to the vestry meeting in November, an unprecedented occurrence at All Saints, to express their dismay about the proposed retirement package. In the course of November, a special committee appointed by the vestry consisting of Dean Hokanson, Doug Hokenstad, Carroll Fredrickson, John Hancock, and Dan Gardner went to work on the problem. It was the wisdom of Carroll Fredrickson which created the solution for the committee. Specifically, a benefit would be paid to Pedersen during the period prior to his turning sixty-five, and his health care insurance would be maintained for him and his wife. In its report to the vestry, the committee stated that "in recent days we have received correspondence and heard comments from parishioners expressing their feeling on a retirement package for Father Pedersen. Since, until today, the committee's report hasn't even been presented to the vestry for consideration, these people's comments are based on pure speculation. Some in the church might say this package is too generous, and others will say it is too lean." When the proposal was presented to the vestry, Tan Creti, who had sat in on the committee's meeting, was asked to attend the vestry meeting as well and comment on the proposal. He said at that time: "While he felt it was not his place to comment on the merits of the proposal, he said it would not jeopardize next year's budget" and that his concern was "that the process of approving the proposal be open and maintain the unity of the parish." Yanney moved that the proposal be accepted. Knudsen, who with Yanney had been most open and assertive about a retirement income, seconded the motion. It carried with two dissents recorded, somewhat unusual for a body that generally acted unanimously.

The package that they approved was that, upon his retirement, Pedersen would receive the following:

1. A cash payment of $10,000, this is compensation to you for the sabbatical which you never were able to take.
2. All Saints is gifting to you the title of the 1991 Buick Electra which you are now driving.
3. All Saints Church will continue to pay for your group medical insurance under the church's group insurance program.
4. Commencing March 1, 1993, All Saints will pay you and Frances $1,500 a month retirement supplement. These payments will continue monthly until you reach age 65.

The Legacy

In the letter of the Retirement Compensation Committee, dated December 8, 1992, the committee offered a summation of what had been accomplished during the Pedersen years as a justification for its unprecedented recommendation. They asked the vestry to look back over the past twenty-two years.

> The total operational budget in 1970 was $80,600, compared to our 1992 budget of $373,000. In 1970 the church had a mortgage on the property. Today the assets of All Saints are mortgage free. In 1970 there were no endowments or special funds established. Today All Saints has a general endowment fund of approximately $500,000, a memorial fund of $64,000,

> an elderly ministry fund of $290,000, a columbarium fund, a scholarship fund of $105,000, an All Saints Village fund, and a capital improvement fund supporting the maintenance and upkeep of our $5.5 million facilities.
>
> Since 1970 All Saints has built and paid for the retreat center, the east wing addition of the church (housing the church offices and chapel), the lower west side addition and the All Saints Village.
>
> Today All Saints is the flagship parish of the Nebraska diocese. Among our lay membership is the chairman of the Finance Committee of the diocese, the chancellor of the diocese, two members of the bishops and trustees, and a member on the standing committee. Never before has All Saints had this level of influence in diocesan affairs.
>
> Since 1970, All Saints has expanded its programs, its teaching, and its staff. It has been innovative in its new programs and service. It has made a commitment to its elderly through the elderly ministry program and to its youth through the scholarship fund, a full-time Christian education director and facilities, such as the retreat center. It has expanded its outreach programs and increased its lay person involvement manyfold. Under Charles Pedersen's direction, this church has enjoyed twenty-two years of growth, accomplishment, service, and witness.

This attempt at stating Pedersen's legacy by the committee was in no sense an exaggeration. Yet it was Pedersen's own version of his legacy, which he had created for the purpose of making his case for the exceptional retirement benefit that he had requested, and things are never quite as simple as they appear. Legacies in the end are quicksilver, and one should be cautious about making over much of them. Above all, there is always the shadow side, which will sooner or later come to light.

Ending in Ambiguity

In fact, as 1992 came to an end, ambiguity abounded. The invincible U.S. economy was sliding into recession, but the country had just elected

Bill Clinton president, presumably because he got it and the old one didn't. Johnny Carson, Nebraska's favorite son, though he was in fact born in Corning, Iowa, had at last retired from *The Tonight Show*; but then there was this new guy, Jay Leno. The city was down from the loss of Enron but valiantly seeking to find new ventures to fuel a belief in its future.

Retirement was staring Pedersen in the face with all its usual ambiguity: loss of status vis-a-vis the gain in freedom, the necessity to get it done vis-a-vis not having to finish anything, the thrill of making it happen vis-a-vis the mystery of watching it happen, to mention a few. The ride was coming to its end, and it was doubly ambiguous because it was coming because of his own decision, which he had made quite abruptly, little more than six months ago, surprising himself perhaps as much as the parish. He found himself with his successor already in place, which deprived him of that period when one coasts out and everyone is saying to you, "We don't know what we will do without you." He worked hard at stepping back to give Tan Creti a head start, handing over the canvass, budgeting, and the annual meeting, which was a relief on the one hand, this being a good start at a list of the things that rectors find least fun; but it was, on the other hand, causing him to experience of loss even before he had actually retired. The original proposal for a life annuity had been shot down. In all likelihood, the prospect of the proposal had as much or more to do with a recognition of his unprecedented accomplishments as it did with his personal financial needs. His retirement annuity for life from the church pension fund would ensure, with built-in cost of living raises, an income that was equal to 80 percent of his salary. When social security kicked in, it would be closer to 95 percent. In addition, the parish had approved a generous package that more than made up for any financial need, but then it fell short of the certification that all retirees look for but seldom find.

Tan Creti had been relieved of a perilous job search. Clergy job search in the Episcopal Church had become particularly problematic in the eighties and nineties as mobility had shut down and the old pipelines maintained by the bishops had shut off. Since April, his career path had been in question, something that put his family's well-being at risk. He now had a job that could be a fitting end to his career, but not without an ambiguity of its own. If Pedersen's coast out was cramped by his presence in the parish, Tan Creti's overly abrupt start was cramped in a different way by the incumbent's presence. He was being asked to be part of validating the retirement proposal, which was not, or should not, have been his business. To this there was the unfinished business of the suspended call process and an incomplete Every Member Canvass bereft of a chairman. Finally, there was the question of the unity of the parish. All Saints had seldom experienced an open division in its ranks and certainly not anything like this since and apart from the issue of Galaty's situation when he was called to active duty in the Korean conflict.

The parish itself was caught in its own ambiguity. On the one hand, it had foreshorten the process of calling a new rector, which is always one of the most stressful things a parish must pass through. In the end, they had called someone who they knew very well, having lived with him for the past sixteen years. They were well acquainted with him as a teacher, a pastoral visitor, and a cook. What they did not know was whether he could administer such a large and complicated operation as All Saints had become. They feared a future by an administrator less effective than Pedersen, but they did not want the conflict and secrecy, which had been used to get things done. In other words, they wanted change, but they also wanted it to be the same.

Still, life is seldom without its ambiguities, and the question is not so much how they are avoided as how individuals go on and deal with them.

Chapter 10

More of the Same but Different: 1993–1994

Out of the Closet

We have reached that point in our story, 107 years after it began, where a number of issues begin to arise. The story, after my arrival in 1977, has begun to present me with so many names and events that have to be passed over in order to advance the story. It is clear to me that without them, the story would have been very different. In retrospect, that has always been true for this narrative, but someone else or time itself had decided to drop some from the narrative. Now with growing difficulty, it will be me who must do so. I have to trust that my reader understands that reality is like a deep flowing river whose surface appears to be what is happening when in fact the greater part of what is happening lies below that surface.

Another issue is the conceit of narrating the story in the third person. It has not been without its difficulties, even in material before 1977, but now it seems to me that I must step out from behind the third person and write in the first person. The narrative has never been without my personal judgments, and I trust that those occasions have been clear. Now it is difficult to make it clear even to myself, so I must forego the language, which seems to make a distinction between fact and personal judgment. This lapse can only be reversed when someday someone else will rewrite an account of this period in the third person.

I have, of course, for some time, been covering my participation in the life of All Saints in the third person. I have justified this in my own mind as a means of minimizing the intrusion of my feelings and opinions in the narration of the Pedersen years in order not to cloud Pedersen's legacy. I am, of course, aware that I have not been entirely free from doing so. Now that we have reached that point in the story where I began serving as the rector of All Saints, it will be considerably more difficult. Perhaps it would have been wise to have simply ended the story in 1992. Certainly it would have been easier. To do so, however, would leave many things that affect the current life of the parish unexplained. So I will, as your author, come out of the closet and shift to the first person. This should make things more straightforward.

In looking for a place to make an end, I have chosen 2001, which is four years short of my actual retirement. Among other things, this choice allows me to avoid the need to talk about the legacy left by these years, the very thing that I am least equipped to do. On the other hand, extending the narrative beyond 1993 will allow a better presentation of Pedersen's legacy, which was, in part, very much involved with the way things turned out in the last decade of the millennium. In reality, Pedersen's and my own legacies are so intertwined that it is doubtful that anyone can or perhaps should try to separate them. That is and was uncomfortable in many different ways. It was, in some degree, a reason why Pedersen was never entirely comfortable with me as his successor.

As he had visited his predecessor, Mark McCallum, I regularly paid visits to him in his new home in the Candlewood Lake Estates. Inevitable it involved a drink. There was always talk of his latest remodeling project on his house. Inevitably, they were always incredible bargains and usually involved his own handiwork. He had, for example, installed a parquet floor in the basement himself. Unfortunately, he had fit the tiles so snug with the wall that the first bit of moisture caused them to pop up! It was one more story to add the list of the fateful Pedersen projects, which his mentors, Father Muller, the Perry's, and Bishop Rauscher loved to tell about him, and if the truth be told, he loved to have stories told on him. Frances inevitable retreated to her part of the house because that what wives did when men settled in for a talk. With these visits, I kept him informed about what was happening in the parish, and he often shared with me information and insights that were helpful to me. We did enjoy each other's company as we had for the past sixteen years.

Pedersen, on the other hand, found it difficult to attend services at All Saints after he retired. He had developed, over the years, a close relationship with St. James, Fremont. Father Muller, who he had counted as mentor since his college days, had been St. James's great long-term rector. During the late seventies and most of the eighties, Pedersen had owned a cabin on one of Fremont's lakes; and whenever he vacationed there, he would worship at St. James. During that time, he had come to know a significant portion of its laity. Before the "Candlewood interlude," his intention was to retire to a home on one of the Fremont Lakes. In fact, when the projects disappeared at Candlewood, he did build his dream home on one of the lakes. Over the next thirteen years of his life, he played a role at St. James, suppling when needed and even working as one of its interims. St. James was like the church in which he had been raised, St. Mary's in Blair. By the nineties, both parishes were struggling because of a number of cultural and economic problems impacting small parishes in the smaller cities across the Midwest. It served, I think, as a kind of surrogate for St. Mary's, and he felt he needed to do something to reverse the outcome.

Periodically, however, he would show up at All Saints for worship. There was never any indication ahead of time when this might happen. He and Frances would come late and leave early. I made frequent attempts to make him feel more at home and invited him to linger for coffee, but I never succeeded. For some reason that I could never understand, it was precisely this idea of lingering that was the most difficult for him to entertain.

For myself, I came, in some degree, to terms with the discomfort of our mingled legacies by recognizing just how strange this thing is that we call legacy. The title I have given to this next section is "More of the Same but Different." Much of what happened in the rest of the nineties had its origin in the eighties. Building projects, such as moving the nursery upstairs, expanding the narthex, remodeling the chapel or the main worship space, had been tossed about and, to various degrees, planned in the eighties. When they were actually done in the nineties, however, it was in a different way with a different result, and in not a few cases, it involved redoing or undoing what had been done in the eighties. The endowment, which expanded so dramatically in the nineties and became a constructive part of the parish's identity, had its origin with the foundation Pedersen established in the eighties, without which growth in the nineties is unlikely to have happened. The same can be said of the building projects of the nineties. They were a continuation of what Pedersen was trying to do, but they too would be different than what was expected and in how they worked.

The programs and the ministries of the nineties were clearly a continuation of those of the eighties: E. F. M., the diaconate, Tuesday Group, the rich array of opportunities for adult education and formation, youth work, youth retreats, and a high-performing church school program. But these also evolved. For example, E. F. M., which I had mentored from its beginning in the eighties, continued forward but under the mentoring of a new group of parish leaders: Judi Yeates, Jean Lewandowski, Judy Gray, and Woody Bradford. Deacons continued their liturgical presence and participation in parish visitations but took on new roles outside of the parish. Mary Sue Sturgeon became progressively more involved in a formal way in the chaplaincy program at Bergan Mercy Hospital. Ernie Bowerman became a leader in the Omaha Police Department's chaplaincy program. Frank and Oral Murphy deepened their involvement with the food bank and homeless shelter and took the parish along with them to an ever greater degree of participation.

Yet if much of what happened in the nineties was fed from the streams that flowed out of the eighties, it was not simply a Pedersen legacy, for I had been a participant in shaping much of what had happened in the eighties as well. As I laid out a mental map for what would happen in the next thirteen years, the time I presumed that I would be rector of All Saints, there was little sense in my mind of what belonged to whom. In fact, it was more than just Pedersen's legacy that was in question, but the legacies of my seven predecessors from Zahner on. Pedersen, who loved to tell stories, had, over the past sixteen years, passed on to me numerous stories about this group of men. He was particularly fond of Mackay stories, which often ended with the observation "the old man had a nose for money." Equally, he loved the Clayton stories, which would inevitably conclude with the observation "Of course, he was a wine bibber and a womanizer." And I would add, "And you, Charles, have managed to own the best of both of these men!" It was not, therefore, lost on me that I was the eighth rector, charting the parish's course out of the twentieth century, and that it had fallen to me to in some ways be a representation of all seven of my predecessors.

The Eighth Rector Goes to Work

That first year began with two back-to-back celebrations. The first celebration was to see that Pedersen was properly honored by an appropriately gracious send-off. It was a little dicey because Pedersen was insisting that he didn't want anything, and at the same time, he was nursing hurt feelings. The celebration to honor him was finally set for Saturday, January 23, 1993, at 6:00 p.m. Ann McConney, who had been a parishioner at All Saints before seeking ordination to the priesthood, covered the story for the *Nebraska Episcopalian*.[218] She wrote:

[218] Curiously, when McConney sought to be a priest in the seventies, Pedersen would not endorse her, a position that was partially obscured by the fact that Bishop Warner would not accept a woman postulant. She had returned to the diocese, and Bishop Krotz had hired her to produce the diocesan newspaper. Her writing and publishing talent was quite remarkable and quite unappreciated in the diocese.

> On February 1, 1971, All Saints Church, Omaha, welcomed Rev. Charles L. R. Pedersen as its rector. On January 23, 1992, it feted him on his retirement with an evening Eucharist shot through with light, woven with music and graced with memories.
>
> During his twenty-two-year tenure, Charles Pedersen—"Father Pete" to more than a generation of church members—introduced the new *Book of Common Prayer*, a new hymnal, pioneered new forms of music, liturgy and Christian service, and was instrumental in bringing an active diaconal order into the diocese.
>
> He saw All Saints grow from a moderately sized urban church into the largest parish in Nebraska . . . and a hotbed of activity, community and spiritual growth that has sent three persons into the priesthood–including his own son–and almost a dozen into the diaconate.
>
> On January 23, the memories were thick, as parishioners and scattered friends returned to pay tribute at a festive Eucharist celebrated by the Rt. Rev. James E. Krotz. In his sermon Krotz refused to enumerate Father Pedersen's accomplishments. ("To do that would only embarrass him"). Instead he called on those present to reflect on both "the unimaginable burden carried by a priest" and on the many times and many ways that Charles Pedersen had affected each individual's life. (This writer could think of any number of times when Father Pete's downright and sometimes blunt wisdom, his sure instinct for the right and healing words, had smoothed the way.) Afterward, the well-wishers gathered for a reception in the All Saints undercroft. The rector elect, Rev. Michael Tan Creti, unveiled an original drawing of Father Pedersen. The drawing was the gift of Bob, Jacqueline and Kristofer Ericson and will be displayed at the church.

The drawing that is mentioned in the article was made by Bob Ericson, who had designed the Centennial Medal and had made numerous others gifts of his artistic talent to the parish.

After the farewell came the question concerning my installation as rector. Pedersen had often boasted that he had not been "installed" as rector at All Saints. When he had arrived, the real work was too pressing, and besides, in his mind, the covenant that constituted his rectorship was between himself and the people of All Saints. It was tempting for me to do as Pedersen had done, for I sympathized with his point of view, and things were very busy. Yet I had a clear sense that I wanted things to be different, so I braced for another visit from the bishop. I scheduled the installation for February 9, a rather low-key Tuesday evening, in order to get the deed done as expediently as possible. More than 310 persons showed up to be part of the new path that All Saints was about to take. The turnout was humbling, and it was a clear indication of the weight of expectation that I had shouldered.

I made a point that evening of adopting a motto as a means of conveying to those gathered and to myself how I regarded these high expectations that we shared. The bulletin cover read "Zeal for your house had consumed me." This is a verse of Psalm 69, which was used by the author of the Gospel of John to explain Jesus's motivation for the cleansing of the temple. It had been a mantra of mine for some time, and now I intended it to be at the center of my life as I took up the work of the rector of All Saints.

A New Assistant

In fact, I had been at work as rector since the past October. The parish had come to the point in its history where it considered a second priest was not merely a good thing but a simple necessity. All Saints had become too large, and its expectations had become too elevated by the past sixteen years for a rector to be able to manage the parish by himself. For that reason, the vestry had empowered me in October, well before I was to assume the office of rector, to begin a search for an assistant.

The national deployment office promptly provided the parish with forty-two names, the gist of which was that all but a handful were marginally viable. Two out that group were invited to come to All Saints. In both cases, the idea that they might be asked to live in the staff house in the parish village was a nonstarter, even though it would have allowed the parish to make them a more generous offer and for their start in the parish less delayed. One of the candidates, who had some attractive skills, confided that his college debt amounted to more than $50,000, which meant that he would struggle with debt his entire ministry! The other candidate was married and was accompanied by his wife. I was advised by the lay committee appointed to help me that his wife had spent a great deal of time answering for her husband and that she had offered her opinion that we were doing a significant number of things wrong with the liturgy. The spokesperson for the committee continued, "Please don't." My conclusion at this point was that the formation being provided by our seminaries had made the idea of living on campus impossible for a candidate to imagine and that it had done little to prepare them to work as an assistant priest. Over the course of time, there has been little to cause me to revise this opinion.

Fortunately, a possibility lay at hand within the parish's own efforts to develop ministry. As the reader may recall, two men within the parish were in the pipeline for the priesthood, and one was an experienced pastor. Emil Belsky was forty-four years old, a graduate of South High. He had received his BA from the College of St. Thomas, St. Paul, Minnesota, and his theological degree from St. Thomas Seminary, Denver, Colorado. He was ordained in the Roman Catholic Church in 1974 and had spent eleven years serving parishes in Omaha. A good deal of his time during this period of ministry was devoted to spiritual direction and counseling. He had served as chaplain to the hospice unit at Montclair Nursing Center from 1981 to 1985, which fit nicely with the interests of the parish.

In 1985, Belsky took a leave of absence from the Roman Catholic Archdiocese because of his discontent with the authoritarian structure under which he worked and with the lack of community in the rectories in which he had lived. He had entered into secular work, and in 1990, he married Cindy Vlcek. Cindy worked as a registered nurse working at the University of Nebraska Medical Center. After attending All Saints for a couple of years, Belsky began the process to be received as a priest of the Episcopal Church. The process was still under way in 1993, so he began his work for All Saints as a "lay assistant" doing everything except presiding at the Eucharist. The diocese required him, as it did Scheiblhofer, to take the national canonical examinations, a rather arduous task, even for the diocese's candidates who had freshly graduated from one of the seminaries of the Episcopal Church. All Saints had, however, an ace in the hole. I had, for several years, been a reader for the National Canonical Examiners, and I knew what was on the exams and knew what the graders were looking for. Since 1992, I had been preparing Belsky and Scheiblhofer for the examination. They both passed the examination comfortably. Belsky's reception to the priesthood was set by Bishop Krotz for the beginning of April.

Emil Belsky's appointment had been announced to the parish at the annual meeting held on January 18, a couple of weeks before I assumed the role of rector, and he went to work the following week. Belsky was clearly a practical answer. It indeed helped the budget since we did not have to deal with moving expenses, and all those added little expenditures of money and times that someone else coming in from outside would have caused. Moreover, he was accustomed to the way things were being done at All Saints and could start making his contribution immediately. This was important because the parish was in a fast-start mode as if it intended to deal with all the issues Pedersen had been carefully sidestepping the past few years, in short order.

Belsky brought into the mix a special ability to work with publications, which made possible a dramatic expansion of the *Witness*, the parish's chief publication. This was a key to making a substantial improvement in parish communications. He had a superior theological education, beyond that of an average diocesan priest, and was an avid buyer of books and a tireless reader. He was particularly good with small groups, in book discussions and in coaching spirituality. These were complements to my own strengths, which ensured that we could broaden the ministry of the parish. He also was an effective and warm pastoral visitor and a definite asset to one of the primary efforts to which the parish was committed. He was thrilled to be back in the ministry, and he was here for the long haul.[219]

Communication

With the practical matter of an assistant out of the way, I could turn to the question of how to deal with the matter of the parish's unity. It is not, of course, uncommon for a search process to open questions about a parish's unity. But on top of the expected anxiety, the debate about a special retirement benefit had brought the issue of the parish's unity to the point of crisis. At the annual meeting on January 18, which I chaired, even though I was not yet the rector, I tried to address the issue of the parish's unity, and I stated that the theme for the coming years was "Communication Communications, Communications." It was clear to me that a good deal of the difficulty with the call process and the retirement benefit discussion had been caused by the lack of communications. This had led first to a reaction of surprise, which then became the suspicion that there could be a lot of other things that might have been hidden from the parish over the course of the past several years.

I had always attempted to be open to anyone's questions, and I was recognized for being candid to a fault. I also made an attempt to go directly

[219] Belsky stayed as assistant past my retirement in January of 2006 and was called as rector of St. Paul's Salt Lake, Utah, where he continued to his retirement in 2013.

to those who had been the center of the opposition, hat in hand, as it was, and make the case for the unity of the parish. Particularly, I went to the main leaders, who had pushed the expansive retirement benefit and lost, and those who had objected most vehemently to a retirement benefit and had also lost. This was, however, more of a short-term attempt at defusing the extremes and would not deal with the larger issue of the quiet centers of opposition, which, in fact, constituted the rest of the iceberg.

I identified the parish publication, the *Witness*, as the most effective tool at my disposal. When I was a young priest in Iowa, it was common for us "young Turks" to make fun of the cardinal rectors, particularly Bill Jacobs, the rector of St. Paul's Des Moines. Jacobs had gone so far as purchasing an offset printing press for his parish office. He was ready to demonstrate it to any young priest that would give him the time of day, and few of us had escaped. It was commonly said among us that he took more pains printing his weekly newsletter than he did visiting his parishioners and, most certainly, more than he did visiting the poor. While I was not exempt for such opinions, I had made a mental note about what he had to say. I was also cognizant of how effective Mackay, All Saints second rector, had used his publication, *Church and Home*, during his tenure to build a sense of parish unity. Alas, I was not, as Mackay was a conversationalist. In that sense, I was more like Dr. Clayton, the third rector, an essayist. Clayton, before finances shut off the parish's ability to sustain a regular publication, had made good use of *Church and Home* by means of essays and book reviews as well as reports on the activities of the parish.

The first thing that was immediately obvious from the first issue of the *Witness* in 1993 was that it was expanded from four pages to twelve pages. The layout was on a three eleven-by-seventeen sheets printed on both sides and folded once to create a magazine, each page being a full eight by eleven inches. This layout was generous and allowed room for articles and notices. It was hoped that it might actually be the kind of thing that one would leave lying around on a coffee table or in a magazine rack and that it might be picked back up for a second look or be seen by a visitor.

The second thing to be noticed was that the first edition published for the first time in the history of the parish the unedited minutes of the last vestry meeting, which had been held on January 12, and the full minutes of the annual meeting, which had been held on January 18. This was a radical innovation, considering that vestry business had previously been communicated only when a decision was made that affected the parish as a whole. Moreover, financial information had never been divulged. In fact, the vestry itself had never seen a report of the growing endowment fund until 1990 when the treasurer Carroll Fredrickson handed the vestry a report for the first time. At the end of the meeting, that report had been collected, lest it fall into the wrong hands and be misinterpreted. Anyone who read this new *Witness* knew precisely what my salary was. A careful reading of the vestry minutes of the eighties, which was for the vestry's eyes only, would have a hard time knowing what Pedersen's salary actually was.

The business manager of the parish, a holdover from the Pedersen years, was quick to tell me that this would not work as I would soon find out. L. K. Muller, who would have been one of those in the parish who would have wondered whether I had the competence to administer the parish, must have founded his doubts deepened in his first week with his new rector. Nevertheless, nothing bad happened, and the general signal that the affairs of the parish would be conducted with a high degree of transparency made a good impression on most. In time, Muller would accede that he had been wrong and was extremely helpful to me in navigating the intricacies of the parish's business. His wife, Lois, who had been the parish bookkeeper since 1971, would be equally helpful. At the time of Lois's death in 1995, I wrote, "My transition to being rector of the parish was facilitated immensely by Lois's service. I don't think the transition could have happened anywhere near as well as it has if she had not been here to keep things on course and to work with me in areas where I felt we needed change."[220]

Gradually, a pattern emerged, in which the front page of the *Witness* was an essay: "The Turning Point of the Year," "Pentecost, Christianity's Third Feast," "Summer Religion," "The State of the Church," "Bearing Reality," to name those first opening essays. Each edition carried an article written by the parish nurse on a particular health issue. Essays by the assistant, Emil Belsky, occurred from time to time, usually about his interest in spirituality or in a new book; and at all the times, Belsky's editorial efforts were the keys to the success of the publication. So was the willingness of the new parish secretary, Sue Norman. She rose to the challenge of mastering the skills of computer publishing necessary for the in-house publishing of the piece. She would extend that mastery of the computer to data management as well, and the parish computerized its bookkeeping well before it was common practice in the church.

The commitment to the parish publication was a team effort and an awful lot of work, but there was a belief in the importance of what we were doing. On the whole, it was communicating to the parish who its ministry and its leadership were and what was on their minds. The degree of readership in the parish was quite extensive and would show itself every once in a while in the form of a comment from a long inactive and presumed disinterested member. It reached, in other words, a hidden

---

220 *Witness*, August 11, 1995, p. 11.

parish. It was also read outside of the parish by the bishop and by a group of diocesan clergy who were on the All Saints list as a matter of courtesy. It was not infrequent that a call would come on Monday mornings from someone expressing his or her interest in what they had read in the last issue of the *Witness*.

The advent of the digital camera soon made it possible to include pictures. The first pictures to appear were a photograph of the staff and a photograph of the parish's hand-carved creche both in the Christmas issue of the *Witness* dated December 15, 1993.

Business and Finances

For some time, Pedersen had held off and/or suppressed a number of issues: smoking in the building; handicap accessibility; the general cleanliness of the building; the progressive alligatoring asphalt in the parking lots; the deterioration of the church's sign on Blondo; the audio system, which had been a problem when the building was opened in 1964; the repair of the organ, which was continuing to degrade; and the new carpet in the chapel, which had stretched shortly after its installation. The result was that from day 1, there were advocates for these various causes knocking on my door, politely pointing out that something had to be done immediately.

In order to help the vestry focus on its fiduciary role and provide a forum for the parish to vocalized its wants and visions for the future, I immediately established a parish council, something that had recently become common in Roman Catholic parishes. The council was made up of fifteen councilors who were to be nominated by the rector, wardens, and the president of ECW and who would subsequently be approved by the annual parish meeting. The council's makeup provided a significantly larger inclusion of women, particularly those who were active in various guilds, taught in the church school, prepared the altar, and served luncheons and dinners.

Again, communication with the women's guilds had not been Pedersen's long suit. He had carried on a set piece battle with St. Mary's Guild over "their money." In part, he had started the battle early on when the finances of the parish were problematic. In part, the guild started it because it wanted to decide how the money was used. The same standoff took place between Pedersen and the head of the newly created parish gift shop. It had been organized by Lannie McNichols, who viewed it as service to the parish and who was of the opinion that any money that it made should be used for the improvement of the shop. My first step was to disavow any claim on the guilds' or the shop's money. It should not, I ruled, be used for the operation of the parish but for such special projects as the organizations that had raised the money saw fit. Once the issue was defused, money began to flow. St. Mary's Guild was particularly generous in contributions to "women in need," a fund that I used for charitable work in the city, which I had cultivated particular among single-parent moms. It was not long before a substantial gift to this fund came from the gift shop as well.

To further raise the profile of the women's contribution to All Saints and to invite them into a broader participation in the parish's problem-solving, I regularly designated a Sunday in late April or early May as Women's Sunday. The first address was made by Jean Lewandowski "My Spiritual Journey," 1995 followed by Barbara Waldron Coffey, 1996.[221]

The role of women in the parish council not only gave them a voice, but it gave them a responsibility in a larger area of the parish's work. The council was charged with the development of programs identified as education, evangelism and fellowship, pastoral care, aging and health, music, arts, outreach, and youth. It soon became the source for a number of efforts to promote the general cleanliness of the building. While I was increasingly working for a better cleaning service, the council responded with the first annual spring cleaning held in March. It involved forty adults and twenty youth from the joint youth group. The pew cushions and kneelers were removed from worship space and vacuumed. Meanwhile, copious amounts of Murphy Oil were being applied to the pews. Deacon Bowerman, who with myself and Willard Gould, a former Omaha Power District lineman, built scaffolding and dusted the beams in the nave, which had been collecting dust for thirty years!

This cleared the way for the vestry to focus on its priorities, the first of which was to secure the results of the unfinished Every Member Canvass. Members of the vestry were assigned to make calls, and by the February meeting, the report read: 329 pledges, totaling $312,559; 93 increases, totaling $19,222; 41 decreases, totaling $20,522; and 41 new pledges, totaling $10,793. This was below the amount budgeted in December and reflected the loss of about $10,000 over the pledges the previous year. That sum was about the amount of pledges lost from the departure of the three or four families, attributable mainly to their feeling that the retirement benefit for Pedersen had been too "lean." The fact that the country had been in recession during 1991 and 1992 must also be included as part of the stress affecting this canvass. In fact, a flat recovery over the next couple

221 Texts of their remarks were published in the *Witness*, May 1995, May 1996.

of years would continue to affect the results of the subsequent canvasses. Nevertheless, the result was quite remarkable considering the turmoil during the last six months.

The parish had been for some time receiving a special gift, which was likely to continue. It was difficult to call this gift a pledge as it was a sizeable cash gift that was made at the end of the year without any prior notice. Pedersen himself had never counted it as a pledge, and it was hard to say if it would continue. It happened at least once more, and it was possible to fund the budget, which had been proposed in December. It was, however, a decidedly lean budget. Clergy salaries were less than the year before, and a number of other items had been carefully trimmed. My own input into this budget process was that it was better to begin with restraint and be proven wrong than the other way around. Having asked ourselves to hold back on our expenses, the vestry felt that it was appropriate to pass the same restraint on to the diocese, and they voted not to accept the full asking that year. Asked for $62,160,[222] the vestry accepted $53,500, which was a slight increase over 1992 acceptance. While the reduction was a rather modest amount, I regretted it for two reasons. First, one of my goals was to change All Saints relationship with the diocese from one of conflict to one of cooperation. During the confrontation precipitated by Bishop Varley in the early seventies, Pedersen had suspended All Saints pledge to the diocese. When the Varley matter was resolved, he restored it but held off the payment of the parish's assessment till the end of the year. "Why should they make interest on our money?" he would ask. By the end of his tenure, he had softened his resolve and had gone to paying half in June and half in December. With the vestry's concurrence, we returned to paying it monthly like everyone else. The second reason for my regret was that it invited division in the parish. For everyone who cheered cutting back on the diocesan pledge, there was someone else who would lament. Of course, most didn't care one way or the other. It also hampered the crucial discussion of how the diocese was using the money and of what way the diocese was responsible for its own money problems. My aim was to get people to look at the long run, which somehow we managed to do in the parish. I was greatly relieved that, with a combined effort of the diocese and the parish, we could, in 2000, begin to meet the full asking.

Part of the diocese's problem was that the return on its endowment funds had been affected by the stock market crash of 1987, the savings and loans collapse in 1989, the reoccurrence of recession of 1991 and 1992, and the lackluster economy that followed. This, of course, also affected the investment return on All Saints new endowment, but the parish's

222 The acceptance was $52,646 in 1991, $52,896 in 1992, and 53,000 in 1993.

investment committee, led by Carroll Fredrickson and his successor as parish treasurer, John Hancock, had managed to do considerably better and at no cost to the parish. The portion designated for elderly ministry went to the support of the parish's new health ministry, and at the present level of return on investment, nothing was left over. The other substantial portion of it was entailed by the retirement commitment to the Pedersens. The result was that the endowment income was spoken for and could hardly cope with the string of capital needs that the building and grounds required after thirty years of wear and tear and impact of the vicissitudes of Mother Nature. However, in the parish, it was possible to look ahead to a more positive picture. The balk of the Pedersen benefit would come to an end in three years, and even with a slow recovery, the return on the endowment and the capacity of parishioners to respond to the needs of the parish would be markedly increased. At that time, the endowment could begin to play a significant role, particularly in dealing with capital needs of the parish. My hope was that transparency about the parish finances would unite the parish behind the course of action that we had adopted.

With the operating budget dealt with, we turned to the problem that the endowment presented. It will be remembered that living as a parish with an endowment was a new experience for All Saints. Pedersen's solution had been to keep the endowment a secret. Only reluctantly had he shared information about the endowment with the members of the vestry, and then they were sworn to secrecy. Pedersen's reasoning was that if the parish knew that it had an endowment, its stewardship would suffer. There was a great deal of evidence to support this view, which I myself shared. Our formation as priests had included a persistent disparagement of endowed parishes, particularly common in Eastern United States. Typically, the laity in an endowed parish cut their giving, and rectors, not needing to press the case for stewardship, cut their accountability, or so we imagined. This was one of those places where Pedersen and I were on the same page.

Where I differed with Pedersen was that I was more optimistic about the ability of people to understand and about my ability to teach. I undertook the responsibility to teach what an endowment should mean to the parish, and in a total reversal of Pedersen's policy, I started making a full disclosure of the size and management of the endowment. That disclosure came at the beginning of the second year in a much-expanded annual report. In that report, I explained:

> For the first time in the past canvass we face the question of the role of an endowment. The endowment grew in the past 10 years at All Saints under the stewardship of Father Pedersen

> and Carroll Fredrickson. There was always the worry that the existence of endowments would inhibit the stewardship of the parish. "Why am I making a sacrifice with my pledge effort when money is stashed way?" The reason is that an endowment is given with a certain trust as to the way it will be used. Breaking that trust is the surest means of ending the long-term giving that All Saints or any place can enjoy. Secondly, like any family, everyday expenses cannot long be met from capital, but must be met from income. The basic program of the parish must be met by our annual giving. That is the only way to know that we have the right program for the right parish.

This was a theme that I had belabored over the past year and had now put into writing. To that I would regularly add in various exchanges that, in reality, being an endowed parish was not so different from any parish because every parish, even the poorest and smallest, have been given a building and grounds by the past, and it was bound out of respect to care for them. Applying that analogy to an endowment, it can be said, I argued, that tapping the endowment for general expenses was selling some of the bricks out of the walls of our building to pay our bills.

My hope was that our stewardship would rise to the occasion to pay for the ministry and programs that we wanted and enjoyed and that the income from the endowment could go for the maintenance of our buildings and grounds, and beyond that, it could allow us to undertake special and experimental ministries, such as our ministry to the elderly. While stewardship was flat going into 1993, by the time we reached the end of the year, it was back on a pattern of growth. Revenue that year had actually exceeded the pledges, and the first canvass, which had been announced as "Staying the Course," had done more than stay the course. Income exceeded the goal of $320,000, and the number of pledges had grown during the year from 329 to 343. Summarizing the result, I wrote in the *Witness*:

> This indicates that we have been successful in building a broad middle base to support the work of the parish . . . This makes possible a budget that sustains the program as we have received it and as we have added to it in the past year. This, it seems to me, is the appropriate goal for a transitional year. We have sought not to incur added expenses with new programs or additional personnel and we made concerted efforts to find operational efficiencies and changes that could bring relief to the 1994 budget without compromising our program.

There was more than enough pressure on it from things that we could not control. These included increases in health insurance and the needs of the dioceses. The cost of health insurance for the coming year was set to increase 25 percent. The diocese, on the other hand, was asking the parish to accept a raise in its assessment from $53,000 to $62,160. The diocese's losses had continued during 1993 due to declining membership as well as declining return on its investments. In an attempt to make up for this loss, it had raised the assessment level to 20 percent. This seemed counterintuitive since the parishes, which the diocese relied upon for its income, needed to invest in their own program in order to stop losing ground, if not to actually reverse their own membership loss. For All Saints, this came at a particularly bad time since the parish was attempting to cross the gap created by the change of leadership without losing the growth that it had experienced during the past fifteen years.

The health insurance problem was, of course, the worse news. It had been a growing problem since the middle of the eighties, regularly increasing 10 percent a year, but the 1994 increase was draconian. The national church's leadership, which had created a most successful pension program, could not solve the health insurance problem. The national group insurance, which we had relied upon, had become progressively more problematic. Large urban dioceses chose to leave the plan, stranding a progressively smaller, less healthy pools of insurees dependent upon the plan. Pedersen had made an abortive attempt to take the parish out of the diocesan plan only to find, that for all its exceptionalism, All Saints could not go it alone. We were caught, as was a large portion of the country, in a long-range problem that would affect the ability of the church to provide full-time ministries, especially in smaller more rural communities. For us, there was nothing to do except to take the losses elsewhere.

The Village

While the financial problems and those of the main building with which the parish faced were daunting, they were not that unusual for a new rector. The really unique problem on the rector's plate was the All Saints Village, which Pedersen had created 1987. There were neither precedents nor words of wisdom passed on as how to approach this problem. Dan Gardener, one of the key senior wardens of the eighties, stopped in my office in January to offer his support. Concluding his remarks, he said, "As for the Village, all I can say is we thought we could keep Charles from doing that and I have no idea what you should do about it."

The problem, as I saw it, was twofold. One, it was an incomplete project, hardly off the ground. Two, it had put the parish into the business of managing residential property, which was something that a rector, parish staff, or a parish office was not equipped to do. Because the units were an indigenous part of the property and because promises had been made to current residents, there was no easy way out of the project. The immediate problem was that one unit was vacant, one unit was involved in a complicated rent-buy agreement, and one unit was occupied by a widow who had lost her husband the past February. She was deeply grieved and was rapidly approaching the point where she would need to be in a nursing home. Moreover, she had no family. The long-range problem was that the project was not properly capitalized, and it was quite obviously going to be a struggle to maintain it.

The resident in need of nursing home care, Edie Wiedner, presented an emotionally difficult problem. The parish nurse, Stephanie Ulrich, in this setting, became instrumental to our success, and we did manage to get Edie into a nursing home during the course of the year. Her anxiety was such that, along with many visitors from parishioners and from the parish's health ministry, I visited her almost daily until her death in September of 1994. On one of these visits, she handed a piece of note paper on which she had written down some of her wishes for her funeral. The note paper had a handsome monogram on it and then the words, "From the Desk of Edith Weidner Benson High School." The misspelling of her name was one easily made by someone not aware of the German origin of the last name and the distinction between the "ee" and "eye" sound in German. But why should such a useful note be discarded when a single stroke of a pen could correct the mistake?

By May, we had secured her permission to auction off her belongings so that the unit could be made available to a new renter. The result was that, on a cold May day that threatened rain, Stephanie Ulrich and I stood among the crowd and watched her things sold off, a dismally sad vigil. However, it was proof that it was possible to carry through on the covenants made with residents that allowed them to stay in their unit as long as they were physically able. It also provided substance to the promise that was made that while a resident was in his or her unit that he or she would be assisted to stay longer than would be possible in their home or apartment. The health minister and many parishioners who made routine visits from the time Mrs. Wiedner's husband had died until she was not capable of living alone had extended her stay well over a year. It was, in fact, a good feeling that was communicated to the parish at large. On May 25, Esther Miller moved into the "Wiedner House" as a renter, and the population of the village was restored. Also for the first time, the village had some income with which it could begin to accrue a reserve for its maintenance.

As early as the annual meeting, I reported that the vestry had authorized me to form "a Village Council to study the structure and future of the All Saints Village." It included three residents from the village, the junior warden and two members of the parish who were experienced in real estate management. The original members included the rector, the junior warden, two realtors who belonged to the parish, Lavonne Anderson and Dick Eckstrom, and three residents, Ellen Black, Jim Wells, and Flo Wells.

At first I had attempted to interest an assistant priest in the unit as part of their compensation, but when Emil Belsky was hired as the assistant, that became a moot point as he and his wife already owned a home in Omaha. I presented the idea to the vestry that Joyce Thomas, the parish's DRE, be given a residency in the staff house as part of her compensation package. Thomas, at this point, had worked for the parish for sixteen years and was way overdue for a raise. The village council had advised that a monthly rent could be calculated as 10 percent of the capital price, which, in this case was $65,000. This meant that the monthly rent should be set at $650. Her salary was raised $325, and the rent deducted from her paycheck. This meant that we were able to give her a small raise, long overdue, and an extremely pleasant living situation. Moreover, the covenant with her was that she would remain in the unit after she retired as "the pension" that the parish owed her for her long excellent service but had never gotten around to arranging for her. She moved in before the end of April. Being a gardener, she immediately managed to establish a large flower garden in front of the unit, and she continued to work on the upkeep of the parish's grounds as long as she was able.[223] The village was full!

A year later we could report:

> Last year at this time All Saints Village, our retirement community, had a number of problems that needed to be addressed quickly. In the course of the year we have managed to fill all the units, created a management plan that reasonably anticipates future needs, and have begun to show the positive budget which can ensure that the Village is self-supporting. Right now we can be pleased to see that the Village is secure. Somewhere in the future we will be able to reopen the question of what direction the Village will take.[224]

223 Mrs. Thomas lived in her unit until the spring of 2013.

224 *Witness*, February 1994.

The village was, of course, conceived of as a service and was specifically not to return any income to the parish. The return to the parish was in the non-tangible value of having people living on its property. On the other hand, the worry was always that it might take money from the parish; and as of June of 1994, there was the first glimmer that this could be avoided.

In the June *Witness*, an article appeared entitled "Common Ground," which articulated a new rationale for the village. The article began by noting that "four years ago, a generous gift was made by an individual which added landscaping to the front portion of our lawn. The donor directed that the gift should be accepted as a memorial to Russell Rauscher's ministry." This gift began to transform the property into an inviting space, which the members of the congregation and their friends ought to regard as their commons, distinct from private property and public property. The way to understand what we share was related in the article to the model of an ancient cathedral close. "Part of the close is often devoted to residences which provide a neighborhood on the cathedral grounds." The result was that distinct from public and private property, which is largely empty most of the time, these grounds are peopled. "This 'on-the-property community' adds to the humanity and security of the property. With the beginning of All Saints Village, this element of 'the close' is realized. The property also holds a retreat center, with adjacent space that, in time, might become a meditation garden, a kind of cloister in which to seek quiet."[225]

This provided a basis for arguing that the way ahead was to reconceive the village as a mutual ministry. The residents ministered through their presence to the parish, and the parish ministered to the residence by providing community and affordable housing. That made it possible to feel that the solution was to expand the village by four or more units in order to make it capable of producing enough income to pay for its own maintenance and management. In the meantime, it necessarily would make demands on the rector's time and on his ingenuity to make do with little. This included more than once clearing the eaves of leaves! My proximate hope was that a second unit would turn over either through a sale, which would have given the project the capital base that it lacked, or by means of a rental, which would have provided the income to grow that capital base. That would not come, in fact, until after I retired.

However, an opportunity to move things forward came in 2004, when Don Erikson began thinking about the possibility of building a unit. Widowed and intrigued with the idea of returning to designing and building something, he was ready to make the move. At the same time,

225 In 2004, the west side of the property was developed as Stations of the Cross in memory of Deacon Frank Murphy.

a couple of unexpected estates made it possible to raise the endowment a million dollars and to have a remainder, which could be used to create a tangible memorial for both individuals. From Doris Lang's estate, $120,000 was dedicated to building a second unit, and so a third duplex was added. This allowed the project to come a step closer to self-sufficiency, but not so far, I fear, as to actually take the issue off the rector's desk.

The Organ Problem

Next on the list of the problems that needed to be addressed in that first year was the parish's pipe organ. At the April vestry meeting, Linda Shirk brought the topic to the attention of the vestry. Shirk had recently been elected to the vestry. She had served as the parish organist from the time of Neubecker's death in 1976 to 1992, so she spoke with knowledge and passion. She began by reminding the vestry:

> In February1992, Deacon Scheiblhofer submitted an excellent report on the state of the organ after careful study and consultation with musical leaders and technicians. Soon after, it was determined that "this is not the time to solicit funds for any major projects." The issue of the deteriorating organ is certainly not a new one. For the past decade concerns have been voiced time and again to be tabled because "the time isn't right." Yet another year has passed and costs of repair or replacement are continuing to rise.

In response to Shirk's apt observation, I proposed that the vestry form a fine arts committee to study and make recommendations "on the inclusion of music, as well as, art and drama in the All Saints mission program." The proposal was aimed at buying some time and placing the problem of the organ in a larger context of the parish's needs.

To this end, a broad well-qualified committee was appointed whose conclusions were neither predictable nor would they be safely ignored. The chair of the committee was Jeff Pirruccello. The committee consisted of Claudianna Todd, Goeff Heiden, Newt Kelley, Oral Couch, Cathy Hufton, and Elenor Plumb. Todd was a soprano who had sung with the choir from the later years of Neubecker's tenure as organ choirmaster. Heiden was a baritone who was rather new to the parish but who had quickly established himself as a leader among the men of the choir. Heiden also was active in the musical arts within the city. Couch, Kelley, Hufton, and Plumb were active laity interested in the church's music. Plumb, even more than Heiden, represented the perspective of the musical arts in the city, long an active board member of Omaha's historic "Tuesday Musical," where her efforts were already legendary. Moreover, she was quite accomplished on the piano and had taught as well, a student and successor to Nancy Benolken, whose name was listed with the music committee that had been appointed in 1948, which had called Neubecker to the post of parish organist and choirmaster.

It was stated in the minutes of the vestry that this study would be deliberate and not rushed. Before long, this committee underwrote a parish survey and began regular articles in the *Witness* reporting on its activity and attempting to educate the parish in respect to the role music played in the life of the parish. This groundwork was important because the issue could have become quite divisive very quickly. There were after all a great many in the parish that seldom heard the organ. There were those who thought of it as a remnant of an antiquated past, and there were indeed those who thought that the organ's voice spoke for no one less than God.

By May of 1994, this committee made its report to the vestry calling for a three-phase program.

1. Immediate repair to the wind chest and contract for a routine maintenance agreement.
2. Repair and/or replace the console.
3. Re-voice the instrument.

Phase 1 was, according to the committee, urgent. As a result, the vestry approved the immediate repair of the wind chest and the removal and storage of the antiphonal organ. The installation of the antiphonal organ was judged by the study to have been seriously flawed, and its future was not so much a question of repairing as rebuilding. The sixteen-foot *trompette en chamade* had sagged for lack of proper support, and the case work, a rough carpenter job at best, interfered with the entrance to the nave not only visually, but also physically. On top of that, it was difficult to find a musically compelling rationale for an antiphonal organ considering the space in which it was housed. To put money into it did not make sense to the committee. The proposal was radical, and it might be expected that the proposal to undo something so recently completed would produce opposition. The process that we had used to make the decision, however, seems to have been the key to the broad acceptance of the decision.

The chests and re-voicing were completed at the cost of $18,462 during the summer of 1994. Problems remained with the electromagnetic console that meant that the full use of the restored pipes was still impossible, and a certain level of unreliability remained. Phase 2 called for the console to be replaced by a completely new, state-of-the-art, electronic console. The flow of things remained more positive than anticipated so that work on the new console was under way in 1995, precisely at the moment that the James Johnson assumed the direction of the parish's music program. This allowed his expert input to help us with the final decisions about the renovation, which needed to be made. The console arrived in October of 1996 at the cost of $85,000, and the necessary work was complete.

When the tile floor in the worship space was completed in 1999 and the last remnants of the blue carpet were removed, it was heralded as the finishing piece of the organ's restoration. The acoustics of the room had never been better. Indeed, the gift that enabled the completion of the floor ended up being more than enough to complete the floor. When I informed the donor, Noni Lundgren, she asked us to please use it for the organ. This allowed a new rank to be installed in the choir organ in 2000, which was a head start on additions to the organ's pipe work identified as phase 3.

And Miscellany

The cascade of urgent problems continued. The speaker system in the church had been criticized from the first Sunday it was used. When the altar was moved in 1982, the altar mike was lost. Pedersen, who had a large voice, made do. Something had to be done. In May of 1994, the vestry approved a contract with Acoustical Design Group of Kansas City. The system had a number of speakers with delayed timing to create an even flow of sound in the space. It also required several wireless mikes to accommodate the growing number of individuals with speaking parts in the service. The installation cost was $20,522.

Most of the remaining items were smaller ticket items: concrete and asphalt repair and the shortening of some pews in the main worship space to provide a permanent location for the baptismal font at the entrance to the worship area, among others. The cuts to the pews were also made in the front and were justified as providing locations for individuals in wheelchairs, something that satisfied the growing lobby in the parish for disability access. In retrospect, these cuts were the beginning of an extensive remodeling of the worship space that would extend on to its completion in 2000.

This stream of capital projects in the two-year transitional period was made possible mainly from memorials and special gifts and a small but growing amount from the endowment fund. The later was made possible by the resolve that endowment income would not be used for the operational expense of the church. This meant lean operating budgets for these opening years but, nevertheless, ones that were getting us to where we needed to be.

The Transition Working

When the annual spaghetti supper came at the end of May, it brought with it a special sense of relief. For some time, this supper had marked the end of the program year, and it had been for some time a comforting thought for me that if I made it through the spaghetti supper, there would be time to catch my breath. It was all the more so this year. The supper had, since its inception, been intended as a benefit for Siena/Francis House, but it was also one good party in which the parish could enjoy who it was. The announcement for the supper in the *Witness* highlighted the purpose of the supper:

> We are proud to have been associated with the work at Siena/ Francis House for the past fourteen years. Members of All Saints that have served on the board have been Don Amsden, Frank Murphy, Jack Kubat, and presently Pamela Finn. Deacon Ernie Bowerman coordinates our work there and buys and delivers the food for the meals that we cook when it is our turn. The past year, we have served four hundred individuals, raised $2,395, and had involved fifty members of the parish.

Since the inception of the supper, my wife, Jane, had gathered a group of women to make the three hundred some pazzelis to be sold for desert at the dinner, and I spent the week prior making the thirty-five some gallons of sauce from an old family recipe. Pedersen often said that every minister has a *shtik*, and mine was cooking. I cooked for the retreats, and I cooked for a newly instituted church night that fed choirs, children, youth, and adults, all of whom went to some particular activity or offering following the meal. It was large and somewhat chaotic, but for some time, it was a dramatic expansion of hours and the variety of persons in the parish mixing with one another.

This initial season as rector, I had, however, one more thing to get done before the summer lull could begin. The bishop was scheduled to make his fifth visit to the parish in that many months. On June 2,

Robert Scheiblhofer was to be ordained to the diaconate. Scheiblhofer had been music director since 1979 and had been prepared in the parish for priesthood. Bishop Krotz felt that he should be placed in a cure of his own, but I managed to persuade the bishop to leave him at All Saints, where he would begin working as an assistant priest. It was a relief that the bishop gave in because it would have been a significant added burden at that point to replace him in the midst of this initial year of the transition. Moreover, Scheiblhofer was a gifted pastoral visitor, and this was an opportunity for him to discover his gift and chance for us to have some relief from the burden that fell to us. As it is often the case, we priests are taught this ministry by someone we are assigned to visit. In Scheiblhofer's case, it was a wonderful old lady named Dorothy Boyles. Dorothy was the sister of James Fields, one the senior wardens that we have met in the course of the story. She never married and had worked her whole life. She literally ran the regional sales office of Proctor and Gamble during the war but was bumped back to secretary when the men returned. She was not one to back down, and she never did get over the injustice of this. She talked his ear off but, nevertheless, gave him a sense of what it meant to be a pastor.

It turned out Scheiblhofer stayed at All Saints until June 1, 1994, when he accepted a call to St. Barnabas. While I regretted, even then, the loss of Scheiblhofer, I was proud that he expanded the list of competent priests whose formation had taken place at All Saints and had gone on to work in the greater church. Scheiblhofer became an effective pastor for those who had remained at St. Barnabas after a number of calamities. In the end, this decision would take him out of the Episcopal Church into the Roman Catholic Church under the particular provision made for accepting Anglican priests in an Anglican Rite as St. Barnabas did itself.[226] It is a puzzle in many ways how this happened, but in a way, what he had learned from Pedersen and me was the sacred value of the pastoral relationship one assumed when one accepted the call of a particular parish. I am rather of the opinion that Scheiblhofer did not so much lead that congregation out of the Episcopal Church as that he found that his ideals as a pastor made leaving the only thing for him to do.

The first six months of my tenure as rector had been extremely intense, and as the summer began, I was, in a sense, still treading water. In a more

---

226 *Catholic Voice* reported that an Anglican parish in Omaha, with a congregation of about fifty people, joined the Catholic Church in a ceremony on July 10, 2013, the first such unification in the archdiocese since Benedict XVI authorized the change in the document "Anglicanorum Coetibus." Scheiblhofer was named parish administer and was scheduled to be ordained a deacon and then a priest.

spiritual mood, I would remind myself of the motto I had chosen at my installation: "Zeal for your house has consumed me." When my mood swung in a more worldly vain, I would describe what I was going through to myself by referring to the expression used in Mario Puzo's *The Godfather*: "going to the mattresses." I was working seven days a week, which never impressed me all that much since that is what my father did and what many business and professional people in the parish were doing as well. Our kids were grown and out of the house.

My wife, Jane, was extremely supportive and made it possible for me to work in the way I thought the call demanded. She was still working as a nurse as she had from the beginning of our marriage, but by the end of 1995, she retired from nursing and became progressively more involved in the art form of writing icons. On our sabbatical leave in 1992, she had made some substantial steps in mastering the techniques of the traditional forms and methods the Eastern Orthodox schools of iconography. By 1999, she was able to begin studying under the discipline of the Prosopon School of Iconography, headed by the master iconographer, Vladislav Andrejev. Shortly after this, she mounted her first professional show at the Hot Shops, an art co-op that had recently been founded in Omaha.

A Pause at Last to Stake Out a Vision

The first pause since October came in the following July. It provided me some time to set out a vision of what I hoped to accomplish during the thirteen years that I expected to be the rector of All Saints. Vision statements were at this time very much in vogue for organizations all the way from governmental agencies to corporate boards. I suppose, in retrospect, that this attempt was a defense, since the statement begins with a number of disclaimers as to the value of vision statements. Nevertheless, I placed it on the front page of the July 21 *Witness*, suggesting the seriousness with which I intended it to be taken:

> My first priority for All Saints is to see the Gospel of Jesus Christ modeled in worship, discipline and government. In all of these essential elements of Christian life, we want to manifest a participatory style that images or reflects the life of the Trinity, the divine life of original and originating love.
>
> Secondly, I should like to see an All Saints that is there for people by means of stability, diversity and openness. . .

> Thirdly, I should like to see an All Saints that reaches out to people in need of the Gospel.
>
> What I envision is not so much a bigger All Saints, as it is an All Saints that is always striving to be more faithful to the Gospel, and to letting God decide whether or not that means a bigger All Saints.

In my recollection, not much was said about the theological argument made in the first point, which was, however, typical of my communications whether in a sermon, class, or general conversation. The parish was used to that by now. I do remember, however, discussions about my mention of diversity. When I spoke about this in other contexts, I asserted that diversity needed to be an intentional policy. I was particularly concerned with racial diversity. I was, after all, a priest whose formation took place precisely when Martin Luther King was repeatedly pointing out that the Sunday morning hour of worship in America was the most segregated hour in American life. I had, by those strange chances that shape a life, become something that I had never imagined being, the rector of a large suburban parish. The basis on which to hope that All Saints could be a diverse, especially a racially diverse community, was slim.

Jeri Anderson Morley was the first African American to join All Saints. She had come to Omaha from Maryland in 1978 to work for InterNorth. When she came to town, she attended Salem Baptist Church; but in 1984, in anticipation of marrying Bob Morley, she set out to find a church for their future together. Somehow that had led her to All Saints. Soon they were taking marriage counseling from me, which was required for them to be married in the Episcopal Church, having discovered in their travels a romantic Episcopal Church in San Francisco. I well remember Jeri's arrival for marriage preparation at All Saints. She was striking, spiritual, energetic, gracious, and bent on a romantic marriage in San Francisco with Bob. We did a lot of marriage counseling for a lot of people that go off and were never seen again. It seemed to us that it was a good work to do regardless, so we tried to do it well whatever the outcome. However, Jeri, with Bob in tow, did come back. She came back to her work in Omaha and to expand the window of equal opportunity in the business world. She worked as well in many other community organizations building bridges to bring racial unity to our city, and Jeri came back to All Saints to worship and to work in the life of this parish. Soon she took on the very heavy commitment of serving in the parish's altar guild and continued to do until the onset of her final illness made it impossible.

Unfortunately, she was diagnosed with cancer in 2000 and died in October of the 2001. In her funeral homily, I said,

> She bore that illness among us with courage and a determination to wring out of life everything it had. That too was a ministry given to us. In a spiritual way, Jeri is a pillar of the parish which extended its roof, which opened up the way for diversity in this parish. She is the first African American to be part of this parish. She has given us a gift which, in the past eighteen years, bore fruit in a growing diversity. She has helped us to be a parish of "the city." I count it a special honor to lead this celebration of the life of Jeri Anderson Morley and to have a hand in committing her remains to the parish's columbarium. In a certain sense, her remains become a part of the fabric of this place.

Jeri's presence, however, was a kind anomaly that scarcely registered. I remember once when I was speaking with a group of more active members in the parish that we could build a more racially inclusive parish by being intentional about diversity. The choice of the word "build" was puzzling for them. How could we build diversity if we didn't have any one of color worshiping at All Saints? How do we know that they would want to? But we did. It was just that it was invisible since Jeri was just another one of us.

In a rather short order, the presence that she had created for us was added to by John Brightman and his daughter Adia joining the parish. John was the son of Rev. Edward Scipio Brightman, who was the last full-time African American priest at St. Phillip's, serving from1963 to 1972. I had met John when All Saints was working at St. Mark's. His daughter was turning eight, the time when Baptists were baptized. Her baptism had been delayed until she could make her own decision of where she would be baptized. Her decision for the Episcopal Church provided me with the privilege of baptizing her. When St. Mark's closed, John and Adia chose to come to All Saints. In 1996, John Brightman was elected to the vestry and served through the crucial period of the building campaign. Soon after I took over as rector, Barbara Coffey joined us, and behind her came the Longs and the Martins. Coffey would be elected to the vestry in 2000 and would serve on the search committee for the new rector in 2005. Bill and Chris Hall came back to Omaha. Chris was a local Omaha girl from the Brown family and Bill, a tall handsome man who had been a Chicago cop, was one of the first black officers on the force. He was a great storyteller and was greatly enjoyed in the parish. Jerry Lucas came to town in 1993 as assistant vice president of the Data Centers of the Union Pacific Railroad. Jerry was born in Brooklyn, New York, and worked his way through Worcester Polytechnic Institute in Worcester, Massachusetts, graduating with a bachelor's degree in engineering. He went on and earned a master's degree in business. With his wife, Melba, they made an immense contribution to the parish. Lucas was elected to the vestry in 2003. Juanita Lowe, whose husband, Darrel, had just been appointed a district court judge, was attracted to the Sunday school. With Juanita as a Sunday school teacher and her young children involved in the church school, I could say by the mid-nineties that there was an African American presence on at every level of the parish life.

While much of this growth had come from personal contacts, it also benefitted from my growing participation in the Urban League of Nebraska. That participation had begun with an invitation in 1993 to participate in an Urban League Fund-raiser called "Men Who Cook." Subsequently, I was elected to the board, and I was particularly privileged to find myself serving on the board with an All Saints parishioner, Barbara Schaefer. Schaefer had been a member of All Saints since the eighties, and she had served on the vestry from 1988 to 1991. She was the Vice President at Union Pacific in charge of human resources and was deeply involved with equal employment activities in her corporation and in the city. Schaefer was slated to become the next president of the Urban League of Nebraska. My own participation on the board continued through 2001.

The State of the Church

How quickly, in the course of 1993, did All Saints change. Within days, Ed Conine died of a sudden heart attack. Conine had been particularly close to Pedersen, and he had been instrumental in reestablishing an effective Every Member Canvass as Pedersen began his tenure as rector. Conine had come with his wife, Sue, to the Saturday night service, and I remember how pleased I was to see him. He was the kind of Pedersen leadership that I wanted to enlist and had already been thinking of him as a future canvass chairman. I scurried out of the service to perform a wedding at Brownell Talbot's chapel, a large social wedding at which I expected to see the Conines again. Ed went home to change and died of a heart attack within hours of the service. During the year, there were four more deaths: Gladys Scott, Bessie Ohle, Jim Paxton, and Mary Bryant each of which signaled that the parish was entering new waters. Gladys Scott was the last of the old school ladies who wore a hat and gloves to the late service every Sunday. Bessie Ohle, who had worked all her life in a cleaning establishment, had been the choir mother for a couple of decades, which meant that she managed, sewed, and cleaned the choir's robes. Jim Paxton was last of the old-style gentlemen, a long-term gracious leader in the parish that was often troubled by change but in the end always managed to find the grace to get on with it. Mary Bryant was the daughter to Guerdon Wattles, that Omaha "capitalist" who had contributed so much to the parish at the turn of the century.[227] The funeral homily for Mary Wattles Bryant was published in the October *Witness*, and in it I tried to suggest how the parish should deal with this change.

> Still, we must mark her loss and the dramatic change that this loss represents. Her physical form, the instrument by which she related to us and we to her, has been taken from us. Across the troubled length of the twentieth century, she gave birth to, preserved, and celebrated a family. She was its gathering point. She was her family's connection to a past strength and a deeply abiding intention formed at the beginning of this century. I speak here both of her biological family and her parish family. Speaking for her parish family, I note that we mark a loss of connection with the earlier building on the hill at Twenty-Sixth and Dewey where this parish used to meet. We know that with Mary's passing, we lose a direct link to our beginnings, someone who remembers where and why and how the walls were built and changed and torn down to be built again elsewhere. Now in a new building a century later, we take comfort in knowing that somehow we shall be able to continue to remember and to receive something from that shared past. We believe this to be the case, for Mary's life was always about nothing other than love, the love of being together. And love endures. Here in a different building and now at a different time, we are still the community that Mary's mother and father helped to build.

These losses were balanced by a significant number of newcomers in that year who would become, in time, significant contributors to the work of the parish: Pamela Barness, Joel Perry, Bruce and Donnie Reid, David

227 Mary's father Gurdon Wattles and her mother gave the money to build the parish hall at Twenty-Sixth and Dewey in 1906 and played an extensive role in the life of the parish until they moved to California.

and Bonnie Linberg, Karen Falconer, Steve Brown, and Joseph and Jean Stothert.[228]

The second year of the transition opened with a further attempt to provide an orientation for the parish to the general climate of the times, which was regarded as dicey. The eighties had ended with a great deal of wallowing in negative news about the church, particularly about the Episcopal Church, and the nineties had opened with an economic recession. In the lead article of the *Witness*, which opened the new year of 1994, I authored an ambitious article that was titled "The State of the Church." January is, of course, the season in which the country prepares to listen to the president speak on the state of the union, and so, I suppose, I thought it appropriate to do so for the church. What I wanted to do is provide a realistic assessment of what we faced as a church so that the actions that we chose to take in the next phase of the parish's life could be meaningful and capable of succeeding.

Turning first to the parish, I said, "It is important to see that All Saints was in a state of transition which had begun a year ago on January 1, 1993, and would hopefully end by the end of the next year, 1994." I argued, I am not sure on what authority, that it was a general rule of thumb that transitions should take two years to accomplish. "In the course of the first year, everything is examined and done once. Doing something once is a big step, but there still remains the question of how much of what worked was pure luck and how much of what didn't work was duly noted to serve as an occasion for learning. This," I wrote, "is what we hope to find out as we do things a second time." The bottom line for the parish was that it is in good shape. It had not lost membership in the eighties, it had not suffered a setback in funding, and the laity seemed to be working very hard at being the church.

I turned then to the state of the diocese, which had lost membership in the eighties, whose income had been depressed and who was struggling to find direction. The diocese was seeking to find a new sense of direction with new church starts, the first of which was under way with St. Martha in Papillion, a sister city to the south of Omaha. Just as it appeared that St. Martha's was taking off, cuts at Offut Air Force Base reduced its membership and raised a big question about its ability to raise the finances to build. Those same cuts also had an impact on its near neighbor, Holy Spirit, Bellevue, as well. The diocese, I pointed out, was talking about a capital drive. The executive council had authorized a fund-raiser, Hillman and Associates of Harrisburg, Pennsylvania, to do the basic study on the

---

[228] Jean Stothert, who taught in the church school while her children were growing up, was elected mayor of the city of Omaha in 2013.

feasibility of a capital fund drive. I said in the article, "I think we need to anticipate and indeed, encourage such a drive to take place, probably in the 1995 calendar year." The key to its success, I suggested, would rest on seeking capital giving for a clear purpose, which can assure a long-term impact.

The state of the national church was even more troubled according to my report, and it was suffering from a continual barrage of bad press. The headline of the eighties regularly heralded the rapid growth of Pentecostal churches and, in contrast, the steep decline in the membership of the mainline churches, including the Episcopal Church. The reports also included stories on a number of disaffected Episcopal parishes in various stages of trying to leave the Episcopal Church. The coverage was not exactly fair. In fact, national church statistics indicated that loss of membership had found some relief the past couple of years. There had been slight increases in membership and substantial increases in stewardship. On the other hand, I argued, the national church was at a crucial juncture. "The great question that the national church faces is whether it will continue to be dominated by a debate on 'rights' or whether it will turn to practical issues that make the institution work." I enumerated a number of these issues and went on to say, "I am not unduly pessimistic, but I do believe it is realistic to focus on the premise that the local church must establish its own integrity and not expect, let alone rely, on dividends from the national church to trickle down from above."

What I was doing with this article was what rectors of All Saints had done from its inception, arguing that All Saints was exceptional and had a distinct destiny of its own. I argued that the parish was poised for some real growth in the next decade in spite of what was happening around it. This did not mean that All Saints would try to separate itself from the diocese or the national church. It would, as it had, work hard in those very structures to the best of its ability, but it would stay focused on the local community within the parish and see its growth and development as the first and best contribution it could make to the diocese and the national church. It had, for example, not been paying its full assessment the past year nor, in fact, would it until the year 2000. It was, however, paying about 95 percent of it on time and in amounts that were growing significantly every year. The parish argued that the cuts in the parish's budget, which would allow accepting the whole asking now, would likely mean less, not more, money for the diocese in the long run. The parish's leadership had developed over time a number of formulas of its own to decide on the level of its support. Noting that it had been paying 10 percent of the diocese's operating budget, it declared that it was committed to continuing to do so. Again, it reasoned that the assessment that was set at 17 percent at the time and that it was, in fact, paying 17 percent of its pledge income. On the other hand, the message to the diocese was that it should be looking at its budget to see if it and its askings were conducive for the long-run well-being of the congregations that made up the diocese.

A New Team

The continued progress with the transition was marked by the election of new wardens at the annual meeting held on January 30, 1994. Dean Hokenson and Douglas Hokenstad were honored for their service to the parish, and Paul Ombruni and Jeff Pirruccello were welcomed on board as the new wardens. Ombruni, the senior warden, was born and raised in Council Bluff. At the time he was elected senior warden, he was a senior engineer at Henningson, Durham and Richardson, Omaha's premier architectural and engineering firm. Ombruni had lived in Omaha for more than forty years with his wife, Jean, and they had just celebrated forty-two years of marriage. Jean was progressively disabled by MS, and Paul had assumed for some time the role of Jean's chief caregiver. His cheerful dedication was not lost on the parish, and his calm and reasonable approach to problems was legendary. He had been at All Saints since 1967. In remarks printed in the *Witness*, he expressed particular interest in the areas of Christian education, care for the elderly, the parish health ministry, and all phases of physical access for the disabled. The latter two issues were of a personal concern since Jean had been in a wheelchair for some time, and her frequent medical crises and bouts in care centers had brought Paul to a deep appreciation for what the health ministry was doing for parishioners.

Jeff Pirruccello was born in Omaha and had joined All Saints in 1987 with his wife, Lynn, who was raised in Cozad, Nebraska. Jeff grew up Roman Catholic, and Lynn as a Presbyterian. They began a search for a common spiritual home as their children were approaching the age when they should be in church school. Both the openness of the parish and the effectiveness of its church school attracted them. Jeff was a lawyer specializing in tax work at Baird and Holm, the firmed founded by C. M. Montgomery, which the reader will remember as one of All Saints early and long-term senior wardens. In 1994, their three children, Ross, Derek, and Erin, were fourteen, eleven, and eight. All their kids were active in youth activities. Pirruccello had served the past year as chairman of the Music and Fine Arts Committee while it wrestled with the organ problem. He also was a member of the standing committee of the diocese.

In an interview for the *Witness*, Jeff gave an expression of his hopes: "We can build upon the excellent program we already have here at All Saints." The article continued, "He wants to support Father Tan Creti in his development of a process for broad-based input from the parish. In addition, Jeff would like us to look for ways to encourage young families to join the parish and participate in its programs and activities."[229]

The balanced experience and competence that these two men brought to their offices sent a message to the parish as well as an enlistment of some crucial competence for making the decisions that lay ahead of the parish. It also, I must admit, provided me with a touch of humor to have the two wardens who shared an Italian heritage along with the rector. Gone for the moment were the Scandinavians! Quick on the heels of the election of the new wardens were two announcements, which would have a significant impact on the parish's financial outlook. Pledge income for the past year had been overpaid by $19,000! Having been trained to expect short falls, this news suggested to me that our pledge base was considerably stronger than we had anticipated. It was also announced to the parish that the Wiedners had left the bulk of their estate to the parish and that it would amount to considerably more than a million dollars.

Yet the maxim holds: The Lord giveth and the Lord taketh. Blessed with a new leadership and a good financial report, we were soon to suffer some significant losses in quick order. In March, Robert Spire died of a sudden and unexpected heart attack. He was living in Lincoln at the time, though he had been in continual contact with us and us with him. During his last hospitalization, I visited him in Lincoln and was encouraged with the thought that he would pull through. It was not to be. His funeral was celebrated at All Saints on March 7, 1994. Senators and governors were among the crowd of more than eight hundred people who attended the funeral and the luncheon served in the undercroft by the women of All Saints, which spoke of the modesty of the Spires and the courage of our women. My hope was dashed that the Spires might soon return to All Saints, a thing to which Spire had hinted at a number of times. I had hoped that he would be of particular value in solving the complicated organ problem since he had been instrumental in its original purchase and installation.

Next came the loss of Robert Scheiblhofer, who had accepted a call to St. Barnabas's. "Scheiblhofer Night was set for May 25," and it occasioned a great outpouring of the parish to thank Scheiblhofer for all that he had given to the parish. The search for an organist choirmaster had begun in January in anticipation of his departure, and after a misfire, Stephen

229 *Witness*, May 22, 1994, p. 4.

Bouma was hired in August. This would prove to be a false start as Bouma's skills on the piano did not carry over to the organ, at which he was less than adequate and with which he was less than comfortable. He, however, bought us a year, and that would prove to be a significant gift, which made up for the painful stumbles during the year.

During the year, we continued to make progress on our list of urgent tasks: $1,000 of concrete work, $4,350 asphalt repair, a new sign on Blondo Street and a new sound system, $20,522, and the first phase of the repair and restoration of the organ, $18,462. It is worth noting that work that proceeds in "phases" was a hallmark of my approach to problems. This was quite different from Pedersen's approach. Pedersen inevitably focused on the way to fix the problem at hand. There are advantages to each approach. People who approach problems by means of "phases" have a tendency to never finish anything. On the other hand, people who work on the basis of a fix-it-now approach tend to compound the problem for what needs to be done next.

By the time the fall came, the Every Member Canvass was announced as "The Next Step Canvass." This was not original. As you will remember shortly after the congregation arrived at Ninety-Third and Blondo it had held a fund drive called the Next Step. While this canvass had its own agenda, namely declaring "the transition" complete, its resonance with past was intentional. The material that introduced the canvass claimed: "One can feel a certain momentum, and one could opt for a comfortable year in 1995. On the other hand, it might be the year to take the next step. Perhaps the next step for All Saints is the addition of another full-time priest on our staff." The theme of "a third priest" replayed a theme that Pedersen had often visited but had never quite accomplished: Miles and Lindeman each had stayed only for a short time. In this new setting, the message was that it was time to make a substantial increase in the parish's reach.

The next step also intended to focus the parish on the larger question of the adequacy of building for the program that it intended. It became progressively clear in the waning days of 1994 that an answer to that question would entail a substantial amount of building.

Chapter 11

Closing the Circle: 1995–2000

What for the parish was a next step was for me a first step. Through 1994, the projects consisted of repairs and remodeling the existing building. That fell within my experience, for as a young priest, I had come to the buildings at St. Andrew's, Clear Lake, and then at St. Paul's, Grinnell, Iowa, which needed fixing. But what lay before us was a substantial addition to the size and capability of the building at All Saints. Actually building something fell outside of my experience, and I never imagined doing so. My formation as a priest in the sixties had been influenced by senior priests who were critical of the building, which the church had done in the past, particularly that which was done in the fifties. It was derisively dubbed by them as the edifice complex. They claimed that many of these buildings were underused and had come at the cost of ministry to the people of the church and to the poor of the world. It was a perspective that I shared, and so there was something ironic about the fact that I found myself leading a parish into a building program.

An article in the *Witness* that was mailed to the parish December 19, 1994, is evidence of my interior turmoil. In it I wrote:

> There is another hidden parish of which I should like us to be aware to some degree. We will not likely see them at our worship, nor will we likely receive a contribution from them to assist our operation budget. While members drive from "all over the city" to be part of All Saints, you will not likely meet these individuals in your neighborhoods, because they live in the "unnoticed city" like a cut off section of 24th Street that

> can hardly be found except by backtracking on Jones Street, at low-numbered addresses on Castelar, a block off the main drag in Carter Lake, or a lost apartment complex set back from Lake, Lakeview, or 108th Street . . . They help us to be whole as a parish. They make our hope more hope than wish, our prayer for the kingdom to come, more a prayer, than ritual.

Nevertheless, as the new year got under way, the vestry and I took the big step of appointing a new committee, which we called the Committee on Architecture and Landscape. Its membership included Paul Ombruni as chair, Helen Amsden, Bob Culver, Mary Culver, Dorothy Eckstrom, Bob Hall, Ibby Hancock, Barb Parker, Marc Ward, and Jim Willour. It was a committee filled with talent, and they all took their task very seriously. Bob Hall was a builder. Bob Culver was a visionary artist. Dorothy Eckstrom was an interior decorator with impeccable taste and an imminently practical knack as a counselor who would help us navigate decisions that committees can't or shouldn't make. Jim Willour was a talented architect from HDR, the same firm at which Ombruni worked. Willour gave us a lot of quiet guidance in dealing with our architects. When Willour suddenly died of a heart attack in March of 1997, the loss to the committee was mitigated by the addition of Ron Schaefer. Schaefer, the husband of Barbara Schaefer, was the building consultant for the University of Nebraska Medical Center, which had embarked on a nonstop building program. Schaefer came on the committee precisely at the moment when the parish was pivoting from planning to construction, and he was again an invaluable council throughout the construction phase of the project.

The committee was charged with producing a ten-year master plan by the fall of 1995! It began its work by calling on help from an old friend of the parish, Bro. William Woegner. Woegner was head of the office for divine worship of the Roman Catholic Archdiocese and was an architectural consultant for the archdiocese. By 1995, he was beginning to be called upon by an ever-widening range of work on church projects across the country.[230] Brother William had acted as a consultant for the parish when Pedersen had relocated the altar in the main worship space in 1982 and when he built the chapel in 1985.

As the building plans were unfolding that year, two major program changes came about, which would have far-reaching effects for the decade. In May, the difficult search for a permanent organ choirmaster came to an end when the parish offered the position to Dr. James Johnson and to his

---

[230] In 2014, Woegner was given a task as primary consultant for the redesign of the Crystal Cathedral in Orange County, California.

wife, Karen, who would serve as the assistant organist and choirmaster, with the particular task of form a youth choir. James grew up in Greenville, South Carolina, and attended the University of Arizona at Tucson, where he studied piano and organ. In 1976, he was awarded a doctorate in musical arts specializing in piano with a minor in music history. While studying in Tucson, he met his future wife, Karen. Karen was born in Iowa and had grown up in Cheyenne, Wyoming. While in Tucson, they joined the Episcopal Church, and James was employed as organist for five years at St. Paul's Episcopal Church on the campus. Karen finished her own bachelor's degree in piano and organ and began working toward a master's degree. Her master's degree program was interrupted in 1983 when James received a position on the faculty of the University of Alaska at Fairbanks. They lived in Fairbanks for twenty years. For fifteen of those years, they directed the music program at the First Methodist Church of Fairbanks. With a change in pastors, they resigned their positions and spent the last five years worshiping at St. Matthew's Cathedral, the small log cabin church, which serves as the cathedral church of the Episcopal Diocese of Alaska. During a sabbatical leave in 1986, James completed a postdoctoral master's degree in church music and organ at Westminster Choir College, Princeton, New Jersey. In 1994, he was hired by the University of Nebraska at Omaha as the Isaacson professor of music and coordinator of keyboard studies.

The "wasted year" with the music program resulted in the parish hiring at a bargain one of the city's most qualified musicians. A year before he was not available, a year later they probably would have been hired by someone with a much larger music program than All Saints had at that time. The Johnsons were incredibly driven and would carry the music program on after my retirement.

The other change that was in the works was with the parish's director of religious education. Joyce Thomas had worked for All Saints for twenty years and turned sixty-five years old. In June, the parish said farewell to Joyce at a grand pig roast, held on the parish grounds in a giant circus tent specially set up for the occasion. Newt Kelly, lifelong member, vestryman, and dentist, was in charge of getting and roasting a pig. It was one of Kelly's specialties. Clearly it was one of the parish's all-time great parties. The crowd included a number of Thomas's family and friends, including two of her favorite Roman Catholic priests, Denny Hanneman and Dick Solick. Joyce would continue to be part of life at All Saints for some time, for the vestry had granted her the rights and privileges of living in one of the houses in the village as long as her health would permit independent living.[231]

---

231 Thomas continued to live in the village until 2013.

The problem created by Thomas's resignation was quickly solved by the presence in the parish of an excellent candidate, Judi Yeates. Yeates had worked in the church school and was preparing for ordination to the priesthood. She brought to the job both continuity and a passionate interest in innovation. Yeates had joined All Saints in 1986 and had taken instruction from Bishop Rauscher. That relationship had a significant effect on both of them. Rauscher quickly recognized in her a call to ministry. In time, that would lead Yeates to seek ordination and Rauscher to the accept the idea of women in the priesthood, a thing that he had not up to then supported. The following year, she was married to Jim Yeates at All Saints. Since that time, both Jim and Judi had been active members of the parish, Jim singing in the choir and participating in the governance of the parish and Judi in the church school and in adult educational opportunities. Their family consisted of Judi's three children—Shannon, Scott, and Sean—and Jim's three children–Michel, Chris, and Cynthia—Shannon being the only one still at home. More recently, they had adopted David, who was now age six.

Judi had taught various levels in the church school, including that ever-notorious level, the seventh and eighth grade.[232] She had been active in adult education and completed four years of EFM. In the last four years, she had completed work toward a double degree at Dana College a degree of bachelor of arts in religion and a master of social work degree. She was just completing a summer practicum with the Visiting Nurse Association's Hospice program. The August *Witness* further explained that Yeates was preparing for ordination to the priesthood and was currently a student in Creighton University in pursuit of a master's degree in theology.

She was prepared to commit to the position of DRE for three years, the time estimated for her to complete her preparation for the priesthood.[233] The time was ripe after twenty years for change in the church school program, and Yeates had both the competence and the people skills to make the change in an effective way. While maintaining the retreat program and the participatory style of the church school, she freshened the curriculum and reenergized its teachers. With Yeates arrival on the staff in the fall of 1995, the parish had a whole new team in place, and a new era was truly under way.

It also helped prepare the way that the substantial remodeling of the chapel was on course to be completed successfully on schedule by the end

232 Joining such notables as Woody Bradford and Florence Van Scoy.

233 Yeates was ordained to the diaconate on April 29, 1998, and to the priesthood on November 1, 1998.

of the year. The project has received an important boost just before the year had begun. Craig Roeder came home to visit his mother. Bobbie Roeder had only recently reactivated herself at All Saints and had become quite active. Craig had not visited All Saints since his days in youth choir and was enthusiastic about what he saw happening in the parish. As a result, I struck up a relationship with him. He had, for some years, been dealing with AIDS, and he was seeing the first signs that his disease was beginning some kind of remission.

Roeder had left Omaha as a young man to seek his fortune and had become a lighting designer with an international reputation. He was due, in fact, to leave the country to do the lighting of a major new museum in Indonesia. A look at the chapel, new since his last visit to All Saints, stirred his imagination, and he left Omaha with some brief notes, promising that his firm would provide a finished lighting design for the chapel as a gift. By the following August, work in the chapel was under way. The bid for the electrical work based on Roeder's design came in at $10,277. A parishioner, Emmett Smith, a recently retired electrical contractor, agreed to supervise the rather elaborate plan, and its success owed much to him.

The work on the floor was a key driver for the other projects in the chapel, and it was nearing completion. It had been decided that the carpet that had stretched and wrinkled would be replaced not with carpet, but with green slate identical to that which had been used in the narthex and on the old altar platform in the main worship area. That choice provided continuity with the original design of the building, and it provided a durability that carpet would not. The cost of the floor came in at $8,752. To enhance the worship space, our consultant, Jean Poulin, suggested that the pews should be in a herringbone pattern, that the altar rail refit in the same pattern, and that the altar itself should be raised on a platform. The rearrangement of the pews, altar rail, and altar platform cost was $4,212. A gift from the estate of Zerlina Lewis allowed this work to begin, and the chapel was to be rededicated as Christ Chapel in her memory.

The funding of the work we had undertaken was completed when Boyd Braman stopped me after a Saturday evening Eucharist. Because of the work in progress, the service had been held in the main worship area, but he had made a point of peeking into the chapel to see the progress. He approached and asked me rather bluntly how much the slate floor was going to cost. When I told him, he proceeded to tell me that he was about to leave on a rather lengthy vacation in California the next day and that he would like to write a check for it then and there. While he was on his trip, he died of a heart attack. Braman had capped his long career in the funeral business by opening what became an incredible, successful funeral home based on low-cost, no-frills, and straight dealing. It was during the time when the costs of funerals were subject to exposé, and funeral directors were still resistant to cremation. His style had appealed to Pedersen, and his funeral home had become the parish's choice replacing long-standing connection with Crosby, Kunold, Burket. In the end, All Saints was his family's choice as the place for his body lie in state and for them to receive visitors. His body lay in the newly finished chapel till his funeral was held in church, after which we drove 135 miles in a most solemn procession across Southern Iowa to bury him in a country cemetery south of Winterset, making history in some strange way.

Craig Roeder, whose lighting design for the chapel was also complete by the end of the year, returned at Christmas quite ecstatic. His doctors had told him that he was AIDS-free. He was quite pleased with the way the chapel lighting had turned out and promised that he would tackle the design for the main worship space. Strangely, in the course of the coming years, he died of a heart attack while on a job in Las Vegas.

The Master Plan

The parish continued to press ahead with a capital improvement budget fashioned out of the endowment income, bequests, special gifts, and memorials. In the coming year, some of the commitments to the Pedersen retirement benefits would be finished; the parish could be more aggressive with its capital improvements. The capital improvement budget for the coming year was set at a record of $73,771. The 1996 capital plan included a major computer and copier upgrade for the office, some landscaping, and the authorizing for our architectural firm, Renaissance Design Group, to create a master plan. The cost for the master plan was $15,000. The RDG principals were Joseph Lang, AIA project master for planning and design, and John A. Sova, AIA project director. They attended and were introduced to the parish at the annual meeting held on January 28, 1996. They began to work the next day on an extensive study, which involved countless meetings with many different groups of the parish and a number of open forums.

By March, we could announce "We're On-Line! all.saints.omaha@ecunet.org." The computer upgrade had been a success, but we noted that the computer revolution brought with it a new ongoing capital expense. Unlike a typewriter, which required a ribbon to be changed from time to time, something a secretary could do herself, lasted forever, but computers required constant attention from specialists and regularly had to be replaced.

By September, the vestry was ready on the basis of the master plan to approve the production of the schematic designs, which included the expansion of the entry, an elevator, the reorganization of space downstairs in order to provide a large gathering space for the church school and for a new parish hall.

When the parish passed on into to 1997, new wardens were elected, Jim Yeates and Pat Perry. Both elections were of particular significance. Yeates was, at the time, working at AGP, a large farm co-op, which was focused on soybean processing. At the time, he was involved with building ethanol plants. Yeates brought to the job of senior warden a great deal of experience in business and construction, just as the parish was about to pivot from its planning process to its building phase. His wife, Judi, was still the parish's DRE and was rapidly approaching ordination. He had been a regular member of the choir and was profoundly interested in youth work and the educational program of the parish. The junior warden was Dr. Patricia Perry, who had previously served on the vestry. Her election made history for the parish as she was the first woman warden.

Dr. Perry was, at the time, the president of Clarkson College and was a skillful administrator particularly knowledgeable about personnel matters, which were becoming more important as we were no longer a parish focused around a rector and some incidental help. Perry had a long history with All Saints. Her name has come up in the course of the Clayton story when she and her husband were students in Omaha. We have also crossed paths with the Perrys because they had hosted Charles Pedersen when he was a seminary intern serving in the small parish in Cozad. They returned to Omaha so Sam could practice in his specialty and so Pat could take on a role in the Clarkson Nursing School. At that time, they had joined McCallum's All Saints. In remarks printed in the *Witness*, Perry said, "I would like to see increased diversity in the church's membership as I believe this strengthens the church. The planned remodeling will ease access and facilitate integration of activities. I would like to see the number of priests and deacons evaluated regularly so we can support the many church responsibilities and activities. Finally, All Saints has become the strongest church in the diocese and should continue to serve as a model for successful programs." In short, it can be said that the vestry and its leadership in 1997 were extraordinarily competent and nicely fit to the task at hand.

The RDG team had come for a second time to an annual meeting, this time with the completed schematic design and with a model that was on displayed in the narthex. Our hope was that some of the work planned for the lower level could be done during the summer of 1997 and that our major focus for the year would be on the Every Member Canvass in the fall of 1997. The success of that canvass was the gateway to launching the capital fund drive necessary to tackle the first phase of the master plan. We agreed that if the canvass was a success, we would launch the capital fund drive in February of 1998.

While the canvass was the key issue, there were some other issues that also needed to be dealt with prior to the expansion of the narthex. These had to do with the educational space and the organ, which had long been postponed, and it was important that they did not appear to be secondary to an elevator and the expansion of the narthex as if we might have to choose one or the other. We felt that we needed to complete these projects in order to sell the more visionary aspects of phase 1. At the top of the list was the long-delayed provision of an activity room for the Sunday school. When the Wiedner estate was finalized, it was clear that it would put the parish's endowment over the $2 million mark, a level that we deemed the appropriate level for the endowment at that time. It was agreed that any remainder could be used to provide a tangible memorial for the Wiedners.

The remainder was about $85,000, and it fit rather nicely to the cost of creating a large gathering area for the church school. RDG's design had solved the problem by redesigning the entry at the north end of the building to the lower level which housed the church school. It made it possible to put two large rooms, previously separated by a hall, together. The new space would be 1,200 square feet, an ample size for the purpose envisioned. Since it was under the altar area of the main church, where the upper floor was raised to form the altar platform, the room would have a twelve-foot ceiling. The result was a multipurpose activity room in which the whole church school could be gathered for a service, audio visual presentations, plays, or other group activities. It would also prove a valuable space of a wide range of adult activities as well. Moreover the design turned a drafty and rather shabby entryway on the north end of the building into a more attractive space, eliminating the blast of cold air that the old design regularly inflicted upon the main gathering space.

The second long-delayed effort was the restoration of the organ. The basic repairs had been made, but that left the replacement of the organ console and the final re-voicing of the instrument. We had authorized Reuters to build a new console, and that was due to arrive at the end of the summer. Installation of the new console required the removal of the old console and refinishing the altar and choir in order to accommodate it. This work was in part simply making the Pedersen's alterations of the altar and choir area of 1982 permanent. While we were doing it, we wanted to put the entire altar rail on the floor level of the nave to accord with our disability access guidelines. We also wanted the blue carpet that

Pedersen had use in the altar and choir area to disappear for aesthetic reason and because it presented a major obstacle to the organs finding it full voice in the space. The bid for the work that summer went to Hawkins Construction Company, and by July 1, the work was begun.

It was the habit of the vestry to do the initial planning for the fall Every Member Canvass at its June meeting so that the canvass was well under way as the summer began. Bob Henrichsen, who had agreed to chair this crucial canvass, was given time during the June meeting to discuss what it would take to make it successful. He said in his opinion it would be crucial for everyone to be contacted in a personal way that not only allowed the parish to ask support, but also for the parishioners to express concerns. The canvass would include a means of recording comments and questions that could be reviewed and responded to by the parish's leadership. Henrichsen was an experienced canvasser, and he was dedicated to making this the most thorough canvass All Saints had ever experienced.

As the work began that summer, I had to leave construction matters in the hands of Jim Yeates, our senior warden, as I was heading for the general convention in Philadelphia. From there, I issued an extensive report to the parish on what was transpiring at the convention. The report, sent by e-mail, was published in a special issue of the *Witness* as events were unfolding. I reported that it was an extremely busy convention. It elected Frank Griswold as presiding bishop, and it passed a Concordat of Agreement, recognizing that the Evangelical Lutheran Church in America "possesses the essentials of the one, Catholic and apostolic faith" and that "the full authenticity of the ordained ministries" presently exists within it. Both of these actions where quite positive and carried with them a great deal of promise for the future. On the other hand, the debate over women's ordination was more negative. It focused on what to do with the four dioceses who would not recognize women priest. That was followed by another painful debate concerning homosexuality. Neither discussion contributed anything to the long-range resolution of these issues.

In explaining that I had voted with a slim majority to withhold, for the time being, approval of the ordination of openly homosexual individuals, I wrote in this report:

> I reject any simple condemnation of homosexuals and insist that the only sins are promiscuity, abuse, infidelity, etc. They are, after all, brothers and sisters trying to live their lives in the same way we all struggle to do. They have a place at the altar with us, confessing their sins and receiving the communion of God's love. Thus far I have voted in the majority against the blessing

> of same-sex relationships and the acceptance of the ordination of practicing homosexuals because thus far we do not know what we are blessing or how this particular life commitment works within the sacramental commitment to priesthood. Clearly this is my limitation, but I must be led by it because it is my only way of being authentic. It becomes a problem only if I refuse to look at new evidence and admit the possibility of new experiences. This commitment to learn and to be open to new experiences is important for all of us to accept.

It was, if I remember it right, when I returned that summer that the new senior warden began to greet me with the question: "Well, Rector, is everything under control?" A lot would continue to be on our plate as we moved into the fall. My reply was, "Just barely." In all likelihood, that is best control can get. The discussion in August reaffirmed the strategy that a successful Every Member Canvass was the essential basis for launching a capital fund drive in February. As we looked ahead to a capital fund drive, there was never any question raised about hiring outside help. The leadership of the parish had been schooled by Pedersen that it could be done with resources within the parish, and his influence on me had convinced me of the same. It fell to me to find the right chairs and then to identify major gifts prior the opening of the drive. These advanced gifts would determine the reach of the drive. Our architectural firm had provided us with an estimate of $800,000 to do phase 1, which consisted of the narthex expansion, the elevator linking the three levels, and a full bathroom core for the upper and lower levels. The upper-level bathroom core was designed to service both a major service in the worship space and a major event in a future parish hall envisioned in phase 2. In addition the new space was to provide a gift shop and a choir room.

The fall of 1998 was intensely busy. We had, among other things, decided to launch a new youth program that fall. Judi Yeates, our DRE, had attended a national church conference on Christian education and was particularly enamored with a new program introduced there called Journey to Adulthood or J2A for short. This required us to look at how it would fit in with our ambitious confirmation program that we had been conducting for the past twenty-some years.

Our confirmation program was built on ten hours of tutorial instruction by one of the priests for each of the seventh and eighth graders in the parish. Focused in the fall, this meant that both Father Belsky and I met students three or four afternoons a week as well as Saturday morning. This program, which was now nearly twenty years old, was built in reaction to the norm across the Episcopal Church of minimal confirmation programs whose outcomes were regularly faulted. The running joke was that three ministers get together for lunch. The Baptist raised the question about trouble with squirrels. "Oh yes," the Methodist said, "we have trouble with squirrels too." The turn fell to the Episcopalian, who replied, "We used to have trouble, but then we started confirming them, and we never see them again." The prayer book revision in the eighties had come very close to eliminating confirmation, something that I considered a serious mistake. There was some indication that J2A was being presented as one more way around confirmation.

After a good deal of study, we, however, came to the conclusion that we could make the two things work together. We launched it on December 14 with the first liturgical "rite of passage." The first pilgrimage was made to San Francisco in 2000. In 2014, the most recent pilgrimage returned from New York City, and it seems clear that this pattern will continue.

At the same time that J2A was being added as follow-up to confirmation, another addition to the youth program was made, which preceded confirmation. It was called All Stars and was led by the parish nurse, Stephanie Ulrich. It took six graders though a ten-week course designed to equip the young person with prevention strategies as they enter the age group, which was exposed to risk behavior. The parish's effort was carried out in collaboration with the Nebraska Council to Prevent Alcohol and Drug Abuse. By February, the first class of kids was presented to the congregation for its "All Stars" reward. This is a good example of the many ways the continuing health ministry was affecting various populations within the parish.

The parish was also active in a wide range of social ministries. These efforts were highlighted, when Jerry Lucas, one of All Saints African Americans members, received the Bishop's Award for Evangelism and Service at annual council. The award recognized his efforts to establish a computerized reading lab in the Omaha metropolitan area to help young children overcome deficiencies in reading. It is difficult to adequately express how much this meant to me and to the parish. On the one hand, here was All Saints being represented at annual council by an African American; and on the other hand, the diocese was recognizing work with the disadvantaged children of the city as evangelism!

These commitments to sustain and expand the programs of the parish actually assisted our push to carry through on the building project because it sent the clear message that we were not focused on building but on being a bigger more active parish. This set the tone for the very crucial Every Member Canvass that was launched in October. We advertised the canvass as the "Clearing the Way Canvass." It started strong, but as canvasses do, it dragged on through the end of the year. Finally, by January 12, 1999, the canvass committee could report to the vestry that as of that date, there was $392,000 pledged by 305 units. This represented a 3.7 percent increase over the previous year. At the annual meeting the following week, the vestry reported that they had adopted an ambitious operating budget for the coming year. The way had been cleared.

Shortly into the new year, we could not only announce that we would proceed with the major building fund drive, we could also make a historic announcement that Judi Yeates had completed her requirements for ordination and would be ordained on April 29 at All Saints. She had accepted our call to stay at All Saints and would serve as the third priest for whom we had long hoped and sought, but to no avail. Moreover, it meant that All Saints would have its first woman priest. Scarcely a decade before, Dr. Kelsey's suggestion to the vestry that the parish should hire a woman priest had been rebuffed, but now the parish would take the step of doing so; and in spite of some reserve on the part of a few individuals, it would do so with enthusiasm. I told the annual meeting in making the announcement, "I think it is especially important that All Saints has the experience of a woman priest and I can think of no candidate more qualified, male or female, to make that happen."[234] Yeates would prove those remarks true. The parish not only was moving into new territory, but it was also keeping a very strong team in tack.

The other thing that the annual meeting heard that year was that we were in the position to undertake an ambitious list of capital improvements for the coming year even while we were pursuing the capital fund drive. The list of these improvements began with moving the nursery to the first floor, something that had been talked about for several years. Even more ambitious, it proposed to redoing the bathrooms on the lower level. They were in poor repair, too small to meet the demand, and made no provision for the disabled. The plan for the bathroom remodel, like that of activity room, was part of the master plan, and getting it done in 1998 was another example of clearing the way for the larger building program proposed for the coming year. The size of the women's bathroom would be doubled, and the men's bathroom would be enlarged by 50 percent. The increase in size was made possible by moving the choir vesting area upstairs and coopting the two choir dressing rooms on the lower level, which were adjacent to the two existing bathrooms. At the same time, the rearrangement of space made it possible to create the hall for the future elevator, which would join

[234] *Witness*, February 13, 1998, p. 6.

the three levels of the building, removing the last set of stairs limiting access.

We were fortunate to have just received funds from Jim Paxton's estate, which we had planned to use for this purpose. The great surprise was an unexpected, very generous donation of $100,000 from a person who insisted on remaining anonymous. This person was motivated by her experience of having been raised with a disabled sister who had been kept out of the public eye as was commonly done during that period. It was the way that these remodels were pointed at facilitating the presence of the disabled among us that had inspired her. This stroke of luck was due very much to Ulrich, our health minister, and her committee's advocacy the past five years for enhancing accessibility to all of the parish's facilities.

Having summarized these projects we expected to complete the coming summer, I added "We are, however, approaching the point where further projects will require a major fund drive." This signaled the launch of a capital fund drive in the fast-approaching spring. In fact, I had never led a major fund drive, and what I knew about it was largely from what I had learned by observing and listening to Charles Pedersen, for whom I had worked for sixteen years. Rule 1, according to Pedersen, was don't pay experts to come in and tell you to do what is obvious. Rule 2, since no one else knows the parish like the rector, it is necessary for the rector to locate those two or three major gifts without which the drive cannot meet its goal. According to Pedersen, this would need to be 20 to 25 percent of the goal. Rule 3, the parish needed to produce a creditable brochure to advertise and explain the project.

Why the vestry was prepared to trust me was not altogether clear. Perhaps it was because they had been schooled by Pedersen to trust the rector. Perhaps it was that I was telegraphing a credible confidence as I had learned in officer leadership school! Freed from any pressure to bring in hired guns, I set to work on the brochure problem by approaching Jack and Dick Barnhart. The result was the gift to the parish from Barnhart Press of the design and printing for an exceptionally fine piece that was attractive, persuasive, and pragmatic. The cover expressed the theme of "a people processing into the twenty-first century." The interior reproduced the key schematics and renderings of the RDG's master plan alongside of a concise but full explanation of the significant additions proposed to our building. The last three pages provided a process for an individual to work toward his or her decision of what form and how much they could contribute to the capital fund. The first step in the process was the examination of one's pledge to the annual operating budget. What was it last year? What would it be for the coming year? What would you like to see it be at the end of five years? The point of this exercise was to drive home the fact that the first and most basic way to support the building project was to support the annual operation of the parish to the best of one's ability. It was stated in the campaign that for some, their way of participating in the building drive was sustaining and strengthening their annual giving. The second step was to review one's ability to give a share of one's capital to the parish. The exercise even presented reasons not to give to the capital fund drive, such as being young and not yet having accumulated capital of one's own, in which case they should concentrate on their annual giving, or being too old and therefore anxious about present and future care costs, in which case they should consider making provision in their will for the parish.

After the brochure, the next task was to identify major gifts and to appoint the chairs for the drive. One of my first visits was to Carroll and Barbara Fredrickson who were, in fact, ready for me. They were prepared to make one of the crucial major gifts, but they did not want any special recognition. They did, however, accept my request that they would serve as honorary chairpersons for the campaign, which was a great help in lending credence to the effort, coming as it did from a couple who was so important to the success of the Pedersen years. Geof Heiden was an obvious choice out of the new leadership of the parish and was quick to say yes. The choice from the other end of the spectrum of the parish, the old parish, was less obvious. My choice was Noni Wells Lundgren. Her husband was one of those "Midwestern work ethic" individuals who made Kiewit Construction an international company capable of punching well above its weight. While they were both well known in the parish, neither she nor he had been involved in the leadership of the parish. She was a Wells and, with her five older brothers, had been raised in the parish. More recently, she was widowed, and my thought was that she just might be ready to step into a leadership role. She not only said yes to my request to chair the drive, but she also surprised me with a major gift that put us over the 20 percent mark. It was clear that we had reached the point where the rest could be done with good solid hard work.

During the course of the summer, the red in the giant cardboard thermometer, which hung on the narthex wall, slowly edged up toward the goal of $850,000. Its success had, in some ways, to do with timing. The 1990s had begun with a recession, and a cautious financial outlook had lingered on long past the time when the recovery had actually begun. When the diocese looked at the possibility of a capital fund drive in 1995, it had decided that economy was too weak to support it. The call was made by the outside consultant, which was unusual since outside consultants are seldom negative about one's prospects. I thought at the time that this assessment was overly pessimistic, for even by then, the country was better off than it thought. In the next three years, the recovery continued, but the country and Omaha, in particular, continued to be cautious. Things, however, were changing and then, and just as we launched our drive, Omaha's Keiwit spun off its fiber optics operation, level 3, in an incredibly successful IPO. This affected a number of individuals in the parish directly, and overall, it gave Omaha a sense of self confidence, which it had lost with Enron's move to Houston in 1986.

All Saints had found the sweet spot for a capital fund drive. We were among the first to launch a major drive, and the drive was concluded and substantially banked before a wave of other drives were launched. Faced again in the fall with another crucial canvass, the chairs were carefully chosen. Our fear was that the success of the capital fund drive might have come at the cost of the annual canvass. Jim Well, Noni Lundgren's brother, was chosen to represent the elderly, and that part of the parish rooted in the old All Saints. He had just turned seventy-eight, and like his sister, he had been raised in the parish but, unlike his sister, had been very involved in parish leadership, frequently serving on the vestries during the McCallum and Pedersen years. He more recently emerged as the very visible and faithful head usher. Also, unlike his sister, he was not in the position to make a capital gift, but he was ready to push his retirement income to the limit to support the parish. The other chair was Debbie Klein, who, at the time, was forty-seven and president of the ECW. Klein was a remarkable parish leader and deserves to be ranked among the exceptional lay leaders in the course of the parish's history. The Kleins were new to the parish and were both raised outside of Sioux City, Iowa. They were new to the Episcopal Church. Debbie was a Clarkson Hospital RN, known in the hospital as a tireless, highly professional, but profoundly compassionate person. Karl worked as a draftsman for a local manufacture, Lozier Corporation. In the parish, Debbie was identified with the compassionate outreach of the parish and particularly with the women-in-need project. She and her husband quietly tithed their income. Together, Klein and Wells gave the parish a strong message about who we were and who we wanted to be. In the wake of the capital fund drive, the Every Member Canvass of 1998 succeeded in continuing the expansion of support for the operation of the parish, which had been increasing since 1995 by 3 to 4 percent annually.

As the year moved to its end, "an Historic Ordination" was scheduled for November 1, All Saints Day, which happened that year to fall on a Sunday. In the morning, a congregation of three hundred gathered for its patronal feast; and again, in the evening at seven, another congregation of three hundred witnessed Bishop Krotz ordain Judi Yeates to the priesthood. The announcement in the October *Witness* read, "This event will represent several firsts: Judi will be the first woman ordained to the priesthood at All Saints and, even more significantly, Judi will also be the first woman priest called to work at All Saints . . . I urge you to be present for this special event. Particularly, I would urge you to bring your children who will then be able to say at some future time, "I was there when . . ."[235]

In the opening issue of 1999, the *Witness* said little about building and finance but was dedicated to healing and health ministries. This was one more attempt at saying that, as significant as the proposed building was, "doing more better," the theme of the past Every Member Canvass, the central thrust of the parish, remained its multifold ministries. The coming season of Epiphany, according to the article, would be devoted "to the mystery of healing," which it contended was particularly appropriate in a year in which the Gospel of Luke would supply most of the readings from the Gospels. The *Witness* went on to explain that on the Sunday that fell on January 24, a special commemoration would be held of God's healing grace as it is expressed in our intercessory prayers for the sick in the celebration of the sacrament of the sick as part of the liturgy and in thanksgiving for the healing vocations of the physicians and nurses of our parish. The ten-thirty celebration of Holy Eucharist was to include a dialogue sermon preached by myself and Dr. Richard Collins, MD. An active member of our parish, Collins was a prominent cardiologist in the city and was well known as a backer of the celebrated Ornish diet. He frequently appeared on Omaha television prompting healthy eating and lifestyles. In the issue of the *Witness*, there were series of other articles on healing: "Recognizing Your Own Need," by myself; "Instruments of Healing," by Stephanie Ulrich; "Elsewhere," by Ann McConney; and "When It Happens to You" by Judith Gray. Dr. Collins returned later that year, on September 26, as "the cooking cardiologist" and provided a cooking class-lecture and dinner for the parish.

Deciding to Build

As our general program for the new year was focusing on health issues, our committee on architecture and landscape was taking one last look at the building plans. Everything seemed good as it was, except the committee advised the vestry that they thought that it would be a good use of the parish's construction dollars to fully excavate the lower level. By then, it was clear

235 *Witness*, October 20, 1998, p. 16.

that our financing was secure, and the additional cost for the three thousand square feet of space would be a bargain. It was easy to see how that space could be developed at some future time as office, storage, and/or classroom space and hard to see when and how it could be had at another time.

When the vestry met in January, it listened to a series of reports. First came the report on the past Every Member Canvass, which had met its goal. Then they heard the report that the past capital campaign showed that pledges now totaled $861,293 and that the campaign had already received and banked $598,517. Finally came the report of the committee on architecture and landscape, which concluded with the recommendation that the vestry accept a bid from Hawkins Construction. The vestry subsequently voted to approve their recommendations, including the contract with Hawkins, whose bid was "cost not to exceed $825,000."

It felt good to have reached this point in the process and particularly good that Hawkins would be our builder. Hawkins had built the original building in 1963 to 1964 and had considerable pride in the work that they had done. Their project manager this time would be Dudley Rinaker, who was, with his family, an active member of the parish. The choice of Hawkins, however, was not based on preference but on the fact that it had presented the best bid in a highly competitive process. Construction was scheduled to begin on May 26, 1999, and was to be completed on October 26, 1999. With a confidence that might seem to have been constructed of more wish than reason, it was announced to the parish that the dedication of the completed project would take place on All Saints Sunday of that year, November 6, 1999.

The new narthex added to the 1964 building in 1999.

Once it was clear that the construction project would go ahead, the vestry entertained the idea that a project of such significance ought to include a substantial work of art. Our architects had suggested to us at an earlier point in the process that we should consider something significant as it was a common practice for major public and corporate projects to designate as much as 2.5 to 5 percent of the construction budget for such a purpose for art. Consequently, we had already begun a conversation with a local sculptor, Littleton Alston, who had recently emerged on the Omaha art scene.[236] His ideas matured into a large figure to be cast in bronze representing "the elder" referred to in the book of Revelation. In December, Alston had been invited to meet with the vestry to discuss his ideas, and he was asked to revisit the vestry in January with a final proposal for "a millennial angle." At the same meeting at which the vestry approved the contract with Hawkins, they approved a contract with Alston, which called for the installation of the sculpture on or before the dedication. Alas, it is one thing to hold builders to deadlines and another to hold artists! *The Elder*, as it turned out, would be installed on March 25, 2000, a delay which gave it its own special moment.

As we moved into the construction season, we tried to remain focused on the management and ministry of our parish life. Father Belsky had, by that time, completed six years as our assistant and was qualified for a sabbatical, a thing that he richly deserved. It helped that Yeates had been ordained and could take on many of his duties. Moreover, the program was scaled back during the coming summer in anticipation of the disruption that would result from construction. The portion of the endowment that had been dedicated to support the clergy had accrued sufficient funds to grant Belsky $10,000 as it had for me in 1992 and Pedersen in 1993. Belsky's sabbatical began on May 1. It consisted of a weeklong spiritual retreat, three courses at Creighton, and a trip to England and Ireland in July, a total absence of three months. Belsky, who was hesitant at first, made excellent use of the time and brought back to the parish and his ministry many valuable gifts.

The spring of 1999 found the interior world of the parish very upbeat, but the world around it was suddenly engulfed in a number of troubling issues. The world was agonized by events in Kosovo, the country, by the castigations of Rev. Jerry Falwell and Richard Reid made against its moral character and the city of Omaha by a bond issue for the Omaha Public School District. It might seem that preoccupation with a capital project

[236] Littleton Alston was a professor of art at Creighton University. For more information about his work and this project, see the discussion in Appendix 1: Landscape, Architecture, and Art at All Saints, p. 492.

the size of which All Saints was undertaking would have been a sufficient excuse for ignoring these issues. It was not the parish's style. We had always insisted that we could walk and chew gum at the same time. The April *Witness* carried a lead article entitled "On Votes and Wars and Other Things." The article announced that on May 9 Dr. Walter Bacon would make a presentation on Kosovo and the Balkan Crisis.[237] In addition, an information session was scheduled at which a number of our professionals involved with OPS would provide information about the bond issue. OPS had in fact been without a capital budget for some time, and the district had been solving building issues by means of temporary structures paid for out of operational funds. The lead article in the *Witness* noted, "It is not the way to run a church, let alone a business." Urging members to vote in the May 11 election, it went on to say, "The Gospel will not tell you how to vote. It will tell you to love the children of this city, all the children of this city, and then to vote the way you see fit. But it is very important that you vote because, whatever your vote is, it will (as we are called to do) infuse the process with love."[238]

Breaking Ground

The spring rain began to taper off as May drew to an end. On May 25, Catherine (Cassie) Hancock walked down the aisle and took Eric Arneson to be her lawfully wedded husband, having the distinction that her wedding had set the date for the construction to begin. The following day was Pentecost Sunday, and as the service ended, an unusual procession formed in front of the altar. Besides the cast of crucifers and acolytes, the choir, ministers of the altar were the wardens, Jim Yeates and Debbie Klein; Nick and Cassandra Boston, representing their grandmother Noni Lundgren; Geof Heiden, the other chair of the Capital Fund Drive; Jane Comstock, representing ECW; Conrad Young and Art Pinkerton, representing the 1963 vestry, which had built the present structure; and Rev. Charles L. R. Pedersen, the former rector of the parish. As they left the building, they were met by Dudley Rinaker, Hawkins's project manager. With him

237 Dr. Walter Bacon was a professor of political science at the University of Nebraska in Omaha and an extremely active member of the parish since the 1970s. He was often called upon to speak of social issues. In 2004, Bacon underwent gender change and continues in the parish as Dr. Meredith Bacon, still active and called upon for her insights.

238 *Witness*, April 16, 1999, pp. 1 and 6.

were Joe Lang, John Sova, and Robert Kroupa, representing RDG, our architectural firm for the past four years. A silver spade was passed among our dignitaries, and ground was broken.

With this began an intense effort to maximize the results of the building project and to bring it home on schedule began. The schedule called for the front doors to be back in use by September 12 "Kick off Sunday." All the remaining construction was supposed to be done by the end of October so the dedication could be celebrated on All Saints Sunday. Those that doubted that this could be done were overlooking the people involved. Since Hawkins's bid was cost not to exceed, they had a strong incentive to work with us and for us to work with them. Hawkins on site manager, John Halford, was an experienced pragmatic builder. He had been involved with our preliminary projects the past two years and had come to like working at All Saints. This was facilitated by Deacon Bowerman, who knew the building inside out and who liked being involved in a building project. Bowerman socialized with John and the crew, seeing that they had what they needed and that they were treated to All Saints hospitality. Bowerman spent several hours daily in the construction area and frequently spotted things that made things easier for Hawkins's or the result more favorable for us. I, myself, visited the construction area daily and was always ready for a briefing from Ernie. We were also blessed with RDG's site manager, Robert Kroupa. He worked very hard at his job and was ready to deal with us about any concern or suggestion that we might have or that Hawkins had.

An example of how this worked was coming to terms with how to finish the area immediately outside of the new front doors, which had been rather vague in the plan. A design emerged from a collaboration of ourselves, Hawkins and RDG, which was able to speed completion and yet to anticipate phase 3. By reducing the plan to a retaining wall at a height required for phase 3 and two parallel walks from each set of the front door, it could be done quickly without steps. The area between the walks and on their flanks would be treated with brick, which we agreed to provide. We, which meant Bowerman and I, laid the pavers and fill the open area with plantings. It was one of many negotiations that made the project come in on time and under budget. As we moved toward the end of the summer with so many things apparently left to finish, the *Witness* published a picture of John Halford, Hawkins on-site manager, with the heading "John Says It Will Be Done!" And it was.

To mark the completion of this effort, we cooked a meal for the construction crew and their families to honor the work they had done.

With Bowerman's help and a few other volunteers, no doubt including my wife, we served them a mini-spaghetti supper and toasted a job well done.

The interior of the new narthex added to the 1964 building in 1999 on a Sunday morning.

Beyond Construction

Life had gone on during the summer of construction. A parish meeting was held for those who might be interested in joining a pilgrimage to the Holy Land the following February. It was to be a part of a sabbatical for me and an experience for the parish, which would add to its identity the concept of being a Pilgrimage community. In July, a planning group readied itself for the Appreciation Day for Police and Firefighters, which had been held for the past several years. The retreat center was opened beginning at 2:00 a.m. for a breakfast for officers on the night shift and for a picnic lunch and dinner for the following shifts. The churchyard was filled with fire trucks and police cruisers during most of the day, and it was even visited that year by the police department's helicopter. As August came, Dr. Bacon reported to the vestry about the work of the parish's Kosovo Committee, which had established a contact with the Islamic Center of Omaha. Father Belsky took on a special role in these contacts, and a significant relationship was established with the Islamic community. This was aided by a parishioner, Karen Falconer, a very bright young woman who was a professor of geography at UNO. Karen, who was raised in St. Luke's Kearney, had recently married a Moslem at a service at All Saints conducted by Father Belsky. The service had included the participation of an imam. A sensitive effort of assistance and dialogue continued for some time.

In that summer, I received an invitation to teach a course at Creighton University because one of the members of the theology department was taking a sabbatical. It was a particularly tempting invitation because it was a new upper-level course, which had not been written and had simply been entitled the Defense of Christianity. This would require me to write thirty-four original lectures, a substantial effort, to prepare for the thirty-four classes, the student conferences, and the assigning of grades that would follow in the fall. I had said yes, so a lot of my spare time that summer was spent writing lectures. It was, in the end, an opportunity to experience the alternative life that I had passed up for the pastoral ministry.

When Labor Day weekend came that year, it rained hard, really hard, and the September *Witness* apologized:

> Sorry to rain on your parade. We did need to schedule rain on the Labor Day weekend in order to assure a dry week following for your construction team. Yes, we will walk through the new front doors on September 12. Yes we will return to the Chapel on September 11. The drive is being laid across the front as this edition of the *Witness* is being put into the mail.

This same *Witness* announced the commencement of my teaching duties at Creighton and offered an explanation of the course.

> What I hope to do is equip students with the ability to invite faith, whether out of themselves or others. If, as I perceive it to be the case, that faith lies in each of us, at the heart of who we are, causing someone to discover what they already have is not a way to have one up on them. It is not a way to gain power over anyone. But then, such a viewpoint is inconsistent with Christianity in the first place.[239]

[239] *Witness*, September 10, 1999, p. 3.

Envisioning a New Century

With the beginning of 2000, it was time for the parish to elect a new senior warden. Jim Yeates, who had been the perfect warden to guide the parish through a season of construction, was replaced by Joe Barker, the perfect warden to lead the parish in an expansion of its vision for the new century. Barker, of course, had been part of the senior leadership of the parish for some time, having played key roles during the McCallum and Pedersen years. He was "an idea man," and with the building issues settled, the time was ripe for challenging new ideas. There would, of course, continue to be a substantial effort to upgrade the parish's working capital. The vestry had accepted a plan in the previous December meeting for the capital projects during 2000, which included more landscaping projects, the expansion of the columbarium, moving the pulpit outside of the altar rail, rebuilding the altar rail, covering the sanctuary floor with ceramic tiles, an adult ed/conference room in the new lower level, an additional parking area, a four octave set of Schulmerich hand bells, a new rank for the pipe organ, and the planning for an expansion of the village.

On February 15, 2000, the pilgrims, fifteen in all, took off for Israel. The group included Barbara Coffey, Joyce Dodrill, Dorothy Harris, Bob and Sula Grace Henrichsen, Millicent Long, Tillie McIntire, Sam and Edna Morford, Alice Tucker, Fred and Stephanie Ulrich, Nancy Wulf, my wife, Jane, and myself. The group was diverse and rich with experience. The two cousins, Barbara and Millicent, had grown up in North Omaha. Tillie McIntire was one of Omaha's first women doctors. She was famous for have climbed over the fence at ASARCO to document the lead presence in the soil on its grounds in the 1950s. An expert on pediatric health care, she had been to Israel several times to speak at international medical conferences, but she, a vibrant eighty, said she wanted to go, as she put it, "for herself." The group had a strong sense of themselves as representatives of the parish and felt themselves under an obligation to bring something back for the parish. Shortly after their return, J2A would leave for a pilgrimage for San Francisco, the first in this new program at All Saints. "It is hoped," I wrote in the *Witness* as we departed, "that we are adding a further dimension to the identity of All Saints as a pilgrimage church."

The sculpture of the elder, which the parish had commissioned as part of it building expansion, arrived five months late on March 25. The sizable group gathered to watch the two-thousand-pound piece of bronze lifted into place, firmly bolted, and blessed. They were convinced that it had been meant to miss its original completion date so not to share its day with anything else. Meanwhile, work had begun on the floor in the main worship area. The goal was to cover the altar area with ceramic tiles. The Italian ceramic travertine, blended with accents of the original slate, which had been used in the narthex and the original altar area. No doubt the original architect had envisioned the entire floor being slate but had to settle for a rather dull gray asbestos laced tile to stay within his budget. In the course of time, much of it had been covered with blue carpet, which severely compromised the room's acoustics. This new application looked to permanence and to an enhancement of the room's acoustics. The hope was that the altar area could be done for Easter so that when the parish made its Easter Communion, the congregation could kneel for a first time at an altar rail that was unimpeded by any steps.

As Easter approached, it appeared that once again we would meet a deadline, if just barely. Lingering after that Easter service, giving the work a redundant inspection, I was approached by the woman who had just completed her duties on the altar guild. "What?" she asked. "What would it take to complete it?' I was a little vague in my mind both from the fatigue of the Easter liturgies and from the press of getting this latest phase of the project finished, but I ventured the guess that it could be completed for another $50,000–$60,000. She replied, "Let's do it. I will make a donation that will more than cover it." It was a startling opportunity and yet humbling for Noni Lundgren, who had already been the chair of the capital fund drive and had already made a major contribution to the building program.

In order to do the nave floor, however, a couple of other issues had to be addressed as well. The stained-glass windows, which Pedersen had been moved out of the bays into the wall line, would need to be put back into the bays and the stored glass restored to them. This presented a risk that Pedersen's insistence that the church could not be properly heated with them in their original position would come back to haunt me. I had, however, never been convinced that was the case. We had made in the last seven years a large number of fixes to the heating and cooling system, which I hoped would solve the problem. Clearly, the enhanced aesthetic in space made the risk worthwhile.

It was also an opportunity to enhance the beauty of the space, not simply from the quality of the tile, but by creating in the floor significant mosaics. We began a conversation with Wilson Tile of Omaha, who had done several significant mosaics in the city. We asked them to develop a proposal for a mosaic in the baptismal area, which would make use of the themes of running water and fish, and for a second mosaic for the crossing, or we have come to call our Gospel area, which was to be a version of the Shield of the Anglican Communion.

With the arrival of Palm Sunday, it was time to seal the "Time Capsule." The date had been chosen because the first service held in the new building in 1964 had been on Palm Sunday. The cover for the time capsule had been made from the end of 1906 cornerstone, which included an incised cross. It was old, used in a new way. The other part of the 1906 cornerstone had already built into the west wall of the new narthex. Together, the time capsule, the 1906 cornerstone across the way from it, and the newly relocated Muller glass with the added panels naming the original vestry of 1885 and the vestry of 1963, which had built the present building, provided a kind of permanent history lesson for the parish. Those who gathered shared a sense that they were hoping to send a message to those who would come here at some distant future and who, upon opening that capsule, would remember them as they were at that moment remembering the many who had gone before them.

The opportunity to complete the floor in the church meant another summer project and another spell in which we would have to make special arrangements for carrying out worship in and around a space under construction. Like the other projects, this one led to others. A finished floor meant painting and repairing the walls. And if we were painting and repairing the walls, some raised the quest if we shouldn't also be installing a permanent set of stations of the cross. For many years, we had been hanging temporary paper stations around the nave during Lent, and a growing group felt that they should be permanent. Part of the support came from the recently returned pilgrims who had walked the Via Dolorosa together and had found it a profoundly moving experience. Incorporating permanent stations in a worship space raised a number of issues. In most cases, stations take on a prominence that overstates their role in the liturgy and are usually out of character with the architecture of the space. The pilgrims had also walked the stations at the Anglican Cathedral of St. George's in Jerusalem, where a new set of stations had been installed for the millennial celebration. They had been done by an Armenian company in Jerusalem known for their ceramic work. The guide at St. George's had told them that a second identical set had been made in case something happened during their installation of the original set, which we had subsequently seen at a visit to the studio. This set seemed an ideal fit for our need, and the arrangement was made to import them from Jerusalem. The new stations were dedicated on September 14, the Feast of the Holy Cross, in memory of Dorothy Harris, one of the participants on the past pilgrimage.

As that summer ended, the vestry endorsed Robert Henrichsen for the diaconate, suggesting that the diaconal program, which had begun in 1980, would continue on well into the new century. The vestry received an extensive report on the health ministry from Stephanie Ulrich, the parish nurse, as she was commonly known in the parish. At general convention the past year, she had been part of the national leadership, which had manned a very successful booth. General convention had gone on to pass a resolution endorsing health care advocacy. With that support behind them, the national church's health ministry organization had begun offering a leadership course for the purpose of educating people for Episcopal Health Ministry and Parish Nursing. This included the creation of a curriculum, which Ulrich had a role in creating.

The renewal of the building continued at a steady pace. A snapshot of where we were at as we entered that fall is provided by some remarks of mine published in the *Witness*:

> With a sense of deep gratitude, I wish to report that we are close to being finished with the lion's share of the work of renovating our church . . . This will allow us to concentrate on the ministries of teaching and visitation which are so crucial to who we are. I am surprised to look into our worship space and see the window bays restored and the slate/ceramic floor in place. These were goals that I had promised to reach before the end of my tenure here. This is not an announcement of the shorting of that tenure, but an announcement that we will search for new goals!

One such goal was to continue to improve our relationship with the diocese. Going into the December meeting, the vestry was informed that the diocese had reduced its asking, which was in line with a new formula that All Saints had been advocating for some time. They responded by approving the acceptance of the full asking, $75,941, and for the first time since the early seventies, All Saints cheerfully met the full asking. That added greatly to our satisfaction when we looked back over seven years of working together.

We challenged ourselves in this final year of the twentieth century to record a set of numbers that would serve as a landmark for future generations to use as they engaged in the continued journey of the parish. Numbers are quixotic, and the picture they portray is little more than the bare bones of a skeleton. They fall far short of portraying the life itself. Still they provide the rack upon which that life hangs, and in the back of my mind, I could hear my predecessor Pedersen saying to me, "Let's do the numbers." At the end of 2000, we counted 1,273 baptized members. During that year, there had been 158 additions to the communicant list and 28 removals due to deaths or transfers. The average Sunday attendance was 390. There had been 310 signed pledges for a total $447,000 pledged income. The operating budget for that year was $546,064. The parish had spent an additional $793,571 in capital improvement, the end of a long series of capital expenditures. Capital spending the first two years of my tenure had been zero while we were getting our feet on the ground. In 1995, an accelerating pace of capital expenditures began. By the end of 2000, the total capital investment in our facility stood at $2,120,160, a sum that seems, in retrospect, hard to believe. I am not sure that I was ever clear about this total at the time, and I remain unclear about how it happened except to say that we had been particularly lucky with our timing, and we worked very hard. In terms of the numbers themselves, the size of the parish had not change that much. As Pedersen had often observed to me with frustration, "It is amazing that the numbers do not change that much."

Standing upon these numbers, however, did not provide or give us any sense of being on solid ground. It had been an election year in America fraught with ambiguity. In September, I found myself trying to deal with the troubling politics that seemed to be washing over the country and clouding the future of the parish. Political language, in the course of the year, had incorporated a great deal of religious language into its own. Joe Liberman, the Democratic Party's nominee for vice president, was Jewish. Like the John Kennedy nomination, it raised speculation of what it would mean to have a Jewish president. The evangelical right, led by Pat Robinson and Jerry Falwell, was holding forth in the national media, claiming that the country stood on the edge of an apocalypse. Nebraskans had an amendment on their ballot to make it unconstitutional for anyone to unite two persons of the same sex in civil union or in a domestic partnership. The irony was that the more religious the language of politics became, the more difficult it was for individuals to be religious.

It seemed to me that what was happening was the fourth great reawakening in American life. These earlier reawakenings had never been very conducive for the well-being of the Episcopal Church. There was much to suggest that this one would also imply that the Episcopal Church was irrelevant and apparently incapable of finding the groove in which it could prosper. In part, this is because the great awakenings have promoted religious conflict. Some religious bodies have a way of thriving on conflict. The Episcopal Church inherited a preference for consensus, as we have previously pointed out, from its mother church in England, and it has never been good at taking sides. If the Episcopal Church, All Saints in particular, was going to continue to thrive in the twenty-first century, it would need to redefine the issue. I was working at this task in my preaching, and it is somewhat surprising to me in retrospect that I had put the issue on the front page of the 2000 September *Witness*. The September issue was always devoted to reenergizing participation in parish programs as they restarted in the fall. The article was entitled "To Be Religious and Political." The article argued

> this reawakening is in part a reaction to a foreign policy that attempted to exempt itself from morality (Vietnam, Chile, Nicaragua) and an economic policy that attempted to exempt itself from questions of justice (racism, sexism and the Reagan–Thatcher economics). The hunger that unites the different parts of this reawakening is the hunger for a sense of community, a hunger which the triumphs of modernity and technology have failed.

The conclusion to which the argument came was

> patience with the political process is the required virtue of the citizen of a just society, even as perseverance with religious conviction is the required virtue of a person of faith. What a religious reawakening should seek out of politics is a fair space to accomplish the work of being together. The future of the family, of morality, and of religion, lies not in legislation, and far less in constitutional edicts, but in the time and effort each of us gives to these endeavors.[240]

All Saints had made good use of the nineties and, for all the uneasiness about the future, there was an even chance that it could do so during the first decade of the twenty-first century. The canvass theme that year was "Greeting the New Millennium," which had been chosen to express that optimism and as a way of pivoting our focus from what we had been and what we had done to what we needed to do and who we were called to be. The lead article in the October *Witness* spoke of "The Century of Opportunity." It explained that "This was not a simplistic hope that the 21st century would somehow turn out to be really new" but rather the

[240] *Witness 2000*, September 8, 2000, pp. 1–2.

conviction that, by means of the proper identification of the mission of the parish, it would prove to be relevant. The article concluded:

> The opportunity at All Saints is to build a community that visits and educates and provides company along the way. This is not a boast that the church can solve the problems of the 21st century, but the announcement of a commitment to use the support of this annual fund drive to build a community that visits you, that provides education, that leads you into community, and participates with you in the great moments of your life; in short, that lives into the Great Commission given by Jesus to the apostles.

EPILOGUE

2001

In the fall of 2000, the Every Member Canvass succeeded one more time, and it seemed that for the most part, the next five years would be a continuation of what we had been doing together for the past ten years, if a little less frenzied than it had been. During the summer of 2001, Judi Yeates, our assistant, with the support of one of our deacons, Lynn Bacon, took the J2A on its first mission trip. The location for the mission was the Dominican Republic, where Deacon Bob Snow and his wife, Eileen, had been serving for some time. Bob was raised at All Saints, and his mother and father were still active in the parish. After being ordained to the diaconate in Lincoln, he and his wife followed a passion for mission, and Bob became the assistant to the bishop of the Dominican Republic. It was an easy choice for a mission experience, and it turned out to be a most successful trip.

Capital improvement projects continued at a reduced pace, but it was projected to amount to $46,000. These projects included a continued reconfiguring of our education space, adding toddler space to the nursery, the replacement of the handbells, and repair of over half of our asphalt surfaces around the church. Attendance ran high, averaging 425 per Sunday, a substantial rise over the previous year and perhaps an all-time high for the parish.

I recruited an EFM class, something I had not done since I had become the rector of the parish. It revisited something that I had enjoyed in the past, and it indicated that I thought my workload would be considerably less than it had been. The four-year commitment on my part felt like a nice way to walk out of the job. It was an excellent group. It was made up of members of the parish, but it also included Juanita Johnson of the Church of Resurrection. I had known Juanita for a long time, having had a pastoral relationship with her mother, Ion Hanger. Her mother was part of the African American age group that played a key role in the advocacy for racial justice in the city, and Ion had been among the most outspoken. Juanita followed her mother in public education. She would go on from EFM and from some tutorial help, which I extended to her to be ordained to the diaconate. She has served at Church of the Resurrection since her ordination. Even though her service was in another parish, it felt like a confirmation that much of what we had set in place would continue.

The fall of 2001 looked to be particularly busy. Our kick-off Sunday, a metaphor from the Pedersen years that could not be shaken, had been particularly successful. In the week that followed, we were preparing for an important staff meeting. We planned to review the launch and to make whatever adjustments that might be required. The meeting was scheduled for the coming Tuesday morning at nine. It was typical for most of the staff to gather for Morning Prayer in the chapel at eight o'clock, and when we finished, we came downstairs with the hopes that we might start a little early if possible. We asked the parish secretary if Linda had come in. Linda Rafael was our director of Christian education who had succeeded Judi Yeates. Sue Norman said yes but that Linda had received a phone call and had gone upstairs to the preschool room to watch something on television. So we went up to see for ourselves with little inklings of what we were about to see. The second tower was coming down. This was September 11, 2001.

We were soon riveted to the screen, as Linda was, except that what was troubling for us was truly painful for Linda. Linda and her husband, Bill, had worked on Wall Street as young business school graduates until opportunities moved them West and ultimately to Omaha. They had friends that still worked there, and Bill's mother lived across town from where the disaster was taking place. We watched for a long time in disbelief and with not a little denial. At last exhausted, we went downstairs and tried to hold a staff meeting.

I remember my first remarks: "Everything is changed." Hastily, we planned to open the church for prayer that day and planned for a special observance for that evening. People wandered in during the day, and a large group showed up for the evening service that we had scheduled. The following Sunday, the church was packed with persons we had not seen in a long time and many we had never met.

And "everything" did change. Like another American president at the beginning of the century, President Bush was pushed into a war mode. Like World War I, September 11 brought on a wave of social responsibility and discipline, but in its wake was the counterflow of fear, which manifested itself in internal surveillance and conflict. Like President Wilson's attorney general, President Bush's attorney general made war on dissents. Wiretapping spread like wildfire. Dragnets were carried out on the basis of racial profiles. Bush, much like Wilson, found himself leading a crusade for democracy, the full impact of which is only now being reckoned with in American life.

The end of the Cold War had brought a peace dividend and a fragile consensus, which seemed like it could provide the country with a chance to repair its social fabric. The peace dividend quickly evaporated, and consensus was replaced with conflict. The country was experiencing one of those swings, which it had gone through before. As we have seen from the beginning, American life has swung between two poles. One pole was its belief in its social solidarity, and the other was its belief in the self-reliance of individuals. Suddenly, perhaps prematurely, American life was swinging toward the pole of individualism. It would be, as it had been before, an age of conflict and of individuals preoccupied with their rights over the needs of society. The Episcopal Church found itself in an age not unlike the one that had begun in 1915 and continued through the end of World War II. Things that the church thought should be solved by means of consensus devolved into crusades. The vision of church growth, which had gone so far as imagining doubling the size of the Episcopal Church by 2020, turned into strategies for stemming loss.

While there was little change on the surface of things at All Saints, it was clear that we were working against an undertow and that sustaining the life and work of the parish was becoming progressively more difficult. The parish, in fact, responded remarkably well as it did in 1915. Capital budgets continued to make improvements to our facility: 2002, $85,755; 2003, $33,136; and 2004, $249,035. The item in 2004 reflects the addition of two units to the village, raising the hope that the village could reach that size where it would be a self-sustaining ministry.

These years also included two unanticipated gifts, which would make a substantial addition to the endowment. Rene Nauman, short of her one hundred sixth birthday, died on March 26, 2003, and left the parish the balk of her estate. She and her husband, Walter, had returned to Omaha in the seventies to live in Skyline, a state-of-the-art retirement home at the time, which promised to care for them to the end of their life. The Naumans had come to All Saints but were put off by Pedersen's brusque manner and because "he wore cowboy boots!" I had begun doing a monthly Eucharist at Skyline in the early nineties, when Fr. William Reid was no longer able to do so. It was a natural thing to do as we had several parishioners who lived there. Through these Eucharists, I came to know the Naumans, and they accepted me as their minister, even though they never joined the parish.

A second significant estate came from Doris Lang, who died on July 9, 2004. She and her husband, Earl, had moved back to Omaha from California to live in Immanuel Village. Here too I was doing a monthly Eucharist, and that had led them to join All Saints. Doris always came on Sundays, but Earl, who had a stroke, received communion in the home, and the little service became an important event for him.

This allowed our endowment to grow to $3 million which seemed like it had reached a new benchmark appropriate for the time. After the contribution from Nauman estate to the endowment fund, there remained sufficient funds to allow the parish to finish a large portion of the new space under the narthex addition. The space was dedicated as a library in memory of Rene's maternal grandfather, Rev. Cannon Burgess, and serves as well as a meeting and classroom. Burgess was one of the early Nebraska priests with scholarly credentials who served at St. Luke's Plattsmouth for decades. One might recall that in our opening page, we read his word of tribute to Bishop Clarkson that he wrote into the minutes of the standing committee in March of 1884.

The surplus in the Lang estate paid for the new unit in the village, which was dedicated as Lang House. Again, like the Wiedners, these two benefactors, who did so much to grow the endowment, were also provided with a tangible memorial. The good fortune of the parish was owed to the work of visitation to which the parish had long been committed.

Pedersen had often remarked that a parish ought to have a capital fund drive every five years. He referred to it as harvesting capital. Not to do so, he argued it would leave something unharvested, which could not be realized otherwise. So in the midst of this uneasy time, there was time for one last capital drive. I called it the Legacy Drive. It was tied in part to the purchase of the three and a half acres of property that had become available along the west line of the parish's property. The protection of our property demanded it, and the prospects, though off in the future, of what the additional space might contribute to the life and ministry of the parish were exciting. It cost $80,000, and the removal of the deteriorating house cost $8,000. To this we added a list of other capital projects, and the hope that it would provide some initial support of the new rector. The drive was set at $480,000. It achieved its goal, rather amazing, considering that I was a lame duck and that the times were progressively more difficult.

These few bones of what happened beyond 2001 are sketchy, and I am overwhelmed by the wealth of stories about the people who moved the parish forward during these final years of my tenure. Progressively, however, I have lost a handle on how to pick and choose between them, so it is now quite clear to me, as it may well have been for some time to the reader, that it is time for me to hand this narrative over for someone else to tell.

Michael J. Tan Creti
September 11, 2014

Appendix 1

Landscape, Architecture, and Art at All Saints

Around the Grounds

It is my intention with this appendix to augment the long historical journey of the first eleven chapters with a shorter, more confined journey around the grounds and through the buildings of All Saints as they exist today. For those who have come all this way, it is a kind of reward where you will be able to take a more extensive look at things you have already encountered. For those who have not yet wadded though the whole, it is a shortcut that will answer your questions about what you regularly encounter on a visit to All Saints, and perhaps it will move you to look back in the narrative to see more of what caused it to be the way it is. Whatever your preparation or motivation, I invite you to start this journey at the west drive of the church, where you can turn off Blondo Street and enter the thirteen-acre campus that is home to All Saints today.

At this entryway, you are near the high point of the property, which falls way to the northeast with a steady but gradual slope. To begin with, I would have you note that construction on this property has done little to alter the original landscape. Aside from a little leveling here and there, it lies just about the way it did before it was claimed by the expanding city of Omaha. It is easy from here to intuit its natural state and the way that it was used by the early farmers who began to work this land at the beginning of the twentieth century.

Another way to state this observation is to say that the church's architect, Charles Morton, intentionally nestled the church's primary building into the landscape. He did this out of respect for the natural landscape, and that respect guided his choice of materials and forms. Morton's intention was enhanced when the parish purchased three acres that ran the length of its west side in 2004. The effect of the additional land was to put the main church building in the center of the property, and the initial experience you have of All Saints is of the open space. If you look west from this point on the drive, one is aware of an open field, running a little over 175 feet to the west. Turning now to look northeast across the large open lawn, approximately the distance of a city block, you have one of the best views of the church. With the advantage of the height and distance, you will be able to see quite clearly the articulation of the building's three units. At the center of your view is the large triangle facade, which forms the west end of the worship space. From the gable, a steeply pitched roof runs for more than 90 feet, striking one as something like an oversized tent. Below and a little near, you will see the low-pitched roof over the west wing, which houses the space that serves the main worship area. A little further east is the new tower built in 1999 to provide a prominent entry into the building. The building doesn't strike one as large or monumental so much as inviting and peaceful.

Leaving this vantage point, you can begin your journey deeper into the campus. In short order, you will come to a small parking area, twenty-two spaces, that was originally intended to serve the office, which was located in the west wing of the building. The office has subsequently been moved to the east side of the building. The west doors remain a convenient entrance to the main worship area and to chapel. These spaces have long been savored by those attending services in the chapel and by seniors and disabled because of the rather short and level access to the building. The parking area is framed by plantings. At the south end of the parking area, there is a flower bed centered on two Japanese maples. They were planted in memory of Bart Brown, a young man of the parish who died in 1993. To the east are plantings that were part of the memorial gift given in memory of Bishop Russell Rauscher, who died in 1989.

Parking in this lot, brings you to a good spot to begin a walk around the campus. You will begin with the long descent down what was once the west side of the property. The descent of a little more than four hundred feet is rather steep, and it will bring you to the lowest point on the property. A path was laid out along this route in 2004 to accommodate stations of the cross. The stations are dedicated to Frank Murphy, a deacon of the parish, who died in 2003. The fourteen brass plaques were purchased from Terra Sancta Guild and were mounted on posts, designed and built by Bob Morley, Don Erikson, and David Linberg. They were installed, and the path was built by the men of the parish, who, at that time, were organized as "Helping Hands." The descent follows an old tree line, mostly cottonwoods, which divided the original farmstead from its western field. A barbed-wire fence once ran along the line and was not fully removed until the nineties due to the insistent work of Joyce Thomas, who had begun living on the property in 1993.

Just past where the stations end are a trellis and bench. It is a great spot to sit down and take a break. At this point, you are six hundred feet from the street, and you will be struck by the quiet. The neighbor to the north is Camelot Apartments, built a couple of years after All Saints was built. While the parish fought the change in zoning, which allowed the apartments to be built, they have turned out to be a good neighbor. Settled on the bench, the most prominent feature before you is the gable of the north end of the worship space. The bottom of the church is twenty feet above you at this point, which means that this view is one of the best for getting a sense of the size of the building. A line of sugar maples shelters this area and has now grown to such a height that they block the view of the steeple, except in winter, when the leaves are down. If you are here in the winter, your eye will likely be fixed on the cross mounted high above upon the slender steeple. It rises seventy feet above the floor of the church and, at this point, has the benefit of an additional thirty feet that you are below the main floor of the church. On a clear day, the simple silver outline is a lovely sight against the blue sky; and occasionally, you see a red-tailed hawk taking its rest upon it.

After your brief stop, you can continue east along the north line of the property. Here you will come to a waterway, precisely where it lay in the original farm field. A great deal of water comes through here in a storm, and an old farm tile that drains into it causes it to continue flowing with water from the south part of the property long after a rain during a wet season. A city storm sewer touches the property at this point and accommodates the runoff, taking it north down Cady Street. A wooden bridge was built over the waterway in 2004 by the same crew who built the stations of the cross. Once across the bridge, you will encounter the retreat center, which was built in 1976. A walk from the back door of the lower level leads up to the front door. Like the main building, the retreat center was built to take advantage of the slope of the land so that the lower level could have windows in each of its twelve sleeping rooms. It was built at the time in the parish's life when thrift was an important consideration, and it is a very practical building. Nevertheless, an effort was made to blend its style and materials with the main building. This is particularly noticeable from the front where the Colorado moss stone was used. Stepping inside of it for a moment, you have an immediate sense of hominess. The room has a low-vaulted ceiling. At the far end of the room is a large fireplace made of Colorado moss stone. This feels like a large family room in a home or like a gathering area in a lodge. The room can be set up with tables to serve fifty or so individuals and still have room for them to mingle in front of the fireplace or, in pleasant weather, to wander out on a spacious deck in the rear. The kitchen and food service area, redone in 2013, is equipped with a very serviceable kitchen and a lovely granite serving counter.

Back outside, you look across a circle drive that serves the rear door of the church. This door goes directly into the church school area and is often used by families with children during the church school year. It is also used when suppers and other events occur in the lower level. Just to the left is an outdoor play area, which was a gift in memory of Kimball Lauritzen given in 2012.

Continuing your walk to the east, you will head down Erskine Plaza. Here you will encounter the village that was founded in 1987. The first unit on Erskine is the "Staff House." It is the west half of the first duplex, and it was built with the idea that it might provide housing for the parish's staff, such as for an assistant priest. It has been lived in by Rev. Thomas Miles and his wife, Susan; Reverend Charles and Frances Pedersen and Joyce Thomas, who was the parish's DRE from 1977 to 1995. It is easy to see that the architecture of these units is much like that of the retreat center. The similar rooflines, the vertical cedar siding, and the accents of Colorado moss rock tie them to the retreat center. The east half of the duplex, known as Black House, was given to the parish by Ellen Black in exchange for being able to live in it as long as she was physically able. It has subsequently been lived in by Rosemary Gammel and Deacon Sam and Edna Morford.

Further down Erskine is a second duplex, Wiedner House and Wells House. The original occupants of Wiedner House were Ed and Edie Wiedner. They were followed by Esther Miller, Oral Murphy, and Jim and Betty White. The Wells House was originally lived in by Jim and Flo Wells. At the end of Erskin Plaza, we will turn to the right to a short run of Ninety-Second Street. Here you will encounter yet another duplex built in 2004, Erikson House and Lang House. It was built by Don Erikson, who remains the resident at this time, and with funds from the estate of Earl and Doris Lang as a memorial for them, and its first residents have been David and Bonnie Linberg.

At this corner, it is a good place to look back at the main building. This location provides the most complete view of the building. From here, it is possible to take in the massive size of the roof over the sanctuary. The roof runs for ninety feet, and it is crowned by a skylight, which runs its entire length. While skylights are meant for the effect they have on the interior, the glass and aluminum, particularly since it was rebuilt in 2013, actually ornaments this roof in a rather stunning way. During the day, its various angles cause interesting things to happen with the sunlight; and at night, it catches moonlight. On the occasion of a nighttime service, it throws off a special glow into the night sky. Turning the corner and walking south past Lang House, you can take another look at the church. From here it is possible to take in the six bays, which hold the stained glass along the east side. If you were here on a night when a service was going on, you would see a pattern of jewellike colors in the windows; but in daylight, what you see is the pattern of the epoxy, which holds the stained glass in place. It looks rather like lacework. The bright white of the bays due to white marble chips imbedded in concrete frames and the intricate white lace marks the windows off from the irregular pattern of the reddish Colorado moss rock that fill the walls around them. From this angle, you are exposed to the size of the building, but even so it seems to remain a part of the natural landscape into which it has been built.

Continuing south, you cross the first of three large parking lots, which together have the capacity to hold more than 250 cars. At the end of this first lot, which was built in 2000, it is possible to find ourselves on another walk. This walk was designated as All Faiths Walk, and it has two memorial flower gardens along it. The first of the gardens was created as a memorial by the family of Margaret Smith, who died in 1987. It is rich with perennials: peonies, roses, lilies, daffodils, hydrangea, and butterfly bush. A stone bench located at its heart is a quiet place to sit and take in the spirit of the surroundings. Sitting on this bench, one looks up through a treed area that was the woodlot for the old farmhouse. The two-storied farmhouse sat just to the south of the woodlot. If you can locate a very large pin oak, now an island in the large parking lot, you can imagine it as marking the farmhouse's front yard. A picnic table has been located in the wooded area, which would have stood behind the farmhouse, and it is another place to take a rest. Looking beyond it, you will see the door to the office.

Going on a little further south along the path, you pass the spot that is the burial sight of Trooper. Trooper is one of the many dogs of All Saints. He regularly came to work with Father Pedersen and spent a great deal of time lying at the west door. As you come to the end of the parking lot, there is a second garden lying on each side of the path. This garden was established in memory of Janet Diehl, who died in 2003. It is maintained by her family. In 2013, the family added a memorial for baby Grace Janet Diehl, a grandchild of Janet's, who was stillborn. Here another bench invites you to sit for a spell. Before you lies the front yard of the church, two hundred feet deep and stretching west for nearly six hundred feet. Over the years on it, kids have hunted Easter eggs, air balloons has been inflated, animals of various sorts have roamed waiting for a blessing on Creation Sundays, and a reception tent seating 250 has been pitched to celebrate a capital fund drive.

Moving further south along the path, the path comes to Blondo Street, which is a very busy thoroughfare. Not so long ago, it was little more than a country farm to market road, but now it carries more than fifty thousand cars a day. As you walk west along Blondo, more of the farm's original woodlot remains on your right, creating a buffer for the property. After a couple of hundred feet, you come to the east drive, which in fact is an extension of Ninety-Third Street. Originally, it was meant to go through to Cady Street, but the development of the apartment complex blocked its extension, turning it into a driveway. Before turning down the drive, you might want to walk on a little farther up Blondo to the center of the property where you can turn and look at the church head-on. Most people who have seen All Saints from the street are surprised at the size of the building the first time they enter it. From here it seems rather diminutive as the architect intended. Looking across the large expanse of green, you will take note first of the tower over the entry with its two sets of red doors. The tower was part of the narthex expansion in 1999. The parish's new architects, RDG, was committed to not compromising Charles Morton original sense of the building. They felt strongly, however, that an entryway ought to have a sufficient prominence as to telegraph the message: this is where you enter this building. At the same time, they were sensitive to the fact that the south end of the main church space was a perfect equilateral triangle. They hoped that they had found the balance between an evident entryway without obscuring the triangular area, which sits behind it. If they succeeded, your eye has moved from the entryway to the triangle behind it, and you are attempting to discern what is on the 221 tiles that make up the structure of the triangle. They are fish, butterflies, sheaves of wheat, doves, divine hands, etc., all symbols of the Christian mystery. If you were third graders, I would urge you to lie down in the lawn about midway between where you are now and the church, as a number of third-grade classes on a retreat called, "Our Church," used to do. They would be challenged to look up at the cross, seventy feet above them, and not get dizzy! Too bad you will just have to fantasize it. If it were night, you would notice that the stained glass in the front wall strikes a passerby with an array of jewellike colors.

When you are finished, backtrack along Blondo and return to the east drive. Looking down the drive, which runs due north, you will be aware of how far off into the distance you are capable of seeing. Your view will take you past Maple Street, where the hill line defines the neighborhood of Maple Village. Down this driveway, you pass a flat area on your left. It was part of the original circular drive intended for dropping off passengers coming to worship at All Saints. It was abandoned in the 1980s in favor of a drive across the front of the building, which brought the drop-off area much closer to the front doors and eliminated a substantial incline between the old drop-off point and the doors. At this point, the church is screened from you by the existence of an early tree line that has been extended and augmented by plantings completed in the late 1980s.

The church begins to come into view in bits and pieces as you start up the drive that runs to the west. Through the screen, consisting of several fifty-year-old pines, you will have a rather good view of the triangular gable with it tiles carrying a variety of Christian symbols. Just past this line of pines, you will see the large bronze figure of *The Elder*. The thirteen-foot-high winged figure has a sweeping gesture intended to draw those walking up this short drive into the worship to join with "all the saints" who habitually gather in this place. Below the sculpture is a tablet on which appear the names of those who were memorialized by this sculpture. They are "all saints" and particularly those who have most recently passed from the parish into the larger life: Mary Noel Culver, Robert Dickerson, William Feeney, Tom Fitzgerald, George Harris, Howard Herrick, Arlene Hinchcliff, the member of William Marsh Family, Myrle Pinkerton, Robert Plumb, Zeda White, and Jerry Wulf.

The sculpture was acquired as part of the parish's renovation in 1999. The primary goals of that renovation were to enlarge the narthex, provide disability access to all of the parish's facilities, and to create an activity room for the church school. In the course of the master plan, the parish decided that the completion of this effort should be celebrated by a significant work of art. It was felt that by incorporating a work of art into the master plan, it would be more than a mere decoration but an integral part of the function of the renewed facility.

The dedication of the parish more than a hundred years before suggested that the themes could be found in Revelation 7, the one of the appointed reading for All Saints Day. The passage makes reference to "a great multitude that no one could count, from every nation, from all tribes and peoples and languages . . ." This heavenly gathering is the archetype of any worship community. The image represents for us, as a Christian community, who we were, who we are, and who we will be! It was this insight that had led those who formed this community in 1885 to choose for its name—All Saints! Already in the Trinity Window in the chapel, the theme of Revelations 7 had been successfully used by the parish.

Taking the theme outside in a different medium made sense to the planners of the 1999 renovation. They found inspiration in Jacob Epstein's marvelous sculpture of St. Michael, the archangel that stands over the entrance to the Anglican Cathedral in Coventry, England. The Gothic cathedral dedicated to St. Michael was destroyed during WWII. After the war, a modern cathedral was built alongside of the ruins of the old one. The ruins were turned in a very dramatic prayer garden dedicated to the ministry of reconciliation in the world. Epstein was chosen to create as stunning sculpture of St. Michael the archangel for the new entryway. The image of the protecting angel fit the needs of those who were making the effort to rebuild a new Coventry Cathedral on the bombed-out rubble of the old cathedral. They found hope in the text "You shall find refuge under his wings" (Psalm 91:4). The experience of passing under the gaze of this figure is so compelling that those who pass there may want to retrace their steps so as to reexperience the effect it has on one.

The scale of the south wall of All Saints current building is hardly that of Coventry Cathedral's entrance. Nevertheless, it provided a similar opportunity. Here the facade presented space for a larger-than-life-size figure to preside over the walkway leading from the parking, on which most of the congregation passes on its way to worship. In the reading from Revelations, we are told that a heavenly elder served as a guide for the seer John on his visionary journey through heaven. He gestures toward a multitude processioning upward to the heavenly throne and challenges the seer, "Who are these?" The intimidated seer responds deferentially to the elder, "Sir, you know." The elder then replies, "These are they who have come out of the great ordeal. They have washed their robes and made them white in the blood of the Lamb."

The artistic challenge given to Alston was to capture this gesture in a way that would cause those coming up the walk to the church to ask themselves the question, "Who are we?" Are we not part of those saints who are coming out of the great ordeal and who are worthy to worship in this place because we have had our robes washed in the blood of the Lamb?

> The sculptor Littleton Alston, a local artist with a growing national reputation, was asked to explore the possibility of an original work of art late in the summer of 1998. At the time, he was the associate professor of sculpture at Creighton University. He had come to Creighton in 1990, where he carried

a full teaching load, mentored a number of young aspiring artists, and maintained his own private studio. To that point in his career, he was known for murals and life-size metallic sculptures of abstract forms. His sculpture *Medusa*, standing on the Creighton Campus, is a good example of his work in this period of his career.

Littleton was born in Petersburg, Virginia and was a student at the Duke Ellington School for the Arts in Washington DC. He was a student of the famous African American sculptor Richard Hunt, and from 1983 to1984, he was artist assistant to Sal Scarpitta. Littleton liked experimenting with different mediums such as oils, bronze, and clay. Metal, however, had progressively become his material of choice.

Littleton's works have been exhibited in galleries and museums worldwide, including the Sheldon Memorial Art Gallery in Lincoln, in Kansas City, Missouri, Brugges and Roeselare, Belgium, and Hagen, Germany. He exhibited work in Black Americanna, the Annual Black Artist Exhibition 1997, and had a monumental piece on the Navy Pier in Chicago for the Pier Walk Show in1998. It was an abstract *Tree of Life*, which began with a pyramid shape and folds out like origami into a towering organic from reaching upward some eighteen to twenty feet. He described it as "a dance of steel." After this piece, which he considered his magnum opus in abstraction, Littleton took a sabbatical, which had allowed him to travel in Europe. He particularly targeted visits to cathedrals and civic spaces in order to observe the interplay of sculpture, space, and the movement of people through those spaces. This had prepared him for the request that All Saints made. He was anxious for an opportunity to move on from abstraction into more classic forms, and his calendar was open! Looking at it from a different perspective, All Saints was extremely fortunate in its timing, and as a result, it managed to receive a valuable piece of art at an exceptional bargain.

After studying the challenge that the parish had presented to him, Littleton proposed a winged elder. The elders' wings were, in his vision, to "support" the roofline, and his gesture was to draw those coming to worship into the sanctuary of the building. The figure was to be twelve to thirteen feet high and cast in 085 aluminum, weighing approximately eight hundred pounds. He created a maquette, which was on view in the narthex for the parish's reaction during that November. On December 15, the commission was authorized by the vestry. Interaction between the parish and artist continued throughout the project. It included a number of visits by the children as well as adults of the parish to the artist's studio. They witnessed the growth of the armature, its filling in with plaster, and the application of the final layer of clay into which the detail of the sculpture was modeled. Finally, they were invited to witness the pouring of the bronze.

Littleton's original intention was to execute the sculpture in aluminum because of the presence of aluminum on the outer surfaces of the building, particularly in the steeple. As the sculpturing in clay proceeded and the detail of the figure began to emerge, the artist recommended that a shift be made to bronze. Not only would the bronze carry the detail that had emerged, but also the spirit of the figure seemed to him to demand the seriousness of bronze. The weight increased from eight hundred to two thousand pounds. Fortunately, we were at a stage in the building where a steel beam could be designed in the wall with interior bracing, which could reach back through the wall that separates the music room from the vesting area, which could handle this weight.

The creation of the sculpture took about eighteen months from the time of the original conversation about its possibility to its actual arrival. It is particularly fitting that its completion has coincided with the two thousandth anniversary of the Annunciation, which calls all humanity to its vocation to be bearing of "the Eternal Word." On that March day in 2000, the sculpture took its place as an integral part of the parish effort to minister to the spiritual longings of the human heart to come home.

Since the completion of this work, Littleton's work has continued to appear around the city. Of particular note are *The Jazz Group*, Twenty-Fourth and Lake; *Martin Luther King* in the plaza in front of the Douglas County Court House, *On the Wings of Angels* in the plaza of the City Building, and *St. Ignatius of Loyola* on the Creighton Campus.

As you pass *The Elder* and turn toward the front door, you will see on the retaining wall beneath the elder's stride a crown. In the vision in the book of Revelation, it is said that the elders cast down their crowns in their act of worship before the throne. The same theme can be seen inside the chapel in the Trinity Window. There, the elders around the throne are in various degrees of casting down their crowns.

Less subtle than the crown is the large limestone Celtic cross, which sits in the center of the courtyard. Referred to as "the old cross," it stood on the pinnacle of the old building on Twenty-Sixth and Dewey. It was moved into the entry courtyard in 1999. It can be seen from the inside as one leaves the high altar and again when you begin your exit from the church. It is a memorial of the old congregation who had worshiped under it in the old building for nearly sixty years, to whom we own so much. The choice in 1906 of a Celtic cross for the top of its new building was an intentional ownership of the attributes of Celtic Christianity as distinct from Latin Christianity. Celtic Christianity existed in the British Isles as early as the fifth century and has a unique and ancient spirituality, which is more affirming than the Latin Spirituality that came in sixth century and dominated the spirituality of the British Isles until the time of the Reformation. The argument of the Celtic cross is that there is a unity between the cross and the circle, the redemptive sacrifice of Christ's death, and the creative power of the world's life. This choice has had a long-lasting impact on All Saints. It can be seen repeated in the Ritchie Window in the chapel, and on the wall of the main church over the altar.

> The courtyard provides an area in which one might linger on a pleasant day for a visit or for a moment of quite. The red benches on either side offer you a place to take some time in your coming or goings as they have often served as a respite for a bride or groom or the member of the family of someone who is being received for burial. They were placed there in memory of Adele Cote Dayton, 1913–1998, by her daughter who continues to worship at All Saints. Adele counted the old location as part of her neighborhood but moved on with the congregation to continue to participate in her church.

Through the Red Doors

You now pass through "the red doors." Red was used for the main doors of the medieval Western churches to mark them off as a place where sanctuary is available. It became a common practice in the Episcopal Church in the later part of the nineteenth century and was adopted by All Saints in 1999, when its front was rebuilt. Once inside the narthex, you can turn back and look at the stained glass placed over the doors. If it is a sunny day, the colors will be quite spectacular. The windows were given by Bea Muller in memory of her husband, Joseph Muller, in 1978. Muller was one of the key leaders in the move from Twenty-Sixth and Dewey. The medium is hammered rock glass embedded in epoxy. This is the same medium used for the stained-glass windows and skylight in the main worship area. This medium recommends itself for contemporary building because it is more durable and heat efficient than traditional stained glass mounted in lead channels. While it is capable of very vivid colors, it lacks the subtly and the ability to represent shapes and objects that is characteristic of traditional stained glass. When it is used to represent figures, they will inevitably be abstract. The glass in these windows is the work of a local artist George Hautzinger. The figures were chosen as a complement to the saints represented elsewhere in the building and are those that frequented the teaching of Father Pedersen and myself in the 1980s. They are Augustine of Hippo, 430; Francis of Assisi, 1126; Lady Julian of Norwich, 1417; Samuel Isaac Joseph Schereschewsky, 1906; Basil 579; Anselm of Canterbury, 1109; and the Blessed Virgin Mary. The choice of saints is from the broad sweep of church history as the dates of their deaths imply and from a wide range of locations wherein they lived, beginning in Nazareth with the Virgin Mary and continuing on to Shanghai, China, where Schereschewsky carried out his ministry. In the center of the saints is the emblem that stands for the Feast of All Saints, a crown over crossed palms and the three stars. It can be seen also at the top of the east panel of the stained-glass window located behind the altar in the chapel.

These windows were installed in the narthex before its expansion in 1999. The expansion moved them south twenty feet and raised them eight-feet, setting them on the upper level of the new entry tower. Raising them created a gap where they had formally been fitted around the original front door. In order to fill this space, a double tablet was executed in rock glass upon which the names of the vestry of 1885 (the founding vestry) and the vestry of 1963 (the vestry that built the new building) were placed in order to create a memorial for past efforts, which have resulted in the present community that worships in and cares for this facility.

> The inscription reads, "The Vestry of 1885: J. M. Woolworth, A. P. Hopkins, Geo. W. Ames, A. H. Bishop, V. S. Montgomery, S. P. Morse, Wm A. Redick and R. R. Ringwalt. The Vestry of 1963: Joseph Muller, Gale Davis, James Canedy, Bernard Combs, John Encell, Darwin Fallis, John Hanley, Neal Hilmes,

> Charles Morton, Arthur Pinkerton, Varro Rhodes, Robert Spire, Lawrence Trickett, Conrad Young, Gilbert Harry." The memorial is extended in a middle panel to all who come through these doors, reading, "To all the witnesses which pass through these doors," which, of course, includes you.

While you are turned back toward the narthex window, it is a good time to look around and note the cornerstone of the new building. It is floor level near to the bulletin board on the west wall. It is a large Colorado moss rock, which was incised with the date of the new building and set into the wall. Originally, this stone was outside of the narthex under the overhang of the roof. If you look to the right of the cornerstone, you can detect a vertical line, which was the line of the exterior windows of the original narthex.

Moving to the left and jumping over the hall onto the wall of the entry tower, you can locate a second cornerstone. This one, a block of limestone, was in the exterior wall of the church building on Twenty-Sixth and Dewey. It carries on it the date 1906, the year in which that building was built. The original cornerstone was quite massive and was incised on two faces. The front with the date 1906 was sliced off the block so that it could be built into the wall of Colorado moss rock. A second slice preserved a cross and was used for a time capsule. You can locate the time capsule by looking across the entryway to the other wall of the entry tower. Shoulder high, it contains the date 2000. It was sealed on Palm Sunday of 2000, memorializing the first Sunday the parish worshiped in the new building in 1964. It contains a number of items saved for another time to view: the bulletin for Passion Sunday, April 15–17, 2000; the current parish directory; the April 14, 2000, issue of the *Witness,* a copy of *The Elder of the Book of Revelation* published April 2000; the parish's Centennial Metal, inscribed: "For Another Century, The Sunday of the Passion, April 16, 2000"; a palm cross; and several U.S. coins (six quarters: 1999, Connecticut; 1999, New Jersey; 1999, Delaware; 1999, Pennsylvania; 2000, Massachusetts; 2000, Maryland; a penny: 2000, Philadelphia; and a gold Sacajawea dollar, 2000.) In the masonry just below the time capsule, there are three small stones, which were brought by Father Belsky from England. There is a small piece from Canterbury Cathedral, a piece of Chilmark stone from Salisbury Cathedral, and a piece of flint stone from St. Andrew's Church Bermerton, where George Herbert, the mystical poet of the Church of England, once served.

Looking across the narthex, you will note a collection of furniture in a Spanish Mission style. These were built for the narthex by Zongkers

Custom Woods Inc., whose shop is located at 1717 S. Third Street. When the parish turned to furnishing the new narthex in 2000, it was decided that the furniture should reflect an informal Western style, which characterizes the narthex. That led to the selection of "mission style." The pursuit through the usual venue for purchasing furniture proved less than satisfactory and expensive. Nini Field surfaced as an interested donor, and she particularly was interested in something that would be of exceptional quality. This led the committee to Zongkers, which is Omaha's premier furniture builder. It turned out that its out-of-the-way location on Third Street was formerly the Metz Brewery. The long association of the Metz family with All Saints seemed to make this a particularly pleasing choice.

The design of the coffee table opened the possibility to add to the artistic content of the building. The parish decided that it should include a tile inset that would honor Standing Bear. The famous Ponca Indian chief stood trial in Omaha in 1878 and defended himself with a stirring speech, which moved the judge to rule that "an Indian is a person." The children of the parish's Sunday school studied the Standing Bear stories and created a set of drawings, which were to be used by the ceramic artist who would make the tiles. The work was done by Bob Wilson and Beth Davis of the Wilson Custom Design Tile Company of Omaha, the same company who created the floor mosaics in the main worship area, which we will visit shortly.

Walking deeper into the narthex, you will notice the large portrait of a priest hanging over the stairwell. It is a portrait of Thomas Jones Mackay, All Saints second rector. Mackay served the parish for nearly thirty years, beginning in 1891 until he died in office in 1920. The portrait was commissioned in 1913 by Dr. and Mrs. Mercier. The artist was J. Laurie Wallace, Omaha's premier portrait painter. It was, of course, a period in which portraits of prominent people were highly valued across the country, and Omaha was no exception.

> J. Laurie Wallace was born in Scotland in 1864, and he was brought to the United States as a boy when his parents immigrated. He studied art in New York City and at the Pennsylvania Academy of Art in Philadelphia under Thomas Eakins. Eakins used Wallace as a model for a number of Eakins well-known works, including *The Crucifixion* (1880), *Arcadia* (1883), and *The Swimming Hole* (1884–85) and for dozens of photographs. Eakins's portrait of Wallace, circa 1883, hangs in the Joslyn Art Museum in Omaha. By 1881, he had become Eakins's assistant, and he continued in this capacity until

> 1891. At that time, he moved to Omaha, Nebraska, to take the position of director of the newly founded Western Art Association. The association soon failed, but Wallace chose to remain in Omaha for over sixty years, becoming a commissioned portrait painter and professor of art. His portraits include such prominent members of the community, such as Fanni Teweles Brandeis, Jonas L. Brandeis, James L. Paxton, and George W. Lininger, which now are property of the Joslyn Art Museum. The inclusion of the rector of All Saints in this pantheon of Omaha early twentieth century notables says something about Mackay's and All Saints' standing in the city at that time.

The portrait hung in the entryway of the church on Twenty-Sixth and Dewey from the time of Mackay's death in 1920 until the parish moved. In 1964, the portrait was brought to Ninety-Third and Blondo and was hung in the undercroft, which was a rather vulnerable and inauspicious place for it to be. In 1999, in the enlarged narthex, it found a place on a wall adequate to its size and in a place of notice so that it plays a role something like the artist intended for it. As members of this congregation come and go to worship, classes and suppers, this portrait seems to extend to them the benediction out of the past from a wise and gentle priest who gave thirty years of his life to the community of which they are a part. If Mackay was not a capital letter S—Saint—he was certainly a saint like you and me, "whom you can meet in shops or at tea."

Through the Holy Doors

Having made the transit of the narthex, you can now pass through the doors at the center of the narthex's north wall and enter into the main worship area. The first thing that you encounter is the baptismal font. This large marble font was given to the church in loving memory of O. A. Patterson, who died in 1905. It was given by his daughter, Mrs. Charles W. Haller, in 1907 as the congregation settled into its new building. It is typical of traditional fonts of the time, and what it lacks in terms of the present preference for large pools of water, it makes up for with its connection with the couple of thousand baptisms that has been performed in it. Most of the year, the baptismal water remains in the font, and many who pass the font coming or going have acquired the custom of touching the water and signing themselves with the cross as a memorial of their own baptism.

In 1995, it was put in this location. In owning the entryway, it reminds those who come into this place that baptism is what qualifies them to be here. As they are leaving, it reminds them of their baptismal ministry to go out into the world to love and to serve the Lord. In order to make its location here possible, it was necessary to form a baptismal area by cutting pews on each side to allow the flow of traffic and to provide space for a family and the ministry to gather for the sacrament of baptism. In 2000, when the floor in the worship area was redone, a mosaic was created to identify the area. The theme for the mosaic came from the biblical imagery of paradise. In the account of the Garden of Eden in Genesis 2, it is said that there are four rivers, the Pishon, Gihon, Tiger, and Euphrates, which flow out of Eden to the four corners of the world. Here, the four rivers are stylized as a cross, and the streams are filled with fish. A fish was used as a symbol of Jesus Christ in the early church. It came from interpreting the Greek word for fish, *ixthus*, as a secret anagram reading *I*, "Jesus"; *X*, "Christ"; *th*, "God's"; *us*, "Son." At the center of the cross, the 1906 baptismal font stands like an image of the Tree of Life.

> The mosaic was created by Wilson Custom Design Tile Company of Omaha, whose studio is located on Twenty-Fourth and Burdette. The principal artists of the company are Bob Wilson and Beth Davis. Their work includes the floor in Bell Tower of Country Side Community Church, wall tiles at Children's Hospital, the Lewis and Clark trail markers, and, more recently, walk plaques at the Gennet Jazz Hall of Fame.

Before you leave the baptismal area, you might note the small slate diamond in the doorway. It is the dedication of the new floor that was installed in 1999 and 2000. It reads, "To the Glory of God and in memory of the Louis Wells Family and Richard Lundgren Family 2000." The entire floor of the worship space is a work of art in its own right. It combines slate accents, which help to tie it to the original slate covering in narthex floor and altar area. Its main fabric is an imported Italian ceramic tile. It is a terrazzo style with elements of greens in it which blends with the slate, yet its dominant color is off-white, which gives the room a brightness that slate by itself could not have given it. It was also a major improvement in the acoustical character of the space, which had been seriously compromised by carpet.

You might also take note, while you are standing here, of the paschal candle stand. It is wrought iron forged by the Loki Forge at Omaha Hot Shops. The choice of wrought iron was an attempt to match the bars in the window bays, the candle stand alongside of the altar rail, and the wrought-iron supports for the altar rail. The design is in the form of Chi Rho, the monogram for Christ. A second one is located in the chapel in association with the font in that space.

Proceeding down the aisle, you will come to another place where pews were cut in order to form an area similar to the baptismal area. In a cathedral, this location in front of the step into the sanctuary would be called the crossing. In this smaller, more intimate space, the area retains something of the feel of an area through which traffic passes. The primary feel, however, is that it creates an area from which the Gospel might customarily be read and, on occasions, preached. It is often used by a preacher when he or she feels in the mood for a more extemporaneous sermon. Like the baptismal area, the space lent itself to a mosaic. It seemed logical that the choice for the theme of this mosaic would be the Anglican Communion's Compass Rose. It was a way of reminding ourselves of the parish's identity with the Anglican Communion, which seemed important. Further exploration of the idea indicated that it would be an ideal place for reading of the Gospel as the points of compass suggest that the Gospel is intended to be dispatched to the four corners of the world.

A Compass Rose had been recently installed in the crossings of Christ Cathedral, Canterbury, England, in 1988; the National Cathedral in Washington DC in 1990; and St. John the Divine, New York City, in 1992. The Compass Rose was originally designed by Canon Edward West in 1954, and it was placed in the floor of St. John the Divine at that time. These more recent installations demonstrated a resurgence in an interest in the Anglican Communion.

The center of the rose holds the Cross of St. George, the patron of England, reminding Anglicans of their origins in the Church of England. The Greek inscription "The Truth Shall Make You Free" (John 8:32) surrounding the cross is a central theme of Anglican Spirituality. From the center, the points of the compass radiate out recalling the spread of Anglican Christianity throughout the world. At the top, on the uppermost point, is a miter, the ceremonial hat of a bishop. It emphasizes the role of the bishop and of the apostolic order of the church that is at the core of the churches of the communion. The Compass Rose is used widely by the family of Anglican/Episcopal churches. It is the logo of the Inter-Anglican Secretariat and is used as the Communion's identifying symbol.

Bob Wilson and Beth Davis Wilson of Custom Design Tile Company of Omaha were commissioned for this work as well. Their sense of the space led them to a unique translation of the Compass Rose, which employed soft earth tones, terra-cotta red and yellow ochre. At the center, the shield of St. George, the patron of England, appears with its single red cross on a white field. It was double glazed to cause it to stand out like a jewel. The text from the Gospel of John was rendered in English to make it accessible for young and old.

Unto the Altar of God

Standing at the center of the Compass Rose, you are squarely in front of the altar. The altar that you are looking at was originally left behind when the congregation moved to this location. It was part of an installation in the old building, which took place in 1924. The Megeath family wanted a significant memorial for their daughter, Mary Virginia. Mary was a splendid young woman known for her charitable work in the city as well as for her charm. In 1919, she was crowned twenty-second queen of Aksarben, and she was anticipating her marriage later that year. Sadly, she contracted influenza and died days before she was to be married. You can see her name carved into the base of the altar: "1896 Mary Virginia Megeath 1919."

The dark-stained oak altar, nine feet by twenty-two inches, is covered by a single slab of white marble, one and a half inches thick. I have seen nine very large men lift this slab off the wood base and shuffle some distance as the base was edged along by a couple of equally strong men. The altar was originally attached to a matching reredos made of the same wood. When the old building was left behind, it was detached from the reredos and put into storage. A new altar table was built for the new church in the spirit of modernity, but it failed to win the approval of the congregation. Dubbed the ironing board, it was put into storage, and the old altar without its reredos was retrieved and was back into service.

On the front of the altar are the Greek letters, Alpha and Omega, symbols of the beginning and the end, the first and the last, which is one of the titles given to Christ. In the center is the monograph consisting of the Greek letters, iota, eta, sigma (i, h, s), which are the initial Greek letters of the name Jesus. On the marble top are incised five crosses representing the five wounds of Jesus. It is located so that the ministers can form a half circle around its backside, and the congregation completes the circle on the other side. Thus having begun as an "east end" altar, a style created by the Latin church during the Middle Ages and revived by the Catholic renewal in the nineteenth century, it found a way to serve the late twentieth century liturgical renewal, which favored a freestanding altar at the center of the worshiper community.

While we could not be a church in the round, the basilica-style building of the early church provided a pattern for us. In the basilica, the clergy were behind the altar face-to-face with the congregation. Moreover, in the basilicas, the chair or *cathedra* for the chief celebrant, usually the bishop of the city, was as prominent a furnishing as the altar or the baptismal font. The bishop taught from the chair, which gave rise to the term of speaking *ex cathedra.* If you raise your eyes and look over the altar, you should identify the great chair, which was designed in 1999 to complete the basilica image. It was made by David Fitzgerald of Wood Specialities of Omaha. It picks up not only the dark-finished oak, but also the blond oak of the figures of the saints as does the cross that hangs on the upper portion of the north wall.

The reredos from which the Megeath altar was detached was carved in a Gothic style in such a way as to create niches for fourteen wooden carvings representing saints of the church. The reredos stayed in "storage," but the fourteen saints that it housed made the move actual before the altar. These figures were hand carved by the German artisan, Alois Lang, 1872–1954. Lang was born in Oberammergau and was part of a family of artists who participated in Oberammergau's world famous passion play. He immigrated in the 1890 to the United States and settled in Detroit. His work was widespread in the 1920s, and a carving of the Last Supper in St. Mark's Pro-cathedral in Hastings, Nebraska, is his work as well. Casady, All Saints rector at the time that the Megeath memorial was executed, clearly had much to do with the design and particularly in the choice of saints included in it. The six large figures are set in the organ screen above the altar. In 2000, two more figures were added as a memorial to Irene Kelley. The idea behind this choice was that they should be New Testament saints as well as the six but that they should represent the role of women in the church. In order to match Lang's artistry, they were ordered from a carver, Josef Albl, whose studio is in Oberammergau. These figures are forty inches high and lightly waxed to bring out the natural color of the oak and to show the grain of the wood. They were meant to be seen close up, and they have suffered some loss in being located so distant from the congregation. It is, however, possible to go up on the platform behind the bell tables and see them close up where the natural grain in the wood can be seen.

As they stand now, they are, from your left, John the Baptist, who holds a disk on which is an image of the Lamb of God; St. Andrew, who holds the chi-shaped cross, which was the means of his martyrdom; St. Matthew, apostle and evangelist who holds a scroll, which represents his authorship of the Gospel of Matthew; and St. Peter, who holds the keys to the kingdom. Across the center line is Mary Magdalene, who holds a vessel of oil; St. John, the apostle and evangelist, who holds a chalice; St.

Paul, the apostle, who holds a sword; and the Virgin Mary, whose feet rest on a crescent moon.

In their new location, they stand in relation to a large wooden cross, which was commissioned in 1963 for the new building. It was given to the parish by Harry H. McDuff in memory of his mother and father, Ethel and Harry McDuff. It is six feet by eighteen feet. The dark-stained oak matches the dark stain used in the woodwork and ceiling. It is set off by a band of carved oak finished with a blond stain. This forms a stunning contrast separating the dark wall and the dark interior of the cross. The blond oak links with the blond oak of the carved statues of the saints below and serves to tie the cross and the saints together. At the center of the cross is a circle, expressing the world as is commonly seen in Celtic crosses, such as "the old cross," which you passed in the courtyard. It is inset with mosaic tiles, which pick up the primary colors—red, blue, and yellow—that occur in the stained-glass window and skylight. The tiles are triangular and seem to point outward as if to express the sense of mission, which is implied by the worship that takes place in this space. It has not been without its critics. The same wags that labeled the new altar, which quickly disappeared, the "ironing board," referred to the mosaic inset in the circle at the center of the cross as "Woolworth Mosaic." While the dime store, which supplied the reference for this name, has disappeared, the cross somehow has remained! Nevertheless, Pedersen struggled with it, moving in up and down in attempt to make it feel more at home, often joking darkly, that perhaps it would fall, and we could start over! I too have had my moments of doubt about it. One of its unusual aspects is the relationship of the vertical and the horizontal, which is not that of Latin Cross, the vertical being extended. My opinion was that what it needs is something more to complete it to better fill the wall and to tie it to the saints.

This is now a good point in you travels for you to turn around and view the stained glass, which gives this space an atmosphere of its own, which continually changes during the day and the seasons of the year. It was designed not so much as to be looked at as it was to alter and transform the light in the space. The stained glass was designed and fabricated by Gabriel Loire in France in 1963. However, the stained glass in the skylight was deferred during the construction in 1964 due to the cost. In 1978, when funds were available, it was fabricated and installed by George Hautzinger of Omaha according to Lorie design.

> Loire was instrumental in the revival of stained glass in the 1930s, which had fallen out of favor and/or had become artless reproductions. According to Lorie, the power of medieval

> stained glass was not so much that it was pictorial as that it created an atmosphere of mysticism in the worship space. The color floated in the air, transforming the space in a way that moved the viewer from a spectator of the natural to a participant in the supernatural. In order to accomplish his vision, Loire altered the medium. He worked with rock glass, where he was able to find the deep hues that he was seeking. The rock glass that he used was three quarters of an inch thick. He used diamond chisels to sculpt each piece of glass to enhance their effect on the light passing through it. He then embedded the pieces of rock glass in epoxy, sometimes in a representational way, but, more often than not, in abstract designs as in the windows at All Saints.
>
> Loire's transformation of stained glass not only accomplished his artistic goals, but it also transformed the practical issues that stained glass presented for modern building. The three-quarter-inch thickness of the glass formed a wall that was much more efficient for heating and cooling a building as modern use required. The thin glass in lead channels, even when tight, allowed for a great deal of heat transfer. The other problem with traditional stained glass was the maintenance that it required. Lead settled and bowed and it, as anyone who has dealt with a building with a great deal of traditional stained glass knows, requires periodic costly maintenance. The rock glass in the epoxy is extremely durable.

It is not easy to understand what would have lead a young architect fresh from the architectural school to include Loire's art glass in his design for his church. The key to this selection seems rather to lie with the new senior partner who had been brought into the architectural firm headed by Steel. Alex Winestein, who joined the firm in the fifties, was an international traveler noted for the originality and artistic flair of his work. Other projects in Omaha with which Winestein was involved used glass from Loire's Studio, including Temple Israel and Pacific Hills Lutheran Church. Temple Israel lost their original glass in the 1975 tornado. All Saints glass should be prized as a world-class work of art, and a description and pictures of it are included in the book by Charles Pratt entitled *Gabriel Loire: Les Vitraux* published in 1996.

The glass is located in twelve bays, the interior dimensions of which are three feet by fifteen feet. The bays are counter-levered so they sit outside of the wall. This adds to the feeling of breath in the space, and it creates an interesting rhythm synchronized with the fourteen pillars. Most important, the position enhances the capacity of the glass to gather light. The interior shape of the bay is trapezoidal so that the light expands into the space. The white marble is reflective and does not alter or dull the light as it passes into the space. From most locations in the space, you are not able to see the glass of more than two or three windows at a time. This was meant to shift the focus from the glass to the transformed light in the room. There is a clear gradation of colors in the windows, beginning with blues and shifting to reds and golds as you move forward to the altar. In the light directly over the altar, the golds predominate. This same gradation takes place in the skylight and is somewhat easier to see.

In addition to the bays and skylight, there is the large triangular gable that forms the south end of the space. This gable has been created by alternating blocks, fourteen inches by fourteen inches, with lancets four inches by fourteen inches. You may recall that on the outside, these blocks are molded with Christian symbols. Remembering that this is exposed to the sun at its zenith in the south, it is possible to understand why the artist rejected a glass wall though which the light would become a single overpowering hot spot. Instead, he chose to make it a solid wall broken by glass lancets, 253 of them, which allowed the vivid colors of light to interplay with the darkness of the wall. The best place to see this is from the central opening in the altar rail about noon on a sunny day. This is, of course, the precise time that ministers and the choir recess form the regular Sunday Eucharist. The colors—the same blues, reds, and yellows—that occur in the bays and skylight make up the triangle and, from an abstract design, suggest raising flames.

Continuing the Walk Around

After one last look around the space for this point, you might move to the east pillar that stands just outside of the altar rail. One of fourteen total, the pillar at which you are presently looking, actually begins deep in the ground below the floor of the lower level. These pillars are, in fact, the working structure that supports the great roof over your head. On this particular pillar is an icon of the Theotokos of Tenderness, which is one of the common forms of the Eastern church's icons of St. Mary the Virgin. It was written by Jane Tan Creti and given to the parish in August of 2001.

Jane Tan Creti had been, for some time, a student of iconography.
In 1999, she became part of the Prosopon School of Iconology.

> The school was founded in the United States by the Russian immigrant, Valdislav Andrevj, in 1988. The school pioneered a unique revival of the techniques of classic Medieval Russian iconography. The medium used is egg tempera and twenty-four-karat gold leaf on a gessoed board. The application is done with a float technique. This produces a particular translucence due to the application of the color in a number of successive layers. In 2001, Andrevj visited All Saints and led a six-day workshop as he did for the next several years. The gift was intended as a thank-you to the parish for hosting the workshop. Tan Creti's work is in a number of churches and homes mainly within the Omaha area.

In front of the icon is a candle rack, which was imported from Sweden. It was the result of a parishioner's visit to Sweden, where such candle racks were common in Lutheran churches. The traveler, Lou Willour, was interested in a memorial for her husband and inquired whether such a rack could be used in an Episcopal church, such as All Saints. Candle racks are generally associated with Roman Catholic churches in this country. Often, they are found in high-church parishes, but they are typically felt to be a little "too precious" for the piety of a pragmatic low-church congregation, such as All Saints. The candle stands, which she had seen, however, seemed different. They combined the image of a tree and the image of the world. The tapers around its circumference seemed to represent a circle of prayer in and for the world. Its association with the icon of the Virgin of Mary, who leads the intercessions of the saints seemed to be fitting. The use of the lamp stand and the icon was readily accepted, and it has made a contribution to the prayer life of the parish. It is dedicated to the memory of Byron James Willour, 1936–1997.

Return now to the crossing and continue west to the opposite pillar located outside of the altar rail. Associated with it are the circular pulpit and the icon of St. Nicholas, the bishop of Myra. This icon was also written by Jane Tan Creti and given to the parish in 2001. St. Nicholas of Myra, circa 343, was an early bishop of the church who was known as a generous provider for the poor. Nicholas's gift giving has made him the patron of charity and has put him at the heart of the Christmas tradition of giving gifts. As a teacher in the early church, he is noted for teaching charity, and his image is a fitting image for this pulpit from which God's love for us all is to be proclaimed.

A second look at the pulpit will reveal four hand-carved figures, which once were contained in the Megeath reredos along with the larger carved figures that you have previously observed at over the altar. They are Ignatius of Antioch, 110; Polycarp of Symrna, 170; Athenatius of Alexandria, 375; and Augustine of Hippo, 430. Their dates provide a time line that leads from the apostles of the New Testament down through the early church fathers, the last of whom coincide with the fall of the Roman Empire and the end of the ancient world. The locations associated with each of the figures mark a journey. Passing out of Palestine, it comes first to Antioch, which was the first great church center outside of Palestine. It is mentioned in the book of Acts as the place where the followers were first called Christians. From here, the journey continues through the Greek cities in Turkey and Egypt and finally arrives in Hippo, a city in the Latin West of North Africa. One might begin to sense that these saints, which Casady had selected, were part of a lecture on church history dear to his heart.

The pulpit's original location was behind the original altar rail. That altar rail ran along a step that was located halfway between the last two pillars, about sixteen feet from the north wall, placing it about even with the present clergy chairs. It was paired with a lectern at the opposite end of the rail. In their original location, these two stations were a remarkable distance from congregation. In 1979, Father Pedersen moved them forward along with the altar rail, which then ran between the third set of pillars, greatly reducing that distance from the congregation. In the remodeling in 1999, two additional changes were made, which were based on insights from the structure of early Christian churches. The first is the insight that early churches had a single station for reading and preaching, which was called an ambo. The division of preaching and reading between a pulpit and lectern in the medieval church implied a hierarchical division within the Word of God, which is misleading. The second insight was that an ambo, the word "ambo" itself has been unable to find any traction, was a station of its own and that it was not to be corralled by an altar rail and made subservient to the altar. The decision was made that All Saints would be best served if the pulpit would serve both tasks and that it should be located outside of the altar rail on the Gospel side. The result was that the opposite side would be open for a piano or other musical instruments.

As a final look at the pulpit, you should note the gold cross that stands above it. The cross was the last altar cross used at the old church. It was given to the parish in 1916 in memory of Victor B. Caldwell Sr., by his son. It is a beautiful piece of brass work, sculpted in the style of the medieval altar cross. The freestanding altar at the new All Saints had no place for an altar cross, and so it had gone into storage. Pedersen took this out of the closet where it had been stored and made it into a processional cross.

Lifted high over this pulpit, it signals that the purpose of this station is to preach the cross.

A Place of Hallowed Rest

The rest of the carving from the reredos can be found by continuing down the west aisle to the columbarium. About two thirds of the way back is a door that opens into the columbarium, which is known as All Souls Chapel. At the far end of the chapel is an altar in whose front are four more carvings from the Megeath reredos. These are Theodore of Canterbury, 690; Stephen Langton of Canterbury, 1228; William White, bishop of Pennsylvania, 1836; and Robert Harper Clarkson, bishop of Nebraska, 1884. Recall that you had ended with St. Augustine at the pulpit. Having entered the Medieval Latin West, the next stop is Canterbury, England. The first archbishop of Canterbury, St. Augustine, was passed over in favor of the second Theodore of Tarsus. Theodore was from the Eastern church, and it was he that ensured that Augustine's shaky start succeeded. In part, this was due to Theodore's respect for the Celtic Christianity that already existed in England and his ability to unite the two traditions. The second choice of an archbishop of Canterbury is also a surprise. Passing over several noted saints in that office, Casady chose Stephen Langton. Langton's fame was that he participated in the signing of the Magna Carta, which established the right of the barons over the king. This document was in some ways a precursor of the U.S. Constitution, and the choice prepares us for a journey to William White, who was consecrated the bishop of Pennsylvania in 1791, second of the American bishops. He became presiding bishop in 1795 and continued so until his death in 1836. Like the second archbishop of Canterbury, he arguably did more to establishing the Episcopal Church in the United States than Seabury or anyone else. From here, the journey comes down to Clarkson the first bishop of Nebraska, 1865–1884. The argument that Casady mounted with the statues was that there was an apostolic succession of teaching and authority that had come down from the church of the apostles to the church in this very place and time.

With the history lesson complete, you can take some time to look around All Souls Chapel. The first columbarium, established by Father Pedersen in 1977, was located in a closet in the sacristy behind the altar. In 1980, he had a door opened from the worship area into the old unused office space. Bishop Rauscher, who was business manager for All Saints at the time, designed the cabinetry and supervised its construction. The original room provided one hundred sixty-eight niches. The space was dignified and yet had been created at a minimal cost. In 1999, a wall was taken down in order to incorporate a second office into the area, doubling the size of the columbarium. This allowed the number of niches to increase to three hundred. By 2014, one hundred seventy niches are filled and another ninety are reserved, making it one of the largest columbaria located in a church in our region. The remains of many notable contributors to the past forty years of the life of All Saints rest in this location. In the southeast corner are the remains of Bishop Rauscher and his wife, Marjorie. Their niche is marked by the pectoral cross that he wore as bishop of Nebraska. In the same corner are the remains of the seventh rector of All Saints, Charles L. R. Pedersen. Others include Patricia Perry, the first woman warden at All Saints, and her husband, Samuel. They referred to the corner niches opposite the door, which they had reserved, as “their sky box.” Avid Nebraska Football fans, they explained that they wanted a niche with a view looking into the church! Other key wardens include Carroll Fredrickson and Deborah Klein. The parish deacons are represented by the remains of Ernie Bowerman and Frank Murphy. The remains of Jeri Morley, the first African American to be an active part of this community, join those of these other notables, which give a special meaning to a visit in this chapel.

Turning to the north wall, which is presently without niches, you will see three stained-glass windows, which were installed in 1999. The parish had five pieces of stained glass in storage at the time. They were two angels, gilded metal sculptures over stained glass, and three symbols of worship: praying hands, an incense pot, and a harp. They were given to the parish in 1957 by Alberta Talbot Pierson in memory of her husband, Ernest R. Pierson. The angels were originally insets in the large front door of the old building and were grouped with the three symbols of worship, which stood in an arch over the doors. It was nice to get them out of storage, and by incorporating them with additional glass, they provide a worshipful sense to the columbarium. The new installation was of a gift Patricia and Samuel Perry.

Turning back to the altar, you will see the large brass altar cross. This was All Saints first altar cross, given to the parish by Richard R. Ringwalt in 1887. Ringwalt was clerk of the vestry that founded the parish in 1885. It was used on the main altar until 1916, when the cross that we have seen above the pulpit replaced it.

Turning around and looking back out of the space, you will see the World War I honor roll in the corner. Created in 1919, it listed all the young men of All Saints who served in the armed forces during that war.

The list includes a number of notable names in the history of Omaha. Only one has a star, Stanley Brooks Mackay. The rector's son was the only one of these young men to die during the war. With the honor roll stands the American flag representing the veteran of all wars, several of whose remains lie in this space, such as Dr. Merrill Musselman, who was a veteran of the Bataan March; Edwin Wiedner, stationed on Attka for the duration of World War II; and Ron Pullen, who served in Korea.

The space has come together by a series of accidents to include material remains of the whole sweep of All Saints history, which make a powerful witness to the continuity and life of All Saints. There is the Ringwalt cross before which Zahner celebrated the first communion service ever held at All Saints. Opposite is the honor roll, which evokes the poignancy of the long Mackay years. The carved figures in the altar represent the 1920s and Casady's ambitions for the parish. The stained glass belongs to the fifties, and McCallum's dogged leadership. Then, of course, there are the honored remains of Rauscher, Pedersen, and many of the great lay leadership of the past forty years.

Continuing on Around

Leaving the chapel, you can continue the walk around the outer perimeter of the main worship space. Crossing through the baptismal square provides you with an opportunity to look up over the door and take note of three carved figures, primitive "sainte" from Spain. The identity of the saints is unclear, though one seems to be St. Peter and another seems to be a Spanish priest. The province of the pieces is unknown, though they were likely part of an altar reredos in a small village in Spain. They were probably sculpted and painted in eighteenth century and replaced others considered more grand. They were brought to Omaha by someone interested in buying antiques on his trips to Europe and passed to a member of the parish, Dorothy Crosby. Dorothy long prized them but wanted them to pass to the church at her death. They have found a home in this inauspicious shelf where they witness the coming and going of those who worship here and, of course, have a particularly good view of the parish's baptisms.

Continue now down the east aisle, past the door into Christ Chapel, all the way up to the front where the stations of the cross begin. Just up the steps is a first tile that identifies that this set of tiles is the Way of the Cross made by Sandouri and dedicated to the memory of Dorothy Harris, 1921–2000. Dorothy Harris, a great parish worker from the 1950s, made the parish's 2000 pilgrimage to Israel and died suddenly and unexpectedly on her return home. When the question was raised at a vestry meeting as to whether the remodeling of the worship area, which was under way at the time, ought to include permanent stations of the cross, there seemed to a ready answer. On the pilgrimage, the participants had seen on their visit to St. George's, the Anglican cathedral in Jerusalem, their new stations of the cross installed for the millennium. They had been made for them by the Sandouri Workshop located in the Armenian Quarter of Jerusalem along the Armenian Patriarchate Road. The priest who led the stations that night observed that a duplicate set had been made to ensure against any accident during installation. A visit to the shop had confirmed this, and so it was proposed that these would be a fitting choice for permanent station at All Saints. Armenian iconography is simple but rich. The blue floral borders are typical. From this point, you might choose to follow the fourteen stations on around the perimeter of the worship space ending at the altar rail just behind the pulpit.

The Chapel Experience

Exiting the central worship area and crossing the narthex to the east, you will find the door to Christ Chapel. The chapel is the upper level of an addition to the building built in 1979. The west wing originally contained a chapel, which was converted into much-needed office space. As a result, the parish had lived without a chapel for some time. It was missed as a venue for worship fitted for weekday services, small wedding and funerals, and a new Saturday night Eucharist. The new chapel not only provides a more intimate space, but it also provides a very different feel. It is considered more traditional. Its most stunning feature is the three traditional stained-glass windows. Each of these was a significant addition to the old building on Twenty-Sixth and Dewey, given as part of the attempt to restore the stained glass that was lost in the 1933 fire. They were too new and too good to leave behind as was done with all of the remaining stained glass in the old building. When they came to the new building, they were located in the glass wall of the narthex. There they had a rather museum-like exposure dissociated with the work of worship with which they had been originally intended. Somewhat as an afterthought, they were incorporated into the design of this chapel, which was built in 1979, and here they have been reengaged with the work of worship.

The All Saints Window

The first of these is located behind the altar. It was the window given in memory of Eunice Arthur Ritchie by her husband in 1949. The window was manufactured by the Willet Studio of Philadelphia under the leadership of Henry Willet, which was, at the time, the premier stained-glass studio in the country. The glass is mouth-blown pot metal glass, which allows for the brilliant colors, especially the blues and the reds that you see in all three of the windows, each of which were manufactured by Willet as part of an extensive series planned to replace all of the side windows in the old building. In addition to high-caliber glass, the artistic embellishments on the glass are those of skilled artists.

The subject matter of this window was strongly influenced by Gordon Galaty, who was the rector of All Saints when it was commissioned. It is a strong statement of centrality of the Eucharist in the mystery of salvation and of the complimentary role of Christ as priest and king. At the center of the window is the Christ figure enthroned, wearing a crown and holding an orb after the manner of a king, and yet he is dressed in the robes of a priest. The earth, a green circle below the figure, is his footstool. It is surrounded by a starry heaven and is mirrored in the circles found along the central vertical line in the window. A circle above surrounds the head of the Christ figure, and at the same time, it forms the circle of the Celtic cross that stands behind the Christ figure. Below the circular shape of the bread held in the hands of the priest below reflects the circle of the earth and circle of the heaven.

Above the Christ figure in each corner are angels with musical instruments with which they accompany the act of worship that is taking place. In the upper realm on each side of the Christ are choirs of saints. On the upper left-hand side are Dorcas, Elijah, Patrick, Isaiah, Francis of Assisi, King David, and the Apostle Peter. Across from them are Hilda of Whitby, Augustine of Canterbury, Thomas Becket of Canterbury, Stephen the Martyr, Ambrose, the Apostle Andrew, and the Apostle Paul. The inclusion of the two women is an interesting touch. Dorcas, also called Tabatha, is mentioned in the book of Acts of the Apostles. She was noted from her needlework, the first head, one might say, of the altar guild. Hilda was a sixth-century Celtic saint who was instrumental in mediating unity between the newly arrived Latin mission from Rome with the remaining Celtic Christians in England. As the saints that Casady chose for the Megeath reredos or Pedersen for the narthex windows, they provide clues to Galaty's spirituality.

A divide is carefully marked in a window by an arch whose lower side seems to be made up of buds on the verge of popping open. Above the arc, the saints represent what was called the Church Triumphant. Below the arc is the church militant, "we feebly struggle, they in glory shine" as we sing in the All Saints hymn: "For all the saints . . ." In the lower left panel is a family—mother, father, children—and on the right are diverse people of the world representing different occupations. In the center is a priest celebrating the Eucharist through which the church militant communes with the saints. The arc that separates the two realms is opened by the upward movement of the chalice and host, an opening that allows for "the communion of the saints." It is, indeed, fitting that the line from the creed was used in the lower level to give a name to the window.

The image of king suggests a reference to the social Gospel an ideal that was current in the theology of the time and most particularly in the theology of Galaty. The image of Christ as a priest suggests the centrality of the Eucharist to the life and work of the church. The Eucharistic image that it portrays is decidedly high church or catholic. This can be gathered by noting that on the altar are two Eucharistic candles, and above it are seven sanctuary lamps. The priest wears a chasuble, a vestment that had not, to that point in time, been worn at All Saints and is flanked by a deacon and subdeacon, both in dalmatics. In the lower story below the priest are a pelican and her babies. The medieval lore about pelicans was that a mother pelican pecked their own breast until she bleed in order to feed her young. The image was used as a symbol to express the idea of "the sacrifice of the mass." These themes suggest something of the reform Galaty had in mind for All Saints, which was interrupted when he was called to active duty in Korea.

There are a few more details that are noteworthy. In the upper story are three shields. Two are the traditional shields of the Feast of All Saints. The other, in the center, was from the Ritchie family's coat of arms. It was also part of Ritchie's influence that the cross behind the Christ figure is a Celtic cross. We have already noted the importance to the Celtic cross to All Saints, which produced the stone cross that once stood at the top of its north gable. The splendid stone Celtic cross in Forest Lawn, which marks the grave of his wife, Eunice, testifies to how much Ritchie thought of it as a symbol of his heritage. While the text in the window refers to "the communion of saints," it is easy to see how this has gained the name of the All Saints Window. It is truly a treasure of the parish, and after a couple of alternative locations, it has found its home behind the altar of the chapel, which it mirrors and explicates.

Trinity Window

The window to the east of the altar on your left is the Trinity Window. It was installed in 1954 on Trinity Sunday in the old building at Twenty-Sixth and Dewey. It was given in the will of the late Dr. Frederick O. Beck in memory of his wife and himself. Like the other stained-glass windows in the chapel, it was manufactured by the Willet Studio of Philadelphia. The quality of this glass and the artistry in this window, if anything, exceeds that of the All Saints Window. It was part of the continuing effort to restore the stained glass that had been lost in the 1933 fire. The execution of this window fell to McCallum. McCallum's churchmanship was very different from that of Galaty. If for Galaty it was the Eucharist that transformed the world, for McCallum it was the Word of God preached by the church that transformed the world. He found the theme for the window in the lectionary of the *Book of Common Prayer*, 1928. The readings for Trinity Sunday are depicted. The Gospel appointed for that Sunday was John 3: the discourse of Jesus with Nicodemus. It is represented in the bottom panel in the center, where Jesus is pictured instructing Nicodemus. The crescent moon and star provide the clue that it is at night. The other proper for that day, the epistle (remember there were no third readings in that lectionary) was taken from Revelations 4. This is the image of the Almighty, the Pantocrator, enthroned in heaven. Here as in the All Saints Window, the earth is portrayed at the feet of the central figure. The central image in this window is more like the icons of the savior found in Eastern Orthodox icons, and it makes an interesting contrast with the Western Latin image of Christ our King. In the icon, it is understood that the face of the Glorified Christ is the face of God, not just the face of the second person.

The four corners of the throne on which the figure sits are formed by four faces: a man, a lion, an ox, and an eagle, representing the Gospels of Matthew, Mark, Luke, and John. In an arc above the throne are twenty-four elders, representing the twelve patriarchs and the twelve apostles. They are in the process of worshiping the lamb, so they are casting down their crowns. A river runs out of heavens, carrying the eternal gospel into the world.

In the lower tier on the left is the Archangel Michael contending with Satan and on the right of the Archangel Gabriel announcing the coming of the kingdom. The window includes the text identified with the heavenly worship, "Holy, Holy, Holy Lord, God Almighty." The thrice holy is a reference to the Trinity, and it is well known as the central act of worship in the Eucharist. In the upper part of each arch are the symbols of Father, Son, and Holy Spirit, a hand, a face, and a dove. The window is, in a sense, a pictorial sermon.

The Ascension Window

This window was originally installed in the old building in 1955. It was given by Gladys Hundley in memory of her parents, Clara and Oscar Goodman. It too was manufactured by the Willet Studio of Philadelphia. McCallum selected the theme for this window as an illustration of the Ascension. The central image in the window is the ascending Christ, Acts 1:9–11. A text from the collect from the Feast of the Ascension from *Book of Common Prayer* appears in the window: "May we also ascend." In the lower story Christ appears among the disciples telling them that he is about to ascend. Above the ascending Christ are angels who are opening the door of heaven, and the apostles look up into the air. In the account in the book of Acts, an angel asks them, "Why do you look up into the air?" The implication is that they should be looking outward to the ends of the world to which they are sent by the Great Commission found in the Gospel of Matthew: "Go baptize all nations . . ." The reference to baptism is implied by the image of a baptismal shell with the three drops of water dripping from it, which appears in the center of the lower tier. It appears that the window was designed to sit over the baptismal font in the old church.

The theme of the Great Commission is emphasized by two additional scenes taken from the Gospel of John at the opposite ends of the lower tier. On the left is the breakfast on the Sea of Galilee, John 21:4–14, and on the right is the commission of Peter, John 21:15–17, "feed my sheep." A rock appears in a panel referring to the fact that Peter is a nickname meaning "rock," which Jesus gave to Simon bar Jonah. The general style of this window is more nineteenth century, and the image of Jesus is perhaps a little saccharine or sentimental. It has sometimes occurred to me that the images of Jesus three windows have a curious sense of history: the one on the left being more primitive and Greek, the one in the middle, Gothic and English, and the one on the left, modern and American. If the Ascension Window falls short of the other two in terms of artistic merit, it is still a very fine piece of work that contributes to the beauty and spirituality of this space.

Other notable items in Christ Chapel are the elaborate brass altar rail, which was a gift of William A. Redick in memory of his father John Irwin

Redick in 1907. Redick was one of All Saints original vestry members, and his father made one of the initial gifts for the founding of the parish. With it is the brass prayer desk, which was part of Redick's gift in 1907. It sat in the center aisle of the old church and was frequently used for litanies and prayers, something which is no longer as prominent as it once was in Anglican churches.

To the right of the altar is an ambry, given in memory of Mary Prince by her daughter Helen Amsden, where the sacrament is reserved. Above it is a sanctuary lamp. Prior to the redecoration of the chapel in 1995, the reserve sacrament was kept in the sacristy behind the main altar. Any sense of devotion to the reserved sacrament was foreign to McCallum. It was important, on the other hand, to Pedersen, though he felt pressure not to impose his devotion on the parish. He experimented with various possibilities, but he never found a solution. It was only with the redecoration of the parish that a prominent location was established, and the parish seemed to readily accept its more public role in the life of the parish.

If you turn now to the back of the chapel, you will see the Baptismal Shell. It is an actual seashell, which was purchased for us in San Diego, California. The stand was built by Bishop Rauscher, and it was dedicated to the memory of Clive Short. Clive Short, a contractor and a federal marshal, was a colorful character and close friend of Rauscher. He had played a big role in Rauscher's "builders for Christ" campaign. Behind it is a Mother and Child terra-cotta, which was given to the parish by Ned and Laura Reynolds. Finally, before you leave the chapel, note the Memorabilia Window. Its featured possession is an autograph book that belonged to Bishop Talbot, the first missionary bishop to serve the Nebraska Territory. Talbot took this autograph book to the first meeting of the House of Bishops following the Civil War. It contains the signatures of all the bishops that came to this meeting, including the Southern bishops, who had been absent during the war. It is a powerful symbol of reconciliation. Talbot gave the book to the mother of Zerlina Lewis, then a young girl. Zerlina gave it to All Saints before she died. The redecoration of the chapel in 1998 was dedicated to her memory, and this keeps us mindful of her and her family's many contributions to the Episcopal Church in Omaha.

As you leave the chapel, on the left is a door, which leads into the choir room. The choir in the new building was originally housed downstairs. Men's and women's vesting rooms where located on each side of the bathrooms, and an office was located across the hall for the organist choirmaster. Rehearsals were held in the hall. When the offices were moved out of the west wing in 1979, they move upstairs in the space that was their own but never designed for rehearsals. In the 1998 building program, one of the goals was to give the choir its own space specifically designed for rehearsals and which was conveniently located in respect to worship area. If you step into this room, you will notice a wall with pictures of the parish's organist choirmasters, which, like its rectors, counts some incredibly long tenures and interesting characters.

If as you leave the chapel you turn to the right, you will find the stairs to the lower level. The lower level can be reached by crossing the narthex and using an elevator. If you continue down the broad stairwell on a third landing, you will be able to walk straight ahead into the office level. Here you will find on your right a large library room, which is home to a sizeable theological library that was given to the parish and the remains of the Diocese of Nebraska's resource library. The room was dedicated to the memory of Rev. Canon Burgess upon the request of Rene Nauman, his granddaughter, whose estate funded the finishing of the room. Burgess was an early scholarly priest of the diocese who has figured in the beginning of our story as he was the secretary of the standing committee when Bishop Clarkson died in 1884. The library is used for classes and various committee meetings as well. In the wall is a miniature portrait of Burgess that was taken at the time of his ordination. You are welcome to spend time in the library and to use it as reading room.

If as you reached the third landing you turned to your left, you would have passed a large office space, which belongs to the organist choirmaster, and another large office, which belongs to the rector. The hall turns at this point and takes you into the main part of the office and out the east door. If you continued down the remaining stairs, you will come to lower level. To the right are the offices, and to the left is the bathroom core for the lower level and the entrance into the parish hall. This parish hall has served the parish for more than fifty years even though it was intended as a temporary solution until a parish hall could be built. It has done remarkably well even though it is undersized and not the most convenient shape for events, being long and narrow. On both sides, the halls are the class rooms, which have been altered and expanded to meet current needs. At the far end of the hall, a large activity room was developed, which allows the entire church school to assemble for worship and audiovisual events. It was dedicated to Edie Wiedner as a memorial to her career in education and to her service to the parish.

If you follow through the hall past the activity room, you will come to the north doors. They are directly across from the retreat center.

The Future of Art at All Saints

All Saints has been privileged over the years to enjoy art and architecture that are world class. That is because there has been a tradition in the parish of supporting the arts. It is particularly satisfying that the parish has made use of significant local Omaha artists, such as Wallace, Alston, and Wilson. Hopefully, the tradition will continue on into the future, and the parish will preserve and add to its artistic heritage.

Appendix 2

The Music Story

The Foundation

In the course of telling All Saints story, there have been many references to the parish's music program, which indicates what a significant role music has played within the greater story of the parish. Looking back over this lengthy tale that has been told, one can, of course, find a number of references to the music program, but it seems that referring a reader to these scattered references would leave untold much of the story within the story. A few quick observations will suggest just how special this story is for understanding All Saints. My first observation is that those who founded the parish in 1885 were of the opinion that growth of the parish was tied to its ability to offer an exceptional music program, an opinion that was held by the parish for some time. My second observation is that the tenures of the directors of the musical program were quite exceptional. Neubecker's twenty-seven years as organist equal that of any of the parish's rectors' tenure, and Simms's fifty-three years exceeds that of any two of them put together! It has drawn out of the parish not only choristers, but also extraordinary and passionate lay leadership, such as Mrs. Hoagland's passionate drive to raise money for a new organ in the thirties or Robert Spire's delft leadership, which saw that the new building in the sixties had a new organ suitable to the building. The music story has been rich, and if the affairs of the rectors and parishioners have been a love story, the music story has been no less so.

I offer, then, this appendix as a means of remedying what is missing in some small way. I venture to do so despite my lack of qualifications when it comes to music and despite the fact that I have been one of the parish's rector. This latter condition means that the music program has inevitably been experienced as a problem. This is because congregations have a wide range of opinions about what music programs should be and do, and a rector inevitably finds himself mediating the difference. You may recall Mackay's story of "The Rector's Nightmare" in the second chapter of our story. In his dream, Mackay said he had died and gone to heaven. Upon arriving in heaven, he finds himself assigned by the on-duty angel to call on new arrivals. His first assignment, he discovered, was to call upon a newly arrived woman, a past parishioner of his, as it turned out, who, back on earth, had recently complained about his lack of visits to her. My rector's nightmare would be that I died and went to heaven and was subsequently put in charge of the heavenly music program.

Let me begin by asking you to imagine that you walked into All Saints in the summer of 1887. You would have heard the sweet-toned sound of a newly installed Roosevelt pipe organ. Its pipes were housed behind the choir on the right side. The building itself had just been completed, and it afforded an expansive space, seating nearly five hundred individuals. Its ceiling was rather low, and hence, the organ pipes had the appearance of being tucked rather tightly into its allotted space. The pipe organ was the gift of James Woolworth, though it was recorded as the gift of his teenage daughter, Meliora, in memory of her little brother, Robert Harper, who had died at the age of five in 1879. The *Excelsior* described it as one of Roosevelt's best instruments "encased in highly polished and carved oak." In a picture taken of the Roosevelt organ in 1905, one can see that the large oak base stood immediately to the right of the altar.

The large pipes rise out of the top of it, reaching to the rather-low ceiling and following its angle of descent to the outer wall.

> The Roosevelt Company of New York City, headed by two pioneering brothers, Hilbourne and Frank Roosevelt, built some five hundred instruments between1875 and 1895. The organ for All Saints was approximately their three hundred fiftieth work and one of the last that Hilbourne worked on as he died in 1886. The cabinet was eighteen feet wide, eighteen feet high, and sixteen feet deep. It had two manuals and twenty-six stops, twenty-one of which were under expression. The sixteen-foot and eight-foot diapasons were not, and one can see them exposed in a picture of the church's interior, tucked under the rather low ceiling on the right-hand side, south side of the building. The voicing of their instrument was described

as gentle, smooth, and lovely. The open diapason was rich, round, and full through its entire compass. It was meant to be the solid "workhorse" of an instrument, while the Aeoline stop was its soft and delicate counterpart. One of the hallmarks of a Roosevelt organ was its Doppelflute. The Doppelflute is a wooden flute stop that is different from other pipes in that it has two mouths, one on the front and one on the back of each pipe. It has a fundamental rich sound. On the other hand, the instrument did not present the organist with a large variety of tonal colors.

The All Saints Roosevelt—1886

8' Open Diapason Bass
8' Open Diapason Treble
8' Salicional Bass
8' Salicional Treble
8' Doppelflute Bass
8' Doppelflute Treble
4' Gemshorn Bass
4' Gemshorn Treble
8' Aeoline Bass
8' Aeoline Treble Bellows Signal

PEDAL (27 notes)

16' Bourdon
Manual Octave coupler
Tremulant

In 1890, Trinity Cathedral installed an almost identical Roosevelt Pipe organ at the cost of $6,400, essentially the same price as All Saints in 1886. Like All Saints, by 1930, it was having trouble with the maintenance and was in touch with the Austin Company, which had succeeded Roosevelt as the dominant manufacturer of pipe organs in America.

The young man at the organ was R. J. Allen, who had recently come to Omaha. Louis Zahner, the new rector of the parish, had brought him with him from Bloomington, Pennsylvania. Their presence was a double coup for the city's new church. Not only had it managed to bring a well-credentialed Episcopal priest to the city, but it had also brought a competent organist to the city, which was perhaps an even greater accomplishment. Allen's salary was a modest $200, but given the fact that the young man would live with the Zahners in the rectory, it was a good place to start out.

When the vested choir processed in, you would have been struck by deep, rich male voices of nearly thirty choristers. They were led by Thomas J. Pennell. Pennell worked as an auditor for the Burlington Railroad, but his passion was music. He belonged to Omaha's Apollo Club, whose purpose was to promote the musical arts in Omaha. The club among other things sponsored a men's choir, which frequently performed concerts for Omaha audiences. Pennell was the club's bass soloist. In 1993, Pennell managed to pull off a major cue for the club. On a business trip to St. Louis, he met and managed to sign Sophia Scalchi, the internationally known opera diva, to a contract to appear in concert in Omaha. Italian-born Scalchi had her debut at the Met in 1885 and was famed for her deep mezzo soprano voice. She sang in Omaha on May 18, 1890, appearing with Adolph Brodsky, violinist and concertmaster of the New York Symphony Orchestra. In 1896, Pennell followed his dream. He quit the railroad and set off to Italy to study music. These aspirations were clearly alive when he began as choirmaster at All Saints.[241]

When Zahner was installed as the rector of All Saints on January 22, 1887, Bishop Worthington had also installed Pennell as choirmaster in a rather unusual addition to the installation service, which indicates that he had already been hired by the parish before Zahner's arrival. The organist who had come with Zahner, however, did not stay long. The vestry accepted his resignation effective November 1, 1887, making his stay at All Saints exactly one year. Perhaps Allen found Omaha too much of a contrast to the picturesque and cultural city of Bloomington, which lies in Pennsylvania's Susquehanna Valley. Perhaps he was not fully qualified for the job. That is, however, unlikely since Zahner's wife was herself a highly trained organist choirmaster and would hardly have allowed her husband to make such a mistake. More likely, Allen found that he was working for Pennell and not the other way around.

Pennell and his sister had been hired in 1883 by Trinity Cathedral in anticipation of the completion of its building program. He and his sister were to receive $500, but there appears to have been a debate at the cathedral whether the parish could afford such an outlay, particularly in view of the expense entailed in its ambitious building program. It is likely that Woolworth was behind the hiring of Pennell at the cathedral, and it

241 *Omaha World-Herald*, June 6, 1897; May 12, 1893, p. 8; August 29, 1896.

is for certain that it was he who brought Pennell to All Saints when he left the cathedral. Pennell's allowance in his new situation was $133.33 a month. That would have allowed him to give himself an annual salary of $500 and to use the remainder to hire an adequate number of male choristers and to buy the necessary music and supplies required by the choir. Allen, the original organist at All Saints, was paid less than $250 a year, which clearly indicates that All Saints saw Pennell as the director of the music program and Allen as part of Pennell's staff. Moreover, Pennell was closely allied with James and Elizabeth Woolworth, who had been the chief force in his being hired, and they continued to be his chief patrons within the parish's music program. Elizabeth Woolworth, Woolworth's second wife, had studied liturgy and church music at Racine, Wisconsin, a small but important Episcopal college. She was a strong-willed person with very definite ideas about church music and would have hardly been a silent patron.

It was not, however, easy to replace Allen. Organists did not grow on trees, at least the trees in Omaha. It took the parish until April of the following year to hire an organist. Its choice was William S. Marshall of Salem, Ohio, and he was offered a salary that was double that of Allen, $500 per year. He seems to have fit in quite well at least for the time being. He had, in fact, been recruited by Pennell, and there would have been no misunderstanding on his part about who was in charge of the music program or what the parish's expectations of him were.

If the vision of musical excellence had originated with James and Elizabeth Woolworth, it was not lost on the new rector, Louis Zahner. We can get an idea of the importance Zahner put in music by looking at announcements he placed in the weekend editions of the *Excelsior*, one of Omaha's secular newspapers at the time. In these ads, Zahner regularly published the music that would be used on the coming Sunday. For example, he placed the following announcement in the *Excelsior* on February 28, 1891:

> On the coming Sunday, the third Sunday in Lent, March 1, the services will be Holy Communion at 11:00 a.m. and a chorale evening song at 4:00 p.m. The music at Holy Communion will be "Litany Hymn, Fiorio; Introit, "O, Savior of the World," Goss; Communion Service in F, Garrett; Offertory, "Come unto Me, Ye Weary," Dykes." At the chorale evening song, the music will be "Canticles, chants, Anthem for tenor solo and chorus, "Withdraw Thou Not Thy Mercy," Attwood; Offertory (unaccompanied) "There is a Green Hill Far Away," Burstall.

Special musical services were a regular offering, and an announcement in 1890 is typical of these special programs.

AT ALL SAINTS

> A special musical service will be held at All Saints Church, Twenty-Sixth and Howard Streets, this evening. This program will be sung: Processional, hymn 203, Magnificat and Nunc Dimittis, Stainer; Anthem, the thirteenth psalm; Mendelssohn, Alto solo and chorus, "How Lord Wilt Thou Forget Me?" Chorale: "Lord My God, Behold and Hear Me." Alto solo and chorus, "Lord, Thy Truth and Loving Kindness." Final chorus, "Lord, With Thankful Exultation." Offertory, "Abide with Me," Barnaby; Recessional, "We Are But Strangers Here," Sullivan. The program will be rendered by the full vested choir of thirty voices, with Miss Elizabeth Pennell as soloist. The seats are free and all are cordially invited to attend the service.

Not all the performances of Evening Song were as elaborate as this, and the availability of Pennell's sister as a soloist made this special. We can see in the selections a hint at the style of music that was favored at the time. The service opened with a solemn processional hymn from the American Episcopal Hymnal, "A Few More Years Shall Roll," a text by H. Bonar, heavy with the thoughts about death. The canticles were sung to new settings by John Stainer. Stainer was the organist of Saint Paul's London and a close friend of Arthur Sullivan, who the reader will recognize from his operettas produced with the librettist W. S. Gilbert. Evening Prayer would have concluded, better put, paused, after a series of three collects for the central musical offering of the evening. This consisted of three chorus anthems from the Mendelssohn oratorio Elijah, which was widely performed in England and America at the time. These selections featured an alto soloist, whose voice would have been a dramatic contrast to the rich deep voices of the all-male choir. After these selections were sung, a collection was taken up during the singing of an offertory hymn. In this case, it was the well-known evening hymn "Abide with Me," which is still in the American Hymnal but, in the later edition, set to a tune by Monk. Barnaby's setting listed here would have given "Abide with Me" a lilt. Following the offertory, a final collect was read and a recessional hymn sung. The recessional was "We Are but Strangers Here" set to a tune composed by Arthur Sullivan, a favored composer of the time.

Like the procession, the theme is heavily weighted with the sense of the transient nature of life. It was, after all, Lent. It would have been thoroughly melancholic, but in a warm and romantic way, suiting Victorian temperament.

Sung Evening Prayer was held regularly at four on Sunday afternoons. These services were well attended and attracted a significant number of individuals from outside of the parish. The draw of these services, which were likely to have enticed an individual to come to church for a second time on Sunday, is hard for us to comprehend. We need to recall that this was a world where music was not a flip of the switch away. A socializing event that allowed one to hear some good music well done was deeply valued. These Evening Prayer services continued on into the 1920s, when American lifestyle was dramatically altered, undercutting the value these services once enjoyed.

When Zahner left in 1891, the music program proceeded unimpaired and was readily supported by Mackay when he arrived as the new rector. Nevertheless, there were approaching clouds. The nineties brought on a number of financial setbacks for the country and for Omaha in particular. This, of course, was felt in the parish, which was itself encumbered with debt and was struggling to make ends meet. No one was prepared to surface the question of whether the music budget was out of proportion to the parish's general budget, but Pennell continually presented the vestry with requests for special expenses beyond his designated budget. Details of the story can be found in chapter 2, but suffice it to say that Woolworth's protection of the music program finally found its limit. On September 10, 1892, the vestry received a communication from Pennell, this time about raising his salary. It was the final straw, and in the absence of Woolworth, the vestry passed the following resolution:

> Whereas it is deemed necessary to reduce the general expenses of the church and to that end reduce the expenses in the sum of $500 per year, by placing the choir under the charge of the organist and otherwise reorganizing the same, therefore be it resolved that from and after October 1, 1892, the services of Mr. T. J. Pennell as choir master be dispensed with and that the secretary notify him of this action.

Beginning a Ministry of Fifty-Three Years

Marshall, who had, earlier that year, himself asked for an increase in his salary, was now being asked to do more for the same salary. Hopkins, the junior warden, was appointed to work things out with Marshall. He must have been successful to a degree because Marshall continued until June of 1895. Marshall lacked the versatility and sense of adventure that had driven Pennell, but for the moment, all Mackay needed was a steady program, which Marshall could supply. However, in June of 1895, Mackay quietly replaced Marshall with James W. Simms. Mackay was not above raiding his old bailey wick, St. Paul's Council Bluff, Iowa. He had already poached a vestry man by inviting A. E. Smith to leave St. Paul's to be on All Saints vestry even though Smith was still living in Council Bluffs. Mackay had hired Simms as the organist for St. Paul's, Council Bluffs, not long before he moved to All Saints. At the time, Simms was unmarried and in his mid-twenties. He had been recommended to Mackay by a friend of his who was traveling in England. The friend, himself an organist, had come across young Simms working at Chichester Cathedral, where he was about to finish his training.

Simms was born and educated in England. His father was an organist at a large parish church in Stourbridge, Sussex. His older brother, Paul, was an organist as well and was working for an Episcopal church in New Orleans. Simms was the "articled student" of Theodore Edward Aylward, the organist of Chichester Cathedral. That meant that he had been invited to live with Aylward while he studied, where he practiced and assisted with the daily cathedral services and choir direction. The result of this kind of training was a student that was steeped in the traditions and techniques of church musicianship. After a year at St. Paul's, Simms's sweetheart, Katherine, joined him; and a year later, they had a daughter, Winifred, their only child. Their marriage would be as quiet and as steady as Simms's career. When Simms died in 1951, she was still at his side, the daughter, Mrs. Harry Gales was living in Jersey City, New Jersey.

When Simms arrived at All Saints, they lived in an apartment on Twenty-Seventh Street across from the church and later moved to 5014 Western. One of his first initiatives was to recruit a boys' choir. One of the boys in the parish to join was Martin Bush. Simms quickly recognized the talents of Bush, and he trained him as an organist and choirmaster. Bush would go to become one of the Omaha prestigious organ choirmasters, serving the expanding music program of First Central Congregational Church. The men became close colleagues in the city, which says as much about Simms's generosity as it does Bush's loyalty. When Simms died, Bush, who was also the music editor for the *Omaha World-Herald*, wrote a tribute to Simms in which he described him by saying his "knowledge of church music both for organ and choirs was vast. One saw him thoroughly acquainted with the music of the Tudor composers. Then the mid-Victorian writers during their vogue, which is about the point of his entree at All Saints." Bush goes on to say that as that vogue passed, Simms "was alert to succeeding styles and schools of church music, even on to modernistic trends of recent years. He avidly read of every new development and, once assured of the new conforming to his ideals of dignity, churchliness and beauty, was willing to accept it." In describing Simms's influence on him, Bush wrote that he had been "inoculated" by him "with the same relentless musical integrity."

However, for all his erudition, Simms was quite personable, affectionately known by his choir as "Simmsy." Bush recalled that he would join the kids in the choir for a half hour of scrub baseball or football preceding weekly afternoon rehearsals. Simms was, in fact, a passionate baseball fan and a player. He was once offered a position on a Des Moines team, which he politely turned down, happy, he said, with Western league. Reluctant to have his picture taken, he was reported to say of the picture he liked best of himself was one that a reporter took of him seated on the third baseline.

The quiet Englishman began to rebuild the music program at All Saints, and with a little over a year behind him, he approached the vestry in November with a modest request for some special music for Christmas. Given that such a request had precipitated Pennell's firing a little over a year before, it provides evidence of the progress that he had made. Mr. Wattles removed any chance that this might initiate a replay of the old debate over the music budget by "kindly consenting to pay the bill for the same." Music returned to the agenda in December. By a unanimous vote, the rector was authorized to maintain the music at its present standard of efficiency until the 1897 midsummer vacation unless sooner instructed to the contrary by the vestry. The budget for the music program for the coming year was $1,800, and the music committee consisting of Mr. Wattles and Mr. Kirkendall, two of the vestry's heavy hitters, agreed to secure such attractions as would make All Saints Choir the best in the city. This is another sign that things were working! The budget was still less than the original music budget, but the results are labeled as quite satisfactory. The businessmen of the vestry provided it with an accolade dear to their hearts but seldom used in regard to music programs. It is commended by them as "efficient," a curious but understandable, appropriate accolade for a music program.

One of the innovations Simms made shortly after his arrival was vesting women as part of the choir. This seems to be an idea that was mutually supported by Mackay and Simms, and it may well be one of the innovations that had produced efficiency. The result of this effort was celebrated with a photograph taken in December of 1897 by Lancaster-Hahnema. In the photograph, we see thirty vested choir members. Twelve of them are women, the only vested women in a choir of the Episcopal Church in Nebraska. The fact was so noteworthy that the *Boston Journal* ran the picture in its *Home Magazine* in the middle of 1898.

As his success in the parish grew, so too did Simms's status in the community. He was one of the founders of the Nebraska chapter of the American Guild of Organists. He was a presence and performer in a wide variety of musical events in the city. For example, in April of 1902, Simms organized a Tuesday evening recital at All Saints. He played and accompanied the soloists, including a featured soloist Madame Myron Smith. Smith had sung in the choir at All Saints before going off to New York for voice lessons and was making a return visit to the city. Mackay reported in *Church and Home*, "She went away a grand singer, she has returned an artist." In the article, he went on to describe the past Tuesday evening event:

> The services at All Saints church were attended by large congregations yesterday. The afternoon musical service was especially fine, and the church was packed to the doors many standing, and numbers of people were unable to gain admittance. Madame Myron Smith's solo was especially fine.[242]

During her visit, Smith sang at several services, including the Easter service, at which she sang an aria from Sir Arthur Sullivan's "Light of the World," "He is risen."[243] The year was topped off with the appearance of another picture of the choir, this time in the *Bee*, accompanied by an article, which declared that it was one of the notable choirs in the city.

As a reward for his hard work, the vestry provided Simms with a trip to England in the summer of 1904. He spent the first part of his vacation is Southern England and on the Isle of Wright, after which he went to Stourbridge, his old home. Mackay reports that "He has been visiting cathedral choirs and no doubt will come back with new ideas and full of enthusiasm for the winter campaign."

The growing range of the choir is evident from a report in *Church and Home* that the choir had sung as the anthem the "Hymn to the Trinity" by Tchaikovsky, the well-known Russian composer. It is impressive that Simms's choice takes him outside of the English choral tradition, asking

242 *Church and Home*, vol. VIII, no. 26, April 12, 1902.

243 *Church and Home*, vol. VIII, no. 27 April 19, 1902.

his choir to sing the piece drawn from the liturgy of the Russian Orthodox Church unaccompanied. The piece would have had a startling Orthodox sound in the ears of the congregation.[244] Mackay's cheerleading, which contributed, in its own way, to the growth of Simm's program, is again in evidence: "We shall want this anthem repeated." He wrote in *Church and Home.*

In 1906, the congregation moved into the new building, which was a substantially larger and more acoustically sophisticated than that of the old wood church that it replaced. Of course, the old Roosevelt pipe organ continued to serve the parish. In the haste of opening the church for the Easter service, much was left undone. Mackay explained,

> The unfinished appearance of our new church may occasion some surprise, but it was a question of whether we should have the building for Easter services, or wait for the entire completion of the work which would take several weeks to accomplish. It was deemed best to postpone the decorations and finishing until later, but our people can see what a beautiful church we shall have when even in the unfinished condition. It is so stately and dignified. The organ could not be fully completed for the Easter services, some of the pipes have been lost in transit.[245]

The Mackay-Simms run continued with considerable success, though after 1915, Simms was progressively more on his own as Mackay began to withdraw. With Mackay's death in 1920, Simms prepared for a dramatic transition. Mackay's successor was indeed quite different in churchmanship and temperament. One result is that there is much less information about the program due in part to Casady's introverted nature, making it difficult to assess Casady's relationship with Simms and the music program. It is probably fair to say that music was not among Casady's priorities. At the top of his list was Christian education for the children of the parish, and then came outreach activities centered on athletics and summer camps and the development of parish administration.

The great shift in American culture was under way in the twenties, and the appeal of special musical events was waning. It was soon clear that it was not possible to sustain the evening service that the parish had since its founding. That depressed Casady because he saw it as a decline in the loyalty of individuals to the church. The loyalty of his parishioners, however,

---

244 *Church and Home*, Vol. XI, No. 2 Oct 20, 1905

245 *Church and Home*, vol. XIII, no. 27, Easter 1907.

was not so much changed as their lives. Suburban life, into which most of his parish had now entered, brought with it new opportunities and new demands both in terms of time and money. Moreover, his parishioners, along with the country, were beginning to listen to music from other sources, not least of which was the radio. In 1926, the All Saints choir was featured in a service, which was broadcast from the Woodman of the Word on February 20.[246] This was felt to be an honor, particularly by Casady, but it was a signal of a change that would affect the way people listened to music. Those who attended live performance would become specialized patrons as indeed would those who performed would become specialized artists. The divide between classic and popular would become not so much a line as a gulf.

The New Era of the Austin

Simms was, however, well established in his position, and he soldiered on without complaint. Casady did not neglect praising the musical program. At the annual meeting in1924, he praised the merits of the parish's various programs and concluded, "The same thing might be said for the musical traditions of the parish which are generally recognized to be the best in the city." At this same annual meeting, Casady challenged the parish to use the coming year to prepare for the parish's fortieth anniversary. A fortieth anniversary might not seem to be such a significant occasion, but Casady was in a hurry, and he used the benchmark as an occasion for announcing his vision for the parish, which included extensive building and the creation of a substantial endowment. His call stirred others to think in a visionary way, and it resulted in a goal that he probably had not anticipated. The new Dundee Guild came up with the idea that the parish needed a new organ.

Mrs. William Hoagland, president of that guild, reported to the parish that her guild, at its final meeting of the year, had had the following discussion: "We have concluded all our plans and pledges for last year, but for some time I have been indulging a dream that one of our organizations might start a fund for a new organ for All Saints Church." In reaction to her remarks, Mrs. D. L. Thomas asked, "How much have we in the treasury?" Upon being informed that it was something more than a hundred dollars, Thomas moved that the guild take $100 and start the organ fund. The first step had been taken. As Hoagland argued, "The parish's organ was old, in bad repair, and only the consummate musicianship of Mr. Simms made any music possible."

The guild's activities were intense, including collecting scrap paper "from Minne Lusa to Bellevue and from Benson to Fairacres to the downtown

246 *Church and Home*, Vol. 29 No. 15

area." In the course of five years, they had accumulated nearly $8,000, which is impressive but far from the goal of $20,000, the price the Austin Company had quoted them in 1924. Casady, by this time, had moved on, and Frederick Clayton had taken his place as rector of the parish. The times were nowise improved, and the prospect of a new organ seemed to be still quite distant. Strangely, in the winter of 1928 to 1929, the parish was approached by the Austin Company with an offer to build the pipe organ for half the original price they had quoted, provided the parish was willing to place its order now. The postwar slowdown was forcing layoffs across American manufacturing, and the Austin Company wanted work so that it would not have to lay off its skilled people.[247] The parish had been experiencing financial difficulties of its own since 1926, and the vestry was not interested. The women's service league was not, however, to be put off and drove a hard bargain with the vestry. They would give the vestry $2,000, immediately solving its debt problem, if the vestry would give the Austin Company the go-ahead on building the new organ! It was an offer they couldn't refuse. Now short $4,000 instead of $2,000, the women increased their frenetic efforts in order to have the money to pay for the organ when it was delivered.

There is no record of Simms's role in all of this, but it is certain that he was involved with the women in their persistence. Moreover, he found his relationship of the new rector, Clayton, greatly improved over his relationship with Casady. If Casady's watchword was "efficiency," Clayton's was "beauty." Both men had been born and educated in England. Moreover, Clayton was an intellectual, with whom Simms could relate, and a man who appreciated good music.

With Clayton's leadership on the matter, the organ was installed and dedicated in 1934. A picture of Simms sitting at the keyboard appeared in the *Omaha World-Herald* under the headline "Organists' Dean Triumphs: after 37 years of service, with only three absences, J. H. Simms to play New Pipe Organ."

The Austin was a three manual pipe organ with twenty-seven ranks, doubling the capacity of the Roosevelt, which it replaced, and with the couplers and combination piston much more versatile than anything the Roosevelt had offered. The console sat somewhat like the Roosevelt to the right of the altar, in the more spacious room of the 1906 building. Its pipe work was divided so that half of it sat on the right with the console and half on the left side of the sanctuary. This provided a considerably better sound for the space than the Roosevelt.

---

247 The Austin Company, for a time the leading manufacturer of pipe organs in the United States, would, in fact, go out of business by 1935, to be reopened later as a craft.

The Austin at All Saints, Omaha, 1934

Great

16' Open Diapason, 73 pipes
8' First Open Diapason 73 pipes
8' Second Open Diapason 12 pipes
8' Doppelflöte, 73 pipes
8' Violoncello, 73 pipes
4' Octave, 73 pipes
2' Fifteenth, 61 pipes
Cymbal III, 122 pipes
8' Tuba, 73 pipes
Chimes

Choir

8' Violin Diapason, 73 pipes
8' Gemshorn, 71 pipes
8' Gemshorn Celeste, 61 pipes
8' Clarion, 12 pipes

Swell

16' Bourdon, 73 pipes
8' Open Diapason, 73 pipes
8' Rohrflöte, 73 pipes
8' Salicional, 73 pipes
8' Voix Celeste
8' Dolce, 73 pipes
8' Dolce Celeste, 61 pipes
4' Flaute Traverse, 73 pipes
2' Falutina, 61 pipes
16' Posaune, 61 pipes
8' Cornopean, 12 pipes
8' Oboe, 73 pipes
8' Vox Humana, 61 pipes
4' Clarion, 12 pipes
8' Violin Diapason, 73 pipes
8' Gemshorn, 73 pipes
8' Gemshorn Celeste, 61 pipes
8' Clarion, 12 pipes

Pedal

16' Open Diapason wood, 32 pipes
16' (Gt) Second Open Diapason, metal 32 pipes
16' Bourdon, 32 pipes
16' (Sw) Lieblich Gedackt, 32 notes
8' Octave, 12 pipes
8' Flute, 22 notes
16' (Sw) Posaune, 32 notes

The dedication recital was played by Simms with his student Martin Bush as a guest performer. Bishop Casady was invited back for the occasion. Mrs. Hoagland commented with her well-known acerbic wit, "With Dr. Clayton's usual courtesy, he insisted that Bishop Casady of Oklahoma be invited to consecrate it to the use of the church services." Bishop Casady, she explained, "was our rector when the fund was started." One gathers that more credit was being given to Clayton's courtesy than to Casady's support for the project!

Shortly after the installation, Simms proudly invited the city to a special Tuesday night program at All Saints to show off the new organ and the skills of his choir. The evening was reviewed by the music editor of the *Omaha World-Herald*, August M. Borgium. Borgium reported:

> Two hymns in descant style illustrated the manner used to create greater interest in the choir and congregational singing. The singing would change from one group to another, men's voices or women's voices, being in reality the first attempt at part writing. The hymns were followed by two choral preludes by Bach, the first expressive of death and the other life showing his mastery in depicting moods.

The program also presented a demonstration of modern liturgical music represented by a Sanctus and Benedictus from the Communion Service in G Minor by T. Tertius Noble, a distinguished Englishman, and an Agnus Dei and Gloria in Excelsis by Arthur Whiting, America's celebrated composer. The program closed with what Borgium described as a beautiful arrangement of a Swiss sacred folk song arranged by Clarence Dickinson. In conclusion, Borgium explains, "Mr. Simms conducted from the organ and increased the pleasure of the evening by his inspired playing and explanatory remarks."

A Choir Scrapbook

A special window to the Simms–Clayton years is opened for us by a scrapbook kept by a choir member, which passed into the parish's archives at the time of her death. Lucia Wood transferred to All Saints in 1919. She grew up in the town of St. Edwards, Nebraska, south of Albion. She came from English stock, which was common in Boone County as can be judged by the place names. Early in her life, she exhibited both a love and a talent for music. At twenty-three, she came to Omaha to pursue her ambitions to learn and teach music. This made All Saints particularly attractive. Simms was well known as a teacher, and from his own music education, he was instilled with the feeling that he owed young people help to develop their talents. By 1919, Simms had many successful students in the city. Moreover, he was a decided English gentleman. Before long, Lucia Wood was not only taking lessons, but she was also singing in the choir, a thing that she did for more than fifty-two years. Her musical contribution to the choir was modest, but her contribution to its identity and sense of community was immense.

The earliest entry in her scrapbook is a clipping which is dated 1922. In her entries, she provides choir pictures, various choir programs, and she records the deaths and marriages of the choir members. She carefully documents Simms's long career and then Neubeckers. The choir brides she mentions are Alice Baker, to marry Mr. Cook, 1924; Ms. Marian Joyce Fisher, to marry Reverend Fullwood, 1930; Ms. Courtney Lois Barner will be wed to Harry William Charman of London, England, 1944; Frandsen–Gibbs Ceremony, 1960; and Linda M. Miller's wedding, August 18, 1962. Linda was an All Saints girl, and she was wedding Arthur Staubitz, an All Saints boy. One senses how thrilled the little woman who never married was with this latest marriage. Then there were the choir funerals: "May Adams, 90, Is Dead," and "Death Comes to Mrs. Munro." Ms. Wood pens in the margin, "Both Mary Adams and Helen Munro were choir members with lovely voices." Munro was well known in the city for the comedic roles in which she acted at the Community Playhouse and with the Brandeis Players. She even, it is noted in the scrapbook, had a run in a Broadway show, which lasted a year.

The scattered record of Lucia Woods hints at one of the mysteries of choirs. Choirs become intense communities deeply connected with one another's personal lives. This explains why they are capable of eliciting commitment from their members, which exceeded that of other parish organizations. It also explains why choirs are the scene of some incredible acts of charity and of some moments of intense pain and anger.

An Impossible Change

When Fr. Gordon Galaty took hold of the reigns at All Saints in 1947, Simms was eighty-five years old, and he had been the parish's organist and choir director for fifty-two years. To say that Simms was an institution would be an understatement. His community profile was so high that whatever Galaty chose to do not only would be intensely reviewed by the members of the parish, but also by the community at large. On the other hand, if the cultural changes of the twenties tested parish music programs, the postwar changes in American cultural life that were well under way by 1947 promised even bigger changes. Simms understood that for him to continue, he would need to live though another revolution. The arrival of a new rector also meant a major change in the way the services would work. His affinity with Clayton, who had resigned in 1947, made this even more difficult to envision himself working with the new man. At long last, Simms was ready to retire.

Galaty was indeed a dramatic change, which the parish was slow to understand. He was much more catholic in his orientation, which meant that he was intent on refocusing the parish's worship on the Eucharist as the principal service on Sunday. In tune with the postwar changes, he also was decidedly family oriented. He quickly instituted a family service, which had a different need for music. In one sense, this meant the music needed to serve the liturgy rather than being a statement in itself. Large thematic anthems were out. In another sense, the music needed to fit the needs of a family, which meant there was less time for music and indeed for preaching. Parishioners in growing numbers did not come to church to listen to music, and they were more likely be accompanied by their children, which introduced the squirm- factor as a measure of likes and dislikes in music.

Clearly, Galaty approached the change with a full understanding of just how important this choice would be for his future at All Saints. He did so by assembling a blue ribbon music committee on April 30, 1948. They consisted of Dr. William Sturges, Mr. Martin Heselund, Ms. Julia Chilton, Mrs. Irving Benolken, Mrs. Conrad Young, and Mr. George Peters. Chilton was a violin soloist with the symphony, and Benolken, a highly regarded piano teacher in the city, with a name that went back into the Mackay years of the parish.[248] The others were also prominent patrons of the music scene in the city as well as that of the parish. At a meeting the following June, they proposed to the vestry that they should be empowered to begin a search for a new organist, preferably a younger man who can work with children. Richard Duncan, who had been hired as an assistant to Simms, seemed to be the obvious choice. By January of 1949, the committee announced that they expected Simms would retire in June and that a search was under way. Simms duly tendered his resignation on February 15, 1949, now being eighty-seven, with an incredible record of fifty-four years of service in the parish. Duncan turned down the position for reasons that are unclear, and so the search was extended outside of the city. The search led through Chicago, where Galaty was from to Eau Claire, Wisconsin. It is not without significance that the small cathedral at Eau Claire, the epicenter of the catholic movement in the Episcopal Church, was where it stopped.

248 Her husband Irving was crucifer for the service in 1906 which consecrated the new building.

At a specially called vestry meeting on July 17, the music committee recommended that the young musician who was working for the cathedral be hired. His name was Cecil Neubecker, recently married and the father of a young boy. He was, they reported, a skilled organist and voice teacher. He was, at the time, pursuing a master's degree, a thing that the contract with All Saints would encourage. The contract was lengthy, including such details as the provision to offer free voice lessons to any child in the parish whose voice was outstanding.

Neubecker arrived on September 1 and stayed in the rectory until the apartment, which the parish had arranged for him in the new Carl Wilson housing development on Florence Boulevard, was ready. Until then, he had left his family, a wife and young son, in Eau Claire. His salary was set at $2,400 per annum, and the vestry agreed to provide his moving expenses. With his arrival, it became apparent that the cost of the apartment would strain his budget, so Galaty provided him with an additional $15 a month from his own discretionary fund, a sum which Galaty hoped that the vestry would assume by increasing Neubecker's pay before long. Galaty introduced him to the parish in a letter dated August 29, 1949, sent to all members of the parish. In the letter, he expressed the high expectations that he had for Neubecker. "Everything possible should be done to encourage members of the congregation to join the choir. Arrangements should be made as early as possible to introduce Mr. and Mrs. Neubecker to the congregation and the community."

Neubecker immediately initiated a strenuous rehearsal program, demanding on him and on the choristers. The senior choir rehearsed Thursdays at 7:30 p.m., the boys' choir 4:00 p.m., on Tuesdays, and the girls 4:00 p.m. on Wednesdays. Neubecker's rehearsals were rigorous and professional. He would point out an individual's error on the spot. He quickly instilled in his choir an immense amount of respect and not little fear. His young wife, Virginia, sang in the choir as well. A tall Nordic-looking blonde, Ginnie served as leaven. She was known for cracking jokes out of Neubecker's apparent hearing and stirring up plans for the next choir party. The same was true for the children's choirs, but for all his strictness, he was also known for being most accommodating, often driving kids across town so they could participate.

When the annual meeting came around in1950, Neubecker made an extensive and detailed report of the past four months. Throughout his career at All Saints, he produced such reports for the annual meeting. The fruits of his labors were soon put on display during Holy Week of 1950. It was announced and advertised in the *Omaha World-Herald* that the All Saints Choir would perform Gabriel Fauré's "Requiem" on Wednesday evening of Holy Week. The announced soloists were Mrs. Louis Murphy, soprano, and Mr. H. D. Sarouian, baritone, both paid section leaders of the choir. The choice of the Latin Mass setting was likely a mutual signal from Neubecker and Galaty that All Saints was going to be more catholic than it had been. The challenging piece was also a signal of Neubecker's intention that the choir would build a new repertoire of sophisticated music that differed from the late nineteenth and early twentieth-century English cathedral music that had been Simms's staple.

Neubecker had hardly settled in when Galaty was called to active duty in 1950 by the outbreak of the Korean War. When Neubecker made his second annual report, again quite detailed, he did so in the presence of a new rector, Mark McCallum. McCallum presented Neubecker with a very different rector than the one that had hired him. McCallum was decidedly low-church and pragmatic. The situation was uncomfortable for both men, and there is some evidence to suggest that they never managed to have a comfortable relationship. The solution that they found was to divide the turf. McCallum did not interfere with the music, and Neubecker did not interfere with the liturgy, which, to McCallum, was primarily the integrity of the sermon.

Neubecker, like Simms, was a teacher with a significant following in the city, and he produced a number of organists who would be leaders in a succeeding generation of organ choirmasters. One of his students in his early years was Dr. Wayne Kalstrom, now director of music at Dundee Presbyterian Church. Kalstrom recalls being one of Neubecker's last students to play their senior recital on the Austin in the old building on Dewey.

An Un-imagined Opportunity

This would not be the last surprise for Neubecker during his tenure at All Saints. It was only in1960 that the rumors that parish might actually move to a different location in the city became remotely credible. Well into that planning process for the move, it was the well-accepted position that the Austin would be moved from the old church to the new one. It was, therefore, only when plans for the new building where actually taking place that Neubecker began to envision a new pipe organ that would exceed the existing Austin in the same incremental proportion as it exceeded the parish's original Roosevelt. McCallum stayed at a distance from the decision, and he deferred, as did the vestry as the whole, to Neubecker and Robert Spire, who emerged as key lay support for the music program. Everyone respected Spire as both musically competent and imminently practical to judge Neubecker's vision. Neubecker and Spire had found a strong ally in Charles Morton the parish's architect. His vision of the church interior was driven by what he called clean lines and envisioned an organ that did not intrude on those lines. He very much wanted the pipes behind a screen. By July of 1962, the vestry gave Neubecker, backed by Spire, the authority to seek bids for a new organ. The vestry's parameters for the project were established as $40,000, to be reserved in the building fund, and whatever else could be raised by the sale of the existing Austin. An independent appraisal suggested that the Austin was worth $10,000–$15,000.

Reuter replied to the parish's inquiry immediately stating that they were interested and that, subsequent to looking at the Austin, they would accept it as partial payment on the price of a new pipe organ. Design work was initiated by Neubecker in cooperation with Frank R. Green of the Reuter Company. Correspondence with Reuter during the process shows that Spire was an active participant in this process, and the actual outcome owes a great deal to his skill and perseverance. On the basis of the resulting design, a contract was signed with the Reuter Organ Company, and work began in Reuters shops in Lawrence, Kansas. The actual installation was made in 1964 by Reuters agents: Timothy Vos, Howard Lang, Frank Creitz, and Roger Banks. The tonal finishing, in what was generally called the classic American style, was completed under the supervision of Mr. Franklin Mitchell, the vice president and tonal director of the Reuter Company.

The installation is described by Reuter as a 38 R458 Reuter Organ and is identified as their Opus no. 1442. In the end, the cost was $53,628. All Saints, as you will recall, budgeted $40,000 for an instrument, and Reuter made that work by allowing $13, 682 for the Austin. The odd sum leads one to think that Reuter was prepared to make the deal work. Subsequently, Reuter sold the Austin to Rock Brook Methodist Church, where it continues to serve nicely. Neubecker was probably justified in arguing that the Austin would not be adequate for the new space particularly if it were placed according to the architect's design behind the screen. The Reuter nearly doubled the size of the Austin, going from twenty-seven ranks to forty-five ranks, from a little under one thousand pipes to a little over two thousand pipes.

The architectural design of the altar end of the church created three large spaces, rooms in effect, twenty feet above the main floor to house the organ chests and pipes behind a screen. The screen is a grill cloth, originally a powder blue, faced and held in place by vertical wooden lattice.[249] This made it possible for the swell and choir sections of the organs to be under expression. Installation proceeded in a timely fashion but not without difficulty. The air channel from the blower, which is located in the lower level of the building leaked, and it was difficult to repair. The ample size that the chambers appeared to provide proved inadequate, the cause of which was never identified. It may well have been failure of the organ builder to build within the constraints of the space or of the architect for not foreseeing what was needed. Suffice it to say that while a visit to the chambers is both possible and interesting, it is not easy to move around once you are there. Moreover, an import rank, an eight-foot Geigen Principal, the gift of Richard Lurth of Mankato, Minnesota, was still in preparation at the time of the dedication and in fact never materialized.

[249] The powder blue color of the grill cloth has been darkened with age and particularly by a fire in the boiler room in 1993 that did extensive smoke damage through out the building.

Stop List Reuter Opus 1442

Organ

1. 16’ Quintaton
2. 8’ Principal
3. 8’ Hohlflöte
4. 8’ Gemshorn
5. 4’ Octave
6. 4’ Spitzflöte
7. 2’ Fifteenth

Choir

8. 16” Dolcan
9. 8’ Bourdon
10. 8’ Dolcan
11. 8’ Dolcan Celeste
12. 4’ Prestant
13. 4’ Dolcan
14. 2’ Spitz Principal

15. III rks. Fourniture chimes
16. 1–1/3 Larigot
17. 1’ Fife
18. 8’ Cromorne

Swell

19. 8’ Viola Pomposa
20. 8’ Chimney Flute
21. 8’ Viola Celeste
22. 4’ Koppelflöte
23. 2–2/3 Nasard
24. 2’ Blockflöte
25. 1–3/5’ Blockflöte
26. Plein Jeu III
27. 16’ Fagotto
28. 8’ Trompette
29. 4’ Rohrschalmei

Tremulant
Pedal

30. 32' Quintbass
31. 16' Principal
32. 16' Bourdon
33. 16' Quintaton
34. 16' Dolcan
35. 8' Octave
36. 4' Choral Bass
37. 4' Bourdon
38. Mixture III
39. 16' Posaune
40. 16' Fagotto
41. 8' Fagotto
42. 4' Fagotto

A dedication concert of the new organ was held on Sunday, October 11, 1964, at 4:00 p.m. It was played by Cecil Neubecker. The playlist was published as follows: Grand Choeur Dialogue, Gigout; Air with Variations, Martini; Sonatina from "God's Time is Best," Bach; Grace Rondo in G, John Bull; The Bells of St. Anne de Beaupre, Russell; Litanies, Alain; Minature, Langlais; The Sun's Evensong, Karg–Elert; and Comes Autumn Time, Sowerby. The range of Neubecker's program, from Bach to Alain, from Bull to Sowerby, was meant as a demonstration of the range of the new instrument. The inclusion of the piece by Russell made use of the chimes, the one thing on the Austin that was brought along to the new church.

The dream come true was not, however, without its cost. No one had fully estimated what a difficult financial circumstance the parish would find itself in the aftermath of construction. The parish's debt stood at $250,000, and the growing of conflict in American life made it progressively more difficult to find a solution to the problem. The new senior warden in 1965, Arthur Pinkerton, would often recall that his first job as senior warden was to tell Cecil Neubecker that there could be no paid soloist for the coming year due to the financial difficulty of the parish. One could tell from his manner of reminiscence that he did not relish the job. The cut, however, did not affect Lois Carlson, who had sung in the choir for some time and was considered an assistant to the choirmaster. From time to time, soloists, particularly male tenors and basses, would reappear, but the age of a paid choir had come to an end. When Neubecker revisited the Fauré "Requiem" in 1971, obviously a favorite of his, the soloist would be Elaine Spire, Robert Spire's wife. Spire was as fine and as well trained a soprano as any that ever sang at All Saints. What was different was that she was volunteer, and she was there because of a sense of ministry.

And Yet a Third Surprise

The third surprise of Neubecker's career at All Saints was to find himself faced with the prospect of working for yet another new rector. Perhaps the surprise was not so much that McCallum retired but that his replacement was Charles Pedersen. Pedersen was about as dramatic a change from McCallum as one could imagine. If Neubecker's relationship with McCallum was parallel, with Pedersen, it was confrontational. Pedersen was even less sympathetic to Neubecker's ambition for the parish's music program than McCallum, but he knew he could not challenge them head-on. Neither man ever figured out how to work with each other, but before long, the problem was solved by Neubecker's sudden death. On March 7, 1976, Cecil Neubecker, who had been organist and choirmaster since 1949, died suddenly of a heart attack. His health had not been good for some time, and the previous September, the parish had given him special recognition at the eleven-o-clock service for his twenty-five years of service as the parish's director of music. At the ceremony, Neubecker was given a paid winter vacation in Phoenix, Arizona, for himself and his wife, Virginia.

Neubecker's death presented Pedersen with a difficult problem since probably next to money, nothing is so perennially contentious in the life of a parish as music. The laity are quick to defer when it comes to theology or ethics, but they are much more secure in offering opinions about dollars and cents and what they like and don't like in music. The choir itself, a significant group within the parish, entered into a time of grieving and was anxious about its future and about whether a prestigious music program would be maintained at All Saints. Pedersen was on the spot. It was an opportunity for him to adjust the music program in the direction that he felt compelled to move the parish. On the other hand, he knew he would face criticism if anything he did implied anything that could be taken as questioning the Neubecker legacy. Quickly, he announced that in the existing music program, the parish had a choir directress who was quite adequate for the time being. This was Lois Carlson, who had served as a paid soloist for some time. In fact, she was one of the choir's brides, having married the choir's baritone. An inquiry on Pedersen's part produced a lead for an organist who had recently returned to the city and had begun playing occasionally at St. Andrew's. Linda Shirk, who had grown up in Wakefield, Nebraska, had been out of the state while her husband was in the service. Both teachers, they returned to Omaha to start a family. With these two appointments, Pedersen bought some time. Less apparent, however, it made a shift from a full-time music director to part-time musicians. This was, in fact, an unprecedented change as All Saints had had a full-time music director since 1891! To Pedersen, the music problem was, above all, a budget issue, and the appointments brought some relief to the considerably stressed budget, making way for things that he considered to be higher priorities.

There had been an alternative service at nine fifteen, with its own music since September of 1973. Until 1978, the music had been supplied by volunteers. The reliability and consistency of volunteer musicians were a problem, particularly for a service that had rapidly grown into a main Sunday service. Pedersen found an answer to this problem through Joyce Thomas, the parish's director of Christian education. Thomas suggested Robert Scheiblhofer, whom she knew through her previous work in the Roman Catholic Church. Scheiblhofer came with a guitar for a small stipend and the right to live in the apartment on the lower level of the building. The music at this service was suddenly infused with a great deal of "Jesuit" music (Dan Schutte, John Foley and Bob Buford) quite popular at the time. "On Eagle's Wings" and "Be Not Afraid" became staples for this congregation.

While the eleven-o-clock service continued in the pattern, Pedersen had worked out with Neubecker, there were growing differences. It was a noticeably smaller service and progressively more liturgical. The incremental elimination of Morning Prayer in itself required a different kind of music. In general, Morning Prayer was rather undersized for a Sunday morning, leaving plenty of room for a twenty-minute sermon and for extensive musical offerings. The music offering consisted of the chants that made up the Morning Prayer service and the classic choir anthem. Both the twenty-minute sermon and the large musical offering presented a problem when the Eucharist was scheduled. When it was once a month, no one thought to blame the preacher or the music people for the service being overly long, and not a few simply avoided communion Sundays.

The issue came to a head on Palm Sunday in 1979. Pedersen was bent on using the new *Book of Common Prayer*'s rite for Palm Sunday as the basis for an elaborate procession at the beginning of the service that would involve the choir. The intension was that the choir would sing an introit at the rear of the church and then process around the congregation singing "All Glory Laud and Honor." At the last minute, the choir baulked, presenting Pedersen with the one thing he was least able to tolerate, a public rebuke. Immediately after Easter, he notified Carlson that her contract as an interim director was terminated and that Robert Scheiblhofer, who had been up to then the music person for the alternative service, had been appointed as the new permanent choirmaster.

The result was that the choir resigned. One who was new to All Saints at that time, remembers being awed by a choir of forty on their first visit and coming back the next Sunday and counting four of five in the choir. Another recollection from within the choir, suggests that only a single member of the choir who chose to remain. This was Claudianna Todd, a highly trained and talented soprano voice who had only recently joined the choir. A small group did, in fact, transfer to Trinity Cathedral and sang in the cathedral choir for some time. A substantial group simply disappeared into the woodwork, so to speak. Much of the old choir had a rather-attenuated relation to congregation. A number of others had, for some time, been ready to retire but could not bear to tell Neubecker and equally, after his death, his widow, who continued in the choir and those with her who had assumed a role in protecting Neubecker's legacy. At any rate the disaffection was not greatly noticed in the parish, and Pedersen and Scheiblhofer immediately went to work at assembling a new choir with a great deal of success.

That success was partly due to the aggressiveness of Pedersen, who asked a number of people quite directly to sing in the choir. For example, he called on Joe Barker to join the choir. Partly it was due to the passiveness of Scheiblhofer who had endeared himself to the people who sang for him at the nine fifteen and who felt, in a certain way, a need to take care of him. Some of them moved into the senior choir, for example, Mary Sue Sturgeon. This group also worked to bring new people into the choir. Sue Fisher was a neighbor of Sturgeon, and her addition to the choir added another well-trained soprano voice. In a short time, a number who identified themselves with "the old choir," such as Gayle Smith, Bud Fankboner, and John and Dorothy Bower, came back. In time, Dorothy Bower became one of Scheiblhofer's enthusiastic supporters. In an article that appeared in the *Witness* in 1992, she is quoted as saying, "We love being in the midst of all that glory Rob brings forth."

The new choir was a new deal. Neubecker's professional practice was replaced by a relaxed community, which was both spiritual and fun. If Scheiblhofer lacked credentials, he made up for it with extraordinary talent. Linda Shirk, who had been the organist since Neubecker's death, found herself working with and for Scheiblhofer. Later, she would testify to Scheiblhofer's talent in the *Witness*. "Rob is able to project his personality and draw together all the voices, he is competent whether dealing with six voices or 1,500.[250] He has the ability to compose music on the organ as he plays and he has written many compositions for the organ, choir, and handbells, all of which we enjoy at All Saints." Shirk continued as organist until 1993, and they were a perfect team. It was difficult to decide which was more exciting, listening to Shirk bringing a piece home with her impeccable keyboard skill or Scheiblhofer taking off with a stunning improvisation.

Scheiblhofer was a graduate of Rummel High School in Omaha and had gone to the Christian Brothers' University in Memphis. He had always been interested in music and excelled at it. He began playing the organ in church in eighth grade, and he continued to develop his skills. His training in the Roman Catholic Church meant that he understood liturgy, and he was able to complement the liturgical direction Pedersen wanted to take All Saints. He quickly shed his guitar and proved to be commanding on the organ and thoroughly competent with classical Anglican hymnology. In the post-Vatican II period, Roman Catholic parishes were scrambling to find hymns to sing with the mass. Scheiblhofer had created a hymnal for the archdiocese, which borrowed heavily from the Anglican world as well as the general run of Protestant music. He also brought to the choir a great deal of fun that had long been missing. By the end of 1979, he was commissioned by parishioners to compose a mass setting for All Saints. This came at the time when the new *Book of Common Prayer* was introducing new translations of the Gloria and the Sanctus and new liturgical texts, such as "Christ Our Passover." New settings were slow in coming and seemed to be less than compelling. His composition made its debut in 1980, and it has remained a hallmark of All Saints until this time.

In 1983, Scheiblhofer became interested in handbells. In a pattern that was now familiar, he threw himself into mastering handbells. A used set of Petit–Fritsen handbells was on sale in nearby Council Bluffs, and he talked Pedersen into buying them. This style of handbell had a unique sound, somewhat of a minor scale, which delighted Scheiblhofer as did the idea that they would set All Saints apart from other bell choirs in the area. They would, however, prove to present a persistent and difficult maintenance problem. A dedicated bell choir emerged with all that amazing loyalty and discipline that choirs seem to produce. This choir was highly thought of

250 Scheiblhofer had conducted a joint choir of Roman Catholic parishes at the Civic Auditorium.

in the parish, and they were used on a progressively more frequent basis to accompany the parish's worship. When Scheiblhofer left the parish in 1995, Jerry Gray, who had been playing in the bell choir and assisting the music program in a number of significant ways, replaced him as the director of the bell choir.

Another part of Scheiblhofer's legacy was the purchase of a Flentrop Positiv Pipe Organ to serve the new chapel. The purchase was made in 1987 from All Souls Episcopal Church of San Diego, where it had served their chapel and was used regularly by the San Diego Symphony and San Diego Masterchorale as well. It was built in 1973 by David Rothe at the Flentrop's shop as a prototype of a Flentrop kit. It has a single manual and three ranks: an 8-foot stop (eleven notes, wooden pipes) built into the back, 4-foot stop and 2-foot stop. The purchase price was $6,500, which made it a bargain. It has proven to be a delightful gem of an instrument and particularly suited for the chapel space. It has continued to serve the chapel, which is the site of a weekday Eucharist, small weddings and funerals, and a weekly Saturday evening Eucharist. On occasions, it has been used in the main church for special recitals in which there was an interest in playing early organ music, which had been composed to be played on just such an instrument. Dr. James Johnson, who would become the parish organist in time, had the keyboard skills to fully utilize the tracker action of this instrument and his play on the instrument made listening to it a particular delight.

The instrument was not, however, without its problems, which had often been identified as a tuning flaw. In 2001, a successful effort was made to correct these flaws. Martin Ott of St. Louis, Missouri, was commissioned to replace the organ blower with a new blower, to add a wind stabilizing system, to repair its action, and to voice and tune the instrument. The cost was not to exceed $5,000. The result, thanks to Martin Ott, was quite successful, and the instrument continues to contribute to the music tradition of the parish.

Perhaps the most sweeping part of Scheiblhofer's legacy, however, was to imbue the choir with a sense of spirituality and with a sense of mission within the liturgy. As a product of the Vatican II reforms, he brought into the choir a repertoire of some of the best Catholic music and best liturgical practices. In the latter period, he became interested in the music of John Rutter, which contributed greatly to the standing of the choir in the parish's eyes. Scheiblhofer's work resonated with Pedersen's and my own approach to liturgy and tastes, modest as they were in music. The result was that the congregation was inspired to see how everything music, sermon, and liturgy worked together. The choir not only was inspired by its own sense of community, but also with its participation in a broad array of ministries within the parish at large.

By 1992, Scheiblhofer was ordained to the diaconate, which began to refocus his interest on a broader scale of the parish activities. Nevertheless, the choir continued to thrive. There was, however, two sources of frustration for the music program. The most obvious problem was the state of the Reuter organ. The other problem was the space provided for the choir for its vesting and rehearsal.

Where Shall They Sing?

In the eighties, Pedersen had taken on a number of attempts to alter the space and position given to the choir in the liturgical setting. What he had inherited was a classic chancel with an antiphonal choir. If the new building had an openness, which felt modern, the tiered choir, four levels on each side, running sixteen feet between the fifth and sixth column, felt monastic, much as the arrangement in medieval cathedrals. The choir mediated between the laity in the nave and the clergy in the sanctuary. Liturgical theory in the latter half of the twentieth century challenged this and attempted to put the laity at the altar and choir with and in the laity. Pedersen, before coming to All Saints, had built a church in Stamford, Connecticut, which followed the new norms. It was an altar-centered church, a church in the round, and the choir was simply a designated section of the pews. From his arrival at All Saints, Pedersen sought to reorder the space in the worship area. In the 1980s, he eliminated the antiphonal choir and covered it with a deck, which allowed the altar to sit between the fifth and sixth column, bringing it thirty-two feet closer to the congregation. Various accommodations for the choir were made behind the altar, all of them rather temporary and makeshift.

I might add at this time to Scheiblhofer's legacy that under his leadership, the choir underwent this experimentation with a great deal of aplomb. Not only was its space in the liturgy shifting, but also its space for rehearsal and robing. Originally, the choir robing area flanked the two bathrooms downstairs. Neubecker had an office on that hall, which now appears to be more of a closet than an office. He was apparently happy to have the space. Rehearsals were held in the parish hall. This presented problems because it was neither acoustically appropriate for rehearsals nor was it adequately heated.

I had, of course, participated in these changes as Pedersen's assistant and was given a good deal of say in what was done. We were in basic agreement as to what we were trying to accomplish. When I inherited the problem in 1993, I was determined that the location around the altar would achieve some permanence and dignity and that the choir would have a dedicated space of its own for rehearsing and robing. Among the various experiments with locating the choir, the one that received the most criticism, was locating the choir head-on. The congregation disliked looking at individuals in the choir, and the choir did not like looking at individuals in the congregation. Moreover, there was a widely shared view that it looked too protestant. The design that we settled on was choir seating on each side of the clergy chairs, forming as close as possible an arc that completed itself with the congregation. The working assumption was the choir regularly had thirty-plus members and would require both sides. On the other hand, the decision was to use choir chairs and not pews in order to ensure flexibility. The bell choir was provided with its own space behind the clergy chairs, which allowed for the ability to use the bell choir multiple times during a month without set up. In 1997, these alterations were made, and the new ceramic tile covering completed the sanctuary for Easter of 2000.

The rehearsal space for the choir was moved upstairs in 1994 into a space in the old office wing. This experiment allowed us to demonstrate the value of a dedicated rehearsal space, and when the design for the narthex expansion was finalized in 1999, it had a room thirty feet by thirty feet with a robing and supply area abutting it.

How Shall They Sing?

The organ had been deteriorating for some time, and Pedersen had continued to resist taking on any major work in regard to the organ. He had, however, allowed Scheiblhofer to explore various possible solutions. Scheiblhofer was convinced that the Reuter could not be repaired and believed very deeply in the idea that it should be replaced with a Casavant, giving the parish a tracker action organ that would be an instrument of distinction. Among the proposals was a plan offered by Rosalis of Casavant Frères, which would cost about $800,000.

No action was taken, and the organ continued to decline. Pedersen's resignation in 1992 handed the problem to his successor, who, as it turned out, was me.

I was convinced that the problem was urgent, and a solution needed at last to be found. With the help of a large committee drawn mainly from the parish's music program, we concluded that the solution was to repair and to rebuild the Reuter. The vestry responded to the report by making a commitment of $100,000, which could be invested in the organ by way of a repair and transformation of the instrument. It expressed the hope that it could be completed in 1997. That decision was, of course, disappointing to Scheiblhofer. Now ordained to priesthood, he left All Saints to become the rector of St. Barnabas's Episcopal Church in Omaha in May of 1994. Clearly, he was at a point in his life where he wanted the opportunity to develop himself as a priest and to leave the musical phase of his life aside. It is not clear to what extent the parish's choice contributed to his choice to leave All Saints, but it is likely to have been a factor.

The Appointment of James and Karen Johnson

If rectors are inclined to complain about the entrenched music programs that they inherit, it is nothing compared to the angst produced by the need to replace one. Scheiblhofer's departure put All Saints in a search mode. With the help of a committee and great deal of work during the summer of 1994, a reasonable prospect was identified, and an offer was made to a young woman with good skills and a promising ability to work with people. She accepted and went back to the Lutheran parish for whom she was currently working to tell them that she was resigning. They offered her a substantial salary increase, and so she reneged, leaving us with the suspicion that we had been used. Late in that summer, an enthusiastic candidate emerged, and we decided to give him a try. By a mutual agreement, it was to be a year trial. The person brought excellent choral skill to the job, but his high level of competence on the piano did cross over to the organ much to his surprise and not a little to our chagrin. It did have the rather surprising result that I experienced the capacity to recognize a wrong note when I heard one, a capacity that up to then had been doubted by many! By a mutual agreement, we terminated the arrangement and faced another summer of searching for an organist-choirmaster.

As it turned out, this unintentional interim paid off. Dr. James Johnson, who had recently accepted an appointment to the UNO faculty as the Isaacson professor of music and coordinator of keyboard studies, was interested in the position. Johnson's skill at the keyboard, whether on a piano or organ, was world class. Johnson had performed and recorded with such orchestras as the Royal Philharmonic, the St. Petersburg Philharmonic, the Prague Chamber Soloists, the Slovenian Radio Symphony, and the Boston Pops. His credentials included a postdoctoral master's degree in church music and organ at Westminster Choir College, Princeton, New

Jersey. As an organist who is a member of All Saints and who has played for a number of different congregations, remarked, "He not just good, he is an artist."

Along with James Johnson's qualifications came those of his wife, Karen. Her skills in choral direction and keyboard were well beyond the level that would suffice for most parish music programs. She was hired as an assistant organist and choirmaster. She had the role of organization and set up so that her husband's time and effort could be maximized. In addition, it was hoped that she could restore an elusive children's choir, something that had not existed at All Saints since the early seventies punctuated by the death of Cecil Neubecker.

Dealing with Change

Not everything changed. The Johnsons brought an astute well-trained sense of liturgical purpose of church music as much in tune with the liturgical understanding that Pedersen and I were trying to develop as Scheiblhofer's. They also approached the choir as a spiritual ministry and opened choir practices with prayer. It should, however, not be lost on the reader that the music program had suddenly moved from being led by an uncredentialed musician to the most highly credentialed musician in the history of the parish. There was, with this, an abrupt change in the visits to the rector's office. The common complaint for some time had been, he never starts a rehearsal on time; and when he does, more time is spent on socializing than on actual working on the music. Now it was "he starts rehearsals exactly on time whether everybody is ready or not. He makes us do warm up exercises and he pushes us so hard on the music that he is going kill one of us."

The Johnsons' work ethic was extraordinary, particularly, considering both carried heavy teaching loads, outside of their church work. They were excited to be back in church work and were overflowing with enthusiasm, which I often found humbling. They had discovered the sophisticated library of choral music that All Saints had acquired over the years, and with additions of their own, they hoped to move the choir to the level where it was executing the greater part of the classic tradition. To add to the challenge, it should be said they never were willing to schedule something for a Sunday that was not securely owned by the choir. There was no "let's see if it will fly."

The struggle in establishing a new children's choir was even more problematic. The expectation that a children's choir was a place where children would learn music skills and that it would serve as a feeder for the senior choir had gone out of existence. In the first year, the children's behavior was rebellious, and the parents' reaction was puzzlement. Wasn't children's choir supposed to offer entertainment for their children?

From the pews, there was a concern that organ, no longer muted and nursed along, was being played in too an assertive manner. For many, this was a welcome change, but it caused a few to bend my ear and to cover theirs.

This first year was as hard on everybody, and at times, it seemed like it was not going to work. I remember a key moment when I asked Goef Heiden to lunch to discuss the music program. Heiden was a member of the choir, a participant on the music committee who had revised the organ and hired the Johnsons, and he was on the vestry. Moreover, he was a person for whom I had the highest regard. At the end of discussion, I asked him what he thought I should do. He looked at me and said, "Father, you know what to do." And that was that. Perseverance paid off, and in the following year, both groups moved ahead dramatically.

Returning to a Strong Tradition

The new choir, which had emerged in 1979, had put an end to the idea of any paid soloists or section leaders; but with time, a new concept emerged of providing scholarships for young people who were voice students. The first such scholarship happened more by accident than by design. Joe Barker, new to the choir, heard a high school student sing at a business luncheon. Brandon Hunt had a stunning voice and was presented to the group as a child living in foster care with much promise for the future but little resources to make it happen. Barker raised the idea that the parish offer Brandon a scholarship for singing in the choir, most of which would accrue in a savings account to be used by him for college tuition. Johnson, who had just arrived, went with Barker for an audition and was pleased with what they heard. This was a win-win idea. Brandon made a significant contribution to the choir, received some really valuable training, and he left in 1999 for college with a significant scholarship augmented by additional gifts from members of the choir. Brandon also found the support from the members of the choir. It was not without work. Brandon needed to be picked up and returned to where he lived in Council Bluffs. Making this happen gave the choir a special sense of purpose.

The Johnsons had access to students at UNO, and during their tenure, a string of exceptional students sang with the choir on a scholarship arrangement. Where a paid soloist or section leader would have raised questions as why volunteers, especially those with trained voices, were not also paid, the scholarship concept had its own built-in explanation. Moreover, it gave the choir the purpose as a place where teaching music was happening, making a contribution to the future church musician. This not only returned to the tradition of the Simms–Neubecker years, but it also fit the persona of the All Saints of the eighties and nineties, which identified itself as "teaching parish."

The Johnsons were active recruiters, and the choir became a growth engine for the church. While their regimen meant that some of the Scheiblhofer's choir dropped out, other came in attracted by the new direction. A good example is Rob and Jan Williamson, a young couple recently married at All Saints who were looking for a means to be active in their new spiritual home. Both were active in community theater musical productions, and they brought well-trained voices to the choir. Rob, whose roles were often comedic, excelling in the role of "the court jester" in Madrigal productions, restored to choir a talent that had lost with the death of Helen Munro, the choir's former theater comic. Most notably, the Johnsons recruiting broadened the diversity of the parish with such families as the Kims and the Wangs, Asian families attracted by the opportunity for their children to learn. They joined Jonathan and Kyoko Fuller's very musical children, who had recently come to Omaha from Minneapolis. In 1997, Millicent Long returned to All Saints and joined the choir, giving it another excellent soprano. Millicent had been raised at St. Philip's and educated at the University of Omaha. The African American color of her solo voice made "Deep River" and "Were You There?" compelling moments for the parish. Along with this growth in diversity came a new kind of choir party. The Johnsons enjoyed and excelled in opening their house to entertain the choir much as they did for their students who were at the university or in their studios.

Giving the Reuter a New Life

The program to restoring the Reuter was under way when the Johnsons were hired, and the essential repair of the chests in swell was under way during their first summer there. In 1992, there had been a strong sentiment that we would be better off scrapping our existing pipe organ and replacing it with a new one. The cost of such an effort would have made it the dominant capital program for some time. Too many other capital issues were competing with it, and the result was to either continue stalling as Pedersen had done or settle for a much smaller or perhaps even an electronic replacement. When I took over in1993, it seemed to me it was no longer possible to keep stalling. Linda Shirk, who was now on the vestry, had made an impassioned plea, which had convinced me that it was time, so I appointed a committee to look at the organ problem in the context of the parish musical needs and to make a recommendation. The committee proposed a three-phase program: (1) the existing problems should be repaired as soon as possible, (2) the console should be replaced, (3) the existing pipe should be reworked with appropriate alterations and additions and then re-voiced.

In the summer of 1994, we were able to make the repairs, putting an end to a set of chronic problems that allowed for tuning and re-voicing of the instrument as best as could be done with what we had. During 1996, the committee looked at various proposals for consoles and for rebuilding the organ with the existing pipework. In the end, there were three proposals before us, one from Reuter, one from Casavant Frères, and one from Wicks. While the proposals were similar in design and cost, they did offer three distinctly different solutions. A good deal of study went into the evaluating what they offered the parish. Comments on the proposals were made by both Scheiblhofer and Johnson. In the end, the committee was convinced that Reuter had offered the most positive proposal, making the best use of what we had and with the most convincing vision of a new voicing for the organ. A contract was signed with the Reuter Company of Lawrence, Kansas, in the spring of 1997 so that work could proceed that summer. The timing was important because work on the organ could be coordinated with work in the church-school spaces directly below the organ, which facilitated rewiring and working on the air supply. At the same time, work was being done that summer on the altar area, which would make the space ready for a new organ console.

By the fall of 1997, the new console arrived. It incorporated the state-of-the-art technology, replacing the electromagnetic switches with solid-state electronics and the wire cabling with a fiber-optic cable to communicate with the organ chests. This promised a longer life for the console and a crisper response between pipe and key. Within the three chambers, the wiring, originally cotton insulated, was all replaced. The pistons, which allow an organist to change the combinations of pipes for different hymns or parts of hymns, were expanded from six, which made a distinctive thunk when used to twelve that make no thunk. Besides being doubled, the computer at the heart of the console allowed the twelve to be set forty different times so that a number of different pieces and a number of different organists could be accommodated without the manual resetting of pistons.

The stops were altered and increased. The choir division of the organ was provided with an eight-foot Geigen Principle. This new rank of sixty-one new pipes gave the division, which is meant to accompany the choir, a clear voice of its own. In the same space, which can be expressed by closing a set of shutters, was added a new eight-foot trumpet. The Great, in the center chamber, was given a new eight-foot open flute. The sixteen-foot Quintaton was removed to make room for the new principal, and plans were made for an addition of sixteen-foot Violone exposed outside of the chambers as part of a phase 3. This was rigorously debated. Scheilhofer was reluctant to give it up, but Johnson was more positive of the new stop list and what was to be gained by the swap.

The Quintaton gave the organ a voice fitted for a Baroque repertoire, which fit the taste the music that was in vogue in the mid-twentieth century. The characteristic of the Quintaton is that it adds a fifth tone to the principal tone. In the march or dance line of a baroque piece, such an overtone felt right; but with the English and French cathedral music, it was a distraction from the principal voice and had probably contributed to the claims that the sound of the 1964 Reuter was mushy. The shift in taste to earlier and later organ music was better served by the versatility of the new principal and future addition of the Violone, at least that was the argument that prevailed at the time.[251]

Other additions to the great were a tremulant and a cymblestern, which furthered the versatility of the organ. There was in Reuters preparation for additional ranks in addition to the Violone, such as an English tuba and for other ranks as well as funding might be available. When the work was completed in September of 1997, it brought to a close a five-year effort to reverse the impact of thirty-four years of aging and change in taste.

[251] Casavant Frères presented a competitive alternation to the Reuter proposal, which preserved the Quintaton. While their bid was not much in excess of Reuter's the committee, felt that the Reuter represent the better value.

Stop List Reuter Opus 1442 Revised-1997

Italics indicates not presently installed.

Great

1. 16' Violone
2. 8' Principal
3. 8' Violone
4. 8' Bourdon
5. 8' Harmonic Flute
6. 4' Octave
7. 4' Spillflute
8. 2' Fifteenth
9. Fourniture IV
10. 8' Fagotto (sw)
11. Tuba (ch.)

Tremulant

Chimes

Swell

12. 8' Rohrflute
13. 8' Viola
14. 8' Voix Celeste
15. 4' Principal
16. 4' Koppelflöte
17. 2–2/3 Nasard
18. 2' Blockflute
19. 1–3/5' Tierce
20. Plein Jeu III
21. 16' Fagotto
23. 8' Trompette
24. 8' Hautbois
25. 4' Fagotto Clarion

Tremulant

Choir

26. 16" Dolcan
27. 8' Geigen Principal
28. 8' Gemshorn
29. 8' Hohlflute
30. 8' Gedeckt
31. 8' Dolcan
32. 8' Dolcan Celeste
33. 4' Prestant
34. 4' Spitzflute
35. 4' Dolcan
36. 2' Spitz Principal
37. 1–1/3 Larigot
38. 1' Fife
39. 8' Trumpet
40. 8' Cromorne
41. 16' Tuba
42. 8' Tuba

Tremulant

Pedal

43. 32' Untersatz
44. 16' Principal
45. 16' Violone (gt)
46. 16' Bourdon
47. 16' Dolcan (ch)
48. 8' Octave
49. 8' Geigen Principal (ch)
50. 8' Violone (gt)
51. 8' Bourdon
52. 8' Dolcan (ch)
53. 4' Octave
54. 4' Bourdon
55. Mixture III
56. 16' Posaune
57. 16' Fagotto (sw)
58. 8' Fagotto (sw)
59. 4' Fagotto (sw)
60. 8' Tuba (ch)

While the work was already under way, James Johnson had input in many of the finishing touches assuring that the Reuter renovation would provide the parish with the greatest possible value. The results were anxiously awaited, particularly now that we had an organist of note, one who played on world class instruments, such as the giant Casavant in the Strauss Auditorium or the Willis organs in a number of English cathedrals. How would Johnson react to the restored Reuter, long maligned as plodding and muffled and fit for the scrap heap. Curiously, Johnson took a great deal of delight in the instrument that emerged, comparing it to the Willis organs that he had played in England.

The electronic midi, with its own mini television screen, was one of the things about the proposal, which least interested Johnson. A guest organist at the university, who had been invited to play a recital on the University's Casavant in the Strauss Auditorium, needed practice time, which was hard to come by at the busy Strauss. We invited her to use our organ, and she recorded one of her sessions. She reported that she was startled when she sat down and listened to it. She realized she had come to play the piece much faster than she had originally or than she wanted to. Johnson would come to the same conclusion about its worth on his own.

In 2000, with the finished narthex, Johnson asked if he might hold his master class at All Saints. Regularly, once a week for the next six years, the narthex was set up for a master class, and a dozen or so of the city's finest piano students gathered to hear one another play and to be critiqued. I often sat in on part of the evenings, particularly when one of the students belonged to the parish as several of his private students did.[252] It was a wonder to hear such sound travel through the building and to add yet another dimension to the parish as a teaching community.

The Sabbatical Year and Master Classes at All Saints.

In 2000, James Johnson was awarded a sabbatical by the university, and he chose to stay in Omaha and spend the time developing his skills on the organ. He set out to perfect a number of pieces, nineteen in all, to add to his own repertoire. The organ that he chose to work on during his sabbatical was the restored Reuter at All Saints, making full use of the new midi for its ability to assist him to critique and develop his own performances. For three months, almost daily, the church was filled with the marvelous sound of the organ. The pieces, nineteen in all, on which he worked, ranged from Widor's Toccata; Langlaise's Prelude on an Anthem; Durufle's Prelude on an Introit for Epiphany; Gigout's Scherzo, Sowerby's Carillion; and Karg Elert's arrangement of Now Thank We All Our God. He called the collection "From Four Centuries and Four Countries." It was not so much that he was unaware of the limits of the Reuter as that he was

252 Rebecca and Benjamin Fuller, Nathan Green, Alex Ritter.

excited about what he could find in it. He would confide it is not the best for Bach, but it can do it.

Dr. Robert Powell came to Omaha at the invitation of Johnson to play a recital at the Strauss Auditorium on the Casavant. Powell was director of music and organist of Christ Church (Episcopal) of Greenville, South Carolina, and was one of the most nationally prominent musicians in Episcopal circles. Johnson had studied with him in South Carolina and was anxious to have him come to Omaha. Trying to make the most of the opportunity of Powell being in town, I asked Johnson if there were any way for us to capitalize on his visit. Johnson suggested that we might commission him to arrange a piece of music for the parish, and after a discussion, we decided that an arrangement of "Sine Nomine" for organ, choir, bells, and brass might be the most appropriate request. The reader may recognize that this is the Ralph Vaughn Williams tune for the hymn, "For All the Saints." It was a favorite of the parish who had long identified with it as its fight song! Powell accepted the commission and produced an arrangement, which was sung for the first time on All Saints Day 2000, a day that had the added significance of celebrating the completion of the building program. The arrangement is quite stunning and has become a regular part of life at All Saints.

The maturity of the senior choir was marked by a unique event in 2001, which stands as a measure of how hard its members had worked since Johnson's arrival in 1995. It is also a vindication of what can happen to the voices of a volunteer choir under proper tutelage. Johnson was due for a faculty recital on the Casavant, and he asked the choir to be part of the recital. It was a remarkable sight to see the full vested choir of All Saints on the stage of the Strauss Auditorium, singing among other things Willan: Praise to the Lord; Ashfields: "Of the Father's Love Begotten;" Powell's arrangement of "For All the Saints:" and Karg-Elert: "Now Thank We Now Our God."

The children's choir, which was known as the Treble Choir, had a similar moment in 2004. The group had become so proficient that there where Sundays, in my estimation, when its anthem outshone the senior choirs in sophistication and execution. I suggested to Mrs. Johnson that it might be interesting to explore some kind of trip to award the choristers for their hard work. After some exploration, she settled on the idea that they might sing at St. James Cathedral in Chicago. The cathedral was pleased to host them. In May 2004, they sang for the Sunday liturgy at Chicago's Cathedral. It was a tremendous experience, which could be seen immediately in the bonding of the children and of their parents with one another.

Alongside of the musical excellence came the growth of community within the choir, which struck me as quite exceptional. As in the past there were "the choir weddings." Perhaps the most warming was the marriage of Gayle Smith and Bryan Watkins in1997. Then came the "choir babies," Francine and Elizabeth Watkins. They often appeared in the midst of the formally robed choir, and they were everybody's goddaughters. There were a series of "choir crises" in which the members ministered to one another. Dramatically, there was an angel flight. When an accident put a choir member near death in a neighboring state, a doctor in the choir, who maintained his own plane and participated in a national angel flight program, brought her home where she could recover. And then there were, of course, "choir deaths." In 2002, Dorothy Bower, who had sung in the choir under Neubecker, Scheiblhofer, and Johnson and who was the proverbial choir mother, was diagnosed with advance cancer. She chose to die in her home in Omaha, where I was regularly visiting with communion. As the end approached, the idea was born that, at one of my visits, some of the choir might come along. As it turned out, it was the whole choir. We made it a home Eucharist and sang our hearts out, and in the following week, we gathered for her funeral at All Saints and sang our hearts out again.

During this period, the bell choir, under the leadership of Jerry Gray, continued to play an important role in the parish's music program. In some ways it was an outlet in which individuals who loved to participate in music but had neither the talent nor the drive that would make them feel at home in the senior choir. Nevertheless, it too made significant advances in the musical sophistication of its offerings. By to 2000, the maintenance problem of the Petit-Fritsen bells was becoming particularly problematic, and the decision was made to purchase a new set of Schulmerich Bells, four octaves, at the cost of $32,000. Like the decision to restore the Reuter Organ, this decision brought with it a host of anxieties at the apparent loss of distinction that the Petit Fritsen bell had provided. As it turned out, the Schulmerich bells were more than just a practical choice. It was quickly agreed that they were easier to play, and their sound was brighter and more versatile and better heard.

The faithfulness of Jerry Gray made the handbells succeed, but over the long period of the past twenty-five years, he supplied an important alternative music source to the parish. A music teacher at Thomas Jefferson High School in Council Bluffs and an active director in community theater, he was used to working with what one got and believed that, with a good dose of enthusiasm, he could make a musician out of anyone, even the orneriest kid in the church school or of the decidedly tone deaf thespian at the community playhouse. He made possible a great deal of music for All Saints kids and various activities, including a couple of rather stunning performance of *Jesus Christ Superstar* in the eighties.

Reflections

There is no such thing, of course, as a perfect music program. There are trade-offs in any music programs, and how to measure their success is in the end mysterious. I never dreamed that I would be working in a ministry, which was accompanied by a musical program of note. On the other hand, the success of the senior and the children's choirs came at the cost of experimenting with an alternative worship service, of the kind that were becoming popular at the time. I kept looking for a window of opportunity, which would allow both, but it never came.

It also is important to say that from the point of view of a rector, at least in my experience, music programs bring with them a need for tending. I found myself with increasing issues to tend as the program matured, but it seemed to me that these demands were well worth the result. In part of my satisfaction was the sense that the music program had reconnected with the parish Simms–Neubecker tradition. The goal was excellence, and part of excellence was the vision that we should be teaching the art and ministry of music. The point was not lost on Virginia Neubecker, Cecil's wife. Long troubled by what had happened to the old choir and what she perceived as the direction or lack of it in the music program, she began to correspond with me. The commitment to the Reuter was part of that, but she also came to believe that the Johnson's music program would have pleased her husband. That pleased me because it contributed to the sense that we were closing the circle as we moved into the twenty-first century. The Simms–Neubecker tradition was being honored.

Index

A

B

C

D

E

N

O

P

R

S

T

U

V

W

Y